THE MACMILLAN DIARIES

The Cabinet Years, 1950–1957

THE

MACMILLAN DIARIES

The Cabinet Years, 1950–1957

Edited and with an Introduction by

PETER CATTERALL

PAN BOOKS

First published 2003 by Macmillan

This edition published 2004 by Pan Books
an imprint of Pan Macmillan Ltd
Pan Macmillan, 20 New Wharf Road, London N1 9RR
Basingstoke and Oxford
Associated companies throughout the world
www.panmacmillan.com

ISBN 978 0 230 76843 7

A CIP catalogue record for this book is available from
the British Library.

Typeset by SetSystems Ltd, Saffron Walden, Essex

All Pan Macmillan titles are available from
www.panmacmillan.com
or from Bookpost by telephoning 01624 677237

For

my mother and father

Contents

1956

521

1957

609

List of Illustrations

Section Three

Acknowledgements

All photos courtesy of Hulton Getty with the exception of the following:

Associated Press: 10, 11, 44. Atlantic Syndication: 20, 24, 25. Camera Press: 16, 29. Daily Express: 23. Macmillan Archive: 14. NATO photos: 6. PA Photos: 28, 48. UN/DPI: 2.

List of Abbreviations

AE	Anthony Eden
ADC	aide de camp
AEU	Amalgamated Engineering Union
AFHQ	Allied Forces Head Quarters (North Africa)
AIOC	Anglo-Iranian Oil Company
ANZUS	Australia/New Zealand/United States pacific security treaty (1951)
AP	Associated Press
ASLEF	Amalgamated Society of Locomotive Engineers and Firemen
BBC	British Broadcasting Corporation
BG	Birch Grove (Macmillan's Sussex home)
BIS	Bank of International Settlement
BMC	British Motor Corporation
BofT	Board of Trade
CAS	Chief of Air Staff
CC	County Council
CDU	Christian Democratic Union (Germany)
CIA	Central Intelligence Agency (USA)
CIC	Capital Issues Committee
CIGS	Chief of the Imperial General Staff
CO	Colonial Office
CofE	Chancellor of the Exchequer
CPC	Conservative Political Centre
CUSA	Macmillan's rendering of Suez Canal Users' Club
D	Dorothy Macmillan
DM	Daniel Macmillan
DSO	Distinguished Service Order
DT	*Daily Telegraph*
ECA	Economic Co-operation Administration (USA)
ECSC	European Coal and Steel Community
EDC	European Defence Community
ELEC	European League for Economic Co-operation

EOKA	Ethniki Organosis Kyprion Agoniston (National Organization of Cypriot Fighters)
EPC	Economic Policy Committee
EPL	Excess Profit Levy
EPU	European Payments Union
FBI	Federation of British Industry
FDR	Franklin Delano Roosevelt
FM	Field Marshal
FO	Foreign Office
FS	Foreign Secretary
FST	Financial Secretary of the Treasury
GATT	General Agreement on Tariffs and Trade
GB	Great Britain
GHQ	General Head Quarters
GOC	General Officer Commanding
HM	Harold Macmillan
HMG	His/Her Majesty's Government
HMM	Harold Macmillan *Memoirs* 6v (London: Macmillan, 1966–73)
HofC	House of Commons
HofL	House of Lords
ICS	Indian Civil Service
IK	Ivone Kirkpatrick
ILP	Independent Labour Party
IMF	International Monetary Fund
IRA	Irish Republican Army
IT	Income Tax
KC	King's Counsel
LCC	London County Council
LG	David Lloyd George
M&Co	Macmillan & Company
ME	Middle East
MofS	Ministry of Supply
MP	Member of Parliament
MRP	Mouvement Républicain Populaire (France)
NATO	North Atlantic Treaty Organisation
NUR	National Union of Railwaymen
OEEC	Organisation of European Economic Co-operation
OSS	Office of Strategic Services (USA)
PM	Prime Minister

PMG	Postmaster-General
PPP	People's Progressive Party (British Guiana)
PPS	Parliamentary Private Secretary
PQ	Parliamentary Question
PR	Proportional Representation
PRO	Public Record Office
PS	Private Secretary
PWLB	Public Works Loan Board
Rab	Richard Austen Butler
RAF	Royal Air Force
SACEUR	Supreme Allied Commander, Europe
SHAPE	Supreme Headquarters, Allied Powers in Europe
SofS	Secretary of State
SPD	Social Democratic Party (Germany)
T&CP	Town and Country Planning
T&GWU	Transport and General Workers Union
TUC	Trades Union Congress
UDC	Urban District Council
UK	United Kingdom
UNO	United Nations Organisation
UP	United Press
USA	United States of America
WAAF	Women's Auxiliary Air Force
WD	Harold Macmillan, *War Diaries: The Mediterranean 1943–1945* (London: Macmillan, 1984)
WEU	Western European Union
WRNS	Women's Royal Naval Service (Wrens)
WSC	Winston Spencer Churchill
WVS	Women's Voluntary Service

Introduction

On 2 September 1955 Harold Macmillan noted in his diary, 'Read *Henry* Greville's diary. It is not as good as <u>Charles</u>, but it is very readable. I have just acquired this book – 4 volumes – (very badly edited, without notes or explanation).' Macmillan was an ardent bibliophile. Publishing was, in any case, in his blood. Throughout his period in office he remained active in the family publishing firm. This business background could also influence his reading. When C. P. Snow switched from Fabers to Macmillan in 1951, Harold read his previous works, concluding: 'I hope we shall be able to arrange with Faber to take over the stock and rights of the old books.' And when reading Manzoni's *The Betrothed* or Churchill's *The Hinge of Fate* he could not forbear from making professional comments on the dust jacket or, in the case of the latter, the fact that, for the general reader, there are 'too many memoranda and minutes printed verbatim. This hinders the flow of the narrative.'[1]

His interest in books, however, was by no means purely professional. He was also a discerning collector, proudly, for instance, acquiring complete sets of Defoe or Bagehot in 1954. But, above all, he was an avid and fast reader. In the period covered by this set of his diaries he read over 400 books, noting carefully the many amongst them published by Macmillan & Co. Even in 1955, when the volume of Foreign Office telegrams would keep him up until the early hours, he still managed 54 books. On 6 November 1955 he commented, 'I have to read for an hour every night, however late, or I get too worked up and cannot sleep.' Plays, films or opera were occasional indulgences, though from his waspish comments on the few he experienced it seems clear he preferred reading plays to watching them. He did not own a television, sometimes going to watch his broadcasts on sets belonging to his tenants. He had no taste for fine wines, indeed spending much of his banquet-filled time as Foreign Secretary trying, mostly with success, to remain teetotal. Shooting was certainly a great pleasure, either on his Birch Grove estate in Sussex or the Bolton Abbey estate of his Cavendish in-laws, whenever time and

---

1. 1 and 5 August 1951.

opportunity permitted. Macmillan's main source of recreation was, however, undoubtedly his books.

To some extent they provided a form of escapism. In times of stress he would revert to old favourites like Trollope, Scott, Dickens or Austen. Generally, however, Macmillan's reading seemed to reflect his intellectual interests. Rarely did this bear a direct relationship to his responsibilities. Insofar as he studied public policy or administration, it was through his extensive reading of history. His interests focused particularly on eighteenth- and nineteenth-century Britain. His reading, however, certainly ranged far more widely than this. One of several books that he twice read in these years was Villari's *Life and Times of Machiavelli*, though whether this book, completed for the second time in the summer of 1956, informed how he handled the succession crisis the following winter can only be a subject of speculation. Occasionally Macmillan was certainly tempted to draw direct analogies from his reading of history to the present, as a perusal of his cabinet memoranda will show. More often, however, he was simply struck by the contrasts between past and present. Above all, what Macmillan looked for from history was explained in his comments on Scott's *Tales from a Grandfather*: 'It is a pleasant form of literature – easy to read, with good stories and the kind of history I like – no economic motive, – all battles and romantic stories of great heroic figures or traitorous villains.'[2] His historical reading was accordingly biased towards biography, which comprised about a quarter of his total reading in these years. Individuals rather than economic motives lay at the heart of Macmillan's reading of history, and insofar as his erudition influenced his career it was in tutoring him to believe that it is the individual with a clear vision of his objectives who makes his own history.

This was not Macmillan's only preference in the reading of history. A particular bête noire was the self-righteous pontificating of liberal historians. Harold preferred his history unvarnished. For instance, in May 1954 when reading Lord John Russell's *Life of Charles James Fox* he comments, 'It is not well written, but full of good material. The great thing about old books is that they give the letters, speeches, diaries etc of their bearers. The new professors give us their own theories. At any age, I prefer the former.'[3] He was, indeed, an avid reader of diaries and letters. Again, this allowed him to focus on the role of personalities in history, their hopes and fears and the mental universes they inhabited. Macmillan was acutely

2. 4 June 1951.
3. 29 May 1954.

conscious of the significance of such factors, not least because winning hearts and minds was so important a part of the cold war in which, during much of this time, he was actively engaged.

Whether this enthusiasm for other people's diaries prompted him to start his own is another matter. He had long been an avid letter-writer. During the First World War he effectively kept a diary in the form of letters to his mother. During his lifetime this and his letters home from his mission in Finland in 1939–40 were in his archives bound as 'diaries' of particular episodes in his life. Macmillan's *War Diaries*, published in 1984, covering his period in North Africa, Greece and Italy during 1943–45, similarly began as letters to his wife, Dorothy. They, however, soon became a regular daily journal, written on any scraps of paper to hand.

This record ended abruptly in 1945. Macmillan provides no explanation why, or why he decided to restart his diary in August 1950 to record the meetings of the Consultative Assembly of the Council of Europe. What is clear is that this diary was far more self-consciously so than his previous efforts. This did not begin as letters. Instead it was from the first laboriously recorded in notebooks. It may be that possible publication was in his mind from the start. After all, following Labour's narrow victory in the February 1950 election, a return to office became possible to contemplate. Twelve years in cabinet, culminating with nearly seven years as Prime Minister would, however, as the diaries make clear, have been beyond Macmillan's wildest expectations in 1950. It is only as he grows more secure in his grasp on office that the diaries become more self-consciously literary and the tone one of recording for posterity rather than for his own purposes.

The first series of these notebooks, covering up to his accession to the premiership in 1957, consists of twenty-two volumes and 459,260 words. The diary would be entered up as and when convenient. Sometimes Macmillan clearly made several entries on a given day, during lulls, for instance, in the Geneva negotiations in 1955. More generally he would write up nightly the events of the previous day. Occasionally pressure of events would ensure that this was not possible. In such circumstances weekends had to suffice to bring the diary up to date. This can lead to problems in ascribing dates to particular entries. Macmillan does not seem to have re-read previous entries very often to check where he had got to. This results in a certain amount of repetition. It can also lead him to incorrectly date particular entries on occasion, or enter the same date twice, a problem I have tried to correct, with appropriate signals, when editing the diaries. Rarely, however, did more than a few days pass before an event was recorded.

The first series of notebooks accordingly form a continuous record of Macmillan's life after August 1950. A few days pass unremarked, but these are usually around the Christmas break. That is, until 4 October 1956. Here volume 22 ends. Volume 23 probably was started, but Macmillan later destroyed it at the request of Anthony Eden. There is therefore no diary record for the process whereby Macmillan changed from hawk to dove over Suez. Instead, a new series of diary volumes started with Macmillan's first entry for 1957, made over the weekend on 3 February. This revisits, after some elapse of time, the process whereby Macmillan became Prime Minister on 10 January 1957, and I have therefore included it in this volume as marking a natural caesura in an account of Macmillan's career. The gap over the latter stages of the Suez crisis, however, remains.

Unfortunate though this is, the diaries are nevertheless still documents of both considerable historical importance and literary merit. Macmillan's official biographer, Alistair Horne, refers to the justifiable acclaim won by the *War Diaries* on publication, 'together, perhaps, with some surprise that they could have been penned by the same author of those six rather stodgy and over-length volumes of memoirs'.[4] Macmillan, ironically given his tastes in history, largely left his personality out of the latter. Their method of composition, in a series of grand thematic chapters, also effectively balkanized the diaries, extracts from which, taken out of context, were scattered throughout. In an attempt to encapsulate the times, the life was too often left out. Hopes and fears, his inner thoughts about his role, even his observations on cabinet government all were sacrificed to the narrative sweep of the memoirs. Macmillan also expunged some of his more immediate and less diplomatic judgements on figures like John Foster Dulles. Similarly, in *Tides of Fortune*, Macmillan comments, 'I was fortunate in having an able, imaginative and generous colleague in the Colonial Secretary, Alan Lennox-Boyd'.[5] This, however, was not what he said at the time, as an examination of the diary entry for 3 April 1955 will show.

Some things, of course, go unrecorded even in the diary. Whilst far more revealing of what their author thought and felt than are the memoirs, family life often remains off limits. Anxieties about the children, especially

---

4. Alistair Horne, *Macmillan 1894–1956* (London: Macmillan, 1988), p. xvii.
5. *HMM* III, p. 664.

Maurice and the youngest daughter, Sarah, are recorded. But the nature of Macmillan's feelings, recorded during a visit to the latter shortly after her marriage, can only be guessed at from the following: 'It was a melancholy day, raining hard, and the rather decayed farm buildings and half built or re-built farm house made a sad sight. How she lives, in such discomfort and dirt, I do not understand. One must be very much in love to marry a poor farmer. But, of course, she is.'[6] Meanwhile, of his wife Dorothy's long affair with his fellow Conservative politician, Bob Boothby – reputedly Sarah's real father – there is next to nothing. The only hints at the affair are some acerbic observations on Boothby as politician and some mock-ironic remarks about the number of divorces amongst his fellow senior Tories.

Notwithstanding such omissions, this is more than a purely political diary. When time permits, the life and work of a country estate are carefully recorded. So are the difficulties of post-war publishing. However, a long account of the sale of the American side of the Macmillan Company, for instance, develops into general observations on the state of Anglo-American relations. Politics, as this example shows, are always at the core of this diary.

Macmillan's political career began when, after Eton and Balliol College, Oxford, he first entered Parliament in 1924. Whilst contemporaries climbed the political ladder, however, he served a long apprenticeship, isolated on the fringes of the Conservative Party and without office, until the outbreak of war gave him an opportunity. After junior positions in the Ministry of Supply and the Colonial Office he was appointed Minister Resident in North West Africa. This role inevitably drew him immediately into the intricacies of inter-Allied negotiations, whilst later involving political oversight in the civil war against Communist insurgents in Greece and of the Allied campaign up the Italian peninsula. He returned to a cabinet post as Secretary of State for Air in Churchill's 1945 caretaker government. After this epiphany, however, came the bitter gall of the 1945 election, in which the Conservatives were routed, Macmillan losing the northern mainly working-class seat of Stockton in the process. Returned at a by-election in the south London suburban constituency of Bromley the following year, Macmillan joined the Conservative opposition's shadow cabinet. At that time shadow cabinet members did not tend to hold particular portfolios, but Macmillan, not surprisingly after his wartime experiences, specialized in defence matters.

6. 28 May 1954.

He was particularly concerned about the vast imbalance in forces in the Soviet favour in Europe. Cooperation through the European army for which Churchill called at the Council of Europe meeting with which the diary commences was seen as a way of tackling this deficiency, whilst the Central and Eastern European section he built with Beddington-Behrens after 1949 was a means of keeping channels open to the peoples of occupied Eastern Europe.

At the same time he saw economic cooperation between Europe and the Commonwealth as a means to rebuild both. What Macmillan seems to have envisaged was some sort of loose association, held together by mutual interest but capable, collectively, of reducing the reliance on the USA that had been all too apparent since the war. By stimulating trade within these blocs, the problems of dollar deficiencies which had bedevilled Britain, Europe and the Commonwealth since 1945, and continued to do so in the early 1950s as the diaries bear witness, might be avoided. What he did not favour was supranational 'constitution-building' of the type envisaged by the 1950 Schuman and Pleven plans.

European issues such as these dominate the period covered by the diaries prior to the Conservatives' narrow success in the general election of October 1951. Understandably they feature rather less subsequently during his tenure as Minister of Housing and Local Government (1951–54), when his coverage of foreign affairs is more shaped by Korea, Indo-China or the British difficulties in the Middle East. However, perhaps more surprisingly, he does not take the opportunities afforded as Minister of Defence (1954–55) or Foreign Secretary (April to December 1955) to return to these earlier enthusiasms. The Messina negotiations of June 1955 that paved the way for the European Economic Community hardly rate a reference in the diaries. The belated British response, the plan for a European Free Trade Area, in contrast was clearly absorbing a fair amount of Macmillan's attention as Chancellor of the Exchequer (1955–57) the following year, even in the midst of the Suez crisis.

In other words, whilst the memoirs may provide post hoc justifications for Macmillan's actions, the diaries reveal what was important to him at the time. They also demonstrate the range of issues with which he was trying to deal at any one time, and the way they interacted. But the diaries do not only reflect Macmillan's responsibilities and priorities. He was also an acute commentator on the wider political scene. Many of the political diarists Macmillan enjoyed were well-placed observers, rather than participants in the political process. Whether or not he was consciously following in their footsteps, he seems to have taken care to record with colour and verve both cabinet meetings and great parliamentary occasions. Of course, the bare accounts of both can be read in the records of the Cabinet Conclusions, or in *Hansard*, but without, for instance, Harold's connoisseur eye for a successful Commons speech. Nor can formal records so fully convey the very different feel of cabinet government under Churchill and Eden.

Macmillan's observations were by no means confined to events within his own party. Academic research into the history of British party politics is often conducted as if the parties operate in hermetically sealed spheres. But how can a rounded picture of a political party emerge unless you examine how they were seen and countered by their opponents? Macmillan certainly had no illusions about the need to know one's opponents, to probe their weaknesses and to exploit every public doubt about their capabilities, even if his heirs in the modern Conservative Party seem to have forgotten these arts. His diaries reveal him as a frequent, acute and, during the Bevanite splits of the 1950s, sometimes gleeful observer of the Labour Party scene. In an era dominated by the two main parties, the Liberals necessarily received much less attention.

The observations in the diaries are by no means confined to the domestic scene. European politics, as previously mentioned, bulk large in the early 1950s. Later in the decade this is equally true of American, Soviet and, to a lesser extent, Commonwealth events. Becoming Foreign Secretary and Chancellor, for instance, afforded Macmillan opportunity to renew his friendship with Eisenhower from North Africa, even if he appears to have presumed too much from that during the Suez crisis. Many of his French and Italian interlocutors were also well known to him from wartime service. Given these contacts, his comments on European affairs in these years were well informed and should not be seen through the prism of hindsight. This is not least because these passages by no means concentrate exclusively on the still unformed 'European idea' or the contemporary debates between federalists and functionalists, but also include reports of lengthy conversations about domestic politics in various European countries, some of which I have been able to include here.

In editing the diaries for publication I have endeavoured to preserve as much of the flavour of the originals as possible. In this I had a certain amount of guidance from Macmillan himself, for whether or not the diaries were originally intended for publication, they eventually came to be used extensively in the preparation of the memoirs. In order to facilitate this Macmillan went through his notebooks marking up passages he wished to have transcribed. These were then typed up, and it was from this 1960s typescript that the selections for the memoirs were made. Around 55 per cent of the diaries for the years 1950–56 were transcribed in this way, and the typescript volumes are now kept with the rest of Macmillan's papers at the Bodleian Library in Oxford.

This, however, still left much of the diaries untranscribed. Furthermore, although Macmillan checked the 1960s transcripts, some errors still crept in. My first task then, was to make an electronic transcript of the diaries in their entirety. The legibility of Macmillan's handwriting was certainly not improved by the bullet through his right hand sustained at the Battle of Loos in September 1915. However, once one is accustomed to it, Macmillan's handwriting becomes increasingly manageable. The most difficult references are inevitably to names and places. I found that, in following his almost annual holidays in Scotland, it was advisable to have a map to hand, but even then it did not always help.

Having produced a transcript, the next task was to make a selection. Whereas Macmillan published the *War Diaries* virtually in toto, there was only space in this volume for about half the original diaries. In making this selection, I tried not to be overly influenced by Macmillan's own. With his publisher's eye, he was undoubtedly an astute judge of which passages to choose and which to leave. The same holds true of his further selection from the 1960s transcripts of passages for inclusion in his memoirs. As a result I would have found it impossible to adopt the approach of Ben Pimlott who, when editing Hugh Dalton's diaries, tended not to reproduce material which had already appeared in Dalton's memoirs. This would have been, at least with some episodes, like telling jokes whilst leaving out the punchlines.

Instead, I tried to approach the diaries as a coherent whole, ignoring as far as possible the fact that passages have already appeared, de-contextualized, elsewhere. When making my selection, therefore, I deliberately did not consult the memoirs. My chief criterion was instead the integrity of the diaries as a work in and of themselves. This involved a rather different selection procedure from Macmillan's own, indeed about a fifth of the material I have selected was excluded by Macmillan himself from the 1960s transcripts. His was primarily a political selection and was generally a good one, though he tended to focus more on events than considered judgements on people or institutions. I have not only felt that the latter certainly deserved inclusion as far as possible. It has also seemed to me important to record a representative sample of the other traffic of his life, such as his comments on recently read works, especially when they develop into more general observations on his interests or on contemporary politics. On the same grounds I have also included passages reflecting his business life, which not only embraced publishing but also, through his inter-war service as a railway company director, no doubt informed his comments on the problem in that industry, and his delight in the gardens at Birch Grove or in long walks through the woods of the estate, the family Christmas or his Scottish tours. Many Sundays Macmillan would read the lessons in his parish church. Whilst his comments on these rarely offer much detailed insight into his religious views, I have included what I hope is a representative sample of such entries. Similarly, a proportion of his shooting parties have been included. The result, I hope, will give a more rounded portrait than the one that emerges from the memoirs.

Whilst including such passages I have, of course, had to exclude others. Here a certain amount of repetition in the diaries has helped. The lengthy discussions over when Churchill might eventually retire from the premiership are a particular example, though it might not seem so from the extent to which they still feature in this volume. I have tried to ensure that none of the vast range of topics to which Macmillan turned his attention has been omitted completely from this edition, although the number of references has usually had to be reduced.

In general I have tried to select passages as a whole, without breaking up the narrative flow. On occasion this has not been possible. Sometimes, for instance, Macmillan would insert parenthetical remarks in the midst of paragraphs that bear little relationship to the surrounding text. These I have usually decided to excise, if only to avoid unnecessary confusion. In other places I have excluded what seemed to me to be superfluous repetition. Ellipsis marks have been used to indicate wherever omissions have been made.

Throughout I have tried to preserve the style of the original manuscript. Some corrections have been made, if only for clarity. One example is Chaudhary Muhammad Ali, whose name Macmillan spells in two different ways, both inaccurate. Other mistakes, such as Macmillan's tendency to abbreviate the Suez Canal Users' Club as CUSA have been left, with an explanatory note. I have also left untouched Macmillan's non-standard transliteration of the Russian leader's name as 'Kruschev', added accents, where appropriate, to French words, and tackled Macmillan's somewhat cavalier approach to the apostrophe. Otherwise punctuation, including Macmillan's idiosyncratic use of the semi-colon, has been left as in the original, except where a quote or bracket needs to be closed. Macmillan's tendency to omit the full stop when a sentence ends with a close bracket has not, for instance, been amended.

Macmillan's abbreviations have also been left as in the original. Most of these should be clear enough. Contractions of proper names have been expanded through the use of square brackets where necessary. In addition, I have provided a full explanatory list of acronyms, and translated the foreign phrases used, except when they can be found in the *Oxford English Dictionary*. Where place names have changed, as with Teh(e)ran, I have retained the contemporary spelling.

The other problem with diaries is a tendency to omit information that is well known to the author, but may be less apparent to later readers. A common omission, for instance, is the reason why Macmillan was travelling to Paris, or Washington, or Blackpool. There are also many places where particular episodes are only incompletely told, without a beginning, or end, or both. The labour disputes in the motor industry in the summer of 1956, for example, disappear from the diaries when they cease to occupy so much of Macmillan's attention. In such instances I have considered it useful to provide brief explanatory footnotes, to expand and contextualize the account appearing in the diaries.

Diaries can, of course, prove partial in more than one sense of the word. Macmillan's are certainly no exception. Although frequently displaying less certainty than his public persona, they nevertheless remain the product of an individual and reflective, consciously or otherwise, of his prejudices and self-interest. Macmillan's diaries are by no means an exercise in hubris. Whilst noting his good speeches, he is equally apt at recording his bad ones. There is, however, somewhat of a tendency to play the cabinets of the early 1950s as gladiatorial contests, which he won, between himself and Chancellor Butler over the capital investment programme – a view which perhaps would not have been entirely endorsed by all of his colleagues. But the diary, necessarily, can only record Macmillan's views, even if other participants in particular events may have had very different recollections. On occasion I have deemed it appropriate to use a footnote to draw attention to these alternative voices.

What I have not generally used footnotes for is biographical purposes. Sometimes, indeed, no footnote is necessary. One hint that Macmillan increasingly envisaged eventual publication of the diaries is the way in which he tended to insert explanatory references in parentheses, whether about people, places or events. This proved very convenient for his later editor. However, for those individuals who appear on a number of occasions without explanation of their role, or where they seem of sufficient significance to require further details either of their career or their relationship with Macmillan, I have provided a lengthy biographical appendix. The difficulty with this, of course, is the sheer range of persons Macmillan refers to in his diaries, which are peopled not just with contemporaries but with the political figures he knew before the war and, through his reading of history, a supporting cast of characters from across the ages. The way I have tried to resolve this dilemma has been through including only contemporaries still alive and in some way active at the time the diaries were written in the biographical appendix. Everyone else, where necessary, has been explained through a biographical footnote.

I am very grateful to the present Earl of Stockton and the other Macmillan trustees for the confidence they placed in me in inviting me to edit Harold Macmillan's diaries. These constitute, in my view, the most important set of political diaries of the twentieth century, and I am acutely conscious of the honour they did me. I hope I have repaid their trust.

Thanks should also go to Anthony Goff of David Higham Associates and Georgina Morley, Nicholas Blake and Stefanie Bierwerth of Macmillan, not least for their patience. This project has taken longer than I initially envisaged. Unlike Pimlott in the 1980s working on the Dalton diaries, I have not benefited from generous funding or teams of supporting researchers. Not the least of the baleful effects of the Research Assessment Exercise that has since been imposed on universities is that now scholarly exercises of this kind, however useful they might prove to both the academic community and the general reader, are at a discount. Harold, I suspect, would not approve.

In consequence this project has had to be fitted in during the interstices of a very busy life. A year in Missouri in 1999–2000 greatly helped to clear the decks and make completion possible, and I would like to thank the Fulbright Commission and all my colleagues at Westminster College, Fulton for their support during that time. The support and encouragement I have received from my colleagues in the library and in the History and Politics Departments at Queen Mary, University of London, and at the Hansard Society, should also be fully acknowledged.

Additionally, I have benefited, over the years, from the advice of many with long experience in the art of editing diaries. To all of them I owe a debt. My gratitude should also be expressed to all those who helped me in chasing up particular footnotes. In particular, I would like to thank Orna Almog, Stuart Ball, John Barnes, Derek Blakeley, Nick Crowson, Alistair Elliot, Matthew Elliot, Tony Gorst, Sue Harris, Peter Hennessy, Lewis Johnman, Charles Loft, Rodney Lowe, Anny Mochel, Mette Peek, Marie-Anne Pegg, John Ramsden and Ken Young.

Finally, I would like to thank my wife and family for cheerfully sharing me with Harold Macmillan over the last few years. One launches on a task like this with trepidation, conscious not least of the author's exacting views on edited diaries. I hope that, whatever his views of the edition of Henry Greville's diaries, this one at least would meet with Harold Macmillan's approval.

PETER CATTERALL
July 2001

1950

6 August (Sunday)

Left Heath Row 11am:[1] an excellent flight to Strasb[o]urg, arriving about 1.15. I am housed in the Maison Rouge, in the suite allocated to but not occupied by Bevin.[2] So, after all the fuss about accommodation, I have the best of all.

Winston arrived by car about 3 . . . .

7[pm] general talk with David Fyfe, Duncan Sandys, David Eccles, and during part of time Ld Layton,[3] on the likely development of the debates. This is important in order to advise WSC as to his speech.

It seems generally agreed that after Monday (which is formal) the debate will be on the Ministers' message to the Assembly, which is in the nature of a King's Speech. Since that message refers to events in Korea,[4] the door is open to a general debate on the state of the world; the state of Europe; and the broad strategic pattern of the defence of Europe. This is in spite of the articles of the Statute against our discussing defence. M. Schuman intends, it seems, to speak on his plan on Thursday.[5]

Dined with W.S.C.[;] Duncan and Diana Sandys; Lady Tweeds-

---

1. Macmillan was flying to attend the meeting of the Council of Europe. The Council had been established as a deliberative gathering of parliamentary delegations from Belgium, Britain, Denmark, France, Ireland, Italy, Luxembourg, the Netherlands, Norway and Sweden the year before. West Germany joined in 1950. Macmillan had been a keen participant in this event, having been a leading light of the United Europe Movement founded by Churchill in 1947. He was to be, at the meetings in 1950 and 1951, effectively the leader of the British Conservative delegation.
2. Ernest Bevin, the British Foreign Secretary, was taken ill and left before the opening session.
3. All of these except Layton, a Liberal, were members of the Tory delegation.
4. The Korean War had broken out two months earlier.
5. That is the Schuman Plan for a European Coal and Steel Community, founded in 1951, and a precursor of the European Union. Britain was not one of the six powers (Belgium, France, Italy, Luxembourg, the Netherlands and West Germany) that formed the ECSC, but it became an associate in November 1955.

muir, David Fyfe. Long discussion. WSC very gloomy about the
defence situation; he was much depressed by his interview the other
day with Attlee. It seems that to scrape together 3000 men and their
equipment for Korea will take two months! Even then the anti-aircraft
guns can only be obtained by taking some of those now in Lincolnshire
defending the American 'atomic' bombers. What have they done with
the war equipment? It would appear that they have thrown it into
the sea.

Arranged that WSC will speak Wednesday.

A long discussion on our proposals on iron, steel and coal; these
are alternatives to the Monnet proposals.[6] Eccles and I have been at
work on them for some time, but could not get the job done in time
for me to submit to the Shadow Cabinet. However, since Oliver
Lyttelton has approved them, and since I had sent copies before leaving
London to all our leading colleagues, WSC is fairly satisfied. The only
question is whether his name is to be put to them or not. If not, he
will give them a broad paternal blessing in his speech. This problem of
how far we can operate here without precise prior agreement with our
colleagues at home is a permanent and often an acute one. But I am
convinced that the Macmillan–Eccles plan can do nothing but good on
the home front. For it will show that Conservatives are as determined
as anyone else to protect British interests, while willing to cooperate
with Europe on a reasonable basis . . . .

7 August

. . . . The Assembly met at 3pm for formal opening. At 4 the opening
session – also formalities. Finally, the election of a President begins.
WSC *has* nominated Spaak; so have many others. But it is clear very
soon that there is a strong and organised opposition. Senator Kerstens
(Dutch Catholic) opens the attack. Several others follow. Mr McEntee
speaks with horror of revolution. (He and his wife are believed to have
murdered a lot of English loyalists, generally by shooting them in the
back!)[7] But the Irish have become very respectable in their dull old
age.

Churchill wisely spoke, shortly but decisively, for Spaak. His line
was that we really could not, as the European assembly, sit in yearly

6. Basically the Macmillan–Eccles plan differed in being shorn of the supranational
   elements favoured by Monnet and Schuman (see *HMM* vol. 3, pp. 201–4).
7. During the Anglo-Irish conflict in 1919–21.

judgement, without information, on the acts of political leaders in their individual countries since our last meeting. Dalton took same line. Spaak's election duly carried, but with a substantial minority (22 or 23). There is no doubt that his action in Brussels is open to criticism. To lead a mob against a government is, at first sight, hardly a suitable occupation for the head of the European assembly. But Spaak is a man of ability and courage. I judge that he regarded the King's return as a tragedy for Belgium and as likely to have far-reaching results on Europe. The only thing to do was to get rid of the King at once. This he has achieved. It was, at heart, a revolution on the model of 1689, not of 1789 . . . .[8]

The whole mind of the Europeans is concentrated on defence. The Germans are afraid of a German army, which they feel will be strong enough to provoke the Russians without being strong enough to repel them. They would accept to be a contingent, on equal terms, in a European army. Philip and others [are] very critical of the European governments, esp Gt Britain. Many French and others feel that to please us they accepted the 'functional' instead of the 'federal' approach;[9] but HMG have not allowed such functional advance as there has been to be associated with the Council of Europe. Of what use then is all this machinery – Committee of Ministers, Consultative assembly and so forth – if it is by-passed . . . .

8 August
At 11.30 I held a press conference on the 'Macmillan–Eccles' proposals. I spoke for about 15–20 minutes, explaining them in detail. E and I then answered questions. It lasted till 1.15, since there were a large number of questions. I thought it went off well.

We decided *not* to put Churchill's name on the resolution, or indeed on any others. First, as leader of the Conservative party, he ought not to be committed to detail; secondly, in this assembly he shd

---

8. King Léopold III of Belgium had refused to go into exile with his government when Belgium was defeated in May 1940. Eventually deported by the Germans, he returned from Switzerland in July 1950, to be greeted by riots which Spaak's socialists took a leading part in fomenting. Eventually he abdicated in July 1951 in favour of Baudouin.

9. For Macmillan this seems to have meant the dichotomy between the pooling of functions in Europe, which he did favour, and what he was later to refer to dismissively as 'constitution-building'.

keep himself a little aloof from detailed controversy. He will give a general blessing to our plan in his speech which is now to be on Thursday.

Lunch with Mr Dulles (brother of Republican politician) Layton, Sandys and others. Dulles was interesting and helpful.

The debate – a sort of general debate on the message of the Committee of Ministers – began at 3pm and lasted till 5.30. Callaghan (Brit Socialist) opened in an agreeable, ministerial sort of speech. Edelman also spoke – a good speech, almost the exact opposite of what he said last year, critical (by implication) of Ministers, esp of HMG. The debate is clearly going to be on defence of Europe. Altho' according to the Statue this is supposed to be out of order, the Ministers' message, by its reference to Korea, opened up this question. A Philip (French Socialist) made a great oratorical performance, very critical of British reluctance to move forward. His important plan was for a European army, to include a German contingent. It is strange how, abroad as well as at home, what Churchill puts forward one year as a daring paradox, becomes an accepted truism a year later . . . .[10]

After dinner (about 10pm) went to Churchill's villa. He had been entertaining 8 or 9 of the German delegates. A long and vitally important discussion followed till after midnight. It was really rather moving. The Germans behaved with simplicity and dignity. . . . They do *not* want a German army; they would join a European army.

9 August

. . . . The speech of the day was, I think, Reynaud's. He is an absolute master – witty, precise, limpid. We have nothing like it now. Perhaps Asquith was the nearest.

Reynaud repeated his figures of Russian strength.[11] He demanded a Minister of War for Europe – and pointed to the one figure who cd fill the bill – Churchill. But he told the British firmly that they must play a European role or at least not obstruct those countries of Europe which were willing and able to combine their efforts.

Early in the morning Bidault had made a speech on the same general lines. It was not, to my mind, so effective – partly because,

---

10. A reference to Churchill's calls for German contributions to European defence at the Council of Europe in 1949.

11. NATO at this time had twelve divisions with which to confront an estimated eighty-plus Soviet divisions, see *HMM*, vol. 3, p. 333.

having been Prime Minister of France for almost a year since the last assembly, he was open to the counter-criticism 'What did you do about it?'

Perhaps the most important speech was that of the first German to address the assembly – Gerstenmaier (C[hristian].D[emocrat])

While disclaiming any German wish for a German army, he accepted the need for a German contribution to European defence. This is the view of the CDU and other parties of the right and centre. It is not the view, I fear, of the Social Democrats. There is a certain O. Schmidt (a sort of fat edition of Dalton) [and] another rat-faced rascally-looking creature (a kind of German Foot or Crossman) who are Schumacher's stooges.[12] Well, if the Germans won't fight, they will be in no-man's-land; this means they will be 'atom-bombed' WSC practically told them this last night.

Lunched with Bill *Donovan*, that ubiquitous and remarkable character who ran OSS[13] and (so far as I can see) is still a sort of unofficial American observer in many parts of the world. He had just been in Asia. The Americans are feeling rather lonely. The fact is, that they are for the first time experiencing the burdens of world responsibility. Being unaccustomed to reverses, they are irritable and impatient. They have conveniently forgotten incidents like Greece, where we fought the Communist revolution of 1944 and they were neutral. They are also beginning to regret all they did to help break up the British Empire in Asia, and their abandonment of the Dutch . . . .[14]

At 10pm went to Churchill's villa . . . . He will *not* speak till Friday. He will move a special emergency resolution, demanding a European army, with contingents from all the member states. He has re-written (in part) his speech with this in view. David Maxwell-Fyfe, Sandys and I went through it and discussed also the terms of the resolution. I think it is really 'out of order' – but Spaak is no hidebound Speaker. He makes the rules as he goes along. (Hence the importance of WSC's support of Spaak the first day) Poor Campion (ex clerk of H of Commons) was dreadfully shocked by this last year. He is still affectionately remembered here under the nickname of

---

12. Michael Foot and Richard Crossman were leading left-wing MPs.
13. Created in June 1942, the Office of Strategic Services functioned as the principal US intelligence organization in the Second World War.
14. After the Second World War left-wing nationalists ejected the colonial power from the Dutch East Indies, which became independent as Indonesia in 1949.

'M. *Pas en Angleterre*!'[15] But in a young and developing constitution like this, Spaak's method is the right one. In any case, we have practically killed our Parliament by a procedure which has effectively throttled the private member . . . .

10 August

. . . . In the afternoon, Schuman made his 'explanation' or 'exposé' of his plan . . . .

He did not really explain the details of his plan, only the 'mystique'. Monnet seems to have dominated him, so far as the actual proposals are concerned. Incidently, I had a long, argumentative, but friendly letter from Monnet.[16] M Schuman made no reference, direct or indirect, to the British Govt or to the Macmillan–Eccles proposals. This was generally regarded as a 'snub'. I am not so sure.

I had a pleasant talk with him in the lobby. 'You have held out your hand. Perhaps one day we shall be able to take it'.

I cannot help thinking that there is a great possibility that one or both of two things may happen. When the Govts (esp Holland and Belgium) get the Monnet proposals, which are still up before the experts only, they will shrink from some aspects of the plan. Secondly, when the French parl and people realise that it means going in *without* Britain, they may shrink from handing over their rather weak and largely obsolescent industry to German control. For, in a few years, that is what it will mean. In any case, I feel sure we shall have done no harm, either at home or abroad, by putting forward our proposals . . . .

11 August

The session opened quietly at 10.30. Churchill spoke – for about 25 minutes – at 11.30, and moved his resolution. The speech was impassioned, both in manner and matter. The little touches of humour found their mark, altho' the technique of speaking to an audience the greater part of which is listening to an indifferent translation through earphones is not an easy one. It is really more like a broadcast than a speech. But then the trouble is that WSC's broadcasts *are* speeches.

. . . . The debate lasted with the usual interval for luncheon and

---

15. 'Mr Not in England'.
16. Macmillan had worked closely with Jean Monnet, one of the principal architects of the Schuman Plan, when he was Minister Resident in North West Africa in 1943.

other adjournments for 'lobbying' until about 9pm. Throughout the day there was a great conflict of view as to whether Churchill would carry the day.[17] The French wd run out, torn by internal dissensions. The Germans would run out, for similar reasons. All the Scandinavians would be hostile. The British Socialists would also be opposed. These reasons and these continual changes of front are part of the interest of this assembly. Since there are no parties (at least no international parties, except the Socialists, and even here many stresses) no whip, no Government, and no set points of view, the argument itself has weight and the balance of arguments swings backwards and forwards (I imagine that a seventeenth or eighteenth century House of Commons was more like this). Everyone listens to nearly all the speeches (This to me is *very* strange). No one is quite sure what turn the debate will take . . . .

Finally, after many points of order and objections (usually by Mr Mitchison KC of the British Socialists) and many 'explications de vote' (which gave the Irish, including de Valera [a chance] to talk about partition and Carlo Schmid to produce a new argument for abstention – viz, the occupation status in Germany) [the vote was held]. As far as I cd see, Dalton and Callaghan abstained (on the ground of ministerial propriety but were favourably disposed); Glenvil Hall voted against. The Irish were against or abstentionist. When the list is published on Monday, a full analysis will be possible.

> *Irish* – Against
> *Brit Socialists* – 2 For (Mackay: Edelman), 1 Against (Glenvil Hall), 6 Abstentions (Dalton and Co)
> *Germany* – 11 For (C.D.U. etc), 7 Abstentions (S.D.)
> *Swedes* – Abstained (owing to Sweden not being in Atlantic Pact)
> *Norwegian* – For: Smister Ingelhartsen, Abstention: Rest
> *Icelanders* – For: One, Abstention: Two

The vote was taken by calling the roll. It was quite a thrilling experience. It ended up as follows

> For the motion 89
> Against   5
> Abstentions   27

---

17. In calling for a European army.

The fact that all the French and a great number of the Germans voted in favour was the true significance of the vote.

I went back and dined with Churchill who was *very* pleased and *very* excited. Since the whole object of the united Europe movement has been to get the reconciliation of France and Germany, he has a right to be pleased. No one but he in Europe could have brought about this result. Without his immense personal prestige, which he has thrown quite recklessly into this campaign, it could not have been achieved. Bed just after midnight . . . .

15 August

The news that Parl is to be recalled on Sept 12th is improved by news of Churchill's demand for an earlier meeting. Another 3 weeks here is a dreadful thought! . . . .

16 August

Telephoned Dorothy in the morning and heard good account of Carol and the baby.[18]

Spaak and others are very keen to finish at the end of next week.

This morning's debate was on the Convention of Human Rights, which Maxwell-Fyfe carried through with his usual efficiency and charm.

In the afternoon, Dalton and full employment. It was rather a flop as a demonstration, because everyone more or less agreed.[19] Boothby made a good speech, in familiar Keynesian terms. But he also pleaded for the Empire and Europe to work together under sterling etc . . . .

All day, in the intervals of the various meetings and sessions, a buzz of excitement about 'the European Army'. Duncan Sandys has got himself appointed 'rapporteur' of a sub-committee of the General Affairs Ctee to consider the structure – European minister of defence etc. Naturally, he has had a row with Callaghan, Socialist Civil Lord of Admiralty. The question of the right of the Assembly or its Ctees to discuss this question has naturally been raised by Callaghan. Sandys accuses C of giving S's 'projet de travail' to the press. C says S gave it (all work in committee is supposed to be secret!) S did not show it to me and told me and his Conservative colleagues nothing about it.

---

18. Macmillan's daughter Carol Faber had just given birth to her second son.
19. This had been Labour's big idea for this session of the Council. Macmillan clearly thought it rather an empty gesture.

Considering that we had a meeting to discuss this yesterday morning, it was rather cool to hand in a 20 clause 'projet' on his own. He seems very embarrassed, so I imagine he has had private instructions from Churchill. My colleagues are alarmed; the shadow cabinet and the party will be angry; I shall get the blame! (Fortunately, David Fyfe is a tower of strength and loyalty)

At 10pm telephone message for Sandys from Winston. It was taken in my room in hotel, to which Sandys came. It is now quite clear to me (as S has admitted) that Winston has been telling Sandys to 'go ahead' and personally giving him instructions, without informing me. Of course, without cyphers, telegrams, 'repeated' messages and all the machinery which surrounds ministers, this cannot altogether be avoided. It is also part of Winston's impetuosity and fondness for acting through a variety of methods and channels. After discussion with David, I have drafted a telegram to WSC, concealing a protest in a request for instructions and telling him that I am sending copy of telegram to Anthony Eden. This is sure to produce something from both of them! . . . .[20]

18 August

. . . . Telegrams from Winston. It is as I thought. He had been sending messages to Duncan Sandys, not known to me. Now he is rather alarmed at the trouble which Sandys has caused and wants to pull back. Like all these minor rows, it will die out if allowed to do so; but I do not want tiresome repercussions. It is clear to me Anthony (who was in London yesterday with Winston) will have been able to play a moderating role . . . .

19 August

. . . . [T]he problems that I have to solve remain two.

First, how to see that Duncan Sandys neither makes a disgraceful retreat from his motion on European army organisation nor a fool-hardy advance. He came to see me. He was penitent and very pleasant; but he is as full of 'projets' as old Monnet himself. He pulls them out of his pocket, written on the backs of envelopes, one after another . . . .

Second how to steer the Schuman plan debate to an agreeable finish when it comes 'out of committee'. The French, dominating the Economic Committee, have put down a resolution which we cannot

---

20. Given Eden's well-known coolness towards the European idea.

accept. I have arranged with Eccles to put down an amendment which gives the guts of the 'Macmillan–Eccles contre-projet' (as it is now termed) Bidault, Maurice Schumann and co are pained. But we will have it on the paper for a bit. If by chance the Dutch and the Belgians support it, the way will be open for a real compromise resolution, which may lead to real results. No hurry about this till Tuesday or Wednesday.

21 August

Introduced a deputation of the representatives of Central and European [sic – Eastern] group of European movement to President Spaak.[21] We had leading representatives of countries 'behind the iron curtain'. It was arranged that 3 speakers should put the case. Those chosen were M Auer (Hungary) Count Razcynski (Poland) M Ripka (Czechoslovakia) There also spoke Senator Pezet (France), one of our vice-Presidents. Spaak made a very good impression and handled the deputation with sympathy and good sense. I think the two resolutions which I proposed about exiles and refugees will probably be formally received by the committee to which they have been sent, and that something will be done in this direction. On the wider aspects of our work, something was said and I hope we may be able to organise the proposed conference next year. It is anyway always worth reminding ourselves (and the public) that (including the 3 Baltic States) there are still 9 countries in Central and Eastern Europe under Totalitarian rule. (Yugoslavia is of course in a peculiar position, but I have had to accept Yug. representatives) . . . .

3pm. Press conference for my C and E Europeans . . . .

When I came out of the Press Conference, I found the usual row had blown up about something new. It seems that, without telling Eccles, Reynaud had arranged a meeting of the Economic Committee for this afternoon. E had gone away for a visit, believing there would be no meeting till tomorrow. As a result, the Committee unanimously passed a resolution about the Schuman plan. E (had he been there) would have announced that we did not ask for any detailed consideration of the Macmillan–Eccles proposals. We were satisfied with having made our proposals public and the sympathetic reception which

---

21. Macmillan had played a leading role in the creation of this group, drawn from countries not eligible to join the Council of Europe, with which he was nevertheless anxious to keep open lines of communication.

they had received in many quarters. But the press (encouraged by some French politicians and some British Socialists) were led to believe that there was a sudden retreat on our part. I did my best to put the matter right and hope I succeeded. It was best to treat it rather lightly. Some of my colleagues are not so prudent. However, it's really rather a bore. But I cannot act as nurse to them all, as well as being leader and whip . . . .

22 August

. . . . 1pm. Luncheon for the C and E Europeans . . . . A very successful party, with few but good speeches – esp Spaak and Reynaud. I presided – in French!

The 'Eccles' row is in full swing. We have a *terribly* bad press. 'Tories run away' etc etc in the London press. I was able to get the *Times* and *Daily Mail* right; all the rest, including the *D.T.* are either hostile or puzzled. We must think of some way to get back . . . .

23 August

Heat grows worse and worse; all day it grew in intensity – I have a streaming cold, a high temperature and a sore throat . . . . [M]eeting of Conservatives, at office at 9am to try and find a way around our many difficulties, esp in relation to Schuman plan. The general view is in favour of an amendment to the Economic Ctee's resolution . . . .

24 August

. . . . We have put our Schuman resolution on the paper. I think it is well drawn.

'That a renewed effort should be made forthwith by all the Governments concerned to find a basis for an agreement which will enable all the principal coal and steel producing countries of Europe to participate fully in the scheme, and stresses the importance of bringing this, like other functional schemes, within the framework of the Council of Europe' . . . .

25 August

I am afraid that the 'Eccles' row has flared up again. It was just dying down and could have been forgotten altogether if we did work in the second debates, when he revived the whole thing by a *most foolish* interview – published in the Continental *Daily Mail*, *New York Herald Tribune*, local French press, and I suppose English dailies. He accused

Reynaud of 'tricking him'; the French generally of having 'deceived him'; and so on. This is to excuse his absence from the Economic Ctee on Monday. He added some most astounding words about Reynaud, saying that he did this because he was angry at not having been asked to the same aristocratic French society party to which they (the Eccles family) had been invited. Nothing cd have been worse or in worse taste.

This agreeable news was broken to me by the Brigadier [Blunt], with that almost sadistic delight in bad news which this charming officer (with many other remarkable qualities) seems to have. Notionally, my line is to know nothing about all this. 'I do not read the newspapers etc etc'. Conservative luncheon party at 1pm (the last, I trust) at which the guests included Parri (one of the Prime Ministers of my Italian Governments) and a fine man with a good 'resistance' record; Carlo Schmid (who seemed very pleased and behaved well); Aiken (the Irish gun man, who is said to have preferred shooting English officers and their wives when in bed in the hotel or billet) the Birkenheads, – and the Eccles! . . . .

3.30–6.45. Economic debate (report from Commission begins). The Schuman plan put off till tomorrow – a great relief. Nothing very important. The British Socialist much vaunted resolution comes back from the committee, firmed and improved. It was debated in a half full assembly, and even Dalton could not boom it or himself into any importance.

I made a very short (and a little teasing speech) congratulating Dalton; reminding him of the great progress made in monetary policy since the days which he and I remembered when the classical theory imposed itself on all parties; dominated even such minds as Churchill and Snowden; when he and I voted for [a] return to [the] Gold Standard.[22] I added a tribute to the memory of Maynard Keynes. He did not like it at all . . . .

26 August

. . . . After a few preliminaries, Schuman plan debate begins with a speech by A Philip, rapporteur of this part of the Economic report. He

---

22. In 1925, when Churchill was Chancellor and Philip Snowden the Shadow Chancellor. The Gold Standard pegged currencies to a fixed value of gold, and was believed to be a self-adjusting regulator of international trade. Britain finally abandoned it in September 1931.

is obviously in a mood of anger against the British as a whole. Being a simple soul, he does not conceal this . . . .

I moved our amendment in a speech, to which I had devoted much care, immediately after Philip.

I sensed the interest – even drama – of the occasion and the settling down of the audience, both in the assembly and galleries, to what was clearly an 'occasion'.

Fortunately, my voice had partially recovered, with the help of much gargling through the night, and lasted throughout the 20 minutes (with a few strange croaks!) The speech was obviously a success. The lighter passages were well received. The argument (at one point necessarily rather complicated) was followed with attention. When I sat down, dripping with perspiration (it is a real Turkish bath day) I felt I had succeeded in spite of the double disadvantage – first, the general continental anger at the British attitude on Schuman; second, the temporary resentment caused by 'l'affair Eccles'.

I was fortunate in being followed by a Durham miner (called Blyton) He made the usual attack on the years 1922–39; and a lot of foolish and untrue statements about Churchill and the Tory party. A good speech for a miner's gala. This, I cd see, began to win us support.

After one or [more] speeches of no great weight except Layton's – on our side – Spaak adjourned the debate, taking some other business (procedure etc) before lunch. Of course he did this benevolently. The interval was well used. Duncan Sandys (who has really been splendid on all this and much improved since his own little trouble earlier) got hold of Reynaud, Philip, Maurice Schumann. It took 20 minutes, in the bar, to do the deal. But it was not easy. R (who is not a good fellow or friend) was very stiff at first and very hostile; Philip (after a lot of bombast) came round; M Schumann (a really good and loyal friend) arrived at the right moment.

I had to put on a bit of an act. R kept saying 'Why do you want this amendment? You know your govt will *not* renew or enter talks. The agreement will be signed in a few weeks. . . . etc etc' (Of course, this revealed the real French anxiety. They know that great difficulties and doubts about Monnet's plan are developing everywhere)

I had to say 'Well – it suits us. I want it. I think after what Churchill has done for you all I have a right to ask it'. (Very stiff and formal!) Then M. S. [Maurice Schumann] said 'Yes; and Macmillan has a right to ask it in his own name. He had done more for France than any man, even including Churchill'.

Then we did the deal for which I had prepared. The amendment had two parts. To the first I attached great importance – for it was really the words we used in our motion in the House of Commons, 'Britain should be there. There should be talks with Britain present'.

The second part was about 'within the structure of the Council of Europe'. I knew they would confuse this expression with the veto of the Committee of Ministers.[23] I abandoned this part; they agreed to recommend acceptance of the amendment, without this phrase.

After luncheon, saw *Spaak*, told him of the arrangement. He approved and wd facilitate.

My only fear was too long a delay and fresh continental propaganda, based on the anti-British prejudice. Against this, a little more time would have enabled us to put some devoted friends among Italians, etc.

Eccles spoke quietly and well. I think he was right to do so. Being chastened, he was more effective than I have ever heard him.

Mackay made a speech attacking everyone (except himself) with indiscriminate vigour. The Socialists (British) lay low, smiling and contented. One or two more speeches; all against our amendment. The British Conservatives would not only be decisively beaten, they would be humiliated. They would get no votes except their own. The Doctor's satanic face glowed with Daltonic gloatings and grinning. He was clearly 'taking the bow'.

Then Reynaud got up. It was really beautifully done. He argued the general case for Schuman; he abandoned no position; yet – with a most handsome tribute to me – if we would help him over part of his difficulty, he would help us. The deal was not only done, but carried out.

Spaak played up well. No more talk. Voting.

In spite of a certain confusion (due to many not quite understanding the position) we got a good result. 66 for; 19 against; 19 abstentions.

After that, more excitement and confusion. The British Socialists had announced their intention (with much sanctimonious righteousness) of voting for the two 'recommendations' of the Economic committee. Now was added the third (the Macmillan amendment) What were they to do on the 'ensemble' – that is, when the whole resolution, now including three parts was put. Usual result, when they have no

---

23. It was interpreted as meaning Britain wanted a veto.

whip to rely on, and sitting in different parts, can only rely on Dalton's gestures. Some voted no; others abstained. The whole was carried, with 32 abstentions.

A complete, dramatic, and to Dalton and his friends baffling reversal of the whole position. Instead of Macmillan's humiliation, Macmillan's triumph. I had a press conference and BBC conference immediately after the division. Of course, I know that all this is very small beer and no one at home takes the slightest interest, but it is rather fun!

I heard a curious piece of news from the Havas agency man.[24] 'The French Govt told them that all the efforts of the British Conservatives were to be played up as far as possible' (these instructions from Guy Mollet – Minister of State – French Socialist) The Monnet negotiations are *not* going well, beneath the surface. The French may want alternative proposals to save their face! . . . .

28 August

A most interesting day. The debate – on a series of resolutions – put forward by the General Affairs Ctee – in reality turned into a debate on the 'Federal' versus the 'Functional' approach. It even changed, as it proceeded, into the real question 'United Europe' *with Britain*, on a loose basis of cooperation; or 'United Europe', *without Britain* (and probably Scandinavia and the Low Countries as well).

. . . . The British Socialists took no part in the main debate (except Federalist Mackay) but sulked and abstained or voted against any move, however modest. The speech of the day came from *Guy Mollet* (French Socialist) He made a very effective and very courageous speech, and I am sure represented the governing opinion in France. 'As a European, as a Socialist, as a Frenchman' he cried 'I will not take any step to split Europe still further'. Of course, this means that the French are beginning to see that to federate with Germany and Italy would be to put France, in due course, under German control. . . . *Bidault* defended the middle position, but with a good deal less fervour than *Mollet*. M.R.P. is very 'United Europe' minded; some are federalist. I got the impression that he was cannily enjoying the break-up of the French Socialist party . . . .

The general impression at the end of the day was that the moderate party had triumphed; that France, when it comes to the point, will not

---

24. The French news agency.

go on without Britain; that all this may lead to a new version of the Schuman plan and other functional schemes, in order to ensure that Britain is associated with France.

What an opportunity for British diplomacy, if it existed!

29 August

A quiet morning; packing, shopping, bill paying etc. And many visits for Continental friends to say 'au revoir'.

Left 3.30, arriving in England (by aeroplane) about 6.30 . . . . Took home a large bag of papers and finished them about 1am.

It is difficult to summarise the impression which S[trasbourg] has made this year. The Assembly was more mature; debate was keener and pressed harder. Last year we were all very polite (except, of course, the British. But even they mainly insulted each other) This year we have grown into a parliament. The British insult everyone equally. Dalton was the worst offender; on our side Eccles is a good 'runner up'.

The debates are more real and more urgent. That is due to two causes – the arrival of 18 Germans and the increasing Russian pressure. Fear, if not quite panic, dominates Europe today.

31 August – 6 September

A very happy holiday at Bolton Abbey.[25] I arrived on Wednesday night, absolutely exhausted. Shot Thursday and Friday; stayed in bed Saturday and Sunday; shot Monday, Tuesday and Wednesday . . . .

12 September

The Prime Minister opened the debate in his usual manner[26] – precise, cold, correct – but with a certain dignity. *The Times* likes this sort of thing because it reminds them of Chamberlain.[27] The weakness is the utter lack of leadership. 'We have done all that is expected of us'; 'We are doing all that our allies have asked'; 'we are doing as much as anyone else'; 'we were asked by the Americans to do so-and-so, and

---

25. One of the estates of Macmillan's brother-in-law, the Duke of Devonshire, where Macmillan had regularly shot since the 1920s.
26. Parliament had been specially recalled to debate Korea.
27. Prime Minister 1937–40. Macmillan had opposed his pro-appeasement policies, not least the surrender of the Sudetenland to the Nazis in the 1938 Munich Agreement.

we responded'. It is rather an uninspiring attitude for the Prime Minister of Great Britain. Sometimes when one shuts one's eyes, one believes oneself back in 1937–1939. The responsible Socialists – sound and trusted men – are put up to make the same sort of speeches which respectable Conservatives used to mouth. Whiteley follows Margesson.[28]

Winston was good – not supreme. His passage on the respective functions of a Government and an opposition was very good indeed – will become the '*locus classicus*'[29] . . . .

15 September

. . . . All this week there has been the usual routine at the office[30] and the usual problems. Production gets no easier. We have some big books competing – the reprint of Feiling, Harrod's *Life of Keynes*, Rowse's *England and Elizabeth*, and others. We have also the problem of the future of the American business, which has meant long conferences, including our legal director, John Archibald. We have been offered a price for all our shares, which (having regard to devaluation)[31] means a lot in pounds, but is really too low a price to be attractive. If Maurice [Macmillan] intends to go seriously into English politics, however, there is a strong argument for getting some security for the family by reducing our commitments in publishing. As I have spent much of my life in obtaining for Macmillan & Co (London) the controlling interest in The Macmillan Co (New York) I should not like to see the shares sold at too low a price.

Some of the papers today believe that whatever the result of Tuesday's division the Government will dissolve in the autumn. It seems difficult to go on very long, with every important vote doubtful and with the strain involved on ministers and members.[32] Government circles are said to be confident of a majority in the autumn. They argue that steel nationalisation pleases the Socialists (as some compensation for rearmament and the two years conscription) and that the country

---

28. Whiteley was then the government Chief Whip, Margesson his predecessor in the Chamberlain government of 1937–40.
29. 'The classic place or example'.
30. Macmillan & Co., the family publishing firm.
31. In 1949 sterling was devalued from a parity of \$4.03 to \$2.80 to the pound.
32. This was following the February 1950 general election, in which the Labour government's majority had been reduced to six.

is not interested in steel. They can still point to full employment and high wages, while the rearmament programme (not having really started) does not yet impinge upon the welfare state.

There certainly does not seem (from our reports) to be any substantial change in our favour. If the Korean war is ended favourably (which seems now not impossible)[33] the Govt will say 'see how well Attlee has managed things! With Churchill you wd have been at war with Russia' . . . .

19 September

The Iron and Steel Debate. Winston opened in a very adroit, and rather unexpected speech. It clearly took the Government aback. For instead of – or, at least, in addition to – the slogging attack which everyone was looking for, he made a well-argued and constructive proposal for an agreed settlement in order to preserve national unity. His suggestion was based on a recent pronouncement by the T.U.C. on the general problem of nationalisation. He also had the authority of the Steel-Masters (Iron and Steel Federation) It was this. To enlarge on the statutory powers of the Iron and Steel Board, which has so successfully presided over the broad planning of the industry. The interval (a year if required) could be used for this negotiation.

Morrison turned this down flat. His speech was successful in rousing the spirits of his party. It was a very poor intellectual perform-ance. Anthony Eden wound up admirably for us; Strauss effectively, though rather ignobly, for them.

Rather a sad day. A lot of party and class feeling was displayed. Perhaps the Socialists felt they must make up for their good behaviour in swallowing national service and rearmament last week. At any rate, Aneurin Bevan (who had been conspicuously absent from the Chamber) sat aggressively next to Morrison all through the debate. He was getting his price for last week. (The paper compared him to Madame Defarge)[34]

The vote was 306 to 300 – the usual scenes, cheering and counter-cheering. It seems to many to mean 'no election this year'; but I am not sure.

---

33. Written after MacArthur's successful Inchon landings, and before Chinese intervention.
34. Charles Dickens' famous archetype of the Parisian women who knitted by the guillotine during the French Revolution in his *A Tale of Two Cities*.

21 September

Went to Foreign Office (with Beddington-Behrens) to discuss future of our Central and Eastern European Section. Saw Roger Makins and Patrick Reilly (both served me in the war) A useful talk; I hope they will decide to help us, though I can see that it is a good deal to expect them to swallow, in view of our connection with the European Movement. Will Bevin agree or turn it down in one of his moods of petty jealousy?

26 September

. . . . I spoke at two meetings at the NE Leicester by-election tonight. We have a huge majority against us but no Liberal. There was a 4000 Liberal vote at the General Election; so it will be interesting to see whether the Liberals in the constituencies will follow the lead given the Liberals in the House of Commons. We are trying to make steel an issue; the Socialists are sticking to full employment and the welfare state . . . .

5 October

The Leicester by-election did not go too badly – the Socialist vote reduced by 5000, on a smaller poll and no Liberal standing.[35] It is clear that there is a great difference between the mere non-intervention of a Liberal and the active support of the Liberal party. If we could get this we could win the General Election. Without it, I fear that there are as many places where no Liberal candidates will injure us as there are constituencies where it will help us. I still feel that we ought to try to get a Liberal alliance, and to offer proportional representation in the big cities in exchange. There is a great deal to be said, in principle, for an experiment in P.R. limited to the great cities.[36] It could do no harm and might do good. How else are the great Socialist 'blocs' to be eaten into? It seems absurd that an immense and dangerous change like steel nationalisation should be made effective by a majority of six. A capital levy, of any extent, could be carried in the same way.[37]

---

35. Leicester NE by-election (28 September 1950), Lab: 18,777; C: 13,642.
36. Churchill had made similar suggestions in the *Daily Mail*, 29 May 1935.
37. At the end of the First World War Labour and some radical Liberals had advocated a capital levy on property worth over £5,000 to try to reduce the National Debt, a proposal rapidly dropped during the recession of the early 1920s.

Ought we not to reconsider the old arguments against P.R. Do we want a 'strong' Govt, if this means a strong Socialist Govt, doing things which can never be undone . . . .

The Margate Conference of the Socialist party seems to have passed off without much excitement. Mr Bevan heads the poll for the executive. Mr Noel-Baker is not elected. These are signs not to be disregarded.

On wages, prices, costs etc a good deal of confusion seemed to exist. The only thing clear was the plan to 'soak the rich' to pay for rearmament. Even Morrison had to accept this. Cripps was away – in his clinic. He is said by some to be ill, by others to be mad. Since he has always been both, I expect him to return and resume his post as Chancellor of the Exchequer.

The 'gas strike' (in the now nationalised gas industry) still continues throughout the North Thames area. The Govt has now issued summons against the strikers under some Victorian law. They also have the Navy standing by. But nothing so far has been done to give the people any gas . . . .

10 October

The Navy took over some of the North Thames gas works, and the strike immediately collapsed. In addition, 10 men have been prosecuted and given 1 month's imprisonment for striking 'without leave'. Curiously enough, the Attorney[-General] did *not* proceed under the Victorian act prohibiting 'lightning strikes' in public utilities. He chose to proceed under the war order (still in force) prohibiting strikes in *all* industries until the matter has been reported to the Minister of Labour. The object of this was of course to gain time for conciliation.

Nevertheless the order is a very unpopular one in trade union circles. It also raises the question as to how a dispute can be reported to the minister, if the officials of the union refuse to report it. In other words, is any strike, or any withdrawal of labour to be illegal, unless the officials of a particular union approve? This at once raises the question of trade unions in nationalised industries when a Labour Govt is in office. Is not every strike then an unofficial strike – a breach of loyalty and all the rest? So we begin to see that, under Socialism, trade unionism begins to fade and wither away. There is also the sentimental point that a) there have been countless 'unofficial' strikes since the war, or at least 'unreported' strikes and the Order has not in fact been enforced; b) that it is unfair to prosecute 10 men out of 1500 men, even if those 10 are members of the strike committee. It is worth reflecting what the Socialist party wd have said to all this had a Conservative Govt been in power.

Maurice has been selected and adopted as 'prospective candidate' for Lincoln. He and Katie arrived back tonight (Sunday) and came to dinner. They are full of enthusiasm . . . .

11 October

Dorothy and I to Blackpool . . . .[38]

12 October

A very large attendance in the conference hall . . . .

I had to reply to the resolution on Communism. I had prepared it carefully, but got it by heart and so did not have to use (or seem to use my notes) The danger was the amendment, which was directed to Communism at home and suggested repressive measures. But by concentrating on the foreign problem and only slipping in a few deprecatory sentences – such as 'we do not want 18B in peace time'[39] – I had no difficulty in getting the amendment withdrawn. This was the desire of my colleagues also, so they were pleased. I had a very great ovation at the end of my speech. After many years of travelling about the country and speaking in a very large number of constituencies, I am now becoming known to them . . . . Dorothy received good accounts from all sides and I feel much more confident of my position in the party. I gather the press will be good and I was told later that my speech came well across the broadcast. But the party is not the country. It is very difficult to build a national reputation out of office, for the House of Commons debates are no longer followed with the same interest as in old days . . . .

13 October

The morning's session was dominated by the Housing question. It is quite obvious that here is something about which everyone feels quite passionately. The delegates reflect not political but human feelings and

---

38. For the Party conference.
39. Regulation 18B was introduced for the duration of the war in 1939 and introduced various controls, including detention, to prevent any particular person 'acting in any manner prejudicial to the public safety or the defence of the realm'.

in their demand for a target of at least 300,000 houses a year, they were really determined as well as excited.

Ld Woolton handled the situation with great skill. We are now committed to this figure. There will be a lot of criticism from the *Economist* etc. But I am glad. The only way we got anything done at the Ministry of Supply in the war was by setting ourselves what seemed impossible targets and then (in some extraordinary way) reaching or even beating them. Moreover, the delegates seem now to be ready to preach the doctrine of 'priorities' . . . .

14 October
Churchill's speech to the mass meeting was very good, both in matter and manner. He devoted most of the speech to Home affairs – especially Cost of Living and Housing, the two issues which worry the majority of ordinary folk. He accepted the 300,000 as a 'target'. No doubt the Socialists will not fail to point out the difference between a 'minimum' and a 'target'. Nevertheless, I think Housing is the one great popular demand . . . .

The general result of the conference was satisfactory. Indeed it was more than that – it was refreshingly good . . . . But the great problems are of course left as they are. There is no sign of a 'swing' and the great mass of our people are so concentrated on the minor difficulties (or pleasures) of daily life that they find it difficult to think of anything else.

17–20 October
. . . . On Friday 20th, a public meeting at Swansea. A good attendance, over 1000, in the fine Brangwyn Hall. I'm afraid Swansea had to listen to the speech which had already served St Helens and Gravesend. One of the advantages of meagre reports in the national press, is that one can repeat oneself in the provinces . . . .

23–30 October
. . . . Owing to the failure of British diplomacy under the vain and ageing Bevin to play any effective role, and the consequent heavy handling of the affair by the still inexperienced Americans, Franco-German relations have undergone a sudden change for the worse. The Americans first persuaded Bevin – who vowing he would ne'er consent, consented. They then offered the Germans an army of ten divisions (with some kind of defence organisation at HQ) The Germans, having

obtained the international recognition of status which they needed (and the German steel industry being no longer alarmed at the prospect of a buyer's market in steel owing to rearmament) at once began to edge away from the Schuman plan. The French ministry (which is not in a strong Parliamentary or electoral position) at once took fright. They have demanded the final acceptance and implementation of the Schuman plan as a first step. After that (basing themselves on the Strasbourg resolution) a European army under a European minister of defence, fully integrated, with battalions or perhaps 'regiments' as the largest national units. So the fat is in the fire. The great range of committees of Atlantic union and Western union[40] are at work – at all levels. What the end will be, it is hard to foresee. All this comes from Attlee's inertia and Bevin's jealousy. If Britain had taken a lead a year ago, when Churchill first raised the question of Germany's contribution to defence, all these matters might have been handled successfully. Now I am much afraid that we are once more in the old dilemma. Are we to woo Germany or repel her. It is the same problem as was unresolved after the first war, and led inevitably to the second. Here (as much as in Russia) lie the seeds of the third.

31 October
.... I missed Churchill's dinner to his colleagues last night, having a long standing engagement to speak at Kings Lynn .... I stayed the night with Ld Fermoy, who rents one of the King's houses in the park at Sandringham. He gave me a brace of partridges to take home. I have never before had anything to show for a political meeting.

6 November
.... I have been reading Mrs Arbuthnot's diary, which we have just published, edited by the Duke of Wellington and Francis Bamford. Mrs A was an intimate friend of the first Duke and her diary has a real historical importance. But it is not, I think, as wide ranging as Greville is.[41]

---

40. That is, NATO. This defence agreement had been signed the previous year by Belgium, Canada, Denmark, France, Iceland, Luxembourg, the Netherlands, Norway, Portugal, the UK and the USA.
41. Macmillan had also recently been reading Charles Greville's diaries. Greville was a very well-connected commentator who kept a political diary from 1817 to 1860.

The Housing amendment to the King's speech. The great duel, so much advertised in the press, between Churchill and Bevan, did not materialise . . . .

The debate was opened for the Conservatives in a very able speech by a Mr Marples, a professional builder, with great knowledge and skill. This was one of the best speeches heard from a back bencher for a long time . . . .

Aneurin Bevan, rather unexpectedly, rose at 5.30 and spoke for some 50 minutes. His speech, so widely advertised beforehand, proved a 'flop'. It was full of old gibes and bitterness; hatred, malice and all uncharitableness. Naturally, many of his sallies were very well received by Govt supporters, but as the speech continued without any constructive policy or anything to comfort the Socialists, they grew more and more despondent. He pinned himself (and them) to the proposition that 200,000 houses a year was the absolute maximum. He ridiculed any idea of an increase. All this is very good for us and very bad for them – and they know it.

Churchill rose at 8.30 and spoke for ¾ of an hour. It was a masterly performance, not so much in matter as in manner. It was urbane, generous, magnanimous, and full of vigour. Without making very much reference to Bevan, he made him seem a small and petty figure . . . .

Churchill took a considerable risk by taking part himself in the Debate – but the gamble certainly came off . . . .

8 November

We beat the Government by 6 on the question of private members' bills. We proposed a return to the so-called 'Ten Minute rule', which Morrison opposed.[42] This was a welcome, if not decisive, victory and it was quite amazing to see Morrison's disgust. We had only a two line whip and encouraged a lot of pairing.[43] This is really our only hope. We shall never win on the wide-advertised 'three line' occasions . . . .

---

42. A number of the rights of MPs had been surrendered during the emergency of war, one of which was the Ten Minute Rule, which allowed an MP briefly to outline a proposal which, if carried, could then go forward as potential legislation. An amendment to restore the Ten Minute Rule was carried by 235 to 229.
43. Pairing is an arrangement between the government and opposition whips to obviate the need for all MPs to vote in all divisions. In a period of low government majorities and controversial legislation between 1950 and 1955, the withdrawal

11 November
A most lovely day – a perfect autumn day – at home. I have never seen
the woods more beautiful. We had an agreeable day's shooting. We
saw a lot of pheasants and killed about 60 . . . .

13 November
A most deplorable debate on the Council of Europe, and the work of
Strasbourg last August. After much haggling, the Govt agreed to have
the debate in Govt time – the obviously correct and the only dignified
position. The motion was a colourless one 'The House takes note etc
etc . . . . ' Davies, the under-secretary opened with an incoherent and
querulous speech, which will be very badly received throughout
Europe. He was offensive, unimaginative, and pedestrian. Sandys
replied in a very well composed and very well argued speech, particularly good on the relation between the European army and the North
Atlantic union. David Fyfe wound up in a short and sensible speech,
which was well received. I thought throughout the debate the Government side seemed restless. Many of them were obviously dissatisfied
with the tone of their own contributions. The Foreign Secretary wound
up with the worst oration I have ever heard, even from him. The first
fifteen minutes were irrelevant; the rest offensive. The chief purpose of
his remarks seemed to be to damn the whole idea of European
cooperation. He made a violent attack on the European movement,
which he accused of 'sabotage' (the favourite Labour party way of
saying that you disagree) 'Arch-saboteur yourself' growled Churchill.

I cannot imagine a more unfortunate day. It can do nothing but
harm. I do not look forward to my week at Strasbourg! It does seem
to me extraordinary that our Govt should be both negative and rude.
In normal life, if one is unable to agree, one tries to be specially
courteous in the manner of the refusal. Even publishers do not insult
the authors whose mss they decline.

16 November
Left London, 7.30am for Northholt. The aeroplane on which we were
to go to Paris, broke down on the run way. As a result, we all had to
disembark and wait for another. However, it is better to develop a

---

of pairing was periodically used by the opposition to increase pressure on the
government.

defect before starting than later. I seem to be something of a Jonah in the matter of flying.[44]

The result of this delay, was that we missed the noon train from Paris to Strasbourg and had to wait for the 6pm. Arrived in the Maison Rouge, where I found my old suite reserved for me, just after midnight.

On the train were various French friends . . . .

. . . . B[idault] fears a sort of unholy alliance between Reynaud and the federalists and the British Socialists – who will be only too delighted to applaud (in principle) a federal Europe without Britain – unconscious of the fact that it hands Europe on a plate to Germany, and destroys in a day the fruits of our hard-won victory in two wars. It incidentally abandons the policy for which we have stood since the Armada, against Spain, France, and Germany successively. B feels that the important thing is to prevent the Assembly going to extremes, either of despair or anti-British action. This wd be playing into Bevin's hands. In spite of Lord Layton (who is friendly to and deceived by Dalton) this is the dearest wish of HMG. They will try to provoke the Assembly to foolish recrimination and desperate action, in the hope of being able to bring the Council of Europe to an end . . . .

18 November

Attended meeting of the so-called 'standing ctee' (*Commission Permanent*) where I acted as substitute for David Maxwell-Fyfe . . . . The Standing Ctee approved the setting up of a special committee to deal with interests of 'those European nations not represented in the Council of Europe' (i.e. Central and Eastern Europe and Spain and Portugal) This followed the resolution which I had proposed in the Assembly in August . . . .

After long discussion (and a vote) it's decided to invite M Robert Schuman to come and speak to the Assembly on 'the European army'[45]. . . . Of course, he cannot speak to the Assembly without the consent of his colleagues on the Committee of Ministers. The opposition to the idea came from those who argued that the whole debate was 'out of order', as well as from some who felt it wrong to invite the Foreign Minister of a particular country . . . .

---

44. See *WD*, pp. 14f.
45. This followed the French launch on 24 October of the Pleven Plan for what became the European Defence Community idea, a very different one from what Churchill and Macmillan saw as a European army.

Spaak announced at the end of the session that the invitation had been sent to Robert Schuman and accepted by him, subject to the consent of his colleagues. By the public announcement, it is made really difficult for old Bevin to interpose his veto. A clever move!

.... In the new circumstances I think it quite likely that Churchill will wish to come himself. My object all along has been to distract the delegates from their eternal (but barren) exercise of constitution making to practical and urgent affairs. In 1949, we made the inclusion of Germany the central theme. In August 1950 we launched the European army. In November 1950, I want to keep the European [army] as the central subject. If both Schuman and Churchill arrive in Strasbourg to discuss it, this can certainly be done.

19 November

.... Dined with Reynaud .... R continues to urge the creation of 'a European authority with limited functions and real powers'. 'Why, oh why', he keeps repeating, 'did the British vote for this in 1949?' The answer is certainly obscure. I never have understood whether Morrison and Dalton knew what they were doing .... R talks, rather glibly, of federation without England and is sceptical about the so-called 'functional approach'.

20 November

.... The usual committee fights and incidents. Mr Callaghan (Socialist) seems to be behaving with characteristic rudeness and offending the continentals almost as much as Mr Morrison and Dr Dalton. (The Doctor is 'souffrant'[46] and has hardly stirred from his bed) The really serious thing is the swing of opinion in the elections which have taken place in *Hesse* and in *Wurtemburg Baden*. The Communist vote has been much reduced. But the Social Democrats have defeated the Christian Socialists [sic] in a sweep which seems almost a landslide, altho' the poll was low.[47]

This will have a considerable effect on the German representatives here. For the Social Democrats are opposed to 'rearmament' and Dr Adenauer and his followers will no doubt be rather shaken ....

---

46. 'Suffering'.
47. Hesse and Würtemburg-Baden were two of the regions of the newly constituted Federal Republic in West Germany. In referring to 'Christian Socialists' Macmillan probably means the right-wing Christian Democrats.

21 November

. . . . There was an excellent debate today in the Assembly on the Schuman plan. It was opened by Reynaud, in a brilliant and convincing speech. I followed. It was not an easy speech to make, but it seems to have been a success and generally approved. The British Socialists were really rather impressed and took a very friendly line – far different from that adopted in August. Dalton was very moderate, and even expansive. A very good debate. I took great pains with my speech, as one must do here. It is also necessary to speak very slowly, to allow time for the translator. The technique is a peculiar one. In this debate, there was much more spontaneity than in the past. Speakers answered each other, instead of delivering 'set' orations . . . .

The general atmosphere was one of hope, even confidence. The Schuman plan will go on; the British will probably end up by joining, if not as full members, at least as associates. All this is very encouraging, especially after the pessimistic talk which has been current here during the last few days.

22–24 November

Three days debate; two days on the constitutional problems – the reform of the statute – and so forth; one day on the 'European army'. The tendency, so marked in August, for the French to shrink from 'partial federation' which means in effect – France, Italy and Germany – continued to show itself . . . .

Far the most interesting and dramatic day was the third. We began by an address from the French foreign minister, Robert Schuman. This strange, melancholy, quixotic figure, half politician, half priest, gave a characteristic address, well phrased, philosophic, and rather impractical. The European army is clearly not so much to fight the Russians as (like the steel and coal pact) to unite Germans and Frenchmen. It is to be accompanied by all the paraphernalia of the Coal and Steel plan; committees of ministers, parliamentary bodies and all the other 'organs' which the French love so much.

. . . . The important question was how the Germans would vote.

. . . . The German opposition[48] – perhaps naturally – has been taking a strong line against German 'rearmament' or even contribution to an European army, except under certain rather drastic conditions – e.g. guaranteed defence of Germany during rearmament (whatever that

---

48. The Social Democrats (SPD).

may mean) and equality not only of military but of political status. This, of course, means an end to the occupation system; a peace treaty and so on. I personally feel that we shall have to do this, but Churchill did not wish me to go beyond equal military status.

My speech was largely an approach to the Germans. It was rather emotional, and delivered with a great air of authority! It seems to have made a very deep impression. This was not due so much to its merits but to the tremendous, and unassuaged, appetite for some kind of British leadership. Our Government representatives sat silent through-out the whole of this vital debate and 'abstained' from voting at the end. This naturally had a deplorable effect.

. . . . The resolution was carried by a much larger majority than I had thought likely . . . . In the end (I forget the actual figures) the two thirds majority was easily obtained . . . .

25 November

Morning and afternoon at a long and rather unpleasant meeting of the Executive of the European movement. After Spaak had resigned his new position as President of the movement owing to the rudeness and absurdity of the Federalists, he was at last brought back into the chair, and the Federalists resigned instead. This is a very good thing. These people are absurd, conceited and quite impossible to work with.

26 November

I got to Birch Grove[49] about 4pm having travelled by night from Strasbourg to Paris and then on by train and boat (owing to bad flying weather). . . . Just as we sat down to tea, Elizabeth Cavendish rang up to tell us of Eddy Devonshire's tragic and sudden death an hour or two before. This is the most terrible blow to the whole family. It is really impossible to believe – it is so sudden and unexpected. Poor Andrew[50] is in Australia.

Dorothy and I thought that the best thing we could do was to go up to London at once and break the news personally to her mother. This we did, getting to her flat about 8.30pm. The firm old lady seemed rather dazed, and hardly able to take it in. I fear it is a very bad affair from every point of view and means a frightful financial

---

49. Macmillan's Sussex estate. The house itself was let 1939–51, and Macmillan was living in Gosses, another house on the estate.
50. Macmillan's nephew, who now succeeded as Duke of Devonshire.

blow to the estate. In these days, every great nobleman who dies is automatically attainted. 85% of his property is forfeit to the Crown.

27 and 28 November
. . . . It is said that Iraq means to follow Egypt in repudiating her treaty with Britain.[51] This may be followed by Persia becoming troublesome. The Russians might then be tempted to start a drive in the Middle East, where the prize is really a great one – the greatest source of oil supply in the Old World.

Meanwhile, with typically British escapism, the House of Commons is thoroughly enjoying itself discussing whether the Festival of Britain amusement park shd or shd not be open on Sunday afternoons.

29 November
The House of Commons met to hear a speech from the Foreign Secretary which appeared to have been written at least a fortnight before. In spite of the sudden and almost overwhelming Chinese Communist counter-attack, ... Mr Bevin dealt, in rather a leisurely way, with a number of topics, including the problem of holding elections in Korea. It is hard to tell from the published news just how bad the problem is . . . . However, there are perhaps more important problems than Proportional Representation in Korea! . . . .

Anthony Eden followed Bevin. He made a good speech, avoiding every danger, and with a great air of wisdom, frankness, fairness, and authority. His speech was very well received by both sides of the House. He is a man of real parts and courage; but he has a greater grasp of the obvious (as Walter Elliot said to me) than any man in public life.

30 November
A very melancholy day. Dorothy, Maurice and I went to Chatsworth[52] . . . .

. . . . As the coffin was lowered into the grave, the sun was setting

---

51. Egypt had been calling for the renegotiation of the 1936 Treaty governing the British bases on her territory since 1945. Under the treaty British troops, which pulled back to the Canal Zone by 1948, were supposed to vacate Egypt by 1956. Iraq had been a British mandated territory after the First World War until 1932, and there were still British bases in the country.
52. The ancestral home of the Dukes of Devonshire.

behind the hill. I fear the sun has gone down on Chatsworth for a long time – perhaps for ever.

Andrew Hartington[53] is expected back tomorrow. It will be a heavy burden for him, with many difficult and painful decisions. For the wreckage of a great estate means a terrible amount of handicap to many individuals, as well as a set back to industry, agriculture and forestry.

I got back to London in time to hear in the club an account of today's sensational (almost panic) scene in the House of Commons. It appears that President Truman, in his usual Press Conference, was asked about the atom bomb. He said 'it is under consideration'. (This was afterwards explained to mean that it, like everything else, was always under consideration) One wd have thought that Parliamentarians wd have taken this well-worn phrase (or cliché) as a synonym for doing nothing. However, it seems to have thrown the Labour Party into something like panic. A circular letter to the Govt soon obtained over 200 protesting signatures. Finally, at the end of a day unlike anything since Munich, the poor little Prime Minister was bolted, like a rabbit, from his hole and is off to Washington (what a picture and what a contrast from the great Churchill days)[54]

. . . . Meanwhile, the news is very bad from Korea. The vast Chinese armies are pouring in and no one seems to know whether the Anglo-American armies will be able to make a defensive line or not. What is to me almost more alarming is the 'wishful thinking' of our people. No one seems to understand the close alliance between Communist China and Communist Russia. I am very sceptical indeed of the idea that China can be detached by kindness . . . .

6 December

. . . . I lunched today with Hamilton Kerr MP. Sir David Kelly and Brigadier Head MP were the other guests. D. K. is our ambassador in Moscow, at present on leave. He believes that the Russians do not want war if they can achieve their purpose without war. They believe (according to the Marxist Bible) that Capitalism must eventually decay.

---

53. The Marquess of Hartington is the courtesy title of the heir of the Duke of Devonshire.
54. This is somewhat unfair on Attlee, who tried very hard on this trip to obtain a presidential agreement not to use the bomb without prior consultation with his allies.

They are not alarmed by Western rearmament. They may even welcome it as likely to precipitate the collapse of Capitalism, owing to the
economic storms involved. But they are seriously alarmed over the
prospect of German re-armament. They feel this to be in a different
category and may well prefer early war to the prospect of a new
German army. He therefore feels that the interval – say two years –
while Western defence is being built up is very dangerous. It wd be
better, in his view, to take this in stages and not to start German
rearmament until we have a strong enough position *without* the
Germans to make the Russians think twice about war.

He does not think that they are deterred from marching to the
Atlantic ports by the atom bomb. He thinks that they prefer to let
the ripe fruit fall into their mouths. War will only be used if this decay
of Capitalism, which is doctrinally regarded as certain by the orthodox,
is unaccountably delayed.

He therefore believes in playing for time. He regards German
rearmament as a big risk, since the Russians (remembering how nearly
beaten they were) are genuinely frightened of the Germans. The rest of
us they regard as amateurs. The Germans have a professional status.
All this is very disquietening, esp if this advice is having any weight
with H.M.G. I regard it as definitely defeatist. Kelly was anyway
'Munichois'[55] and all this falls into line.

Kelly is of course very opposed to the American eastern policy. He
believes that China is not a satellite country (like the others) but can
even now be detached from Russia if we follow the prudent line . . . .

At the meeting of the 'shadow cabinet' tonight Churchill began
to soliloquise on the crisis. There is no doubt that a powerful case can
be made against the British Government for their laxity and lack of
vision . . . . Thus the close relations between U.S. and U.K. have not
continued, esp during the time when HMG toyed with the 'third force'
idea. Even the Churchill–Roosevelt treaty about the use of the atom
bomb (under which neither power might use it without the agreement
of the other) has been allowed to lapse.[56]

---

55. That is, an appeaser in the 1930s.
56. Not actually a treaty, which the US Congress would have had to ratify, but the
    secret wartime agreement signed in Québec in 1943. This was followed up by
    the equally secret 1944 Hyde Park aide-memoire promising full Anglo-American
    cooperation in atomic energy for military and commercial purposes. Very few in
    the Roosevelt administration were aware of either document.

Meanwhile, here is the dilemma. If we wait for the show-down with Russia, we may well be weaker (relatively) in 3 years than we are now. For the degree (if any) that we have caught up in conventional weapons may be more than balanced by Russia's increased power in unconventional weapons. Should we then hurry on the conference and the show-down now. Peace by ultimatum! Either you agree to our terms, covering the whole field, including Central and Eastern Europe – or we destroy you! . . . .

After the meeting, I was made to agree to become chairman of the party Housing committee. I resisted as much as I could, but was overborne. It really is a great bore, as I am already overworked and since I know absolutely *nothing* of the matter, it will mean a lot of work. But it seems that the party are in revolt against Walter Elliot. This adds one additional complication for me, for we are very old friends.

It seems that Shinwell's extraordinary attack on MacArthur has done him and his party a good deal of harm at home, but has *not* been widely reported in the American press . . . . [T]he truth is that Shinwell was probably right in saying that MacArthur went beyond his instructions.[57] The real gravamen of the charge is, however, not against MacArthur but against HMG (and to some extent the American administration) for having no clearly stated directives and no effective consultation and control, such as the Combined Chiefs of Staff had in the war . . . .

Meanwhile, the retreat continues. It is still uncertain whether strong points can be held in Korea or complete evacuation will become necessary. My 'hunch' is that our troops will hold on somehow to something . . . .

11 December

. . . . WSC and others are terribly alarmed at the prospect of being 'bogged down' in the East while we are so weak in the West. But is not this weakness a curious and paradoxical source of strength? For a Russian attack in the West means an atom bomb right away. Is not the greater danger that of Europe being gradually driven in on herself, as first the Far East and then the Middle East are overrun or so dominated by fear of the Communist powers that all our influence disappears . . . .

---

57. In pushing beyond the 38th parallel in Korea up towards the Chinese border.

13 December

.... The [Foreign Affairs] Committee met in a spirit of some discontent, I thought, with the Opposition front bench. They do not feel that either Churchill or Eden gave a sufficiently clear lead in the last debate. I have been pressing this view on my colleagues and was therefore pleased by the tone of the rank and file. I feel that we have put too much emphasis on the strategic advantage of disengagement in the East. We have not sufficiently emphasised the moral issue – the unprovoked aggression – and so forth. Nor have we given strong enough warnings against an Eastern 'Munich'. Whatever might be the technical advantages of not 'getting bogged down' (as the phrase goes) in Korea, I am sure that a moral defeat would mean the end of the white man's position in the East and that the moral collapse might easily spread to the West.

If Indo China goes, Siam follows. Then Malaya falls. Hong-Kong is of course indefensible in such circumstances. Burma goes next, and Communism may easily seize India. Churchill has put too much emphasis on the purely military needs of Europe. Europe's supremacy in the world largely depends on her position in Africa and Asia.

At 6pm we had a shadow cabinet .... The 'Prof' (Ld Cherwell) observed at some point in tonight's meeting that if the British had not yet succeeded in making an atom bomb, at least they can claim to have taught both the Americans and the Russians how to make it! ....[58]

14 December

.... The debate today was interesting ....

Churchill made a fine speech, and got exactly the balance which was required between the East and the West. His speech was just what I was hoping for. At the end, he put in an appeal to the Govt to drop steel nationalisation. This was the signal for a tremendous coming together of the divided Socialists, who booed and stormed in good style. I am not sure whether Churchill intended this or not. If the

---

58. A reference to both the British participation in the Manhattan Project and to Klaus Fuchs. He was a German physicist who had become a naturalized British subject and had worked on the atomic bomb programme both in England and at Los Alamos, meanwhile regularly supplying the Russians with information. In January 1950 he was arrested in London and sentenced to fourteen years in prison.

object of a speech is to divide the other side or exploit divisions which are showing themselves, it was not adroit. But I think it will encourage many of our supporters in the country, who are perhaps beginning to feel that we are giving almost too much support to the Govt, without the slightest thanks or gratitude in return.

I think that perhaps Churchill's main purpose was to make it clear that if there was to be any talk of coalition, we shd demand that the steel 'take-over' should be shelved . . . .

Anthony Eden wound up the debate with his usual clear, deft and competent speech. Bevin in reply was very dull while he stuck to his text. Occasionally, he improvised, much to the dismay of the Foreign Office representatives in the box. One of his curious revelations was that General MacArthur received his instructions not from any UNO staff organisation, or from any Anglo-American staff organisation, but from the American Chiefs of Staff. We had made representations about our views as to advancing beyond the 'waist'; but they had not been accepted. What a terrible admission of how the British Govt has sunk! We are treated worse than General de Gaulle or exiled governments in the war! . . . .

19 December

. . . . The Brussels meeting seems to have been a success. The Foreign Secretaries of USA, UK, and France have reached a general agreement regarding German rearmament. It remains to be seen what the Germans will now ask in exchange. I am sure the price will be much higher than it would have been when Churchill raised the issue, many months ago . . . .

20 December

Lunched with Massigli at the French Embassy. We were alone. He was very indignant about an article in today's *Herald-Tribune* (by Alsop) in which it is alleged that Winston wants an immediate 'show-down' with Russia, while we still have atomic superiority. The article, very cleverly written, certainly reflects a good deal that I have heard Churchill say in private conversation. (But it shd certainly not be published) Massigli (reflecting extreme French nervosity) was horrified . . . .

. . . . M is still much alarmed about German rearmament and at the heavy price which the Germans will ask. I told him frankly that I thought we ought to have made all these political concessions long ago. But I am sure the French (as after the 1914–18 war) will haggle on every point and repeat all the mistakes which they made before.

.... Above all we must avoid a German '*volunteer*' army. This is what the Weimar republic had to endure. Such an army today wd consist of nothing but officers and non-commissioned officers of the old Nazi army. Within a few years they wd threaten the whole state. If they have a '*conscript*' army (even if only one man in ten is actually called up), it may remain a democratic army, loyal to the regime. There is no doubt at all that nothing has really been settled at Brussels about the 'European army'. There are two quite different conceptions of Western defence. The first regards America as the lynch-pin (as England was in the Coalition against Louis XIV) If, for any reason – either a Russian withdrawal or some kind of so-called agreement or a wave of isolationism or 'Asialationism' in America – the USA shd drop out, then either the whole defence system wd collapse or (worse still) Germany be left in a dominant position. The second conception (disapproved by HMG and ridiculed by Lord Beaverbrook's papers)[59] regards the whole defence force – under General Eisenhower's command – as a field army falling into 3 groups. There wd be an American contingent, a Canadian contingent and the European army. If the first two were to be withdrawn, the third wd remain, a guarantee against the return of German militarism and German military domination of Europe. There are, of course, many who feel that it is unrealistic even to contemplate the dangers of German aggression at any point in near time. But of course Americans and British are (in their different ways) more detached from this problem than the French, who are haunted by it. It would certainly help the French very much if the 'European army' conception was maintained; still more, if some British contingent were joined to it. But I can see the technical and 'logistical' difficulties, which will be urged by the French. At the same time, there are such immense difficulties in any scheme which involves re-building the power of Germany, that bold and imaginative decisions are necessary. My feeling is that these will not be forthcoming.

21 December

Herr Schlange-Schöningen came to see me this morning at 90 Piccadilly[60]. Prussian, protestant, gentleman – and pretty sly. I liked him;

---

59. Principally the *Daily Express*, *Sunday Express* and the London *Evening Standard*.
60. Macmillan's London flat.

for he said some delightfully sincere things. 'The British and Germans – they will fight the Russians. That is so. The rest, the French and others, will run away. But we will not run away'. His home was near Stettin '3000 acres; stolen by Russians; very bad'. He had always been against the Nazis. 'Hitler was very ignoble' (I think he meant by this 'not a gentleman') One of his sons was farming in Brazil (where he had bought land in 1936, foreseeing what Hitler wd do) another was carried off to a prison camp in Siberia and had not been heard of for 2 years . . . .

Christmas

It has been a pleasant Christmas-time at home. Maurice, Katie and my 3 grandsons went to the Harlechs, to Brogyntyn.[61] Carol's family were with us much of each day; Catherine and Julian Amery came down on Boxing Day to stay.

The weather has been quite good – cold, but no rain. I have stayed in bed a good deal and rested. I have read the first 3 volumes of Gibbon[62] and pondered much on the parallel between the fifth century and today.

The King's speech struck a very sombre note.[63] It will have alarmed the people a good deal and rightly so. He will be seen to have more courage than the politicians.

Alan Lascelles (whom I saw on Dec 27th at the Beefsteak Club) said that he felt the monarch could not make the usual genial 'happy Christmas' speech. Something more was expected; if things went worse, he wd at least get the credit for having revealed some of the truth.

He also said that H[is] M[ajesty] was much incensed by the theft of the Scottish Coronation Stone from Westminster Abbey. Lascelles managed to keep the news from him until after the Christmas broadcast was safely over. He wanted to go on the air to appeal for its return!

It seems that silly 'practical jokers' or (more likely) 'Scottish

---

61. The family seat of Lord Harlech, in Oswestry, Shropshire. Maurice Macmillan's wife, Katie, was daughter to the 4th Baron, who had been a colleague of Macmillan on the Conservative benches in the Commons before he succeeded to the title in 1938.
62. Edward Gibbon's *Decline and Fall of the Roman Empire*.
63. The King's Christmas broadcast.

Nationalists' carried out the exploit on Christmas Day (early in the morning). It was brought to London by Edward Ist in 1296. It should have been returned by the English after some treaty or other early in the 14th century, but this clause was not carried out. Lascelles seemed quite incensed at the 'theft', and still more at the Duke of Montrose's approval. I hazarded the opinion that if it were found in Scotland, it would not in fact go back to Westminster. What a strange and delightful interlude in the great world tragedy – a sort of Scottish harlequinade.[64]

---

64. The Stone was taken to Arbroath Abbey by a group of Scottish nationalists. It was returned to Westminster Abbey in time for the 1953 Coronation.

1951

3 January

. . . . The weather continues cold. There has been almost continuous snow and ice since a week before Christmas. The usual result is now upon us – a coal crisis. It will be 1947 all over again, except that I suppose that this time the 'cuts' will be imposed more rapidly. The P.M. assembled the Trade Union leaders of the industry to Downing Street[1] this morning. It is said that he told them that 'Our government' (the government of the working-class by the intelligentsia) will have to resign unless the miners play up. Then they will once more become the victims of the wicked Tories and Capitalists!

I dined with Massigli (at the French Embassy). The only guest was Brisson (Editor of the *Figaro*). . . . A discussion took place on the 'European army' as the conception has emerged from Strasbourg and as it has been presented by M Schuman. I urged with all the strength I cd command that the French Govt shd abandon all the complicated constitution with which the French Foreign Secretary had tried to surround this simple conception. The British wd never accept a Parliamentary control by a sort of sub-committee of the European Assembly. What was important was that a British contingent shd be included in the European Army, even if the greater part of the British contribution was made direct to the Atlantic force. If we were to persuade our people to accept this, the system must be simple and elastic . . . .

Unless Britain plays some part in the European army, I feel sure that France and Germany can never work amicably together. They will always be suspicious of each other. It is the British function to act as the solvent of these ancient fears and hatreds. We have no right to abdicate from this position; if we do, the defence of Western Europe will be mutilated and ineffective . . . .

Massagli said that for the first time for many years, British and French policy on the right attitude towards Russia were in complete harmony. When he had taken the text of the proposed French reply to

---

1. 10 Downing Street is the official London residence of the Prime Minister.

the F.O. William Strang had exclaimed 'But this is almost word for word like our draft' I thought (but did not say) that this sounds rather ominous to me. Is it appeasement? I should be happier if I felt sure about our Govt. There is no doubt immense pressure in the Labour party in favour of a 'sell-out'.[2]

4 January

The Prime Minister, the Foreign Secretary, the Chancellor of the Exchequer, and the Minister of Fuel and Power received the leaders of the Miners Federation yesterday at Downing Street. It is clear that the Government have promised the men more wages. But the trouble is that the Government, and the Miners' leaders are well aware that if the wages go up the output of coal will go down. This tantalising dilemma is typical of socialism in action, where high taxation and shortage of commodities, with rising prices has destroyed all incentive either to earn or to save . . . .

5 January

Lunched with William Bullitt (formerly US ambassador to France 1940) . . . .

His account of conditions in Washington was fantastic. If half of what he said is true, the American administration is as woolly and incompetent as ours . . . .

. . . . I asked him about the British ambassador. He said he made no impact at all. Halifax, without anything like this position of intimacy with the administration, was a fine ambassador and deeply respected. Franks is well liked, but gives the impression that he merely passes on his Government's views. He is not a creative ambassador . . . .

We heard from the Bank of England this morning that they have given their consent to our proposals both for the flotation of the greater part of our American shares and for the reinvestment of the proceeds (if we desire it) in American bonds. This is very satisfactory and marks the end of a long negotiation. It now remains to be seen whether the under-writers will be prepared to go ahead in present conditions . . . .

---

2. The French at the time were very concerned about plans to rearm Germany and about being committed through membership of NATO to anti-communism without sufficient guarantee of French security (see Alan Bullock, *Ernest Bevin: Foreign Secretary 1945–51* (Oxford: Oxford University Press, 1983), p. 760).

13 January

A pleasant little day at home. We got 22 cock pheasants – all very high and very difficult. The Commonwealth Prime Ministers have issued a very woolly and sentimental declaration. I wish they would all talk less about the desire for Peace and do more to ensure it by getting on with our defences . . . .

15 January

Dined with Julius Holmes, formerly of AFHQ, now American Minister in London. The party was to meet General Eisenhower, ... He was more encouraged by the French than he had expected . . . . The Belgians were quite good. The Dutch awful; the Danes frightened. Here there was a good spirit, but much confusion. Of course, this was a very hurried visit and first impression.

Ike has no staff[3] – beyond Al Gruenther (a *very* able man) an ADC and an orderly. He seemed quite ignorant of the Council of Europe and all the arguments that have raged round and about the European army. I don't know how he is going to get political advice. That certainly seems a great gap in his 'set-up'.

16 January

We signed the contract today for the sale to a group of New York underwriters of the shares in Macmillan Co of New York held by Macmillan & Co London. It seems now almost certain that the deal will go through. Per contra, we buy a block of shares in the Canadian company, which will give us 75% of the equity.

It was rather a solemn affair, carried through by telephone to New York and simultaneous signing of the contract in New York and London. I am not yet sure of the precise sum which will be raised, owing to the commission, expenses etc being not exactly fixed . . . .

17 January

. . . . Dined with Woolton. Bob Menzies (Prime Minister of Australia) Holland (Prime Minister of New Zealand) Anthony Eden, David Maxwell Fyfe, Oliver Lyttelton. A very good party and very free talk . . . .

A great part of the evening was taken up with discussing the

---

3. In his position as Supreme Allied Commander, Europe. It was not until February 1951 that SHAPE was set up.

possibility of a Coalition or National Govt and the attitude which the Tory party ought to take. It was generally agreed that we ought at least now to be thinking out our conditions. The steel question of course looms large.

While we were at dinner the news came through of the Chinese refusal to consider the 'cease-fire' offer which UNO had proposed, largely at the suggestion of the British Commonwealth. There was a general sense of relief, for a conference might have proved very dangerous for the Anglo-American alliance.

There was also a general agreement that we shd now concentrate on the campaign and try to hold some part of Korea. There did not seem much point in a resolution at UNO to condemn the Chinese. This would probably only lead to fresh disagreement between the Allies. A little reticence about our policy might keep the Chinese guessing. Menzies gave us an extraordinary, and rather alarming, account of his recent visit to Tokyo and his interviews with Mac-Arthur. The General seems to live in a more and more fantastic atmosphere of royal pomp, surrounded by obsequious 'yes-men'. His political and military plans are not revealed to anyone – least of all, to Washington.

During the evening, we heard the news of the Govt reshuffle. A poor hand cannot really be improved by re-arranging the cards. Poor Isaacs, the present weak and incompetent Minister of Labour, fades into the very suitable portfolio of Minister of Pensions. The surprise is Aneurin Bevan, who succeeds him. There is a certain sardonic humour in Attlee's choice of this man, who defies him so often in language but never in deeds. The Ministry of Health is (rightly, I think) divided into two. The Housing part goes to Dalton. Bevin remains; but even so, I prefer this vain and incompetent old man to the 'smart-alecs' who might succeed him like Hartley Shawcross.

At the same time, the account which Menzies and Holland gave of Bevin's performance at the conference of [Commonwealth] Prime Ministers was terrifying. He 'babbled o' green fields'[4]. But he keeps somehow and mysteriously alive and afloat . . . .

21 January
Have got the 'flu', which is a great bore, as I have a tremendously full week ahead . . . .

---

4. From Shakespeare's *Henry V*, Act II Scene III, of the death of Sir John Falstaff.

22 January

.... There does not seem to be much news. As far as I can see there are 3 ways of dealing with the Chinese reply to the UNO cease-fire proposals

1. To brand China as aggressor; and to threaten economic and military sanctions

2. To brand China as aggressor; but to think again what ought to be done

3. To say that the Chinese reply leaves a loop-hole (however small) for negotiation and to think of a reply on these lines.

The American public fiercely demands 1. The American Govt would like 1. The British Commonwealth (less India) would adopt 2. India, the Arab states etc are for 3.

It is tragic that at such a moment we shd have Attlee and Bevin, and thus be able to exercise very little leadership. Churchill is still painting in Marrakesh!

The remarks which I had made on Saturday night at Bromley, asking not for a national government but for a national policy had a good press – *Observer*, *Times* and *Daily Telegraph*. There may have been others, but we do not get all the papers in Sussex. But the *Daily Express* has a leading article attacking me for having suggested a 'steel compromise'. This, of course, is Max's spite. The terms of the compromise are those which Churchill put forward in the debate in the House. But facts don't worry Max Beaverbrook . . . .

23 January

.... Today's papers have, in a few instances, a paragraph dealing with the purchase of our American shares by the underwriting groups. It seems that the price is about 3 million dollars. It is nice to know this . . . .

24 January

.... Now that the sale of shares is through, one has the natural inclination to argue it all out again and go over the old ground. It is, of course, a wrench and a certain sense of having betrayed a trust. But the American business was only a business, or rather only an investment. It was not, as is M&Co for us, a way of life. We could not direct (for the last 30 to 40 years) its publishing policy. The fact that we gave up trying, coupled with the fact that in the Bretts we found 3 generations of able and loyal men, whose interests (since we gave them large amounts of shares) were [the] same as ours, resulted in the growth of the American company from a small depot to sell English books to a large mature business to manufacture and sell American books. Moreover, we are entirely in the hands of George Brett and his successors. If he were to die, it would be difficult to find the right man. If we had to make a forced sale of our shares – either because of such an event, or to raise funds for British death duties, we should be in a very poor position and the shares would have a low value. By this arrangement, the pressure to buy is American; we are not particularly keen sellers; we sell on something like a 5%–7½% basis; and we sell at a time when, if we convert into sterling, we get a 40% bonus. Maurice, because of his health, his large family, his political ambitions and so forth, will find it quite enough to manage the English company. He could not be responsible for the American as well. Curiously enough, altho' the American company has shewn good profits, the margin of profit is small – only about 5%. Bad – or even less good – management, coupled with bad luck and the inevitably high American overheads, can easily turn that into a loss. Writing from my bed at Gosses (Birch Grove) I have not the figures by me. But the result of the whole transaction will be that M&Co will retain 5000 advisory shares in the American company, selling just over 150,000 shares. My father's 12,000 shares (which are in trust) will remain – also various blocks in some settlements of Uncle Fred. I think the English shareholders could still marshal about 20–25,000 shares out of the 287,000. If the flotation is highly successful, and a large number of small buyers get a large number of small blocks of shares, we may still – in fact – dominate the position, if we should wish to do so!

Of course, the broad consideration which makes this change desirable is of wider than purely family or personal interest. Before 1914, and even before 1939, American public opinion saw nothing unusual, and certainly nothing improper, in a big American manufacturer, wholesaler, or retailer being partly or wholly English-owned. After all, most of the public utilities – harbours, docks, railways, etc of America were built by British investors. But when the relation between the two countries was changed – partially by the first and wholly by the second war – an English connection became a handicap, instead of an advantage. For instance, a rival publisher in a text book adoption territory could argue – 'Why should we make loans to the Limeys and then let them get the profits of sales of books to American schools'.

'Why should you give American money to these shysters twice over'. Technically, the M&Co of New York, being British owned (or controlled) could not share in ECA or similar orders of the American Govt or its agencies. All this pressure was beginning to tell on George Brett. Instead of his father's position, which was the proud associate of a great English firm, he was injured not benefited by the connection. He was tied up with a lot of Socialist and decadent, feet-dragging, British partners, sitting on top of him, and (since in decay they had retained, like the Old Turks, their extraordinary subtlety) plotting and scheming to undermine him and the true interests of the United States. (Of course, all this sounds absurd in London or even New York. But translate it to the arena of a great text-book adoption in the South, with perhaps 100 competing publishers. Or think of it in terms of the old accusation about a history series of ours – that George Vth was re-writing history to corrupt the pure minds of the children of the Chicago schools. Anyone who has fought even a British General Election will agree with me. Chinese Slavery, as a cry against Balfour,[5] had far less foundation than these doubts of the loyalties of a British controlled American book publisher operating so widely in the educational field)

25 January

The news is bad. The anti-Communist forces in UNO are allowing themselves to be bamboozled and divided. A lot of subtle oriental finesse is putting Nehru into the position of arbiter. (How strangely differently he sees Kashmir and Korea)[6] The Americans will soon begin to get very angry indeed. The British Govt has almost ceased to function. The P.M. doodles or talks platitudes; the Foreign Secretary has pneumonia; there is no rearmament plan, no economic plan, and now – no coal . . . .

. . . . *The Times* is playing as unpatriotic a role (from the highest motives) as it did in Mr Chamberlain's days. The truth is that they prefer Mr Attlee to Mr Churchill. He is more like dear Mr Chamberlain.

---

5. A reference to the agitation against the use of Chinese indentured labour in the South African mines raised by the Liberals in the 1906 general election. A. J. Balfour was then the Conservative leader.
6. A reference to Nehru's determination to hold on to as much as possible of his native province of Kashmir, divided with Pakistan at the partition of India in 1947, in contrast to his indifference to the post-war partitioning of Korea.

26 January

Got up in afternoon. Although I am rather 'wobbly', the enforced rest has done me good. We don't get any proper time to think nowadays. It is one of the terrible results of 'time-saving' devices – the telegram, radio, telephone, aviation and all the rest. One can only get away from it by being ill.

27 January

The P.M. has made a good speech, accusing the Russians. What a lot they have learned in 5 years! It is queer to think that Smuts accused me (to Churchill) of being too anti-Russian. That was in 1943, after a visit to Algiers. I must say that he made a handsome retraction in 1946 . . . .

31 January

Luncheon party at Italian Embassy . . . . A large party, mostly of politicians. I sat on the ambassador's right; next to me A L Rowse. The chief talk is now openly about whether the Russians will attack Yugoslavia this summer. The ambassador tells me that the Yugoslavs now think this less certain than they had thought some months ago. The Korean affair has made the Russians think a bit. They did not expect any American reaction . . . .

1 February

Colonel 'Monty' Woodhouse came to see me today. He is to do a book for us on 'Resistance' based on his experiences in Greece, where he was the chief British officer in the movement[7]. . . . He is now attached to the Western union planning staff, soon – no doubt – to be transferred to Atlantic Union, under General Eisenhower. This secret work is really planning a possible revival of Special Operations after the Russian conquest of Western Europe.[8] According to W, the present operational plan is that the line of the Rhine wd fall at D+21; the Russians wd reach the channel ports at D+60. The only planning is on

---

7. Macmillan had first met Woodhouse in 1944, not least in his efforts to achieve a settlement in a Greece descending into civil war. See *WD* p. 480 (4 July 1944) and *HMM* II, p. 592.

8. A reference to the Special Operations Executive, charged with encouraging sabotage and resistance throughout Nazi-occupied Europe during the Second World War. 'Western union' refers to the Brussels Pact organization then being subserved in NATO.

this defeatist basis, and of course this is known throughout all the political and military circles in Europe. Hence Europe is completely defeatist.

The plan therefore is 1940 over again, with the far greater danger to this island which must result from modern weapons. The S.O. plan (which the Americans are prepared to back on a very large scale) is the rather hopeless one of getting together resistance groups in occupied Europe with probable great losses and perhaps total destruction of the will and power to resist. For resistance, without a real base, is not an easy thing.

Such a base, says the Colonel, is ready to hand if we will only look for it. It is not in the Pyrenees; it is at the very centre of Europe, comprising every great European country. It is the Alpine massif – Switzerland; Savoy; S Germany; Tyrol and N Italy; and (if the arm of defence can be flung so wide) Yugoslavia and prob Greece. The basis of the armed redoubt (the Germans had something of the idea) would be the strong highland and independent tradition. Frenchmen, Germans, Italians, Austrians, Swiss – and, finally, the Slav peoples of the Balkans. (If the area could be held, it would give a great advantage)

The Russians, ignorant of the science of mountain warfare, wd be frustrated. They could reduce this European fortress. It would be difficult to attack by land; hard to harness by air. It would be supplied by air, from Britain and North Africa . . . . It would be forged on the anvil of heroic but highly skilful resistance. Instead of the futile exiled governments, in Washington and Ottawa, becoming (as time went on) more and more remote from their peoples and more and more quarrelsome and difficult for their hosts to handle, the Government of Europe would actually come into being in this mountain redoubt. Mr Churchill might decide to leave the government of Britain to Mr Eden, in order personally to preside over the government of Europe . . . .

The Colonel developed this theme with gravity and precision. Fantastic as it appears at first sight, he makes it (so lucid and matter of fact is his exposition) appear both obvious and zany. I did venture to ask whether the Swiss would agree; but he did not appear to regard this as a serious difficulty. They would be subjected to a gentle but admiring coercion. On reflection, they would see in this less dangers than in the permanent and final occupation of the whole of Europe by the Communist barbarians.

. . . . A resolution of mild disapproval of China – not for aggression but for assisting aggressors – has finally been passed through UNO.

The Americans seem a little calmer on the surface, altho' I shd guess that there was a deep resentment among both officials and the mass of the people at the crassly stupid way in which HMG has handled this affair. What is amusing, is the rapidity with which the French have 'cashed in'. The Prime Minister (Pleven) has had an immensely successful visit to Washington (in great contrast to Attlee's) and by instructing their delegates at UNO to support the Americans instead of lecturing them, France has gained additional prestige . . . .

9 February (Friday)
This has been a week of quiet activity and excitement in the House of Commons. Churchill led the attack on steel [nationalization], in a speech of remarkable power, knowledge and wit . . . . The Govt (after all the newspaper speculation as to the possible effect of influenza) won by 10 votes; seven Liberals voted with us. The figures were 308 to 298. Every vote (save one) was accounted for. These are really extraordinary figures – such as no one remembers – and indicate the growing strain on all sides. (Even more or less ordinary divisions on the committee stage of a second-rate bill are working out at 450–500 members present) On these 3 line whip occasions there are, of course, no ordinary pairs. Only the dying are paired nowadays! . . . .

The following day (Thursday 8th) we had another 'go' – this time on meat. The Government benches were a great contrast to the previous day. The people do not go into the little shops every week end to buy a piece of steel. But they do grumble every week-end about their minute portion of meat. Harry Crookshank opened with a magnificent Parliamentary performance. Cool, incisive, witty, well-argued, it was a masterpiece. It was by far the best speech he has ever made. I was particularly pleased, because it may make a good deal of difference to his political future . . . . This time the majority fell to 8 (two more Government supporters have fallen ill) . . . . Of course, some may die; but unless those with uncertain seats chose to die, it's no good. There is said to be one dying now; but, with a majority of 20,000, it makes a farce of it. Moreover, those who are older and presumably most likely to collapse under the strain, generally have the safest seats, in mining or similar constituencies . . . .

12 February
Debate on foreign affairs – opened by Eden in a very well balanced and effective speech. He is certainly a most talented and experienced

Parliamentarian. If he never says anything very striking, he is never guilty of a 'gaffe' or even of an indiscretion.

Winston sent for me to 'consult' me about the latest phase of his controversy with Attlee about the 'atomic' agreement made in the war between himself and Roosevelt. As was admitted in a little passage between them in the House the other day, this agreement (which was very favourable to us) was allowed to come to an end a year or two ago. It was, in fact, abrogated by the McMahon Act [in 1946], which Congress passed on the advice, no doubt, of the administration. The Churchill–Roosevelt agreement was secret. It has not been published since. Presumably Congress was not informed of its terms, though possibly of its existence. It was not a binding treaty, but it was a 'gentleman's agreement'. A treaty could not have been made in 1943 without disclosing the secret to Congress. But, of course, our position now is much injured. We have not now the right to equal share in discoveries and developments. (Since the Fuchs case,[9] I imagine the Americans are pretty scared of us) Moreover, we no longer have the protection of the original agreement, by which neither we nor the Americans have the right to use the atom bomb without the agreement of the other. With the American bombers on the East Coast, armed with the atom bomb, and ready to take off at any moment, this is an important point . . . .

25 February
All the grandchildren (except Adam Macmillan and baby Mark Faber) in church this morning. I read the lessons as usual. The children enjoyed Genesis 37 (Joseph and his brethren) . . . . Finished *The Old Curiosity Shop*. I still love Dickens . . . .

1 March
The most absurd storm in a teacup has blown up. In a moment of irritation, Churchill leaned across the table and said to Shinwell 'Oh, shut up. Go and talk to the Italians; that's all you're fit for'. (The new loud-speakers of course pick up and exaggerate these *sotto voce* observations that in old days did not go beyond the first rows of the stalls)

The *Daily Herald* has worked this up into an international drama. Miss Jenny Lee (Mrs Aneurin Bevan) has got 100 socialist signatures

9. See above, p. 38.

to a telegram of national apology to De Gasperi and Sforza; and even the sweet Italian ambassador (Galliatti Scotti) kept ringing me up, asking to see me. I saw him and explained that what had irritated Churchill had been an interview which Shinwell had given to the press attacking the whole idea of German 'rearmament' – which we prefer to call 'German contribution to Western defence'.

Of course, Churchill dealt with the whole thing effectively by issuing a dignified and complete apology. The Italians are absurdly sensitive as a rule, but I thought the Ambassador quite sensible about it . . . .

2 March

We beat the Govt on a private members' resolution by 4 votes. Since this was a very important subject – shortage of raw materials – and the President of the Board of Trade chose to deliver a great speech, this defeat was a blow . . . .

4 March

Left Northolt at 10.30am, with Dr Gordon Lang MP (with whom I am 'paired' for a week) We arrived at Stockholm at about 6pm (with a short stop at Copenhagen).

Our purpose is a short tour of Sweden and Norway on behalf of the European movement. Dr Lang, although a member of the Labour Party, has been joint secretary of United Europe since it began and has suffered a sort of Pauline persecution from Morrison, Dalton & Co . . . .

6 March

. . . . 10.30. Dr Lang and I called upon the Foreign Minister, M. Unden. I had been told something of the character of this statesman both by Retsinger (in a note which he gave me before leaving London) and by the British Ambassador. He is a precise, intelligent, and I have no doubt high-minded radical lawyer (notionally Socialist) of a type reminiscent of many Victorian figures. I should take him to be scrupulously honest, both in public and private affairs. He received us politely, but by no means effusively. I thought the conversation might be difficult. It did not prove so. Mr U began by observing that there had been a good deal of confusion as to what functions should really be entrusted to the Council of Europe. He felt that at any rate it should become responsible for those joint financial and economic efforts which were now being operated by OEEC.[10] This large staff, operating at Paris, but international in character, could well serve and make its reports to the Council of Europe; both to ministers and the assembly.

I asked whether it was not the fact that his Govt favoured such a plan and meant to put it forward. He said, yes. He himself would be going to Paris next week for a meeting of OEEC, to be followed by a meeting of the Committee of Ministers. At the latter meeting, he would propose a committee to study the possibility of fusing OEEC and the Council of Europe. He observed, in passing, that Strasbourg was really a very inconvenient place for ministers. They had not the help of their legations (as in a capital) and not even cyphers for their telegrams.

M Unden seemed much more favourably disposed to the European movement than we had been led to suppose. Naturally, the policy of neutrality is the accepted policy. But, in practice, I shd judge that Unden wd favour any amount of cooperation with other European countries so long as their neutrality was formally respected. He wd avoid, naturally enough, anything that cd be a cause of complaint by the Russians. He expressed the view . . . . that in general the Swedes agreed with the British in their preference for some practical results, by ad hoc methods, over facile but unreal constitution making. So far, he did not reveal anything of his real feelings or fears. I made some remark about the usefulness of the Consultative Assembly in acting as a 'sounding board' for Europe. The great debates on Germany, on the Schuman plan, and (although strictly out of order) on defence have done good and helped to educate public opinion . . . . The Minister agreed to this – more readily than I shd have supposed.

M Unden . . . . thought that the only thing of which the Russians were really afraid was 'German re-armament'. For the first time, therefore, since the war the Western powers had a really good card in their hands. Could they use it to force the Russians step by step to relinquish their hold on Eastern Germany. The withdrawal of the occupying armies, of both sides, must be gradual. Otherwise, there was the danger of a coup to impose Communism. But if it were a slow process, matched by a parallel building of a genuine democratic German government, firmly established, it could perhaps be used by the Western powers to bring about their purpose. The strengthening of Germany would go on all the time. As for Poland and the other satellites, M Unden did not believe that the Russians would give up

---

10. The body established in 1948 to administer Marshall Aid to Western Europe.

their control. Sweden had considerable trade and other contacts with Poland. His impression was that the Russians were tightening their grip. For instance, the military control, following a new purge, was now absolute. We did not actually approach the 'defence' question or the Swedish policy of neutrality. But I felt that M Unden was glad to see the efforts of the Western powers, with American aid, to build up their military strength. His attitude was correct, but by no means unfriendly . . . .

In general, this was more than a courtesy visit. The Minister seemed glad of the opportunity of an informal talk; he was more generally favourable to the European idea than I had been led to expect; he struck us as less pedantic than I had been told he was apt to be. Whether he is a man who has any real 'guts' or 'fire in his belly', I shd doubt. He would always act honourably. Will he ever act boldly?

I am sure that his daily prayer must be not to be put to the test. The interview lasted about 30–40 minutes. We were next taken to see the Prime Minister, M Erlander. I was not so favourably impressed by this gentleman as by his colleague. He did not seem very anxious to discuss [the] foreign situation . . . . He seemed to be more apprehensive of a revived German militarism than M Unden. I reminded him of the fate of the Weimar Republic, and he agreed that we ought not to make the same mistake with the Bonn Republic. M Erlander seemed to me almost hostile (or at least sceptical) about the European movement. He seemed to be more like our Labour isolationists at home than M Unden. He is very Scandinavian, and I shd think rather timid, except upon the platform. He asked a good deal about Dr Dalton, and his attitude to the European question. I do not think we shall get much out of M Erlander . . . .

At 5.30 M Rei (former Prime Minister of Estonia) called for me and took me to a meeting of exiles from the 3 Baltic states, leaders of parties and notabilities of various kinds, living in Stockholm. I explained to them the work and purpose of the Central and Eastern Section of the European movement which I founded. They were very impressive in their calm acceptance of their position. The women spoke bitterly of the Yalta betrayal (not that this had anything to do with the Baltic states) but with this exception they were calm and serious people.[11] I am bound to admit that I find it difficult to imagine conditions in which Russia will evacuate these territories . . . .

---

11. The Yalta conference in February 1945 could be seen as a betrayal through

11 March

[A]rrived England about 4.30. We were refused in London (owing to fog) and had to land at Marston (near Margate)

. . . . I feel pretty doubtful about the Swedes. They are not unnaturally encouraged by their successful neutrality in the past. But many of the most intelligent of them would like to have at least 'staff talks' and some prepared plan if the worst should occur. As long as the present Govt lasts, this will not happen, in my opinion.

12–17 March

This has been a very busy, even hectic week. I returned to find the House of Commons completely out of control, like an unruly class under a weak French master . . . .

Every day there is a row about something – a question of privilege is the favourite Socialist method of provoking trouble; 'prayers' against Government 'orders in council', which come on after 10pm and can be prolonged night after night after night till any hour in the morning are the main weapons in the Conservative armoury.

Interspersed with these less serious matters, a fresh stream of Government follies is poured out – Gambian eggs, another million for the Festival of Britain Fun Fair, and so forth. I do not remember quite such a sense of strain between the parties since the old days of the General Strike and the Trade Disputes Bill.[12]

To add to this confusion, Mr Speaker is clearly breaking up.[13] He has always regarded a late sitting as a sort of personal affront (I don't think that when he was a private member he would have enjoyed them much) and he has always been a weak and insignificant Speaker. He was made Speaker during the war, against the wishes both of Churchill and Eden, by the pressure of the Tory Party. Churchill, who then rode magnificently in the saddle of the state but uneasily in that of the party, gave in. Of course, Gwilym Lloyd George (who was the

---

Western recognition of Soviet predominance in Eastern Europe, though this was no more than a reflection of the military reality at the time.

12. Following the 1926 General Strike the Conservative government in 1927 passed a Trade Disputes and Trades Unions Act outlawing secondary strike action and undermining, through changing the trade union levy, the financial basis of the Labour Party.

13. D. Clifton Brown retired as Speaker of the House of Commons the following year.

alternative) would have been far better. Now Mr Speaker has begun to lose control of the House. His rulings are attacked and argued about and he allows general talk about them to go on, for sometimes half an hour at a time. Late at night, he alternates between weak appeals, and weaker threats . . . .

20 March

More rows; more scenes; more confusion. Mr Ede (he was Leader of the House) is trying to be moderate and conciliatory. This is embarrassing to us, especially as it seems that the country is not reacting well to our new line in Parliamentary opposition. The truth is that the power of Parliament has fallen so low and the people have become so accustomed to regard the power of the Executive as sacrosanct that a form of opposition which some twenty years ago would have been thought mild is now considered as a sort of *'lese-majesté'*[14] . . . .

At the same time, there [has] been today a serious and important debate on the Government's handling of the Egyptian problem: Anthony Eden opened in a very moderate and well-balanced speech. It certainly seems rather feeble to make a new agreement involving large new 'unrequited exports' to Egypt, including a priority for sterling-acquired oil, at a time when Egypt is (contrary to international agreement) closing the canal to our tankers on their way to Haifa.[15] The Chancellor of the Exchequer (Gaitskell) was in a difficulty in replying, since no speaker, on either side of the House, had supported him. His reply was not effective. The Government majority fell to 3 votes . . . .

Good Friday

. . . . I have read *'The Eustace Diamonds'* – which I consider the best Trollope of all . . . .

I have now read quite a good American book (Gail Brightfield) on John Wilson Croker (where like so much American academic writing, it is the material for a book rather than a book) But it certainly produces some most interesting material. It gives quite a different picture to that which casual readers of *Coningsby* or of *Vanity Fair* (where Croker is caricatured and even libelled as Rigby and Newham)

---

14. 'An affront to sovereignty'.
15. To prevent oil supplies reaching Israel.

would have in their mind's eye. One is always astonished at how hard these people write the vast quantities of books, and the millions of words which they write with their own hands. We have become a race of '*flaneurs*'[16] now; we write no letters, only the phone; dictate ill-thought out minutes and memoranda; and employ a mass of secretaries, personal assistants and the like, to do half of what men like the Duke of Wellington would achieve by himself, practically without staff or amanuensis. Croker seems, in his sphere, to have been a second Pepys at the Admiralty; . . . .[17]

Easter Sunday

Church at 8am; very well attended, over 60. Our little parson, Mr Eastham, gets gradually higher and higher. Having some knowledge of liturgy (from old Oxford days and Ronnie Knox and so forth) I am amused to see his slow but steady upward progress! . . . .[18]

Easter Monday

. . . . Lord and Lady Woolton to luncheon. Lord W was in very good form. He described with great humour the difficulty of inducing a Lancashire Conservative association to adopt Sir Arthur Salter as Conservative candidate. They wanted a farmer, who would live in the district. They had to be persuaded to take an economist who lived in London. The committee was brought to London; entertained by Lord W in the Lords and by Churchill in his room in the Commons, given drinks and cigars (which they wd not smoke but took away as keepsakes) and finally agreed. 'But he isn't a tea party, is he?' was the unrepentant view of the women's representative . . . .

31 March

I have had a delightfully lazy week. Late breakfast in bed; long walks; grandchildren to tea; reading quietly in the evening. I had a nice walk

---

16. 'Idlers'.
17. This passage illustrates both Macmillan's passion for nineteenth-century novels (in this case by Disraeli and Thackeray respectively), and for the political history of the late eighteenth and early nineteenth century. Croker was Secretary of the Admiralty 1808–30, an essayist and diarist.
18. Under Knox's influence Macmillan had undergone a similar progress before the First World War, but had not followed Knox in converting to Catholicism. See Alistair Horne, *Macmillan 1894–1956* (London: Macmillan, 1988), pp. 24–34.

which took me to Steynings, and tea with the Caroes on Wednesday (I use the train to start me off and get me back) I have finished M Troyat's immense novel – '*Tant que la terre durera*'[19]. 850 pages of close type, demy octavo. It is certainly very readable and the characters are living. I have started on the sequel (which begins with 1914) '*Le Sac et la Cendre*'[20] . . . .

The Prime Minister gave a 'party' broadcast tonight. Very 'party' it was; and I thought, pretty feeble. There was an attack on Churchill, and the rest was an apology in the Baldwin manner. What a long way from the enthusiasm and fire of Socialism in 1945! The most effective plea was that the Labour Govt have 'planned' full employment, in contrast to the Tory misrule after the First World War. This was reinforced by a long passage about Tory mismanagement after the battle of Waterloo! . . . .

1 April

. . . . All the news from Middle and Far East is gloomy. Persia seems almost in a state of anarchy. India and Pakistan are no nearer a settlement of the Kashmir dispute, and are therefore turned inwards against each other, instead of outwards against Communism. The frontiers are not any longer guarded by British power and prestige. The 'new deal' in Nepal looks like threatening the last remnants of our military strength, by making Gurkha recruitment less secure. When one thinks of the state of the world, the P.M.'s broadcast last night seems very thin – almost puerile . . . .

6 April

Left by air from Heathrow at 8.15am for Brussels. All day at a meeting of ELEC. A most interesting and useful discussion. Tomorrow will be still more important, for we must prepare the precise agenda for the Dominions Conference . . . .

We were given luncheon (20 to 30 in all) at the Automobile Club. Dinner at Baron Boel's house.

Once more, one is ashamed at the wonderful hospitality one receives abroad and the little one can do when foreign friends come to England . . . .

---

19. 'While the Earth Endures'. Sir Olaf Caroe was a former adviser to the Viceroy of India.
20. 'Sackcloth and Ashes'.

7 April

10–1; 3–5.30. Meeting of the Central Council of ELEC. Again most interesting and useful discussion. This is really the only section of the European movement which functions effectively. It consists of serious people; economists, bankers, industrialists, a few good Trade Union leaders, and some serious politicians. But ELEC has always really been run by the economists and bankers and has therefore done some excellent work. The present European Payments Union is based on the ELEC proposals of two years ago.[21] One of the chief items for decision (which occupied most of the afternoon) was the organisation in detail of the Conference between European nations and the Commonwealth which is to take place, partly in London, partly in Brussels, at the end of May. This will be of great importance; for, if successful, it will be a complete answer to those who have argued that Britain's obligations to the Commonwealth and Empire preclude her from a European policy. We hope, by detailed study of the question of trade relations (including Tariffs and Preferences) and of monetary policy (including widening and strengthening of the sterling area) to prove our case that Europe and the Commonwealth should be complementary and mutually supporting in a dollar-dominated world.

Luncheon was given to us all by the Minister of Overseas Trade (in the absence of the Foreign Minister, M Van Zeeland in Paris) This function was held in the Foreign Office, in agreeable and even sumptuous surroundings. Food and wine were consummate. Lady Rhys-Williams, Sir David Waley and I left for airport at 7.45pm (in M Camn's car, which he again put at my disposal) and arrived in London airport about 9.30pm (British time) I got home to Sussex by train from Victoria about midnight. Two tiring, but useful and most interesting days.

The general morale of the people we have met in the last day or two seems higher than last year. The French believe that they will be able to maintain the present Governmental coalition against the Communists and Gaullists, even after the Election. The Belgian constitutional crisis has been more or less surmounted. Italians are pleased with the set-back to Communism. Germans (although full of the usual self-pity and lack of responsibility) are looking forwards not backwards. There is a feeling that perhaps the Russians are not so strong after all.

---

21. See *HMM* III, p. 154.

Against this, in spite of immense arguments about the economic consequences of re-armament, it is difficult to find any evidence of anything serious having been started. Everyone laughs at the NATO organisation, on the supply as well as the service side, as ludicrously top-heavy. 'Never were so few commanded by so many!' Or, as Reynaud has written in the *Figaro* 'We cannot be defended by the staff officers alone, numerous as they are!'

Meanwhile, the acute continental mind is aware of the American weakness and confusion. There is no clear idea of what we are trying to do in Korea or who is in charge. MacArthur is domineering, but at least knows what he wants – which is to engage and defeat Communist China as soon as possible (like Churchill with Bolshevik Russia in 1920) Truman vacillates; Marshall is said to be senile and ineffective. The British Govt, weak and divided, exercise little or no influence on events. Everyone is beginning to contrast the present situation with that during the war, when the Roosevelt–Churchill combination, served by a closely-knit staff, ran the war. Whatever mistakes may have been made then, now seem very small compared with this vast chaos.

Rain and storm still continue. It has rained more or less steadily since Christmas . . . .

10 April

Mr Gaitskell, the new Chancellor of the Exchequer, was a pupil of Dr Dalton. He has imitated his rather pedantic style, tedious exposition of the obvious, weak gestures and irritating smile. But if he is Dalton-esque in manner, he is Crippsian in matter. The [Budget] speech was a success; having all the elements which make a speech successful today. It was like a very good lecture to a Working Man's Club. The broadcast was even better. The Budget itself is, nowadays, not so important as the general economic policy which it has to follow. Owing to the reckless finance and vast muddles of the last few years, there is no fat left. Taxation has been pushed, in time of peace, to the limit. Many taxes (such as those on tobacco and drink) are already subject to the law of diminishing returns. So – 6d more on income tax; 50% instead of 30% on distribution profits; double the purchase tax on motor-cars; 4d more on petrol – and there we are, *en principe*. The inflating gap of £170m is closed! All this assumes

a) that on a national income of £12,000m and a Government expenditure of £4000m the margin can be calculated down to £150m.

b) that these new taxes can raise the additional money without a corresponding (or nearly corresponding) reduction of private saving, whether individual or corporate.

If b) occurs, the whole calculation, so clearly built up before a breathless audience, falls to the ground like a pack of cards.

The real human interest today lies in Mr Bevan's position. He declared a few days ago that 'he would never be a member of a Government which made charges under the National Health Service for a patient'. The Budget proposes that the patient shd pay half the cost of the spectacles and half the cost of the dentures supplied at present gratis. What will Bevan do?

There were strong rumours, after his visit accompanied by Wilson (President of Bd of Trade) to Attlee, that both had resigned. For my part, I feel sure that they will both stay.

11 April
Bevan has definitely resigned. So I was told at noon. Wilson also. If this is true, the Government must fall and a General Election follow . . . .

12 April
The sale of our American shares, the purchase of American bonds with the proceeds; the sale of these bonds; the transfer of the proceeds from the Guaranty Trust to W Coutts & Co – all this is now complete. So M&Co have today £1,200,000 odd in their a/c at Coutts. I went in to see Seymour Egerton (acting for Jasper Ridley) to consider what to do with this money. It is quite a problem. Should we buy gilt-edged (in an inflationary situation) or equities (which are over-taxed) or land (which we don't know how to manage)? . . . .

The Budget has had a good reception on the whole. I think it is really a mood of 'It might have been worse'. Nevertheless, as the new imposts begin to be paid and as prices continue to rise, I think the public will be disillusioned. Bevan has now definitely decided to stay – also Wilson. It is said that Strauss (Minister of Supply) and Freeman (Parl Secy to MofS) were also in the plot. The event will, of course, correspondingly improve Gaitskell's position. It is something to have stood up to Bevan and scored off him . . . .

16 April
Maurice and the boys were playing with what they believed to be a

grass snake. It was quiet and harmless and they took it into the house. Alexander even put it round his neck. They proposed to keep it as a pet. Then suddenly it bit Maurice in the finger. It was an adder! This happened about tea-time yesterday (Sunday) Katie took him in to see the doctor at East Grinstead, who did not take it very seriously. By dinner time his arm was terribly swollen and he was in great pain. Dorothy insisted that his doctor should obtain some proper 'serum', which was difficult to do on a Sunday evening. Finally, this was obtained from East Grinstead hospital and the Dr came out again and made the injection. Maurice is better today but had to go in the afternoon to get the finger lanced. The poison seems to have stayed in the arm, and is now draining out.

Mr Bevin died on Saturday. The House of Commons tributes were made today, after questions. In Attlee's absence (in hospital, with duodenal ulcers) Morrison did this – very clumsily and inartistically. Churchill was in Sheffield (receiving the freedom of the city) so Eden made the tribute on behalf of the Opposition. He did this quite beautifully, in the best House of Commons style. Bevin was in many respects a very bad Foreign Secretary. His Palestine policy was absurd, for he succeeded in the almost impossible result of becoming equally odious to Jew and Arab. His attitude to united Europe was petty. But he has done one immense service to Britain and to the world. He has imposed upon an unwilling and hesitant party a policy of resistance to Soviet Russia and to Communism. A Tory Foreign Secretary (in the immediate post-war years) could not have done this.

In Churchill's absence, Eden was asked to see the leading ministers about Thursday's debate on the arrangements for naval command etc in the Atlantic and elsewhere. He asked me to go with him – also our Chief Whip. We found Ede (Leader of the House) Morrison (Foreign Secretary) Shinwell (Minister of Defence) and the Govt Chief Whip. They seemed rather upset and confused, but it seems that they have prepared a 'white paper' on the military, naval and air force commands etc to set up under NATO (North Atlantic Treaty Organisation) They had intended to publish this tomorrow. It makes it clear that the supreme naval commander of the Atlantic would be an American, with an Eastern section (comprising North Sea, the Western approaches etc) under a British and the Western section under an American officer. In return, there would be a British 'supremo' in the Mediterranean, with flag officers in each of the 3 or perhaps 4 sections. (The North African coast etc wd be a Frenchman) But there is a complication here. As far as I could understand (though Shinwell was rather obscure about this) an American naval officer would be in command of any American 'task force' that might be operating (in support of land forces and landings) in the Mediterranean. It seemed uncertain whether this officer wd be entirely independent, or would be under the British 'supremo'; I think the former. In any event, telegrams from Washington indicated that the Americans now had doubts about publishing the 'set-up' (although agreed with us and the other partners to NATO) Tedder has sent a telegram urging that any public discussion would be very undesirable at the moment, since American public opinion is much excited by MacArthur's dismissal alleged by Republicans to be due to sinister British intrigues. According to Ministers, the American doubts are due to their feeling

a) dubious about the Mediterranean arrangement

b) uncertain whether they have been wise to surrender the Eastern Atlantic . . . .

18 April

. . . . Lunch with Churchill at the Savoy. Some discussion, continued later at the Shadow Cabinet, on the general situation, with special reference to Bevan's position and how we shd approach the Govt's plan to impose charges for teeth and spectacles in the National Health Service. We tried a vote tonight in a 'prayer', but failed by 9 votes.

19 April

Primrose day.[22] My father's birthday. A very busy morning at the office. Book sales have shewn a marked falling off (in totals) since Christmas, in spite of the increase in prices. I do not see how we can remedy this, at least in the general trade. We have very heavy commitments and very large overheads, compared to pre-war days. Fortunately, we have pursued a most conservative policy during these years. We have put large sums to reserve and divided only a fraction of our profits. Our cash position, in spite of huge increase of costs, is therefore pretty good . . . .

---

22. The Primrose League, as a vehicle for popular Toryism, was established in 1883, and named after the favourite flower of the late party leader, Benjamin Disraeli. 19 April was the date both of Disraeli's death in 1881 and of Macmillan's father's birth in 1853.

23 April

After a week-end of tension, in which all the political world has been speculating and guessing, Aneurin Bevan's resignation was announced this morning. The interchange of letters was in the new style – 'My dear Clem', 'My dear Nye'. But these endearments could not conceal the bitter hostility between the two men. Bevan made his personal statement this afternoon. I have heard many such statements, from Eden, Cranborne (Salisbury), Duff Cooper, Sam Hoare, and so on. Eden was so careful to spare his colleagues that it was obscure to many people just what was his quarrel with Chamberlain. Cranborne was restrained, but severe. Duff Cooper was truculent, but in classical language. Sam Hoare almost burst into tears.[23] Bevan's 'apologia' was certainly novel in manner, if not in matter. It was a violent castigation of his colleagues, delivered with incredible asperity, not to say malice. Up to a certain point it was well done; but he lost the House at the end. Members were shocked by his explanation of why he agreed to the 1/-[24] contribution towards prescription and the 25,000 cut in house-building last year. He had only agreed because he knew these measures were impracticable and could not in fact be carried out. He out-manoeuvred – not to say, 'double-crossed' his colleagues.

It was the talk last night that Bevan had 'done for himself'. I am not sure. He said things which a large majority of the Socialist party like to hear their leaders say. His anti-Americanism is really a popular line. The attack on the Budget was liked by many of them. The Socialists are very angry at his 'disloyalty' – which threatens their own seats and pockets. But really they agree with his sentiments 'Why not a Capital Levy'.[25]

I think Attlee will survive the immediate storm. But 'how long can he last?' is [the] question on every lip. No one believes it can be beyond the autumn. Wilson, President of the Board of Trade, has also resigned and will presumably speak tomorrow. It is said that Freeman

---

23. Eden and Cranborne both resigned from the Foreign Office in February 1938, Duff Cooper (from the Admiralty) later that year over the Munich Crisis, and Hoare resigned as Foreign Secretary in 1935 over his handling of the Abyssinian crisis.
24. Before decimalization in 1971 there were twenty shillings in a pound, and twelve pence in a shilling.
25. That is, instead of prescription charges.

(who is Under Secretary at Ministry of Supply) is resigning. This will make it awkward for Strauss, who is still shivering on the brink. I predict that both he and Strachey will betray Bevan when it comes to the point.

24 April

Bevan has had what is called 'a very bad press'. Such cynical disloyalty seems to have shocked the sensitive reporters and leader-writers. I still believe that he may be a formidable and dangerous demagogue. The speech was directed to the election of 1955 or 1956 – not that of 1951 or 2. Of course, this kind of long distance calculation may not 'come off'. Mosley, for instance, tried the same thing. He also was a demagogue, more on Caesarian than on Aristophanian lines – but a demagogue. Bevan is pure 'sausage-seller' . . . .[26]

Maurice . . . . has had every sort of doctor and surgeon to look at him and tonight seems rather better. It is a very anxious time, however, and will be for several days . . . .

25 April

We are to put a motion forward next Tuesday on the raw material situation.[27] This will not be a vote of censure; yet, if it was carried, I think the Govt wd fall. It has been carefully framed to make it very difficult for Bevan, Wilson, Freeman etc to vote against it.

The Chinese have launched a new offensive in Korea. We have given a good deal of ground, but this seems the new method of mobile defence. I fear that our British brigade has had a tough time. But they have covered themselves with glory. Churchill is to speak at a Albert Hall meeting on Friday. 'If I were to call the Prime Minister "this lion-hearted limpet", would that be offensive?' In view of Attlee's illness, it was suggested that he might widen the front [to] 'this bunch of lion-hearted limpets!'

---

26. The implication is that Macmillan saw Sir Oswald Mosley, the leader of the 1930s British Union of Fascists, as a more autocratic demagogue than Bevan. Bevan, in contrast, is compared with the Sausage-Seller, one of the leading characters in Aristophanes' political comedy *The Knights*. This play, first performed in 424 BC, was a vicious attack on the populist Athenian demagogue Cleon.
27. With regard to the deficiencies of supply to the war effort in Korea.

26 April

. . . . Maurice is better today. The poison seems to be gradually yielding to treatment. But it may be necessary to open the arm again.

I dined a night or two ago with the Amerys. Leo and Julian; Catherine as hostess; the Yugoslav Ambassador as the chief guest. I made an appeal (or attack) after dinner, as arranged with Julian, telling him that Marshal Tito ought to release a number of the political prisoners – particularly those who had worked loyally with us in the Mihaelovitch [sic] and other resistance movements against the Germans.[28] I told him that the English were not really interested in the politics of the matter. But they could not bear to see their friends in trouble. Any help – financial or military – which we might be asked to give,[29] wd come from our people with a much better grace if we cd be reassured about these men. Why can they not be let out of prison now? (I had a list of names, and gave some as examples) The Ambassador took it very well, I thought. He explained the need for going circumspectly. But he explained also the various 'liberalising' plans which were being proposed and would gradually be implemented. Even journalists wd be encouraged to write freely their opinions, altho' he admitted that they had lost the habit and the power to do so! I have sent a report of the conversation to Sir William Strang (at the Foreign Office) with details (supplied by Julian Amery) of the people about whom we ought to feel specially concerned. Julian is going to send the list to the Ambassador. Let us hope that something will come of it . . . .

1 May

Debate on raw materials. Our motion was very carefully drawn, and being itself an amendment to the motion that 'Mr Speaker do now leave the chair' it cd *not* be amended. We asked the House to express 'anxiety' about the chance of carrying though the defence programme

---

28. The Chetnik resistance movement, royalist and Serbian, to the German invaders, had begun in Yugoslavia in 1941 under General Dragoljub Mihailovíc. By 1944 the British government had, however, decided to support Tito's more powerful Communist partisans. Despite the creation of a united government in Yugoslavia at the end of the Second World War, Tito consolidated his power in the November 1945 elections. Former royalists were imprisoned or, in the case of Mihailovíc in May 1946, shot.
29. For instance, in the event of a Russian invasion of Yugoslavia.

because of shortage of raw materials etc, as revealed by 'Minister Concerned'. It seemed hardly possible that Bevan, Wilson and co would vote *against* this motion, as it was couched almost in their own words. However Bevan announced (in a few words only and reserving his right to speak later on the whole subject) that he would vote for the Govt. This took away all interest from the division but not from the discussion . . . . Shinwell wound up for the Govt. The second half of his speech was good and really courageous. The Govt won by 13. The Liberals abstained . . . .

2 May

. . . . In the course of a very rushed day, I had to motor to Bromley for a civic luncheon to inaugurate the Festival of Britain. Dorothy came from Sussex. How we shall learn to hate this Festival by the time the year is over . . . .

4 May

Went with Dorothy to the opening of the Festival of Britain (South Bank) It rained hard. I left her with some friends and went to the office, where I had much to do. All is now arranged for Lazards to manage our investments and there will be the first meeting at the Board on May 22nd.

Left HofC by bus; special aircraft to Strasbourg, with most of delegates etc . . . .

5 May

. . . . In the afternoon, general meeting of the Assembly[30] – election of officers etc. Spaak and all the vice presidents elected without contest – a great contrast to the historic fight over Layton in 1949. Our only anxiety is a proposed motion by Reynaud, inviting USA and Canada to send observers from their Congress and Parlt to our next meeting.

(a) I do not like U.S. and Canada being joined like this – it all results, I know, from that wretched North Atlantic pact, calculated to break up the integrity of the British Empire

(b) Since we have already invited observers from the Dominion parliaments (who have not yet appeared owing to the lack of enthusiasm

---

30. Of the Council of Europe.

shewn by Dominions Office at home) I don't want Americans on the same level as our own people . . . .[31]

7 May

. . . . It was arranged for today to be chiefly on the message from the Ctee of Ministers (or Speech from the Throne, as we shd say) Tomorrow and Wednesday will be the economic debate etc . . . .

. . . . No British Socialist spoke. Few attended. This year their line seems to be to treat the whole thing with silent contempt.

8 May

The economic debate was made memorable by a truly magnificent speech by Lord Layton. I have never heard him speak so well. He spoke 'as one having authority'.[32] Apart from a most admirable account of the work of OEEC and a demand for some more ambitious plans in the future, he dealt admirably with raw materials and thus spiked poor Edelman's much advertised guns. He also made a powerful plea for arms standardisation, backed up with the experience of two wars.

Edelman, who had prepared a great Socialist demonstration (with press conferences, circulated speeches etc) spoke in the afternoon. The famous resolution, signed by all the Socialists in the Assembly, is an attempt to re-build that international socialist front which Bevin, Morrison, Dalton and Co have shattered since 1945.[33] It was a gallant attempt; but rather thin. The trouble is that there is no future for Socialism in countries where Communism has siezed the left position. It can only continue (as in Scandinavia etc) by abandoning Socialism and becoming a sort of mild radicalism. Perhaps this is now happening in Britain? . . . .

10 May

. . . . André Philip introduced the Schuman plan report and resolution.

---

31. Technically speaking, the term Dominion had ceased to be used officially to describe the self-governing states of the Commonwealth in 1947. Macmillan here not only continued to use the term, he also clearly wished to maintain the military leadership of the Commonwealth which Britain had hitherto exercised. The American-led NATO clearly undermined the significance of this relationship.
32. Quoting Matthew 7: v. 29.
33. It proposed the creation of an Atlantic Joint Resources and Purchasing Board.

He made a fair speech, with more power of lucid exposition than I expected from him. Nölting (German Socialist) made a clever and purely partisan speech, the object of which was obviously rather to embarrass Dr Adenauer than for any other purpose. I followed, with a speech which seemed well received. I tried to set out the Conservative attitude, and was able to have a little fun with the extraordinary phenomenon by which modern Socialism, both in Britain and now in Germany, had become nationalist and isolationist.

Blyton, speaking for the British Labour party, made a characteristic contribution. After a few minutes of a very robust and amusing attack on me (in his own language) he read out 30 minutes of a jesuitical and casuistic essay written by a certain Healey. He is the adviser of the Labour party on foreign affairs . . . . B is a good honest miners' member for County Durham. He cd not be guilty of the subtleties and falsehoods supplied to him. Reynaud summed up in a truly brilliant parliamentary speech, witty, and charming, but also deadly in its analysis of modern Socialism in Britain and in Germany. He ended with a moving peroration in the best style. Duncan Sandys made a short but crushing reply to Blyton, quoting the famous resolution of the Socialist party in 1948, demanding a supra-national authority for steel and coal! . . . .

11 May

. . . . The debate on the Schuman plan was resumed this morning. A Philip wound up with a brilliant speech, attacking the German Socialists and gently rebuking the British Socialists. I doubt if International Socialism can really survive this affair.

The voting followed. Everyone votes for the motion, except the German socialists (who voted against) and the British socialists (who abstained).

The conduct of the British Socialists is very queer. They hardly even bother to attend the debates at all . . . .

In the afternoon, a long and confused debate on a motion of Paul Reynaud; about making contact with U.S. Congress. Introducing the motion provided Reynaud with the occasion for a brilliant attack on international socialism. 'The only thing they have successfully nationalised is socialism itself' . . . .

12 May

. . . . [I]t was agreed to have a general debate on the 'defence' problem, without specific relation to any particular resolution and without a vote. On the whole, this was wise. For I fear that the Sandys resolution is too robust to commend itself to an Assembly where defeatism and pacifism are pretty strong.

. . . . Duncan Sandys presented his view (and those of all the stout-hearted elements) in an admirable speech – moderate, grave, and well-argued. A Dutch Socialist followed with a pacifist and defeatist contribution, but he was well taken up by a Greek delegate. We adjourned for luncheon in a rather tense atmosphere. The British Socialists are plotting a 'Churchill the war-monger' campaign . . . .[34]

Turks and Greeks spoke this afternoon. The failure to include them either in the Atlantic Pact or in a special Eastern Mediterranean pact is unforgivable.[35] The results may be quite serious. Turkey can easily be made a most valuable help to us in our present difficulty and weakness in the Middle East. I wish the Foreign Office would fall into the hands of someone who had some knowledge of world affairs. Bevin (except for first learning to mistrust the Russians and then teaching the working men of Britain to do the same) has been a disaster. Morrison looks like being futile or dishonest . . . .

13 May
The defence debate will be resumed tomorrow. After a lazy morning and afternoon, I went out with Julian Amery to a garden party given by General and Madame Gruss at their country house at St Leonards [St-Léonard], some 20 miles or so from Strasbourg . . . . On returning to S, we found that Dorothy and Catherine had arrived safely by car. I need hardly say that they had
    a) broken the hand-brake
    b) blown a tyre –
otherwise all well . . . .

14 May
Glenvil Hall opened the renewed debate on defence, with a very poor speech, (written by Denis Healey) After some most interesting speeches, esp by Turks and Greeks, and one or two quite robust Swedes and

---

34. This, indeed, was to be characteristic of Labour's campaign during the forthcoming 1951 general election campaign, not least in the famous *Daily Mirror* headline on the eve of poll on 24 October 1951, 'Whose finger on the trigger?'.
35. Greece and Turkey joined NATO in 1952.

Danes of the right kind, and a fine address by a German (Gerstenmaier, Christian Democrat) I wound up with an extensive speech. This was generally applauded and I think was the most effective speech I have made in the Assembly. Certainly, as one joins in, one seems to get the ear of one's colleagues. It was difficult at first, but I have now got the hang of the place (building, technique of two languages, etc etc) . . . .

(The general view is that the British Socialists have done even worse than usual. Dalton's absence has not been such an advantage to them as I wd have thought. With all his faults, he was a 'character' an experienced 'conferencier'[36], and brought a certain glamour. Now the Socialists are dull, petty and ineffective)

The report of my Committee for Nations not Represented in the Council of Europe was presented this afternoon by Mr Pfleiderer (German C.D.U.) He did so in an agreeable speech. The form, though not the substance of the report came under some criticism from Serranens (Dutch Socialist) and others. Mr Mitchison KC MP (Brit Socialist) made a violent personal attack on me and Beddington-Behrens and the Eastern and Central Commission of the European movement. This was very badly received and my reply to him was scarcely needed . . . .

15 May

Resumed debate on my 'commission'. Interesting speeches were made by Hollis and Henry Hopkinson. The latter spoke entirely on Portugal. Of course it is an inherent difficulty of my 'commission' that it deals with countries which are not included in C[ouncil]ofE[urope] for such very divergent reasons, e.g. Switzerland, Spain, Portugal and the 'Iron Curtain' countries . . . . After debate, the 'recommendation to the ministers' was postponed (on my motion) till the autumn . . . .

It is not easy for me to take an objective view of this session of the Consultative Assembly. I have myself found it of absorbing interest. But then I like foreigners; I like listening to their speeches; and I am beginning to understand, after a good many years of experience, their way of thinking. I find their speeches much more interesting and witty than those I have to listen to in the House of Commons. Their method of thought is at least logical. They try to argue a case, where we are content with mere assertions. Apart from these personal

---

36. 'Speaker'.

predilictions, I must also admit that I like the life at Strasbourg. How much has the Assembly achieved. Of course, the Press say that it has been a complete failure. But that is because they want news – a story; if possible, a scandal. This time, especially in Churchill's absence, there has been no news-story. Moreover, the wrong press representatives are here. They always send the local correspondents not the lobby correspondents. None of the press understand or take any interest in Parly debate. But I think the Assembly, in spite of many difficulties, has done some solid work. We have had very few and very intermittent French attendances, owing to the forthcoming French elections. There have been few Italians, for they are immersed in local and provincial elections of great significance. The Irish (except for 2 or 3 senators acting as 'alternatives') have been absent. Nevertheless, we have had some excellent and valuable debates. That on the Schuman plan was on a very high level; that on defence turned out pretty well; and some of the economic debates have been good. It is true that the great emotional hopes of the early period have been dashed. But solid progress is being made.

The Commonwealth has entered into our discussions and has also begun to be understood by Europeans as never before. We got this idea into almost every discussion and decision. The picture of the Commonwealth and Europe, acting in a very close economic and monetary alliance, is getting clearer. The idea that in this way an organisation might be formed which can meet USA on equal terms, is beginning to seem quite practicable. With regard to US many Europeans are frankly out to get what they can while the going is good – that is, while USA are so frightened of Russia that they must somehow keep the old world afloat. But more wise and more imaginative minds are beginning to be attracted by the idea of Europe and British Empire and Commonwealth getting together, and so reproducing something like the American wealth and power. This has been our Conservative theme whenever we cd put it forward or introduce it, with reasonable discretion . . . .

17 May
Left by car for Italy. The Gothard pass was closed, but we drove to Göschener, where we put the car on the train, emerging at the other side of the tunnel at Airolo. It was a beautiful morning, but unfortunately on the southern side of the pass, the clouds came down and rather spoilt the view. As we approached Bellinzona this turned to

heavy rain. Just outside the town we unfortunately blew a tyre. As the spare tyre was also punctured, this led to a tiresome delay. However, Julian is a most useful person to travel with, as he seems to speak all languages and most dialects with useful and sufficient fluency.

We got a Swiss paper at Lucerne. I do not like the news from Persia;[37] still less the rather unfriendly American attitude. Acheson (Secretary of State) appeals to Britain and to Persia to keep calm! As if we were two Balkan countries being lectured in 1911 by Sir Edward Grey! . . . .

20 May

Flew from Milan to London. A wonderful flight over the Alps – the whole being covered by thick white cumulus, out of which stood, like islands, the summits of Monte Rosa, Mont Blanc, the Matterhorn and a few larger peaks . . . .

23 May

It is now alleged that the Foreign Secretary has informed the Persian Govt that he has no objection to nationalisation of oil 'in principle'. If so, there will be a first-class row. The British people do not understand that in normal diplomacy, to agree to something 'en principe' means that you have no intention whatever of agreeing in practice . . . .

26 May

. . . . I have finished an article for the *Daily Telegraph* about our Commonwealth–Europe conference, which will give it some useful publicity.

27 May (Sunday)

. . . . At 3pm we had the first (informal) meeting of the Commonwealth delegates. About 4 delegates for each member (7 countries in all)

---

37. This was Macmillan's first reference to the Abadan crisis, the recent attempt by the nationalist Iranian Prime Minister, Dr Mossadeq, to nationalize the vast oil interests in southern Iran of the Anglo-Iranian Oil Company, in which the British government then held a controlling block of shares. As Macmillan's subsequent entries were to make clear, it was the strategic and political significance of these holdings that was at issue both for him and the government. NB: the official name of the country became Iran in 1935, but it continued to be referred to as Persia.

At 8pm a dinner in their honour given by Leo Amery and myself . . . .

29 May
. . . . The quality of the overseas delegates is high, but they are (perhaps naturally) ignorant about Europe and especially about the work of European institutions like OEEC and EPU . . . .

31 May–2 June
The Conference has met in plenary session; in committee; and finally in plenary session. It has had buffet luncheons and dinners, with Baron Boel, with the British Embassy, and with the Belgian Govt. It has been addressed by M Spaak and M Van Zeeland (these two are *'en delicatesse'*[38] and it is regarded as a great triumph that they appeared on the same platform. Altogether the conference has had a good time and felt contented but exhausted at the end. There were the usual crises and the usual rows and the usual reconciliations. Mr Stacey May (American 'observer') was thought to be doing a good deal more than 'observing'. But I think really he played a useful role. The Amerys (father and son) were respected and feared for they still believe in the British Empire, Imperial Preference, Britain as the financial centre of the world – indeed, a lot of things which are painful to Americans.[39]

The Commonwealth representatives underwent many changes of emotional and even of intellectual position during the week. The orientals were uniformly friendly and helpful. They really do *not* like Americans! I think because they have even worse manners than the English! The Canadians seemed almost entirely 'sold out' to the Americans, but gradually changed from this extreme position. The Australian leader, Sir Douglas Copland was tough, cheery and friendly. A 'Free Trader' of the school of Victorian economists under whom no doubt he studied, he is nevertheless a stout-hearted and breezy 'imperialist' in the best sense. The Australians and the New Zealanders naturally stick together. The South African representatives

---

38. 'Not on speaking terms'.
39. The Americans had, for instance, made clear during and after the Second World War their hostility to preferential trading regimes such as then (since the Ottawa conference in 1932) existed within the Commonwealth.

were (I think) all political opponents of the Malan Govt.[40] They were loyal, friendly, and intelligent.

The general impression which I formed was that all these people, before coming to London, had formed the view that England was finished. Some were very sorry, some less sorry. But all agreed that the sun had set. I think we may have done a little during this week to give them some hope and to make them feel that there is another England, besides that of Morrison, Bevan, Kingsley Martin and the like. I think they may also have been impressed by the extent to which Europe still pines for English leadership and even by the authority which some of us, as individuals, have acquired in the European movement . . . .

5 June
The Persian situation has undergone a change; whether for the better or not, is hard to say. The Company have now agreed to send representatives to discuss the situation with the Persian Govt. This is, of course, at once hailed as a great moral victory for the Persians. For

a) it is said to accept the principle of 'nationalisation'

b) it accepts that it is a matter only for the company and not for HMG.

However, the Foreign Secretary has reasserted the right of HMG to be interested in this affair in the House yesterday. It is, of course, possible that with this 'moral' victory to support his waning prestige, the Persian Prime Minister may now be content and that some sensible negotiation will be possible.

Without intimate knowledge of the position it is not easy to say whether we have done a wise or a foolish thing. [J. H. Le] Rougetel (formerly British Ambassador in Teheran – during the 1947 crisis[41] – and now in Brussels) told me last Saturday that the Russians were really behind the whole thing, and used the so-called Persian patriots

---

40. The National Party government elected in South Africa in 1948, which went on to introduce apartheid.
41. Iran was occupied in the north by the Soviet Union and in the oil-rich south by Britain during the Second World War. In August 1946 there was a general strike against the AIOC and Britain was accused by the communist Tudeh party of fomenting separatism. Although Soviet troops left in May 1946, separatist movements in the north had to be crushed, and although this was achieved it left a legacy of political instability and growing anti-British feeling that culminated in the Abadan crisis.

or nationalists as much as the 'Tudeh' or left wing party. He seemed to favour a very firm line.

6–8 June

. . . . We have had almost a record sitting; from 2.30 on Thursday to 12.15*pm* on Friday (nearly 22 hours) The Government majority was between 8–20 (mostly about 10) all through. Churchill stuck it out, much to the delight of the party, and voted in every division. Two casualties so far, though I have no doubt there will be other. Harrison (Socialist, Nottingham) has had a fit. Majority 2100. Walter Fletcher (Conservative, Bury) has had a haemorrhage (majority – a few hundreds) . . . .

After it was over, I went to the office. It is rather satisfactory that Keith Feiling's *History of England* has now been twice reprinted, and will at last begin to repay the heavy outlay.

Julian Amery's 'Vol 4 of J[oseph] Chamberlain'[42] is published today and has some good reviews. Of course, Garvin planned this biography on an extravagant scale and this must now be followed to the end . . . .

9 June

Ld Woolton has urged me to send, even at the last moment, extracts from speeches we may be making at the week-end for the Sunday papers. He has arranged for a stenographer to be on duty for this purpose. Accordingly, I rang up from Sussex this morning. There seemed some uncertainty at the other end. I gave my name. Still some doubts. I demanded to be put through to the publicity officer and began to dictate my piece. All went well at first; a passage about Europe and the Empire. Then I went on to something about Socialism being the product of a weak intellect and a diseased and rancorous attitude to life etc etc. A weak voice interposed 'I suppose you know this is the Home Office' 'What number?' 'Whitehall 8100, perhaps you want the Conservative Central Office – Whitehall 8181?' I began to apologise profusely, but added 'I hope you don't disagree' 'Look – perhaps I'd better not say'!! . . . .

11–14 June

The House has been in almost continuous session. From Monday

---

42. The first three volumes, by J. L. Garvin, were published 1932–4.

afternoon, we continued till Tuesday 10pm without a break; I believe the longest continual session since 1881. Moreover, since there was no pairing (or practically none) the House was full in every part. The Committee stage of the Finance Bill was allocated 4 days. At the end of this tussle, the Government gave in completely. 3 more days are being allotted, perhaps 4. This, with the all-night sittings, amounts to 10 to 11 days. There was no charge of obstruction – indeed, with very few exceptions, there was no frivolity or excessive repetition. Our young men in particular, put up a very fine show.

Ede, who was much cracked up as an astute and wily tactician, has been completely out-manoeuvred by Churchill. The latter has been quick to realise the value of this to him personally, conscious that many people feel that he is too old to form a Govt and that this will probably be used as a cry against him at the Election, he has used these days to give a demonstration of energy and vitality. He has voted in every division; made a series of brilliant little speeches; shewn all his qualities of humour and sarcasm; and crowned all by a remarkable breakfast (at 7.30am) of eggs, bacon, sausages and coffee, followed by a large whisky and soda and a huge cigar. This latter fact commanded general admiration. He has been praised every day for all this by Lord Beaverbrook's newspapers; he has driven in and out of Palace Yard among groups of admiring and cheering sight-seers, and altogether nothing remains except for Colonist 2nd to win the Ascot Gold Cup this afternoon.

The only snag in all this is that we have not succeeded in defeating the Govt on any issue and the wicked clauses of this penal Finance Bill remain unchanged. The result will gradually be the elimination of London as a financial and commercial centre. It is almost impossible to imagine anyone registering a company again in London to trade abroad.[43] The Treasury put up no real defence, and clearly preferred to rely on the solid vote of their men. The truth is that argument has ceased to matter at all in this modern Parliament. The Socialist leaders hold their people by the same sort of financial control as the King and Lord North held their supremacy. In spite of the opposition of all the brains and oratorical power of the period, the King and his minister succeeded in losing the first British Empire.[44] The analogy is disturbing, as one sees the second being dissipated.

---

43. A reference to the clauses restricting overseas investment in the 1951 Finance Bill.
44. A reference to the loss of the American colonies during the premiership of Lord North (1770–82).

20 June

The Persians have refused the Company's (and therefore the British Govt's) counter-offer. It would seem, therefore, that the crisis has now been reached, although one never knows how these affairs may work out and none of us (in the Opposition) have any information except in general terms. The expectation is that HMG (as Churchill observed to me) have taken the firm and resolute decision 'to do a bunk'. It seems that they are proposing to abandon Abadan and the fields and to retire. In the event of dangers to life, they will cover this oil Dunkirk by a show of force. But they will not use force to protect this immense property.

In drawing this distinction between life and property, they are of course altogether overlooking the effects on British prestige in the Middle East and the probable developments in Persia. It may well be that the whole Persian economy will collapse. But in that case, a Russian controlled Communist government will take over Persia, and a huge new gain made by expanding Russian Communism. There is really no middle course to be followed in this affair. We might have taken a very generous line, offered to give them the whole concern. In that event, we cd almost certainly have an arrangement to manage the concern for the Persians on an *agency* basis. (It would be like changing over a book from a royalty to a commission basis) The profits would have been considerable, if not quite so large. The oil would have physically remained in our hands in peace – and in war.

Alternatively, we could have landed troops to protect our property. This would have led – not to war – but to partition. The Russians would have held the north and we the south of Persia, divided by the great mountain range.[45]

The course which HMG has followed will, I believe, lead (unless corrected) to a Communisation of *all* Persia, following the economic and financial collapse which will result from the decay of the oil industry on which Persia depends.

With all these matters reaching a crisis, the Opposition asked for a debate. A day has been given – tomorrow. This has meant a lot of discussion all through the evening by various groups. The 'back-bench' Conservatives are incensed with HMG and would like to recommend, even demand, immediate despatch of troops. Churchill is unwilling to

---

45. Much as Persia had been divided into British and Russian zones of influence before the First World War and during the Second. See above, p 77n.

commit himself to details of any military operation on the facts of which he (and we) are quite ignorant. He is also very conscious that Morrison and Co are just waiting to fix the 'warmonger' accusation upon him. They care so much more about a by-election than an Empire,[46] that this gang wd willingly lose Persia to the Russians if they could keep their precarious hold on office and its sweets. After hours of discussion in the Shadow Cabinet and in a smaller group, it was decided at this stage merely to oppose 'evacuation' in any form. 'We must not abandon the Anglo-Iranian enterprise' – that shd be our demand. How the Govt achieves this, must be their affair – whether by bluff, bribery, or force.

21 June

An interesting morning at the office. We are still in a great tangle with lawyers and accountants about the structure of the company and how to deal with the sterling proceeds of our American sale. Almost everything that one can do seems to attract penal taxation. The only thing that it is agreed we can do with absolute safety, is to sell the whole of our business and retire to private life to live extravagantly on the capital . . . .

In spite of the 'slump' in the book trade; which applies only to 'general' books at home, our foreign trade is growing. We are beginning to develop a lot more areas than India for school books – both in English and in the vernacular . . . .

The debate on Persia took place today . . . .

. . . . When the Foreign Secretary came to reply, it became clear enough why he had not opened the debate. He had nothing to say. HMG clearly make a great distinction between defence of 'life and limb' and defence of property. They have no plan, except to appeal to the Hague Court[47] and to hope that, when it comes to the point, the Persians will not be so mad as to destroy their only source of revenue. I confess I have more hopes of the second than the first of these.

In form and manner the Foreign Secretary's [words] were contemptible. In all the years I have been in the House, I have heard

---

46. The following day Labour held Westhoughton in a by-election.
47. The government had referred the nationalization to the International Court of Justice in The Hague in May 1951. Two months later, however, the court decided that it had no jurisdiction in the matter.

nothing like it from a Foreign Secretary at such a moment. Poor old Bevin had a kind of patriarchal dignity. If his pronouncements were obscure and often meaningless, they were never vulgar or paltry. This dirty little cockney guttersnipe has at last revealed himself for what he is 'a third-rate Tammany boss'. The House was astonished and ashamed. When he sat down, there was not a single cheer from the Govt benches . . . .

24 June (Sunday)
Church at 11am (St John the Baptist's day. Lessons Ecclesiasticus 48: 1–10 and Luke 3: 1–20) After church went to see Blake[48] and found him in a state of great depression. We are raising a few pheasants for the first time since the war. Alas! The last few days of cold, wet weather have started up 'gapes' [a poultry disease] and I fear we shall lose most of them . . . .

27 June
After questions, Churchill asked if the P.M. wd receive him and some of his friends for a private talk about Persia. P.M. at once agreed. Churchill, Eden and Salisbury are to have a meeting with Ministers this afternoon. This is a good move, for two reasons. First, the mass of the public will be rather shocked to learn that no such private talks have been initiated already by Attlee and Co; secondly, it will be easier to decide our line on a little more precise information . . . .

Churchill told me that the meeting with Ministers had taken place. The tanker position is good, 94% of the world's tankers being agreed to a boycott. 'Panama' tankers[49] (sort of pirate lines) cannot appear in less than 5 weeks and wd be altogether insufficient. Troop concentration and arrangements are getting slowly under way. There seemed to be in his mind a hope (although no more) that the Govt might do the right thing – that is defend the property, not merely British lives, in evacuation conditions. But there is no doubt also that the game may be a longer one than seemed at first sight and that it may be wise to let internal pressures develop. I could only have a few words with him. No doubt we shall have a more comprehensive discussion amongst ourselves today and tomorrow. He has made a preliminary report to

---

48. Macmillan's gamekeeper.
49. Tankers registered in Panama as a flag of convenience.

the 'shadow' cabinet today, but I was not there as I was on the [parliamentary] bench.

28 June

Sir Orme Sargent, formerly permanent secretary at the F.O., to lunch. He told me that there was some doubt about sending Gladwyn Jebb to America, (as British representative to UNO) on account of his rudeness. By a stroke of luck, his only task has been to be rude to the Russians. He has done this with such skill and energy, that he has become the most popular figure in the United States. He also told me that Bevin used to tell him that he would stick to the F.O. till he could hand over to Anthony. 'Never to Morrison, except over my dead body'. So it has proved.

Churchill came to the 1922 Ctee (party meeting)[50] and spoke with great moderation and caution about Persia. It is clear that he thinks there may be a change for the better and that it wd be foolish for the Tory Party to 'stick its neck' out. This was not to the taste of some of his audience . . . .

29 June

. . . . I have read carefully now Julian Amery's vol 4 of Chamberlain's life. It is really very well done. I am still reading and enjoying [Sir Walter] Scott's *Tales of a Grandfather*. This has been a heavy week, with 2 elaborate speeches to prepare and deliver in the HofC. Tomorrow I have 2 speeches in Somersetshire.

2 July

Lunched with Arthur Salter, to meet Mr Royal Tyler; this gentleman is running the American 'Free Europe' committee in Paris. It is important that the Central and Eastern European Commission of the European movement (of which I am chairman) shd work in close cooperation with him and his group.

D and I dined with the Andersons and went on to a ball at Syon House, given by the Haddingtons. It was a wonderful sight and a most unusual experience in these days. To see a great house, in full order and party, with its pictures, furniture, carpets, chandeliers, books etc is a vast pleasure. The lighting of the house and garden by flood lights was very lovely. It was a perfect June [sic] night, which added to the

---

50. Of backbench Conservative MPs.

pleasure. It was also fun to see all the remaining tiaras, necklaces, etc out of the banks for one night!

3 July
Dinner for General Eisenhower given by the English-Speaking Union. Ld Salisbury presided. General E made a very remarkable speech, a plea for the United Europe movement and a tribute to Churchill. This speech was quite exceptional and may prove of real political import-ance. Attlee and Morrison seemed surprised and even alarmed. Churchill made a short, but very moving reply. I have obtained a copy of General E's speech which shd certainly be used by the European movement. Reading between the lines, this speech reveals a great sense of frustration, almost desperation . . . .

5 July
. . . . The Persian situation drags on. The Conservative party is getting very restive about Churchill's continued inactivity. Salisbury spoke out in the Lords yesterday and this may 'force the pace'. Winston is naturally (and properly) very anxious not to be called a warmonger. But he must not risk being called an 'appeaser'.

6 July
. . . . Evening at Bromley, with a deputation from the Trades Council, to complain about the rising cost of living, esp bus and train fares! They almost sighed for the good old days of Tory misrule! . . . .

9 July
Beaverbrook devotes the whole leading article in the *Daily Express* (this time) to a bitter personal attack on Eden and me – for thinking too much about Europe! Great pressure is being exerted by the party on Churchill over Persia.

10–12 July
. . . . The Egyptian Govt, with its powerful navy, has now started to stop our ships at sea. This, and still more the nonchalant attitude of the Foreign Secretary, infuriated the Tories and even some of the Socialists (esp the Jews) Meanwhile, Churchill remains in a very cautious mood over Persia. The latest move is the announcement that (contrary to their first decision) Dr Mossadeq and the Persian Govt are willing to 'discuss' the oil crisis with Averill Harriman, President

Truman's 'adviser'. This certainly supports Churchill's waiting policy . . . .

On Monday night and again last night I have had to propose the toast of first, the American ambassador and then, of visiting American senators. One of the latter explained neatly why the Senate had a 'Foreign Relations' committee and the House of Representatives a 'Foreign Affairs' Ctee. 'Senators', he observed gravely, 'are too old and too respectable to have affairs'; they are reduced to relations! . . . .

16 July

Dr Richardson seems very concerned about my health. I have no organic disease, so far as he can tell. Heart, stomach, blood pressure, kidneys etc are all in good shape. But I am over-tired and overdone and must have a month's complete holiday if I am to avoid a collapse! What am I to do? There is no doubt I must do something. The trouble is to plan a holiday for a month in the course of which one will not be either bored or ruined.

Harriman has arrived in Teheran, to be greeted by Communist riots. I don't like the situation at all. He says he is not a 'mediator', but of course he is. He is the Runciman of today.[51] How ridiculous that he shd mediate between Britain and Persia, between an ally and a most doubtful and crooked pawn in the Russian game.

. . . . Harriman's adventure is, of course, a great blessing for Churchill, for it means that the debate is postponed . . . . No one dares do anything but wait for 'something to turn up'. Micawberism is universal.[52]

. . . . Anthony Eden and I lunched with the Italian Ambassador (no other guests) The De Gasperi Govt is in difficulties, chiefly from pressure from the right and the revived 'patriotic' or 'neo-Nazi' movements. They would like two things to help them in this predicament – first, a revision of that part of the Treaty which limits the size of the Italian armed forces; second, some forward movement regarding Trieste.

We told the ambassador that we thought the first could only be done (since Russia is a signatory to the Treaty) by a declaration by

51. Lord Runciman was sent to try to resolve the Czechoslovakia crisis in the summer of 1938.
52. A reference to the characteristic attitude of the impecunious Mr Micawber in Charles Dickens' novel *David Copperfield*.

Britain, France, and USA that they would not regard an extension of Italian forces beyond the figure named as a breach of the Treaty. Trieste is a more difficult question. In fact, it is greatly to the interest of Italy that British and American forces shd remain in Trieste. Originally placed there to prevent a Yugoslav occupation, they now act as a deterrent to a Russian move. It might perhaps be possible to associate the Italians with the other 2 powers in some way. But the Italians must remember that it is not easy for Tito at one and the same time to abandon Communist orthodoxy and Yugoslav expansionism. He has his difficulties, no doubt, as well as De Gasperi . . . .

18 July

. . . . The Americans are said to be negotiating with Spain for 'air bases' and perhaps for [the] inclusion of Spain in NATO. As a first step, they may offer a unilateral defence pact. The French and British Govts are put into a quandary by this – for internal political reasons. But the Americans seem determined to go ahead. I have always thought that it might be better to get NATO defence (and esp General Eisenhower's actual forces in Europe) more developed before thinking about the Spaniards. French opinion is much more sensitive to this talk about 'retiring on the bastion of the Pyrenees' than to purely political considerations about Franco and Falangism.[53] Of course, there is something rather ridiculous about British and French 'doctrinal' objections. Franco is just as respectable as Tito!

19 July

The Royal Garden party. A very hot and even oppressive day, but good for a garden party. The King was not present. All sorts of rumours are going about again concerning the King's health. Many people believe that the disease cannot be cured, only delayed. Meanwhile, the Queen and the Princesses grow daily more popular. It is amazing to remember that in 1937, Mr Attlee, Mr Ede and the whole Labour party voted against the civil list. Now, hardly a voice is raised against the Bill, introduced this week, to give the Princess Margaret £6000 a year.

---

53. Thus effectively giving up any attempt to defend France in the face of a Russian invasion. Falangism was the Spanish variant of fascism, an important element in the autocratic regime established by General Franco after his victory in the Spanish Civil War of 1936–9.

Dined at the Other Club. Sat between FM Ld Alexander and Gwilym Lloyd George. A large party, to do honour to 'Alex', on leave from Canada. The company included Lords Camrose, Leathers, de la Warr, Oaksey, Vansittart, Asquith (Cy Asquith) Ismay; Churchill, Walter Elliot, Leslie Cowan; ex Ambassador L Douglas. Winston really is 'The Other Club' today. Founded by him and F E Smith during the 1906–1911 Parliament, its object was to comprise an equal number of Conservatives and Liberals who, though politically opposed, were socially friends. As the bitterness of party rancour increased during those years to a degree we hardly realise today, 'The Other Club' played the role that 'Grillions' had played many years before as between Whigs and Tories.

But 'The Other Club', like 'Grillions', has changed its character. In 'Grillions' we have tried to have a few Socialists, but we do not succeed in getting many. Lord Jowitt, who is a sort of legal vicar of Bray,[54] hardly counts. In 'The Other Club' we have none.

Nevertheless, though the old idea has gone, we have a very interesting and pleasant company and usually good talk and much argument . . . .

20 July

C P Snow lunched with us at the office today. This author has come to us from Fabers. His work 'The Masters' is published today and looks like being quite a success, as we have sold over 8000 copies before publication.

I have now finished all the volumes of Scott's 'Tales of a Grand-father' which deal with Scottish history. There are two more about French history wh I have not embarked upon. I have read Mr Snow's novel; also The Small House at Allington and Dr Thorne. I'm afraid Trollope is become rather a drug to me. It is such a wonderful change from modern life; so wise and tolerant and witty; and with such refinement and delicacy of touch. It is amazing how observant he is and with what a sure hand he deals with people and institutions of which he can have seen but little . . . .

---

54. 'The Vicar of Bray' is an eighteenth-century folksong (author unknown) poking fun at a clergyman's ability to trim his principles to fit in with whatever ecclesiastical policy was in favour from the reign of Charles II to that of George I.

23 July

The last – or at least the penultimate – week of a very laborious session. By really wonderful discipline the Govt have survived all serious attacks. We have won on a few minor divisions – but that is all . . . . Bevan seems to be increasing his power both in Parlt and in the constituencies and playing his hand with great skill and show of moderation.

24 July

Trollope is a drug. I have now had to read '*Dr Thorne*', '*Framley Parsonage*' and have begun again at the beginning with '*The Warden*'.

A great dinner at the Mansion House, for united Europe. Spaak and Churchill made the principal speeches – the latter superb – robust, audacious, and tender . . . .

25 July

It seems that Averill Harriman has achieved something. It is reported that the Persian Govt are now prepared to 'negotiate' with the British Govt. To this is added the obscure condition 'The basis for the negotiations would [be] the principle of nationalisation'. Does 'basis' mean 'subject matter' or does it mean that 'nationalisation' is accepted and the negotiation is about how to make it effective? The press says this morning that Lord Jowitt (Lord Chancellor) is to represent British interests. This gives me no confidence. There is nothing and nobody that he would not betray. However, the turn of events will no doubt benefit HMG politically. It will also immensely strengthen Churchill's position in the Conservative Party . . . .

26 July

. . . . I gave a luncheon party at the HofC for the German Consul General – Herr Dr Schlange-Schöningen. He is a real Prussian stick, and did not tell us much of interest. He seems to prefer the American to the Pleven plan for German rearmament,[55] and did not conceal his ill-will toward the French. 'They are always thinking about Paris', he observed 'and seem to fear another capture of their city'. I could

---

55. The Americans had proposed American reinforcements to Europe and changes to the NATO structure in return for German rearmament, rather than the EDC proposals of the Pleven Plan.

not help saying that my sympathy was with the French. He did not seem to mind. Ld Swinton suggests that General Eisenhower shd be asked to adjudicate, quite objectively, between the various plans. The important thing was to have a co-ordinated and integrated general staff, as to operations, intelligence and supply, leaving only the adjutant general's dept in national hands. Thus a revival of the old German general staff (wh the guest said he feared as much as anyone) might be avoided.

I went back to the flat to work after luncheon and so missed the economic debate – or, at least, its beginning.

It is clear from the Chancellor of the Exchequer's speech that he hopes to keep wages in control by attacking profits and dividends. This is not unnatural but I doubt if it will succeed. There will, of course, be a lot of bad results and great complications from a statutory dividend freeze. In any case, it is clear that the proposals to deal with the financial situation are quite inadequate. More restriction will not result in more production . . . .

At 6pm I went to the 1922 Ctee, where there was a discussion as to the line to be taken in Monday's debate on the Middle East, and esp Persia. I thought the ardent spirits, demanding armed intervention etc, were a good deal damped in comparison with a few weeks ago. Churchill has certainly been wise and the back-benchers are beginning to realise this . . . . Meanwhile, the position of the Company's employees is becoming almost intolerable . . . .

29 July

Went over to luncheon with Churchill. He was alone, exc[ept] for Brigadier Blunt (of the research dept) We went through the speech for tomorrow's debate. With his usual skill, WSC has prepared an oration, ⅚ of which will stand whatever may happen in the next 24 hours . . . .

Having spent nearly 16 hours (all Friday afternoon and evening and most of Saturday) compiling my own speech, I am rather distressed at the skill with wh Churchill has avoided the difficulty into wh I have fallen. For if Morrison announces with triumph that negotiations are to be resumed, much of my speech will have to be altered . . . .

Churchill gave me a copy of vol 4 'The Hinge of Fate'; and inscribed it. He showed me a letter from Ld Woolton. According to some information which we have received, they are now planning the Election for September. I find it hard to believe this, for polling in

September would be regarded as interfering with holidays etc. On the other hand, they might find that this wd be to their advantage. However, I do not think an October Election is unlikely; indeed it is probable. The dissolution might take place before Parlt meets; or there might be a short session to draw attention to a number of electioneering measures, such as controls, limitation of dividends and so on, putting us into the dilemma of accepting them reluctantly or voting against them. If there is peace in Korea; a settlement in Persia; and pure 'soak-the-rich' demagogery at home, I wd say that the Socialists have a good chance of getting back.

30 July

Debate on Middle East. Morrison opened with a speech of nearly an hour, even drearier than his speech last week. It was all written by the F.O. As Churchill observed, it would be nearly better if the F.O. were to write the speech he made to the Durham miners (accusing the Tories of wanting war) and he were to write his own speeches for the HofC. Churchill replied in one of his most devastating and polished efforts. (It was much improved on the version he had completed on Sunday) He was in tremendous form and under a mass of chaff and invective covered the only weakness of his position – that is, the brake which he has put during the last 6 weeks on the more ardent Tory spirits. He thus established a complete ascendancy over the party and indeed over the House. His only error was being led into too long a passage of arms with Morrison about the Durham speech, which delayed his own considerably. His opening passages about the changed position of Britain since the war and the loss of prestige etc in the world, which cd (however) be to some extent rebuilt with American partnership was very fine. Also his account of the functions of an Opposition (based on a dictum of Ld Lansdowne) They might caution against, but they shd be very chary of demanding particular military operations. This was the task of Govt. A very good day for us, for by the end the division was not in our ranks but in those of Tuscany.[56]

Crossman followed with a clever speech, trying to separate Churchill from his party, both on the Persian and on the Palestine question. But, as usual, it was over-subtle. After attacking us for a bit, he turned his heavier guns on his own party (I picked up this point in

---

56. Quoting Macaulay, *Lays of Ancient Rome, Horatius,* LX.

my reply) Julian Amery made a good speech on our side; so did Fitzroy MacLean.

I wound up for us. A empty house when I began (earlier than usual, as the guillotine[57] falls at 9.30) but it filled well and was full (without being crowded) before the end. I spoke for 40 minutes, and sat down at 9pm sharp. The peroration or rather conclusion – 7 minutes of 'high-falutin' stuff about war-mongering was risky. But it came off. Had it crashed, it would have done so badly – like an aeroplane, not like a motor-car! However, I think it made some of the Socialists rather ashamed of themselves and our boys liked it well enough. The P.M. ended up in that pawky imitation of Baldwin which he does so well. He really took far the best line in answering Churchill that he cd do, and is expert at lowering the temperature and generally reducing the whole thing to a pleasant Sunday afternoon at the boys club. He sat down at 9.27 without answering any question (except on my interruptions about Egypt and about the Sudan) I then got up and said 'What about evacuation'. He got up and said 'Oh yes! Evacuation. We do not intend to evacuate Abadan'. This is what the whole row in the Conservative Party; the uncertainty in the Labour Party; the anxiety in the whole nation has been about these last 6 weeks! There was some applause and some silence from the Govt benches; hearty applause from ours. The clock struck. The debate was over. This is certainly an odd and haphazard sort of country . . . .

31 July
. . . . Left Northholt at 3pm for Paris, and on (by train, alas) to Strasbourg, which I reached at midnight. Very hot and stuffy . . . .

2 August
. . . . The 'Joint Ctee'[58] met at 11am . . . .

The chief thing we had to ask them, or inform them, about was the proposed meeting with Congress. It was clear that they did not like it and especially did not like the proposed agenda. We met them again at 7pm to get their answer, which was favourable to the idea but (no doubt under British pressure) wanted to leave out 'defence'. Anybody who seriously thinks that 14 American congressmen and senators are going to Strasbourg (or Paris) for a week and *not* discuss defence must

---

57. A procedural device to curtail, by timetabling, the length of debate.
58. That is, with the ministers represented at the Council of Europe.

be crazy. They really knew this, but wanted their views 'on the record' .... Morrison hardly spoke and looked very white and glum. He doesn't like 'abroad'.

Left midnight. The heat stifling. Got to Paris at 7.30am.

3 August

Left Le Bourget 10.30 plane. Lunched at the office ....

.... Got home in the afternoon. I am by way of having a month's complete holiday; no work, public or private. It will be very agreeable ....

4 August

Walked in woods for about 5 hours; felt better. Read Winston Churchill's volume 4 'The Hinge of Fate' ....

5 August

With the holidays, come news which wd excite immense attention at any other time; but we are all too languid and exhausted to bother with newspapers. The 'Stokes' mission has left for Teheran,[59] as far as I can see without any satisfactory guarantees about the British employees of the company. HMG has reaffirmed its acceptance of 'the principle of nationalisation' – as I said in my speech, a foolish and fatal phrase, wh will cause an infinity of trouble ....

6 August

I have a letter from Lazards this morning about investing at least some of our 'US' money. It is proposed to invest about £½ million, and a scheme is being prepared. This means that I must break my holiday and go to London on the 8th.

Miss Gertrude Tuckwell has died, aged 90. I got to know her in the 1924 Parlt and never lost touch with her.[60] She and Ld Henry Bentinck taught me much, and their circle (for in these matters of social reform Ld H.B. was an enthusiastic if sometimes eccentric worker) included J J Mallon and others who were never political partisans and always generous friends ....

---

59. Richard Stokes was then Lord Privy Seal.
60. A niece of the radical Liberal MP Sir Charles Dilke, though never an MP herself, she was especially active on women's and social insurance issues.

7 August

A fine day, with occasional storms. Spent most of the day in the woods with the agent, Mr Streatfield, making plans for the winter work. There is a great deal of thinking to be done – mostly of the plantation in the old Birch Grove property, which my mother made . . . .

The work is progressing, indeed almost finished, at B.G. House. The furniture is being unpacked and the vast confusion of 12 years (we left it to [a] Nursery School in 1939 and to a preparatory school in 1945) is being sorted out. On the whole, the damage is less than I expected . . . .

Both Korea and Persia are in a state of suspense, which suits the holiday spirit. I feel better already – but I am still mentally and physically tired. But I spend most of the time when I am not walking in the woods in bed with my book . . . .

9 August

London, for the day. A lot of work at the office had piled up, wh I despatched . . . .

Very little news; . . . . Mr Shinwell (Minister of Defence) has taken his new .280 rifle to Washington, for comparison with the American and Canadian rifle; but he had to return to Durham County to judge at a beauty contest at Easington, so the standardisation of the rifle remains unsettled. The Duke of Edinburgh has made a much acclaimed speech to the British Association, about science in industry; patents and price rings, which seems to please the 'Left' very much. I fear this young man is going to be as big a bore as Prince Albert and as great a trouble. Let us hope that the King may live to a great age and the power of the Mountbattens (the Orléanists of Britain) be cashed accordingly.[61] Lord and Lady Mountbatten have done enough harm by their conduct in India to last a long time. But I feel sure that they hope to exercise great influence in Britain through the Duke. What does the Duke of Edinburgh know about patent law? It was significant that the passage accusing industrialists of buying up patents in order to suppress them, was itself 'suppressed' by the wish of the royal advisers (in the 2nd press release) but of course printed with approval by the *D Herald*. I suppose he will speak about the 'net book agreement' at his next effort. It was really much better when royalty

---

61. The House of Orleáns was a junior branch of the French royal family that briefly held the throne, from 1830 to 1848.

were just pleasant and polite, with the appropriate courtesies or the simple truths which both George V and VI have done so well.

10 August

[T]he Central and Eastern Committee of the European movement, of which I am chairman and Beddington-Behrens is rapporteur . . . . is getting too big for us alone. After months of negotiation, in spite of the general wish of the office, the FS (under the Prime Minister's direction) has prevented any official (or even unofficial) support. I offered to resign the chairmanship in favour of a Socialist, such as Mayhew, or a neutral. But from a mixture of timidity and jealousy, the Socialist Govt wd not help. So I got Arthur Greenwood (Treasurer of the Labour Party) who hates Morrison, to become Vice-President . . . . We can also, through our American contacts, provide most of the material for 'Free Europe' and the vast American radio organisation now beginning to work into the occupied countries. Moreover, as the Russian 'peace offensive' develops, it is more and more certain that the future of the satellite and occupied countries will become the central point in the struggle between the Communist and the Free World . . . .

Finished . . . . another novel by C P Snow (the first of the series) called '*Strangers and Brothers*'. This man can certainly write. I am glad he has become a 'Macmillan' author. For he is still young and will write more and probably better books.

We are busy on the house; a great part of the furniture is now unpacked and re-arranged. Not very much damage, after 12 years being packed away, except (I fear) by moth etc in upholstered chairs and sofas.

11 August

. . . . Finished Dizzy volume 4.[62] What a tragedy that the Whig nonentities, like Russell, Palmerston and so forth, could have kept this great genius out of office and power for nearly 20 years (roughly

---

62. Macmillan was reading Monypenny and Buckle's monumental biography of Benjamin Disraeli, Conservative Prime Minister 1868 and 1874–80. The Earl of Derby being castigated here was leader of the Conservative Party 1846–66 and a descendant of the Lord Stanley who, at the Battle of Bosworth in 1485, failed to support Richard III and was rewarded by being made Earl of Derby by the victor, Henry VII. Most of the other people mentioned in this passage were Prime Ministers in the nineteenth or early twentieth centuries.

1855–1874) at the creative period of his life. Even Gladstone was lacking in the impulsive efforts wh might have altered our century. What happened to Dizzy for 20 years, happened to Churchill for 10. In Dizzy's case, the fault was partly Derby's poltroonery. As Eddy Devonshire used to say, 'The Stanleys ran away at the Battle of Bosworth and they have been running ever since'. . . . The truth is that Disraelis and Churchills are not liked by Parliaments or People. They prefer (in our system) Russells, Aberdeens, Palmerstons, Gladstones, Baldwins, Neville Chamberlains. For they can understand these sort of people. Of course, Gladstone was an eagle among all these; nevertheless, he had not that imagination and creative mind which makes men belong not to their own time only but to all. This quality Disraeli had. Churchill has it. Of the Chamberlains only Joe had it.

12 August

It is sad to think of Eddy's death, since last year and Bolton Abbey let. I suppose it will either have to go, or be let for a very long time. Except for the war, I think I have been there almost every year for 30 years[63] . . . .

15 August

Lunch at the office with Dan and Maurice. We have agreed to invest £500,000 according to Lazards' advice, leaving over for the present whether the investments purchased are to be owned directly by M&Co or indirectly by an investment company, wh wd be a subsidiary of M&Co . . . .

Dorothy and I leave tomorrow, for the rest of my holiday, – a round of Scottish visits . . . . I have read Mr Snow's 3 previous novels. None of them has sold above 7000. The one we have just published has gone beyond that. I hope we shall be able to arrange with Faber to take over the stock and rights of the old books . . . .

21 August

. . . . I have brought with me volume 6 of Dizzy's life – the last vol wh I did not finish before leaving. It is fascinating, mainly about the 'Eastern' (wh means the 'Russian' question) According to the wireless, Stokes has 'ordered his train' (like Dizzy at Berlin). Will the gesture (really an ultimatum – 'take it or leave it') be as successful in Teheran.

---

63. For the shooting season, which begins on 12 August.

If it comes off, it will be a great coup for him and the Socialist Govt. Dr Mossadeq may have in his hands the political fate of Mr Attlee. Strange! . . . .

24 August

A most enjoyable day. D and I left Rothesay at 10am, arriving at Lochranza (Arran) at noon. The boat called at Millport, Largs etc on the way. By a piece of good luck, the rain which had been falling early, cleared away by 10.30, and for the rest of the day we had a most glorious, sunny, perfect summer day. The splendid Arran hills; the islands of Bute, Cumbrae etc; the whole of the mainland (more or less) from Kintyre to Loch Lomond – were in view. On arriving at Lochranza (which was much less spoiled by development than I had feared) we took the path across the hill to the Cock. It was a lovely day and the colours quite beautiful. We reached the Cock farm, now deserted and ruined, and got back to Lochranza in about 3 hours walking. We then visited the churchyard, with the tomb-stones of my great-great-grandfather Malcolm Macmillan (tradesman of the Cock) and many other Macmillans, Kerrs, etc – all forebears of mine – intact and in good order. Mr Hay keeps the churchyard with all the fervour of Old Mortality.[64]

25 August

. . . . The Persian situation is unchanged . . . . Attlee naturally hopes to get through without the use of 'force'. But it is clear that the Company's officers are in a very angry mood, and feel that they have been thoroughly let down by HMG, and it may be difficult to keep them there without support, suffering the kind of indignities which they have had to undergo. Yet immediately a force is landed, it means the summoning of Parliament and the danger of trouble from the Left, led by Bevan and his friends. The Korean deadlock continues. All this may mean 'no election'!

26 August

. . . . David Eccles seems (by the newspapers) to be busily engaged in writing the new policy for the Tory Party. Good luck to him! I agree

---

64. A reference to the care of the churchyard by the name character in Sir Walter Scott's novel *Old Mortality*.

with it all. A sense of new life and energy in the party (such as we tried to give in 1924–1929) will do a lot of good . . . .

29 August

. . . . Drove to dinner with James and Rachel Stuart. They inhabit a tiny flat or cottage at Findhorn, surrounded by wind and waves. James thinks they have decided for an autumn election. He thinks we shall win. Churchill in that event will form as 'broad' a Govt as he can; but he will not get much in the way of left-wing recruits. He will retire in a year. James does not think we shall get through the next period without a Coalition. Lord Woolton will be Ld President; Sir John Anderson, Chancellor of the Exchequer, if a seat can be found for him. Eden will insist on leading the House *and* taking the F.O. – which will soon prove impossible. Alternatively, Salisbury for F.O. Lyttelton will be Minister of Defence. J.S. sees a lot of Churchill – so all this has some importance. He also approves strongly of the 'Eccles' policy. This means Churchill does also. If he wants it, James can be Secretary of State for Scotland, and will be a very good and popular minister. He says he cannot and will not do it. But I hope he will – for every reason, private and public . . . .

30 August

. . . . *The Economist* – which becomes more and more pontifical – disapproves now altogether of the Socialists; has a mixture of fear and middle-class jealousy towards the Conservatives; recognises that the Liberals are finished – and so has nothing left to believe in but itself . . . . Crowther is a clever editor and in the collapse of the daily press (esp *The Times*) he is becoming almost the Delane[65] of the day. How Trollope would laugh at him! . . . .

3 September

. . . . We made a wonderfully interesting expedition today to Dunnet Head and the beautiful coast between Thurso and John of Groats. It was a glorious day, with fine views of the Orkneys. On the way back we called to see the Sinclairs, in the Highland retreat to which the leader of the Liberal Party retired in 1945 (like Achilles) and from which he seldom emerges. Marigold has aged much since I saw her; Archie is grey but handsome, as theatrical as ever. They live in a small

---

65. J. T. Delane (1817–79), editor of *The Times* 1841–77.

house, under very squalid conditions, in the middle of a desert of heather and bog, completely flat country, without much charm to any but a native. Archie said he had heard from Max Beaverbrook, who said first, that Churchill wd have a resounding victory at the Election; (which Archie devoutly hoped wd turn out true); secondly, that the Election wd be in October (which he thought improbable owing to both Korea and Persia having apparently gone sour)

6 September
I shot a stag, after a short but exhausting stalk. Fourteen stone; a poor head . . . .

According to the 'Gallup' poll, the Conservatives are regaining and even increasing their lead. Eden leads over Churchill; esp among Liberals. This seems rather hard after all C has done to woo the Liberals . . . . Gaitskell has made a very gloomy speech to the T.U.C., ... but his prestige has been much injured by the 'dividend limitation' policy – which is pure pandering to the mob, as he knows . . . .

8 September
Left Langwell by car. D put me down at Inverness, where I got [a] train for London. She continues visits in Scotland for another week . . . .

10 September–16 September
A busy week at the office; mostly details. My brother is on holiday. General book sales are not good; but the schoolbooks and text books seem all right. Sales for July down on 1950; those for August up – the result about level. We have some good general books coming this autumn, including some 'selling' novels which will help. But for the first time for many years, we need a good deal of finance. We have had to borrow £65,000 from the investment a/c for the trading a/c to meet authors' payments etc . . . .

18 September
. . . . Great progress at Birch Grove. Went out before dinner and shot a duck. An excellent dinner, with venison from Langwell. I was so tired after dinner that I treated myself to my favourite vice – and read 'Rob Roy'.

. . . . In Persia, it is clear that it will be a test between bankruptcy (on wh HMG are relying) and a more or less revolutionary position by

Dr Mossadeq and his supporters . . . . The situation at Abadan is deteriorating, and at the end of the month the Co will cease to pay the Persian employees. It may still be necessary to take action to protect Abadan and the remaining British staff.

Pre-election fever is growing in intensity. The Press on both sides is beginning to clamour for an early election. Attlee is lying low, like Brer Rabbit, and sayin' nuffin'.[66] Anyway, he has got lumbago . . . .

19 September

The evening papers – on their own responsibility or as the result of a leak (there was a Cabinet this morning) have announced October 25th as polling day! . . . Meanwhile, the situation in Persia continues to get worse.

At 9.15 the P.M. came on the BBC. He told us that the King had agreed to dissolve the Parliament on October 5th – polling day to be October 25th. It was all done in 2 minutes! So that's that! . . . .

20 September

Lunch with Churchill. Eden is still abroad. Woolton, Lyttelton, Butler, Bracken and Chief Whip (Buchan-Hepburn) It was decided to cancel the Conservative conference in Scarborough. The policy paper already prepared could stand. A short manifesto (to be written by Churchill) would be issued about Oct 1st. C wd also make the first broadcast; Eden the last. We have 3 others. One woman (Dr [Isobel] Barnett) and then a choice between Hill (the Radio Doctor) [W. J.] Brown and Gammans.[67] We have a fifth; wh shd be a party leader – perh Salisbury. An optimistic note prevailed, although it was recognised that the Gallup poll would swing back against us as the election proceeded. (This is the return to the fold of the wavering Socialists) C is to make 5 speeches, Eden to fill in the main cities he leaves out.

---

66. A slightly odd choice of simile (though reused in the entry for 2 March 1955), as Brer Rabbit always outsmarted his foes in the children's stories *Uncle Remus: His Songs and His Sayings* by Joel Chandler Harris, first published 1880.

67. Except for the Tory MP Sir Leonard Gammans, all of these were well-known broadcasters. Brown had also been an Independent MP from 1942 to 1950 (and previously a Labour MP) who stood as an Independent with Conservative support in 1951. In the end none of them was used except Hill, with the other slots being taken by Woolton and Pat Hornsby-Smith, MP for Chislehurst 1950–66, 1970–74.

The rest of us will contribute as best we can. C persuaded me to return for dinner. This was alone with him. Somebody had sent him some caviare which put him in a good temper. He has finished volume 5 of the War History completely . . . . Vol 6 (the final volume) is in type and practically ready . . . . But . . . . must not be published till after the Presidential election of 1952, since it deals very frankly with C's disagreement with Truman about Russia at the end of the war . . . .

He hopes for a majority of 90 – will be satisfied with 50. He is very conscious of the difficulties which wd face any Conservative administration, both at home and abroad. He could not add to his own reputation; he cd only hazard it. His plan would be to group ministries under a senior minister – e.g. Food and Agriculture under Woolton; Fuel & Power and Transport under Leathers; and so on. He is worried by the French defeatism and sloppiness. Their idea of a European army is a woolly organisation singing some new international tune . . . . Patriotisms must be united in a common purpose, not merged in a general mess.

After dinner, he began to dictate the manifesto, but did not make much progress. He was not in the mood. He could not 'see' it. For it must be not a speech, but an essay; with crisp and simple phrases . . . .

21 September
. . . . Gwilym Lloyd George to lunch . . . . He told me that he had heard (on very good authority) that Attlee's decision to dissolve was quite suddenly taken, and that neither Morrison nor Gaitskell were consulted, even by telephone (They are in USA) At the rising of Parlt, all ministers, except Dalton, were against holding it now. But Bevan has, in effect, blackmailed Attlee by threatening to withdraw his support unless the Parlt were dissolved. According to L.G. there is much despondency in the Socialist ranks. Nevertheless, wherever I have been, I am impressed by the class solidarity of the Labour vote. They grouse, and tell the Gallup poll man that they will never vote Socialist again – but when the election comes, they vote the party ticket. For my part, I think we should do *very* well if we get a majority of 50; it may well be 10 to 20. In all these calculations much depends on

a) how many Liberal candidates go to the polls. Last time there were 450; this time it may be only 150

b) what will happen to the Liberal vote where there is no Liberal candidate. This may actually be the decisive factor in the whole election . . . .

22 September

Shadow Cabinet at 11am at Churchill's house . . . . The chief business done (apart for discussion of arrangements for broadcasts and speeches for the Election) was with regard to the proposed 'manifesto' by Churchill . . . . But he raised one most important question of policy. He felt concern about the stock exchange boom and the general feeling which might be created, and exploited, by the Socialists that the Conservative party was that of business and profits and dividends. Something must be done (from the political point of view) to counter this. Could a plan be devised which would be politically advantageous and at the same time economically sound. What about a restoration, in a modified form, of the Excess Profits Tax during the rearmament period? A long discussion followed. Strangely enough, everyone seemed to agree with this proposal – Lyttelton strongly, Sir John Anderson more guardedly. Naturally, this would have to be accompanied by a 'review' or 'recasting' of the present system of taxation of profits, whether distributed or retained. Dividend limitation by statute would also be dropped. A committee was formed to produce a definition. This committee (Sir John Anderson, Butler, Lyttelton and myself) met after lunch and rapidly produced a draft. This certainly seems an important political note and may prove very effective – provided it does not cause too much alarm among our own supporters.

23 September

This morning's papers carry the news of the serious operation performed yesterday on the King. No precise medical details are given, except that the operation was on the lung . . . .

Dorothy and I dined with the Wooltons, in their house near Haywards Heath. George Christ (of the Central Office) was there: we worked till midnight on Churchill's draft. The first part was excellent; the second part much weaker and requiring a lot of alteration.

24 September

At office all the morning. Left by air from Paris at 3. . . . The operation on the King had taken nearly 3 hours. His condition would be critical for some days to come. It certainly seems very strange that the P.M.

shd have launched the Election at this moment. What will happen if the King dies? . . . .

27 September

. . . . It seems that Churchill is to see Attlee today, after the Cabinet has met to hear the result of Attlee's last minute appeal to Truman. Mossadeq has ordered all the British to leave Teheran by October 4th (the day our Parliament is to meet and be dissolved) M certainly has a sense of humour and has realised that there is no limit to the loss and indignity which Britain will accept under her present rulers. Morrison and co are only thinking how to pin 'war-mongering' on to the Tories and so perhaps snatch electoral victory out of defeat. Since Attlee gave me a most explicit assurance at the end of the debate (July 30th) that we would *not* evacuate Abadan, I don't see how he is going to execute this further retreat without some loss of face . . . .

A car was sent to the Hotel Lotti for me by General Eisenhower at 11pm . . . . An hour's conversation followed. He is confident that he can make progress, but is naturally worried at the slow rate. The European army, a wonderful conception, must not be allowed to disintegrate into 'constitution-building'. Jean Monnet's ideas are too detailed and too precise. The purpose (which is to make German rearmament safe for the world) must be kept in mind . . . . Nor must national and even local patriotism be forgotten, if troops are to fight. The main thing is to organise the structure and chain of command in such a way as to be proof against German disloyalty or 'double-crossing'. This can also be done (he agreed with me) by the control of munitions productions and of 'supply' (esp oil) General E asked a great deal about Churchill, to whom he is devoted. Is he really physically able to take up the work of Government? Why does not he announce that, after setting up things on the right lines, he will give up the reins to younger hands? . . . .

We then reverted to the NATO set-up and the problem of finding some semi-military, semi-political authority or institute to which the nations could transfer a great deal of their individual and sovereign power. He thought it wd be difficult to develop the present staff system in Washington to be as efficient as the old Combined Chiefs. There are now too many countries. Even the present system – America, British and French – can hardly continue *after* Germany comes in. E is clearly playing with the idea of becoming this semi-political, semi-military authority himself; with all and perhaps more than the powers now

allowed to the council of NATO or the committee of deputies . . . .
There is no doubt that he has enormously developed in stature and
confidence since the old days of AFHQ. He seems to find no difficulty
in getting on with 'the Field Marshal' (as 'Monty' is referred to here)
He paid a most generous tribute to him as the finest trainer of troops
and builder of morale there has ever been . . . .

Flew back to England, arriving Northholt 10pm. I found a mass of
stuff to be done on my arrival, but finished it all (including my election
address for the printer) before going to bed at 1.30am.

28 September

. . . . The Persian situation is as bad as it could be. HMG have decided
to appeal to UNO. Nothing can prevent, as far as one can see, total
evacuation in spite of the P.M.'s and the Lord Chancellor's very
definite pledges. What a collapse! However, there is nothing we can do
to alter the sequence of events. The important thing is to get power
and make a fresh start, when perhaps the Persians will begin to realise
their immense loss of revenue. Dalton is said to have expressed the
view (so Churchill said to us) that if they can only fight the election on
'Peace or War' in Persia, they may still win! . . . .

Victor Mallet dined with me. He returns to Rome in a day or two.
He does not change – a good, loyal friend from Balliol days . . . . He is
what foreigners like a British ambassador to be – hearty, sincere,
straightforward, not too clever, but with a wife richer and cleverer
than himself . . . . The Italians think we are playing up to Tito too
much – as indeed we are. The endless flow of Socialist ministers and
under-secretaries, as well as resigned ministers (like Bevan) to Tito's
court has upset Italian opinion and will no doubt turn Tito's head.
Meanwhile, Bevin's pledge about Trieste etc (given in the famous
Italian general election to help de Gasperi) hangs like a stone round all
our necks . . . . We are pledged to both Zone A *and* Zone B reverting
to Italy yet the Italian Govt knows that a deal ought to be done (and
very nearly was done) on terms more favourable to the Yugoslavs . . . .

Went home after dinner, with Maurice – returned from Lincoln.
It seems that there will not be a Liberal candidate at Lincoln . . . . So I
doubt if Maurice can hope for more than a *'succes d'estime'*.[68] I am
starting a cold – which is a great bore . . . .

---

68. 'Success with the critics', though not with the voters.

30 September

In bed all day. Finished 'The Antiquary'. Scott is better than Party pamphlets. What a horrible 3 weeks and more lies before us! I hate elections more and more.

1 October

. . . . [M]y throat is very bad – which is not a good condition to *start* an election!

2 October

I woke feeling better. I must unfortunately go to London, on the way to Bromley, to correct proofs etc of my election address. This is not very different from that of 1950 – simple, well-spaced, and short. Most candidates put too much into the address and make the type too small. They forget that 80 years of full and compulsory education have produced an electorate that is practically illiterate and cannot understand any but the simplest words . . . .

The evacuation of Abadan, in spite of Attlee's pledge and the Lord Chancellor's bold promise, seems now to be inevitable. Never was a great issue so badly or ineptly handled . . . . The evacuation is now to take place immediately, and in the most humiliating manner imaginable. The Persians refuse to allow the British cruiser to come alongside the pier (which is British property) so that the last 350 odd British employees may go aboard. These men and women will not even be taken out in the launches belonging to the cruiser. They will be ferried out by Persian launches, 30 at a time, in the presence of an immense crowd of Persians, Indians etc, employees of the company. It is difficult to conceive any procedure more calculated to destroy the last vestige of British prestige.

The news came through during the afternoon that in the election to the Socialist executive Bevan tops the list by an immense majority. Shinwell is thrown off, after 15 years service, and replaced by Mrs Castle, a Bevanite. Shinwell immediately left Scarborough in a rage, and it is rumoured that he has cancelled his speaking engagements for the party! Of course, he will not stick to this, but it is amusing and perhaps important. If it is clear that 'Bevanism' is in the ascendant, a lot of Liberal and middle-class votes may cross over to us . . . .

3 October

Churchill opened the campaign last night in Liverpool with what reads like a fine speech. He has scotched one lie that is going round – that, if returned, he will increase the national service period to 3 years. I gather from what he said about Persia, that the evacuation of Abadan *while* the matter was before UNO and therefore 'sub judice' had not been communicated to him by the P.M. . . . .

Addressed two meetings – first in Romford, second in Brentwood. I spoke for nearly an hour at each. The speech was well received, but I am not quite satisfied with it. It was rather too long and too closely argued – almost a House of Commons speech in certain points. It is always difficult to switch from one style to the other. But I think at the beginning of a campaign – when the meetings tend to be mainly one's own supporters – it is better not to be afraid of a solid and reasoned argument. The chief object is to provide arguments for our canvassers and helpers. But I must work at it to get it shorter and simpler. The advantage of having a good many meetings is that one can adapt and change. Romford was won back by us, by a small majority, at the last election. Owing to certain shifts of population and new housing estates, it will not be too easy to hold. I felt that our people were not unduly frightened by the 'warmongering' stunt. They certainly enjoyed its 'debunking' . . . .

I fear that the evacuation of the Suez Canal zone will soon follow the evacuation of Abadan. The whole Middle East position will be threatened unless, with American help, we can undo some of the damage. The only hope I can see now is an International Company, with joint Anglo-American control.

4 October
. . . . I had a talk with Brendan Bracken in his house this evening. He seems to be in the thick of things. According to his account, Churchill intends to stay a year or 18 months as P.M. (not more) in the event of a victory at the polls (Incidentally, B.B. is quite confident about victory) 'Eden will go to Foreign Office; Butler to the Exchequer; Lyttelton to Production. What would I like? The service departments will be under-secretaries in effect, as in war. Brig Head; J H Thomas; and perh a peer for the air. Wd Bill de L'Isle do?'

Churchill's present idea is to ask F.M. Alexander to be Minister of Defence. B.B. is against this. He is not flexible enough and anyway shd not enter a party government in peace time. But C is set on it. The alternative wd be to have a permanent chairman of Chiefs of Staff

Ctee – this to be Alex – as an official, reporting to and advising a Minister of Defence – this to be Macmillan. This is, in effect, the American system, with Omar Bradley as permanent head. Alternatively, there is the leadership of the Commons, with Anthony at the F.O., this is important. Wd I like that? A strange conversation! The most interesting revelation is

a) Butler, not Lyttelton, at the Exechequer

b) the list corresponds in every detail, except for Lord Ismay instead of Ld Alexander as Minister of Defence, with that published in last week's *Sunday Express*.

It looks as if the Churchill–Beaverbrook axis was pretty re-established through Bracken. One or two other posts were mentioned – 'C wd like Maxwell Fyfe as Minister of Labour, at least during the first period of the Govt. This means that he must give up the office of Lord Chancellor, to which he has a right. Cd somebody be got to hold it for him? Not so easy. Strange as it seems, lawyers seem to have both pride and conscience. Cyr Asquith wd be a fine Lord Chancellor, but just has not the health. Walter Elliot must have a post, for it would break his heart to be left out. He will do as Minister of Health, with Housing etc in a separate office. Fred Leathers has gone to S Africa. But he will be wanted to get some sense into Coal and Transport. John Anderson ought to go to Scotland, an honour to both. A good young man is wanted as Minister of State for Anthony. Duncan Sandys will not do. He wd not work well with Eden and has played too big a part in European affairs. Salisbury will lead the Lords and have the Dominions Office if he wants it.'

5 October

Travelled to Birmingham. A large and enthusiastic meeting at Brierley Hill. This is a Socialist seat, about which we have hopes. Stayed night in Birmingham.

6 October

Travelled back from B. The train nearly an hour late, but this is the rule nowadays rather than the exception. Dr Retsinger called no. 90 Picc. to see me. He thinks Labour will win the election. He says the Ministers do *not* think so; but he clings to his view. He talked about the possibility of raising an army out of the exiles and refugees from behind the Iron Curtain . . . .

8 October

Travelled to Preston. At 7.30, joint meeting for Julian Amery and Billy Maclean – very enthusiastic. Left at 8.10, motored at break-neck speed from the hall to Lancaster – 30 miles or so in 30 minutes. Here I found a huge audience – 2,500 or more – in an immense hall, with a large and empty platform. Fitzroy and Veronica McLean and the chairman! My speech was better at the second performance, altho' there was one moment when I was not sure I shd get through. Two speeches of 45 minutes each, carefully rehearsed as they may be, are really fatiguing. I fear that RAB (Butler) has been rather late over the school question and allowed the Socialists to steal a march on us. He has not yet produced his policy – but I gave out mine and I know it will be in the local press in Lancashire . . . .

9 October

. . . . My first public meeting (since the adoption) at Bromley. It was in the Burnt Ash Lane schools – part of the constituency which takes in some of the L.C.C. housing estates of Downham and has a large Labour vote. A good, boisterous meeting, with a fair attendance of the opposition party and plenty of questions. Our people seemed in good heart. The school-room was packed to overflowing. All (or nearly all) the questions were on the 'war-mongering' or 'finger on the trigger' theme. This seems to be the *mot d'ordre*.[69] How successful the tactic will be in the long run is hard to say. It may wear a little thin at the end. Dingle Foot, giving a Liberal broadcast, seems to have made a bitter attack on Churchill. I suppose this is intended to counter-balance Clem Davies, whose broadcast was much more anti-Government. How the Liberal vote will be divided is the real enigma of the whole affair . . . .

11 October

A good meeting at Hayes (part of Bromley) This is one of the most solidly Conservative parts of the constituency. It seems that Iraq now wants 'Treaty Revision'. I'm afraid the whole Middle East is in a turmoil. It will not be easy to intro[duce] calm and goodwill. The Americans are beginning to get alarmed – as well they may be. They have done us immense harm all these years by their sentimental anti-Imperialist doctrines. Now they are beginning to understand what

---

69. 'Slogan'.

happens when British prestige is undermined. They learn – but in the course of their learning much harm may be done . . . .

13 October

Wrote article for *Daily Chronicle* [*News Chronicle*], for next week on the theme 'Peace'. Morrison is to write a parallel article to appear alongside. Wrote a new speech – or part of one – for next week since the present one, in spite of various changes and interpretations is wearing a bit thin!

A very good meeting indeed at the Central Hall, Bromley. It was very well attended – indeed many were turned away. Dorothy drove me home to Gosses afterwards. Read a little of *Waverley* before going to bed. Scott is becoming more and more of a drug. But it really does take my mind off all this, as modern novels cannot do.

14 October

I have had to give up church-going during this election and use Sunday mornings to rest in bed. Finished draft of speech. Ld and Lady Woolton to luncheon. He asked himself, seeing the need of company. During an election, the HQ have all the loneliness of a commander during a battle. W stays at head office and does not go about the country, like Churchill. He also has to deal with C. He told me that C rang him up nine times in one day – the day he (Woolton) was trying to prepare his broadcast . . . .

W seems to think we shall get a majority, but there is no great swing. There is probably, at the moment, a swing back in favour of the Socialists. All the same, I think what Churchill calls a 'demure' election may suit us. If they are not stirred up too much, quite a number of Socialists may abstain . . . .

19 October

The dreary, long-drawn out fight goes on. I had meetings yesterday at Brigg, Gainsborough and Lincoln. The last was really a wonderful meeting – the hall packed to over-flowing and large crowds outside. I came in while Maurice was speaking. Of course, he had never faced so large an audience, but I thought he did very well. My speech was rather long, but it 'went' well. It was well delivered and well acted. There were, I should think, about ⅓ of the other side, which is good sign . . . .

. . . . The Gallup poll has narrowed further against us. But on the figures we should be home. However, it is all on the knees of the Gods.

A small thing might influence the vital 2% or 3% one way or the other . . . .

20 October

Travelled by train to Swindon. A large meeting in a theatre – packed and a small crowd outside. There was a good deal of interruption and a fight in the gallery, with old-fashioned fisticuffs . . . .

The *Daily Mirror* has published a ridiculous story, with a vile leading article, accusing Churchill of having plotted with Eisenhower and the French Govt to deliver an ultimatum to Stalin. Can you see the French Govt doing this anyway? But, of course, the 4 million people who read the *Mirror* and its mixture of bunk and bawdiness will prob believe there is something in it. 'They read it in the paper'. So elections progress, to the much-awaited finish. This has been a particularly tiring one (with so much travelling) but quite interesting. I still get the impression, in spite of all the Gallup and other polls, that a lot of people are still wavering. I have never experienced audiences so ready to listen to reasoned and often heavy argument. Only a little wit and a few mild jokes are necessary, to coat the pill.

24 October

The last day! Holidays tomorrow! A fine meeting at Chislehurst last night, in support of Miss Pat Hornsby-Smith; a good little meeting at Bromley Common afterwards. Before this, a heavy day at the office with Board meetings all the morning and at lunch, the first report by Lazard's representatives about our investments . . . .

Churchill made a fine and moving protest at Plymouth agst the 'war-mongering' campaign. I still believe it may recoil on the Socialists. It was, of course, planned a long time ago by Herbert Morrison, who is the meanest man I know. He is utterly incapable of magnanimity. I remember when I was his Parly Sec at the Ministry of Supply in the 1940 Govt, how despised he was. Poor Admiral Brown cd hardly stomach him at all, for all his courtesy and generosity of mind. For in addition to the physical cowardice wh used to send him down to the deep dug-out at the Ministry as soon as it was dark, not to re-emerge till morning, Morrison was the kind of man who would never take the blame for what went wrong – only the credit for what went right. He thought more about publicity than armaments. His genius for this was remarkable. He invented 'Go to it' and 'Keep at it'. I used to say that his real motto was 'Get away with it' . . . .

25 October

The usual polling day routine, driving round committee rooms and polling stations. Went to Moucher (Devonshire) to hear results. These were disappointing. D went to the great Camrose party at the Savoy; but I felt I cd not stand it. I do not like the Noel Cowards etc. It is equally bad whether we win or lose. By 3am, it was clear that there had really been no swing at all for us – or, perhaps, that the clever Morrison propaganda had brought back into the fold all the hesitating and doubtful voters. On the other hand, we have lost no seats. It will be a stalemate, or a small Tory majority.

Poor Maurice has not been able to make any impression on Lincoln. He has got half the Liberal votes; de Freitas (his Socialist ministerial opponent) the other half.[70]

26 October

Went to Bromley with D for the count. We are in, easily. Majority about 2000 higher. Our Liberals were 5000 last time. 1000 have abstained; 2000 to me and 1000 to my opponent. This gives me over 12000 majority.[71] Spent the afternoon listening to results on radio . . . . Altogether, 23 seats gained by Conservatives.[72] No losses, except 1 in Belfast. Megan Lloyd George is out, which is a very good thing. Clem Davies will not be so frightened if she is not there to bully him! . . . .

27 October

. . . . Attlee went to the King as soon as we topped 313 members of the new House! This seems rather strange. How relieved he must be. So Churchill must have kissed hands at about 6pm last night to form his third administration . . . .

The process of Cabinet making, always difficult, seems to have begun. According to the 6 o'clock news the following ministers have been appointed.

P.M. First Lord *and* Minister of Defence – Churchill
Foreign Secretary *and* Leader of Commons – Eden
Ld President – (with control of Food and Agriculture) – Woolton
Ld Privy Seal *and* Leader of Lords – Salisbury

---

70. G. S. de Freitas (Lab): 23,400; M. V. Macmillan (C): 19,840.
71. M. H. Macmillan (C): 25,710; T. E. M. McKitterick (Lab): 13,585.
72. The overall result was Conservatives 321, Labour 295, Liberals 6, Others 3.

Home Secretary – Maxwell Fyfe
Minister of Labour – Sir W Monckton
Dominions Secretary – Ld Ismay
Chancellor of the Exchequer – R A Butler
Colonial Secretary – O Lyttelton
These ministers were sworn in tonight.

This seems an extraordinarily maladroit move – I should say the combined effort of Bracken and Beaverbrook. It is just folly for Churchill to become Minister of Defence. It almost justifies the *Daily Mirror*! He should have been Prime Minister only, thus showing that he is as interested in economic and social affairs, as in military matters. This is a major blunder and may have most serious results. It might even endanger the ministry, because I think a difficult by-election after this gaffe cd easily be lost. It is also surprising that Eden shd demand to lead the House as well as take the Foreign Office. It is obvious that this cannot be an effective management. There was a hint by the 'Parliamentary commentator' that a deputy leader may be appointed. Lyttelton's appointment is odd, and will (I fear) be a disappointment to him. He had worked hard to fit himself for economic and trade affairs. Fyfe's appointment is a good one. He will be a better Home Secretary than Minister of Labour. His speeches and writings thoroughly frightened the unions, and in spite of Churchill's denials during the campaign, made them alarmed and caused them to rally their forces. He will be a good Home Secretary. It seems he is also to be Minister for Wales. This means, I suppose, that Clem Davies has refused to come in. I have heard nothing, as I have stayed in Sussex all day resting. Monckton's appointment is unexpected, but good. He has a more subtle and a more flexible mind than Fyfe. He shd do very well. Ld Ismay's appointment as Minister of Defence was generally expected and was explicable. His appointment as Dominions Secretary is unexpected and inexplicable.

Harry Crookshank spoke to me on the phone. He seemed much concerned about these announcements. Apart from mistakes over the Ministry of Defence, this method of announcing half a Cabinet seemed unusual. Harry thinks that it may prove to be the *whole* cabinet. If that is so, it raises serious issues. 'The Nine Bright Shiners',[73] they will be called. I do not think this can really be the intention, but it will

---

73. From the nursery rhyme 'Green Grow the Rushes, O'.

cause a lot of misunderstanding. No more on the 9 o'clock news. I rang up Ld Woolton (in Sussex) to congratulate him. He said very little. He also seemed unhappy over the Ministry of Defence. He said that he had told Churchill that I was not particularly keen on the Colonies. I judge from this that some offer will be coming along; but it seems all the same a queer way of doing things.

Maurice and Katie got back from Lincoln. They were tired but not at all depressed. They seem to have enjoyed the election and have quite obviously fought an excellent campaign. He must wait now for a safe and permanent seat, to which he is entitled. I am so thankful that the majority was not so small against him as to make him bound in honour to go back to Lincoln. Finished *Waverley*. What a grand story, and what a noble story! . . . .

28 October (Sunday)

. . . . It is now possible to form a view of what has happened at this election. The nation is evenly divided – almost exactly even. For if allowance is made for unopposed returns, the votes cast on either side are just about the same. The Liberal party has practically disappeared in the House of Commons. But whereas last time they polled over 2 million votes in the country, this time (since they had only 100 odd candidates) the Liberals have had only the choice of abstention, voting Conservative, or voting Socialist in 500 odd constituencies. As far as one can see, north of the River Trent they have gone 2 to 1 – 2 Conservatives, to 1 Socialist. This is very marked in Scotland, and in places like Durham and North Yorkshire which have suffered under the Socialist tyranny. By this means both Middlesborough and Darling-ton were won by us. In the midlands, the Liberal vote has either abstained, or gone fifty-fifty or even worse. This explains Lincoln, Birmingham, Nottingham etc. The Liberals of this area have too much of the Civil War radical and roundhead tradition to join a cavalier vote. In suburban constituencies, like Bromley, the Liberals have split on a class basis. The bourgeois Liberal, pillars of chapel and League of Nations Union and all that, voted for me. (2 to 1 was about the figure, but ¾ only voted – the rest abstained.)

So the result is, once again, a moral stalemate. This follows a long innings by a Govt wh has made a tremendous number of mistakes; has had egregious failures in administration; and has been thrown about, like a rudderless ship in a storm, from crisis to crisis. At first sight, therefore, one can only form the most gloomy forebodings about the future. What will happen, after 3 or 4 years of Tory Govt, with the inevitable mistakes and failures? Moreover, what will happen with so many almost insoluble problems crowding on us, at home and abroad? Will there be a terrible reaction at the next election, and another 200 majority for Labour, with Bevan this time (not Attlee) at the head?

Against this, is the remarkable fact that our seats have been very steady. We have not lost one. Even seats which we held by 30 or 40 votes, have improved. The truth is that the Socialists have fought the election (very astutely) not on Socialism but on Fear. Fear of unemployment; fear of reduced wages; fear of reduced social benefits; fear of war. These four fears have been brilliantly, if unscrupulously, exploited. If, before the next election, none of these fears have proved reasonable, we may be able to force the Opposition to fight on Socialism. Then we can win.

It follows, therefore, that our chief anxiety must be to disprove and destroy the efficacy of Fear. We must, in addition, try to increase the property holding of the people. The only way I can think of is to get more of them to own their houses. This ought to be really seriously studied at once. Meanwhile, the Foreign Secretary – poor Anthony – starts with Persia and Egypt. What a heritage!

Message from Churchill to come out to Chartwell.[74] I expected this. On arrival, at 3pm, found him in a most pleasant and rather tearful mood. He asked me to 'build the houses for the people'. What an assignment! I know nothing whatever about these matters, having spent 6 years now either on defence or foreign affairs. I had, of course, hoped to be Minister of Defence and said this frankly to Churchill. But he is determined to keep it in his own hands. I gather the reason is the frightful muddle in which defence has been allowed to fall. In this 'set-up' the service ministers become in effect under-secretaries (in spite of their grand titles) and will *not* be members of the Cabinet. I asked Churchill what was the present housing 'set-up'. He said he hadn't an idea. But the boys would know. So the boys (Sir Edward Bridges, Head of the Civil Service and Sir Norman Brook, Secretary to the Cabinet) were sent for – also some whisky. It seems that there is much confusion in all this business. Broadly speaking, the old Ministry of Town and Country Planning retains these functions, but is now called Ministry of Local Government and Planning. All the functions of supervising local govt in general remain with it. It also has to

---

74. Churchill's house in Kent.

administer the ill-fated [1947] Town and Country Planning Act. It is also responsible for housing. But the actual agent, which controls all building, whether for housing or other purposes, is the Ministry of Works. (This also does the work of the old Office of Works) The building priorities or allocations are made by the Cabinet. It was at once clear that the Ministry must be re-christened, in order to pin the housing flag firmly to the mast-head. It will therefore be called 'Ministry of Housing and Local Government'. (Planning can be dropped. It is part of local govt) It is also clear that this Minister will be in the Cabinet. The Minister of Works will not. But can we build 300,000 houses? That is what we are pledged to do. Churchill offers me the task – or alternatively, the Board of Trade. The latter is routine; the former a great adventure. We then discussed who shd be Minister of Works. He will be very important. Would Eccles do? No. He will be too flashy. Why not Swinton. He really can run a show. But would Swinton (who has held almost every high office in the State) agree to serve as Minister of Works outside the Cabinet? Could he be deputy leader of the House of Lords? Will Salisbury agree to this? And so it goes on. Who will be under-secretary to me, if I take the job? Marples. Yes, Marples will do. He is said to know something about housing. Churchill says it is a gamble – make or mar my political career. But every humble home will bless my name, if I succeed. I said I would think about it. So I went and had a talk with Bridges and Brook. Then with Dorothy (who drove me over and was in the garden with Mrs C) On the whole, it seems impossible to refuse – but, oh dear, it is not my cup of tea. Harry Crookshank arrives – he is to be Minister of Health and help Eden as deputy-leader of the House of Commons. This suits him. He thinks I had better take it on. So I accept . . . . Meanwhile Clem Davies has come and gone. Will he be Minister of Education? He would love this, but what about the Liberal Party? He will try to persuade them, but Megan L George and Ld Samuel will resist. He leaves for the meeting. (We learn later – on the wireless – that the Liberals will not play) Then much talk about junior offices . . . .

In all this confusion, there is a plan. First, the selection of the main problems – *Defence, finance, supply, food and agriculture*, the business ministries (transport, coal, electricity) *houses* for the people. A Cabinet minister in charge of each – Churchill, Butler, Anderson, Woolton, Leathers, Macmillan. These, with Dominions, Colonial Office, Labour, Home Office, and Leader in Lords from the Cabinet. (Health and Board of Trade (probably Thorneycroft) also) Then there must be new blood in the Cabinet. There must also be a suppression (or reduction) of departments (the number of 9 or 10 is aimed at) Then there must be men of all types and classes . . . . Then the ministers must have £4000 instead of £5000 and no individual cars . . . .

. . . . When I get home, I begin to realise what a terrible burden I have undertaken. Churchill is grateful and will back me; but I really haven't a clue how to set about the job. (Among other minor problems, James Stuart, who is motoring south, has disappeared! But he is wanted, to be Secretary of State for Scotland. Nobody can say the Tories stand about waiting for office. It is a job to get hold of them!)

Went in to talk all this over with Maurice. Carol came to dinner. (I have now a lot to arrange – first of all, with my brother and affairs at St Martin's St)[75] So to bed. What a day! . . . .

30 October

At the palace at 12 noon to kiss hands. Ld W (Ld President) and Lord Leathers, James Stuart, Harry Crookshank and myself taking office, with 2 new Privy Councillors being sworn . . . .

A Cabinet (the first Cabinet) at 3. Churchill in great form. He was anxious to get Peter Bennett as Parl Secy to Labour. 'Tho a Wesleyan and a teetotaller, he is none the less a most agreeable character, respected and even loved by the trade union leaders'. This is certainly true. The P.M. opened with a review of the defence situation. It is quite deplorable. No formation remains in the island except the 6th Armoured Divn, and this is promised to General Eisenhower. He cannot let it go. Territorial divisions will have to be called up in turn, and the Home Guard got together again. He will prob tell the whole story to the House in secret session. Butler (Chancellor of the Exchequer) gave a review of the financial and economic position. This is shattering. A paper had been prepared by the Heads of Departments, but apparently the late Govt ignored the facts. Eden told us something about the Middle East, where a desperately difficult situation has been allowed to develop. Woolton told us about food. The stocks are very low – meat worse than at any time in the war, both as to current landing and reserves. Ld Leathers said that the transport system may collapse this winter and there is no coal. He is getting 1 million tons at once from America – the largest amount that can be dealt with by ships and ports. A committee was appointed to meet the Chancellor of

---

75. Then the M&Co head office in London.

the Exchequer and discuss cuts, of which I am a member. Another, of which I am also a member, to draft the King's speech . . . .

At the Treasury Ctee, it looks as if I shall lose even the timber and steel I hoped to get on the 200,000 house basis! What a start! . . . .

2 November

. . . . Sir Graham Cunningham (Chairman: Triplex Glass and lately Controller-General, Ministry of Supply) came; at my request, to see me. He advised me (as I hoped) to get a business set-up. We can never build the houses with the men we have. It is just possible I cd get Cunningham for the job; though he advised me to try Sir Percy Mills. I am already in touch with him. He is coming from Birmingham to see me on Sunday. (He was Machine Tool Controller all the war and is a first class man) . . . .

5–9 November

. . . . I am working through the chief officers of the Ministry in turn. This takes quite a time, as I like to encourage them to talk quite freely. There have been 2 Cabinets. I have seen also the representatives of the building unions (Coppock and Fawcett) and of the Builders (Hudson). Coppock and Fawcett were very pleasant. I told them that I knew little or nothing about the problem. They were much amused by this. 'The last ministers knew everything. It was no good trying to talk to them. They talked at us'. This referred to Bevan and Dalton. The union leaders support the Labour party. But they have very little affection for the political leaders. I gave C and F tea in the House of Commons. F (who is a fine hearty fellow, weighing 15 to 16 stone, I shd say) consumed cream buns at a prodigious rate . . . .

The Americans have and are treating us very badly over Persia. It is obvious that it was Washington that frightened London out of strong action at the critical time . . . .

I am still struggling to get a man to run housing. It is quite clear to me that neither Sir Thomas Sheepshanks (Secretary) or Sir John Wrigley (Deputy) will build many houses . . . .

My Parl Under-Secretary, Ernest Marples, is very good and very keen.

I have to speak in the debate on Tuesday. I heard Dalton on housing on Thursday. He was quite moderate. But, of course, we have that 300,000 'target' (often, I fear, turned into a 'promise') round our necks.

Timber and steel are the bottlenecks and with the economic crisis and rearmament will get worse . . . .

10 November

A very useful morning with Lord Swinton. It is clear that we must have *proper* system of steel allocation as soon as possible. Even if the decision is taken now, it will not be possible to get into working order before February. Lord S is to propose this at Monday's cabinet. He is also in favour of returning the *buying* of timber to private hands at once. Everyone seems to agree, so this also shd be settled on Monday. Of course, the amount wh can be spent and the currencies will have to be fixed by the Treasury. But the bulk buying has broken down, because the timber control cannot do it properly. I am in hopes that by this method we may get more and more suitable timber, better cut and graded, than by the old method . . . .

12 November

A good Cabinet this morning. Steel allocation is now agreed, to start on Feb 5th . . . .

14 November

. . . . The maze of difficulty and confusion grows daily more baffling. As far as I can see, the former Govt held a broad meeting once a year, when a capital programme in terms of money was agreed; after that, everything was left to civil servants. This might work in a free liberal economy, where goods always are there to match money. It makes no sense in the siege economy in wh we are today. The Treasury planners may be very clever – but they have got us into 3 major crises since the war. If I am to have any success, we must have flexibility and adaptation.

15 November

An interesting meeting between Minister of Works and his people; Lord Swinton; and myself. We are trying to work out a machinery to manage the *whole* building programme; this is the only way to see that house-building, repairs, factory building, schools etc are regarded as a whole and carried through with mutual goodwill and common sense.

A long Cabinet. Eden reported on the German situation. The chief problem now thrown up is who is to pay the cost of the Allied armies

stationed in Germany. The so-called 'occupation costs' are enormous
– much inflated, probably, by the Germans themselves. But we cannot
afford this extra charge; yet, if Germany joins the European army,
it is hardly reasonable for her to pay the allied occupation costs as
well . . . .

      . . . . Dinner with Beddington-Behrens, to wind up the Central and
Eastern section so far as I am concerned. I have written to Eden to
explain the position about all this. I fear he will still think that I am
trying to interfere in foreign affairs, for he is very sensitive about this.
Nor did he ever much like the European movement.

16 November

'Rent restrictions' all the morning. 'Housing policy' and paper for
Cabinet all the afternoon. The latter is now ready and I hope to get
everyone to agree to the ministerial building ctee. The paper has been
drawn up with the approval of Ministry of Works. The first part of
the paper deals with things under my direct control – ratio between
council and private building; smaller houses; sale of existing council
houses to the sitting tenants. All these will excite the utmost disapproval among the Socialists. So I expect there will be a row in the
House, altho' the principles are simple, the machinery has to be pretty
complicated to prevent abuse. For instance, re-sale of a private house
cannot be allowed within a period . . . .

19–24 November

A heavy week, with 2 Cabinets . . . . My poor housing seems very
uncertain. The first steel allocation meeting shows a deficit of a million
tons. I am having trouble with the civil servants about Percy Mills.
They want him to be advisory; I want him to be executive. Things
are much changed since I was in office before. The 'Trade Union'
of officials is back in power. The Treasury planners are supreme.
Ministers are treated very politely, but with firmness, as temporary
nuisances . . . .

Sunday 25 [November]

Last meeting with Central and Eastern section of European movement.
I have done my best to get the F.O. to help them. It was rather a
moving occasion. It seems odd that Strasbourg starts tomorrow and
that, for the first time, I shall not be there. There was a short, but

interesting and even strained discussion at last week's cabinet about Europe. David Fyfe is going to lead our team, altho' I fancy he will only stay a few days. But, as a member of the Cabinet, what he says must carry great weight. Every word will be scrutinised. Churchill wd like, obviously, to be loyal to the European movement, wh he founded. Salisbury and Lyttelton, for different reasons, are temperamentally opposed. Fyfe wished to suggest that we shd say something about our being associated with the Schuman Iron and Steel plan. Churchill agreed, rather weakly I thought. But Churchill has his own plan for a European army, to which it is clear that he believes we shd contribute. Many of the Cabinet will fight this. I said that I thought the Schuman plan wd collapse and that de Gaulle wd [not] like the European army at least as planned by Pleven, with all its political paraphernalia. The way wd then be open (and the last opportunity presented) for Britain to give a lead to Europe. The subject dropped; but in a certain atmosphere of doubt.

26 November

. . . . I have now arranged to bring in Percy Mills, on terms agreed with the Cabinet ministers and the civil servants concerned. This is a triumph . . . .

27 November

. . . . I introduced, in answer to several arranged questions, my new policy, on [the] ratio between council and private building, 1 for 1 instead of 1 for 5; sale of council houses to tenants; thirdly, the simpler house. A storm of supplementaries followed my pronouncement; but I think the Opposition were really rather stunned. Attlee and Morrison both rose to supplementaries, which is unusual. They will probably ask for a debate; even perhaps a vote of censure. The party seemed very pleased and I have received much congratulation . . . .

28 November

A very good press on my housing plan in all except *Daily Herald* and *Daily Worker*. Even *Daily Mirror* fair and on the whole favourable. The *News Chronicle* and the *Manchester Guardian* friendly; the Tory press very good. The *Daily Express* ecstatic. Is it the 'kiss of death'?

10.30–12. A press conference at the ministry on the new plans. I announced the appointment of Percy Mills. The evening press favourable. An emergency Cabinet at 6pm to hear a report from the

Chancellor of the Exchequer on the financial and economic position. This continues to be bad; the drain on our gold and dollar reserves continues at an alarming rate. Drastic remedies will be called for. I pray we shall not take several bites at it; all the unpleasant things should be done rapidly and ruthlessly. Butler's first cuts were insufficient to achieve any real result . . . .

29 November
Eden has stated definitely in Rome (in a press conference) that we shall not join the European army. Maxwell-Fyfe has stated definitely in Strasbourg that we may do so. Reynaud says that no French assembly will vote for a European army in which Britain is not represented. But how can Britain be represented in the devitalised and denationalised army which Pleven and Monnet plan to make – no national uniform but a common uniform; no national tunes; only an American jazz. Such an army will never be formed and if formed will not fight. So fall to the ground, it seems, all the hopes of 2 to 3 years work in the European movement. Schuman and Monnet have made the same errors with the army as with Iron and Steel. It is curious but, I fear, was inevitable, since one is a mystic and the other a superplanner. From de Gaulle's speech, it is clear that all this will be destroyed, if he can do so. All the more – if the Iron and Steel plan is doomed, and the Army is doomed, ought we to take the lead to create a Europe which *will* work. If we stated our terms, they wd be accepted. So far, the Foreign Secretary has attended only one Cabinet since the Govt was formed. We are able, of course, to read the F.O. telegrams. But we have no real picture of the policy he is following . . . .

The Opposition put down what amounted to a vote of censure on the refusal to give a 'Christmas Bonus' for forces. I did not hear LG's speech. Charles Hill (the Radio Doctor) wound up in great style facing courageously a storm of noisy abuse. Our majority 37. (It is curious how badly the Socialists are voting in the House. Our majorities – even on 3 line whips – are running at about 40.) . . . .

30 November
. . . . The Opposition motion on housing is now on the paper. Of my three proposals, it condemns two and says nothing about the third (simpler houses) I have drafted an amendment and got James Stuart and Crookshank (as Leader of the House) to agree . . . .

4 December

At the Cabinet this morning Churchill gave us some indication of what he would say about the European army etc on Thursday. Eden took the view that, since HMG had refused to take part in the negotiations, it was too late to do so now. The military negotiation was complete; the political one remained. Eisenhower had strongly urged us not to enter the European Community – that is European army on the Pleven model, with the whole superstructure of supra-national authority; Parliament; etc. If we did so, we shd delay everything. The French politicians (and the others) were now hesitating. We should urge them to go ahead on the course they had planned. Churchill (after this explanation of Eden's) read his passage. He then turned to me and Maxwell Fyfe (his fellow-conspirators at Strasbourg!) and asked if we were satisfied. I said that I thought the present position tragic, but that, in view of what Eden had said, we must accept it. But I thought that both the Schuman plan and the European army (on the Pleven–Monnet model) might break down. But was there not a danger that if it went through, the position in ten years would be still worse. There would be a European Community which would dominate Europe and would be roughly equal to Hitler's Europe of 1940. If we stay out, we risk that German domination of Europe which we have fought two wars to prevent . . . .

The vote of censure on my housing plans announced a week ago was rather a flop. Dalton began, with a speech in very moderate tone. I followed. The speech was well received and I think made some of the points intelligible; but it was rather too long (largely due to interruption) Dalton was very scornful of the phrase 'comparable housing need'. What could it mean? (This was as between applicants for houses to buy and houses to let) In answering, I was able to say that the words were the text of the last Government's formula. Curiously enough, Bevan (who followed me) fell into the same trap (about another paragraph) I let him work himself up into a great show of indignation about another phrase. What could these enigmatic words signify? They were a trap, a swindle, etc etc. I then got up and said 'I am afraid I must ask you to explain their meaning. Once again I have been guilty of plagiarism. They are your words, taken from your circular of 1948' . . . .

5 December

Housing meeting[76] – Parl Sec; Wrigley; Mills; Wilkinson, to discuss

---

76. In the Ministry.

next steps. First, we must free ourselves from the shackles of the so-called 'Capital Investment Programme'. Secondly, we must get materials. Thirdly, we must look into the system of making housing allocations to the local authorities. On the first, it means a row with Treasury – perhaps leading to Cabinet row. The second depends on the success of the Cabinet Building Ctee (and its working sub-committees) which met for the first time last Monday. The third is a real weakness, I feel . . . .

Dinner at 1 Carlton Gardens[77] for Adenauer . . . . The Germans are determined to 'federate' Europe, and speak about it quite confidently. Rather naively, one said that if they did not achieve united Europe, there was a danger of the revival of bad men and bad things in Germany . . . .

6 December

Churchill's long awaited speech on defence. Either by design or by mistake, the debate ended in a great demonstration of national unity. C praised the Socialists for conscription, for the atomic decision (including the American atomic bombers in E Anglia) for the efforts at rearmament etc. Altho' he indicated the serious position of the air service, he did not press any charge of neglect. Shinwell tore up his speech; C got up, tears in his eyes, and praised Shinwell as a patriot. All this left the Tories rather dazed. But what a strange end to a warmongering election! Perhaps this was partly C's purpose. Also, no doubt, to lay to the foundation of a national position when he goes to Washington . . . .

7 December

. . . . Cabinet at 12 . . . . A row between Eden and Churchill about the release of German political prisoners – Kesselring etc. . . . . E was very upset and nearly what you call 'flounced out'. Eden is a queer man. He has great charm and some great gifts. He is a really first-class negotiator. But he is almost childishly jealous – hence his dislike for me, for David Fyfe, for Sandys and for all of us who have dared to show an interest in foreign affairs. He specially dislikes me, altho' I really like and admire him. If he had the first place, he might easily rise above all these faults. It may really be that he has been Prince of Wales too long.

---

77. The official residence of the Foreign Secretary.

Beddington-Behrens came to lunch with me. The F.O. are behaving badly about the Central and Eastern European Commission and the proposed conference in London. One side of the F.O. likes the movement. 'C'[78] even supplies a secretary and other help. But Eden (I suppose because of my having started it) is very sticky. Duff Cooper had promised to preside in my place, but is so angry with Eden (and Churchill) about their foreign policy, that he has now chucked . . . .

8 December

. . . . Went to see Leo Amery. Churchill has offered him a peerage. I did all I cd to dissuade him. It is a most selfish act. He is 78 and will ruin poor Julian's life.[79] No money; no career; and a peerage! Catherine is distraught. Julian is in Strasbourg and can do nothing. He is to consult with Salisbury tomorrow. Leo has persuaded himself that the HofLords will be reformed. But this is most unlikely. Anyway, he had better wait until it is. I rang up S when I got home to Sussex and urged him to stop Leo if he could. To ruin his son's life just for the chance of making a few more speeches to some bored noblemen! What folly!

9 December

Leo Amery has abandoned his idea of taking a peerage. I am much relieved.

15 December

Got to B.G. after a very heavy week. We are making considerable progress in creating a mechanism and in strengthening our liaison with other departments interested in building. But everything depends upon the cabinet's decision on my paper, printed and circulated today. I ask for authority to get away from all this annual planning and this grandmotherly control by the Treasury. I want to build 800,000 houses during the next 3 years. I shd expect to do 230,000 in 1952; 265,000 in 1953; 300,000 in 1954. If I can get this authority, the Minister of Works and I can plan together the necessary supply of building materials. By reducing flats; by having more 2 bedroomed houses; by

---

78. The traditional name for the head of Britain's Secret Intelligence Service.

79. Except for the law lords all peerages were hereditary until 1958. Macmillan feared that his son-in-law's inheriting a peerage would ruin a promising political career, since he would not be able to sit in the Commons.

having smaller houses, we can get the 300,000 with a remarkably small increase of steel. We shall have difficulties and bottlenecks. But the Treasury don't want us even to try.

A good day's shooting at home – 65 pheasants, 1 woodcock and lovely weather . . . .

20 December
The Cabinet met at 11am. There was a very full agenda – so protracted that my two items were only reached about 1.15. Most of the time was taken up with the economies on Health and Education. The P.M. was obviously concerned with the broadcast wh he has to make on Saturday. His influence on economies is always in favour of one big cut, rather than a lot of niggling ones. I had only time to expand my main paper shortly. The CofE suggested a further meeting between himself and me. This was agreed.

21 December
The meeting took place in the CofE's room at 3pm. Present; Butler, Swinton, Stuart, Eccles and self, with a number of officials. I made a grand assault on the Treasury planners. I felt that, on the whole, we were on a winning line. In a talk, after the officials had left, I made it clear to Butler that I wd resign if my plan of working up to 300,000 by 1954 was not accepted. A further report has to be made on 28th. Meanwhile, more meetings of officials. I asked, and obtained, that Swinton shd preside over this and that it shd be only to work out money (esp dollars) involved in timber imports etc. The policy of 230, 260, and then 300 thousand houses must be accepted. So far as Rab [Butler] (who is a good diplomatist) can be pinned down, he seemed to accept this . . . .

. . . . Slept at Birch Grove House – the first time for 12 years!

28 December
Cabinet 11–1.15. My housing paper was second item and quickly reached. The Chancellor of the Exchequer was conciliatory, but still wanted another committee and another Cabinet paper. But he admitted the political (if no other) need to work up to 300,000. But he still seemed to cling to the precise planning conceptions of the annual Capital Investment Programme. The P.M. asked me if I were satisfied. I replied 'No. Another committee means another month. I have already wasted 2 months getting started. I must begin to organise the

builders and above all the makers of building materials. I would ask the Cabinet to accept a formal approval of my broad plan'. I then read out the points in sequence from a paper which I had prepared with Percy Mills last night summarising the Cabinet decision which I required. There was no 'come-back' from the CofE. There was general approval by the Cabinet . . . . There was then much discussion about the financial agreement with Egypt.[80] The Treasury want to carry it out and transfer £15m on Jan 1st to the free a/c. Considering what has happened recently in Egypt and that we came within 3 votes of defeating the last Govt on the agreement itself, the P.M. (as I expected) exploded in wrath and indignation. The Foreign Secretary, with much ingenuity, argued that the argument was only to transfer this sum 'in the course of the year 1952'. So why do it on Jan 1st. It wd be a good thing to keep the Egyptians waiting, and get entangled in a long argument on interpretation. This shd be done quietly (without publicity) in order not to provoke the Egyptian Govt to reprisals on cotton. The cotton position is quite good for a time. We have in England all our purchases of last season's Sudan crop and a good deal of Egypt's. Nor will the Egyptian cotton millionaires be in a hurry to stop business, since they cannot easily find alternative markets. So this course was approved. The Cabinet were rather distressed to be told that another meeting is called for tomorrow (Saturday). Since most wanted to go out shooting tomorrow, faces lengthened as the morning went by, ...

29 December

. . . . Cabinet at 11am. The first paper was from the F.S. and gave a draft announcement to be made if and when the Paris negotiations about the European Army prove successful. This statement will go a long way and will associate us in a very complete manner with the life and work, though not with the constitutional mechanisms of the European Army . . . . I gather that Churchill has been putting a good deal of pressure on Eden over this . . . .

The Cabinet was chiefly concerned with the payment due to Egypt under the Sterling Release Agreement. It was now clear that £5m (out of the £15m) had to be paid on January 1st. It was only the £10m that could be paid 'in the course' of 1952. So yesterday's plan wd require

---

80. The Sterling Release Agreement negotiated earlier in the year, to release Egyptian sterling funds for trade and related payments.

modification. A very long and even sharp debate took place. Churchill, supported by Salisbury, Lyttelton, Cherwell, and Fyfe were against paying; on the ground that Egypt had repudiated her treaty with us and was allowing our soldiers to be murdered.[81] The CofE was for paying, to protect the credit of sterling. The F.S. was clearly *for* paying, because of the recent more favourable turn of events and his desire to help, not embarrass the King[82] at this moment. I supported the F.S. I felt that he was playing the hand and ought to be able to play it as he thought best. The final decision was adjourned till the afternoon. After sitting from 11 to 1.30, the Cabinet resumed at 3.30. P.M. was in rather a black mood and proposed that the whole £15m shd be paid to a special account, until the murderous attacks on our soldiers ceased etc etc. Eden clearly did not like this. After much discussion, in wh I again supported Eden, the Cabinet began to come round to this view. It also emerged that the more important of the two agreements with Egypt, which gave them facilities for their general use of sterling for trading purposes over a very wide field, wd lapse on Dec 31st.[83] It was this agreement wh was much more important to them than the 'release' agreement. It was finally decided to allow the £5m to be transferred from our a/c to the others (in accordance with the agreement; *not* to do the same with the £10m (which we need not do at once according to the letter of the agreement) and to refuse to renew the wider and more important agreement about sterling payments generally. Facilities wd continue to be granted, under strict Treasury and F.O. supervision, but the screw cd be tightened at any moment and to any degree. Thus, we keep our agreement (£5m); keep *within* the agreement (£10m) and by not renewing the lapsed agreement covering the wider problem, hold a continual and efficacious threat over the Egyptian economy. I am sure this was the right decision . . . .

30 December (Sunday)
. . . . D tells me that many of her friends think that I have been put

---

81. In October 1951 Egypt had repudiated the 1936 treaty governing the stationing of British troops in Egypt. Meanwhile there was increasing terrorist activity against the British bases in the Canal Zone.
82. King Farouk of Egypt.
83. This was the Sterling Payments Agreement, which provided for trade between Egypt and the sterling area and the use of sterling by Egypt outside the sterling area.

into the housing job in order to fail and finish my political career. Malcolm McCorquodale told her this at her luncheon party. 'He must be tough – very tough' – 'for you know', he went on, 'who wd like to see him out of the way'. All this is very mysterious and to me very unpleasant. It is always said that, in politics, there are no friendships at the top. I suppose Eden and Butler are those indicated . . . .

1952

1–4 January

A short, but very heavy week. The battle of the Capital Investment Programme is still being waged,[1] but on a more restricted front. Having got freedom for Housing, I have now to fight for water and sewage – more especially for water schemes *not* primarily for housing but for industrial needs. In this of course, I can rely on help from their departments. We have also had a great departmental issue to decide – the future of the Regional system. Sir P Mills is very anxious to set up Regional Housing Production Boards, with M of Labour and M of Works officials and representatives of labour and builders. This frightens the dept; but I have decided in favour of Sir Percy's plan . . . .

8 January

The dept still worries about Percy Mills, tho' what we shd do without him, I shudder to think. He approaches every problem with realism and precision; his suggestions are at once bold and ingenious; and he has a quiet persistence which enables him to get his way . . . . Yet they are suspicious, particularly of the speed with which he works . . . .

9 January

The first meeting of the Ministerial Council this afternoon – Secretary; two deputy secretaries (Sir J Wrigley and Dame E Sharp) Sir Percy Mills; Mr Wilkinson; Parl Secy; and myself. We made real progress. 40,000 new allocations are to be issued forthwith, as well as the 28,000 for special departmental needs . . . .

One of the tiresome and wasteful duties of a minister is seeing individuals and deputations. They take much time and achieve little wh is useful.

---

1. That is, the Treasury efforts to manage capital spending in order to combat balance of payments problems.

10 January

. . . . [A] Cabinet, presided over by Harry Crookshank – mostly routine business, varied by a statement by CofE on the Commonwealth Finance Ministers meeting. I do not feel that Rab has really grasped this nettle. The real question is – 'Can Gt Britain ever become a going concern on present lines?' I shd like to see the whole monetary policy of the Empire unified and strengthened . . . .

12 January

A pleasant shoot in glorious weather – sunny, frosty, and still. We got 50 pheasants and a woodcock. Our woods were quite beautiful. Lord and Lady Woolton, Col and Mrs Clarke, Sarah and Andrew Heath, Maurice to dinner. This was our first attempt to give a dinner since we went back to B.G. Dorothy enjoyed it and had worked hard on the restoration of the house. W was in good form, full of good stories about the war period. I fear we all hark back (in this Cabinet) to those inspiring days. Can we recreate that spirit?

It is evident that Churchill and Eden are having a successful time in USA and Canada. I am rather distressed at Anthony's continual and very marked emphasis on Britain's detachment from Europe in any organic sense. Churchill seems to have given in to the predominant F.O. and party view. The F.O. have circulated a quite dreadful paper on European unity. Altho' it will infuriate Anthony, I think I shall circulate a reply. I will get Julian Amery to help in drafting it . . . .

14 January

Went to Hemel Hempstead New Town. I was pleased with the progress and the enthusiasm. I thought the lay-out rather extravagant. I laid the foundation stone to a factory (Rotax) and for the first time in my life received a silver trowel! . . . .

16 January

It is fairly certain that Churchill has now invited Alexander (the General, not the cooperative leader)[2] to become Minister of Defence. This means another peer, but I don't suppose the public will mind.

---

2. A reference to the Labour Minister of Defence (1946–50), Earl Alexander of Hillsborough, who was also leader of the Co-operative affiliate of the Labour Party.

I am not so sure about Alex's power to do the Parly side or even the office side. What he excels in is the diplomatic side. He will be quite excellent for all the NATO work, relations with European Army etc . . . .

Dined with Lords Brand and Salisbury at Brooks! Lord B was pessimistic about our prospects of 'doing the right thing' as to the financial crisis . . . . Lord S felt it would end up with a strong demand for a 'National Govt'. He fears coalitions – or, rather, the aftermath of coalitions.

17 January
. . . . The Cabinet today was interesting. Eden gave us his general impressions of the American visit. He had been forcibly struck – indeed horrified – at the way we are treated by the Americans today. They are polite; listen to what we have to say; but make (on most issues) their own decisions. Till we can recover our financial and economic independence, this is bound to continue . . . .

The reforms in the management of NATO went well. Unfortunately, they insist on Paris, not London, for HQ. (Can you blame them?) We lost out on the Atlantic Command. It was too late. Had the former Govt pressed it earlier, the Americans wd have agreed . . . . On Egypt, the Americans are pressing us to come to terms with the King, before it is too late . . . .

On Persia, they are spoiling everything by their restlessness. Instead of allowing the economic pressure to become effective, they are allowing themselves to be blackmailed by Mossadeq's threats that Persia will go Communist without American aid . . . .

The Americans are pressing all the time for a reduction of trade with China by us. They have, in fact, done great injury to Hong Kong.[3] Meanwhile, they buy very largely from China, paying in gold or dollars. But they say buying is not the same as selling! 'What do the Chinese do with the dollars?', the mere Englishman wd be inclined to ask . . . .

---

3. Having spent much of the war trying to encourage Britain to hand Hong Kong over to the Nationalist regime which was overthrown by Mao's People's Liberation Army in 1949. The new People's Republic of China on the mainland was recognized by Britain in 1950. However, diplomatic relations with the US were not established until 1978.

18 January

A long meeting of the Home Affairs Ctee. The problem of the
insurance structure in present inflationary conditions was discussed at
length. The pensions, which were intended originally to be sufficient
for the pensioner's modest needs, are now only worth half what they
should be. So nearly 2 million people draw Poor Law – now called
National Assistance . . . .

22 January

9.45am. Legislative Committee. My Town Development Bill[4] (which is
absolutely essential to my Housing Programme) was rather knocked
about by the Committee. Salisbury was the leader in the attack. I cd
not get agreement and must try again next Tuesday . . . .

11–1. Cabinet. A most gloomy affair. The 'balance of payments'
position grows daily worse. More cuts are to be made in imports, and
we must in addition draw heavily on stockpiles. Foreign travel is to be
cut to £25 allowance . . . .

. . . . Left for Nottingham, when I delivered my Housing speech –
the whole programme – expansion, housing boards, etc etc. A very
large audience in the Albert Hall accepted the speech with much
enthusiasm – which surprised me, as much of it was dull and rather
technical. Slept at Nottingham.

23 January

A wonderful press!! We have really hit the headlines. On the whole, a
very friendly reception. The *Manchester Guardian* a bit sniffy, as the
Times will no doubt be tomorrow. The *Daily Herald*, as I expected,
hostile but rather silly about 'way clear for the jerry-builder'. But all
the press gives it big space and I hope this will help to create the sense
of urgency which is so necessary. Left Nottingham at 9am and drove
through Leicester to a little village called Desford. Here had descended
(like locusts) a host of photographers, BBC men, television, news-reel
reporters and the like – all to see me open 2 houses – the first built to
the new simplified designs. (Incidentally, they have cost less than £1000
a piece, which is very good for 3 bed-room houses in these days.)

Got back to London in time for meeting of the Ministerial Council
(the new organ of my own Ministry wh meets alternative Wednesdays

---

4. To allow expansion of existing towns.

and in an attempt to get the Housing and the Planning parts of the Ministry together). A useful discussion on

a) London housing problems and the New Towns
b) The Town Development Bill and how to meet objections
c) The need for more 'unconventional' houses
d) steel shortages and water and sewage schemes . . . .

24 January

Cabinet at 11.15 . . . . Egypt, not on agenda, but first item. Eden (presiding in Churchill's absence) made a statement. The position is growing hourly worse, and the Cabinet may be asked to agree to the drastic steps which are all prepared . . . . After this, a long discussion as to how to get the further £150m of savings on imports which we must make, in order to save a collapse of sterling and to do our part in the general Commonwealth arrangement . . . .

I was not so impressed by the CofE today. No doubt he is tired. He seemed not to have a real grip of the situation, and to move too rapidly from one opinion to another. He seems to start firmly, on the basis of the Treasury brief. Then, as the discussion proceeds, he is driven to see how thin, unimaginative, and pedantic these briefs often are. I do not believe the Treasury has ever been so badly served as now. There is no man of any real value left. Leslie Rowan is the best; but he has become intolerably conceited. Eady is delightful but ineffective. Bridges is a good head of the civil service and a charming fellow, but worked out. There is no one who has a real grasp. I suspect the same is true of the Bank. I cannot believe that Cobbold is a big man, or even a clever man. We ought to put Sir John Anderson at the head of the Bank. There is a man for you.

At the end of a long agenda, Lord Swinton's paper on the raw materials etc wh wd be required for the Housing programme came before the Cabinet. All through recent meetings I have been expecting an attack on my timber imports. But an exhausted Cabinet accepted the paper and adjourned . . . .

25 January

We have now lived for six weeks or more, without the House of Commons, but in almost daily conference, either in full Cabinet or in Cabinet committees. The absence (recently) of the P.M. has made ministers more forthcoming and more natural. For, although he is less prone to monologue than in 1945, nevertheless [the] P.M. does do a lot of the talking. We are getting to grips with things – and beginning to weigh up the importance and strength of individual ministers. In the Cabinet itself, Salisbury carries great weight. Thorneycroft talks too much and addresses the Cabinet as if it were a public meeting. Crookshank is master of all Parliamentary questions. Eden has presided well in Churchill's absence. When P.M. is there, he betrays his impatience . . . .

27 January

. . . . This has been an exceptionally heavy period for us all. I have taken considerable risks in the 'Housing' field; but I have been lucky in getting all my publicity into a period when there was a lull in *announcement* of general policy, tho' great activity in framing it. To plump for an *expansionist* housing programme, (wh I have carried in the teeth of the Treasury, the Bd of Trade and the Service departments) in a restrictionist and deflationist atmosphere is bold and may prove disastrous. But it wd be equally fatal to stand by and see the housing programme whittled away . . . .

. . . . Dr Retsinger called to see me on Friday and stayed over an hour. This is his theme . . . . 'Unless England takes the lead, there will be a gradual weakening of European morale and the will to resist . . . .

. . . . '[I]f we take the lead, the British Empire–European bloc can be made independent of America and Russia – a real and beneficient third force. Then a deal can be made and he is convinced that Russia will give in without war – even to the extent of retiring to her frontiers. Nothing could be a greater guarantee to Russia than the emergence of a Europe–Empire group *not* subservient to America. The Russians are absolutely convinced that Britain and Europe are as much satellite states as her own . . . .

'Churchill understands all this – but is too old to break through the prison of English tradition. Eden understands it not so well, but he is too ambitious for the succession (the only thing he thinks about) to risk any bold policy. He is a prematurely aged man. He had moments almost of genius during the war. Now he is very conventional. He is not sure of himself. This is why he is so jealous. He is an ageing woman, with a morbid fear of any younger or more attractive rival.

'War is almost certain, unless Britain leads Europe. The Americans have the wealth and the material power – but they have no experience and no patience.'

This is a précis of his talk. I listened, with hardly an intervention.

I must say that I thought it a pretty shrewd summary of the world situation – and a pretty frightening one . . . .

28 January

. . . . The Cabinet (Eden presiding) was given an account of the weekend in Egypt. It was not a very good story and I think Eden has handled it well in trying circumstances. The military, who have always been confident that the operations to occupy Alexandria and Cairo could, if necessary, easily be put into action, suddenly got cold feet when the time approached . . . .

In any event, the end of this story would be ludicrous if it were not clouded by the tragic events in Cairo – the burning of the Shepheard's Hotel and the brutal massacre in the Turf Club. For, however frightened we may have been of them, it appears that they were still more frightened of us. So when the news leaked that the British Army was on the move, the King gave way and dismissed his Government. (What a good thing that he could not read the teleprinter messages between the War Office and GHQ Egypt!)[5] Thus a new situation has been created. No solution of the great problem is in sight. But the fall of Nahas Pasha and his Govt must be a good thing. That his fall was due

a) to the riots and the fear of the palace that real revolution was starting

b) to the British threat, is clear enough.

What follows next, is more obscure . . . .

29 January

9.45am Legislative Committee. I carried (by one or two judicious concessions) my Town Development Bill . . . .

31 January

Deputation from L.C.C. The Socialists (I was informed) intended to run their campaign on the cry that the Ministry of Housing, under Tory management, was frustrating their efforts to re-house the people, in out-town sites particularly. I took the exact opposite line to what

---

5. A reference to 'Black Saturday'. Following escalating violence against terrorists in the Canal Zone, culminating in British forces killing some fifty Egyptian auxiliary police, the Cairo masses rioted, killing numerous Europeans. There had been a plan for the full-scale re-occupation of Egypt in such an eventuality, code-named 'Rodeo', but the army decided that it was too risky.

they expected (much to the delight of Henry Brooke, leader of the Tory Opposition on the Council) and pressed all kinds of sites on them. They retired a little puzzled . . . . Some of the more responsible Labour men spoke to me (esp Arthur Henderson) deploring the situation. They feel that we are to blame for trying to charge them with the full responsibility for the bad turn of affairs, wh they think unfair. They say it plays into the hands of their extremists and makes a movement for national concentration more difficult. Many of them still favour a national Government . . . .

1 February
Daniel's birthday (66 years) I sent him a note in the [ministerial] bag. I lunched with him at Macmillans on Wed. He is in great form . . . .

2 February
I travelled to Swinton (where I spoke to a course of some 100 students at the Conservative college) in the company of Gaitskell (as far as Leeds) . . . .

. . . . [H]e fears that these crises in the sterling–dollar situation are endemic. Things will improve, and then perh another crisis in 18 months. Our problem is how to get a large enough reserve of gold and dollars to stand the pressure. If the Americans were to raise the price of gold it wd be the easiest way out. But

a) they wd hardly do this during a boom in U.S. It is a measure reserved for a slump

b) there is a danger that it might lead to a popular outcry agst buying gold at all.

We had some talk about Bevan, whom G obviously despises as well as dislikes. He thought his speech in the debate this week quite deplorable. I said I thought he made the Parly mistake of having no fixed place in the House (as Chamberlain, Churchill, Ll George and other figures had when they were no longer on the *front* bench) G thought that perh he did not wish to take quite so definite a position against the official party as that wd imply. I shd think G was essentially a moderate, by temperament as well as conviction. He is able, and agreeable . . . .

3 February
Lunched with Lady Swinton and party of Yorkshire neighbours. The house is hideous; built by Lady S's grandfather in a very bad mixture

of early Victorian (mahogany and gold) and Gothic battlements. The stables (about 1720) are very good – rather like those at Chatsworth. There was a lovely Queen Anne house before . . . .

5 February

. . . . The Cabinet was today long and rather desultory . . . . We had a passage of arms about rates of interest and the effect of the new P.W.L.B. on housing and the housing subsidy. The P.M. cd not understand what [it] was all about; the CofE did not like my argument. I still maintain that the object of raising bank rates is to stop people doing unnecessary things. If HMG want to stop more houses being built, they have only to say so. It's quite easy. But to try to encourage local authorities and private individuals to build more – then to raise rates to build more – then to raise rates against them is folly. I told the Cabinet that it was just masochism. The discussion died away without any clear decision; this means that the Treasury wins and the P.W.L.B. rate goes up to 4¼% at once and perh to a higher figure later on . . . .

6 February

This has been a most extraordinary day. I was receiving a deputation of advertisers at 10.30am, when my P.S. came in to tell me that an emergency Cabinet had been summoned for 11. He whispered to me 'The King is dead. No public announcement yet'. As I walked from the Ministry to Downing Street, I was told that the news is now public.

The P.M. spoke a few simple and very moving words. Business then began. The Ld Chancellor and Mr Speaker (who attended the Cabinet) were asked as to procedure and the Ld President (Woolton) was asked to deal with the immediate problem of the Accession Council. The last time that a monarch was proclaimed in absentia was on the death of Queen Anne, under rather more perilous circumstances than today, so far as the succession is concerned. The last time a Queen, already married, succeeded was Queen Anne herself.

It was decided to hold the Accession Council at 5pm at St James. The summons to the appropriate people were to be sent out at once. It was decided to adjourn each House until 7pm, when members wd start the process of taking the oath of allegiance.

. . . . At 2.45 there was a meeting of the Cabinet in the P.M.'s room at the House of Commons and quite an important discussion took place on the form of the proclamation. The old form included expressions like 'the Crown Imperial' which (since their real meaning is forgotten or obscured) cause difficulties in the new situation of the Commonwealth and Empire. (Imperial Crown meant originally a king who owed fealty to no Emperor) The words 'Head of the Commonwealth' were introduced into the recital of titles, and the expression 'with representatives of other members of the Commonwealth' inserted among the list of people composing this strange and ancient body, the last relic of the commune conciliar or Witan.[6] It includes 'Lords Spiritual and Temporal', the Privy Council, and 'other Principal Gentlemen of Quality, with the Lord Mayor, Aldermen, and Citizens of London'. These changes made the presence of all the High Commissioners, including the High Commissioner for India both regular and possible . . . .

At 5pm we assembled at St James Palace, entering by Ambassador's Court. The meeting of the Council took place in the large room upstairs – and very fine it is. Ld Woolton (as Ld P) presided. There was a very large assembly of Peers, Ministers, ex-Ministers, Privy Councillors, High Commissioners etc. The Lord Mayor and the Aldermen were present in their robes – all others in morning clothes. The Lord P read the draft declaration, proclaiming Queen Elizabeth 2nd (The Scots, of course, will argue that she shd be Elizabeth 2nd of England and 1st of Scotland)[7] Various other draft orders were read, including instructions to the Lord Mayor, to the Secretary of State etc, for proclaiming the Queen, firing guns, sending 'circular letters' (presumably to Lords Lieutenants) etc etc. After this, we all signed the great parchment scrolls, which were laid out for the purpose. A remarkable and rather impressive ceremony. We hear that the Queen is expected back tomorrow evening. She will be met by a small number of notables, including the leaders of the Socialists and Liberals in the HofC. At 7pm the Speaker took the chair. He proceeded to take the oath of allegiance, and was followed by ministers, led by the P.M.

7 February
Cabinet at 12.30. Churchill was not present. (He did not wake till after 10am, being much tired with the emotion of yesterday) Eden presided. Certain matters were arranged regarding the funeral, as well as some other business. The city is dead; a strange hush. I worked

---

6. The Anglo-Saxon royal council.
7. Churchill compromised by deciding that the Royal style in Scotland would be ER (for Elizabeth Regina).

quietly at the flat on a lot of departmental papers. Finished Greville volume 6. (It is strange to have read so recently G's account of Queen Victoria's accession council.)

Churchill's broadcast was superb. It was the best piece of prose I have heard or read from him. Some phrases will live long – such as 'During these last months, the King walked with Death as if Death were a companion, an acquaintance whom he recognised and did not fear. In the end, Death came as a friend.' His references to the Queen Mother and Queen Mary were very fine. The last sentence was memorable 'I, whose youth was passed in the august, unchallenged, and tranquil glare of the Victorian Era, may well feel a thrill in invoking once more the prayer and anthem "God Save the Queen"'.

8 February
'The Lords and others of Her Majesty's Most Honourable Privy Council' gathered early this morning at St James' Palace. We entered by Ambassador's Court, and assembled in the old Levée room. Punctually, at the stroke of 10, the ceremony began by the Lord President nominating a small number, including P.M. and Attlee, 'to wait upon Her Majesty'. (Unfortunately, 10am is not a good hour for the P.M. and he was a minute or two late).

The Queen's entrance; the low bows of her councillors; the firm, yet charming voice in which she pronounced her allocution and went through the various ceremonious forms of the ritual (including the oath to maintain the Scottish Church) produced a profound impression on us all. A large number of notables were present. Of course, the effect wd have been much more brilliant if we had all been in full dress. The officers of the Brigade and Household Cavalry; the Earl Marshal; Lord Halifax (as High Steward of Westminster) and one or two others were in full dress and very fine they looked. But a lot of politicians in dark coats and striped trousers present rather a scruffy, scrubby appearance . . . .

A question arose about foreign troops at the State funeral. It seems that Lord Mountbatten has made some suggestion about Norwegian and Danish sailors. This was at the Earl Marshal's meeting. 'Why was he present?' grumbled P.M. 'As Fourth Sea Lord, I suppose', replied Eden 'and also as a member of the Family'. I could see that P.M. did not much like this early sign of the role wh I have no doubt the Mountbattens will aspire to play. He was much in evidence at the Council and will have much opportunity for interference if he (and she) wish to be (as I think they will) the power behind the Throne . . . .

11 February

. . . . After the speeches, we moved in procession to Westminster Hall. The Peers, led by the Ld Chancellor did the same. We lined the South and they the North side. I will not describe the ceremony, which was most moving in its simplicity and sincerity. The lying-in-state is a wonderful ceremony and a great opportunity to the people to show their loyalty.

At 5pm a Cabinet . . . . We discussed the date of the Coronation. There was general agreement that it shd not be this year. This year the bailiffs may be in; the Crown itself may be in pawn. 'It'll have a steadying effect next year' said Churchill. 'Anyway, it'll beat the Festival of Britain'. But the Queen might well make the Australian visit this winter, before a Coronation next May. 'Of course' he added 'with a young Queen there are always other aspects to be borne in mind'. Churchill, who was in good form, chaffed James Stuart very much about the Scottish pedantries regarding Elizabeth 2nd or 1st. There was a paper before the Cabinet about the Stone of Scone. We decided to take it out of the cellar in which it is now guarded, and put it back in its place . . . .[8]

12 February

. . . . The mass of paper continues. One cannot finish one's 'home-work' till very late each night. It seems that there are immense queues of people waiting to pass through Westminster Hall. It is cold, but fortunately not raining. The internal sorrows and confusion have taken our minds off external problems for the moment. But these are piling up. Germany is beginning to raise her price ominously; France is having doubts about the European army. America is angry about the delay. The next few weeks may be the turning point . . . .

Churchill says he has at the back of his mind an old saying 'When there will be 3 Queens of England, England's troubles will be over and all go well'.[9] Can anyone trace this? It must certainly be a rare event. Henry 8th took his own precautions, but perhaps at some moment it may have happened . . . .

---

8. On the theft of the Stone of Scone see above, pp. 39–40.

9. I have been unable to find a source for this quote.

14 February

. . . . Lunched at St Martin's St. After lunch took Daniel and Betty, Arthur and Peggy (Macmillan) and Elizabeth (Cavendish) to Westminster Hall. Then Carol and her children and some maids from home; then Sarah and Alexander and Joshua (Macmillan) and more maids from home. The children were impressed, I think. The crowds keep growing, orderly but immense and persistent. Last night the Hall had to be kept open till 2am; tonight it will be 6am.

The Secretary, (Sheepshanks) who never liked or understood the necessity for Sir Percy Mills, is behaving in a petty and rather old-maidish way. Mills, who is courteous but frank, has had it out with him and this may do good. It is incredible how narrow is the world in which these old-fashioned civil servants move. Nor have they any sense of time at all. Urgency is a word they cannot understand . . . .

Steel is a tangle of prices and quotas. My chief anxiety is that the new prices (when announced) shd give a sufficient encouragement to steel makers to give us the reinforcing bars and wire necessary to the reinforced concrete wh I want to see replacing sectional steel building. I think Churchill understood the point. Unless the price differential is sufficient steel-makers will continue to refuse to make enough of these rather fiddling products and my programme (and that of all building) will either go wrong or consume an unnecessary amount of sectional steel . . . .

15 February

. . . . I was able to arrange 3 separate parties to see the funeral; my room at the Ministry, to which I invited all former ministers and their wives and children . . . . my room at the HofC (wh overlooks New Palace Yard) to which I invited directors and officers of Macmillans; my flat in Piccadilly, to which came a lot of children, grandchildren, cousins etc etc.

D and I saw the procession from 90 Piccadilly, then motored to Paddington. It struck me that the crowds were not very large. I think the police had frightened them away, with the barriers and closing so many approach streets . . . .

By train, with Cabinet etc, to Windsor . . . . The service was short but very beautiful. The display of wreaths was astonishing. Returned by train, arriving about 4.30. Went to the ministry and worked late. At supper in Pratts found Randolph Churchill, full of wild diatribes agst the Mountbattens . . . .

18 February

Somebody said after the ten days during which George V was lying in state and being buried, 'Le roman est fini; l'histoire commence'.[10] This is very true.

The Cabinet met twice today, at 11.30 to 1.30; at 10pm to nearly midnight. The European army hangs in the balance; . . . . Eden, at tonight's Cabinet, seemed hopeful of some compromise being reached. But, of course, the facts of European life remain. The French are frightened of the Germans; the Germans are frightened of themselves. (For they know that Hyde is there, always ready to replace Jekyll) This is the reason why, at the last minute, the French are ready to jettison any or all of the complicated constitutional machinery which Pleven has built up round the conception of the European Army, if only they can get the British in. (A lot of this has already gone, as a result of pressure from the Benelux countries)

Churchill seems to make no effort for the European conception. His eyes are on Russia. He is impatient with the French, and does not seem to understand their hesitations. For him, there can be but one enemy of Europe at a time. Eden, therefore, and the F.O. and the majority of the Cabinet – all of whom have always been against the European movement – are taking full advantage of C's strange unwillingness to defend the ideas and ideals wh he did so much to promote. I suspect that they regard his change of front as pure opportunism. Europe has served his purpose while he was in opposition; now he need not worry. This is not, I believe, the truth. His mind is now much more obsessed with the practical need of getting some genuine defences into being and with keeping the Americans in the ring. For him, these are the first things wh we must pursue . . . .

21 February

. . . . At 4.30 meeting with the representatives of the various associations of local authorities to 'consult' them on the new subsidy rates. They were very courteous and seemed really quite pleased with what we were doing for them (so they ought to be. The Economist attacks me violently for giving them so much, 'Sabotage by Subsidy') . . . .

Saturday 23 February

The first spring day; a really lovely day. I woke with the sun streaming

---

10. 'The novel is finished, history begins'.

in to my big bedroom (wh was my mother's) Worked till 11. Then got up and went for a walk. Catherine (Amery) arrived for luncheon. Sarah is here; also Quintin Crewe. Walked with Catherine later in the woods. Blake's plantation is finished, to my great delight. Alexander (Macmillan) and Anne (Faber) to tea. Worked after tea till dinner and after dinner till bed-time, partly on the Foreign Affairs speech. I have received a rare brief from the F.O . . . .

25 February

Building Committee of Cabinet at 11. A useful meeting. There is considerable progress in the reinforcing rods (or bars) problem. After this, a meeting on possible amendments to the Town and Country Planning Act. I had to introduce the Town Development Bill, ... I moved the 2nd Reading in a speech about which I had taken a great deal of trouble and will read well in the record. But it was dull to deliver and I shd imagine very dull to listen to. Dalton supported in a few words; Bevan made a patronising and rather silly attack on the bill as a paltry one and said I shewed lack of courage in not dealing with all local government. (This was not well received, as he did nothing in 5 years about it) But he approved of the one clause which I thought he might oppose – that giving power to local authorities to sell freehold of land in their estate, subject to ministerial approval.

A good many of our county members are disturbed about the Bill and we shall have to pacify them in Committee . . . .

27 February

Cabinet at 11 . . . . There was a long argument about the B.C.C. [scil. BBC] charter. The party seems to be anxious to break the [television] monopoly. 'Free' or 'sponsored' programmes might easily fall into the hands of the Cooperative or the Communist party. For they have the money. But it is difficult to resist the party pressure.[11] 'I am undecided' said Churchill with his disarming smile 'because I don't know which view is the more popular'. It was finally decided that Lords Salisbury and Woolton shd see the 1922 Committee and talk it all over . . . .

The Socialists have put down a motion protesting agst Anderson's

---

11. This refers to pressure within the Conservative Party to break the BBC's monopoly over television broadcasting, eventually realized, despite opposition from Churchill and others, with the creation of ITV in 1955. Macmillan, who did not own a television set at this time, was himself very ambivalent about the idea.

(Ld Waverley's) appointment to the Income Tax Commission on the grounds of his political partisanship. Actually, he has always refused to join any party. Moreover, if we choose we can explode another little mine under Attlee, who issued the most pressing invitations to Anderson to join his Cabinet in 1945 . . . .

29 February

From last night's Cabinet till tonight has been the most extraordinary 24 hours I have ever spent. I was dining last night with Arthur Penn at the Turf. At 8.30 a call from Sir N Brook's secy announcing a Cabinet at 10pm and asking if he cd bring me personally some most secret papers. The messenger duly arrived at 9pm.

When the Cabinet began, it was clear that something quite unusual was in the air. The papers sent to me were the outline of a startling and quite dramatic proposal by the Chancellor of the Exchequer.[12] Although written very badly and in the confusing jargon of the Treasury etc, the proposal amounts to this. In spite of all our efforts to save imports, cut internal expenditure and generally do all the right things at home, we are going to be ruined by our customers in our capacity as bankers. The drain on sterling cannot be stopped unless something drastic is done about this. Australia is the worst offender – but there are others.

It was at once apparent that an inner circle of ministers had been discussing this situation amid the proposed plan for some days. To me, to the Lord Chancellor, to Ld Salisbury, to Sir W Monckton, and to several others it was a surprise. To the P.M. the CofE (of course) Crookshank, Woolton, Cherwell, Eden etc it was a matter wh had already been discussed up to a point. The CofE expounded this plan – this was (roughly) to block or fund (at nominal interest) all sterling balances up to 90% for 'foreigners' (Egypt, etc) and 80% for the independent study area members (Australia etc) The 10% and 20% to be convertible but at no fixed rate. A market in transferable sterling to be opened and a free gold market in London. The reserves to be used, if necessary, to hold up the free market.

After an exposition (not very clear) from the CofE (who seemed very exhausted) the P.M. asked everyone to speak in turn. At that stage, 'for' were Crookshank, Stuart, Lyttelton (strongly) and (with

12. Operation Robot. This was a plan to float the exchange rate and make some sterling holdings convertible.

reservations) Thorneycroft. Woolton rather uncertain; Leathers (who seemed not to have been in on the secret) doubtful, inclining against; Cherwell against (strongly) Monckton and I refused to give a view at such short notice. Apparently, the idea was to act at the same time as the Budget – hence, the postponement of the Budget by a week. Telegrams to Commonwealth etc wd have to go at once. The Cabinet adjourned at about midnight . . . .

At this meeting, it was clear that the P.M. had turned against the plan . . . . Butler seemed very tired and very uncertain of himself. I sensed that Churchill had encouraged the plan at the early stages, but had been intellectually put off by Cherwell's advice and politically alarmed by Eden's clearly hostile view . . . .

When we reassembled at 3, we went through an alternative plan put up [by] the Treasury – viz another £150m of general cuts (mostly dollar) and £50m of European cuts. The end of my housing efforts!

A long and rather desultory argument about re-armament and other matters. Churchill (who had been rather restrained) in tremendous and boisterous form, cracking every sort of joke. It was clear that he had made up his mind – and against the plan, at least as regards the suggested timing. By 5 o'clock it was all over.

Woolton, Crookshank and I went off together to talk it over. I feel very angry at the Cabinet being treated in this way. How can one agree or disagree in 12 hours to a most revolutionary and vital decision. The Treasury ought to have warned us for the last 4 months that the 'cuts' wd not do the trick so long as the leakage (through our banking customers) was allowed to go on. All their estimates have been proved wrong. It is not worth while making all these tiresome and unpopular cuts, if the leakage keeps going on through the Commonwealth etc. We might do better to wind up the sterling area (except for the U.K. and the Colonies) altogether.[13]

. . . . But the more I think of it the more I feel that, in essence, the plan may be right. However, this is really what *was* settled. It cannot be *rushed*, to coincide with our Budget. (The Commonwealth Finance

---

13. The Sterling Area had developed after Britain abandoned the Gold Standard in 1931, incorporating the formal empire (except Canada and British Honduras) and those European, Asian and Latin American countries with a heavy dependence on British trade and credit. Whilst the sterling balances built up by these countries in London could effectively furnish cheap loans to Britain, dollar purchases, in this case by Australia, could start to undermine the currency.

Ministers are just reaching home and it wd certainly surprise them to have the whole London plan torn up so quickly and, as they might think, so frivolously.) But it is very likely that we shall come to this in April or May. But that wd be after some show (at last) of consultation and discussion; not as a panic matter, amounting to default (or 90% and 80% default).

.... Anyway, it's no good 'panicking' or we shall be in real trouble, and perhaps revolution. If the people are both unemployed and hungry under a Tory government, they will be very angry .... I think Churchill (although he does not understand the niceties or so-called technique of finance etc.) understands in a dim way the salient features of the problem. He is evidently disappointed in Butler, who is really *too* agreeable; *too* pliant; and *too* ready to go from plan to plan, accepting perhaps too readily the rejection of each. If he believed in his 'Grand Design' he shd have fought harder for it ....

1 March

.... I feel very unhappy about the way things have been managed .... For, if the plan was right, it was right in November. Really, it was right in 1945! For the whole basis of the plan is that it is impossible to carry on a central banking business as large as that of the Bank of England with such slender resources. To have nearly £3000m 'at call' and to have some of the huge debt by the Bank to its customers funded, is an impossible position. (This has been the basis of Churchill's long and instinctive feeling that the 'sterling balances' must be dealt with) The position has been, to some extent, dealt with by the release agreements. This at least regulated the calls made by customers. But the Australian position has been built up, quite suddenly, by the high wool prices. After all, we have had the dollars wh they paid into the pool. It is therefore not unnatural that they should be drawing heavily on their account at the Bank. Even so, you wd have thought that some effort wd have been made to arrange a definite release agreement with Australia. What shocked the Cabinet on the first impact of the plan (wh most of them only heard of on Tuesday night for the first time) was the recollection that *all* the finance ministers of the Commonwealth customers of the Bank were here for discussion of this very problem a few weeks ago; some of them have only just got home; yet *no* discussion or even hint of such a solution was ever put forward. Surely then was the time to have put the whole thing through. Neither the Bank nor the Treasury seem even to have contemplated any drastic remedy then. This sudden change of front appears to be due to the fact that February's losses of gold and dollars are just as bad as previous months. But the cuts wh we made in imports (since contracts have *not* been repudiated) have scarcely had time to become effective, and the Commonwealth cuts have hardly started. There is not sign of any real grip of affairs by any of the authorities concerned.

.... After the morning meeting yesterday, Eden walked with me from No. 10. He was strongly against the plan, on political grounds. 'The country are not ready', according to him, 'to cast away the whole effort of years and return to "Montagu Normanism" without a struggle.[14] For (apart from the writing off or funding the Bank's debt) the plan is really one to restore solvency by bankruptcy; large scale unemployment etc. How could a huge armament programme survive the semi-revolutionary situation wh wd follow'.

Woolton told me after the afternoon meeting, that Eden had threatened resignation on this issue. If this is really so, it wd explain Churchill's sudden change of front and abandonment of Butler. Arthur Salter (Minister of State at the Treasury) is against the plan. He thinks it may be forced upon us. That will be a different thing. 'You mean you think we ought to go bankrupt in a genteel way' was Lyttelton's retort to this ....

Sunday 2 March
Church in the morning, took Alexander and Joshua (Macmillan) and Anne and Michael (Faber). A large congregation of boy scouts; girl guides; brownies, cubs etc. We had the hymn 'All things bright and beautiful', but in deference to modern political thought the third verse was omitted (viz. 'The rich man in his castle / The poor man at his gate / God made them, high or lowly / And ordered their estate'). What rot! ....

3 March
.... Spent the morning at the Ideal Home Exhibition at Olympia, where we are shewing examples of 'The People's House'. They are very attractive. Dorothy and Mrs Churchill go tomorrow ....

---

14. Montagu Norman was the autocratic Governor of the Bank of England from 1920 to 1944.

Wednesday 5 March

. . . . The new rate of housing subsidy (to cover [the] rise in interest rates) was violently, and very unfairly, attacked in the *Times*. This has had a bad effect on some of our members, and shewed itself in the Housing ctee of the party which I attended today. Of course, the Opposition will attack the subsidy from the opposite point of view, so the criticising will, in some degree, cancel each other.

6 March

P.M. began the Cabinet this morning by giving us an account of his audience with the Queen on the subject of the proposed declaration, drafted by the Ld Chancellor, and approved by the Cabinet, regarding the name and style of the dynasty . . . . Poor Churchill, who wants to adopt a paternal and fatherly attitude to the Queen, was clearly much distressed himself – and a little alarmed for the future. Behind all this, clearly lies the figure of the Queen Mother, who of course favours the name of Windsor and all the emphasis on the truly British and native character of the Royal Family. It is also clear that the Duke has the normal attitude of many men towards a mother-in-law of strong character, accentuated by the peculiar circumstances of his position . . . . It is more than likely that he has been told that we are suspicious of him on political grounds. It is still more probable that the Mountbattens are exercising their influence pretty strongly. Altogether, it is rather tiresome and had it happened at a time when the Crown had more real power, might prove very dangerous. In present conditions, it should not be worse than 'tiresome' . . . .

7 March

. . . . I am having a great struggle to keep some of my big water schemes going. Manchester, Hull, and now Tees-side have all sent deputations. The growth of the needs of Tees-side for industrial water is just staggering . . . .

The great Socialist schism is developing. Attlee (it is said) will ask the party meeting (wh takes place on Tuesday) for authority to issue an ultimatum to the rebels. They must either accept majority decisions, or be deprived of the whip and expelled from the 'Parliamentary' party . . . . Bevan, with some skill, having got wind of this manoeuvre, decided to anticipate it by an appeal to the 'Executive' (the Inquisitors themselves, one wd presume) wh meets on Thursday. B complains that the whole thing is a plot, got up by Attlee and co, to force a rift. Of course, much – indeed almost everything – turns on the way the great unions go. For they are powerful in the Executive, and by their influence, in the party. The Trade Union leaders are like the great Whig houses – (Russells, Cavendishes, etc) for they have the same kind of power that the territorial magnates used to have. Most of them, like their Whig predecessors, are moderates. But there are others more radical (equivalent to the Lambtons etc) like the A.E.U. and some of the miners. It is a most interesting situation, full of possibilities. Many shrewd observers believe that, in the long run, 'Bevanism' will win, but not Bevan. That wd be very Whig!

I have finished volume 1 of the correspondence between Princess de Lieven and Lord Grey. This covers 1824–1830. I am now in volume 2. It is a fascinating correspondence, if one knows the history of those years reasonably well. Having just read all Greville, and a selection of Creevey, I am fairly well equipped. I found these volumes at B Grove, but had never before read them. They were published by Bentley in 1890.

9 March (Sunday)

.... The Town Development Bill was due to start in committee 'upstairs' on Tuesday. I have received an urgent request from Dr Dalton that it shd be postponed till later, owing to the great 'party meeting' of the Labour Party on Tuesday morning. I have told our whips that we ought to agree to this. It will simplify matters to treat them with courtesy over this.

Dorothy lunched with the Churchills on Tuesday, before going with Mrs C to the Ideal Home Exhibition at Olympia. C was in a vile temper. Mrs C confirmed to D afterwards that it was 'Philip'. I think he is much distressed at the situation developing in the Palace, for he is very 'loyal' in the best and the old-fashioned sense of the word. He feels that personal and sentimental loyalty to the King or Queen wh all the Victorian aristocracy felt in the second half of the 19th century – a great contrast to the normal view of the grandees fifty years before ....

12 March

The Budget has had a very good press. The Cabinet continued at 11am [with] a lot of foreign affairs stuff left over. Egypt in particular. Eden

seems to me absolutely right in wanting to make some verbal concessions to this new Govt to get the negotiations started on a good
wicket. Churchill and most of the Cabinet were, I thought, rather
unreasonable. Crookshank and I supported Eden. Unfortunately, there
was not time to do more than begin a discussion on the future of the
Council of Europe. On this, Eden and the F.O. are quite unrepentant.
They clearly mean to destroy Strasbourg. My paper (which is, I think,
very powerful and rather damning) has been circulated. But I don't
think many of the ministers had read it . . . .

13 March
The Cabinet (without Eden, who is away convalescing from influenza)
discussed the Council of Europe. Anthony Nutting represented Eden.
I was allowed to explain my position and develop my argument, without any interruption but without any assistance. Salisbury restrained,
but very hostile. Maxwell-Fyfe loyally favourable, but not powerful in
his discussion. The rest, largely ignorant. Lord Alexander (to whom
the P.M. now turns for an opinion on everything) charming, but naïf
and obviously unaware of the great issues. Churchill, clearly uneasy,
did nothing at all to help. Nevertheless, I think, as a result, the F.S.
will not be able to take quite so devastating a line at the Committee of
Ministers next week at Strasbourg as he had intended . . . .

15 March
A quiet day. Stayed in bed till luncheon, working at my boxes. I have
put the whole of the 'Council of Europe' papers in order. I still am not
sure what best to do. Resignation is no good and wd delight those
who are against us – at least, so I feel. But Churchill must be pressed,
and warned. I don't believe he realises the sense of disappointment or
even anger of those whom he led in 5 years work in the European
movement.

    Walked with Dorothy in the woods – a lovely day, but cold . . . .

    Andrew Heath, to whom Sarah was to be married on April 26th,
has been taken seriously ill, with pleurisy and a tubercular abcess
on the lung. He was operated on yesterday. This is a terrible blow to
her; there can be no question of the marriage for a long time to come.

16 March
. . . . I have composed a minute to Churchill, restating my views on
European unity etc . . . .

17 March

I have sent off my minute to Churchill. This closes this phase of the matter. I leave world politics and return to my 'rabbit hutches' (as he will call 'The People's House')

18 March

.... Butler made a fine speech at the end of the Budget debate; Lyttelton made a poor one. He has no real sense of the H of Commons, having come too late into it and gone straight into office. Butler's stock is, at the moment, very high.

19 March

All morning in Ctee of Town Development Bill. Only got half-way through Clause 2. There is a good deal of difficulty in steering this so-called 'non-controversial' Bill through Committee, hearing all members, of all parties, combine against the minister in charge in almost every amendment. Give me a good partisan Bill. It is much easier.

Percy Mills and I lunched with the editor (Crowther) and some of the staff of the *Economist*. The swing over of economists from the left to the extreme (liberal) right is extraordinary. Geoffrey Crowther is like the small boy in the bath, in the old Pears advertisement. He reaches after unemployment as that chubby child did after the cake of soap. 'He won't be happy till he gets it' ....

21 March

A sort of royal visit to Birmingham – Lord Mayor, Aldermen, Council-lors etc – informal luncheon, formal banquet and all the rest. Their housing is at last beginning to make some progress under the energetic direction of a young and active man, Alderman Burman. D came with me; also Sir Percy and Lady Mills. After the banquet, motored to Creighton Court to stay with the Mills.

23 March

.... Our visit to Creighton Castle was very enjoyable. Sir P Mills and Lady Mills occupy one wing; the owners, Lady Throgmorton (or Throckmorton) and her son, Sir Robert, occupy the other. The centre, which is about 1500, is open to the public. It is rather a sad, but a memorable house – full of sorrow, and loyalty, and fierce reli-gious feuds. When the Gunpowder Plot had failed, the messengers rode to Creighton. The ladies then hid away or spirited away the

Throckmortons; the Catesbys could not be saved. Among other relics, is the shift in wh Mary, Queen of Scots was executed. These families of Catholic gentlemen suffered much for the faith – but they somehow survived their fines; their pains and penalties. Now Cavaliers and Roundheads; Tories and Whigs; Catholics and Protestants are all equally overwhelmed in the crushing burden of the Death Duties. No king, however absolute or tyrannical, ever dared take 85% of his subjects' property or 19/6 in the £ [sic] of his income.

Sat 29 March

. . . . A very heavy week, in and out of Parliament. Two days in committee of the Town Development Bill – and very slow progress. A speech in the House on the Ealing Corporation Bill. It was a free vote, but the House followed the line I wanted, and defeated the Bill.

. . . . An adjournment of the House on the 'urgent' question of Seretse Khama and his wife.[15] The Cabinet supported the decision to bar him 'for ever' (instead of for 5 years) from the Chieftainship. Seretse told the newspapers that he had believed that in England a man could marry the woman he loved. Curious that he should have used the very words of a King who lost his throne on this account . . . .[16]

Eden, in spite of having received from P.M. my bitter minute of complaint (or perhaps because of it) seems to have quite changed his position about Europe. He was very charming to me and very nice about Julian (Amery). It is all rather queer.

I feel that we are in for a pretty rough time. If we escape collapse over the 'balance of payments', it will only be to plunge into a degree of unemployment which the people (after years of over-full employment) will regard as intolerable and will be told has been deliberately organised by the Tories. I think we are making progress in the Ministry. The Housing policy is developing. We have reached much more flexibility and a greater measure of freedom. We have over half

---

15. Seretse Khama, the hereditary chief of the Bamangwato in the Bechuanaland protectorate, married an English girl in 1949. After pressure from South Africa he had been exiled on the grounds that the tribe was split over whether a chief with a white bride was acceptable. He remained in exile until he renounced his claims in 1956. After the territory became independent as Botswana in 1966 he served as president until his death in 1980.
16. Edward VIII, who abdicated in 1936.

a million houses 'on order' – instead of less than 200,000. Will the materials and labour be there? Labour, certainly; materials, for the moment – but next year will be very difficult. Sir Percy Mills, with his quiet but inflexible will, has really moulded the whole Ministry to our purpose. I could have done nothing without him. I have now put before the Secretary a plan for re-modelling the rest of the Ministry on the same lines. He will *not* like it and will put up the sort of obstinate resistance which is innate in the Civil Service. But I shall force him to agree, in the long run. The trouble is, one wastes so much precious time . . . .

31 March
The Secretary (Sir T Sheepshanks) is deeply offended. He says my proposals are unconstitutional. The Secretary (and only the Secretary) can advise the Minister. He must consult Sir Edward Bridges, head of the civil service. So the Bishop[17] consults the Archbishop! What a lark! . . . .

3 April
The P.M. informed the Cabinet this morning that the Queen has agreed the terms of the proposed declaration about the name of the Royal Family and the surname of her children. This is to be Windsor. It is clear that this has been a painful episode, but it is a very good thing that the influence of the Consort and his family shd have had an early rebuff . . . .

The Bishop has capitulated; but I have saved his face by dividing the new proposal into two. The first part will be put into force at once; the second part will be further discussed after Easter. He will give in again later on . . . .

The Opposition have embarked during recent days on a steady plan of obstruction. This is the more embarrassing because any agreement reached 'through the usual channels' with the Attlee-ites is at once repudiated by the Bevan-ites. In spite, however, of the nuisance to me, I think all this really serves to increase the split in their ranks. Since my P.P.S. (Bevins) is extraordinarily good at getting me a pair, I have up to now had no very late nights.

At the Economic Policy Ctee on Wednesday, a paper was produced by the Treasury Planners attacking (more or less overtly) my Housing

---

17. Sheepshanks was the son of a former Bishop of Norwich.

Programme. I cd only stay for a few minutes (owing to the committee stage of the Town Development Bill) This enabled me to put on a dramatic act of protest and then withdraw. After rather tedious debates, the situation in the Standing Ctee suddenly changed, and we got the whole Bill through – which is a great relief . . . .

4 April
Another Cabinet today . . . .

. . . . The farmers are still dissatisfied with the very handsome offer they have been made. We decided (and I am sure rightly) not to be blackmailed any further. The figure of £52½m stands, if it can be an *agreed* figure. If not, there will be an *imposed* figure at another level. What this should be, is not to be disclosed. Nothing cd be more unpopular than to surrender to the farmers. With this new ceiling on food subsidies, any increase goes on to food. This means more wage demands. Moreover, the agricultural wages wd probably have to rise again and a new inflationary spiral begin . . . .

5 April
. . . . I ought to have recorded a short, but very important discussion on Europe at the Cabinet yesterday. A paper had been circulated by the F.O. giving the British Embassy's new appreciation of the situation in Paris. It cannot have escaped the attention of ministers that this entirely confirmed (about 6 weeks later) the information which I had given in my paper. There now seems only the most slender chance of the French assembly passing the European Defence Community plan and the European army, unless Britain is more directly associated. Unwilling to join ourselves, we are therefore reduced to the old policy of 'guarantee'. The history of the guarantee, when one thinks of Belgium, and Roumania seems hardly encouraging. But the French seem to like it and the Cabinet agreed. How odd it is that we undertake these obligations in this rather haphazard way! Of course, it is right and really commits us to no new position. But I still feel we should have taken the lead ourselves in Europe, instead of adopting this method, wh does not save us from the risks but deprives us of the control . . . .

7 April
. . . . Left at lunch time for Stevenage. This, the first of the new towns, has made the best progress. It has been the plaything of politicians and

amateurs. Now (under its fifth chairman in 5 years) it is making some progress.

Cabinet at 5.30, on the textile situation. The Cabinet decided on refusing to abolish Purchase Tax, but to bring forward military orders to the tune of £25m. I expressed the view that it wd be impossible to maintain Purchase Tax much longer. Purchase Tax was invented in war as an instrument to stop or reduce production. But it now has become just a sales tax. If we want to stimulate Lancashire sales, purchase tax will have to go, sooner or later. No one agreed with this view, except the Prime Minister . . . .

8–10 April
. . . . Everything goes on in rather a whirl of difficulty. The party is stunned by the set-back in the County Council elections and looks forward with much apprehension to the Borough elections in May. Meanwhile, prices rise, unemployment grows, Lancashire is in something like collapse, food gets less and more expensive, and the 'cuts' are vigorously opposed and exploited by the Socialists. At the same time, the balance of payments problem, though slightly eased, is by no means solved. It looks as if the critical months will be July to September. American aid is almost completely cut off, and they are doing all they can to force down the prices of rubber and tin. There is no hope of any short term solution of the Persian question, and an immense loss to the balance of payments follows. For Egypt, negotiations have not yet begun. We wrangle for hours in the Cabinet on a formula wh will prob not be accepted and which is, in any case, only the beginning of a negotiation. In the House of Commons, the Opposition have managed to run a very effective 'filibustering', wh has prevented all progress with business. When we return, it will be necessary to have a 'guillotine' motion both for the Health Bill and the Finance Bill. The Budget, popular at first, is now under fire from both sides – Purchase Tax and Excess Profits Levy. The latter has been drawn up so badly by the Treasury, that one almost suspects sabotage. Altogether, we are not at a good point in our fortunes. When we get a bit of 'Anti-Socialism' going – the Steel Bill, the Road Haulage Bill [denationalizing these industries], etc, things will improve . . . .

14 April (Easter Monday)
Worked at a speech for Manchester from 10am till 7.30pm (with

intervals of walks in the garden) *and finished it*. A glorious warm and sunny day. These speeches are a great burden – but I think it's worth while taking trouble about them. I call this 'Housing: Progress Report'. I hope it may help for the Borough Elections . . . .

22 April

. . . . Worked all the evening at the House, waiting for the Committee stage of the New Towns Bill, which was never reached.

I am beginning to get very worried about my steel supplies. If these are cut down for Period 3, my Housing will be much embarrassed.

23 April

Another long Cabinet in the morning, revising the white paper on Transport and discussing plan for Monday's debate on railway fares. We have taken a strong action in giving 'directions' to the Transport Commission.[18] We may even be challenged in the courts. All the same, I think (properly handled) it will be a winner.

Introduced 2nd Reading of the Housing Subsidy Bill. The speech was long and necessarily complicated with figures; but it was success-ful. De Freitas in replying got into a tangle with his figures, and retreated under my interruption. Bevan (who spoke at 5.30) was more formidable and tried to bully me. But I bullied him back (wh is the right way) with interruptions, and I think I successfully drove him from point to point. His speech was not a success. The great thing with Bevan is to stand up to him and not be frightened of him. Like all bullies, he is easily put out if you fight him back. In the end, we carried our Bill without a division.

24 April

. . . . I have had a good press over yesterday's debate – the *Manchester Guardian* particularly friendly and describes my duel with Bevan very favourably for me. The day and night look like being taken up with a dreary debate on the guillotine motion for the Health Bill.

27 April (Sunday)

. . . . It looks as if we are in for a lot of trouble. I shall have to take a

18. Established by the 1947 Transport Act, the British Transport Commission was responsible for all inland transport. It was abolished in 1962.

very strong line about 'steel'. If I cannot get more from the allocation, its goodbye to my Housing. But I will take it to the Cabinet and have a first-class battle. I honestly don't think the Govt cd survive my resignation. But the Chancellor of the Exchequer and the Treasury 'planners' will put up a big fight.

Our garden at B.G. is really making a wonderful scenery. The new Scotch gardener, Mason, is excellent. The weather has been very good, and everything is at the best. The daffodils have been very fine. Now all the blossom is coming out; the wild cherries in the woods are superb . . . .

29 April

A very interesting Cabinet today. In Korea, the protracted negotiations for the armistice continue. It was thought that the Communists wd break off on the question of the return of prisoners, but this has not yet happened. The truth is that some 70,000 of the prisoners captured by the UN forces have a strong objection to going back. Still more curious, this is specially true of the Chinese. It would seem very wrong to send them back against their will, but we are proposing some independent method of scrutiny.

As regards Egypt, the British ambassador in Cairo (Ralph Stevenson) and the Gov-General of Sudan have both been home for consultation. A formula has been worked out about the Sudan, wh is satisfactory to the Gov-Gen but Ralph S thinks that the Egyptian Government will not accept . . . .[19]

The Americans are not very friendly over this, and do not understand our sense of duty to the Sudanese. At the same time, they are behaving very badly to us in Persia by giving more money to Mossadeq. If only they would hold off altogether, M wd fall and some business might be done . . . .

The rest of the Cabinet was taken up with the B.B.C. 'monopoly'. A compromise suggestion has been put forward, wh envisages 'competition' at some future date in the realm of television. I do not like it and said so – wh is rare for one at Cabinet. I was supported by

19. Under an agreement of 1899 Sudan was an Anglo-Egyptian condominium, though effectively British run. With negotiations proceeding towards Sudanese self-government, Farouk of Egypt was attempting to claim the kingship of the Sudan. On the formula mentioned here see Anthony Eden, *Full Circle* (London: Cassell, 1960), p. 234.

Salisbury and Crookshank. P.M. is also worried. However, some of the party are very insistent and maybe the formula will not seem too bad. After all, a white paper is not a Bill. Its object is partly to test public opinion . . . .

I think opinion is veering back a little towards the Govt. The 'fares' question has helped, for it has at least shewn the power to do something.[20] I shall announce the Housing figures for the first three months of 1952 on Friday. They will be quite good.

1 May

. . . . During late afternoon and evening, a long talk with Percy Mills, to review a large number of difficulties. The American Steel Strike, if it leads to our 1m tons from US being cut off, will have [a] catastrophic effect on us. Actually, I believe 300,000 have been shipped before the embargo.

I went yesterday to the 'New Town' of Basildon – in Essex. This struck me as pure *Martin Chuzzlewit*. It was 'Little Eden' again.[21] What a mad venture – without any of the facilities. No water; no sewerage; no river to pollute (except the Crouch, wh cannot be polluted because of its oyster bed) no industry – and jolly few houses. I felt sorry for Sir Launcelot Keay, struggling manfully as chairman of the corporation . . . .

The Health Bill [to extend charging] passed all the stages under guillotine – all very quiet. I think the Opposition mean to change their tactics and leave off 'filibustering' for the present.

2 May

The Housing figures are out today – completions 22% up, starts and houses building up by similar percentages. I went to Hatfield and Welwyn and gave the figures in a short speech . . . .

---

20. The Transport Commission had intended to put fares up in London and then the rest of the country, prompting outrage. With the London County Council elections coming up Churchill stopped this, a decision which also meant that the government's Transport Bill had to be amended, dropping the provision to allow the Commission greater discretion in setting fares. It also undermined the Transport Commission's financial viability for the rest of the 1950s.

21. Charles Dickens' Martin Chuzzlewit goes to the US and seeks his fortune in setting up a firm in the newly planned town of Eden which, when he gets there, turns out to exist only on paper.

6–7 May

Two long mornings on Standing Committee on Housing Bill. We got Clause 1 without difficulty, but an immense argument developed on Clause 2, dealing with repairs of 'Tied Cottages'[22] . . . .

9 May

. . . . The Borough elections have resulted in a good many Labour gains. But, when analysed the swing-over is not really as large as I feared. I think there was bound to be this reaction, esp in Lancashire and Yorkshire with all the troubles of the cotton and wool trades . . . .

Sunday 11 May

Sir Thomas and Lady Sheepshanks for the week-end. He is 'sweet' – but not an effective figure. 'Small' in every sense of the word – even 'petty'. What will happen when Sir Percy Mills leaves me I shudder to think. Poor S wd have made a fine canon, or even archdeacon – but Permanent Secretary of the Ministry of Housing – oh no! . . . .

13 May

Committee stage, (Standing Committee) Housing Bill. We have not yet got Clause 2. I hope it will go a bit faster tomorrow. I have now read 3 volumes of L.G.'s *War Memoirs*. It is most interesting to re-read them after all these years and to compare some of the 2nd war and post-war problems with those of the First War. The most striking change is pyschological. 40 years ago, there was free money, free exchange and a really free economy. Rationing was a horrible idea. Government control, even for war purposes, was repugnant. Now there is almost as much difference between Britain in 1914 and Britain in 1950, as between Britain 1950 and (say) a Communist or Satellite country. It is hardly credible. How delicately the Govt had to tread in the first war in any interference with property or liberty.

The back-bench members of the House of Commons are very disgruntled. First, they dislike a Cabinet of peers. Secondly, they dislike ministers who scarcely ever come into the smoking room and rarely speak to them. Thirdly, they think our publicity very bad and our decisions muddled. Fourthly, they think we are losing popularity very fast and they are fearfully rattled by the local elections. All this they

---

22. Housing linked to employment, usually on farms.

confide to me over a glass of gin, after the standing committee has adjourned . . . .

14 May

Committee stage (Standing Ctee) Housing Bill. We [at] least got Clause 2 and started on Clause 3 (sale of council houses) I hope we can finish by Whitsun . . . .

15 May

A long Cabinet, and a very painful discussion about Europe and Strasbourg. The politicians in the Cabinet (of wh there are still a few) are divided, Salisbury being almost a disciple of Beaverbrook in his isolationism. The functionaries (of which there are almost a majority) cannot make out what it is all about. The P.M. is puzzled and unhappy. It seems to me now that he turns avidly to minor problems (like railway fares) because he cannot grasp – or at any rate sees no way out of – the big ones.

16 May

We have been scurrying round all this week in a desperate search for timber and steel. Our men are working so well in the housebuilding industry that they are working themselves out of materials. The new timber allocation does not start till July 1st. So we have the absurd position of risking a stoppage in June! This is restriction planning in the best Crippsian style![23] . . . . The steel battle was postponed till Monday, when there will be a great 'show-down' at the Economic Policy Ctee of the Cabinet. If I cannot get my demands, I shall appeal to the Cabinet. If I am turned down there, I shall have to resign. But I don't think it will come to that . . . .

30 May

The last weeks have been very busy – after 8 morning sittings and one long afternoon, I have succeeded in getting the Housing Bill through Standing Committee. As we have only a majority of 1, and not enough to move the closure, this has had to be done by kindness. I am glad it is over.

In addition, I have been to Bromley, to Folkestone, and to Somer-

---

23. A reference to the austerity controls of Sir Stafford Cripps, Labour Chancellor of the Exchequer 1947–50.

setshire for speeches, as well as many Cabinets and committees of the Cabinet. Now a few days rest at home. I get quite exhausted at the end of each week, and depend entirely on one day at least at home. The peace and comfort of being back at Birch Grove House are a great help; for I have mother's bedroom as a bed-sitting room, and here I can read and rest undisturbed. The garden has been lovely and is much improving under the care of our Scottish gardener, Mason. It is wonderful how much he has done. There has been lots of young people and some old friends to stay, including the Leepers. It was pleasant to have them and talk about the 'siege of Athens' which we underwent together [in 1944]. I have read Lloyd George's 4 volumes of war memoirs and 2 volumes about the Peace Treaties; also Duff Cooper's *Talleyrand*; Aldous Huxley's '*Brave New World*'; one or two new novels; and have started on Busch's Bismarck Papers (wh I had not read before).

The position of the Govt is not an easy one. According to the series of papers circulated by the Chancellor of the Exchequer, each of which is more depressing than the one before, ruin stares us in the face. But the public is not told this and would not believe it if they were. Every Govt since the war has, in a sense, deceived the public, alternating with occasional attempts to make their flesh creep. But something has always come along to save the situation at the last moment. So, this curious combination of the philosophy of Cripps and Micawber has gone on, without actual disaster.

The Treasury say we must increase our exports, moving to non-sterling areas, by 20% in order to survive. This seems such an extravagant hope as to be quite unrealistic.

The truth is that we must find another policy altogether. Armament expenditure must be re-directed. (Here the Field Marshal [Alexander] will help us) useless weapons (like anti-aircraft guns) must be abandoned. We must concentrate on the new and unconventional weapons by which alone (if war came) we could hope to resist the Russian masses. We must take a much stronger line with the Americans. We must substitute a sort of mixture of Beaverbrook and Lord Layton for the Cripps–Micawber attitude. For it is only by making a rival force that we can resist the American imperialism, so strongly mixed up with their internationalism. 'The Empire and Europe' – it is the old Strasbourg theme. Meanwhile, the Cabinet are rather in the position of directors of a rapidly deteriorating concern. They dare not tell the shareholders the facts, for fear of destroying the credit of the company so completely as to destroy all hopes of recovery. They do not know quite how to reconstruct the company – or there is a divergence of view and approach to the problem in the Board. So things drift on.

The E.D.C. and the German agreements and the whole complex of undertakings and guarantees have been successfully negotiated – a great triumph for Eden. But I do not think they will be ratified by the French or German parliaments. Will this be a disaster, or does it give Britain another chance?

4 June
My holiday is coming to an end; . . . . I go back to London tomorrow to Houses, Sewers, Local authorities, Blitzed Cities, Rents, Rates, development charges and Local Govt reform – as well as the approaching national crisis, for wh I carry some degree of responsibility . . . .

14 June
A very interesting day in Durham County, first at Aycliffe and then at Peterlee. These two New Towns have undoubtedly caught the imagination of the north, esp the latter . . . .

15 June
Got home by 11am, after travelling overnight from Durham. Found Catherine Amery and her daughter Louise (aged about a year) at Birch Grove. Julian A came down and we worked all day on my paper for the Cabinet on the economic situation. I call it 'the Grand Design') . . . .

17 June
A most interesting Cabinet, at which Mr Menzies, Prime Minister of Australia, was present. After . . . . an explanation of some of the small concessions (very few) wh Australia cd make in relation to the actual working of the import cuts,[24] it seemed as if no real advance wd be possible, except on some arrangements for Australia accepting various types of armaments (chiefly tanks and airplanes) from us, instead of trying to duplicate their manufacture . . . .

It was finally agreed to aim at a November meeting; to appoint a 'steering' or 'management' committee as soon as possible to direct the research; to seek agreement of the Dominion Govts to a meeting in

---

24. In order to tackle the dollar shortages in the sterling area.

1. Members of the Conservative
Shadow Cabinet, 11 January 1950.
From left to right they are
Macmillan, Lord Salisbury, Harry
Crookshank, Lord Woolton,
Sir David Maxwell-Fyfe, Anthony
Eden and Rab Butler.

2. Iranian Prime Minister Mossadeq
(left) and Britain's representative at
the UN, Sir Gladwyn Jebb, shake
hands before the first meeting of the
Security Council on the Abadan
Crisis, 15 October 1951.

3. Macmillan, the founding chairman of the Central and Eastern European Section, on 21 January 1952 at the conference at Church House, Westminster. One hundred delegates from behind the Iron Curtain attended.

4. The Minister of Housing and Local Government opening a block of 'people's houses' on a new estate at Eastcote, Middlesex, 7 March 1952.

5. The sort of housing the Minister was looking to replace.

6. General Eisenhower's farewell speech to NATO staff at the Palais de Chaillot in Paris on 21 May 1952.

7. Macmillan exploring the flood damage at Lynmouth, 19 August 1952.

8. Egypt's Revolutionary Council, 20 August 1952. Nasser is at the left end of the couch, with Neguib to the immediate right

9. Churchill thanks Russian Ambassador Andrei Gromyko on the steps of 10 Downing Street for the Russian gift of £90,000 towards the Flood Relief Fund, 23 February 1953.

10. Macmillan leaving St Thomas's Hospital, London, after his gallstone operation, 24 July 1953.

11. About to give away the bride at Sarah Macmillan's wedding to Andrew Heath at Horsted Keynes parish church, Sussex, 30 July 1953.

12. Showing the Queen a new housing development just off London's Oxford Street, 13 July 1954.

13. Anglo-French talks at Chartwell, 23 August 1954, with, from left to right, René Massigli, Anthony Eden, Pierre Mendes-France and Sir Winston Churchill.

14. The head of the family firm, Daniel Macmillan.

15. Churchill's final Cabinet, 6 April 1955. Left to right, standing, are Osbert Peake, Peter Thorneycroft, Sir Walter Monckton, James Stuart, Gwilym Lloyd George, Alan Lennox-Boyd, Duncan Sandys, Derick Heathcoat Amory, Sir David Eccles and Sir Norman Brook (Cabinet Secretary); sitting are Macmillan, Lord Woolton, Lord Kilmuir, Sir Anthony Eden, Sir Winston Churchill, Lord Salisbury, Rab Butler, Lord Swinton and Harry Crookshank.

16. The new Foreign Secretary at his desk, April 1955.

November or December (it was important to have it in 1952) and the P.M. of Australia would be glad to come himself.

All this discussion was of the greatest interest to me (although I took no part in it) for it is a good preliminary to my paper (which I have now sent to be printed as a Cabinet paper and christened 'The Grand Design' . . . .

21 June

. . . . The more I reflect on the situation, the more dangerous the present drift of H.M.G. seems to be. Churchill doesn't know what to do. Eden has now become aware of the danger. Butler is caught up in all the Treasury confusion and timidity. What am I to do? If I campaign openly for my ideas, (without some argument with P.M. or Eden) I shall injure the Govt, perhaps fatally. If I do nothing, and stick to my Housing, I shall do my departmental but not my Cabinet duty. Perh we shall make a little progress next week. So far, P.M. is obviously postponing decisions, and Butler is also (I think) playing for time . . . . Meanwhile, we drift – like our predecessors . . . .

24 June

My reform of the Town and Country Planning Act, wh started fairly smoothly, has run into rough weather. Salisbury, Fyfe, Thorneycroft, and others against; Crookshank for; Monckton on the whole for. But Walter (in the chair) was weak and so everything is again postponed.

. . . . My paper on 'The Grand Design' has got a lot of support in the Cabinet and from other ministers and under-secretaries who have read it. But the Cabinet never discusses these great matters, or only in a desultory way. There is talk of a committee under Eden to deal with 'Home Affairs', while P.M. is to remain 'in general charge'. This is reminiscent of 1916 and the attempt to turn Asquith from a First Minister into a President. I don't feel that this will appeal to Churchill . . . .

26 June

The bombing of the Chinese power station in N Korea has caused a great flare up. We had not, it seems, been told by the Americans about it. Since both F.M. Alexander and the Minister of State (Selwyn Lloyd) were around, it seemed odd – if not, contemptuous – treatment. Of course, the Pentagon and the State Dept never tell each other anything and so we are the sufferers . . . .

27–28 June

. . . . The Housing progress both in Liverpool and in Lancashire is remarkable. Liverpool is still controlled by the Conservatives; Lancashire CC has just been captured by the Socialists. But there was nothing but friendly rivalry to get on with the job and I was received as courteously and as warmly in the County as in the City. I think we have now really got going something of the spirit of a crusade. It will indeed be a tragedy if it has to stop owing to economic difficulties or Treasury planning. There is a new plot hatching among the Treasury and Bank of England boys, of which (in one way or another) Housing will be the target and (they hope) the victim.

I have finished Villari's '*Age of Machiavelli*' – a good book, but horribly written. I then read '*Boswell in Holland*' – the second volume of the Boswell papers – very dull. As a treat (being very hard worked and tired) I have allowed myself a Trollope novel. '*The Vicar of Bullhampton*'. T is very restful during a financial and economic crisis! A new one is now threatening, to culminate in great decisions wh the Cabinet is to take next week . . . .

30 June – 4 July

This has really been a most extraordinary week. A most secret meeting was called in the P.M.'s room in the House of Commons on Monday 30th. This followed a meeting of certain ministers in the Foreign Secretary's room early in the day. The F.S. is laid up with jaundice – a most unfortunate moment, so dangerous and so explosive is the situation, altho (as always in a Tory crisis) marked by quasi-good humour and affected calm. (We do not go rushing round, whining, babbling, and gossiping like the Socialists) . . . .

We discussed first 'the Capital Investment Programme' for 1953. This seemed rather an academic introduction to an immediate financial crisis, but it is [the] 'Little Planner's way'. Then we came to the real point, how to reduce imports by £175m in July–Dec 1952. This plan, deemed necessary by the Treasury and the Bank to avoid too great a loss of reserves – of course involves savage cuts in imports – of food and raw materials. On raw materials it is proposed *not* to issue the outstanding licences for the (at present agreed) import programme. This means a saving of only £5½m (it would have been £8m but for the fall in timber prices) but it involves a loss of 85,000 standards[25]

---

25. A standard was 40 cubic feet of timber.

and a proposed diminution (the planners say) of 50,000 houses. Of course, in fact it would mean something much worse – the virtual collapse of the whole programme, and the loss of that confidence in the building industry which Eccles and I have built up. No decisions were taken at this meeting, which was held in appalling conditions of heat and humidity. (We are having a real heat-wave, with for England, very high temperatures).

The ministers present were Butler, Cherwell, Woolton, Thorneycroft, Swinton, Eccles – with Makins representing Eden.

At 10pm a meeting was held in the Prime Minister's room in the House of Commons. The P.M.; Lord Woolton; Ld Cherwell; Lyttelton; Butler; Thorneycroft; Crookshank; Ld Salisbury; and myself, with Edward Boyle and Norman Brook. The choice of ministers was, I suppose, meant to distinguish the meeting from a full and ordinary Cabinet. All (except, curiously enough, Crookshank) had received (in the most secret fashion) a paper by the Chancellor of the Exchequer, advocating a) more import cuts b) immediate convertibility of sterling, with a scheme called 'External Sterling' not dissimilar than the one we had discussed and rejected in February. We had also received a paper from Cherwell, bitterly opposing the scheme. (It was a terribly hot night, and very oppressive. The 'Prof' (Cherwell) had an automatic hand-fan, wh we felt must be running on atomic energy)

Butler opened, with a grave statement; at times he shewed an unusual emotion. He has clearly been under a very great strain. His paper referred to the advice of the Bank of England. He repeated this phrase, which was taken up subsequently by Salisbury, and led to a sharp exchange between them. P.M. poured oil on the waters. He was clearly anxious for unanimity, and unwilling to impose a view. Everyone in turn was asked for an opinion. The general view was sceptical of the possibility of success and almost universal against the timing. Lyttelton was for the scheme at first, but seemed to waver later in the discussion. It was a very *good* discussion – calm, sensible, and balanced.

Butler pressed for a decision at the full Cabinet on Thursday. Churchill was doubtful as to this. The meeting broke up soon after midnight. I went home with Harry Crookshank (to Pont Street) and we talked it all over till nearly 2am. We are both against, chiefly on timing. We must try to hold out till the Commonwealth conference in November. To do this unilaterally now wd (we think) wreck the conference.

1 July

I have produced a paper on the crisis, with special relation to Housing, but some broader considerations and sent it to Norman Brook for circulation. It is becoming very difficult to maintain 'the Housing Drive' without a sense of unreality, knowing as I do the determination of the Treasury to stop it by any means they can.

2 July

A final meeting of the Home Affairs Committee has approved my scheme for amendment of the Town and Country Planning Act (Development charge etc) and sent it to the Cabinet. Although the Financial Secretary has attended every meeting since March, without apparent dissent, I am told that the Chancellor of the Exchequer will oppose the scheme.[26] A message came from Brook that the CofE has withdrawn his 'convertibility of floating rate' scheme. Nevertheless I wrote and circulated my paper. It is called 'The Great Debate' – the sub-titles are 1. 'The Bankers Ramp' 2. 'The Housing Cut' 3. 'The Grand Design' 4. 'Action this Day'. I think it's a pretty good paper – racy and readable.

3 July

Half the Cabinet, not 'in the know' came expecting what the Lord Chancellor called smilingly 'a battle of Giants' – viz Butler v Macmillan. But it was all called off, and sent back to the committees of the Cabinet for study.

The new Treasury attack is to ask for 85,000 standards of timber (not yet ordered) *not* to be bought. This wd (they say) reduce houses by 30,000. Of course, this absurd mathematical method of arguing takes no account at all of either the houses now in construction or the flow of production. Actually, such a step wd wreck the whole housing effort. We are hard at work trying to design the 'timberless' house (I call it 'the boneless wonder') but even if this succeeds it cannot seriously affect the 1953 programme, the houses for completion by the first half of which are already started.

---

26. This was because whilst Macmillan wanted to abolish the development charge imposed by the 1947 Town and Country Planning Act, Butler simply wanted to reduce it to 50 or 60 per cent. See Paul Bridgen and Rodney Lowe, *Welfare Policy under the Conservatives 1951–1964* (London: PRO Publications, 1998), p. 235.

4 July

A morning at Stevenage, opening a factory. Collected another silver trowel. A long and dreary meeting in the Chancellor's room – Butler, Woolton, Swinton, Eccles and I. I have offered to take some cut in purchase of timber this 6 months, *on the understanding* that there is *no* reduction in the pace of building; we must let stocks run down . . . .

9 July

. . . . Rather a good meeting of the Ministerial Council on the problem of 'Rent Restriction'. Marples had written an excellent paper.[27] I am beginning to see a little daylight. But it will not be easy to raise the rents of some 8,000,000 houses (or perh 16–20m people) without political disaster!

10 July

I dictated a draft paper on the Investment programme. The CofE has called a further meeting and circulated a paper demanding the stabilisation of the 1953 Housing programme at 230,000. This, of course, I cannot accept. Meanwhile, a great triumph. P.M. has appointed a Committee of Ministers to study 'The Grand Design' (ie the plans for the November Commonwealth Conference) . . . . I have been appointed to the new and much stronger Ministerial Committee.

Cabinet at 11.30. The last item was my paper on amendment of the T&C Planning Act. It was clear that the Chancellor of the Exchequer was anxious to postpone the discussion and did a good deal of stone-walling on earlier items. I think Churchill (who realises that Butler has had some rough handling) was helping. So there was a good deal of desultory talk on items *not* on the agenda . . . .

. . . . At last, at 10 minutes before 1, the huge subject of T&CP came on and was duly postponed. Fortunately, the CofE did (in a short intervention) disclose the Treasury view. He asked for a special meeting with me to discuss his proposals. This was a particularly Jesuitical move. I could not help retorting that there had already been at least a dozen ministerial meetings, at every one of which the Financial Secretary of the Treasury had been present. It would have

---

27. The Rent Restriction Acts were felt to distort the market by (a) keeping rents artificially low and (b) providing disincentives for private landlords to repair properties. Macmillan's response, later in the year, was to propose legislation linking rent increases and repairs.

been most helpful if he had ever expressed any view at any of these meetings . . . .

It is rather a bore that the Permanent Secretary, Sir Thomas Sheepshanks, is so useless. I think he is the most ineffective man I have ever met in any walk of life . . . . Of course, as long as Percy Mills is there, it's not so bad. But I don't know what will happen when Percy goes . . . .

As I expected, Walter Monckton is proving one of the best ministers in the Government. He is handling the trade union leaders with consummate skill. His support in a Cabinet will be important.

11 July

The great Housing battle continued. At 3pm a meeting of ministers (Chancellor of the Exchequer presiding) Thorneycroft, Cherwell, Ld Alexander (with defence ministers like destroyers flanking a battleship) Swinton, Lloyd George, Eccles, etc. The Protean Chancellor is impossible to pin down to any precise statement. He twists and turns, like the Old Man of the Sea.[28] He seems never to abandon his brief, which he cons like a breviary. This afternoon we started on the old 'Capital Investment' argument. I had put in a paper proving the absurdity of all this prolonged argument about what is to be done (measured by money) in 1952–3. No one can accurately estimate what will be the output of the Building industry. The planners say (with a sort of Olympian certainty) £1600m. If the whole claims of all Departments are admitted in full, there is a 10% difference. If on the slightly lower scale of their revised claims, a 5% difference. So why go on arguing about this completely theoretical point? All the ministers really agree with this. The CofE, after a good deal of vague talk, then changed his ground again. He said he wd propose to the Cabinet that my Ministry shd be allocated in 1953, the actual quantities of *timber* and *steel* which we had got in 1952.

I said 'What about cement?' '1.9m tons of cement must be exported', was the reply. 'But can we push up cement production. After all, cement is indigenous. Its only Thames mud and chalk'. 'But that would require capital investment'. And so it goes on. I don't really think that Butler can believe in all this. I feel that he is using this to force a crisis and prove and assert his authority. (What a pity Oliver

28. The sea god in the *Arabian Nights* who forces Sinbad the Sailor to carry him on his shoulders and wriggled to avoid being thrown off.

Lyttelton, who has humour and courage, was not put at the Treasury!) . . . .

The CofE will make now (so he says) definite proposals on 'Housing in 1953' for Thursday's Cabinet. The meeting ended at 5pm. I got hold of Marples and Mills and we prepared the draft of our reply. I want to find out just what we could do with the timber and steel suggested. In order to win, (without actual threat of resignation) I shd like to prove that we are being very reasonable and prepared to use all our ingenuity to get all that is possible out of our allocations . . . .

13 July

Church; all the Macmillans. Took Alexander for a walk to the woods and saw Blake. Pheasants doing well so far . . . . Worked at two great bags of papers in the evening . . . .

Both the *'Times'* and the *'Economist'* newspapers attack me, continuously and petulantly. They talk of 'subsidies' and 'rents'. But the first thing is to demonstrate our powers to build the houses. On a basis of public confidence, we might move to reform.

The campaign by the *Times* against 'empty rooms' and 'under-occupied houses' seems dangerous. It might recoil on the Proprietor. Hever Castle is definitely 'under-occupied'.[29] Poor Astors; they are so charming, but so ineffective.

14 July

A heavy morning; the Chancellor of the Exchequer is (a) attacking our Housing programme (b) attacking our proposals on Town and Country Planning. Worked all the morning on our counter-attack. I believe we shall win on (a) and lose on (b). We can help him a long way on (a) (as the 'boneless wonder' develops) On (b) the Treasury are under the influence of Gilbert, who is old and obstinate. Rab does not appear to have any views on anything himself. He simply follows the line of his advisors. Even in Cabinet, he usually reads out the brief . . . .

6pm. Special Cabinet meeting, to decide whether or not (a) to go on with the de-nationalisation of Iron and Steel (b) whether to publish the white paper now (and so commit ourselves definitely) or whether to keep ourselves free till the Autumn.

---

29. *The Times* was owned (1922–66) by the Astor family, who also owned a Kentish stately home, Hever Castle.

Ld Salisbury opened. He was for abandoning the 'Iron and Steel' Bill, in view of the great financial and economic dangers of the moment and the immediate future, and as a contribution to 'National Unity'. Monckton (M of Lab) took the same line, in order to keep 'Labour' sweet. Lord Chancellor agreed. Ld Privy Seal (Crookshank) also for delay, chiefly in hope of getting a permanent compromise by agreement. Sandys (M of Supply) and the minister in charge (tho' not in Cabinet) was present and put forward a powerful argument for going on in order (a) to shew strength of purpose (b) from that position of strength possibly reach a settlement.

As the hour was now seven, I had to go to the House of Commons for a debate starting at that time on my supply vote. This made it necessary for me to give a view before leaving. I plumped strongly for going on. After I had left, I gathered that Lyttelton (Colonial Secretary) and Fyfe (Home Secretary) took the same view. Actually, before I left Butler expressed his view for going on – so I was glad to be able (for once in a way) to be on his side. This did not influence my decision, but made me able to say with much earnestness that I felt (since the economic crisis had been used as an excuse for inaction) that the CofE's attitude was really decisive.

P.M. restrained himself very well through all this, except for one 'interim outburst' (as he called it) He is clearly determined to force the Bill through. He spat out the contemptuous words 'If you abandon your principles, you will get not thanks but mockery. It will not be the White Paper, but the White Flag' . . . .

The most interesting thing the P.M. said (and the wisest) was that if things got so bad as to make a Coalition possible or desirable, the Tory Party must have something to give away (apart from himself) He would stand aside willingly. But Transport and Iron & Steel would be going their way through Parliament. They might be abandoned then – as the price of and as a contribution to National Unity. In such circumstances, this sacrifice might be most effective. Made prematurely, it would be thrown away. I am sure that this is true. (It's just like bargaining with a literary agent) . . . .

15 July

After last night's preliminary talks the situation has today culminated in the first real clash in the Cabinet. Shall we or shall we not proceed with the Iron and Steel Bill? It is not really time to say that this is a 'Denationalisation' Bill. It is far more and far less. It is a Bill . . . . on lines put forward by myself and my friends before the war, in '*The Middle Way*' and the '*Next Five Years*'.[30] The Board which is to be set up for the broad strategic control of the industry, is exactly what progressive Conservatives have recommended. Its composition will be wide (including representation of managers, trade unionists, and consumers). Its powers will extend over the *whole* industry (whether publicly or privately owned) and deal with prices, development and so forth. The shares of the nationalised concerns will be vested in an agency or trust, which will be charged with the duty of selling these concerns, in whole or in part, over a series of years, to the investing public.

. . . . Finally, David Fyfe, Duncan Sandys and I were charged with the task of drawing up a draft statement.

We went at 6pm and did this. But I added a note on the general situation, intended to meet the fears of the hesitant ministers. I argued in this a) that there could be no negotiated settlement (with Labour) except at a moment of grave foreign and economic crisis b) that, even so, it wd be better to have both Steel and Transport Bills to bargain with c) that in the event of no crisis and a Socialist Govt at the next election, the Socialists wd find that a) the Board – which they rather liked – was in being b) that we had only succeeded in selling a third or so of the industry. It was certain that they wd leave the Board alone. It was doubtful if they wd incur also the odium of confiscating the shares wh had been resold; that it was more likely that they wd merely content themselves with stopping any more sales. Thus a kind of 'de facto' settlement wd have come into being – viz, a regulating Board and a mixed system of actual ownership . . . .

17 July

After a feverish week of preparation, the Housing issue was brought to a head at today's Cabinet . . . .

Two hours' attack on the Housing Programme. Two hours' resistance. At the end, no ground lost. The Treasury planners cannot be made to understand that a) 1953 Programme is all arranged and

---

30. *The Next Five Years: An Essay in Political Agreement* (London: Macmillan, 1935) emerged from a cross-party ginger group looking towards planning as a means of tackling unemployment. Macmillan followed this up with his *The Middle Way: A Study of the Problems of Economic and Social Progress in a Free and Democratic Society* (London: Macmillan, 1938).

contracted for now b) that no change in design can become effective until (say) end of 1953 c) that the slightest hint of any 'cut' wd wreck the whole programme. Butler kept changing his ground, from the 'money ceiling' to the balance of payments. The first is sheer Crippsian nonsense; the second is important. But I can keep the whole programme going at full speed, at an additional cost of £4½[m] of timber imports (at present prices) Prices are still falling. In 1954 (if 'the boneless wonder' comes off) we can build 300,000 houses with the timber used for 230,000 in 1952. We *must* have a chance. I did not mention the 'political' argument but only the industrial and technical. I thought it wiser to leave that to others. P.M. was firm, yet very unwilling to upset Butler. I thought he kept the balance well. But he made it clear that he thought it wd be political suicide to abandon Housing. Lyttelton supported me on the absurdity of the whole conception of the rigid capital ceiling. Prof (Cherwell) agreed on this, but thought Housing took too much materials. It shd be halted and the men sent down the mines – only you can't do that in a democracy. Crookshank was for the political argument – so was Woolton. Thorneycroft (Board of Trade) sided with Butler. Nothing was agreed, but nothing conceded. Butler is to meet me and Eccles for a further talk. But by July 28th and 29th great and far-reaching decisions are to be announced in the House. I suppose they will be made on the night of the 27th. However, I have everything to gain by stonewalling. The Treasury (through Mr Leslie – alias Lazarus – the chief publicity officer) will no doubt get to work on the press to attack me. *The Times, Economist, Observer*[31] and so on will of course respond.

It has been an exhausting period – fighting for my own political life and that of the party. I do *not* feel it wrong to fight – for I feel sure that the additional strain upon the exchequer (£4 or £5 million) will be amply compensated by the prestige wh HMG will gain if they succeed in something.

I cannot help feeling that there is a certain piquancy in the struggle, because Butler dislikes and fears me. The absence of Anthony Eden[32] has complicated the issue. I think he is now more friendly to me than 6 months ago. He has been particularly agreeable lately. The F.O. has decided to back my old 'Central and European Commission' (wh they

31. *The Observer* was also then owned by the Astors.
32. Owing to illness.

had so bitterly opposed) and Dick Law is to take the chair. In several other ways he has gone out of his way to give me information and talk to me about Foreign Affairs. He has been particularly nice and appreciative about Julian Amery's work.

I like both Butler and Eden. They both have great charm. But it has been cruelly said that in politics there are no friends at the top. I fear it is so . . . .

23 July

. . . . [Butler] now wants to 'cut' the Housing programme, not by a direct cut in the target of houses, but indirectly through the capital investment programme. In other words, first he says 230,000 not 260,000 next year. When the Cabinet supports me on this, he turns and says 'I'll cut your timber and steel'. When I say 'All right. I'll build with less timber and steel', then he takes another twist and says 'All right; I'll cut your money' . . . .

24 July

. . . . In Egypt, a military coup d'etat (which may prove healthy) has intimidated the King, the corrupt old politicians, and the corrupt old generals. It remains to be seen how soon the 'Young Egyptian' movement will itself be corrupted.

The Cabinet was today attended by the Chiefs of Staff. There were some rather alarmist telegrams from our Minister in Alexandria, suggesting that the new General may prove to be the instrument of extremist forces, both of the right and the left, such as are supporting Mossadeq and threatening the Shah . . . . P.M. was very sound, I thought, and very calm. He was against any military measures by us wh might cause alarm or the accusation that 'British Imperialism' was trying to interfere in an internal Egyptian dispute. We might, in the long run, stand to gain as well as to lose by all this. He would not intervene to save Farouk either as King of Egypt or King of the Sudan . . . . If we had later to move, it must be obviously only to prevent disorder and protect British lives and property.

After some other items, the postponed contest between Chancellor of the Exchequer and the Minister of Housing came on. An equal fight on the whole, but I think the Minister of Housing won on points. No clear decision was reached; everything depends on the referee (Sir Norman Brook) who writes the minutes . . . .

25 July

. . . . [A] heavy day at the Ministry, chiefly sorting things out after our victory over the Treasury, and beginning to think out some of the next forward moves wh will now be possible, based on an expanding programme. The most important of these are (i) to reduce the swollen river of 'subsidised' house-building and increase the trickle of 'private' building (ii) to deal with 'rents', and therefore 'repairs' (iii) to get rid of 'development charge' . . . .

27 July

. . . . King Farouk, of Egypt and the Sudan, is gone – abdicated and disgraced. What will come next is hard to say. Will the General (Neguib) be a Cromwell or a tool in the hands of clever and unscrupulous men.

Mossadeq has equally triumphed over the Shah, who is humiliated but not yet deposed. Meanwhile, M has sent for our Minister and begun to talk about a compromise. He is doing some propaganda to this effect over here. The *Observer* has, of course, swallowed it, hook, line and sinker. I suppose the Americans will do the same. 'Do treat us nicely, or I shall go Bolshevist'. Yes; but Persia might equally be partitioned, and that might suit us well enough. It will be interesting to see what line the Cabinet will take.

Meanwhile, I have been reading the reports of the officials about 'The Grand Design'. They are not encouraging. 'They murmured as they took their fees, There is no cure for this Disease'.[33] Perhaps it would be better to give up the struggle and ask to become the 49th state. But then, what wd happen to the officials? The Americans would not take them on.

30 July

A long Cabinet yesterday. Both Egypt and Persia seem to me deteriorating. Eden (back after his sharp attack of jaundice) was in good form. In Egypt, it is too soon to be sure, but it looks as if the ingenious general will fall victim to the wiles of the politicians. The *Wafd*[34] will return to power – that is my forecast . . . .

The two days debate on the economic situation has gone badly for

---

33. From Hilaire Belloc's 'Henry King' in his *Cautionary Tales*.
34. The Egyptian nationalist party. Contrary to Macmillan's prediction the Wafd, along with all other Egyptian parties, was dissolved in January 1953.

the Govt. Butler made a dull, lifeless, and academic speech, full of lofty platitudes, but saying and doing nothing . . . .

31 July
. . . . [W]e had an incident without parallel. Attlee got up after questions to make a 'personal' statement. (This procedure is usually to defend oneself, not to attack somebody else) He said that Bevan had disclosed Cabinet secrets and broken the tradition which bound colleagues on this. (This was in connection with the beginning of the rearmament plan during the Labour Govt) Bevan was *not* in the House, but Ellis Smith (Lab) got up and asked if notice had been given to him by Attlee. The reply was 'yes' – but it seems that either by accident or design the letter did not reach him. Bevan will make a statement tomorrow . . . .

The Devonshire estate has lost in the first court. This was expected. I imagine the case will go right up to the Lords.

1 August
Bevan's statement in the Commons, in reply to Attlee, was made in a very full house. It was admirably done. He dwelt at some length on the strongest part of his case, viz, Attlee's fatuity and incompetence in not making sure that his letter to Bevan was delivered before he spoke yesterday. Merely to give a note, at 1.30, to the messenger on the door was an incredibly casual method . . . .

2 August
To London early; a good deal of work from the Ministry. I still cannot get a decision on the reform of the Town and Country Planning Act. But after my last talk with Butler, I am more hopeful. I have done a new paper, with instructions to the Dept to work on it, which may help to remedy the chief political weakness of my scheme – viz, the fear of a renewed attack on 'unearned increment', if development rights, even on a circumscribed basis, are returned to landowners.

There are more telegrams today from and about Persia. I am sorry to see that Acheson is still hankering after an agreement with Mossadeq. This is surely dangerous. It will merely prolong the agony. The Americans are an impatient people. They will never allow a situation to develop. Mossadeq hopes to get American money to support his tottering regime, by the bogey of Communism. But if Persia was to go Communist, it wd inevitably lead to our re-occupation of Southern

Persia. I do not think this wd lead to war. It might lead to a much stronger position to us in the Middle East . . . .

Travelled to Harrogate and thence to Swinton with Lord Swinton. We are to devote two days to trying to write an agenda and a plan for the Commonwealth conference . . . .

4 August

Worked in bed till luncheon. I have finished the paper for the Commonwealth Economic Conference – in draft. It is a start. Drove out to the moor with Philip Swinton and had a good walk. There has been some rain at last; but it was a fine, gusty afternoon, with sun and racing clouds. Worked with S after dinner and finished the paper. I will get it circulated tomorrow for the meeting of the Cabinet committee on Thursday.

Having finished volume 1, of [John] Bodley's *France*,[35] read volume 2. An excellent book; if it were not so 'dated' it could with advantage be reprinted. For it is as true and as revealing of the end of the 3rd Republic and the beginning of the 4th, as it is of the first 25 years of the 3rd . . . .

5 August

Left Swinton at 9am, arriving Kings Cross at 2.35pm. Found a lot of work in the Ministry – Capital Investment Programme (other than housing); Town and Country development etc etc. We work hard enough on all this, but make (against strong Treasury pressure) very little progress . . . .

6 August

A deputation from Southampton in the morning about Capital Investment for their 'blitzed' city. If they only knew to what a low figure the Chancellor of the Exchequer is trying to cut our total programme on this!

Opened a block of flats in the afternoon; I took the opportunity to give the Housing figures for the first 6 months of 1952 in the form of a progress report. I think there should be a good press coverage tomorrow. (The BBC had a good report on the 9pm news, wh I heard at Birch Grove) At 6pm a further conference with Butler and his officials on Town and Country Planning amendment. Very little pro-

---

35. A Macmillan book that went through three editions in 1898–1902.

gress. Dorothy, who was in London for the day, motored me home. We arrived at 8.15pm . . . . (The Housing figures show good results: *Completion* up by 22%; *under construction* up by 18%; *new starts* up by 31%).

7 August
At 10.30, and again at 3pm the committee of ministers to prepare for the Commonwealth Economic Conference met at the Foreign Office, under Anthony Eden's chairmanship. The paper which I had prepared at Swinton; Lord Swinton's own paper; and Lord Cherwell's paper were the basis of the discussions.

The Foreign Secretary is a very good chairman, and clever at getting the best out of the members. Although the whole tone is rather subdued, I am not without hope that we shall make some progress. My paper (which made these definite suggestions – viz, Commonwealth consultation; (Bank of England court to be enlarged) Commonwealth protection (discrimination until reserves built up by honest savings) and Commonwealth development (the Investment Trust) was not received with quite the hostility I expected) . . . . Ld Cherwell's idea of a sort of extended E.P.U. (to include Canada and America) is well worth considering. But they all seem to me to think too much in terms of 'money' and 'currency' and 'convertibility'. They do not think enough (it seems) of the realities – that is a balanced trade and the development of real wealth – which these currencies all merely reflect.

At 5.30 there was a Cabinet which lasted two hours . . . . It seems quite hopeless to expect any agreement with Mossadeq. Yet the longer he goes on, the more likely it is that Persia will ultimately fall into Communist hands. The Shah is no good – a strangely helpless monarch. It is strange how often the son of a powerful and self-made tyrant turns out to be no good.

8 August
Stayed in bed most of the day. Read '*Madame Bovary*', which I had [not] read for many years. (It is difficult French, full of hard words) A large party of young people (Sarah's friends) in the house, but alas! The Macmillan boys have gone off for a holiday to the Harlechs. I miss them very much . . . .

9 August
. . . . Having finished Flaubert's masterpiece, I have started on Hugo's.

'*Les Miserables*' has the advantage of being written in very clear and easy French. Worked on the bags, wh keep arriving from London . . . .

12 August
It is sad to start a grouse-shooting season and not to be or look forward to being at Bolton Abbey. Except for the war, and one year I was at Strasbourg, I think I have [been] every year since about 1922. What will happen now remains to be seen. But after the judgment in the Devonshire case, it does not look very hopeful.

13–15 August
I see that 300 brace were got yesterday on the Bardon beat at Bolton Abbey. Worked yesterday and the rest of the week at the Ministry without much interruption . . . . We are chiefly engaged on two problems. The first, the amendment of the Town and Country Planning Act so as to abolish development charge. Here the Chancellor of the Exchequer has now definitely declared himself, whereas before he had shewn a certain degree of hesitation. He is against me and for retaining charge, tho' at a lower rate. He starts at 80% but wd go to 60%. This, of course, is the most futile suggestion of all, esp in the case of arbitrary valuations. It wd be better to stand by the act. But it sounds a sort of 'compromise' and will probably appeal to the Cabinet. I'm afraid it means another great struggle with Butler and the Treasury at next week's Cabinet . . . .

Eden's marriage (to Churchill's niece) has much excited the '*Daily Mirror*' reading world – it's extraordinary how much 'glamour' he still has and how popular he is. Churchill is admired, but on the whole disliked. Of no other Tory, have they ever heard. Eden has still all the usual accompaniments of film-star success – fan mails and all the rest.

The *Church Times* has attacked the marriage, drawing a comparison with the fate of Edward VIII. This is unfair (whatever may be the orthodox view of divorce) because Eden was abandoned by his wife and Miss Churchill cannot be compared with Mrs Simpson, who had had two husbands . . . .

The other problem on which we have been working has been that of how to get more private and unsubsidised building into the programme. After much thought, I have decided to get some extra (if we can) by administrative means during the rest of the year. This we can do, at least in the case of friendly authorities, through the present system of licensing. Then, in the New Year, I would like to abolish licensing altogether and free the market for private builders. But the success of this will depend (apart from the political battle with the Socialists) on the end of Development Charge and some decent stimulus to private effort . . . .

16 August

I do not like the Persian telegrams, whether from Teheran or Washington. Those from Washington are the most dangerous. These restless people are determined to save Mossadeq and prop him up, ... No doubt this is all partly due to the Presidential election. The Democrats cannot risk the chance of a Tudeh coup in Persia and yet another country falling under Russian control, after the disastrous failure of their policy in China . . . .[36]

17 August

. . . . On getting back from Church, I found the Sunday papers, and the account of the tragic disaster at Lynmouth (in North Devon) and in other Devon and Somerset villages. It seems that something in the nature of a cloudburst over Exmoor, with 9 inches of rain in a short period, so flooded the river Lynn (and other smaller streams) that immense damage has been done. Deaths about 30 in Lynmouth, the holiday makers and the villagers equally in flood. Much loss of property and so on. I rang up the Secretary (Sir Thomas Sheepshanks) and said we must do something. Apparently this happened on Friday night, but was not in Saturday's newspapers. As we never listen to the wireless, I had not heard the BBC account on Saturday night.

18 August

. . . . I had made up my mind yesterday to go to Devonshire today. So I rang Ld Fortescue, and arranged to leave London at 1pm. Arrived at Barnstaple at 6.45 and drove to Lord Fortescue's house, where I spent the night. Lord F is Ld Lieutenant and seems very competent and sensible . . . .

19 August

A long and tiring day. We left at 8.45 and drove to Lynton, with short

---

36. The collapse of their Kuomintang clients and the accession to power in China of Mao's communists in 1949 was to permanently embarrass the Truman administration with the 'Who Lost China?' tag.

stops at two villages on the way, which had also been injured. The urban district consists of two separate towns – each of about 1000 inhabitants – one, Lynton, on the hill; the other, Lynmouth, on the shore. The damage was to Lynmouth, and caused by the tremendous flood forcing the river out of its bed, so that what was the High Street is now the river. The immense quantity of boulders (said to be 40,000 tons) destroyed the bridges. The problems of reconstruction are very considerable; the major cost will be in roads and bridges. I met all the local councillors (whose resources are naturally very limited) the County Council authorities; and the heads of the Army, Police and of the voluntary services (Red X; W.V.S. etc) at a conference in the little Town Hall after the tour of the town (This took till 12.30 or later) . . . .

Naturally the locals are wanting immediate promises as to Government grants for reconstruction. I told them I wd consider this with the ministers concerned, but persuaded them to concentrate on getting immediate work done before arguing as to exactly who is to pay. Anyway, in addition to grant-aided services (like roads) there is need for generous response to the fund raised by the Lord Lieutenant. Finally, some kind of orderly operation of the various services under a steering committee was agreed and I have no doubt things will begin to improve. One of the problems is to look after all the people evacuated from Lynmouth (about 1000) without altogether destroying the economic life of Lynton as well. So it was agreed not to take over the remaining hotels, but to encourage visitors.

Left Lynton–Lynmouth about 2 and drove to Dulverton, stopping at one or two villages (such as Exford) on the way, where a good deal of damage had been done. At Dulverton (though on a small scale) the damage was quite severe and a good deal of property was lost including one large garage . . . .

The chief danger now is a) at Lynmouth by the high tide early in Sept b) in the villages of collapse of buildings etc. a) is quite serious. It will need hard work between now and then to build up a sea wall wh can keep out the sea if there should be a strong westerly wind with the next tide.

Drove to Taunton and got train for London, arriving at 9.30pm.

20 August

The Press; the news-reel; and the B.B.C. have been full of N Devon and esp Lynmouth. My decision to go was obviously a wise one, and has been very well received . . . . Cabinet at 3.30. We began with the Devon disaster. HMG will give £25,000 to the fund. But of course the big expenditure falling on the exchequer will be the grant-aided services – roads, bridges, etc. I expect we shall have to make 100% grants in many cases . . . .

After Persia, the Cabinet approached – rather gingerly and with evident distaste – the amendment of the Town and Country Planning Act. P.M. had no intention of reaching any decision. A desultory discussion (after rather a fierce opening encounter between the Chancellor of the Ex and myself) led to the usual postponement . . . .

23 August
Arrived at Gleneagles at 10am on night train from London. Here I found Dorothy (with the car) Played a good round of golf with her . . . .

24 August
A round of golf at 9.15 . . . . Motored on later, ... to Gavin Astor's new Scottish property where we are to shoot grouse and stay a week.

. . . . This is a glorious place, with a magnificent view (rare in Scotland, at any rate in shooting places) across a wide expanse of mixed ground – arable, woodland, moorland – towards the mountains of Invermouth etc . . . .

31 August
A week's shooting is a wonderful rest. All thought of politics, business, family troubles and all the rest is put aside, and for some 8 hours a day everything is concentrated on the vastly exciting and infinitely various problems of trying to kill grouse. When – as during this week – each day has been one of very high winds, the grouse fly very fast and every graduation of feeling, from despair to triumph, is undergone by the shooter. I shot fairly well on the whole; at some drives very badly, at other almost brilliantly. Down wind the birds flew at tremendous speeds; I shot the highest and fastest I have ever killed . . . .

1–5 September
Back in London – a very hectic four or five days. Apart from a long Cabinet on the 4th, we have had long meetings of the committee of Ministers to prepare for the Dominion conference . . . .

Our view had been a) multilateral trading, convertibility and all the rest *only* when the reserves have reached a figure (say $3000 millions or more) wh makes it possible to contemplate. Also, this figure to be genuinely earned by the strength of the sterling area, not merely resulting from loans from America. b) until then, discrimination, imperial preference, and all the rest. I was quite happy with this. But now the majority of the officials have gone once more whoring after the 19th century stuff – immediate convertibility and all the rest. (Of course, carefully guarded with all sorts of reservations, but this is what it comes to) Butler, who seemed quite happy with the previous decisions, has equally happily swallowed the new line . . . .

Lunched at St Martin's St on the 5th, with Daniel, Maurice, and Rache Lovat Dickson. Our new venture in the USA seems to be starting pretty well. In England, the book trade is not good – overseas, we are still doing well. But the margin of profit is shrinking and the cash needs of the business growing all the time, as prices and costs still continue to rise.

6–10 September
. . . . I was told to do a 'party political' broadcast in September. I have fixed the date for Sept 20th and had a rehearsal etc at Party H.Q.; . . . .

Anne Bentinck told me a good story about Lady Cholmondley (née Sassoon) She went with her pearls to the jeweller. 'No, Lady C. I really cannot advise you to sell. I cd hardly get a price for them. Pearls have fallen dreadfully in value' etc, etc, by the poor jeweller, who had been asked by Lady C to dispose of her fine pearls. After a good flow of this talk, she turned on him and said 'Let me see all the pearls you have to *sell*. I want to buy'. The Oriental does not change!

This broadcast is a bore, but an opportunity. I have never done a broadcast of this kind or this importance. I have decided to take only fifteen minutes (instead of the twenty minutes wh I am allowed) I feel it will be better not to bore the listeners with too much 'politics' at this time. I also think I [don't] want to make it 'party political' at all and I have drafted it as 'Housing Report' . . . .

19 September
The *Evening Standard* started off a great story about my having set up a full enquiry into Rents and Repairs. The *Evening News* and *Star* followed. This [was] apparently begun by Fife Clarke (the Government publicity officer) who gave rather an injudicious reply to a lobby correspondent at his daily meeting. Anyway, this has started them all

off, and today they are in full cry. Every paper this morning has starred this news, giving most circumstantial accounts of a 'departmental' (or sometimes an 'interdepartmental') enquiry wh does not, in fact, exist! My speech at Folkestone (with a short reference to rents and repairs) is singled out and starred. It is rather a bore – for all my colleagues will think I have started all this off! . . . .

20 September
. . . . Read [Charles Dickens'] *Dombey and Son*. At 8.30pm went to BBC and was finally delivered of the broadcast at 9.15. I now know what a mother feels when at last the wretched baby is born . . . .

22 September
The reports on the broadcast are coming in, and seem all to be good. There is a general view that I was wise to make it so 'non-political'.

24 September
A very full day at Plymouth . . . . We visited Housing Sites all the morning; visited the 'Blitzed' areas all the afternoon, ending with a conference with the reconstruction committee. I cd give out no news about reconstruction; . . . . This 'Capital Investment Programme' is really intolerable. It is especially silly in a place like Plymouth, where there are no armament or export factories – or indeed any factories – to build. Plymouth's factory is the Royal Naval Dockyard. So – if I lose my battle with the Treasury, now transferred to the Cabinet – a lot of people will be unemployed at Plymouth, including (after the next election) the Hon J J Astor . . . .

25 September
When I got to London, I was in the grip of a really bad chill . . . .

26 September
I felt a little better this morning, but did not get up till Cabinet at 11.30am . . . .

There was a difficult discussion about UNO, one part of which insists on discussing 'racial problems' – esp S Africa, British colonial policy etc. I'm afraid a lot of these fine plans (like UNO) with all their immense value in general, lead to a lot of trouble in detail . . . .

A long meeting of the Local Government (Party) Advisory Committee at Conservative Central Office. Lord Woolton, Miss Horsburgh and I attended, and listened to the valuable and on the whole reasonable criticism of the Govt by the delegates. My stock is high now; but wait till I disappoint them on Blitzed Cities, and on Development Charge – and start to put up everybody's rent! Then I shall be leaving mass meetings (like Lloyd George in the Boer War) disguised as a policeman and by the back door! . . . .[37]

27 September

. . . . The political situation is rather uncertain and obscure. There is a general feeling that the Tories have recovered a good deal of ground in the last few months. Certainly, ministers have settled down. Lord Swinton (the one really *efficient* and *experienced* politician in the Govt) has transformed the Public Relations position. The Trade Union leaders, frightened of Communism and not on very good personal terms with their colleagues in the political wing of the party, are anxious to 'play ball' with us. (Walter Monckton is first-class as Minister of Labour) . . . .

All the same, there is a distrust and even fear of the Tories, which is based on the suspicion and jealousy of the 'proletariat', now come into its own, and determined to maintain its standard of '*panem et circenses*'[38] at all costs. If '*panem*' is rather scarce, '*circenses*' are all the more vital. 2/- or 3/- on the rent, to keep the house from falling down, will be bitterly resented and probably fought to the end. But 12/6 a week on the 'never, never' system to buy the television set is a necessity.

One of the embarrassing legacies of war is the change in the pattern of spending. Since necessities, like food, are short and many luxuries, like music-halls and circuses impossible in the black-out, with clothing, dancing, travel, holidays etc rationed or impracticable, all the inflationary wages of the people are spent on the few available luxuries or pleasures. Roughly, those are tobacco, alcohol – and (for the war) books. (Now television, cinemas, dancing etc are taking the place of books) . . . .

Meanwhile, although the public position of the Govt may have improved, I don't think it has got any nearer to a central theme or purpose . . . . [T]he Prime Minister is 78; although still as brilliant as

37. A consequence of David Lloyd George's pro-Boer sentiments during the South African War of 1899–1902.
38. 'Bread and circuses'.

ever, he is lost (perhaps we all are) in this strange post-war world, at home and abroad. The Foreign Secretary, admirable technically, cannot really act as Prime Minister. Time will show whether, if he gets the opportunity, he will rise to it. The Chancellor of the Exchequer (Butler) has time on his side, and can afford to wait. The Colonial Secretary (Lyttelton) is disgruntled and cynical. The Dominions Secretary (Salisbury) is quite glad to see nothing happen in particular, because Cecils[39] by nature are against things happening. The President of the Board of Trade (Thorneycroft) has his heart in the right place, but he has no head without the Tory reformers (like Quintin Hogg) who supplied that deficiency for him. The Lord President (Woolton) is a splendid wreck – he is worn out. Lord Cherwell is a critic, not a creator. Lord Alexander, excellent in his own sphere, can add nothing outside it. The Lord Privy Seal (Crookshank) is sensible, efficient, honourable, but not creative. (He is the most admirable, valuable colleague we have, with great experience and absolute loyalty) The Minister of Labour is first-class, but rarely contributes anything to general political problems. The Lord Chancellor is sensible and sound. Lord Leathers, apart from an emotional dislike of the Lord President, is sound and sensible, but has no political experience or political sense. The Home Secretary, (Maxwell Fyfe) so powerful a figure in opposition, seems to have become almost insignificant in office. Altogether, a strange Cabinet . . . .

Perhaps the most noticeable, and painful, difference between our position now and when we were last in office (1945) is our relationship to US. Then we were on an equal footing – a respected ally. Then it was the Churchill–Roosevelt combination (or its aftermath) Now we are treated by the Americans with a mixture of patronising pity and contempt. They treat us worse than they do any country in Europe. They undermine our political and commercial influence all over the world. Yet all this they do (so ambivalent is their policy) with only one half of their mind and purpose. The other half is just as friendly and loyal as in the days of the war. They are really a strange people. Perhaps the mistake we make is to continue to regard them as an Anglo-Saxon people. That blood is very much watered down now; they are a Latin–Slav mixture, with a fair amount of German and Irish. They are impatient, mercurial, panicky. But, while capable of terribly narrow views and incredible breaches of decency and decorum,

---

39. The family name of the Marquesses of Salisbury.

they are also capable of broad and generous sentiments and really big-hearted generosity . . . .

5 October (Sunday)

. . . . There was an adjourned meeting of some ministers (without the CofEx) on Wednesday afternoon, but no real progress was made. This, with another house-opening ceremony on Friday; a speech at Bromley Friday evening; a meeting with the Bletchley U.D.C. on Saturday; a political speech at Bletchley on Saturday evening made a real dreadful week . . . .

6 October

Drove to Brighton from Birch Grove. The usual ceremonies – opening 3000th house, tour of housing estates, luncheon, speech, opening of People's House exhibition etc etc . . . .

Got to London at 4.30, for meeting with Percy Mills and after that with Walter Monckton. Percy Mills (owing to the illness and timidity of the chairman) has now become, de facto, head of the Engineering Employers Federation, now engaged in [a] most difficult and complex situation. The Engineering Unions, largely under Communist influence, after receiving 11/- increase in Nov 1951, immediately after Butler's Budget put forward a ridiculous demand for £2 increase on basic wages.

I had only time for a short talk, as Mills had to go to Birmingham, and I had to go to a meeting on development charge at 5.45pm . . . . Over and over again the same arguments were deployed. But one great advance was made. Ld Salisbury withdrew his opposition to the 'Limited Compensation' scheme and this helped a great deal. It was decided to go back to the Cabinet with *all* my scheme approved, and the only question to be settled – should Development Charge be reduced to 50% or abolished? . . . .

9 October

. . . . I rang up Percy Mills, who told me that the Employers had agreed (under great pressure from him) to recommend negotiation without any strings, and that the ban on overtime, threatened for October 20th, would be removed. This is good news . . . .

10 October

The first resolutions at the [Party] Conference today were on Housing and kindred subjects. When I rose to reply there was a tremendous demonstration. It was really quite moving . . . .

The applause at the end was even greater. It really is rather comic, after all the years of conflict and unpopularity![40] But it will not last. It is all right to put up the houses. But the next job is to put up the rents!

I gave a large luncheon party today for the delegates from Bromley, Stockton and Preston.[41] Catherine Amery (since Dorothy has not come to the Conference this year) acted as hostess.

Tonight I addressed another large meeting of the C.P.C. (the educational movement of the party) This is really doing very good work. It is creating something of the character of the Fabian Society and helping enormously in the task of appealing to the universities and the 'intellectuals' . . . .

13 October

Building Committee. This little piece of organisation wh we started is doing good, but unobtrusive work. The 'steel-saving' propaganda etc is going well, and the production of reinforcing rods is going well too. Now we have started on methods of saving cement.

A meeting in Catford Town Hall (3 Lewisham seats) The hall was full and it was quite a good meeting, but rather 'dead' and unresponsive. I am making too many speeches and feel very tired.

14 October

Cabinet. At last we have a decision on Town and Country Planning (esp development charge) My plan was accepted entire – exactly as first presented last March. Development charge is to be abolished. The Chancellor of the Exchequer did not fight unduly hard for his 50%. P.M. was clearly for abolition – so were Harry Crookshank, Monckton, and others . . . .

15 October

. . . . In theory, the Attlee–Bevan split should weaken the Socialists. But it may do no such thing but rather give publicity and a sense of

---

40. Between June 1936 and July 1937 Macmillan resigned the Conservative whip, whilst his critical attitude towards the leadership over appeasement did not endear him to the party faithful.
41. Respectively Macmillan's constituency (since 1946), his former constituency (1924–29, 1931–45) and the constituency of his son-in-law, Julian Amery.

excitement and interest. There is nothing like 'publicity' nowadays. The High Wycombe election, (following Waldorf Astor's death and Bill Astor's succession to H of Lords) will be the first (and a most important) test. If we hold the seat, it will have a very good effect on our party all through the country. If we lose it, it will weaken us very considerably. It will be difficult to maintain that we have the 'moral' right to govern, if no seat under 2000 majority can be held. So this is really a vital election.

I have the Housing returns for September. The completions are good – 22,000 odd against 17,000 odd in September 1951. It looks as if we shall get 230,000 for 1952, which was the figure I gave the Cabinet as the target as long ago as last Christmas. But what will happen when Sir Percy leaves? That is really a great tragedy and the time is very near. However, I hope he will be able to give some help even when he is no longer 'full-time'. The Permanent Secretary, Sir Thomas Sheepshanks, becomes more futile and ineffective every day. He is utterly useless – yet I cannot get rid of him . . . .

19 October
Missed Church again – to my regret. A large tea-party of grand-children, and Maurice and Katie to dinner. A wet, misty sort of day. Except for a short walk, worked all day on 'The Housing Plan'. This is an attempt to bring together in a single paper all that we have done, are doing, and plan to do in the Housing field. It is very ambitious and cannot be completed except over a long period. But it will be useful to have a plan, covering all the different aspects of the question . . . .

22 October
I went to see Dr Richardson – who looked after me so well in Africa – and is now a Harley Street consultant for what is called a 'check-up'. He took a large number of tests and photographs and there are more to be done. When these are ready, he will know how many diseases I have . . . .

24 October
. . . . 11 to 1 – 'Ministerial Council'. A very good discussion on the question of private licenses and the next 'jump to freedom'. Mills, Wilkinson, Dame Evelyn and Marples all made useful and valuable contributions. There are all sorts of tricky problems – political, legal, and administrative. In order to control the size etc of houses, we must

have a 'licence'. Can we arrange for it to be issued automatically, like a passport. Of course, we shall be violently attacked by the Socialists if we depart in any way from the 'comparable needs' test . . . .[42]

25 October

. . . . The result of the by-election at Cleveland (Yorkshire) is not discouraging. The Socialist vote and our vote are both down – but theirs more in proportion. Socialist majority is reduced by 1500 votes.[43] This may, of course, have been affected by the Bevanite schism – now, at least in theory, at an end, ...[44]

A fresh attack (so my officials tell me) is about to be launched upon us by the Treasury. We are building too many houses! They seem to think we can turn them on and off like water out of a tap.

26 October

. . . . I went to London yesterday to meet M Spaak – at the Amerys . . . . He was still hoping that the French would ratify E.D.C., but he thought this much less probable than it had seemed a few months ago . . . . For, when it came to the point, a European army where German generals ordered French troops, and where the great French army (the finest in Europe) had to be merged in a European force, took a lot of swallowing. In most countries, the European movement had been an intellectual movement of the few. The mass of people did not yet realise its implications, if it approached realisation.

31 October

Another heavy week; . . . . The people insist on the Coronation being televised and the Cabinet have had to climb down as gracefully as possible. Meanwhile, the session has ended and we are preparing for a new one on Tuesday. Our main legislation is fixed – steel, transport, and my T&C planning amendment bill. All are doubtful and controversial . . . .

---

42. Macmillan was concerned to shift away steadily from the massive preponderance the public sector then enjoyed in house building, an objective frustrated by (a) the limited number of licences for building being given by local authorities to private builders and (b) the 'comparable need' test that had to be passed before they could be issued.
43. Cleveland by-election (23 October 1952), Lab: 25,985; C: 22,064.
44. After the recent Labour Party conference.

I lunched (alone) with René Massigli at the French embassy today. He is very worried about the position in France regarding EDC. He thinks it now very doubtful whether the Assembly will ratify (or ought to ratify) Frenchmen are only just beginning to realise (with a shock) what is involved in 'Federation'. Far better had they followed our original plan for 'Confederation'. Moreover, with the French army so much committed in Asia,[45] will not Germany soon regain the old leadership? . . . .

1 November

Rained all day; worked at papers and also at a speech for High Wycombe election. Rowland Clark and Streatfield came in the morning to discuss the position of the Birch Grove Estate Company. As usual, it is short of cash. Read *'Mansfield Park'*. What a relief it is to have Jane Austen to fall back upon in this troubled world! . . . .

3 November

The 'eve of poll' meeting at High Wycombe was quite in the old style. How Dizzy would have liked it![46] . . . . There were 1300 to 1400 people crammed into a hall which holds 1000 – and about 1000–1500 outside, listening to the relay. About $1/7$ of the audience inside was hostile and I think they vaguely intended to break up the meeting. However, all went [well] and I think it was a very successful effort, with the proper variations from grave to gay and a good lot of 'back-chat' between platform and hecklers . . . .

5 November

We have won the Wycombe election by an increased majority.[47] People are saying nice things about the contribution made by the Housing programme and by my speech. Actually, our housing figures are out for the third quarter and are very good. September is the best month since the war.

---

45. In the losing struggle to remain in Indo-China, an endeavour the French were forced to withdraw from in 1954.
46. Benjamin Disraeli's country residence, Hughendon Manor, was in High Wycombe, Buckinghamshire, the county which he represented in the Commons 1847–76.
47. Wycombe by-election (4 November 1952), C: 27,084; Lab: 25,331.

8 November

A very good day's shooting at home. We got 214 pheasants – they flew very well . . . . We had a wonderful bonfire and fire-work display, to which all the Macmillan and Faber children and all the people and children from the Estate came . . . .

The success of the Tories at Wycombe is of great political importance . . . . The press puts (I think) too much stress on the Bevanite split. I think it is more due to a certain disillusionment about Socialism and the post-war utopia . . . . The settlement of the engineering dispute without trouble (largely due to Percy Mills) is another symptom. In spite of much extremist and Communist pressure, the T.[rade] U.[nion] leaders are keeping their heads. It may well be that we shall get through this session without too much trouble . . . .

11 November

The *Times* leader today is a violent and very malignant attack on me and my housing record. It minimises our achievements and goes on about subsidies and rents in the usual style. I suppose the inspiration for this has come from the Treasury . . . .

12 November

Two meetings this morning. The first – the Economic Policy Committee – under the CofE's chairmanship. A desultory and not very satisfactory discussion. However, we decided to raise the limit for *unlicensed* repairs to £500 – and for industrial and agricultural building to £2000. I tried – but failed – to get a similar concession for local authorities. However, I have no doubt we shall get it in a few months time . . . .

At 11.30, a meeting of a Cabinet committee on the management of our atomic undertakings. A most valuable and interesting discussion – Crookshank, Monckton and I form the Ctee. Sandys (on Ministry of Supply) and Ld Cherwell gave their evidence. The problem is how to free the undertaking from civil service control . . . .

13 November

A very long Cabinet in the morning – so long that my vital item – final approval of the Town and Country Planning Amending Bill and of the immense white paper – was not reached . . . .

The Cabinet dragged on – and lunch time came. However, the

P.M. came to the rescue. A special Cabinet was fixed for 5.30 at the House of Commons. 3.30pm I introduced a Bill to postpone the rating valuations, supposed to be completed by the end of this year. I wisely refrained from dwelling too much on the real reason – viz, that the plan of valuation laid down in the 1948 Act, has proved quite unworkable in practice (T&CP over again!)

The debate that followed was interesting, but not acrimonious . . . . The Labour party is so divided that, even on a subject like this, the rift shows itself. To be studiously polite to Bevan (which is an attitude he finds very disarming) upsets the Attleeites no end. It seems that they are now having a new row – about the method of voting to be adopted for the 'Shadow Cabinet'. This was carried through (without notice) by an Attleeite majority at a sparsely attended Party meeting. The Bevanites are correspondingly enraged.

I managed to escape from the debate at 5.30, and leave Ernest Marples to hold the fort. The Cabinet met in the P.M.'s room at the HofC, and went through my Bill and White Paper. I accepted a few amendments and left one clause in the White Paper to be finally settled tomorrow morning between my officials and the Treasury. The Bill and White Paper were approved. So ends a nine month struggle – with the Treasury against me all the time . . . . The P.M. was complimentary and enthusiastic about the scheme. I am now a little staggered and beginning to have doubts and hesitations . . . . It will be very exciting to see what the Press will do. The *Times* is sure to be critical and prob[ably] also the *Manchester Guardian*. I think the rest of the Press will be friendly . . . .

18 November
At the opening of the Cabinet today, P.M. posed the question of the Duke of Windsor. There was unanimity in the view that he could not come to the Coronation *with* the Duchess and that he *would* not come without her . . . . I was much congratulated on the good Press we had for our Town and Country Planning Amendment Bill, published this morning. I held a lobby conference yesterday morning, and explained it all very carefully to the lobby correspondents. By distributing (a) a hand-out giving a clear account of the new purposes (b) a large number of questions and answers on particular points, I was able to ensure that the Press had a very good objective account – even in the opposition papers . . . .

24 November

. . . . At 4pm a meeting – the final one before the Conference – of the Ministerial Committee. It seemed to me, and to Lds Cherwell and Swinton, that the whole thing was beginning to slide towards the Treasury and Bank of England passion for 'convertibility' at all costs . . . . I restated the position as follows

(1) No convertibility with a fixed exchange. 'If you [are] to be free, you must float'

(2) Convertibility must be sustained on its own merits – that is, it must represent real conditions of stability, due to genuinely improved production in the non-dollar world

(3) quantitative restrictions etc cannot be removed till it is safe; in danger, we must be free to reimpose, unilaterally, the protective measures we need.

Everyone seemed to agree . . . .

Thursday 27 November

After a day's delay the Second Reading of the Steel Bill was resumed this afternoon. Freeman (a Bevanite Socialist) opened with a very able speech . . . . The debate dragged on in a desultory sort of way till 9pm when Jones (Socialist) wound up in a glorious platform, tub-thumping, emotional speech, tears in his eyes – but all, or nearly all, fake emotion. The contrast between the icy precision of Freeman (scholar; intellectual; gentleman) and Jones (steel workers' union) was very interesting. On the whole I prefer Jones . . . .

During most of the debate there were not more than 10 members on the Opposition side present. The House filled up (as usual) for the 'wind-up' speeches – and the vote. I wound up for the Government in a ½ hour speech. The first part boisterous and racy, and was very well received by our people and quite amused the comrades. The second part was a serious and philosophic argument – a restatement of '*The Middle Way*' and a plea for the view that Govt 'supervision' of a great industry could be better done without 'ownership'. I was told by many members, on both sides, that this was the best speech I have made in the House. It was not that – but I think it just suited the occasion . . . .

I had to stay up and wait for the committee stage of my little 'Rating and Valuation' Bill. This ultimately came on at about 8am on

28 November

The Bill went through without amendment and got 3rd Reading also.

After that, business ended and the House adjourned about 9.15am. It was not worth going to bed . . . .

1 December

After all these long struggles and disputes in the Cabinet, the great day came when the Bill and White Paper on the reform of the financial provisions of the Town and Country Planning Acts were presented.

I rose at 3.30 and finished at 4.35. It was a *good* speech; lucid and well presented, with a touch of humour here and there. The House listened very well. Dalton attacked – but very mildly. The debate was not very lively. Dick Stokes wound up for the Opposition with the pure orthodoxy of Henry George's doctrines.[48] This seemed rather odd, as these are not the official views of the Labour party. There was some rumbling about 'Land Nationalisation' – which need not be taken too seriously. Marples answered the debate very well indeed. We got a majority of 30.

2 December

A very good press today – esp from the [Liberal] *Manchester Guardian,* which is important . . . .

Now that we have the Town and Country Planning Bill launched, the next thing is to get on with freeing private building. I hope to get a statement in the House on December 16th.

3 December

A good day – after a very tiresome night in the House. We did not finish the Expiring Laws till 5.15am, and then only by a closure. The whole night was spent on pure 'filibustering' – as the Opposition moved to omit every Act from the schedule, in order to spend an hour or two on each explaining why they ought to be retained! . . . .

D and I went to a 'farewell' party for Roger Makins, who leaves shortly to be Ambassador in Washington. All the young men I had in the Mediterranean have done well – Makins, Caccia, Rumbold and Halford . . . .

---

48. A late-nineteenth-century American radical, Henry George publicized his ideas of a single tax on land values on both sides of the Atlantic, not least through his book *Progress and Poverty* (1879). By 1905 it had sold an estimated 5 million copies around the world. The abolition of development charge would no doubt be seen by someone like Stokes as offending against Georgist principles.

4 December

A very good meeting of the Building Committee. There were two subjects for discussion –

    1) the restrictive practices in the industry, both of masters and men

    2) the materials position.

On the first, the recent 'revelations' about the operations of Sir Alfred Hurst and the London Builders 'Ring' and of Mr Girdwood and his committee about the low production of the men have created quite an impression on public opinion . . . .[49]

As for materials, I can see that both with bricks and cement we shall have difficulties, in spite of the considerable increases we have achieved. David Eccles has done and is doing very well for me. Lord Swinton has left our committee – instead we have the new Minister of Materials, Arthur Salter. Swinton is a great loss, for he has real practical knowledge of business . . . .

At 11am there was a full Cabinet, with the Commonwealth Prime Ministers and representatives . . . .

. . . . I don't think the Conference is going very well when you come down to the brass tacks. Judging by the minutes, all the safe-guards which alone made me and others agree to Butler's 'convertibility' are in danger of being whittled away. A 'free' rate, is become a 'flexible' rate; tariffs and preferences are not going to be a sufficient protection, once quantitative restrictions have gone; the sterling area will not even keep together, since some of the Commonwealth countries will not link their currency to a floating sterling. The whole approach has been lacking in emotional appeal . . . . Another 1947 fiasco would be fatal.[50] Nor can the Conservative party survive another Montagu Norman – with excessive deflation and millions of unemployed.

The Opposition censure motion was taken today. Churchill just crushed Attlee. Bevan (unwisely) wound up for them. He started well, but ended with a flop . . . . Harry Crookshank made a fine reply. He

---

49. Sir Alfred Hurst was the Independent Chairman of the London Builders' Conference. The Girdwood committee had been set up in 1947 by Aneurin Bevan to investigate the costs of house-building. In its second report in 1950 it pointed out that productivity was still well below that of the pre-war period and that substantial cost savings would not be made without affecting size or equipment – hence the reduced size of Macmillan's 'People's Houses'.

50. A reference to Labour's failed attempt to restore convertibility.

was really quite angry and this made his speech powerful, as well as witty and well-argued. Of course, the truth is that our modern Parly system is not devised for small majorities. In the middle of the last century, when parties were more fluid, the convention of a government defeat on any issue being practically a vote of no confidence, had not arisen. Now all members are 'kept in' all the time, and they cannot stand the strain.

5 December
Dorothy and I had a most fatiguing round of parties . . . . This side of political life is a great bore, but it must be endured . . . .

7 December
. . . . Sarah is, I'm afraid, rather worried about her future. I have had a talk with her and must now see her Andrew Heath. It is no good their getting married until he is really well and even if the tuberculosis is definitely stopped, I feel he must have at least a year (or nine months) since it shewed itself to be safe. All this means a difficult time for her, poor child. But she is being very reasonable about it. It would be perhaps a little easier if he had any money. He has some capital – all sunk in his farm. So he depends on his health and power to earn enough to keep himself and a wife and family. The capacity of the Macmillans for making money in business is certainly not matched by any corresponding facility for finding it in matrimony . . . .

8 December
Cabinet called for noon. This was sad, as I had intended to shoot at Birch Grove. Another lovely day in the country, with impenetrable fog in London. The ostensible reason for the Cabinet was a difficulty – of the first order – which had arisen in the discussion of the 'Collective Approach' to the USA. It seems that some of the Commonwealth countries, notably India, would like to see their own currency, in the event of convertibility, no longer attached to the new 'floating' sterling rate, but to the dollar rate. If we agreed to this, Australia would follow. It would, in fact, be the end of the sterling area. At the same time, it was clear that the Indian delegates did not expect or want this to happen. Indeed, they felt 90% sure that the rupee would in fact follow sterling. But they could make no definite undertaking. (Of course, they were under instructions not to do so) . . . .

Sir Percy Mills to see me in the afternoon to say 'goodbye'. He has completed his year of service. This was a melancholy occasion and it will make things much more difficult. But I am very lucky to have had him, and he has given us a good start . . . .

12 December

. . . . Yesterday (as Marples was away) I took the Housing Policy Committee myself. Bricks, cement, tiles. We decided for a dual drive – to save these precious commodities on the one hand and to give orders well ahead to the producers, so as to help increase production on the other . . . .

The situation in Kenya is ugly.[51] It could, no doubt, be dealt with quickly and effectively by absolute firmness, even ruthlessness. Under our system, this is impossible. So, while the settlers grow restive and blame the local government for its weakness, poor Oliver Lyttelton is represented here as a sort of monster of tyranny. There will be a difficult debate next week . . . .

19 December

This has been a tremendous week. Harry Crookshank achieved a great victory in the House. In the battle of wills, he has prevailed. In spite of days wasted with 2 votes of censure and so forth, he has carried the whole of the business which the Government set out to get. The Committee stage of the Transport Bill was carried through;[52] our majority fell to 10 on one division on Thursday, but we emerged well over 20. The Chief Whip is entitled to immense credit, and the party has been splendid. Ordinary members, with none of the minor comforts which ministers get (e.g. a room to sit, read, work or sleep in) have been most faithful.

I carried my Town and Country Planning Bill in the committee upstairs, in two mornings and without a division . . . .

On Tuesday, ...

. . . . the Kenya debates, on which I had to make the winding up speech for the Government. On this, fortunately for me Oliver Lyttelton had already made an excellent reply to Griffiths – the best speech I have ever heard him make . . . . My task was not too difficult and the speech was regarded as a great success . . . . We won the Kenyan

---

51. A reference to the Mau Mau conflict, which had recently broken out in the colony and lasted until 1956.
52. This was the Bill to denationalize road haulage.

division by 23. Many, almost half we are told, of the Socialists did not want to press the division.

The Press has been very friendly to the new housing scheme. Except for the *Daily Worker* and the *Daily Herald*, there has been no adverse comment. I went on Wednesday (17th) to the party Housing Committee, who seemed very pleased. Although they mean a great deal of extra work, I like to do these outside speeches, for they add to my position, and therefore power, in the party and in the Government. Both the Steel and the Kenya speeches have done me good . . . .

Among other activities, was a luncheon given by David Eccles to the heads of the architects, the quantity surveyors, and the builders, to see whether a reform of the tendering system can be achieved, with a voluntary abandonment of the 'ring' system.

On Friday (19th) I got all the P.R.O's (Principal Regional Officers) to a meeting on Bricks . . . . Apart from saving on the use of bricks, the local authorities – and other users – can but help by ordering work ahead and in some cases paying in advance. For the small brickyards are often short of credit . . . .

23 December

. . . . There was a Cabinet yesterday – all foreign affairs and all insoluble, or nearly so . . . .

We decided to go ahead with African Federation,[53] in spite of Mr Attlee and Mr Griffiths. But all depends, of course, on the result of the Rhodesian plebescite . . . .

Christmas Day

A very happy day. D and I went to Communion at 8am. Afterwards to matins, with 4 grandchildren (and parents) The Macmillans have gone to Brogyntyn – but the Fabers are here in force and Louise Amery (aged 20 months) came to church for the first hymn and then was taken out.

Boxing Day

. . . . I worked all day, and have produced with much labour, the paper

---

53. Labour had approved in principle the idea of a Central African Federation, consisting of North and South Rhodesia and Nyasaland, when in office, but had now turned against it. The Federation was established by the Conservative government in 1953.

on Housing Policy which I have had for a long time in my mind. It sets out a comprehensive policy – a Rent Bill (short term); a Rent Bill (long term); a valuation Bill; a Bill for taking over (without payment) the derelict houses and repairing them to last 5–15 years, till they can be destroyed; and a long term co-ownership housing Bill. Of course, we cannot do more than the short-term Rents Bill (probably) this session. But if we could present this measure in a great and ambitious frame, it wd alter the whole psychological and political approach . . . .

30 December
David Eccles came to see me at the Ministry about Bricks. He had a bad cold and seemed tired. However, he had plans for increasing production. This unlucky Coronation takes all his time and I want Bricks and Cement, not Coronation seats . . . .

1953

6 January

A long Cabinet, presided over by Eden in Churchill's absence. The Americans are quite determined to sustain Dr Mossadeq. They want to give him $100m in return for an undertaking to agree to an arbitration on the oil dispute. They want to pay him $50m down (wh is said to be enough to keep him going for a year, prob 2 years) and then take delivery of oil from Abadan for American military needs. 25% of the value of this wd be paid to us, as instalments of the compensation. At a later date (if the claims of some speculator who says he has an agreement with M for all Persian oil can be set aside) an operating company of an international character will be formed to market the oil, with Anglo-Iranian an 70% equity holder. The Prof (Lord Cherwell) points out that Mossadeq has left himself plenty of loop-holes (e.g. need for ratification by the Majlis or Parliament) and will probably 'renege' on the whole affair as soon as he has got $50m. We want the Americans to pay in instalments, and in accordance with the progress of the negotiations for the arbitration. Of course, Acheson wants to have a success before going. I shd have thought we might have held on till Ike takes over.[1] After nearly an hour's talk, it was decided – oh, I forget what! But Sir Norman Brook will have it very accurately and logically set out in the minutes.

After Persia, Africa. The Cabinet decide to agree to certain modifications in the Federal plan (regarding the African Board etc) which Huggins and co want.[2] Actually, I think the change will make a better

---

1. Eisenhower had just won the US Presidential election, and took office on 20 January 1953.
2. A federation of Central Africa (comprising North and South Rhodesia and Nyasaland – now respectively Zambia, Zimbabwe and Malawi) had been agreed in the late 1940s. In early 1953 concessions were granted to the Prime Minister of South Rhodesia, Sir Godfrey Huggins, reducing the representation of the 6 million Africans in the federation parliament and on the African Affairs Board (which had the power to refer federal laws in London if they were felt

guarantee for African rights. But since it is a change, it will certainly be represented as a concession to Europeans by the Socialists etc. Finally, the everlasting question of bus and railway fares in London. This absurd nationalised industry wants higher fares every six months. We discussed only the tactics of presentation. Fortunately a very unpleasant Socialist peer, called Lord Latham, is chairman of London Passenger Transport. So let him be the whipping boy! . . . .

In the afternoon, a long and most encouraging discussion with officials of my paper 'Houses Old and New'. The Secretary was less damning than usual; the Dame was enthusiastic; the others (Wilkinson and Symon) helpful. Although everyone began by saying that the time-table was impossible, after about 2 hours it seemed almost practicable. I am not without hope . . . .

7 January

. . . . [A] meeting with Sir Percy Mills (who has come back to help with bricks!) . . . . (British brick production is of the order of 7000m) . . . . Our expected gap is only two or three hundred million – so with savings, foreign purchases, and extra production at home, we ought to be able to do it.

Came home on the 5.20. D met me. She brought Catherine (Amery) down yesterday from the hospital. She will be better at B.G. but she is naturally very weak and rather depressed. This is the second miscarriage – which is a little alarming. And she has had a bad time and lost a great deal of blood. I hope she will pick up soon here . . . .

I went from B.G. on Sunday (Jan 4th) to see poor Lord Woolton. (He lives near Haywards Heath) He was remarkably better than I expected to see him. He nearly died twice, in spite of, (or perhaps, because of) all the doctors. His illness was a series of disasters. First, it had been wrongly diagnosed for years as colitis, when it was really appendicitis. Next, when he was taken ill late at night at the Scarborough conference, altho' the local doctors and surgeon diagnosed correctly, they would not operate without another (Leeds) opinion. Before this could be got (the following afternoon) the appendix burst, and peritonitis followed. If he had been an unknown person, they would prob have operated at once. (I comforted Lady W by reminding her that under our wonderful health scheme, you cannot get an

---

to discriminate against Africans). After a referendum in South Rhodesia the federation was inaugurated in October 1953.

operation, however urgent, till you have taken your turn in the queue and done some 'fair shares for all' – probably 3 months) The poison went all over his body; lung, ribs etc had all to be dealt with to get it drained away. At the final stage, the doctors gave him up. He was dying. But Lady W had procured another surgeon (a young man from Birmingham) He took one look at him as he lay dying, rolling up his sleeves, stuck a torch in his mouth, applied a local anaesthetic, and stuck a dagger in his side – there and then, just like that, on the bed not the operating table. He struck the right spot; the poison poured like an oil gusher, and W's life was saved . . . .

. . . . Lady W told me a strange story. Towards the end of Oct (when W was still so ill as to [be] incapable of anything) he got a letter from Winston. He could not read the letter; he was engaged in dying, not resigning. The letter preremptorily demanded his resignation as Lord President and offered him the Chancellor of the Duchy . . . .

The reason which P.M. gave for the need for an *immediate* decision was the Commonwealth Conference. It was absolutely vital that Ld Salisbury shd become Ld President and Ld Swinton become Commonwealth Secretary, in order that Lord S shd have time to prepare himself for the heavy task of presiding at the Commonwealth Economic Conference which was to meet in a month's time. Judge by Lady W's surprise and the indignation of the now recovering Lord W to learn that nothing of the kind actually happened . . . .

The Wooltons are very upset and I think will never quite forgive the P.M. I quoted to her what Cyr Asquith had said to me about him 'He was always an appreciative, but never a considerate colleague' . . . .

12 January

. . . . The Persian problem is looming up again, and I was called in (with Oliver Lyttelton and F.M. Alexander) to join the Persian Committee . . . .

I did not like the proposed terms for the arbitration and said so forcibly. They wd have led, easily enough, to a basis of compensation wh wd be quite unacceptable . . . .

16 January

. . . . Anthony Eden, and his new wife Clarissa, (Churchill's niece) came to stay for a night. They were both very agreeable. Since they wanted no party, we had only the family. After dinner and the next morning

17 January

We had much open and useful talk. He is much less nervous and much less easily offended (or frightened) than he used to be. I think he notices that we all want him to succeed to the Throne, and that no one is intriguing to supplant him. Of course, week by week, Ld Beaverbrook's papers instil all the poison possible into the position – but no one takes much notice. There is no doubt at all that, if and when Churchill goes, Eden will succeed. Even Eden believes that. But when *will* Churchill go? At one moment, he seems inclined to lay down the burden. At another, he clings to the job like a leech. Anthony at one time thought 'after the Coronation'. Now he doubts it. Meanwhile, all kinds of decisions are taken – or not taken . . . . What will Eden do as P.M.? He told me frankly that the Foreign Office must go to Salisbury or to me. (It is clear that he would prefer S) But he doubts whether the HofC will stand an F.S. in the Lords . . . . Could I be Privy Seal and Chairman of the Party? (This idea really sprang from something I had said about the importance of a strong successor to Lord Woolton) . . . . Of course, the Lords Leathers, Woolton, Cherwell would go. Also old men like Salter. What about Alex? Would the Field Marshal want to stay? Ought we to want him to stay? He gives distinction. What else does he give? Geoffrey Lloyd – no good. Dugdale (agriculture) good; but is he good enough? Anyway, there are lots of young people. Walter Monckton (who has proved such an admirable Minister of Labour) wants to be Attorney and then Lord Chief Justice (what odd things people want!) Who should succeed? It is a key post. Perhaps Selwyn Lloyd? Yes. A very good man . . . .

Eden agreed that in the last few months – or weeks – the political situation had changed. A Socialist victory at the next general election was no longer inevitable. All this made it all the more important to get the change in the Premiership before any radical alteration in the atmosphere. Just before he died, the King (so the Queen had told Eden) had made up his mind (no doubt stimulated by the Queen) to have a talk with Churchill about his plans. He had, of course, only just come in. But that made it really easier to discuss plans quite freely. The King's death meant, of course, that this conversation never took place . . . .

The visit was both pleasant and useful. We seemed to understand one another better than ever before . . . .

18 January
. . . . Worked hard at Housing policy. The *new* houses aren't too bad. We've just got the final figures for 1952. 240,000 odd against 195,000 for 1951. And about 280,000 building. But the *old* houses are a problem. It is really impossible, amid all the confusion and illogical character of our rent system, twice interfered with by war and scarcity, to devise any scheme to increase rents which will even appear rational, still less equitable. However, I worked away at the papers for the Cabinet, which *must* be printed soon.

19 January
A good morning at the Ministry. Went through all the Rent scheme with officials. Several improvements and easements were suggested. I have had to re-write all the papers – over and over again. If I hand it to the officials, we get more or less unintelligible officialese . . . .

20 January
A long Cabinet, very well presided over by Eden. The question of Japanese admittance to GATT came up. So far, we have managed to 'stall' on this, but it does not seem possible to go on 'stalling' indefinitely. What between US and Lancashire, HMG are in a difficulty! . . . .[3]

22 January
Another Cabinet. The chief business (as indeed on Tuesday) was to receive reports of various unsolved problems – Sudan and Egypt, Persia; Germany and France; etc etc. I am not sure that I really want to be Foreign Secretary!

Besides this, the main business has been to support the National Coal Board in resisting fresh demands, pressed very hard, from the mineworkers unions for more wages. The coal industry, as a national monopoly, is threatening the whole national economy, by ever-

---

3. The Americans were keen sponsors of Japanese participation in the international trade negotiations conducted under GATT. Lancashire textile interests were hostile, which placed ministers in a quandary as Lancashire contained many marginal seats.

increasing prices. It is really necessary to call a halt. Of course, the men will (just as if it were a private and not a nationalised industry!) appeal to the Govt over the heads of the Board – but what will happen when the P.M. returns from America, I don't know . . . .

25 January
. . . . Katie took some of the children to church. We have Anne, Michael and Mark Faber staying at Birch Grove, while Julian and Carol (their parents) are in America. Alexander (Macmillan) has gone to school – away from home for the first time – leaving us all (esp Joshua) very disconsolate . . . .

1 February
We got back late on Saturday night from a Bromley Young Conservatives 'do'. The wind and rain were terrific. Naturally we thought little of it; but this afternoon (Sunday) I was rung up (partly by the Press and partly from officials) and told the news.

It was very hard to make out just what was the extent of the Great Flood. But it was clear that it was a terrible calamity, ranging from Yorkshire to Kent, and that the effect on urban and rural life would be considerable in the areas concerned.

I had been in bed most of the day, trying to get rid of my cold. But I naturally went to London, after first making what arrangements were possible from here.

2 February
Churchill has [been] very insistent through the night on the telephone, but came to stop soon after midnight. As no one else seemed to take the lead, I summoned a conference at 11am today, at my Ministry, of all departments concerned. It was most useful, and we got a proper procedure going – viz, a committee of officials under Sir Frank Newsam (Home Office) and a small committee of Ministers, under David Maxwell Fyfe (Home Secretary) Having thus successfully voted myself out of the chair, I prepared a statement for the P.M. and David and I went to see him with it at 1pm. The statement was well received in the House, although the Socialists will certainly try to exploit the position. Morrison suggested that we had cut expenditure on sea defences – which is untrue. We cut expenditure on sea erosion. But a cliff may crumble away without letting in the sea!

3 February

Left Hendon at 10am in an Anson. I took Beddoe and Symon with me. We flew first to Manly airfield and managed to get a car to take us to Mablethorpe and Sutton. The sea had burst through the sea defences (the sand dunes etc) and flooded both these resorts and a good deal of agricultural land. About 6000 people had been evacuated – their houses being uninhabitable. The water was not very deep (as it was low tide) but wd rise again with the tide to 3 or 4 feet. We went about in a 'Duck'⁴ and saw everything. The Chairman, Town Clerk, surveyor and other officials seemed to have done well. All the people had gone to Louth or to villages in the county.

From Manly, we flew to *Scalthorpe* (now being used by the American air force) There was a fine array of Generals, Eagle Colonels⁵ etc and great kindness. The first car broke; so it was decided to 'motivate alternative transportation'. We drove to Hunstanton (to which we used to go as children) and saw similar (but much more limited) damage there. Unfortunately, the loss of life was high, owing to the sea having broken through the sea wall and swept away a number of little bungalows. These were largely occupied by officers and non-commissioned officers of the American Air Force. About 26 or so were drowned, in spite of some very gallant rescue work.

At Hunstanton, I got a telephone call (the telephone had just been repaired) about a row in the House of Commons in my absence – poor Marples had (it seems) a rough time. The Socialists are still trying to make capital out of the disaster, of course. We got back to London about 9pm, when I heard all about the trouble, which was caused by Mr Dodds (MP for Dartford), arising from my unwillingness to allow a general seizure of empty houses on the excuse of flood victims.

4 February

I made a statement after questions today, and I think dealt satisfactorily with yesterday's troubles. The Opposition seemed rather ashamed of themselves. A very full day, with every sort of flood problem.

5 February

.... The flood problems are sorting themselves out a bit – the official

---

4. An amphibious US military vehicle.
5. An American forces' nickname for full colonels, from the eagle with spread wings that forms their insignia.

committee (under Newsam) is doing very good work. The chief problem is still about the evacuees. We do not think that they amount to a very large number; but there are more than can be handled either in rest centres or by private hospitality without *some* payment. Dame Evelyn and the other Ministries have worked out a scheme for a 'billeting' allowance. The Treasury (that is, Sir Bernard Gilbert) are rather doubtful. Yet we *must* have a definite statement by tomorrow (Friday) This is 'Budget Day' in every working class household. Unless we can make an announcement, these people will drift back from private houses and crowd, perhaps overwhelm, the centres. It is really remarkable how kindly neighbours have been. In Whitstable (Kent) about 6000 people are homeless, yet only 50 are in the 'rest centres'. All the rest have found a home in Kentish towns and villages . . . .

6 February

At the meeting of the *small* Ministerial Flood Committee this morning (Home Secy; Minister of Health; Minister of Agric; and myself) we settled today's statement, and included in it a repudiation and refutation of the lie started by Morrison and Bevan about our having 'cut' the coast defence work. Of course, we shan't catch up with this lie, but we will try to scotch it. The next point was the 'billeting' allowance. The Treasury was represented by F.S.T. (Boyd Carpenter) who delivered us a pontifical lecture, in the most irritating terms, about the danger of rapid decisions and the importance of clearing all questions involving expenditure in the normal way. (But what is an emergency procedure for? And is not the Treasury represented both at official and ministerial levels?) I lost my temper and even my staid colleagues were highly indignant. We managed to get the Chancellor of the E on the telephone, and he promised an answer by lunch time. The odd thing is that the Treasury has agreed to millions of pounds of emergency expenditure (troops etc) without a murmur. This odd £60,000 or so alarms them!

However, the answer came (a complete surrender) and I was able to make the announcement at 4pm (before the House rose) The details will be on the radio and in the press. We shall pay 10/6 a head lodging allowance for each adult; 5/- for each child. I am sure this will help enormously and prob save us money on more schools, halls, emergency hospitals etc in the long run . . . .

11 February

Stayed in bed all day. My cough is better, but still troublesome. It looks from the telegrams as if we shall reach some agreement on the Sudan with Egypt. It will be ill received here, esp by the Tories. But the truth is that the Sudanese are only thinking of getting rid of the Egyptian claim of 'sovereignty' and are anxious to close at almost any price.

Read Trevelyan's *'George 3rd and Charles James Fox'*. Very readable, but of course very prejudiced. It is the pure milk of whiggery. Finished the first volume.

12 February

Snow, wind and cold. Got up in my bedroom for luncheon. The Secretary (Sir Thomas Sheepshanks) came. He lunched downstairs with Dorothy; came up afterwards. He was most helpful, but I cannot find much use for him. Nothing is put clearly or dealt with succinctly. But he is doing his best. We are certainly a weak team. We have only Dame Evelyn Sharp who is really first-rate . . . .

I have been following the telegrams and struck by the weakening of the Egyptians at the end. Of course the truth of it is something like this. The Sudanese (Northern) want to get rid both of the British and of the Egyptians. They do not want to miss the chance of hitting both birds with one stone. The Egyptians want to get rid of the British, and feel that (although promising the contrary) they can somehow get back into Sudan later, by bribery or force. The Sudanese (who despise the Egyptians) are contemptuous of this danger – probably too much so. The British (as usual) are honest, and trying to do the best for everybody and would be accused of betraying everybody. The only people who may be sacrificed are the Southern Sudanese. But this is the same story whenever [we] leave a country to enjoy its 'independence' . . . .

13 February

My temperature is now down to normal and the pains in my chest and body are less. But I still have a most troublesome cough. So I keep my room, except to go down for luncheon with Dorothy while my room is done . . . . The weather is quite horrible; cold north-east wind and drifting snow, fine and now beginning to cover the landscape. This means no work in the woods or in the gardens.

Finished Lucas' *'Life of Lord North'* – a bad book, but with some interesting things in it. What a queer figure! And how these types repeat themselves – honourable, lazy, and disastrous. Baldwin was just such another, the 20th century Lord North.

Judging from the radio news (to wh we scarcely ever listen but did so last night), Eden 'got away with' his Sudan announcement pretty well in the House yesterday.[6] I have not yet seen the papers; for they still do not reach Birch Grove House till lunch-time – and this 40 miles from London! . . . .

19 February

Debate on the Floods. Home Secretary opened, in the grand manner. I wound up, in a more work-a-day mood, answering minor points etc. We got away all right, and I think there is a general feeling that the Govt have handled the whole matter expeditiously and effectively. The only weak spot is the Lord Mayor's Fund. There will be a demand for compensation as of right, not by charity. This will have to be resisted, for the sums involved would be large; the principle of insurance wd be endangered; and there would, in the end, be public indignation against I.C.I., Unilever, and other large corporations receiving 'compensation' from H.M.G. in respect of risks against which they could have insured . . . .

Sat 21 February

Dorothy and I motored to Chequers,[7] arriving before dinner. P.M.; Mrs Churchill; Mary and Christopher Soames; Brendan Bracken; Jim Thomas. The house has not changed since I was there last (in 1945) but I think I looked on it then with a less critical eye. It was pleasant enough (in war-time) to be home and one did not bother too much about the sham panelling, the fake decoration, the 'antique' furniture, and the over-painted and over-varnished pictures. However, I was very comfortable and it is wonderful to see masses of servants – all WAAFs or WRENs or whatever they are – like a chorus of excellent parlour-maids and house-maids. We had a pleasant evening, Winston in a beneficent and patriarchal mood, very flattering to Dorothy about me etc etc.

---

6. Regarding an agreement with the Egyptians on the right of the Sudan to self-determination.

7. The country residence of the Prime Minister.

Sunday 22 February

. . . . The P.M. was (I thought) rather sombre . . . .

He talked a good deal about American foreign policy – the atom bomb – and the hydrogen bomb.[8] Will the Americans be prepared to wait or will they force the issue? Will they wait until, either by their own skill or by treachery, the Russians have learned the secret of the hydrogen, as they have of the atom, bomb . . . .

23–26 February

A very rushed week, with a mass of engagements and very little achieved – except the 3rd reading of my T&Country Planning Bill. I had all the Chairmen of the Regional Production Boards and their founder, Sir Percy Mills, to luncheon at the HofC. We had a good meeting after luncheon, and even the Ministry officials (like Wilkinson) now admit that these boards (the creation of wh they so deplored) have done a lot of good . . . .

2 March

Went to the 'Press' Pre-view of the Ideal Home Exhibition at Olympia. We have an *extremely* good Ministry of Housing exhibit – better than last year. We show 2 'People's Houses' (one 3 bedroom, one 2 bedroom) One of these is the new 'open' design, which will (I think) be popular in the South and with young people. It gives them a large sitting room and dining room and 'lounge' all in one room, from wh the stairs go up. (This in place of the old 'front parlour' where no one ever sat and which was reserved for the 'corpse') . . . .

3 March

A long Cabinet. I got caught for a 'sub committee' on Farm prices (which is a bore) . . . .

My private problems – Rents, Repairs, 'Operation Rescue'[9] etc are making slow but steady progress. When [one] gets into the details, the difficulties multiply. It is very difficult to see how we can get away politically with rises in rent of the order of 50% – 60% in some cases

---

8. The US were to explode the first H-Bomb on 1 March 1954.

9. This was to tackle the dilapidated and condemned privately rented accommodation not covered by Macmillan's rent and repairs proposals, by giving local authorities powers to upgrade these dwellings.

(the old controlled rents) But I can't see how anything less will allow the repairs to be done . . . .

6 March

Stalin's death is today officially announced by the Kremlin. All through yesterday the strangest bulletins, with an extraordinary wealth of detail, both as to the illness and its treatment, were published to Russia and to the world. It appeared as if all the doctors were heavily insuring themselves against accusations of incompetence or treachery.

There is no indication yet of where power will now reside. Will it be a committee of public safety? Will it be an individual? If the latter, will it be Molotov, Malenkov, Beria, or another? Malenkov is said to be a particularly bitter and intransigent Communist, who has never left Russia and scarcely met a foreigner.

The government got a majority of 40 in the defence debate last night. The Opposition continues to 'splinter'. Mr Shinwell did not accept the 'party' line. Nigel Birch, in winding up for the Govt, had an amusing passage about 'lapsed Attleeites' . . . .

7 March

. . . . Walked in the woods from 11–5 (taking my sandwiches) This did me a lot of good. I found Blake, his son, Lucas and Stevenson engaged in shooting grey squirrels. This they do by either poking out the 'drays' with a long rod (like a drain rod) or (if the dray is too high up) shooting it up. In the first place, if the animal is at home (wh at this time it is likely to be, for it is sleeping) it runs out and is shot (or shot at, for they run fast and jerkily) In the second, it may be killed in the dray but you can't be sure. Nor do you get the little beast itself – wh is important, for the Govt will give 2 cartridges for every tail. It was quite good sport and very necessary – for they do great damage to trees, shoots etc as well as to game.

Worked at boxes all the evening . . . . The papers announce the succession of Malenkov to the position of Augustus, with Beria (the secret police) as Caesar. Molotov is foreign minister, but seems no longer of the Imperial family. I have a foreboding that Stalin's death (and these successors) will bring still more miseries on the world . . . .

This week has been a week of luncheons, dinners etc. How I hate these speeches. However, as a change from Housing etc, I did one at the London Rotary Club on Foreign Affairs. I hope there was no report to the F.O . . . .

10 March

. . . . At the Cabinet this morning more news about America and Egypt . . . . There is to be a 'joint approach' by the US and British Governments to the Egyptians, suggesting a joint negotiation. But General Neguib has been behaving in a very truculent way both about the Sudan (where they are accusing us of breaking the Treaty) and about 'unconditional evacuation'.[10] However, he may not dare to flout the two Governments, if they are clearly acting together. Besides, he is desperately in need of money . . . .

14 March

. . . . Lady Rhys Williams to luncheon – much talk about the poor European movement and the follies of the F.O. Will E.D.C. be ratified by the French? If not, we have a new opportunity to lead Europe. But if EDC passes and the 6 power Federal Europe comes into being, Germany has it all handed to her on a plate . . . .

18 March

. . . . The Egyptian business has now reached a complete impasse. As one might have expected, the Egyptian Govt rejected the 'joint approach' from US and GB. US immediately ran out and the position is really worse than before . . . .

19 March

Another tiresome morning in Standing Committee. But we made better progress. I worked all the rest of the day on this terrible 'Rents and Repairs' Bill (for the Bill is now taking shape) The Cabinet Ctee is making very little progress and is beginning to get alarmed. I am not surprised. As a technical problem, it is as bad a tangle as the Town and Country Planning Bill. But, unlike my decision then, whatever we do positively will be (we are told) unpopular and may be fatal . . . .

22 March (Sunday)

. . . . The Germans have ratified E.D.C.[11] This will not, I think,

---

10. Of the Suez Canal base. The future of the base remained a fraught issue until agreement was finally reached in July 1954 that the base would be evacuated in 1956, with a number of British civilians remaining to service it so that it could be reactivated in the event of war.

11. Three days earlier in a cabinet memorandum (PRO: CAB129/60, C(53)108)

encourage the French. Rumour says that the Americans intend to bribe the French deputies. (Joseph Retsinger tells me that Ambassador Bruce – Ambassador at large – is employed on this and that most of the deputies are only too anxious to be bribed.) I have circulated a paper to the Cabinet raising doubts as to the '6 power Federation of Europe' from the point of view of British interests. Swinton (the ablest of our colleagues) agrees. The fact is that we are just drifting. P.M. does not now do more than act decisively and effectively on separate and individual issues. He is incapable of devising or pursuing any long-term coherent policy on economic or political matters.

The Russians (as I expected) have started to blow soft and seem more reasonable. This (as I expected) is proving very awkward for US and British Govts. A change of heart (if one cd believe in it) one wd welcome. But we must beware of a mere change of tactics . . . .

23 March

. . . . A long and boring debate on 'Floods'. 3.30–9pm (when the debate collapsed) The Opposition made a great error in choosing this as a subject for attack. Fortunately for them they had realised this in time; so little Chuter Ede, who opened, 'roared like any sucking dove'.[12] David Fyfe made a masterly exposition of what HMG had done, was doing, and intended to do. This virtually finished the debate. A few members (from both sides) fired off speeches directed at their constituents, not the House, and when I came to wind up there was little to be done.

24 March

10.30–1. Standing Committee. We got on a bit faster and will (I hope) finish on Thursday. I had to go to the P.M.'s room after questions (3.30pm) to talk over some points on my Housing plans and to try to get him to understand something of the Rent and Repairs proposals. He was very friendly, but very distracted. I then learned that the death of Queen Mary was to be expected at any moment. P.M. was much

---

Macmillan had expressed his misgivings about this development and asked: 'Are we really sure that we want to see a Six Power Federal Europe, with a common army, a common iron and steel industry (Schuman Plan) ending with a common currency and monetary policy?'

12. A slight misquote from Act 1, scene 2 of Shakespeare's *A Midsummer Night's Dream*.

concerned, because of his loyalty and attachment to the Throne. Also, I felt, because of the passing of yet another of the great figures of his life. There was much argument about whether the House shd be adjourned or not, immediately the news became known. However, since it did not take place till 10.20pm, it was decided to say nothing till the end of the debate (on the proposed African Federation) which, owing to an hour's extension, did not occur till 11pm. Unfortunately, the news became known to members while Henry Hopkinson was winding up for the Govt (with bad effects on his speech) The Govt had a majority of 40. Immediately after the division, P.M. announced the news, and gave notice that after questions tomorrow he wd move a vote of condolence and that the House wd then adjourn.

25 March

Queen Mary's death has filled the press with tributes and (as far as one can see) the people's hearts with genuine sorrow.

The P.M. moved the vote of condolence in a short, and well phrased speech. Attlee seconded. The House adjourned at once. I went home in the car . . . .

28 March

D and I went at 10.30 to the Cadogan Pier, to go on board the Port of London authority launch. This is an annual 'outing' for the Varsity Boat race given by Lord Waverley (Sir John Anderson) It was a very cheerful and very mixed party. At about 12.30, a terrible pain seized me, from which I had to suffer agonies and hope not to be observed till the boat got back to Cadogan Pier. We had left our car there, and D motored me to the flat. The pain increased – a sort of terrible griping of my belly. Fortunately, she found my good Dr Richardson at home. He very kindly came out and took me to St Thomas' Hospital where I was put in a private room, and drugged, doped and generally dealt with . . . .

1 April

. . . . After much discussion, it was decided to issue a bulletin about me from the Ministry. This really became necessary because I had to decide to cancel quite a lot of speaking engagements up and down the country. The announcement ran as follows:–

'Mr H.M., Minister of Housing and Local Government, who became unwell during the week-end, is in St Thomas's Hospital,

London, under observation. He is suffering from an affection [sic] of the gall bladder. He is continuing to receive official papers, and hopes to resume his Parliamentary duties shortly. He has, however, cancelled his outside engagements for the next few weeks'.

This has duly appeared, in various and mainly shortened forms, in all the press this morning. 'Macmillan ill' is the usual formula. The object was to avoid raising too many hopes among young and ambitious members (by suggesting an incurable and dangerous malady) and yet to placate the angry chairmen of all the local associations etc whom I must disappoint.

Dr Richardson (even if the best of the possible diagnoses is made next week, when the tests are taken) is emphatic that I should cut down the *strain* of work – apart altogether from the work itself. I certainly have found preparation and delivery of these speeches a heavy labour . . . .

Good Friday
A bad day. The pain came on about 10.30 and grew more and more intense . . . .

We think that all these attacks of violent pain point to more than colic and suggest a gall-stone trying to force the way from the gall-bladder (where it is formed) into the intestine. Anyway, all this adds to the doctor's knowledge and our power of decision next week. The chief difference between this attack and the previous one was that there was *no* fever. My temperature remained normal throughout – indeed, by a curious paradox, it was the first day since coming into hospital, that it did *not* go up in the evening . . . .

4 April
A quiet and peaceful day – no secretaries, no 'bags', and no visitors except dear Carol, returned yesterday from America . . . .

The nine Russian doctors, arrested and accused of foul murder of Communist leaders a few months ago, have now been released and those who accused them have been arrested instead. The only embarrassing thing is that everybody has, of course, confessed to everything, however contradictory, at some stage or other of this strange affair.

All the Russian news is odd. Tito thought that the struggle for supremacy was by no means over – indeed, had scarcely begun. Malenkov and Beria had made a duum-virate. Would it last? Meanwhile, either with full Russian support or on their own, the Chinese (and the Russians behind them) are calmly accepting the position about compulsory repatriation of prisoners in Korea which we have demanded for over a year. This, with all kinds of other signs, big and small – in Berlin and elsewhere – are generally regarded as the first moves in a Russian 'peace drive'. What is the purpose of the peace drive? How should we meet it? . . . .

However, it may be that there are some 'benefices'[13] to be got from the present internal position in Russia. We might even get an end of the Korean war. But we have no guarantee that this will not mean renewed pressure in Indo-China and Malaya . . . .

Easter Monday
According to the paper, Anthony Eden has got the same disease as I have, only worse. They have decided to take his gall bladder out right away. It's a great bore for him, esp at this time, when his position in the party is weakened and so many opportunities as well as difficulties, lie ahead. It will be interesting to see how long it will be before he is back at work . . . .

7 April
The Russo-Chinese game still seems 'a peace offensive'. They are now (with great applause from the 'left' in every country) graciously accepting the precise proposals for exchange of prisoners (injured or sick) in Korea, as they rejected flatly a year ago. This is called 'Communist peace move'. Really, the democracies sicken one with their folly and their cant.

A quiet day, spent chiefly in being photographed. Dr Richardson came in the evening, and after studying the x-rays, seemed to think that I had better have the gall-bladder removed. The only question is 'when'. We decided to leave this over till next week.

If the Cabinet decides to go ahead with *Rents* and press through the Bill this session, then I will take a chance of lasting out till the end of July. If they will not take the hurdle, then I will have the operation done at once . . . .

8 April
Left St Thomas's at 10am. The nurses and sisters have been remarkably

---

13. 'Benefits'.

kind to me. Motored to Birch Grove House, arriving for luncheon. The garden quite lovely, all the daffodils being at about their best . . . .

9 April

Stayed in bed in the morning, reading and working. P.M. rang up and asked for some housing 'dope' for a speech he is to make next week in Scotland. He seemed very excited about 'Housing Subsidies' and 'millions of houses falling down because the landlords cannot do the repairs' . . . .

10 April

. . . . Lord and Lady Woolton came to tea today. He is much exercised about the Chairmanship of the Party. Winston has practically told him to go and has (very impulsively) offered the job to Malcolm McCorquodale (without telling Woolton or Eden!) Now, I think, he wishes he hadn't! Woolton clearly doesn't want to go, except in his own way in in his own time . . . .

13 April

Motored to London, arriving for Cabinet at 4pm. The Chancellor of the Exchequer gave us the broad outline of his Budget. Its main theme is, I think, right. A fillip to industry. Hence, he proposes to restore 20% (half the original) initial allowances for new plant; he will bring EPL to an end on a fixed date; he will cut all purchase tax (at whatever rate) by a quarter; he will take 6d off the income tax. This, of course, will be called a 'Capitalist' Budget. But then we believe in Capitalism as the best instrument for the prosperity of the people. As a sop, a few minor income tax adjustments and sugar to be 'off the ration'. (This has been done by buying a million tons of surplus Cuban sugar at a very good price) A good Budget. I wish EPL cd be dropped forthwith; but even so, I think the announcement will help our Brick and Cement people to get going . . . .

14 April

A very stimulating Cabinet. The P.M. gave us an account of a considerable interchange of telegrams – on a personal and private basis – which he had been having with President Eisenhower.

It seems that the President is due to make a speech on the 16th in which he is to review the general international situation. But his welcome to the Russian thaw (if thaw it be) seemed to the P.M. unduly freezing. He proposed to state minimum conditions for peace. Back to the Yalu river (with a neutral zone this side of it);[14] free elections in a united Korea under UNO supervision; peace in Austria; free elections in Satellite countries and effective re-union of Europe; a united Germany; disarmament – including a clause preventing any country from using more than a fixed proportion of its steel on armaments; the Baruch plan for control and inspection of atomic production.[15] The P.M. replied that although all these things were right in principle, to state them so baldly (not to say crudely) might be thought by world public opinion as rather a negative act at the moment. It would seem as if a sudden frost had nipped spring in the bud – even if it were no real spring. (I am bound to say that I was personally very glad that President Eisenhower had such robust and such sound views. This is altogether apart from the tactical question) It seems as if the President will soften the language and accept many of the P.M.'s proposed amendments. (Ike had sent him the text of the speech, or the relevant parts) Churchill seemed very pleased to have re-established this very friendly and useful contact; this certainly [is] all to the good. He reminded the President of the uncertainty as to how the Russian internal situation might develop. There was an old saying – 'the most dangerous moment for evil Governments is when they begin to reform' . . . .

16 April

Cabinet today approved *all* my proposals for dealing with the *old* houses – rents, repairs, operation rescue and all the rest. Harry Crookshank's committee, with Chief Whip added, to report on procedure, timing etc. I was really pleased with getting all this through. The P.M. asked me to explain it in two sentences. I replied, 'I'm afraid that's not possible. I will do it in ten minutes'. I had prepared a text – every word and all the figures, and provided them with charts and tables. This is really the only way with these complicated matters. I'm afraid it is beginning to look as if we shall have to put off the 'Rent

---

14. Presumably Macmillan meant not the Yalu River (the border with China) but the pre-war frontier of the 38th parallel.

15. The Baruch Plan had been put forward by the US in 1946 for the complete international ownership and control of the sources of nuclear energy. With the USSR wanting the US to destroy its existing weapons first and only offering limited inspection rights the plan was soon dropped.

and Repairs' Bill till the autumn. In that case, we will do the Rating Bill this session. Anyway, we can now work on all this aspect of the Grand Design with the knowledge that we shall be able to carry it out without going back to the Cabinet. This is a much better position than I had last year on Town and Country Planning, where I never got a final Cabinet decision until a few days before the publication of the white paper and the Bill . . . .

After the Cabinet, I went back to rest at the Ministry, before going to St Thomas's Hospital for further x-rays – this time of my stomach. Dr Richardson was there, to test the x-ray and to view the demonstration of various foods going through my inside! (I had had no food since last night) Afterwards, we had a talk about what is to be done. It seems he feels that it will be the wise course to have the operation. But if I keep to a strict diet and reduce some of the more fatiguing of my activities, I think he feels I can last out (with luck) till the end of July. This will be much better for my work and preparing for the heavy winter programme.

17 April

Home affairs at 10am. Not a very exciting, but rather a long agenda. At 11.30 a meeting of the committee on 'the collective approach' presided over by Butler.[16] The Treasury have prepared a most persuasive, indeed a most damning, paper to explain to the Americans the wickedness and folly of Protection. (The latest symptoms are the story of the Seattle Dam, where an English company underbid all the Americans by £100,000; and the story of the wheat pool, where the Americans are demanding a fantastic price by monopoly powers) I'm afraid I am very sceptical about any change in American policy. They will talk; but they won't act. No American Govt dare do so. My only contributions were to present the Chancellor with a motto for his paper (which is to be given to Mr Humphrey, US Secretary of the Treasury) and to express the hope that we should now begin to study the alternative policies, based on the Commonwealth and Europe, which Swinton, Cherwell and I had put forward at the beginning but which the Treasury experts have always ridiculed. Rather to my surprise, the Chancellor of the Exchequer thought we ought to study this alternative, as a matter of urgency . . . .

---

16. See below, entry for 20 May 1953.

19 April

My father's birthday. He was born 100 years ago today. Church in the morning; Maurice and the 3 boys; Carol and Anne Faber were there. The second lesson was Corinthians XV 35 to end – the splendid passage wh ends with 'O, death, where is thy sting?' etc.

John and Ava Waverley to luncheon. We walked in the woods and collected primrose roots for them to take home. Worked with Marples between tea and dinner – he went home and we went to dine with the de la Warrs . . . .

22 April

Bricks and cement are still our chief worry. The long drought has resulted in an unprecedented consumption of materials for building for this time of year. Moreover, we lost some cement production in the floods and had to divert concrete to the sea walls. We are doing all we can in our Ministry to slow down starts (in order to concentrate materials for the next two or three months on the houses already started) and to save bricks (by cutting out extravagant plans etc) Ministry of Works are doing their best (and we are helping) to increase production and to get some imports from the continent. I think there will be a lot of troubles, but I believe the programme (which is now a little out of balance in relation to materials) will get back into balance by the end of the summer and early autumn . . . .

5.30. Meeting of the Cabinet Committee on 'Houses – Old and New'. We decided to abandon the idea of doing the Rent and Repairs Bill this session. We shall try to do the Rating and Valuation Bill instead. This is really a better plan, tho' rather a disappointment in some ways. But with the new filibustering mood of the Socialists (who are keeping us up on Lords amendments to the Transport Bill by pure obstruction) it would hardly be possible to go for the original plan . . . .

23 April

. . . . Lunched with Ld Beaverbrook. No other guests. I had not seen him for two or three years. He looked young and well. He was not changed in his conversational methods either. He thought Churchill ought to dissolve now and had told him so. But he won't. 'The cat has been twice singed'. Anyway Churchill says 'The only election you lose is the one you have'. Max did his usual charm, flattery, insinuation, and 'pumping'. He wants me now to become Minister of Agriculture and has told Churchill so. 'Keep out of the Foreign Office. Churchill will always dominate foreign policy while he lives, esp with a new F Secy'. 'When Churchill goes there will be a contest for the leadership of the Party. There will be an Eden section; there will be a Butler section. You may easily slip in, as Bonar Law did between Austen Chamberlain and Walter Long'. 'Yes' I replied, 'but who is to be my Max Aitken'.[17] He laughed at this. Quite an amusing and stimulating medicine, to be taken in very small DOSES, at two or three year intervals . . . .

24 April
A very satisfactory meeting with the brick makers, conducted by David Eccles (as Minister of Works) and by Ernest Marples (representing Minister of Housing). They have accepted – or indeed, proposed of their own accord – precisely the plan for brick deliveries during the next 3 months which we desire. That is, to keep fed with bricks the houses which *have* started and are building; to quote longer delivery dates for houses which have *not* yet started. If they will do this; they will get the programme into balance far better than we could by any administrative means . . . .

27 April
I had intended to leave London at 8.30am, with David Eccles and Marples, to go to Basingstoke, to open 'The Boneless Wonder' – that is, the houses built either without *any timber*, or with varying degrees of *timber-saving*. But as I had a good deal of pain during the night and a temperature last night (I suppose more imflammation of this cursed gall-bladder and liver) I decided not to go but to rest in bed . . . . Lunch with a committee of United Europe and European movement, who are trying to organise another economic conference (like the Westminster conference, which was so successful) . . . .

René Massigli was very charming and very interesting. He was also very frank. In his view, the French assembly will never ratify E.D.C. Indeed, under the impact of the new Russian peace moves (which M takes very seriously, as a genuine change of policy as well as of tactics) it is less likely than ever before that the French will accept 'federation' and 'supra-nationalism' now that they are brought up against it.

What then is to happen? The President of the Republic is consid-

---

17. Bonar Law became leader of the Conservative Party in 1911. Max Aitken was Beaverbrook's given name.

ering a gesture on his own. But of what kind? Well, really, to revert to the original Churchill conception, for which the British Conservatives argued so consistently at Strasbourg – in a word, to have a 'confeder-ation' and a European army, which we could join and which would not involve any merging of sovereignty, but a treaty or alliance. At the same time, any Russian negotiation will be terribly dangerous if Germany is not tied up definitely with the West. But France is terrified of a German–French merger, without Britain, which leaves them at the mercy of Germany. All this is quite interesting, but really tragic. If 3 or 4 precious years had not been wasted; . . . . Shall I ever be Foreign Secretary? If I can, shall I be able, so late, to prevail? It makes me think a bit, anyway. Better stick to houses, than have a title and no power. We seem at least to be able to get on with our houses.

28 April
Winston's first appearance at Cabinet since he received the Garter. We all made respectful noises . . . .

After the Cabinet, Churchill kept me back and talked to me about my health. Anthony would not be back nearly till October. I asked him, straight out, did he propose to handle the F.O. till then. He said 'yes'. If he were to appoint another minister he would only have to learn to work him etc. All the issues (Russia, Egypt etc) were so great that the Prime Minister had to take a great hand in this anyway. He urged me to have the operation done before getting into a really bad state – like poor Anthony . . . .

1 May
. . . . [A]t the opening of an LCC estate in Woolwich (and a very fine one) I was given the opportunity for announcing the quarter's Housing figures. They are very good – 69000 against 53000 last year. At this rate of increase (if all goes well) we shd be not far off the 300,000. 'Pourvu que ça dure!'.[18] I am still worried about May, June or July. The brick people will help as only they can, and if they concentrate their deliveries in the way they have agreed, we ought to get through without too much trouble. Cement will be more difficult. The floods meant a considerable loss of production and wastage in use . . . .

---

18. 'Let's hope that this lasts!'

2 May

.... In Korea, the American general, Harrison, seems to be of the bungling type so familiar to us in the Mediterranean.[19] In demanding Switzerland as the neutral country to take care of the disputed prisoners (in itself reasonable) he has succeeded in insulting every Asiatic country, – India, Pakistan, Ceylon, etc – by saying that no Asiatic country, even if neutral, could be considered! Mr Dulles – who appears to be the most dunder-headed man alive – equally moves from blunder to blunder. Poor Ike strives to be dignified and noble, but Senator McCarthy throws in his bit of fascist nonsense every now and then, just to bring comic relief.[20] I suppose it's the result of the 20 years of opposition and the ignorance of the Republicans and their inexperience. Let's hope they learn. There *is* hope of that. When I worked with them, I found the Americans very quick to learn – especially from their mistakes.

The French are having a very rough time in Indo-China. They are still reluctant to 'inter-nationalise' the war, for they fear the Americans and the effect of bringing the whole struggle into the UNO arena. It would mean full steam ahead with 'colonialism', 'imperialism', and all the rest. But, if the offensive to which the Chinese seem to be giving increasing support, develops with increasing pressure, it may well be that France will not be able to sustain the burden. What wd be the effect on Malaya? Well, judging from the Japanese invasion, it wd become untenable . . . .[21]

Read Arthur Bryant's *'Samuel Pepys: the Saviour of the Navy'* –

---

19. When Macmillan was Minister Resident in North West Africa in 1942–45.
20. Joseph McCarthy, a Republican senator from Wisconsin, as chairman of the US Senate's sub-committee on investigations, accused many Democrats and liberals of communist sympathies. He went too far for Eisenhower when he turned his attention to the army, and a Senate motion of censure in 1954 destroyed his career.
21. The Malayan 'Emergency', in which British and Commonwealth troops confronted communist insurgents, began in 1948. This was a not dissimilar problem to that facing the French in nearby Vietnam. Although the tactics pursued by General Templer in the mid-1950s effectively contained the threat, it was not until 1960 that the insurgents were considered defeated. Macmillan clearly felt that the swiftness of the Japanese advance down the Indo-Chinese peninsula in 1941–2 was an alarming precedent for a domino-style collapse to communism in the region.

very readable, and a pleasure to read (for a change) a Tory historian.[22] What harm Macaulay did! And how long it has taken for the other side even to be understood! Disraeli began it, but was not taken seriously by the 'intelligensia' until this century. 'How I wish I cd be as sure of anything as Mr Macaulay is of everything!'. Who said this? . . . .[23]

3 May (Sunday)
Church in the morning. Isaiah 60 and Luke 3 . . . . (Alexander, to my regret, has gone back to his boarding school. I miss him greatly)

The news from the Far East is bad. The Russians and Chinese are quibbling about the Korean truce, in the old familiar style. Meanwhile, the pressure on Indo-China grows. The French Govt are obviously uncertain and divided. It really looks as if the purpose of the Communist 'peace offensive' may have been to act as cover for this new (and most dangerous) war offensive in SE Asia . . . .

4 May
Cement and Bricks – Bricks and Cement – these fill the day, morning, noon and evening – till far into the night! After a great struggle we have got the Treasury to agree to the purchase of another 200,000 tons from abroad. Now can we scrape together another 50–100,000 tons. This wd see us through, even if this phenomenal building weather lasts. How I wish Percy Mills were here . . . .

5 May
. . . . I heard today that Sir Percy Mills' name has gone forward for a baronetcy. This is very good of the P.M. and I am delighted. But I

---

22. Bryant was an extremely popular historian at the time, equally admired by people like Attlee.

23. Perhaps these thoughts subsequently prompted Macmillan to re-read some of the works of the Whig politician, essayist and historian Thomas Babington Macaulay (1800–59). On 5 August 1953 he noted in his diaries 'Read Macaulay's Essays. I had not looked at them for years. I read 'Horace Walpole' – *very* bad. Also *William Pitt* (to end of George 2nd) – not so bad, but hopelessly prejudiced. He even admires Henry Fox, who was a crook, a miser and a coward. The Macaulay style does not wear well. It is brilliant, but hard and without depth.' Incidentally the quote, which should read 'I wish I was as cocksure of anything as Tom Macaulay is of everything', comes from Lord Melbourne, Whig Prime Minister 1834 and 1835–41.

wish he wd come back. I feel he wd help me to get this Housing programme – approvals, starts, houses building and all the rest – and the position of materials (bricks and cement!) into the right perspective. My civil service advisers have not the business experience . . . .

6 May

The first day of the Local Govt elections (Urban District Councils) shews very little change. The swing to the left, which was so marked last year, seems arrested. It will be more interesting when we get to the Boroughs, and the Counties. Lancashire, the control of which was lost last year, is very important.

Negotiations still drag along in Korea. In Laos and Indo-China generally, the French are anxiously awaiting the rainy season to give them a respite. In Egypt, there is to be an interval for a fortnight. No doubt the Egyptians (who already rely on the American ambassador, Caffery – a very bad Irish type) are hoping to get something out of Dulles – who is due to arrive in a day or two. Dunder-headed Dulles is sure to make a 'gaffe' if it is possible to do so . . . .

The Opposition vote of censure was a very sham fight yesterday. The electorate is bored by all this manoeuvring in the House of Commons, wh seems to them somewhat ridiculous. When we did it in opposition, we gained nothing by it. Nor do the Socialists today. For the moment, the Govt are in a favourable position – the balance of payments [deficit] reduced, taxation reduced, full employment maintained. But it wd only take a very small change in the economic climate, to produce very dirty weather in the political. In this situation, will Churchill dissolve? He is being constantly urged to do so by Beaverbrook. It is very tempting. For a victory wd give him a lease of power probably for his life – or at least, his active life. But a defeat? That would indeed be a terrible anti-climax. I must say that if I were he, I wd play out time. But he is and has always been a gambler . . . .

6 May [sic]

The Urban District Council elections are finished. We have gained 40 seats and lost 40. Socialists have gained 53 and lost 28. (The independent losses account for the difference) Since we are comparing with 1949 (a *very* favourable moment for us) and in contrast to what happened last year (when we lost heavily) this is a good result. Lancashire is particularly good – which is significant . . . .

7 May

Went with D to the presentation of new colours by the Queen to the 1st and 2nd Battalions Grenadier Guards. The ceremony took place on the lawn, in the palace gardens. It was a beautiful bit of drill – more like a ballet, and executed with marvellous precision. There being 4 (four) Grenadier officers in the Cabinet, as well as the Colonel of the Irish Guards,[24] we demanded that the Cabinet should be put off. It can never have happened before and it is unlikely to happen again . . . .

12 May

Churchill made a 'great' speech yesterday on Foreign Affairs. 'Great' as a Parliamentary performance; 'great' as the effort of a 78 year old Prime Minister taking on the additional job of Foreign Secretary;[25] and 'great' as in the sequence of the prewar, war and post-war speeches which have profoundly affected public opinion in the world.

At the same time, he is taking big risks. His Egyptian policy (about which the Cabinet has had very little recent information) is a gamble on provoking a situation which leads to the collapse of Neguib's regime. Alternatively, if we fail in Egypt, we shall have to hold our position in the Sudan. A breach with Egypt wd bring the treaty about the Sudan to an end. All this reverses altogether Eden's policy.

But while P.M. is tough in the Middle East, he is all for an accommodation in the Far East. (The Americans are pursuing the exact opposite policy) Churchill almost takes the Korean armistice for granted, and sweeps away all the American and Chinese hair-splitting. (Meanwhile, the President sends a present to Col Neguib of a revolver!)

But the high light of Churchill's speech was the offer of a 3 power talk (or so it amounted to) on the old Roosevelt, Stalin, Churchill model. This excited the enthusiastic support of the opposition, the less vociferous approval of the Conservatives, the interest and sympathy of all Europe and the Commonwealth but, of course, the alarm of Washington.

D and I dined last night with Michael and Pamela Berry. The American ambassador and Mrs Aldrich were there. The Ambassador (without the slightest regard to discretion) criticised – or rather attacked – the Secretary of State, Dulles. He was in 100% disagreement

---

24. The four were Churchill, Crookshank, Lyttelton and Macmillan, all due to service during the First World War. The colonel of the Irish Guards was Alexander.
25. During Eden's illness.

with him. Either he or Dulles would have to go. It was also clear, that Julius Holmes (his Minister) and the rest of his 'boys' in the Embassy had listened to Churchill's speech with alarm and indignation. The Ambassador thought it 'great stuff' and was in almost complete agreement.

This now means that on questions of finance, trade, economics, and foreign policy we and the Americans are now in total disagreement. This may please Silverman and Co,[26] but I regret it very much. The President is very naive and inexperienced; Dulles is ignorant and stupid; some of the old Republicans are hopelessly reactionary – but we have *got* to get along with them. Malenkov has made a breach in the Anglo-American front such as Stalin never succeeded in doing. Does Churchill know what he wants as a settlement with Russia? Will Central and Eastern Europe be 'sold out' in a super-Munich? All these things are very worrying. At present I can do nothing in the Cabinet. But I shall *not* stay if we are now to seek 'appeasement' and call it Peace. Churchill may know what he is doing, but he has not told the Cabinet as a whole . . . .

14 May

The Sunderland by-election (announced late last night) will have a considerable effect. A minority of 300 turned into a majority of 1100 (despite the intervention of a Liberal candidate) and a seat won from the Opposition by the Government, is a sensational event.[27] Such a victory has not happened for many years. It will certainly upset the Socialists and they will begin to quarrel still more. At the Cabinet this morning, there was a very genial atmosphere.

Meanwhile, ... Churchill's speech (while a brilliant effort) has no doubt puzzled a lot of people. They have read into it an attitude of 'appeasement' which is not really, or not necessarily, implied in it . . . .

David Eccles and I met the representatives of the Cement Industry at 5.30. They have appointed Sir Malcolm Trustram Eve as their chairman. We had a useful talk. They will take up the additional 200,000 tons of imports. They will consider letting exports drop a little behind. They will try to get the cement when it is most wanted. Meanwhile, *we* will try (on the Housing side) to get a system going by

---

26. Sidney Silverman and other far left members of the Parliamentary Labour Party.
27. Sunderland South by-election result (13 May 1953), C: 23,114; Lab: 21,939; Lib: 2,524.

which serious and urgent needs can be passed on and met. While our problem is by no means solved, I feel happier about it, chiefly because everyone concerned is being so helpful and trying so hard to solve it. It will be, of course, a narrow squeeze, until we can bring our programme into a little better balance . . . .

18 May

A long and tiresome discussion about Gatwick air-field (calculated, if gone on with, to ruin Crawley New Town) at a committee under the Lord Chancellor. I managed to get further delay. But I fear the Committee will report in favour of the scheme. Carried through the Lords amendments to my Town and Country Planning Bill. What a long time ago it seems since I introduced the Bill – before Christmas. The legislation mill grinds very slowly . . . .

20 May

Quite a useful discussion at the Economic Policy Committee, initiated by the Chancellor. The so-called 'Collective Approach' was decently buried. It remains an 'objective'. But no one really believes that non-discrimination, multilateral trading in the Free Trade sense, and convertible currencies with the dollar are really practical politics. So we must work at a new plan. We must particularly try to protect ourselves from an American recession. Rab [Butler], Cherwell, Swinton, Thorneycroft, Salter, Monckton all spoke. I said nothing, which seemed to alarm them all!

A very good meeting of my Ministerial Council after luncheon. Sir Percy Mills came, for the first time for some months. He dined with me last night – in excellent form, after his journey round the world. Our chief problems in the Housing field are a) shortage of materials – long term as well as short term b) the programme.

On the first, the measures we have taken for *saving* in design are helping – esp with bricks. As usual the NE coast (Durham County etc) won't play. But generally the whole country has done wonderfully. The arrangements we have made with brick manufacturers and cement distributors are also working well. Long term measures are more difficult. But with the state of confidence that pervades the building industry and with the abolition of Excess Profit Levy, I have hopes of new kilns and even new cement works.

The building programme presents quite a problem. It must not be too empty; but it must not be too full. Once local authority schemes are 'approved' we lose all control of them. We cannot run a 'starting date' system with so many diverse schemes. We have got the order book a bit *too* full and we have got to work it down by the end of the year. But to what figure? This is difficult to assess accurately, because we don't know how many private enterprise starts there will be. On the whole, we must take a cautious view. We may *just* scrape through this year. It would be a bad mistake to have the programme overloaded next year.

21 May

At Cabinet this morning the P.M. was in a mood of almost schoolboy excitement. He has been invited (with the French Prime Minister) to meet President Eisenhower. The meeting is to be in Bermuda. This is *much* better than Washington. The P.M. is immensely pleased at this turn of events. He announced it this afternoon to the House of Commons. It was well received by all parties. But it has not saved M Mayer, the P.M. of France. He was voted out by the Assembly today.

2nd Reading of our Rating and Valuation Bill . . . .

A good debate, on a tiresome and unpopular subject. Marples introduced it in a good speech. [John] Edwards made a very good attack on our plan, but not so good a defence of the 1948 system. Dalton wound up with a heavily genial speech; I replied with as light a touch as I could manage. I think the House liked my approach. We carried it by 20 odd votes. But we shall have a lot of trouble in Committee; and, unless it's very carefully handled, it may prove 'political dynamite' – as have all previous efforts to get any uniform system of assessment for rating throughout the country. People don't like 'averaging' when it means 'averaging up' . . . .

28 May

Worked all the morning on a paper for the new 'Trade and Employment' Committee. This is really a successor to the 'Committee on Commonwealth Conference and the Collective Approach to US' which dominated the late summer and autumn of last year, and resulted in the abortive visit of Eden and Butler to Washington.[28] The new committee (of much the same ministers under the Chancellor of the

---

28. They returned on 18 March 1953. Butler failed to win any alleviation of Britain's balance of payments problems.

Exchequer) will, I trust, be more successful than the former one. We are also to be more practical, I hope. Anyway, we are to study the possible American 'recession' and its effect.

. . . . The sooner we get down to cultivating our Empire and our potential European garden, instead of trying to persuade the USA to adopt Free Trade, the better it will be . . . .

29 May

. . . . [T]he Rating and Valuation Bill is going to be very difficult in the Committee. The main thing will be absolute refusal on my part to give figures which can be misinterpreted at the General Election. But it's a tricky subject, with a tricky history. We had a meeting with all our people (Secretary etc) and the Inland Revenue people after Wednesday's Cabinet. I hope to be able to get them to draft one or two amendments which will help to define 'free market'. This may help. But, of course, the public will not judge by definitions, but by whether their assessments go up and by how much.

1–7 June

This has been a week of celebrating and of ceremonies. The actual Coronation was very impressive, and in spite of the rain, so was the procession. The enthusiasm of the people has been extraordinary – a sort of outpouring of pent-up emotion. D and I had excellent seats in the Abbey, with a view almost to the altar. We were in the North transept, so we could see the Royal box, with the Queen Mother etc. Moucher (Devonshire) was very dignified as Mistress of the Robes, and the little grandson (Peregrine Hartington) did very well too. We saw the procession from the bridge (between the Abbey and the Houses of Parlt)

The rest of the week has been a series of luncheons, dinners, and banquets. We went to Buckingham Palace on Wednesday night. I wore again; as in the abbey, my Privy Councillor's costume, hired from Morris Angel, theatrical costumiers! The footmen (in splendid 18th century liveries) and the plate were the best part. I have lunched with the *Finns*, the *Pakistanis*, and the *Italians* and *Austrians*. At the Italian Embassy, I was between two of my old friends – Signor Pella (Finance Minister) and dear Count Casati. I think my reception by these Italians (hugs, embraces etc) rather astonished my English colleagues. On Thursday, D and I dined with the *French*, where the Ambassador was as kind and friendly as ever. On Saturday, we went to the Derby, in all the luxury of the Jockey Club box. (I have never been to this event before) . . . .

. . . . Ld Salisbury (Ld President) told me (at the Derby!) that he thought Churchill meant to go ahead with a meeting with the Russians, *whether the Americans agreed or not*. I said that I thought this a *most* serious step, which cd *not* be taken without specific Cabinet approval. Lord S assented, and deplored once more (what we are all beginning to realise) the absence of Eden. (Eden left on Friday in this memorable week for Britain, for his operation – the third) There is a two-fold danger in all this – a serious rift in the Anglo-American politico-military alliance; and the collapse of the European effort. Both in Germany and in France, there are many people only too anxious for 'appeasement', and only too ready to clutch at any excuse to relax defensive measures. The French political crisis is partly due to the inherent weakness of their constitution. But it is also largely due to the unwillingness of anyone to take a final and definite line about European unity (or federation) and German re-armament.

Churchill (freed from Eden's influence) is playing a big game. But it is strange how little he tells his colleagues, or at least, the Cabinet as a whole. Lord S agreed with me (and so did Maxwell Fyfe) that we must really ask for more to be told us . . . .

9 June

. . . . After the Finance Bill today (or rather, about midnight) the financial resolution of my Rating and Valuation Bill came on . . . . Aneurin Bevan, supported by his little gang, started a long and boring wrangle . . . . In the course of the evening, Bevan called me a cad! He accused me of revealing what he had told me in private conversations – although it had all been in the newspapers. The fact is that like all bullies, he is a coward. He spluttered with rage; withdrew his words, about foaming at the mouth. I think he was rather drunk.

10 June

I expected a repetition of the Bevan incident on Report stage tonight. But the musketeers were caught napping – or rather drinking – in the smoking room. So the Report stage went 'on the nod' as the Bevanites came rushing in – too late! . . . .

14 June

. . . . The foreign situation gets more and more complicated. It looks as if Europe was breaking up under Malenkov's sunshine. Stalin's icy blasts kept it together. France is still without a Govt; Italy has swung violently to the left, leaving de Gasperi just in a majority; Germany is puzzled by the sudden and even spectacular change of front in the Eastern zone. It is now solemnly announced that the Russians are to demobilize an army of 120,000, the existence of which they have always denied! . . . .

17 June
The first day of the 'Rating and Valuation' Bill passed off well in Committee. We got clause 1 (which repeals the 1948 system) by lunchtime . . . . Meanwhile T.V. (sponsored or not) fills the whole political world. There are violent opinions, for and against. The B.B.C. and the *Times* newspaper (now edited by Haley, former head of the B.B.C.) are putting up a tremendous fight to defend their monopoly. They have got Lords Halifax, Waverley and Brand – and, of course, the Bishops – to form a society for their support. The alleged American 'vulgarity' and esp their handling of the Coronation has been whipped up into a great cry against sponsoring. With all this and a minute Party majority, the Govt's position is rather serious. For this is just one of the things about which people get very exciting [sic]. After all the tedious economic problems which no one can understand or solve, this is one issue on which everyone can have an opinion. I was not at the Cabinet (owing to my Bill) but I understand that the discussion was adjourned. The P.M. is wavering (owing to Lady Violet Bonham Carter) and I think most of the experienced politicians scent danger . . . . (Eden has left a sort of last will and testament, strongly *against* sponsored television. But he never said so at any point that I can remember!) . . . .

21 June
The Macmillan boys to Church today, Alexander having been back from school 'in quarantine' for something. He returns today. Ernest Marples came and we worked all the afternoon . . . . A great scare has been worked up about 'slum' schools and a great attack on Miss Florence Horsburgh (Minister of Education) It is really directed to a denigration of my housing record.[29] Ernest and I worked on a reply.

---

29. The accusation was that scarce building materials were going into housing and not schools.

23 June

We made fair progress with the Valuation Bill in Standing Committee. The Opposition asked to be let off sitting tomorrow, to which I agreed, on the understanding that we would definitely finish the Bill next week. The 'television' contest still rages and will be decided (in theory) at tomorrow's Cabinet. I have circulated a paper *against* 'sponsored' television *unless* it can be brought about in 6 or 9 months. A prolongation of the controversy without any practical test wd be fatal for us. Lords Halifax, Waverley, and Brand (Church, Kirk, and Counting-House) are a formidable combination. Nor do I believe that younger people want it very much, or any advertisers except the very large ones. But the real cause of the feeling against it is a desire to remain different from the Americans . . . .

26 June

Lunched with Lord Leathers and Mr Jensen (Tunnel Portland Cement) We discussed ways and means of getting more cement. It is the lack of bricks and cement to grow to the full extent of our need, which will be the limiting factor to building expansion. Yet this could very easily be overcome, if it were not for recession taxation and fear of socialism. The truth is that no particular firm in industry wants to get too big or too successful. If it does, it is 'ripe for nationalisation' . . . .

27 June

. . . . It seems that the P.M. (who looked bad at the Cabinet on Wed) has got worse. A communiqué has been agreed and will be put out this afternoon. Butler and Crookshank will act for him in the Commons; Salisbury at the F.O. It says he is 'overtired' and must rest for at least a month.

Arrived at Birch Grove late in the afternoon and went to bed, feeling quite worn out.

28 June (Sunday)

I did not feel up to going to Church, but stayed in bed all morning. The pain (from my gall bladder) keeps threatening me. I have had no very acute attack, but feel it all the time . . . .

4 July (Saturday)

This has been a most extraordinary week – full of drama. I have had no time at all to write the diary till today . . . .

Monday morning the Cabinet was summoned for 12 noon. Butler took the chair . . . . He told us of the visit which he and Salisbury had paid to Chartwell on Friday, where they found the P.M. in poor health, but very gallant. With the greatest tact and the lightest of touches, he revealed to us (what we did not know) the nature of his illness. 'The speech was not very clear; the movements were not too easy'. (In fact, he had had a 'stroke' – the left leg and arm were paralysed and the left side of the face)

It was a terrible shock to us all, although revealed so discreetly. Many of us were in tears, or found it difficult to restrain them . . . .

Lunched with Lady Pamela Berry – James Stuart was there. I was interested to find that she knew the whole story. But if the press know (she is Lord Camrose's daughter in law and Ld Birkenhead's daughter) can it be kept a secret indefinitely . . . . Lady Pamela is a devoted friend of Anthony Eden. She fears that Churchill will not be able to hold on till Eden is ready. This (she thinks) cannot be till October. But can the P.M. last so long and can the truth be concealed so long. All this was rather a shock to me. I had not (till this conversation) got such an impression of critical illness (This proved later to be a correct impression)

After questions, a talk with Harry Crookshank – my best, oldest and staunchest friend. He told me how the Salisbury arrangement has broken down. The pressure from Attlee and the House as a whole was too great to be resisted – somebody must be in charge of foreign affairs. So after some telephoning to Chartwell, this was arranged. Ld S is appointed 'acting Foreign Secretary'. (There are precedents for this both in Ld Balfour's and Ld Curzon's time)[30]

Harry seemed rather concerned about my going off too all this time. So (he said) was Rab [Butler]. Could the operation possibly be postponed till August? Later in the afternoon, I saw Rab (on some departmental matter) and he made the same suggestion.

So I went out (after dinner with the County Councils Association!) to see my Dr Richardson. He examined me. But he was quite firm. No more delay, or I might become very ill. We had left it too long already.

July 1st was a very heavy day. I had (fortunately) broken the back of preparations for the wind up in the great debate . . . .

The debate dragged on,[31] without a very full or a very empty

---

30. A. J. Balfour was Foreign Secretary 1916–19, and Lord Curzon 1919–24.
31. A supply debate on school buildings.

house, until the end. I had a crammed house at 9.30 and made the best Parliamentary and debating speech I have ever made. I got a tremendous ovation at the end . . . .

On *July 2nd*, I went early to the Ministry. The Press on my speech was excellent. The *Daily Mail* gave a whole front page. The papers also carried the news which I had put out officially the night before – that I would go to hospital on Monday, and that an operation wd prob be necessary . . . .

At 7pm I left by car for Chartwell for dinner. This invitation had come the day before. I put on a dinner jacket and arrived at 8pm. This was a dramatic evening . . . .

The Churchills are using the 'flat' upstairs. When I went into the sitting room, only Lord Moran was there. He told me that he was very satisfied – more than satisfied – at the progress made. But he feared I might be rather shocked at P.M.'s appearance, although he was much better in the last two days . . . .

P.M. was wheeled in, and as he entered the room cried out 'I must congratulate you on a magnificent Parliamentary triumph. It was a masterpiece'. I sat down beside his chair, and he began to talk with great animation about the debate. He spoke without any difficulty and apparently without any particular slurring of words (more than his usual lisp) Since he had done 3 hours or more talking and dictating already, Lord Moran had warned me that the speech might get very indistinct. (This did happen, later in the evening, but not till about 10pm) As far as I could see, his left arm was by no means helpless. He tried to get out of the chair and walk in to dinner, but was persuaded to go in the chair.

At dinner, he talked so much at the beginning that he slobbered over his soup. He poured out some champagne with a steady hand and cried out 'you see, I don't spill precious liquor'.

The atmosphere was not oppressive (as it used to be at Chatsworth) but positively gay. It was a kind of conspiracy we were all in – and it was rather fun to have such respectable people as Salisbury, Butler and Co as fellow-conspirators. He said 'you know, I have had a stroke. Did you know it was the second. I had one in 1949, and fought two elections after that.' He then described how he had gone from Strasbourg to Ld Beaverbrook's villa in the South of France and had had a seizure after bathing. He said his arm was almost restored and his leg much better. There were certainly times, at and after the dinner, when I thought he was putting on an act – but it was a jolly brave one, anyhow. I was, at many times in the evening, nearer to tears than he. We discussed the possibility of a dissolution; death and Dr Johnson's fear of it; Buddhism and Christianity; Pol Roger – a wine, a woman, and a horse; and many other topics. But he talked most of Germany and Europe . . . .

After he had gone, I had a talk with Christopher Soames, who gave me the story of the week.

The attack was at the Gasperi dinner[32] – on Tuesday June 23rd. It was slight and the P.M. was got off to bed. Lord Moran cd not be got till the next morning. He got to the Cabinet without too much difficulty and got through the Cabinet meeting without disclosing what had happened . . . .

They got him to Chartwell on Wed afternoon. He got much worse – the clot seemed to grow and his arm and leg movements got worse. It seems, therefore, not to have been a sudden incapacitating paralytic stroke, but something which began fairly gently and grew steadily worse . . . .

On Saturday he got much worse and they thought he wd die. Then he rallied – and has been getting steadily better since Monday or Tuesday. On Monday he was telephoning and so on. Today I could see his state – a sick but a very gay man. Christopher and his family have taken a great responsibility and will need support. If he gets worse – there may be another and fatal seizure – it will all come out. If he gets much better, and he can be photographed walking or can do a short statement on the news, all will be well. If he just drifts on, about the same, unable to appear or function, there may be open criticism and the accusation that there has been something like a conspiracy. However, it was really the only thing to do and I told Christopher that I thought they had done quite right. It is only fair that Churchill shd have a few weeks to make up his mind. He had two courses. He can go on till October and then hand on to Eden. Or he can go on till October – and then, if he is all right – go on 'till the pub closes'. It is clear that the old man has this in mind. Out of chivalry to Eden and in repayment of all that he owes him, he must not hand over now to Butler, unless he feels in conscience unable to serve the Queen efficiently *in the essential work of the First Minister*. To do this it is not necessary to walk or make speeches – I mean, for a few weeks. I told C that, of course, if this had happened in February, it would have

---

32. For the visit of the Italian Prime Minister.

presented much greater difficulties. But we have only a few weeks left of the session . . . .

The situation is really fascinating. Butler is, of course, playing a winning game . . . . Churchill cannot really last very long. Reflecting on it all, I feel it unlikely that he will be able to do more than keep going till he can hand over to Eden. In any case, I think he will *not* want to go on unless he can get well enough to undertake meetings with Eisenhower and then Malenkov. His only purpose in remaining must be the foreign situation and the sense of mission to be the 'peacemaker' . . . . But can Eden last? No one has any real experience of the subsequent effects of his operation . . . .

. . . . [W]hat will Butler do if Eden has to give up. Then he will have to appoint a Chancellor of the Exchequer.

In modern conditions, a CofE dominates almost any Govt. Neville did so, with Baldwin.[33] Cripps did so, even over Bevin as F.S. Who wd Butler wish to see? I am sure not a strong chancellor. Not Lyttelton; not Macmillan; not Eccles . . . .

6 July

Lunched with Oliver Lyttelton at the Turf Club. He was very incensed by the proceedings of last week. Although he was in London the whole time, he received no information of any kind about Churchill till the Monday Cabinet. We discussed a very significant article which appeared in yesterday's '*Observer*'. This said that Macmillan would be favourite for Foreign Secretary, if it were not for the break-down in his health. He would be facing an operation *at the end of this session.*

Considering that the whole press last Thursday carried the announcement that my operation wd take place almost at once, this was purely malicious.

The article went on to boost Monckton and Fyfe. This exactly conforms to my theory, and strengthens the view that it is Butler's. For he is, and has been for years, notoriously close to Massingham and the *Observer*. It seems likely that this article was inspired by him. Oliver [Lyttelton] would be unlikely to stay on in a Butler govt, but would certainly serve Eden. It will be a tragedy if Oliver goes; without his courage, we might by now have lost Malaya and be on the way to losing Africa. One of the uncertainties would be Monckton. He told me that his only desire is to become Lord Chief Justice. He told

---

33. Neville Chamberlain was Chancellor of the Exchequer 1931–37.

Lyttelton that he would always serve Churchill, but would not serve 'a slab of cold fish' (Butler) This is too hard on Butler – who is able and sincere, but wildly and almost pathologically ambitious.

Cabinet at 5.30. Lord Salisbury gave a very good – even masterly – account of the foreign situation and the line he proposed to take in Washington. It is still our policy to press the French to ratify E.D.C. (However, they won't do this, and I doubt whether it is to their or our long-term interest that they should do so) . . . .

I spoke briefly, and I think impressed my colleagues, at least by my moderation. I was very careful, but I think got to the main point. The future of Germany – that is the whole issue. She *must*, be kept from isolation and neutralism. That means the Stalin–Ribbentrop Pact over again in the long run.[34] She must be bound to the West. If E.D.C. is the best method, well and good. Personally I prefer 'Greater Europe' to 'Little Europe' for in EDC Germany may become too strong. Instead of being bound to the West, she may bind the West to her . . . .

At about 8pm (after the Cabinet and a final talk with my P.S.) I came to St Thomas's hospital, and settled myself in to a nice little room off Arthur ward. This – I suppose – will be my home for some time to come. Telegrams, letters and flowers have begun to stream in – which is rather encouraging.

When I write this diary, I feel it best to put down quite truthfully what is in my mind. Whether it will (in future years) be of any historical value, depends on absolute sincerity . . . .

7 July

A day of rest, but not of repose. A continual 'va et vient'[35] – both of nurses and doctors. It seems an operation is like a minuet – or an execution! The doctor calls; the surgeon calls; the surgeon's two assistants call; the anaesthetist calls. These may be regarded as ceremonial calls. Then there is the blood-test man; the radio photographer (for the chest) the barber, to shave the hairs for the affected part; and the physiotherapist, to give breathing lessons (to prevent pneumonia after the operation) and knee and toe exercises (to prevent thrombosis) . . . .

---

34. A reference to the non-aggression pact between the Soviet Union and Nazi Germany concluded on 23 August 1939.
35. 'Coming and going'.

14 July

After being more or less knocked out for a week, I am slowly coming to. The operation was done on the 8th (by Mr Boggan) and was (it seems) successful. It was also necessary and even overdue. Owing to the gall bladder being full of stones, it was necessary to probe the main bile duct (to make sure that no obstruction had got there) This means that I have to have a tube, to take away the bile from the liver until it forms the habit of passing direct through the duct. This is rather a bore, but we hope it will be possible to get rid of the tube in another week.

I have received such a mass of letters, telegrams, messages and flowers from all kinds of persons, known to me and unknown as to be quite touching. Among others, I had yesterday a charming letter from Butler, wh made me rather ashamed of my suspicions of last week. Perhaps these were the product of my physical condition, wh (now that I reflect on it and have heard about it from the doctors and surgeons) must have been very bad . . . .

16 July

The usual hospital routine. Rogerson (my P.S.) came about Gatwick. Marples came for a general talk in the afternoon. D came also for a few minutes. My brain is recovering, but rather slowly. The first 6 months housing figures (estimates) have been sent to me (not for publication) The number will be over 145,000 – so we are on the way! The meeting of Foreign Secretaries has finished (at Washington) and decided on an invitation to Russia to discuss the future of Germany etc. But it is a very jejeune note, obviously written by the Americans, and full of omissions. It's a long way from the Churchill idea of a talk between heads of states, with no fuss and no agenda . . . .

19 July (Sunday)

A very quiet day. We had a very nice little service in the ward at 9.15 – a few prayers read by the sister, and a few hymns. I came in on a chair to take part . . . .

It doesn't seem probable that Churchill will want to go on after October – at least that seems the general view. Alex[ander of Tunis] seemed to take it for granted. But I would not be too certain, myself. He is of course saying to himself *now* that he is keeping the place warm for Eden. But if, when the time comes, he feels completely restored to health, he may well decide to go on . . . . Again, I think this depends on whether he can see any opening in the foreign situation, which he could hope to explore and exploit.

Considering that it is only about 10 days since I had this severe operation, I feel remarkably well. If, as I hope, they decide to take the tube out in a day or two, I should be able to get home by the end of this week . . . .

22 July

I have had several visitors in the last two days, including David Maxwell Fyfe and David Eccles. The position is still being held, of governing without a Prime Minister or a Foreign Secretary – but only just. However, every member of the House wants to get away. They are tired out by this constant attendance, insufficient pairing, and all the rest.

I am reading Voltaire's 'Siècle de Louis Quatorze',[36] with great pleasure. How much easier classical French is than modern French. There are no hard words!

D has been in to see me. They are all working hard for Sarah's wedding. Altho' the church is so small, they seem to have asked a great number of people. I suppose they will cram in somehow.

James Stuart came in. We talked Housing and Rents, as well as gossip. He doubts whether Churchill can go on beyond the autumn; he also doubts whether, after Churchill's departure, the Govt can go on without a General Election.

23 July

Philip Swinton came in late last night. He thinks it possible that Churchill will go on, for the latest reports are that he is practically restored to normal . . . . But if he does go on, there must be a complete overhaul of the Govt. There must also be some new themes – esp in the line of foreign trade . . . .

24 July

René Massigli, the French ambassador, came to see me. He told me that there could be no question of *any* French Govt being able to persuade the French Assembly to ratify E.D.C. so long as there was any chance of talks with Russia. He said that the French Govt were convinced that the Russians wanted a détente. Malik, the Russian

---

36. 'Century of Louis XIV'.

Ambassador in London, had been to luncheon with him. He was rabid against the Americans. The Americans were determined on war, to destroy Russia. Why did the Western European powers allow themselves to be dragged along behind America. Russia could reach agreement with Europe etc etc. Massigli said also that Americans, having no historical sense, were quite unaware of the potential danger of Germany . . . .

Massigli thought that, except during the short period of Churchill's reign of F.S., the officials at the F.O. made the policy. The most powerful was now not Strang but Roberts. Roberts was bitterly opposed to the Churchill policy . . . . I fear that all Europe will believe the Attlee–Beaverbrook story. For, strangely enough and from quite different motives, both Attlee and Beaverbrook assert that Churchill has been 'let down', if not betrayed by the Cabinet during his absence.

At 4pm I left the Hospital by car for Birch Grove. I had a great battery of press photographers at the hospital. Got home about 6pm and was very glad to be back . . . .

26 July (Sunday)

Stayed in bed till luncheon. Worked on the White Paper on the 'Autumn Housing Plan' (this is the name we have for 'Rents' and for 'Operation Rescue') I am to go to London for Tuesday's Cabinet where I am to expound the scheme and the progress made. A bag of other stuff from the Ministry kept me pretty busy. Also wrote letters to all the doctors, surgeons, nurses and sisters who have looked after me so well . . . . The garden has been made very spick and span, largely for Sarah's wedding. I *do* hope for a fine day on Thursday.

27 July

Churchill has had a fine photograph of himself, looking very well, in all the papers on Saturday. (Many of them had one of me saying 'goodbye' to the Sister) Anthony Eden arrived yesterday from America. He gave a press conference yesterday; the papers carry it today. He looks pretty well in the pictures, though a good [deal] thinner. He told the reporters that he had lost a stone and a half. He also said that he hoped to be back at work 'for the end of the Parliamentary recess'. I suppose this means the beginning of October.

Lord Woolton was here to tea yesterday. He thought that Churchill now had it in mind to go on. In that case, there would be some rearrangement of posts in the Government, but no Election. Lord de la

Warr, who came over between tea and dinner, thought that we ought to go on without an election, whether Churchill resigned or not.

The Truce has at last been signed in Korea. Syngman Rhee has promised to 'co-operate in the armistice, but not to endorse it' – an obscure phrase. An even more difficult problem is 'Where do we go from here?' It is not an easy hand to play, either for the Americans or for us.

28 July

Cabinet at 11am . . . . Ld Salisbury explained some of the difficulties and complications following the Truce in Korea . . . . The Americans have lost many men and spent a vast sum of money. One can hardly blame them for being alarmed at the possible loss of what they went to war for – esp their 'interests' in the Far East generally. It is as if, at the end of the Boer War, the delegates of 20 or 30 nations had started to discuss the future of S Africa . . . . At this Cabinet, the first since my illness wh I have attended, I had a warm welcome from my colleagues. I gave them a review of the Housing position to date; future plans for new house-building; the rent and repairs plan; 'Operation Rescue'; and all the rest. (The six months new housing figures will be published after August bank holiday. It will be 145,000 for first 6 months of 1953, as agst 110,000 for 1952 and 91,000 for 1951)

I warned them that if ever the 'white paper' (which will be circulated – in first draft – to the Cabinet tomorrow) is actually published, we must 'see it through'. In other words, if the plan is launched, there can be no dissolution this autumn – or indeed for two years . . . .[37]

30 July

Sarah's wedding. A most happy and successful day. The little church looked lovely, with flowers which D and her sisters had arranged. It was quite full. Andrew Heath and his best man were there when I arrived. I went down early and waited for Sarah in the porch. Maurice brought her. After one or two storms in the morning, the rain stopped, the sun came out, and from one o'clock onwards it was a perfect day.

The service was very well done, with a choir from Reigate, who sang beautifully. The Archdeacon of Lewes and our rector officiated.

---

37. Macmillan felt that politically controversial proposals on such matters as housing rents would have to be enacted and accepted before an election could be risked.

At the house, to save me the effort, Maurice received the guests with his mother. All those in the Church came; also another 30 or more – came to the house only. This included many of the Macmillan people (the seniors were invited to the Church) and the tenants, foresters, gardeners etc.

Moucher Devonshire came – Andrew [Duke of Devonshire] could not come; Nancy Astor came; and told René Massigli (French Ambassador) that she really approved of him because he was a Protestant! It was most fortunate that it was fine, for it made the house less crowded, since many walked in the garden. Altogether, it was a tremendous success, and a very jolly combination of friends and relations, country neighbours, estate tenants and servants, and Macmillan & Co staff. I confess I was tired out when it was over, and glad to get into bed at about 7 o'clock.

31 July
. . . . The Socialists are beginning to realise their danger. They have now elevated Churchill into the 'angel of Peace' – they have beatified, if not sanctified, him. What if he recovers after all – or worse still, dissolves on the cry 'Peace with Russia'? . . . . The amusing result is that it will certainly encourage Churchill to go on. For the 'warmonger' who nearly lost us the last election, is now the 'peacemaker' who may win us the next! . . . .

2 August
. . . . I read all the recent Foreign debates in both Houses . . . . There are many Conservatives *and* many Socialists (like Denis Healey) who clearly regard Churchill's speech of May 11th as a blunder. In any event, it is tragic that (if he really knew what he was trying to do) he was not able to follow through . . . .

I was amused to see that Nutting, winding up the debate, stated categorically that Churchill had consulted the Cabinet *before* the May 11th speech. So far as I can recall, this is *not* true. He told us about it afterwards . . . .

3 August (Bank Holiday)
The best day we have had this summer. Sat in the garden in different places according to the sun – reading and dozing . . . . Dined with the Wooltons – the first time I have attempted this since the operation. W says that, if Churchill retires, there should be an election; if he stays,

there shd be no election. But, without Churchill the Peacemaker, (St Churchill) should we win an election? More important, we discussed the Foreign policy and the situation wh Churchill's speech has created. I tried out my idea 'All non-Europeans to leave Europe' – for this purpose, Russians and Americans both count as non-Europeans. W rather liked it. His guest, Sir G [sic] Stopford – Vice-Chancellor of Manchester University – liked it very much. But it is a dangerous idea, and could only work if the Americans proposed something of the kind. We must *at all costs* avoid the Grand Alliance being split. That is the risk of the Churchill approach, as all his colleagues know well.

4 August

. . . . Went to London and had luncheon with Anthony Eden. We lunched in his flat at No 1 Carlton Gardens.

I was delighted to find him so well. He is very thin; he has lost more weight than I have. But his colour is good; he moves well (better than I do yet) and seemed 10 years younger. Instead of a nervous, highly-strung, irritable and self-centred man – and that is what he has seemed during recent years – he was quiet, courteous, charming, and very calm and collected . . . .

Nor have I ever known him (except on the day he stayed at Birch Grove in the winter) so friendly and so anxious to work with me as a partner and friend. There seemed no sense of rivalry or suspicion.

He had been the 'week-end' at Chequers. Not having seen Churchill for so long, he was naturally shocked at his appearance. It would seem that he has not really made much progress in recent weeks. He still drags the left leg; the arm is not right yet; the mouth is down on one side, and he sometimes – though by no means always – speaks thickly. He could not make a public appearance at present; he might do a 'broadcast', but this would be risky. He is back to the usual consumption of champagne, brandy etc and the doctors (no doubt wisely) think this the better course or, at least, do not stop it . . . .

Meanwhile, he is not really functioning as Prime Minister. He works – but slowly and for no great part of the day . . . . In a word, Anthony thought that Churchill was now the wreck of a great man – a tragic wreck of one of the greatest men in our history . . . .

. . . . Crookshank has written to him a letter which C asked him to destroy. But he gave me an indication of his views . . . . our fellows were beginning to ask 'What is the truth about C?' Very soon, had the session gone on, the Opposition leaders would have demanded to know the truth. We are dangerously near being parties to a conspiracy. There has, after all, never been a medical bulletin given [which] gave the facts about his illness. This cannot go on in the new session. Either the P.M. (by October) must appear or resign. This is all C[rookshank]'s view. He thinks (I understand) that he shd resign.

Anthony thinks – from something C said – that he will not resign if he feels he can go on with his foreign policy . . . .

But what is his foreign policy? Anthony says he wants 'talks', but he has not thought out any plan. He would improvise. (Naturally, Anthony feels that the May 11th speech – though brilliant – was dangerous, and if pressed too hard, might be fatal) It is a reflection on Anthony's policy, whose author feels was proving its success – the policy of sustained pressure on Russia and the building up of strength in Europe . . . .

If (as on the whole seems the most likely) C resigns, what does E do. He forms a Govt in early October . . . .

Eden spoke very frankly and sincerely about such a Govt. It could not be formed, like the present one, without any real consultation among the leading members. We must work together. (This was good news) He said frankly that there were only two possible Foreign Secretarys – Salisbury and myself. Naturally, he had a long association and partnership with S going back to the Chamberlain days and the joint resignation.[38] He also had great confidence in his judgment, and intellectual power and integrity. But he was in the Lords. This would mean that Eden himself, although P.M., would have to do all the F.O. questions and debates in the Commons. He did not want to go on being sort of F.S. for the Commons. If he was to be P.M., he wanted really to study *and to lead* in economic, and other internal questions wh Churchill had left entirely to the Chancellor of the Exchequer and the Economic Committee of the Cabinet.

I said that I must honestly say that with Eden's knowledge and experience of Foreign Affairs, a F.S. in the Lords (ordinarily impossible today) *would* be possible. I knew Crookshank thought so too. Eden agreed, but repeated his objection. This subject was then dropped.

The next point was the Board of Trade. It was *very* weak now. Cd Thorneycroft go to Transport? Was there a good young man (another McLeod [sic]) he could promote? I suggested Eccles, but wd Butler agree? Then about Housing? I said it depended on whether we went

---

38. From the Foreign Office in February 1938.

on or dissolved. If we went on, we needed a pretty strong minister, to do the great autumn scheme (Rents and Repairs) *and* the Town and Country Planning. If I was not wanted for something else, I had better finish the job . . . .

7 August

A heavy day, which tired me. I am still easily tired. Went out from 10.30 to 1pm with Streatfield, mostly with planting to be done this autumn in the Park; also with various minor improvements in the garden, the home woods, and the farm yard etc. At 1pm Miss Ursula Branson (the Foreign Affairs expert in the Conservative Research Dept) Miss Miller, my Ministry typist, also came . . . .

Meanwhile, the bag from London brought Salisbury's preliminary telegram to Makins in Washington; a telegram from Paris and Washington giving their first views. Curiously enough, the Quai D'Orsay[39] was rather pessimistic; the State Department was rather hopeful. The latter want us to accept the rather grudging Russian acceptance and to have the meeting of 4 Foreign Ministers . . . .

A great deal of Ministry stuff came down – so I had to work late again. We are building too many houses! So we have got to squeeze the L[ocal] Authorities' programme a bit – esp with Private enterprise going ahead so well. This is not easy; but we must 'stabilise' the programme at about 300,000, for there aren't enough bricks or cement for more, *and* the offices, factories, schools etc . . . .

8 August

Woke early, having slept badly. Worked on a bag, which I got off to London about 9am. The Parl Sec has written a powerful minute, asking [for] still further reduction in 'approvals' for Local Authority building. Mr Wilkinson has written a reply, saying that we cannot 'stabilise' too quickly, or there will be an intolerable row with LAs. We must not be impatient. New 'starts' will be rather too high for the next 2 or 3 months, since they represent tenders let 6 months ago. The effect of our 'tightening up' (which only began in May) will be progressively felt. Sir Percy Mills, on the whole, agrees with Wilkinson. In making my decision, I have been influenced by two considerations. First, it *is* possible (or at least in the case of large authorities and sizeable housing projects) to give approvals for houses on the under-

39. The French Foreign Ministry.

standing that they do not start till (say) December 1953, or better still, Spring 1954. This is really controlling 'starts' (in these larger projects) which ordinarily cannot be done for administrative reasons. You can have starting dates for a few hundred schools or factories. It's not possible to do so for hundreds of thousands of houses – at least as a general rule. Secondly, we have arranged (and this can be tightened up) with the suppliers of the main materials (bricks and cement) to give priority in their deliveries to houses already under construction. They can quote long forward dates – 6 months or so – for new projects. This means that the suppliers of materials will in effect control the starting dates. There will be outcries about 'shortages' – but that doesn't matter. We have 314,000 houses building – and that's the answer to our critics. It's more than 50% better than the Socialists.

So I wrote my decision this morning – which is to go on as we are for another 2 months or so. We can see where we have got to about the middle of October. Anyway, I dislike sending out continually changing instructions to our Regional officers. It destroys their confidence in me and the confidence of the local authorities in them.

Read Macaulay . . . .

. . . . M seems not to have realised that the main problem of every monarch after Elizabeth was financial. He was expected to run the country out of his Royal estates or *fixed* revenues, granted by Parl at beginning of a reign. The falling value of money and the inflation taxed on the New World, made this impossible . . . .

9 August

A vast 'bag' arrived last night. Our own Ministry's problems seem to grow rather than diminish. The very success of the Housing drive brings new ones. Bricks and cement are still insufficient; we *must* curtail the programme. We cannot touch the Private Enterprise or unsubsidised part. The greater this is, the better for the economic and financial position of the nation. We cannot restrict New Towns; or special houses for miners; or other Govt needs. So any restriction must fall on the Local Authority schemes – and they don't like it. I hope that if we go on with the great slum clearance and Operation Rescue scheme in the autumn, L.A.s will be ready to begin to switch their activities. But there must be a gap – perh a year – to make new plans. If we could only get enough cement, we could get through. For we could have a special quota for 'New Tradition' houses. Will there ever come an end to pouring cement into the ground for American bombers?

A long paper on New Towns which I must read, correct, and put in to the Cabinet. A problem about a proposed Royal Commission on the use for land – I hate R.C.s: if you want a thing done, do it yourself. R.C.s are only good for stopping things . . . .

10 August

. . . . 3pm. A most important Cabinet. We discussed at great length a long telegram to Washington, of wh F.O. produced first one, then a second draft. I did not at all like either of them . . . .

. . . . I suggested cutting the F.O. draft in two – but unequal parts. A short telegram shd be sent saying

a) we agree with Paris that there is no hurry about sending our reply

b) we welcome the acceptance by the Soviets of our invitation to the conference of *four repeat four* foreign ministers. (This gets rid of China)

c) Suggest end of Sept or beginning of Oct. Suggest Switzerland.

d) Add that great care will be necessary to avoid seeming by implication to accept the Russian thesis. d) is what the three allied powers should now consider carefully. After some discussion, and the point that the P.M. wd certainly like this, this plan was agreed . . . .

The most serious results of his illness are that tho' the old flashes of genius and brilliant grasp of a problem all remain, there is a good deal of tiresome and even perverse repetition . . . . S says that the P.M. is more charming and delightful than ever – but he ought to resign as soon as Anthony is ready.

We then discussed the timing of all this. It seemed to us both that the Conservative Conference (Oct 8th) was the crucial date. It must be attended by a) the P.M. b) a Foreign Secretary. This means that Eden ought really to be back towards the end of September and try to get a definite decision out of Churchill . . . . Another complication was the Queen. She cd agree to a dissolution by telegram. But suppose a deadlock! Was the Crown to be unable (through absence of the Monarch) to intervene in just one of those rare crises where the Crown has still a great role to play. I fancy that Churchill may use this as an argument for his going on till May, when the Queen returns . . . .[40]

---

40. From her post-coronation Commonwealth tour.

16 August

. . . . There has blown up a tremendous row about the publication (on August 8) – after Parliament had risen – of the 16 power declaration about what wd happen if the Chinese or N Koreans were to break the armistice agreement.[41] Since no mention of this was made by Butler or Salisbury; since, indeed, the whole tone of the Govt statements was quite different, they are accused of bad faith. Butler did mention an article in the *D Herald* at the last Cabinet, to wh he took exception. He said he wd arrange (with Salisbury's agreement) for some guidance to editors by the F.O. (never a very successful method of correcting anything, tho' an admirable technique for starting it off right) . . . .

Then suddenly the old man appears in Downing St; (like Tiberius returning from Capri)[42] he dictates a devastating and typically Churchillian reply; recalls the Socialist record and the debate of Feb 1952 (I remember it well, for I wound up for the Govt with a 'whose finger on the trigger' jibe, wh brought me the deepest roar of cheering I have ever got in the HofC) and, after this terrific broadside, which all the Press (including [the *News*] *Chronicle* accept as overwhelming – except the *Times* which ignores it altogether) the old P.M. is more firmly seated than ever, and while his colleagues are having a brief holiday, chooses this moment to reassert his authority and his pre-eminence in political wisdom and courage . . . .

18 August

. . . . Lunched with Harry Crookshank . . . .

Harry was clear that we could not have a repetition of the closing weeks of July. The Govt only just scraped through. The Opposition saw their advantage and pressed it. With no P.M.; no F.S.; and most other ministers in the House of Lords, they demanded discussions on Foreign Affairs, Defence and similar topics in order to embarrass the Front Bench in the Commons. There was also the struggle in their own party, and Attlee and co used the situation with considerable address to restore their prestige and authority vis-à-vis the Bevanites . . . .

---

41. The UN alliance had previously agreed in December 1951 to warn the communists of the consequences of renewed hostilities. By summer 1953, however, it was feared that this might (a) end the Soviet thaw and (b) encourage Syngman Rhee to wreck the armistice. Accordingly the warning was slipped out as a declaration in support of General Mark Clark's report to the UN on 7 August 1953.
42. The Roman emperor Tiberius (AD 14–37).

5–6.45pm. Cabinet. The first Cabinet over which Churchill has presided since the end of June. There was a large crowd in Downing Street. Ministers were much applauded on arriving and on leaving. Churchill was looking remarkably well, (*much* better than when I had seen him) He was, of course, sitting down and I did not see him stand or walk. But he was in tremendous form, full of quips and epigrams. 'Do not call it "Biological Warfare". Call it "anti-Biological warfare". You cannot be accused of arson for providing yourself with a fire-engine.' . . . . P.M. was really very good throughout this long and serious sitting. On Egypt, he was moderate and fair. I'm afraid the party, especially the Julian Amerys and Fitzroy Macleans, will be critical. But, really, we must try to get a settlement which reduces our commitment in time of peace. If we get the 10 years (or virtually 10 years) use of the base wh we ask for *and* the right of re-entry, we shall have done well. Of course, there will be quibbling about the right of re-entry. But, in the event of war, there will be no quibbling. We shd in fact go in, and the Americans wd support us . . . .

19 August
. . . . The 'stabilisation' process – that is, getting down the number of houses 'authorised and approved but not started' has now begun to be pretty effective. The curve is flattening out, at least so far as those houses which we control – that is, Local Authorities, New Towns, and Government building (such as Coal Board) In this field, the 'starts' are not now greater than the completions. But 'private enterprise' are going ahead rather more rapidly than we anticipated. Whether this will go on or not, we cannot tell. We certainly do not want to reintroduce controls here, for our policy is to encourage unsubsidised houses. Indeed, we are hoping for 80,000 in 1954. But this element of uncertainty makes it difficult for us to manage the programme, and we are now in danger of too many 'starts' in relation to bricks and cement available. Moreover, now that all factories are automatically licensed, and that much more office and other building is being done (as well as schools) the materials problem in 1954 will be very acute. The M of Works (and, I am afraid the Minister) take too sanguine a view. I do not see brick or cement production rising very much in 1954.

However, our discussion today was useful and we decided on new steps, esp to try to increase the rate of completions to get the 300,000 this year. I still think we shall do it, but it will be 'a damned close-run thing' . . . .

The American ambassador and Mrs Aldrich came to tea. Carol and her children; Arthur and Peggy Macmillan and the Waverleys. The Aldrichs are really very charming people – the nice, simple, rich, and rather old-fashioned Americans one likes so much. He is a great friend of Eisenhower – I understand he was the Lord Woolton of the campaign (at least so far as collecting money is concerned) It was a glorious day; we walked in the garden etc. After tea, I had a short talk alone with the Ambassador (Aldrich). He told me that he had recently lunched with Churchill, who had talked to him freely about his illness. According to the Ambassador, the real cause of his illness is arteriosclerosis. The blood does not reach the head properly, and this condition is now more or less permanent. Hence the repetition and occasional loss of sequence in his thought. However, he certainly has made a wonderful recovery, although A did not think he could – or ought – to go on. A then said that the President was so devoted to Churchill that he was much distressed, first by his condition and secondly by the apparent drifting apart of Anglo-American policy. He thought that the May 11th speech, with all its merits, was a mistake (I remembered, but did not remind him that he had expressed a different view at Lady Pamela Berry's house immediately after the speech) The Churchill–Eisenhower correspondence was also embarrassing to the President. He was too kind to let Churchill feel it; always sent copies of his replies to the Ambassador. I said 'did not C also send him copies of his own letters?' This he admitted was the case. But it is clear that C is making an error in trying to revive the Churchill–Roosevelt relationship. We are at Peace, more or less, not at war. And F.D.R. was (like C) an artist and a politician. E is neither. In any case, an informal and unorthodox method of approach shd be reserved for very exceptional occasions. A is, of course, very pro-English. He has a great admiration and affection for Salisbury. He hopes that either he or I will be F.S. in a reconstruction. Of course, Eisenhower (so he said) has a great regard and affection for me. I said that I thought he and the American administration must recognise that, whether they liked the speech of May 11th or not, it was a world event of great importance. Nothing could put us or our policy back into the pre-May stagnation . . . .

20 August
. . . . Iain Macleod (Minister of Health) and his wife to luncheon. They are both very pleasant. M thinks a) that P.M. shd resign b) that Eden

shd form a Govt and dissolve. His reasons are a) that Churchill is not really fit and unlikely to last till the Queen returns in May b) that Eden cannot return to the F.O. He cd become Deputy Prime Minister, but there is no such post and nothing to do (Against this I quoted the Balfour–Salisbury precedent)[43] c) that half the Govt is too old and ought to be replaced with a new lot of faces. He thought we shd win now; if we waited 2 years, we shd prob lose. There wd be no novelty about a Govt in 2 years time; . . . .

I recalled Disraeli's failure to dissolve after the Treaty of Berlin[44] (when he wd prob have won) and his defeat two years later.

M also feels that there must be changes in the under-secretaries. The older ones, if they can never make the Cabinet grade, shd make way for the brilliant young men we have, who shd be given a chance. I was glad that he included Julian Amery among these. He agreed with me that *Education* was a key post. We shd give it to a successful minister. He shd be in the Cabinet.

21 August

Arthur and Peggy Macmillan left. Carol and the children came up; they are all very nice and I love having them about. The Macmillan boys are coming to stay at B.G. on Monday; Louise Amery (aged 2) is here. So there will be *all* the grandchildren. Walked in woods with Blake (keeper) from 11 to 2 . . . . We saw a good many wild birds on the Buttocks Bank side. I fear there are very few at the top end (garden etc) The foxes have had them all; when we are rearing, it's almost impossible to protect the wild birds from vermin. Perhaps next year we won't rear any tame pheasants and really have a go at vermin of all kinds – human included! But I never think the human poachers (unless really organised like some of the Wiltshire gangs) do as much harm as animal ones.

After supper, worked till rather late. There seems to be a large number of very difficult Compulsory Purchase Orders. I hate these 'semi-judicial' functions . . . .

------

43. Balfour was not formally designated Deputy Prime Minister, but was the last non-Premier to hold the post of First Lord of the Treasury, in 1891–92 and 1895–1902, after which he succeeded the 3rd Marquess of Salisbury as Prime Minister.
44. In 1878.

23 August

Church in morning. A good service by the Rector of Cuckfield. Julian and 2 Fabers ([II] Kings 18 v 13 to end – Rabshakeh's blasphemy [–] and the Epistle to Philemon) . . . .

I have at last finished my new suggestions – incorporating some of David Eccles' – for the white paper. This is certainly going to be a tricky exercise, if it goes forward. To raise the rents of some millions (say 5 or 6m) of people, with a majority in the HofC of 18, and to come into force with increasing tempo just before a General Election! Even the editor of the *Economist* will not be able to accuse us of lack of courage! . . . .

25 August

. . . . Late in the morning Walter Monckton came to see me.

He told me that he had dined with Churchill last night. From his conversation, it was clear that he was contemplating reorganising his Government during the next few weeks. The 'overlords' were to go;[45] Eden was to be Lord President and 'Deputy Prime Minister' – a post wh does not exist – and so forth. M said that, altho' the P.M. did not say this in so many words, it was implied. Anyway, he has made up his mind to go on and not resign . . . .

I would judge from what Monckton said, that Winston has pressed M very hard to stay on and has offered him the Foreign Secretary-ship. M told me that he was convinced that Winston ought to resign; that Anthony ought to form a government and dissolve; that if this was not done, the party wd 'miss the 'bus' . . . .

I had luncheon at St Martin's St today. Publishing problems are very great nowadays – rising costs, falling sales, and slender margins of profit . . . .

26 August

Went for a long walk in the woods, taking sandwiches. Worked

---

45. Churchill had been interested in the idea of modifying the cabinet system by the incorporation of co-ordinating ministers since at least the First World War. When he came into office in 1951 to head his only peacetime administration he put this idea into operation by establishing a number of ministerial 'overlords' covering wide areas of policy. The experiment was not deemed a success and was formally brought to an end in September 1953.

afterwards and read Acton.[46] A wonderful dinner party – Alexander (9) Joshua (8) Anne (9) Michael (8) – also Maurice and Katie. The dinner was very formal and very successful. After dinner, hilarious games, indoors and in the garden. A lovely moonlight.

In reading the evening papers this evening, I see that Monckton is going to Chequers; to stay a night or two with Churchill. It is said (by the *Evening News*) that he is to be Foreign Secretary, 'which will surprise politicians, who expected Mr Harold Macmillan to be chosen' . . . . Anyway, all my own autumn plans are well advanced; and if C means to go on as P.M., I shall be able to go on with Rent Reform and Operation Rescue and all the rest. But, what is much more serious, we shall almost certainly lose an election in 2 years time. We could win today with a new team . . . . I have no doubt that Churchill is saying to himself that he will retire when the Queen returns in May. But that forces us to remain in office *over* the winter 1954, or else drop the Rent Bill in the winter of 1953. We can hardly dissolve 2 or 3 months after everybody's rent goes up . . . .

27 August

Another glorious day. I have never seen Birch Grove so lovely. The garden is beautiful and now very well kept, altho' by such a very reduced staff compared with old days. Dorothy returns tomorrow night – which will be very welcome. It never seems anything but empty and rather forlorn when she is away.

30 August (Sunday)

. . . . [T]here have been great comings and goings, culminating in a much-advertised visit this week-end to Chequers of Walter Monckton and his wife, and the Chief Whip (Buchan Hepburn) and his wife. An invitation for me and Dorothy for tomorrow (Monday) I have accepted for myself; Dorothy doesn't want to go as Sarah returns here tomorrow with her husband from their honeymoon. (I am not sorry, for it is really rather a bore for her, and if necessary, I can refuse to do anything without consulting her)

The papers all believe that a reconstruction of the Government is going on. Harry Crookshank telephoned from Eastbourne, where he is staying. He and Butler have been invited for Wednesday. He cannot believe that all this activity is purely social, but is puzzled as to Eden's

---

46. The nineteenth-century British historian, Lord Acton.

position. Since he is still cruising in the Greek islands, he cannot have been consulted, except by telegram . . . .

31 August
I have now, with the help of Wilkinson and others in the department, completed a third (or perhaps fourth) draft of the white paper . . . . I had hoped we might have done the 'Rents' Bill this summer, but the Coronation lost us nearly a fortnight and we could not get the time. If I go on with the job, we shall have to have the 'Rents' Bill this autumn; also a Bill to authorise 'Operation Rescue' (it is possible that we may get both these into *one* comprehensive Bill) We must also have the second (and most formidable part of the Town and Country Planning (Financial Provisions) Amendment Bill, consequential on the abolition of development charge last year. (This will be an immensely long and technical measure) In addition, I may have to have a New Towns Bill. It will really be better to have an election!

Left Birch Grove by car, and after a short stay at the Ministry in London, went on to Chequers – where I arrived about 6.15 . . . .

The P.M. appeared about 6.30 and watched us play a game of 'golf-croquet'.

I had not seen him since I dined with him at Chartwell, about a week after the attack – except, of course, at the two Cabinet meetings. But in the open, and moving, is a more severe test. His recovery has certainly been remarkable. He walks pretty well, although he still drags the left leg slightly. The arm seems recovered; the face shows no or little sign. The speech is as clear as before – and it was always thick. On the other hand, if you happen to look towards him when he is off his guard, he looks – as he is – a very old man. I chanced to notice him sitting hunched up on a stool or garden chair. He seemed very feeble. He is 'bad on his pins' (to use his own words) Nevertheless, it *is* a very wonderful recovery, brought about, I have no doubt, largely by his own extraordinary courage.

. . . . We did not go to bed till 1.30am – and still we had scarcely got to any major point.

The only indication of his determination to 'hang on' as P.M. was his reference to some minor Governmental changes. All these (with one exception) could be called consequential on the decision to end the 'overlord' system and the amalgamation or ending of certain departments . . . .

The Ministry of Materials, successively under Ld Swinton and Sir Arthur Salter, has very successfully 'organised itself out of a job'. Nearly 90% of its functions have gone to the free market, and private enterprise has taken the place of public buying. It was high time! For owing to the fall in prices, very large losses must necessarily be shewn. This means, in terms of men, that my old friend and colleague, Sir Arthur Salter, ceases to be a Minister and becomes a Peer. All these are minor changes, consequential on changes of function or reorganisation of the posts themselves.

P.M. also said he intended to replace Miss Horsburgh at the Ministry of Education. In her place, he wd bring in Walter Elliot – who has made good speeches and given us good support from the back benches – to be in the Cabinet. I asked him, 'was this all'. 'Yes – for the present'. There will be three stages. The first is this one – mainly simplification, and compression – also to give Cabinet status to Food; Agriculture; and Education.

Then, there will be a reshuffle of under-secretaries and parl secretaries, to bring in new blood. Finally, there will (or may) be the great change – when he knows better how things are with himself and with Anthony.

I asked whether Anthony [Eden] knew what he was doing. For if he only saw the newspapers, he might be rather concerned. P.M. said he had sent him a telegram and a letter . . . .

1 September

Went in to see P.M. at 9.45 (at his request) He was in bed – and no one else in the room . . . .

We first discussed the changes . . . .

I said I like them all, except the change at Education, of which I approved in principle, but not the timing . . . . The public, who had been led by the press, to expect a great reconstruction of the Govt, would be bewildered. The Opposition wd be scornful. All this fuss! All this coming and going! All these visits to Chequers, by all the most important and influential ministers! and then – an elderly governess goes out and an elderly lecturer comes in! . . . . Moreover (here I threw a fly) it was a really key post today. If there was a change of Prime Ministers, or a major reconstruction, then was the time. He agreed with this, and immediately got on to the Chief Whip, with a view to undoing this. Alas! He cannot undo the poor Chief Whip's painful 3 hour interview, with a sobbing Miss Horsburgh, who refused to be comforted from leaving office and the House of Commons by £5,000 a year at the [National] Assistance Board.

We then, at last, had a conversation – for over an hour – about the real point of my visit. He was charming in manner (he is much softer than he used to be) but very slow in diction. The following is a summary of a lot of soliloquy; cross-questioning; and normal discussion.

(a) The P.M. intends to remain P.M. as long as he can 'face' the Party Conference and the House of Commons. 'Face' means, of course, meet the physical strain . . . .

(b) His purpose is not merely (or so he protests and no doubt persuades himself) to prolong his tenure of office. He thinks he can contribute something – perhaps something vital in the next 6 months or so to the World Situation. (This means, he wants to go on till May 1954, when the Queen returns from her visit to Australia etc)

(c) Eden can either return to F.O. or become Lord President (owing to the Act of 1947[47] he cannot – as did Mr Balfour in 1900 – be First Lord of the Treasury. This office is now definitely merged in that of P.M.) As Ld P he would be definitely Prime Minister in action – which he cannot be if absorbed in F.O.

(d) In that event, having taken from Lord S the high office of Lord P he would have to compensate him with the F.O. (This seems a strange idea)

(e) If Anthony stays at F.O. no changes of importance will be required.

(f) If he (Churchill) cannot meet the Party Conference, he will resign. Then Anthony can form a Govt, and of course every office will be available to him.

(g) There is nothing in the story of Walter Monckton going to the F.O. He wants to be Lord Chief Justice, 'but I cannot spare him yet'.

Churchill said 'I suppose you want the F.O.' I said 'Of course'. He asked 'Why?' I said 'Because I think I could contribute something to the World Situation!'

He laughed, and said he supposed I felt he had rather let down the European movement. But it was inevitable. We had got in too late, and things had hardened.

---

47. Macmillan means the Ministers of the Crown Act 1937, which specifically links the offices of Prime Minister and First Lord of the Treasury, ensuring that they could henceforth only be held by one and the same person.

We then had some interesting talk about France, Germany, EDC etc. He knows that EDC will not be signed. He is thinking out an alternative. A partially armed Germany, in our general camp, but a 'guarantee' by America, Britain and Western Europe to Russia against German aggression. 'The only thing the Russians fear is a re-armed Germany'. 'Yes', I said, 'Everyone keeps saying that. But does it not follow that it's the only card we have to play?' He agreed.

I said that if the F.O. did not become available, I wd prefer to stay where I was and finish my job . . . .

We then talked about Eisenhower. I tried to give him the picture of E as I had known him and to make the P.M. realise that E wd never willingly go to a 'high-level' meeting. He would not trust himself. He likes to work through the staff, in the orthodox way. Although I was a Minister of Cabinet rank, I always dealt with the Chief of Staff Gen Bedell Smith, in Algiers and seldom direct with Ike. Men had their different ways of working. This was his way, and I thought it a prudent one . . . .

I saw Harry Crookshank later in the day. He agreed with me about the proposed changes. He and Rab go to Chequers and will support my view. To throw over Miss Horsburgh now – and almost alone – would be a sign that we accepted the adverse criticisms. It would be better to promote her to Cabinet rank!

Harry still feels – and very strongly – that Churchill ought to resign. It is not a question (he thinks) of his 'recovery' since June. For over a year he has, in fact, been unable to perform his functions properly. (Of course, Harry, as Leader of the Commons, sees him continuously and experiences daily his maddening hesitations and incapacity or unwillingness to transact ordinary routine business. I have not had any 'business' relations with him since I took office. He has given me full support, but I have not had any details to discuss with him)

He feels unhappy that history will accuse us all – Rab, Bobbety [Salisbury], and the politicians in the Cabinet – of weakness and cowardice. We know the Emperor has no clothes, and we dare not say so . . . .

3 September

D and I left by train at 9am for Chesterfield where we were met by our car and luggage . . . . This saves a tedious part of the road, and

somehow starts us off on our September holiday less exhausted . . . .
In the afternoon, we motored to Chatsworth. I had not been there – or
scarcely been there – since the war. It was then a melancholy sight,
occupied by a school, and terribly neglected. Now (whatever may be
the final situation of the estate after the tremendous death duties are
paid) it is quite beautifully kept, inside and out. All the rooms are in
perfect order; pictures, books, and furniture in fine condition; tap-
estries, carpets, curtains, rugs – all set out as if for a Royal visit. The
Royalty are represented by the Public – 200,000 of them have been
over the house in seven months. The gardens are also in fine condition,
indeed much improved. A good deal of timber was cut – and replanted
– in and after the war. The views of the hills are really improved by
cutting . . . .

After dinner we went back to Chatsworth to see the 'flood-lighting'
of the house and gardens – Andrew's latest venture. The people came
well at first – 30,000 in a month, but have dropped off lately. The
effect is really lovely – a golden light on the house, which brings out
the warmth and beauty of the stone. The cascade and fountains are
also lit very effectively, and many features of the garden – the Italian
garden; the Wellington rock; the fountain tree; and many of the statues
and urns, as well as Flora's temple . . . .

4 September

Stayed in bed, reading and writing, till luncheon. The changes in Govt
have now come out. I see that P.M. has taken my advice, which I have
no doubt Harry Crookshank and Rab [Butler] reinforced. So Miss
Horsburgh, who was dismissed on Monday, in a flood of tears, is
promoted on Friday to Cabinet rank! . . . .

All the same, she really must go soon . . . .

5 September

A pouch arrived at 8.30. A special Cabinet to deal with my 'White
Paper' on Sept 17th. (Right in the middle of my Scottish holiday. I
shall be in Morayshire!) . . . .

7 September

A lot of letters – no bag. Dr Charles Hill (Parl Sec Ministry of Food)
gave some interesting figures of food consumption. In first 7 months of
1953, meat up by 50% and bacon up by 24% on 1951. Sweets are
running at 60% increase. So, in spite of the high cost, the people *are*

eating more. Normally it's not the millionaires who eat the sweets. Everyone knows that they only eat caviare! . . . .

13 September

. . . . Churchill's appearance at the [St] Leger[48] and his visit to Balmoral[49] have been reported at length and fill the press. But we are losing in the Gallup poll – not dangerously, but significantly. A few months ago, the public felt that we were in command of events. Now they are not so sure. The P.M.'s illness and the F.S.'s prolonged absence have caused a vague sense of alarm. Fortunately, the divisions in the Socialist party show no sign of being healed . . . .

16 September

A very heavy day. Breakfast at Admiralty House[50] at 9am (where James Stuart lives with Jim Thomas) Since the Inverness train was late, James did not arrive till after 9.30. We settled some of the outstanding points of difference between England and Scotland, as regards the Slum Clearance policy in particular. On the obligation of the landlord to do 'repairs', Scotland is still against us. Then Sir F Lee (head of BofT) at my office, for some advice. Then further talk about some details of the plan. Then, the Cabinet meeting at 11.30.

The Housing Paper (Rents: Repairs: Slum Clearance etc) was item 1. There was a very useful discussion. Churchill had read – or at least glanced – at the paper, but had not really mastered it. Most of the Cabinet had read it very carefully – also other ministers present – Health, Education, Works etc. James Stuart said very little, sticking more than loyally to the agreement we had made. Lord Salisbury raised two questions which were vital

a) Was the rise in permitted rents enough? Why should it be restricted to one and a half times the statutory deduction? If the Girdwood figures were right, it ought logically to be twice.[51]

b) Was the second condition too hard on the good landlord? (that is, the proof of actual expenditure)

---

48. One of the premier events in the British horseracing calendar.
49. The monarch's Scottish home, to which Prime Ministers are traditionally invited during the summer holidays.
50. A building at the end of The Mall in London used for ministerial accommodation.
51. The figures on how much to allow for landlords' spending on repairs were based on the Girdwood report on building costs.

I had to answer that there was no real logic in (a) and if the Cabinet felt it right to go further, it could be done. It would be 'fairer' to the landlords; but it might put very heavy percentage increases – more than double – on the low rents. But I must hold to the repairs condition. I wd more willingly yield on the amount of the increase. For, without the repairs condition, the scheme became really an ordinary 'increase of rents to Landlords Bill'. I was anxious to make it 'a help to repairs Bill'. The repairs were what people wanted. Monckton (Labour) supported the scheme, but warned that it might affect cost of living figures and thus wage claims. I replied that it would be very difficult to get any actuarial figure of the actual rent increase under my scheme. It would be staggered in time and it would be uneven in effect (unlike a percentage increase) Butler warmly supported the scheme, but observed that it might make it more difficult to deal with the remaining food subsidies. Maxwell Fyfe supported the scheme, generously and vigorously. The P.M. summed up in favour, and so it will be recorded.

But he carefully avoided any reference to my opening remarks and to the problem which was in everybody's mind. I had only asked for approval of the scheme, if it was decided to have a scheme at all. That was what the Cabinet thought it was discussing. For whether we have the scheme at all is a question of higher strategy – on which Eden, for instance, might have some views. But once the white paper is published, we are committed and must go on . . . .

Caught the 7.15pm to Scotland. James Stuart travelled with me . . . .

19 September

Good weather; good golf; good food; and much sleep. All these make a good holiday. The papers are full of the disappearance of Mrs Maclean, the wife of Donald Maclean of the Foreign Office, who (with Burgess) disappeared last year.[52] The *Express* is especially enjoying it!

We dined with James and Rachel Stuart, at their little house at Findhorn. A very pleasant evening – with excellent food (cooked by Rachel and Davina) and drink (provided by James) . . . .

---

52. Guy Burgess and Donald Maclean, two senior British diplomats, disappeared on 25 May 1951. Having defected to the Soviet Union they confirmed that they had been long-term communist agents.

21 September
Worked in the morning. Drove to Ballindarroch (nr Inverness) to luncheon with my sister-in-law, Maud Baillie . . . .

Dorothy loves this part of Scotland, where she has many friends and relations. This is a very pleasant way of seeing them (from the hotel as a base) without putting too much strain on them. One can only *stay* nowadays in the few remaining houses of the very rich.

Read Trevelyan's '*English Social History*' – a very good book. I had read it when published some years ago. It is well worth re-reading.

22 September
. . . . It is now recognised that the Russians may really believe that the Germano-American alliance (France and Britain they disregard and know to be pacific, if not decadent) is about to attack them and drive them by force out of Eastern Germany and Central and Eastern Europe. Can some guarantee be given or some 'pact' entered into which will calm their apprehensions? This is being studied by 'our side' in London, Paris and Washington. (I am supposed to be on a committee of ministers to study it, but I just *had* to finish my holiday)

Yet how can such a 'pact' be made (which wd, of course require a united Germany as the minimum Russian concession) without formally abandoning Poland, Czechoslovakia, Hungary and all the rest? A 'de facto' recognition of the Russian invasion is one thing; a 'de jure' acceptance is another.

Nor do I think that the Russians will pay much regard to or set much store by pacts and treaties of non-aggression. They have never been incommoded by regard to a treaty or their pledged word. Nations, like individuals, judge all others by themselves . . . .

23 September
Left Nairn at noon and motored to Comrie. We came by Loch Tay and Loch Earn – a really lovely drive, in beautiful weather, sun and cloud and an occasional storm. At Blair Atholl we drove up to the Castle, now – like all the houses of the grandees – abandoned to the tourists, more or less . . . .

A pouch arrived, containing a very gloomy letter from Julian – though very well written – from Strasbourg. He fears Germany more than Russia, and above all fears E.D.C. and handing the leadership of Europe to Germany on a platter.

. . . . [T]his balance of fears is a most difficult problem to decide. It has always recurred in our history. For instance, Spain or France. Cromwell got it wrong, and out of pure conservatism continued his fear of Spain, and failed to observe the rise of France. It may be that Germany is no longer the potential master of Europe and that we are right in thinking only of the Russian menace. But – if we are wrong – there will be a heavy price to pay . . . .

5 October (Sunday)

This has been an exhausting, and remarkable week. I left Perth on Sunday night (a week ago); this was the end of my holiday. One always feels like a schoolboy, going back reluctantly to school. I have been rather troubled to find that I am still rather easily tired and even 'shaky' when it comes to any but written work. One still feels tired by people – esp the continuous succession of people whom one must see and deal with as a minister. I spoke at a Rotary luncheon at Stockton, and did not get on very well. I also had to speak at a Licensed Victuallers Dinner (in London) and had the same experience. I forgot altogether on more than one occasion what I had intended to say, altho' I don't think it was very noticeable . . . .

We have worked all the week at the final touches to the White Paper. I shall call it 'Houses: The Next Step'. I think this is a humbler and more defensible claim than Housing: A Comprehensive Plan (wh it certainly is not) We have also been hard at work on the materials problem, with the never-failing aid of Percy Mills. The prospects for 1954 look better than we had feared. I think RAF use of cement shd be reduced, as the great radar installations are being completed . . . .

And then, the Cabinet! Churchill excelled himself, in control of the situation and in showmanship. Eden had got back on the Wednesday, and issued a vague statement that his future rested with 'his colleagues' – or some such phrase. He did no such thing. Except for 'the Big Four', who seem to have dined at length on the problem on Thursday (that is, Churchill, Eden, Salisbury, Butler) no one knew anything. The Cabinet met at 11.30 on Friday. P.M. welcomed the F.S. on his return to duty, and we proceeded with business. Ld S acted as spokesman for F.O. items, but Eden took part.

Egypt. Things do not look so good and the Egyptian govt, in spite of the wise precaution of shutting up most of their critics, seems to be hanging back and asking for more concessions. It was decided to refuse any more.

Trieste. The original Eden plan of last year has been revived – that is, a 'de facto' settlement, by the British and Americans merely withdrawing their troops. Then, in fact, the Yugoslavs wd be left in occupation of one zone, the Italians of another. The State Department has got rather cold feet about it . . . .

11 October (Sunday)

The Margate [Party] Conference is safely over. It was a real success. Butler and Eden made admirable speeches and had tremendous welcomes. To my amazement, I had the same. My speech on the Friday, with some light touches and a reply to Bevan, pleased the audience. Eden, in a more serious vein, as suited his subject, had a really triumphant 'come-back'. But, of course, amid all the speeches and amusement of the Conference, the excitement was concentrated on the Saturday afternoon. How wd Churchill come through his ordeal?

The answer was really magnificent. He spoke for 50 minutes, in the best Churchillian vein. The asides and impromptus were as good as ever. His voice seemed sometimes a little weak, and once or twice flagged. But this happens to everybody in the course of a long speech. At the end, he was (of course) completely done. But he soon recovered and seemed none the worse . . . .

17 October

. . . . [P]oor Maurice has had very bad luck. After so nearly getting the East Grinstead division, he has been 'runner-up' in two other places . . . .

19 October

Building Committee in the morning – I presided. The Beaver report on the design etc of Power stations is now available. They have certainly done a fine job. If Fuel and Power are strong enough to lobby Ld Citrine and the British Electricity Authority to accept these proposals, it will be an immense saving in Bricks, Cement and above all, money . . . .

A long Cabinet at 4pm. Trieste, Egypt, Israel–Jordan, Korea – nothing but trouble everywhere . . . .

21 October

Dined as Charles Morgan's guest at the Salisbury Club. M André Simon presided. The dinner was in the Vintners' Hall. I'm afraid

I don't know enough about wines to appreciate them; but it was a pleasant enough occasion.

22 October

. . . . A very long day in the House. Oliver Lyttelton opened the debate on British Guiana with a fine and well-reasoned speech.[53] Griffiths followed, oozing insincerity. He is a sort of super-Pecksniff.[54] I did not think the Socialists very happy either about the speech, or their 'amendment' – wh was a compromise, meant to satisfy the two wings of the party and thus pleased neither. As Lyttelton said, the Socialist amendment accepted the premises (the wicked behaviour and Communist tendencies) of the P.P.P. leaders, but recoiled from the conclusion. The debate went on all day, without any very notable contribution, except from McGovern. (He used to be ILP but has now rejoined the Labour Party) M denounced the Communists, and announced his intention of voting for the Gov[ernment], *against* the Socialist amendment. Attlee, who seemed very nervous and jumpy all day (he made some foolish interruptions – very unlike him) wound up in a short, ill-tempered, but not ineffective speech (from his point of view) It at least seemed to bring his two wings together. I replied for the Govt – 35 minutes. There was a great deal of interruption (which I am bound to say I 'asked for') esp from Attlee. It was my first HofC speech since my illness. I was very nervous, and rather lost control in the middle. But the beginning and end were good, and the party seemed satisfied. Both Oliver and P.M. were generous in praise. We had a good division – majority of 38.

23 October

6000 transport men, who move oil, have gone on strike. This means that London and the London area will soon be immobilised.

The meetings of 'emergency' ministers (as in the floods) have now started.

Troops will go in tomorrow, altho' there is, of course, a risk that this will spread the strike. However, since the action of the men is 'unofficial' and altogether contrary to the wishes of the leaders of the

---

53. After Cheddi Jagan's PPP had won the first adult suffrage elections in British Guiana (Guyana) in April 1953 Britain had on 9 October 1953 suspended the constitution claiming that Jagan's government were communists.
54. A pompous and hypocritical character in Charles Dickens' *Martin Chuzzlewit.*

union, this may not happen. The strike seems directed at the union leaders – esp Arthur Deakin – rather than at the employers . . . .

25 October
Church in morning; took Anne Faber and Adam Macmillan. Ezekiel 14 and Peter 1.4 . . . . The strike continues, but so far has not spread, in spite of the use of troops to distribute oil.

The ministry has produced a paper on 'Housing Subsidies' – very strong meat. But we must wait till the 'Rent and Repairs' Bill is launched. We must not bite off too much at a time . . . .

5 November
The last few days have been very hectic. After immense labours, and with all kinds of 'public relations' efforts, the white paper on '*Houses: The Next Step*' was launched on Tuesday 3rd.

It was mentioned in the Queen's Speech. I held a Lobby Conference immediately afterwards, to explain the details. P.M. referred to it in his speech, and it was in the vote office when he sat down. He made a very fine speech – one of his best. But I fear that, in spite of all his efforts, the Russian reply to the last allied note is the worst of the series.

The press received the Rents Plan etc pretty well. Anyway, they set it out objectively.

Morrison opened the debate yesterday afternoon – very mildly. He complained of the popular version of '*Houses – the Next Step*' which we called 'Operation Rescue'. Otherwise, he left the attack to Bevan, in order that the Opposition speaker shd be able to speak after me. I was able to laugh off his complaint. Later, when Bevan repeated it in a more offensive form, I was armed with some of the Socialist Govt's own productions – far more propagandist and better illustrated than my humble effort! As I pointed out 'The Budget and You' in 1949 even had a strip cartoon!

My speech was long and complicated – and therefore difficult to deliver. But it was necessary to get it on the record.

Bevan's reply was poor. It was really encouraging to find that so skilful a speaker had so little to say. He spent half his speech trying to prove that he had really built more houses than I had. When he came to rents etc, his only remedy was that the L[ocal] Authorities shd take over and repair *all* the houses. This did not seem a very practical course.

I was glad when this day had past. The party have taken my plan very well, even those with marginal seats. They feel that it may work out all right in the long run.

Churchill's performance on Nov 3rd was really remarkable. It was the first speech he had made in the HofC since May 11th. He was far more confident of himself than at Margate. Indeed, he was complete master of himself and of the House. It seems incredible that this man was struck down by a second stroke at the beginning of July. I wd not have believed it possible at any time during the summer or even in the early autumn.

We had a good day at Birch Grove on Saturday. We killed 244 pheasants. On Monday it rained, but we got 27 before we had to stop . . . .

6 November

. . . . 'The grand design' has been launched, and at present all seems quiet. Churchill was in very good form at the Cabinet yesterday. He said that to Bevan's great theme 'Any fool can build 300,000' there was an obvious retort. 'I know one fool who couldn't'. As to their attack, they must declare (as on the Turf) which horse was the pace-maker and which was being ridden to win. Is it 'A gift to the Landlords' or 'A mouldy turnip to the Landlords' (the concluding phrase of Bevan's speech) On the argument that the increased consumption of meat has gone to the rich, he asked for a reply. Maxwell-Fyfe said that it had been calculated that if no extra consumption this year had gone to people with £2000 a year (the sur-taxable) each of them wd have had to eat an additional hundred-weight a week! This pleased him immensely.

On the question as to whether politics or religion were to be banned or not from 'sponsored' television, he said 'The Archbishop of Canterbury versus Cardinal Griffin would be rather good!' Then, turning sweetly to Ld de la Warr (Postmaster General) 'could we have it coloured?' This matter was summed up admirably by Oliver Lyttelton. 'I don't see how we can say that private enterprise must be restricted to Sport and Sex, and Politics and Religion must be nationalised!'

There was a desultory talk about the House of Lords. The P.M. issued a solemn warning against meddling with it. 'You must destroy it altogether, if you touch it. What does it matter that the Peers don't come? They are like the Home Guard, ready in case of danger'.

At the end of the Cabinet, he asked me to stay to luncheon. I couldn't, for I was due to Lady Pamela Berry (and I had been forced to put her off the day before) He pouted, like a child – 'but I shall be alone'. I'm afraid he is sometimes rather a spoilt child, and expects everything and everybody to suit his convenience. But it is so simple and even naive, that one doesn't resent it . . . .

I have been so long with launching '*Houses – the Next Step*' and all the work involved, that I have hardly noticed or attended to the foreign situation . . . .

11 November

On Wednesday (Nov 11th) a large dinner given by the P.M. for the American ambassador and Mrs Aldrich . . . . No serious row seems yet to be boiling up about my '*Houses – the Next Step*'. But I fear it will not help us in the by-elections . . . .

13 November

Travelled to Middlesborough for a public meeting. We had a fine meeting in the Town Hall, and a lot of Stockton and Thornaby people came especially to see me – which was rather touching. Before going back on the night train, I went over to the old club which I started in Thornaby many years ago.

Read Duff Cooper's autobiography '*Old Men Forget*'. A *very* good book. The picture of pre-1914 Oxford and London is awfully good. So is the account of the battle in which he got his DSO. The Munich story is excellently told.

15 November

I have just got the October Housing figures – over 30,000 – a postwar record. The 300,000 shd be 'in the bag' now. We have only 45 to get in the last two months. The Treasury statisticians are beginning to get very alarmed! . . . .

The reaction agst the 'Rent' Bill is beginning to work up. The *Herald* is starting to attack the scheme, following Crossman in yesterday's *Sunday Pictorial*. It will be interesting to see the effect on the voting at Holborn,[55] where I go to speak on Wednesday . . . .

Ld Beaverbrook is beginning to work up a campaign agst the proposed Egyptian treaty. He did this both in yesterday's '*Sunday*

---

55. There was a mild pro-Labour swing of 1.9 per cent.

Express' and today's '*Daily Express*'. This is largely because of his vendetta against Eden. Walter Monckton, with whom I had some talk today, fears that the discontent in the party may grow, esp if the Sudan elections turn out very badly.[56]

17 November

D and I dined with the American ambassador. I sat next to a certain Mrs Oppenheimer. Her husband, Dr O, is a nuclear physicist – an American Jew. She told me that she was a niece of Keitel.... who was lickspittle to Hitler and whom [sic] was very properly hanged. It was a difficult conversational gambit, I thought. One did not know quite the mood in which to treat it!

18 November

My ministry has produced a scheme to cut down the housing subsidies. But it is not a good scheme. We had a long meeting in which they explained it to me. But one must not do these things except as part of a larger plan – e.g. reform of Local Govt finance. Standing alone, they are just crude attacks (so the Socialists will say) on the Welfare State. My rents proposals would have no chance by themselves. The reason why they are not going too badly at present is because it's all mixed up with Slum Clearance etc . . . .

21 November

D and I are staying at Edensor House with Andrew and Debo Devonshire. It was really kind of them to ask us. We had a very good day's shooting . . . .

The Govt have made the mistake of starting too many hares. T.V. will do us no good. Now David Fyfe wants us to begin on legalised betting.[57] All this is folly in our parliamentary position. We should stick to the essential economic and strategic needs of the country. The most urgent of all is to study the implications of an American recession, which the *Manchester Guardian* and Professor Colin Clark seem to regard as inevitable. But we really have no plan at all . . . .

Sunday 22 November

. . . . Drove in the afternoon over some of the High Peak country –

---

56. The pro-Egyptian Sudanese National Unionist Party won a small majority.

57. Off-course ready money betting was legalized in 1960.

most of the estate will, alas, be sold. I had a long talk this evening with Andrew about the Death Duties etc. To hand over ⅘ of a property is not easy, when its character is so varied, ranging from shares, town property, rural estates, houses, woods, quarries and the like, to statues, pictures and books. A very small change in price levels between probate and realisation may be disastrous. It takes 400 years to save and build such a property. It disappeared on a winter afternoon at Couples Place, Eastbourne, when my brother-in-law, the 10th Duke, died suddenly in the garden.

26 November

Great storms have blown up suddenly, and the Govt is threatened with defeat. It has all arisen from an old dispute about the pensions of some 336 retired officers – mostly generals etc – now surviving, whose pensions were stabilised at the 1935 level, or 9½% *below* that granted to them (on a sliding scale basis) in 1919. Altogether we have had 3 Cabinets *before* the decision, and one *after* the storm in the House.

The Cabinet supported the CofEx (against Ld Alexander and the service ministers, *and* the Cabinet Secy) on the ground that this wd open up a whole series of claims, amounting not to £200,000 or even £400,000, but to £30 millions, or even £40 millions, in the first instance.

There wd then be a challenge to all pensions etc wh had ever been stabilised, whether in 1935 or 1946, on a price basis lower than that ruling today. The only safe course was to stick to the principle of the 1952 Act, and deal with 'hardship'. This, in effect, means that additions are given to lower pensions of lower ranks – captains, majors and colonels, while higher ranks get little or none. A number of Tories took the P.M.'s announcement on Tuesday very badly, even shouting 'Shame'. He was very much put out and very angry. As one might expect, he took on himself the full responsibility and his attitude has been much strengthened by the insulting attack on him.

The Socialists (who when in office took the same line) are trying to stimulate the row. Of course, they hoped we wd grant this concession to these old officers, and then exploit it to the full. 'What! £100 a year and more extra for generals and nothing for private soldiers and serjeants'. It wd have been (and is) a good manoeuvre, and with the help of old age pensioners and [the] British Legion[58] might prove disastrously successful . . . .

---

58. Ex-servicemen's organization.

There was a desultory discussion on Egypt. The P.M. is toying with a new idea – an Anglo-American 'package deal' for an Anglo-American base in Egypt, as representative of NATO. He is obviously much worried about the 'prestige' and political effects, at home and abroad, if the Treaty goes through. But if it doesn't go through, what do we do? Sit here indefinitely, at huge expense, with 80,000 browned off troops?.

. . . . We had a very interesting talk about EDC. The French are asking still more guarantees. This we shall refuse. The question arose what to do if France rejects EDC. I put forward again my old thesis in favour of 'confederation' and against the 6 Power Federation. Some of the Cabinet, notably Salisbury and Crookshank are beginning to be rather alarmed by the German recovery and power. This was not removed by the Field Marshal [Alexander] assuring us that they were all ready, and if they got the word 'go', they would have 12 divisions in 2 years. Eden was very sympathetic and friendly to me. He himself is perplexed and regrets the way all this has worked out. For if France is so weak, Germany will be masters of EDC and all that this implies. Why could not all the Federal Assembly and Senate and so on be dropped, and only the army come into being? This is perhaps a way out. Eden said – very fairly – that Germany in NATO wd be free to start atomic work, which she cannot do (under the rules) in EDC. So really EDC is better for France than NATO. But will Germany, if the 6 Power Federation comes into being, be strong enough to 'waive the rules'. What will happen when Adenauer goes? All this was a very different discussion than that which we had 18 months ago, when I wrote my Cabinet paper. I thought the Cabinet noticed the change and listened to me much more sympathetically . . . .

1 December

A Cabinet in the morning, on the Sudan, Egypt, and the generals' pensions – all chiefly from the Parliamentary point of view. Julian Amery is being very active (and very troublesome) over Egypt. I wound up the debate on the 2nd reading of my Bill, following Herbert Morrison. He made a poor speech, entirely about the Slum Clearance part of the Bill. He read out a long brief (from the LCC) about the Finance. He also attacked the 'deferred demolition' proposals.[59] His

---

59. Slums, Macmillan recognized, ought to be demolished, but this was not an
    immediate option because of the housing shortage. The Bill therefore allowed

chief skill was in avoiding altogether the Bevan alternative – that the Local Authorities should 'take over' 7 million houses or so. I pressed this in reply, but of course got no answer. I spoke for 45 minutes. At the end, I announced that we had reached the Housing target – from Nov 1st 1952 to October 31st 1953 we had built 301,000 houses. Therefore we had done the job in the second full year of the Government's administration. This was received with great applause by Govt supporters, and made a good note to end on – esp as Churchill came in for the end of my speech . . . .

4 December

. . . . The revolt of some of the party, under Charles Waterhouse, Ralph Assheton etc (with active support of Fitzroy Maclean and Julian Amery) was discussed. They threaten to put down a motion about Egypt. However, it seems that they have now reached the view that we must get out of Egypt, at least as far as the bulk of the 80,000 troops are concerned. But they favour leaving a brigade, as a strong point, but *without* an agreement. This seems the worst of both worlds, at least as long as there is any chance of a reasonable agreement.

Meanwhile Persia has asked for the restoration of diplomatic relations, and has accepted quite a reasonable preliminary formula about oil nationalisation and the principle of compensation.[60]

5 December

A nice day's shooting at home, with lovely weather. We got 120 pheasants, mostly cocks. This is good for the 3rd time over . . . .

6 December

. . . . We did a lot of M&Co and family business last Thursday, when I lunched at St Martin's St with Daniel, Maurice, and John Archibald. Maurice is really beginning to take hold of things very well, and to be a real help. He came to see me for a good talk this evening.

D and I walked in the garden and park. We are planting some

---

local authorities to requisition privately rented accommodation for patching up, paying only the site value to the landlords, thereby deferring demolition.

60. Mossadeq had been overthrown on 19 August 1953 and the new government agreed to restore diplomatic relations, broken during the Abadan crisis, on 5 December 1953.

more trees in the park. I shall not live to see them, but I hope Alexander will still be living here when they begin to make a show. Anyhow, one must go on as if continuity were assured.

7–10 December

A week of great activity on the local government front. The Socialist LCC is leading a campaign against the financial proposals of my Bill. During the first two days of the Local Govt conference at the Friends House, there was a lot of criticism. However, I was very well received after my speech by the 1500 delegates and I think things will quiet down – esp if we postpone the Financial Resolution till after Christmas . . . .

10 December

Left on night train for Leeds. A useful Dec 11th morning going round Leeds 'slums' and housing estates. The special problem of the 'back-to-back' houses is very acute in Leeds, as in some other Yorkshire towns. There are over 30,000 of them in Leeds – some very old and some of quite recent date . . . .

12 December

Sheffield housing plans and a tour round during the morning. The architect, (Wormersley) seemed very good. Some new flats (on the hill) should be very good.

Drove from Sheffield to Bradford. Here I had a political meeting in the St George's Hall. This was not quite (but very nearly) full. As it holds about 2500, this was not bad for a political meeting nowadays, esp on a Saturday evening . . . .

14 December

Cabinet in the afternoon. The Railway Strike seems pretty likely . . . .

15 December

A heavy day. Home Affairs; Cabinet; Parliamentary Questions; speech and dinner at Constitutional Club; 3 line whip on Television. The last proved rather a fiasco, since David Maxwell Fyfe by mistake went on to just after 10pm, and so 'talked out' the Govt motion. (I have nearly done this myself and have seen others nearly do it – but I have never seen it done before) . . . .

17 December
The strike is off. Monckton (M of Labour) has done wonderfully well. There will be quite a price to pay – but we all had the impression that public opinion favoured the railwaymen. The only real justification for the terms (which involve still greater losses) is that General Robertson must be given a chance to get some sense into the railway structure and management, wh have been fatally injured by nationalisation.

I was made to act as substitute for Anthony Eden at an Albert Hall rally, organised by the UN Ass[ociation]. This was indescribly dreary, and not relieved by the presence or speech of the Secretary General, M Hammarskjöld.

The Foreign Affairs debate in the HofC was, on the other hand, quite a lively affair. P.M. spoke shortly, but with his usual mixture of humour and serious, even prophetic, declaration. Attlee followed in a pawky, witty, but fundamentally kind and useful speech. The Tory rebels (on Suez and the proposed Egyptian treaty) were led by Charles Waterhouse. He is a bad speaker – falls into all the traps, but effective because he is sincere. He and his friends were bitterly attacked by Lord Lambton, in a brilliant and very offensive speech . . . .

18 December
The November housing figures amount to 29000. So the total is 285,000. December has only to be 15000 for us to make the target. It will be at least 25000, I shd say. The Treasury are terribly concerned and still more about next year. Sir Percy Mills came in. The railway settlement cannot but have an unfavourable reaction of the Engineering claim . . . .

19 December
. . . . The Walter Moncktons have come (last night) to stay till Monday. He is quite exhausted, since he had influenza during all the railway crisis . . . .

20 December
Stayed in bed till luncheon; so did Walter M. Philip Swinton (Dominions Secretary) came to luncheon. We had a long talk. These were the conclusions

(i) *Churchill* has now decided to stay until the Queen returns (May) S says he practically told him he wd go then. I said (and M agreed) that this was too late. It wd be impossible to make large changes in the govt – both ministers and under-secretaries – before then. Without changes, we shall find it hard to carry on. Younger men are getting bitter, and feel that their careers are sacrificed to one old man's vanity. S said that Churchill has now really given up his hopes about Russia. M said he doubted if he cd last physically till May. S said that he found him much weaker (on his return from his Empire trip) than he expected.

(ii) If the present *system of Govt* goes on, (apart from question of P.M.) it is so ill-organised in its methods, that we shall drift to disaster. No great issue – trade, economics, future of Empire etc – is really grasped. But M and S were very critical of the Economic Policy Ctee, and Rab's methods of avoiding issues.

(iii) *On Egypt* – if we get a treaty on the present proposals – we shall carry the party, but with 20 or 30 voting against. This might mean that Eden's position wd be gravely compromised and Churchill fortified to stay on indefinitely. S was very clear that the Treaty was right. We ought not to worry when we have done right. It is when we are doing wrong, *or doing nothing*, that we risk the future of the party.

If we don't get a treaty, we shall have to put into effect a plan of voluntary concentration and partial or complete evacuation. Since in the early stages it will be the plan prepared by the rebels, there will be no political trouble. But there will be a difficult situation locally, wh may lead – through someone's folly – to an explosion.

(iv) The *Railway* settlement will encourage the Engineers, the Building operatives and all the rest. M said we must be firm about the Engineers. He wd like to be in touch on Wednesday with S and myself, Churchill and Butler were so weak! They wanted peace at any price! (This rather surprised me) This was perhaps natural. The old man thought about himself; the Chancellor of the Ex about his Budget! . . . .

23 December

A busy morning, with a number of troublesome ministry problems. We had our Council at 3 – Sir Percy Mills was there. Next year's completions look like being 350,000. We shall now cut them down a bit. 300,000 ought to be the 1955 figure, for by that time repairs, slum clearance, and other building (now freely licensed) will take up all the available resources. Dined with Walter and Biddy Monckton. He is bitter – but very tired. Now the Engineering trouble is coming along. The Confederation (that is the 39 unions) have declared a ban on piece work and overtime to begin on the 18th of January. W.M. had been down to luncheon at Chequers. He thought P.M. much weaker. He talked of his approaching resignation.

24 December

Motored home, arriving for luncheon. Alexander, Joshua and I walked in the woods. A glorious sunny day. We have Maurice and Katie and their 3 boys; Julian and Catherine Amery and Louise; Sarah and Andrew Heath. So the house is like old days – quite full. All the children seem very well. Anne and Michael Faber came to tea – so we had all 7 grandchildren, for the first time for many months . . . . D and the girls sat up half the night, filling stockings, preparing presents and the like. The big Christmas tree in the Hall (by the stairs) is very fine. The children spent the evening decorating it. The three cats, and two dogs (which we now have around) were obstructive. Altogether, a good old-fashioned Christmas.

Christmas Day 1953

Dorothy, most of the children (Maurice, Katie, Carol etc) went to Communion at 8am. The grandchildren were awake and dealing with their 'stockings' from 4.45am. Since D and her daughters did not get to bed till the early hours of the morning, they were rather short of sleep. This is the first Christmas for some years when we have all been together – for Maurice, Katie and the boys have generally been to Brogyntyn – to the Harlechs.

The tree in the Hall was very fine – reaching almost to the top of the house. The decorations were very good on the tree and in every room. Supplementary trees in the boys' bedroom; in the nursery; in the servants' hall.

The church was very full at matins. I read the lessons as usual. We had two full pews – D and I; my four children; their wives and husbands; my seven grand-children; . . . .

After tea, the presents to all – including indoor servants. After luncheon, D and the girls took round the presents to all the children on the estate.

Altogether the whole ritual in its full form!

Very good charades and dumb-crambo after dinner, in which I always take part. This also is part of the now accepted ritual. Fortunately, it was a fine day. Alexander and I went for a walk in the woods in the afternoon.

Boxing Day

. . . . Worked in the evening and made good progress. I am trying to repeat what I did last year, and produce a 'Comprehensive Plan' or 'Grand Design: Second Phase' for 1954–5. This is to cover all the outstanding problems – Housing Subsidies; help to owner occupiers; de-rating of industry to be amended; New Towns to be reorganised; Valuation for Rating to be amended; requisitioned houses to be dealt with; Local Government reform to be at least adumbrated – quite a programme. It would require a White Paper in September 1954, with legislation on all these matters in the 1954–5 session.

27 December

The Russians have accepted the 4 Power conference. But they propose that the date suggested Jan 4th shd be postponed. It is now proposed to start on Jan 25th . . . .

It is not easy to see what the Russians aim at. I never could understand why they did not accept the earlier suggestions for a 4 Power conference . . . .

29 December

. . . . I lunched with Swinton at the Carlton Club. He says that the Americans have now told Rab [Butler] quite frankly that there is little hope of anything coming out of the Randall Commission.[61] (1) They will *not* lower their tariffs (2) They will *not* simplify their tariff procedure (3) They will *not*, through I.M.F. or in any other way put up a fund to back sterling and thus assist us to go for convertibility. So the great Treasury dream is over! We had better get back to Tariffs and to the Commonwealth–Europe plan.

Cabinet at 3pm . . . . P.M. is more and more worried about Egypt. He keeps saying 'things should be brought to a head' – by which, of course, he means 'to a break'.

. . . . Churchill observed 'If there is a break, we have them in the hollow of our hands. 8000 Egyptians on the wrong side of the canal, to be starved into a rapid surrender; all Egypt at our mercy if we turn off the oil. The CIGS is confident'. Eden agreed to produce a paper, showing the 'pros and cons'. This, no doubt, will be discussed next week . . . .

---

61. The Randall Commission had been set up by the US Congress to investigate means of encouraging freer trade and convertibility. Butler had recently appeared before it.

The Cabinet agreed to my proposal, supported by Rab, that the new rating system must be postponed till 1956 – *after* the election. This is not mere politics. It is the only hope of any Government being strong enough to see it through. In any case, still further legislation is necessary to deal with questions like gas, the rating of charities, and so forth. Also to alter the procedure, to ensure that the new assessments and the new poundage rates come out together. Always before, the householder and shopkeeper has had the shock of the new assessment six months before the (probably) lower poundage rate is published.[62]

After the Cabinet, Eden, Butler and I had a talk in No 11.[63] Poor Anthony is finding things pretty difficult. The P.M. (who talked of staying till the Queen's return) now talks of staying till 6 months before the election – that is, March 1955. (Hence his interest in my rating problem and the date of the election) We feel that this does not give a new administration the chance to develop and present a new line of policy.

As P.M. had asked me to dinner, I undertook to try some probing. But it was not very successful. He countered every leading question; had Christopher Soames there all the time; and then gave me a wonderful box of cigars as a New Year's present!

He is a remarkable character, and yet in a way simple. He cannot bear to abandon power. Of course, he will not risk another defeat – so he will resign before a dissolution. But he will go on as long as he can, always having a date ahead, which (when reached) can be extended for a new reason . . . . But it must be difficult for Eden, and I fear that he will be driven to physical collapse or resignation within a short time if this goes on . . . .

31 December
Left B.G. early. Went to Barnet, where I opened the last house of 1953 – thought to be about no. 310,000. The B.B.C. TV and movietone people were there, and we got good publicity . . . .

---

62. The rates are a property tax used to fund local government. Properties are periodically assessed on their notional rental value. These revaluations can prove politically unpopular, hence Macmillan's anxiety to postpone the next valuation until after the election. Local authorities then set a poundage, effectively the proportion of their rental value that property owners are required to pay in a given tax year.

63. 11 Downing Street, the official London residence of the Chancellor of the Exchequer.

1954

1 January
A lovely day. Walked in the woods with Streatfield (agent) all the morning and with Catherine in the afternoon.

Some very queer Honours in the afternoon, including a peerage for Hore-Belisha. This will not be well received by the Tory party . . . .[1]

According to Ralph Stevenson's telegram, very little progress is being made in Cairo. The reasons are (i) the Neguib regime is afraid of an attempted *coup d'état* by the Moslem Brotherhood. It must therefore keep up its xenophobia. (ii) Caffery, the American ambassador, continues to give him aid and comfort. (iii) Bevan, Crossman and co have told him that HMG will have to give in. Caffery's behaviour is really too bad, because it is not what the President or even the State Dept really intend . . . .

3 January
. . . . The news of Duff Cooper's sudden death has just come. He was a very remarkable man – the perfect amateur. I always found him an agreeable companion and a very loyal friend. His contempt of the Chamberlain–Halifax 'gang' was genuine and effective. His was one of the great resignations . . . .[2]

4 January
The Russians have now definitely accepted Jan 25th for the meeting of the 4 Foreign ministers. It is also announced (from Moscow) that 'atomic' talks have begun. The game is obvious – get America out of Europe; have no German re-armament; play on French fears and jealousies and exploit the sense of uncertainty wh Churchill has

---

1. Hore-Belisha, a former Liberal National MP and Secretary of State for War 1937–40, had been widely disliked on the pre-war backbenches, not least because he was Jewish. The award was in the annual New Year's Honours List.
2. From the Admiralty over the Munich agreement in October 1938.

unwittingly created. But is it for Peace or is it for ultimate Communist expansion? Is it a change of heart or of tactic? . . . .

12 January

. . . . Before the Cabinet, lunched with Ld Swinton. Salisbury and Maxwell Fyfe were there. Swinton said that Churchill told him recently that he had definitely decided to resign after the Queen's return . . . . Both Swinton and Salisbury felt that the people were growing conscious of a lack of grip. The strikes – or threatened strikes; the 'guerrilla warfare' in certain industries; the admitted communist leadership; the growing sense of the possibility – even probability – of a trade slump – all this was contrasted in the public mind with the absence of any reference to these matters by ministers. Salisbury said that Eden was very conscious of this. He wd like to revive the general policies of '*The Industrial Charter*'[3] and to take some lead in all this, with the covert, if not the open, approval of the moderate T.U. leaders. I suggested that what the people wanted was a) a realistic and objective appraisal of the economic situation, esp with regard to our exports and foreign competition b) some kind of lead as the spiritual or at least psychological means by wh capital and labour cd be got to face these problems together. Could not Butler do a) immediately on his return from the Queensland conference.[4] Then Eden cd follow with b). Swinton suggested that the P.M. might do a national appeal on the broadcast. Salisbury felt that he was only thinking about Russia (except for Suez) He doubted whether he wd be willing or able to contribute to these problems in his present mood. Maxwell Fyfe thought we must not neglect some of the information available which made one fear that the Communist leaders were determined, by one means or another, to create a situation wh wd lead to a General Strike . . . .

16 January

. . . . It looks as if we shall have to give in to the Russians about the 'place' of meeting in Berlin. East and West is the slogan, with alternate meetings in East and West Berlin. It is wise to give in; questions of protocol are not really important. No doubt the Russians wd like to

---

3. The policy document on industrial partnership produced by the Conservative Research Department in 1947.

4. Of Commonwealth finance ministers.

postpone the meeting and so prolong the French uncertainty about
E.D.C. The meeting of Commonwealth ministers has ended in a
prodigious communiqué – 3000 odd words, and all the same platitudes
about Free Trade, 'Convertibility', GATT and IMF. It will make the
Tory party as angry with Butler as they are already with Eden[5]. . . .
Next week the HofC resumes, and with it my Rent and Repairs Bill. It
will be a dreary affair and I am sure the Labour Party will 'obstruct'
as much as possible. I don't see how we shall get it through without a
'guillotine'. After that, the Town and Country Planning Bill, with 70
odd clauses!

Eden's broadcast was very good and very firm. NATO, now and
in the future; German elections *before* a German Govt; no surrender
but willingness to agree with Russia – that was the theme. The only
fear I have is that he does not (living so largely in official circles) realise
that the Americans are treating us like poor relations, not partners.
This is instinctively felt and resented. Moreover, their business methods
are becoming more and more crudely imperialistic, both at home and
abroad. There has been another flagrant case of the rejection of a
British tender (which was the lowest) on some trumped up excuse.

18 January
Eden explained to the Cabinet all the absurd and protracted arguments
about the plan of meeting in Berlin, and the preparation of meetings
in East and West Berlin. The Russians have been intolerable and
obstinate . . . .

There was an interesting dialogue (between P.M. and Eden) on
Egypt. There is a growing alarm in Egypt that they are being left on
one side. They are the 2nd line of defence, and the Arab League is not
so strong as it was. We might consider now withdrawing our offers
on the Treaty revision, and let Egypt stew a bit in her own juice.
Meanwhile the new policy of 'neutralism' has infuriated the Americans. The Wafd has been 'liquidated'; now the Moslem Brotherhood
has gone the same way (perhaps both have gone underground) So the
Committee of Revolution are getting a little lonely . . . .

There was a good discussion on East–West trade. The Americans
are very tiresome and very selfish about this. It is quite absurd to limit
the sales to Russia of British controlled rubber. Russia can get all the

---

5. Over the proposed Egyptian treaty.

rubber she needs from other sources. We are merely injuring ourselves to please the Americans and to no good purpose . . . .

19 January
Financial resolution on Rent and Repairs Bill . . . . We won (quite unexpectedly) by 44 majority. We wd have been satisfied with 7 or 8. But I expect they will make up for it by being very tiresome in the Standing Committee!

20 January
Standing Committee started. We got 2 lines of Clause 1! So they are being very tiresome . . . .

26 January
We had another 2½ hours in standing committee and got clause 1 . . . .

27 January
. . . . Molotov demanded an agenda which the western powers thought it best to accept, in order to avoid unnecessary argument. This clearly surprised Molotov.

28 January
2½ hours standing committee. Bevan was today really 'obstructing'. We have not quite got Clause 2 . . . .

6 February
After 2 more days in standing committe, we have got 3 clauses. It doesn't seem likely that we can get the Rent and Repairs Bill without a guillotine. However, I suppose we shall have to go on for another week at least before resorting to a time-table. It's a very tedious business. I went yesterday to Birmingham, to open some flats, and took the occasion for announcing the 1953 figures – 319,779 houses. Even the *Times* calls it 'the Minister of Housing's triumph' . . . .

On Wednesday we had a 'cocktail party' at the Ministry to celebrate the Housing figures. I invited about 50 people, including representatives from the Scottish Office and the Ministry of Works.

The news from Berlin is very bleak. Molotov has relapsed into the old negatives. Meanwhile, the icy wind from Russia has prolonged the frost all this week. We have had frost and ice for a fortnight now.

Read Henry James – '*The Awkward Age*'. How remote all this

world seems now! And how strange all these refinements and romances of human behaviour! But rather restful, because so artificial . . . . The newspaper campaign against Churchill is growing. The *Daily Mirror* is scurrilous, but not altogether with skill in its attack. The [*News*] *Chronicle* had a Gallup poll which turned out (against the views of the paper itself) in favour of C's resignation. It is all rather sad and I think worries and pains him. Meanwhile the party in the HofC is restless and bewildered. But the by-elections (so far) show little swing either way. The American economic situation is uncertain. A serious 'recession' would have formidable effects on the old world. Nor is it clear what Butler's policy really is. We have removed so many 'controls' that a bad storm wd be difficult to ride. Yet a bold policy of freedom and expansion of trade seems to many people a better bet than restriction. I confess that I am very baffled and uncertain. Vast Treasury papers and memoranda are circulated to us in shoals. But one is not much wiser when one has read them . . . .

The Cabinet day has been changed to Wednesday, wh allowed me to go this week. But nothing much happened . . . .

There is an easier position (for the moment) in the world of organised labour. The Communist led Electrical Union is making itself unpopular and slightly ridiculous by its tactics of 'guerrilla' strikes, and it looks as if the men are getting sick of it . . . .

The tax on flooring tiles, wh the Treasury put on (a purchase tax order) without any consultation with me is causing a frightful row. I saw Rab [Butler] about this on Saturday (6th) and agreed with him that he shd try to see it through, since he conceives his 'face' is at stake. But I fear there will be trouble on Tuesday in the HofC when the debate takes place. However, I have warned him.

14 February (Sunday)

A terrible week. Two days on Standing Committee and practically no progress. On Thursday I gave notice that I shd move to sit on Wednesdays – a great bore for everybody. If we are still 'stuck', we shall have to resort to 'guillotine' or 'time-table'. I think the Leader of the House and the whips now recognise that this will be necessary. Alderman Key (Labour MP and member of the Standing Ctee) has expressed (privately) the same view. If there is to be a guillotine, it will be better tactics to start it while we are still on Part 1 (Slums) and *before* we pass to Part 2 (Rent increases)

The Chancellor of the Ex 'got away' with his purchase tax debates very skilfully. I sat through the debate (in 'loyal' support) but I am nevertheless annoyed about the affair. It makes us look foolish in the eyes of those who know the facts.

Wednesday was a tremendous day, beginning with 'Legislation Committee' at 9.45am and followed by a very long Cabinet. The Legislation Committee approved my immense Town and Country Planning Bill. This was partly because Dame Evelyn Sharp had provided me with such a lucid exposition – partly because I had taken the precaution of sending the Bill – and the exposition – to Lord Salisbury and to the Lord Chancellor some 10 days before. There only remains the great battle with the Chancellor of the Ex about the finance of the Bill. I thought I had definitely won this in the Cabinet, but the Treasury have somehow managed to keep the issue alive. I suppose it means another struggle.

The Cabinet was very long – but interesting. The Services have forced the Treasury to increase pay by a very substantial amount. Whether this will deal successfully with the serious position, in all the Services, remains to be seen. The warrant officers; petty officers; serjeants etc are *all* leaving in shoals. For myself, I believe the trouble is that being either in Germany or on the Canal they are separated from their wives. All this pay question has got mixed up with the trade union wage demands; the pensions of first-war officers; the salaries of Judges; the payment of members of Parliament and so on. The best hope of carrying it all seems to be a 'package' arrangement – a proper combination of jam and medicine . . . .

Some rather gloomy telegrams from Berlin. But P.M. still feels this will be an age of continuous and more or less ineffective conferences. This is better than war . . . .

. . . . A very long (and valuable) discussion followed on Egypt, in wh (at P.M.'s request) I ventured to take some part – altho' I do not much like doing so in Eden's absence. But it is really necessary (however anxious the F.O. may be for the agreement) to think out an alternative policy if no honourable agreement can be got and carried through the HofC. Such an alternative is possible. I think the Chiefs of Staff have been very remiss in not working at it in detail at an earlier date . . . .

On Thursday night I went to Manchester, and got back home (to Birch Grove House) on Saturday afternoon . . . . Two speeches – one at a luncheon of supporters and subscribers, (Manchester business men) the other an open meeting at night. Both were quite good, but tiring. We had the hall full at night, which was good for nowadays. With T.V. and all the rest, the people won't go to meetings any more.

20 February

Another heavy week. 3 mornings of our Bill in Standing Committee. We decided to have a Time-table, and announced this to the House on Thursday. There was a great show of noisy indignation (rather synthetic) and I have no doubt there will be a very noisy debate on Monday . . . .

The Berlin Conference is over. It has failed in every European question. No settlement in Germany; no Austrian Treaty. But the truculence of Molotov is much less dangerous than a show of moderation. The neutralist forces in France and Italy have been correspondingly weakened. M Bidault's reputation has grown, and with it the probability of EDC being finally agreed by the French Parliament.

On the Eastern side, there *is* to be a conference in April of the Powers (including China) to discuss Korea and Indo-China. This represents a concession by Dulles and a success for Eden . . . .

Meeting at Bromley Friday evening, at the Central Hall. It was quite well attended. I spoke on Foreign affairs and the Berlin Conference. They seemed to like this; I have not strayed from my narrow home field for some time. The proper approach, I feel sure, at these kind of meetings and with these audiences is a 'lecture', not a political speech. I am so tired with all this that I have reverted to Trollope. Read '*The Warden*'.

A select committee of the HofC has reported – unanimously it seems – in favour of raising the salary of MPs from £1000 to £1500, with divers other 'perks' and a non-contributory pension after 10 years service. This puts us in a difficulty. If the Govt carry out the report, we shall be execrated by the people; if we decline to do so, it will be said (quite untruly) that the Tories are the rich party. Perhaps we wd do best to postpone the whole thing till after the General Election. At least that wd involve no breach of contract.

My battle with the Chancellor of the Ex about the financial clauses of the T&C Planning Bill will be taken again on Monday, at the Cabinet. As I have to be in the House all the afternoon and evening (on the Guillotine motion) it won't be too easy. Cabinet is to meet at 4pm . . . .

22 February

The 'time-table' or 'guillotine' debate took place. My speech was perhaps too carefully prepared and allowed Bevan to do the usual retort about 'midnight oil'. Then anything properly done is out of date today – like hand-made clothes or furniture, it is 'reactionary'. To finish your sentences; to put in verbs; to worry about neat turns of phrase or apt and appropriate adjectives – all this is 'undemocratic' and 'Victorian'. Nevertheless, my speech was a general success . . . . After Bevan's reply, the debate fizzled out. His right-wing colleagues (Attlee; Morrison and co) left him completely 'out on a limb'. They absented themselves from the whole debate; we won the first division by over 100 – the second by over 20. Considering that the Liberals voted against us, as they always do on closure or guillotine motions, this was very good. There was a Cabinet in the HofC (Prime Minister's room) at 4pm. I got to it at about 6pm, in time for another round in my fight with the Treasury about the financial provisions of the Town and Country Planning Act. It was very stormy, but I think we shall get what may be called a compromise in the end. So long as this gives me what I want (as I told the CofE) I shall be happy!

23 February
10.30–1pm. Standing Committee on the Housing Repairs and Rents Bill. The 'guillotine' is not yet effective. At 4.30 we had the 'Business Ctee' (of the Standing Committee) which, under the new procedure, has to work out a programme of work so as to finish the Committee stage by the date appointed by the House of Commons. This date (in accordance with yesterday's Resolution) is March 18th. It follows, therefore, that in theory one could do this in the maximum or the minimum of sittings of the Standing Committee. One could sit morning, afternoon and evening for five days a week between now and March 18th. Or one could sit only twice a week. So it worked out that Bevan and co proposed another 22 sittings – or 55 hours more talk. I proposed 11 sittings. As we have a majority of 1 on the Business Ctee, we carried our proposal. The next thing is to divide up the sitting between the clauses. We agreed to fix only the next few and meet again for a review of the progress made. The Opposition, of course, affected great indignation. But they would have been much more indignant if we had accepted their 22 sittings!

24 February
Standing Committee 10.30–1pm. We finished Part 1 of the Bill, in a gallop, and scarcely a clause or amendment was in fact 'guillotined'.

3.15. Minister's Council. Sir P Mills attended. It is a great help to have him still available for advice. The housing figures – under construction, starts, completions, licensed – all seem to be following more or less the pattern wh we want. The only uncertainty is always the figure of 'unsubsidised' private enterprise houses. I was glad to see that the applications for license (which are now formal and available as of right) reached 8600 in January – a record for January and indeed for any month. We had an interesting discussion on the problem of the 'back-to-back' houses – in Leeds, Sheffield, Bradford etc. Many of these, of course, are very old and must be demolished as 'slums'. But many are quite new, some post 1914 war. We must try to find a method of so 'improving' them, esp by improving the ventilation, as to make them suitable for another generation at least. We hope to be able to do this, chiefly by the modern means of 'fan' ventilators which can be fitted nowadays . . . .

25 February
. . . . I lunched with Rex Leeper, at the offices of the Anglo-American Corporation of S Africa. (This is a grand word for Oppenheimer, Joel and Co) Harry Oppenheimer, (who largely financed the United Party in S[outh]A[frica] and wd have held high office if they had got in)[6] telephoned yesterday to say that Dr Malan is meditating some drastic action about the Protectorates[7] – indeed, has decided on such action. This, of course, in view of British feeling about S African policy to the natives, wd put us in a very bad position. I was asked whether it wd be a good thing for Mr O (who comes over frequently on business) to come to London and get into touch with someone who cd tell us what it's all about, (For, he naturally cd not send any details of what he has heard either by telephone or cable) O had seen Ld Salisbury last summer, and knew both Lyttelton and Swinton. I said I wd find out. It's amusing to see the scholarly ambassador whom I knew in Greece now metamorphosised into a city pundit. Rex is chairman of this and I think other companies. He presides and keeps the peace and if

---

6. The United Party had lost power in South Africa to Malan's National Party in 1948, and lost again in 1953.
7. The British High Commission territories of Bechuanaland (now Botswana), Basutoland (now Lesotho) and Swaziland had long been coveted by the Union of South Africa. All three became independent in 1966.

necessary adjudicates. His great successes are with the companies run entirely by Jews.

3.30pm. A long discussion with my Conservatives on the Standing Committee, about amendments they want. I find it best to see them 'behind the scenes'. This saves a lot of time and looks better when we come to Standing Ctee itself. At 5.30 I went off to see Ld Swinton. By chance, I found O Lyttelton in his room at the HofLords. The general view was that it wd be very helpful for us to see Oppenheimer. Since he came so frequently to London on business, there wd be nothing marked in his leaving S Africa for a short trip. I telephoned this to Leeper and it will no doubt be arranged . . . .

26 February

10am. Cabinet. My agreement with the Treasury was formally ratified. Rab [Butler] began to explain it – not at all objectively. I stopped him. 'Be careful' I said. 'We have made an agreement. But if you start to explain it, we shall have another quarrel.'

There was a very long agenda. The Agricultural Price review – or one aspect of it – had to be discussed and certain decisions reached. We then went through the whole text of the Television Bill. (I am much afraid this will be rather a muddle. No one has really been in charge of the Bill. Buck de la Warr is agreeable, but neither very clever nor a strong character)

Then we had a desultory discussion on the Teacher Superannuation Bill (another muddle: 'Auntie Flo' as Miss Horsburgh is irreverently called, is also a very poor politician). This led to judges' salaries, General pensions, British Legion pensions – and a number of allied subjects . . . .

These minor political problems are matters – above all – of 'timing' and 'presentation'. The great issues – large questions in economic or foreign policy – can't yield to such treatment. But the small ones can. Yet no one really studies the art of 'public-relations' . . . .

27 February

This has been a very important week politically. No record of inner politics cd be at all fair – not to say complete – without reference to the extraordinary situation *inside* the so-called 'Labour Movement'. After much searching of heart and great intrigue, the Parly Labour Party decided by majorities of 2 (and another vote [of] 9) to support the views of its leaders on foreign affairs. It is said that even that result was only obtained with the help of the Labour peers.

The issue wh has at last forced the Labour party to come to a decision was that of E.D.C. and esp German re-armament . . . . Of course, there are a lot of Labour members, who are not 'Bevanites', finding themselves on this question supporting Bevan. There are the old pacifists and radicals – lay preachers etc. Nevertheless it is a great triumph for Bevan. Perhaps even more significant was the voting on the National Executive of the Labour party. Altho' Attlee and co won by a good majority, it is said that Bevan is now beginning to get strong trade union support. Even the [Transport &] General Workers (Bev*in*'s old union) are said to be on his side. At the Wednesday morning meeting of our Bill, I said to him 'Why don't you leave me alone? You are after much bigger game!' He blushed delightedly. There is no doubt a great fight going on. Nevertheless, if there were a General Election, they would all come together again 'for the duration', and quarrel afterwards.

On Tuesday night, I dined alone with Churchill . . . . he saw no reason for a General Election till the spring of 1956. (This is, of course, to allow a good excuse to himself for going on till Christmas!)

. . . . Churchill broods a great deal about the atomic and hydrogen bomb. The destructive power of the latter is frightful. All London in one night. The Russians have not got it – but will in a year or two. It is the story of the atom bomb again. Will the Americans put off the 'show down' again until the Russians have caught them up for a second time? or will they go for pre-emptive war? We talked about Suez; the Foreign Office, and Eden. The fall of Neguib will make things worse for British interests; but it makes a new situation, easier perhaps politically at home. He said he thought Eden sometimes shrank from anything except the F.O. (wh he understands so well) I said I thought he had been in the difficult position of 'heir' for too long . . . .

28 February

A new change in the Egyptian scene. Neguib – dismissed on Tuesday, is back on Friday. It all looks very confused and bad for any sense of security or peaceful arrangement. There is to be a Cabinet on Egypt tomorrow . . . .

1 March

.... Lyttelton has telegraphed from Kenya encouraging news. With the help of the captured 'General China' – who seems ready to 'work his passage' – there seems a chance of a fairly large-scale surrender of Mau Mau rank and file. The terms of the 'amnesty' wd have to be open. This involves not the pardon, but the substitute of 'detention during H.M.'s pleasure' for the death penalty. But (in spite of some expected clamour from some of the Europeans) the price is clearly worth paying . . . .

4 March

.... 4.30–6. A meeting of selected Ministers to discuss the vexed question of members' salaries. The P.M. tried hard to force through his plan – which is, in effect, to accept the Committee's scheme of an immediate increase to £1500 pa. I spoke strongly on 3 points, which most of the others seemed to accept. a) whatever is done, the Government will be held responsible. We cannot shelter behind the committee or take any comfort from the Opposition's support. b) We cannot win any votes; we may lose a lot. c) no rise of salary shd take place in this Parliament – but we might improve the facilities (e.g. postage) and allowances.

It was finally decided that the Chancellor of the Ex shd propose a scheme on c). This is a most dangerous question and wants most careful handling.

At 6pm the full Cabinet met to discuss the situation in the Sudan. This lasted for 1½ hours. A very strong telegram was agreed to be sent to the Governor General – who is, it seems, a very weak man. Fortunately Selwyn Lloyd, who went out as Minister of State to attend the opening of the first Sudanese parliament, originally arranged for March 10th, is in Khartoum.

We have only *one* battalion in K. There was a long discussion about reinforcements. I ventured to ask how far the airfield was from the palace, and how 500 to 600 men cd guard both. Alex and Churchill (remembering Athens, as I did)[8] took up this point quite vigorously. Churchill called a special meeting of the Chiefs of Staff later in the evening – so I assume that all this will be dealt with.

---

8. On the siege of Athens in December 1944 see *HMM* II, pp. 607f.

5 March

. . . . I went to see Dr Richardson. He says that the pains I feel are not significant – only 'adhesions' and normal after so serious an operation. But he says I am over-worked and must reduce the pressure. Easy to say!

6 March

. . . . I have been reading more Trollope this week – and have now finished all the Barchester series – very good they are too. '*Dr Thorne*' I like very much, and '*The Small House at Allington*'.

There was a lot of work waiting for me. I finished 'The Grand Design' (2nd edition). But I have re-christened it 'Operation Round-Up'. It tries to pick up and produce some kind of policy for all the remaining problems in the Ministry of Housing. These are – Local Govt Reform; (structure) Local Govt Finance; ('De-rating' of industry etc) Equalisation Grants; Housing Subsidies; Requisitioned Houses; and so on. If Churchill goes on, it will be my task for the 1954–5 session. If he goes, and I go to another office, it will be of great value to my successor. For he will find a programme ready-made (and perhaps agreed in principle by the Cabinet) . . . .

10 March

A very long Cabinet in the morning. P.M. tried to move the payment of members, about wh we had agreed to wait for the Treasury paper. I spoke up against him, wh he did not altogether like. But the others did.

Eden had a paper on E.D.C. In the hope of getting the French to take the plunge, we are offering almost everything but marriage. We are even to put an armoured division under command of the G.O.C. European army.

The news wh Oppenheimer gave us about Malan's intention has not yet been confirmed. But it looks as if he will make a formal demand for the Protectorates. This will lead to a very grave, even perilous, situation if the demand is pressed . . . .

11 March

10.30–1pm. Standing Committee. We carried all the Govt new clauses. So we have really finished the Committee stage of the Bill. Now we have only to sit patiently through another 7½ hours of talk, while

Aneurin Bevan (by the media of new clauses) develops his great ideas of Housing reform. These he will try to pin on the reluctant Attlee, Morrison and co. He is trying to force the Labour Party to accept his principle of public – or at least municipal – ownership of all houses now owned by landlords . . . .

15 March

Town and Country Planning Bill – 2nd reading. I introduced the Bill with a very long speech (over an hour) It was, I think, very clear. Dame Evelyn Sharp had really composed it. It was a very poor house all day; only the experts attended. We had a good division. I had to leave the bench for 2 hours for a very long Cabinet on Egypt and the Sudan. The P.M. was in remarkably good form and very robust. I think (and ventured to say) that the real question is not whether we shd adopt this or that plan at the moment, but whether we can negotiate at all with the present Egyptian govt . . . .

17 March

A very long Cabinet – lasting till 1.45, and ranging from Homo-sexuality to the price of milk. At the end, Eden came in with some bad news about the negotiations for the Consortium to take over the Anglo-Iranian interests in Persia. The British Company and the Americans have reached a deadlock

a) as to the terms on which the consortium shd be formed – that is, in effect, the value of the 60% rights in the Persian concession wh Anglo-Iranian are to sell, keeping 40% for themselves.

b) The compensation to be claimed by Anglo-Iranian from the Persian Government.

Lord Woolton and I were 'delegated' the job of trying to sort this out . . . .

18 March

We finished the Standing Committee on the Repairs and Rents Bill. Altho' the Opposition had to make the usual protests about the guillotine, the time allowed was more than ample. We have had 22 sessions in committee; that is 55 hours of talk . . . .

7–9.30 Luton Bill. This was a bill to give County Borough status to Luton. It was a 'free vote' and rather a good debate – county versus borough – and cutting right across party lines. I was anxious to defeat the Bill, because it would be a bore to have these separate bills ahead

of a general reorganisation of local government. We just succeeded –
by 20 votes.

20 March

A long meeting at the Foreign Office, Sir W Fraser, chairman of AIOC,
has, under considerable pressure from us, come to terms with the
American oil interests . . . .

22 March

. . . . A Cabinet at 5.30. On Egypt, ... Negotiations are not to be
resumed 'until confidence has been created'. But why don't we decide
what we want to do, irrespective of the Egyptians? Everything drags
on – the P.M. is pleased, in his heart, because negotiations are 'broken
off'. Every time he said this, the F.S. said 'suspended'. There was a
long discussion about the reply which the P.M. shd make to some
P.Q.s on the use of the atom or hydrogen bomb and the agreement, if
any, which we had with the Americans.

It was rather a desultory discussion, but a fairly clear decision was
taken. The P.M. must do more than answer in a correct and formal
way. He must make something of a general statement, esp about the
appearance of this new horror, the hydrogen bomb. Then there are
clearly different degrees of understanding with USA. As to the use of
our bases in UK, we have a *written* agreement, made by Attlee.[9] As to
retaliation or action by US as a NATO power or acting on behalf of
UN there are 'understandings' and 'contacts'. The trouble is that we
are really largely in the hands of the Americans . . . .

24 March

A long Cabinet, with a varied agenda, and the usual discussions which
were not on the agenda at all . . . .

Butler put forward two Budget ideas for discussion – the first,
a levy on flour to help to pay for the subsidy on bread; the second, a
start with 'Equal Pay'. There was a long, often almost heated and quite
inconclusive discussion . . . . (For my part, I cannot see the sense of
taxing and subsidising a commodity at one and the same time. But
that is what the so-called 'levy-subsidy' would really do) 'Equal Pay',
if introduced into Civil Service, local govt service etc would cost

---

9. US Air Force bases were re-established in 1948 at the time of the Berlin Airlift
   and further deployment was made in 1950.

£37m. (of which £9m on rates) These are formidable sums. But if we don't *do something* (and Butler's idea is to do it by instalments over – say – 7, 5, 4, or 3 years) the Socialists will *promise everything.*

Monckton (M of Labour) did not seem unduly concerned about industrial repercussions. Thorneycroft (B of Trade) was strongly against. The money wd be better spent by tax reliefs.

The trouble is that the Chancellor has nothing to offer in this Budget. It will be perhaps a wholesome, but not an appetising pie. So he wants a plum to put in. Attended a luncheon at the Hyde Park Hotel – the Leather Federation. Dorothy came with me. I made a speech, about the new phase of Housing policy. First year, expansion; second year, achievement; third year, stabilisation. I hope this will help to keep the local authorities reasonably quiet during the period of transition. Of course, I want private and unsubsidised building to go ahead unchecked. Subsidised building ought gradually to change over to slum-clearance and dealing with over-crowding in its various forms . . . .

26 March
Annual General Meeting of the Bromley [Conservative] Association. A very good turn-out. The organisation has now nearly 9000 members, wh is pretty good . . . .

28 March
. . . . It is obvious that there is tremendous interest, almost panic, in many parts of the world, about the Hydrogen Bomb. P.M. has summoned a meeting of ministers for 5.30 tomorrow in his room.

29 March
A long meeting, to draft P.M.'s statement. This was not easy, because we must give away to the American public that we have *in fact* been receiving information from US Govt going rather beyond the strict interpretation of the McMahon law . . . .

30 March
P.M. made his statement on H bomb. The Labour Party was very confused and divided, but managed to make a good uproar. They obviously feel (or at least the left) that they are 'on a good thing' . . . .

31 March
The Hydrogen Bomb panic is spreading. The *Daily Mirror* attacks the P.M. with headings similar to the Election ones. 'CHURCHILL CON-FESSES' etc. The *Daily Herald* is almost as violent. It is obvious that the Opposition – or the less responsible part of it – feel that at last they have found something to cling on to . . . .

But I have no doubt that Churchill will accept the challenge, and perhaps tell the true story of the Atomic Bomb (Tube Alloys) which he has kept locked in his heart all these years. If he does, it will be devastating for Attlee . . . .[10]

1 April
10am. I had to go to the meeting of the Economic Committee, for a very stupid and desultory discussion on New Towns, and overspill. Nothing happened – except that I lost my temper with Thorneycroft (B of Trade) – a very stupid fellow, who will talk to Cabinet committees as if they were public meetings . . . .

5 April
Cabinet at 12 noon. Butler expounded his Budget. There was nothing in it; but it will do in a non-election year (if it proves a non-election year!) P.M. gave us his speech and the text of the Churchill–Roosevelt agreement of 1943, on Atom bomb, by which we definitely retained a veto on its use. This was removed by the McMahon Act apparently without any protest, certainly any effective or public protest, from H.M.G. By 1948 we had to make a new agreement, formally abandoning all that Churchill had secured in 1943. It is, of course, true that C gave up any formal claim to the goodwill of any industrial or commercial value in the work to be done by the Americans in the war. But what matters is the veto, and that has gone.

During the discussion on the Chancellor's proposals (which included his postponing, but not abandoning the question of Equal Pay and increased Old Age Pensions) I passed this note to Eden, 'Old Age Pensions: Equal Pay. I suppose both these *could* be done in the Autumn, *before* the election, should you decide to have an election this year? Thus the double opportunity is preserved. Is this right?'

---

10. A reference to the secret atomic bomb programme during the Second World War, code-named Tube Alloys. Attlee, however, although the then Deputy Prime Minister, seems to have played little part in and known less about this programme.

He replied with 'Yes – you have guessed my thoughts (I cannot call them plans!)'

The *Daily Mirror* and the *Daily Herald* have come out with most violent attacks on Churchill 'powerless to deal with USA' and all that. There is sure to be a row this afternoon.

6 April

There *was* 'one hell of a row' yesterday afternoon. It was really a very strange performance. Attlee made a speech wh commanded general approval and respect – with a 'non party' approach and full of worthy sentiments. But of course it did not touch the real problem. It was a strange contrast to the flood of partisan questions last week, and violent attacks on the P.M. by Michael Foot on the T.V. and by Crossman in the *Sunday Pictorial*. The House (and the press) expected that the P.M. wd make a similar sort of speech – perhaps a little more realistic and better phrased, but on the same note. This he did for the first part of his speech. Then he started on the story of the Churchill–Roosevelt agreement of 1943, and its 'abandonment' by the Socialist Govt. In other words, we had a veto on the use of the atomic or any other nuclear bomb by USA. Now the veto has gone. This sudden change of tone infuriated the Opposition, and shocked the Government back-benchers. A long and angry scene followed. Attlee made some effective interventions, and Churchill muddled his case in answering. He was thrown off his balance by the violence of the reaction. After about 20 minutes of storm and cries of 'resign' 'dirty' and all the rest, he was able to finish the speech, the latter part of which was in the tone wh had been expected, but coming after the attack, was ineffective and not appreciated, even where good points were made. Bob Boothby, with a characteristic gesture of disloyalty, walked out – apparently to show his disapproval of Churchill. It was the greatest failure – on the surface at least – since Churchill's speech on the abdication of King Edward VIII.

The debate dragged on after this – with a very thin House – until Eden's wind up. He made a splendid defence of Churchill, restating the story of the Quebec agreement very effectively. The second half of his speech was a masterly review of the broad problem of rearmament. By this speech, Eden immensely increased his hold on the party and on the House.

Churchill's failure was due to two things. First, the contrast between the general 'non-partisan' character of the debate and the damaging revelation was too horribly made and was inartistically led up to. Secondly, his power of recovery has gone. His hearing is bad; he was rather staggered by the noise; he was temporarily 'knocked off his perch'. All he could do was to force his way through the delivery of his prepared text. Of course he has never been very mobile and his method of speaking (with every word prepared) has this inherent danger. But, of course, a few years ago he wd have been able to readjust himself to the situation . . . .

6 April [sic]

The press has been bad – though not quite as bad as I feared. The *D Telegraph* loyal; the *Times* insufferably pontifical; the *Express* and *Mail* in full support; the *Chronicle* and *M Guardian* fair; the *Daily Mirror* vile. Yet, with all the criticism, I feel that the main strategic purpose has been secured. Eden's speech received much praise.

I lunched at Carlton Gardens – a party for the oil companies representatives who are to go to Teheran to try to negotiate a new agreement on behalf of the consortium wh has been formed. After luncheon, I had a talk with Eden. We both feel it to be absolutely vital for the change to come soon. The trouble is that (after yesterday) it may be delayed. Churchill's natural reaction will be to fight on. He wd like an oratorical triumph – not a failure – as his last effort. But we are losing time and losing any real unity of purpose and method. The Cabinet is often chaotic, and always intolerably slow. (From Eden's attitude, I feel that he has now decided to offer me the Foreign Office)

7 April

The 'stand put' 'carry on' or 'chicory' Budget has been pretty well received. The chief criticism is about the continued increase of expenditure. Yet how to reduce it is a puzzle. The main items are a) service of debt b) defence c) welfare state. No one wants to reduce any of them. Economy is popular in principle. In practice, everyone demands more expenditure – for instance, on Old Age Pensions or on 'Equal Pay' . . . .

11am. Cabinet. A very long meeting, lasting till 1.45. The Parliamentary business included the problem of the Teachers Pension Bill. The original idea was to take 2nd reading on Tuesday of next week, with Wednesday as the 3rd reading of my Housing Repairs and Rents Bill. But the Chief Whip took rather a gloomy view. We have 20 sick; several ministers away; and some determined 'abstainers' or opponents

of the Bill on our side. It was quite likely, he thought, that we shd
be defeated . . . . I protested that it wd not be possible to have the
3rd reading of my Bill the day after a defeat. It wd be tragic to sacrifice the result of such great efforts over so long a period. Then the
Minister of Education naturally protested in her turn – and so the
debate went on. The P.M. was in good form and obviously felt that
the whole question of the Teachers Bill has been thoroughly muddled
– as it has been. It was not worth risking the life of the Govt for
it . . . .

Dinner at Carlton Gardens, for the Persian ambassador and his
staff, to celebrate the restoration of our relations. After all the work
which has been done to create the 'consortium', the Americans have
suddenly discovered that it may be contrary to the Sherman anti-trust
law! Can you conceive such folly and incompetence? The State Dept
only discover this – having been the protagonists of this plan for 3
months and more – just as the agreements are to be initialised! . . . .

9 April

After our recent electoral successes the tide has turned. We had a *very
bad* result in East Edinburgh – a swing of between 3% and 4% away
from us.[11] I think [it] is partly the Budget, which is a disappointment
to many; partly a sense that [the] P.M. is failing; partly the panic and
hysteria being worked up about the Hydrogen bomb . . . .

12 April

Lunch at Carlton Gardens . . . .

The negotiation – or talk – with Dulles began last night. By lunch-
time good progress had been made . . . . So far, we have no American
guarantee of any kind for our Eastern interests – Hong Kong; Malaya
etc. We are not members of ANZUS (which is very shaming for us)
Now there is a chance of getting a sort of Far-Eastern duplication
of NATO. Of course, the problem of Indo-China remains. Can it be
recovered for the French? Can it be partitioned, (like Germany and
Korea)? Can a firm line of defence be organised anywhere if Indo-
China is lost? I said to Eden that, with democracies, one could never
lock the stable door until some at least of the horses had escaped.
(e.g. the Western Front. It was only after the rape of Czechoslovakia –
following the loss of Poland, Hungary etc – that British and other

---

11. Edinburgh East by-election (8 April 1954), Lab: 18,950; C: 13,922.

Western European opinion was shocked into resistance) In the same way, half Korea; half or perhaps all Indo-China must go, before British opinion will face saying 'Thus far, and no further' . . . .

Butler wound up the Budget debate with a very good little speech. But the Budget is not popular although probably the reaction against its 'dullness' will begin to subside. There is no real feeling about 'Equal Pay'. But there is a real trouble about the 'Old Age Pensioners'.

13 April

9.30am. A short meeting of some ministers – Swinton; Butler; Thorney-croft (B of Trade) and self to organise some policy of reductions in Govt expenditure – to take effect for 1955–6. The 'automatic' rise in expenditure is really alarming, and threatens to engulf us if nothing can be done . . . .

After questions, the Foreign Secretary made a statement, embodying the agreement with Dulles. This was very well done. Attlee asked one or two mild and more or less friendly questions. Then came a few offensive and extreme questions or statements, from back-bench 'fellow-travellers'. After one or two 'moderate' front-benchers, Bevan suddenly stalked to the box (treading on as many front bench toes as possible – physically as well as metaphorically) and made three statements (in the form of questions) of a most violent kind. The offence, of course was against Attlee, not against us . . . .

14 April

I went to a meeting of the Commission for Central and Eastern Europe (European movement) of which – before taking office – I was President, and Beddington Behrens was rapporteur. After he and I resigned, it was allowed by the F.O. to crash, altho' they supported it for a time. But Dick Law and Kelly killed it – whether purposely or not, I do not know.

Anyway, Retsinger has got it going again (with French money, and perhaps some Dutch and Belgian support) and Senator de la Vallée Poussin has become Chairman. I have been elected '*Président à titre d'honneur*'.[12] All this I have explained to the Foreign Secretary, who seems to approve.

Another curious scene in the House . . . . [A] debate was started by

12. 'Honorary president'.

the Bevanites on the motion for the Easter adjournment, to protest against the Foreign Secretary's new statement on E.D.C., as well as yesterday's statement about the Far East. This was kept up by the left-wingers, until it was closured. The official Labour whips did not 'tell' in the division and the Front Bench boycotted the debate. Yet over 100 voted (out of 230 subsequently revealed – by a division on Budget resolutions) to be present in the House. This may shew about the strength of the Bevanites.

Later in the evening came the news of a great scene and Bevan's resignation from the Opposition 'Shadow Cabinet'. It is not clear whether this was a previously 'planned' manoeuvre, or the result of a flare up . . . .

Easter Monday
Arthur and Peggy [Macmillan] came down to stay for a few days. Lovely weather continues. Read Lord Mahon's *History of England* – very readable. I *do* like *detailed* history. The Wooltons came over to see the garden . . . .

21 April (our wedding day)
. . . . Worked on speeches for Liverpool and Nottingham. Read Mahon, and finished volume 2. The weather is unbroken; the garden was wonderful in the evening sun – a splendid show of daffodils. Our quarterly housing figures are very good – nearly 10,000 up on last year. Now I am working on 'Operation Round-up' and how to persuade the Cabinet committee to accept the plans. They may lead not only to improvements but to substantial economies. The newspapers are full of the Petrov drama. M Petrov (2nd secretary in Russian embassy at Canberra) has 'come over' to us, with a full account of the Soviet spy organisation in Canberra. His wife was on her way home (ordered back by the Soviet Govt) but rescued at Pt Darwen [sic]. She also seeks asylum. The account of how the Russian thugs tried to terrorise her and were disarmed at the airfield by the Australian police is more like a piece of popular fiction than real life. It will be interesting to see whether Menzies will be helped by all this at the forthcoming General Election in Australia. Apparently there are a number of 'left-wing' figures who may be implicated if the full story comes out. It won't make the Soviet Govt any more tractable at Geneva. I think it will have a good effect at home, where people tend to forget how horrible Communism really is . . . .

23 April

Liverpool and Sheffield. Stayed at Welbeck Woodhouse, with the Portlands, who were as charming as ever. Meeting at Nottingham – for the county divisions. A poor meeting, the hall being too big and not full. (The usual folly about charging for tickets) . . . .

25 April

A telephone call early this morning to come to London for an urgent meeting of ministers. This was not possible, since the only train from Retford did not arrive till 3.20. However, on reaching London, I found that a second meeting was being held at 4pm.

Present: P.M.; Eden; Lyttelton; Alexander; Selwyn Lloyd; also Chief of Staff and First Sea Lord. This is the story. Eden flew over (from Paris) last night. He is being pressed by the Americans (and now the French) to sign a 'Declaration of Intention' by the 3 powers, saying that they will not allow Indo-China or SE Asia to go Communist. (This is really a revival of the proposal which Dulles made *before* his visit to London and agreed to modify) Armed with this document, the President will obtain permission from Congress to use American air power immediately. The excuse will be to help the beleaguered French garrison at Dien Bien Phu. But, since it is impossible to bomb the attacking forces without also bombing the defending troops (they are 500–1000 yards apart) this is only an excuse. As Admiral Radford admitted, the Fleet Air Arm will attack 'second-line targets' – that is Chinese air bases etc (the frontier is only 100 miles or so from Dien Bien Phu) This will produce a 'show down' – in other words, either Russia must come to the aid of China (this means World War 3) or abandon China (this means an almost fatal blow to Russian prestige) The French Govt, in desperation, clutch at this American straw to save themselves – and perhaps the 4th Republic. The garrison, in spite of a fine defence, must fall in a few days. The French Govt can hardly, at such a moment, refuse the offer of *direct* intervention. (At present, the American aid has been indirect – money and material) But, even so, Bidault seemed at first reluctant to accept the American plan.

Eden had no doubt that we ought to refuse to take part in this rather amateurish plan. First, he resents having no direct American approach. All the details have reached us by French talks in Washington with Bedell Smith and State Department . . . . Secondly, there is *no* method by which the garrison can be rescued. Bombing will not help it. Bombing is only intended as a 'blind', and the emotional feeling in

France about the garrison is just being exploited by the Americans. Thirdly, a new declaration of policy, if it is to be effective and (which is vital) carry *Asian* support, must emerge from – not precede – Geneva. Fourthly, such a bare-faced plan could not get the support of the House of Commons or the country or the Commonwealth . . . .

26 April

On thinking over yesterday's talks and the whole of this strange story, it is terrifying to realise how dangerous the Americans can be without good advice. They mean well and their heart is in the right place – but their head! . . . . The alarming thing is that the story is bound to leak – from French or American sources. It is all the more worrying because our reluctance to accept a bad plan of action may lead the Americans to think that we are 'dragging our feet'. That is not so. We *must* make a stand, at the right place and the right time, with a well-thought out and carefully matured plan. But no one cd call the Dien Bien Phu adventure anything but a last minute 'bright idea' . . . .

28 April

. . . . The F.S. has made a good start in Geneva, and clearly established a sort of 'honest broker' position between East and West. The fact that the late Govt afforded recognition to Communist China may perhaps now prove of some use at Geneva.

I dined with Brendan Bracken, alone. He said that Churchill had taken the decision (a few days ago) to resign when the Queen returned (if Eden was back from Geneva) or anyway at Whitsun. Now he was inclined – in view of the grave international situation – to go on. I said that this wd be impossible, without considerable changes in the Cabinet. There was no drive; no central direction, and no control of the Home side. B agreed instancing the failure to sell the steel business, or the lorries, or to deal with transport, coal etc. He suggested that if Churchill stayed on, I shd become 'Coordinator of Home Front' – as Privy Seal or Ld P[resident] or Minister of State. I said I still thought Churchill ought to go. There was only just time to pull ourselves together and recover the ground which we were losing . . . . Oliver Lyttelton can wait no longer and means to go back to his electrical business at the end of May. It's a great tragedy and ought not to be allowed . . . . Alan Lennox Boyd will have to go to the Colonies, but he is nothing compared with Lyttelton. Monckton ought to be Lord Chancellor. Then Lloyd George (or possible Heathcoat Amory) shd be

Minister of Labour. If Lyttelton wd stay he would be a fine Minister of Defence. Sandys for Board of Trade. Eccles for Housing, combining this with half of Works, and shedding the Museums, Palaces etc, to a revived Commissioner of Works . . . .

4 May

A dreary morning on Standing Ctee. We waded through a couple of clauses. At question time, I announced the new schemes, worked out with the Building Societies and the Local Authorities for reducing the deposit on house purchase to 10% – or for houses of £2000 or less – 5%. I went straight from the House to a Press Conference on the same subject.

5 May

We got a *very* good 'Press' on the new house-ownership scheme.

A very long Cabinet. After much discussion it was decided *not* to proceed (at least at present) with the Teachers Bill . . . .

(That the decision was right was proved later on in the day, for our majority fell to 3!) . . . .

6 May

. . . . Dinner at the Other Club . . . . Much talk about atomic, Hydrogen and Cobalt bombs. Archie Sinclair (walking very badly after his stroke, but quite gay) told the story of Adrian Bethell saying to him in August 1914 (as they embarked for France) 'I say, old chap, we never thought, did we, that it would come to this when we joined the Life Guards!'

14 May

Left on night train for Edinburgh. I am to act as deputy for a deputy at the conference of the Scottish Unionist Party. Churchill 'chucked' because of the Queen; Eden had to stay in Geneva . . . .

15 May

A very successful meeting. My speech 'went well' – indeed, it was the best reception I have ever had. Left on the night train.

16 May

Got to Birch Grove by 9am (by car from Kings Cross) I am utterly exhausted, with a good deal of pain (where my gall bladder used to be and my liver presumably still is) Stayed in bed till luncheon. We are alone, which is good. Read a mass of papers, which had arrived and kept arriving . . . .

20 May

Another 2½ hours on 'Standing Committee'. We got one clause. We have now done 24 clauses out of 72 clauses and 8 schedules! I have had a talk with Ungoed Thomas, Lindgren and co. I am hoping they will agree to finish the Bill in 6 more sessions. If not, we shall have to take sterner measures, or our whole Parliamentary programme will be thrown out of gear. Left on night train for Whitehaven.

21 May

. . . . We started at 10am with visits to Housing estates; slum clearance schemes; new chemical factories; and so forth. Then we went out to Ennerdale Lake – a splendid luncheon, with lake trout, chips, apple tart, cheese and beer at the charming little Anglers Hotel. Then the official opening of the new water scheme, by which the lake water will be taken for the Borough, and esp the new industries which are springing up.

. . . . (The Whitehaven 'fathers' plan to destroy the charming little inn; build a large and vulgar hotel; turn the lake into a lido, and generally 'improve' the landscape. This will, I trust, be prevented by the National Park people and myself and my successors) . . . .

22 May

According to the papers, Eden plans to fly back to London today . . . . [I]t is clear that Eden is making a tremendous effort to get some kind of truce in Indo-China. He is the central figure and Britain the leading country in the Geneva conference. This is good, because so unusual . . . .

24 May

Cabinet at 10am. Eden in great form – clear, effective, sure of himself. He had circulated a paper, which was also much more incisively drafted than the usual F.O. stuff. He thinks there is a fifty-fifty chance of bringing off an armistice or 'cease-fire' in Indo-China.

25 May

. . . . The House of Commons voted last night about members' salaries.

A coalition of the *whole* of the Labour Party and some 30 Conservatives, defeated a motion for 'allowances' in favour of a straight increase of £500pa. This will 'put the cat among the pigeons' . . . .

26 May

. . . . Cabinet at 11am – very long and rather acrimonious. I had sent Churchill a note the night before, asking for a final decision upon Parl salaries to be deferred till Eden's return . . . . Churchill has *not* played the game over this. While nominally supporting the Government's view in favour of an 'allowance' system, and voting for this, he has let it be known that he favours the flat increase. He has talked openly on these lines in the Smoking Room. So the 30 Tory members who voted this way (against all the Government and against Butler's advice) are quoting P.M. as their leader . . . . Butler seemed to favour delay – perhaps till the autumn. But as Churchill wants the increase of salaries to be his parting gift, this wd have the appalling result of delaying his departure. Woolton also wanted delay, at least till we cd do something for old age pensions. P.M. reacted violently against this, tho' strongly in favour of increased old age pensions. Butler pointed out that all the provincial press was in favour of his scheme (allowances) as well as the *Times* and other London papers . . . .

In the afternoon, I went to a meeting of the Conservative Women's Conference. There was a 'housing' resolution, about which I had to speak. After I had left, there was an 'emergency' resolution about MPs' salaries. Mrs Prior-Palmer (wife of a Tory MP) was 'howled down'. All the women were excitedly and violently *against* the rise . . . .

29 May

. . . . I have started on Lord John Russell's '*Life of Charles James Fox*' (3 volumes) . . . . It is not well written, but full of good material. The great thing about old books is that they give the letters, speeches, diaries etc of their bearers. The new professors give us their own theories. At any age, I prefer the former.

Whitsunday, 6 June

This has been a very interesting week, but a very full one. Two meetings of our Standing Committee have us still at clause 43; there are 72 clauses and 8 schedules in the Bill. However, I hope that we may be able to finish in something between 2 and 4 sessions. The trouble is that we depend entirely on the goodwill of the Opposition . . . . The party is torn with bitter wrangles about the MPs' salaries. There is a very strong feeling about the P.M. I have never heard it expressed so openly before. What is particularly resented is his open support of the salary rise – in the smoking room and elsewhere – while the Cabinet was supposed to be united behind an alternative method – expenses etc. We had two Cabinets on Wednesday – morning and evening. The evening Cabinet was entirely devoted to the salary problem. It was arranged by me with Harry Crookshank and the Chief Whip to come out strong *against* . . . . From Churchill's opening phrases, it was clear that he was going to give in. So all seemed easy. It would be just a matter of 'face saving' . . . .

However, we were no sooner safe from Scylla, than we were about to lurch against Charybdis.[13] 'Rab' started to parade his conscience, which (alas) he doesn't treat quite as much *'en bon camarade'*[14] as Winston. According to his account, he had committed himself – and by his own intention, the Government – to *accept* as final the free vote of the House. So he thought it 'dishonourable' to do anything but vote the £1500 salary forthwith.

Lyttelton strongly denied that the Govt had any intention – on that fatal evening – of doing more than seek the freely-expressed opinion of the House for its own guidance. Maxwell-Fyfe strongly supported this. The Lord Chancellor said this was the clear meaning of Butler's speech 'as a whole', whatever some individual phrases might seem to imply. Churchill, rather enjoying all this hair-splitting, rallied to the side of Butler and we were off again.

I weighed in to implore for a course wh wd preserve the unity of the party in the House; and of the Cabinet. We should take no decision today, but reflect on all that had been said. Finally, about 8pm, the Cabinet broke up on this note, having sat for 2 hours. Meanwhile, there are other storms blowing up, among them 'Crichel Down'.[15] We had a long committee again on this, and reached the best conclusions

---

13. In Greek legend Scylla was a sea monster and Charybdis a whirlpool separated by a narrow channel of relative safety.
14. 'As a good friend'.
15. The refusal of Ministry of Agriculture officials to allow the three pre-war owners to buy back this 725 acres of Dorset farmland, compulsorily purchased for an airfield in 1938, became a scandal when their decision was publicly criticized at an inquiry by Sir Arthur Clark QC. The Minister of Agriculture and Fisheries, Sir Thomas Dugdale, was eventually to resign over the affair.

possible, which the Cabinet accepted. The report will be published *after* Whitsun, and the debate follow. I think myself that Tommy Dugdale (Minister of Agriculture) ought to offer his resignation. There is nothing wh the House likes so much as an opportunity to be generous. He wd be universally admired, as a hero. If he tries to 'blarney' it out, I fear that he may be in great trouble. He will then almost certainly be 'dropped' from the next Government. On *Saturday* (June 5th), in high contrast with all these petty internal squabbles, we had a most interesting summary and review of the strange international situation from the Foreign Secretary. He had arrived from Geneva the night before. The Cabinet met at 11am, in an empty Whitehall, in an emptier London. It was a glorious June day, such as only an English June day can be. As far as I can understand it, this is the position (i) The conference cannot do any[thing] but fail on *Korea*. The important thing from our point of view is that we should choose the right issue to break on. Obviously, as in Germany, it should be on 'free elections'.[16] The Americans, so far, don't agree, but probably will. But Korea is not the vital issue. The line is stabilised in Korea. The 'partition' exists, *de facto* if not *de jure*.

(ii) *Indo-China*. Vietnam is ⅚ gone. Free elections wd perhaps result in a victory for the Communists. But if the line could be 'stabilised' in any way, this would avert the disaster which is impending – the fall of Hanoi; possible large-scale massacre of Europeans; collapse of all and any French Governments; bitter recriminations between Britain and US; the fall, in due course, of Laos in north and Cambodia in south, which are by no means Communists but good people; great pressure on Siam and all the rest . . . . If the French were quite sure that the Americans wd not intervene, they wd make a 'standstill' agreement on the best terms they cd get. It seems as if Russia wd use quite a lot of pressure on China and Vietminh[17] to agree. Indeed, if the French had accepted the Colombo Powers as supervisors of the arrangement,[18] the thing could have been clinched

---

16. As a precondition for reunification.

17. The Communist-led Vietnamese nationalist movement founded by Ho Chi Minh in 1941.

18. Eden had wanted the five Colombo powers of India, Pakistan, Ceylon, Burma and Indonesia to supervise the Indo-China armistice. They were so called after the Colombo conference of November 1950 to promote economic development and cooperation in Asia.

this week. But whenever Bidault accepts with his *brain* the realities of the situation, Dulles – sometimes through Bedell Smith, sometimes by other means, tempts and seduces the French heart. They will land 2 or 3 divisions – either of troops or of marines. They will save Indo-China, if the French will stand firm. Of course, the French find the idea that the Americans shd reconquer their colonial empire for them quite agreeable. But the Americans (as Bedell Smith admits) have *no* military plan at all . . . . The Chinese (who are not *officially* at all in the civil war in Vietnam) would certainly react, for they wd naturally feel that the only conceivable American purpose in occupying Indo-China etc was as a base for a war in China. A Chinese reaction, and an appeal to the Russo-Chinese alliance might mean the Third World War. The French alternatively face the facts and think they will settle; then are tempted by American talk, and shrink from a division. At the very moment when Eden was explaining all this, vital and dramatic telegrams from Makins (in Washington) were brought to the Cabinet. From this it seems that Dulles has now decided to 'call his own bluff'. He has delivered a formal note to us, to Canada, to Australia and to N Zealand, which, in effect, says that there will be *no* American intervention by troops etc in *Indo-China*, unless *China* intervenes . . . .

Churchill has for some time been exchanging telegrams with President Eisenhower, suggesting a visit by the P.M. to Washington. He longs to do this (i) because he enormously enjoys these jaunts (ii) because he wants very much to get a good arrangement on atomic secrets etc. He feels strongly about all this. It has now been arranged for about June 20th.

But the Cabinet was (tho' almost mute at first) frankly horrified at the idea of Churchill going off on his own (with Ld Cherwell, who is not even in the Cabinet any longer) on a mission which will certainly be misunderstood or misrepresented. If Geneva is over, Eden must go too. If Geneva is *not* over, Churchill's visit must be postponed . . . .

After all this, there was a short – but constructive talk about home affairs, including the everlasting problem of MPs' salaries. Harry Crookshank had put in a paper, based on a draft which I sent the Chief Whip on Thursday last. This recommended (a) no salary increase as such (b) a London subsistence allowance, based on 4 nights a week while Parliament was in session. Prob[ably] about £230 a year for those who chose to claim it. Butler still seemed hesitant, but obviously intends to bow to the wishes of the Cabinet and the Party. I have a feeling that the worst is over on all this . . . .

I went to the F.O. immediately after luncheon. Eden was in good form and *very* pleasant. He is worried about Clarissa – otherwise he is well and buoyant. He told me that Churchill now means to retire at the end of July . . . .

Tuesday, 15 June
D and I got back to England last night from a week's trip to Germany. We had a very interesting time – first at Bonn and then at Berlin. We stopped for a few hours at Hamburg on the way back. We were the guests of the High Commissioner, Sir Frederick Hoyer Millar. Lady HM was, as well as her husband, a very kind hostess. The main purpose – or at least the official purpose of the visit was to see Housing in Germany. This we did with considerable thoroughness – in the Ruhr, in Berlin and in Hamburg. I was very much impressed by two things – the similarity of the problems in each country, and the generally similar solutions with which each started and were now moving away from. Rent control is even worse in Germany than at home. The worker in Germany is paying only 8% – 9% of his wages as rent. Herr Preusker – the Federal Housing Minister – is contemplating a Bill not unlike our Rent and Repairs Bill. Then the subsidy in Germany, though paid differently, is as large as ours. They subsidise mortgage rates etc, chiefly by the so-called 'tax incentives'. We subsidise by way of the local authorities. This system we hope to deal with a) by reduced, and perhaps by differential subsidies b) by ever increasing 'private enterprise' or unsubsidised building. They are working at similar schemes. As regards technical methods and output, there is not a great deal to learn. The [German] workman works harder and longer hours; but the industry is not so mechanised as ours. Also, they work harder than our people partly because of unemployment (especially in Berlin) Their costs are rather higher than ours; their output is certainly higher. They quite rightly (with the huge size of the gap to be filled) concentrate on number of 'accommodation units', rather than on quality. For, in addition to the loss of homes through bombing, there has been an influx of 10 million refugees into West Germany from the East. They are still coming at the average rate of 300,000 to 400,000 a year.

They have been very clever in using salvaged materials – all the bricks are carefully recovered which can be used again. Some of the rubble is ground down, mixed with cement, and made into a sort of 'breeze block'. What cannot be utilised has been, in many cases, turned into a hill on a flat disused or empty site – covered with soil, and planted with trees . . . .

It is hard to form any very useful judgment in so short a time. But I felt that these people are at once extremely formidable and extremely childish. There lies the danger. They like being 'told'. They like a leader. At present, the Chancellor tells them. He is a good, and much respected, leader. He had impressed upon them a European policy of cooperation with France. But if France finally refuses to play, what happens to Adenauer or his successors? (He is nearly 80 years of age) The other thing wh is alarming is the rather 'smarmy' attitude of some of the business men and administrators towards us. One feels that behind this veneer, there is a good deal of real dislike for us.

Since the 'officer class' and the landed gentry have more or less disappeared – or at least do not come to these sort of parties, one only sees one type. It is as if one came to England and saw chiefly L.C.C. members and officials, as well as some City bankers or merchants. Nevertheless, in spite of all the dangers, I am sure we want the Germans 'on our side' and on the side of decency and freedom. If we all (USA and France with us) play our hand well, it should be possible to keep them looking westward.

Naturally, the partition presents a baffling situation. But it has its corresponding advantages, and we ought to use them fully.

We certainly could not have been received with greater courtesy and often (I felt) genuine pleasure. There is a very good side to these people. It is our job to see that Dr Jekyll remains in possession . . . .

16 June

. . . . There was a dinner at No. 10 for Herr Rabb, Austrian Chancellor. After the guests had left, the P.M. took me into the Cabinet room and began to speak of the future. He had intended to resign in July. But how could he go to negotiate with the President with the sense of only having a few weeks more of power. It would deprive him of authority. Yet we were perhaps coming at last to a climax. After talking with the President, he might be able (with the President's approval) to see Malenkoff. All this would take time. So he would prefer to wait for the changeover till the end of September.

I asked about Lyttelton – who means to go anyway at the end of July. He said it would mean some slight re-shuffle but it could be kept as limited as possible. Lennox-Boyd could go to the Colonies. Would I like Transport. I said I wd do whatever he and Anthony wanted. But

I doubted whether we could *do* very much in 3 months. It was pretty clear to me that this was 'sounding' me, and that he has not yet broken the news to Eden. Of course, if he goes on to September, the next move will be to wait till the Christmas holiday – and so on . . . .

20 June

Church in morning. Maurice and Katie, Julian and Catherine Amery and Sarah Heath are staying in the House. Carol and the Fabers are near – so the family is almost complete. I went to London after dinner, to see Anthony Eden – who returned today from Geneva. We had a useful talk. He is very unhappy about Churchill's indecision.

21 June

. . . . Anthony and Churchill had a bit of a difference about Egypt. A.E. is anxious to renew negotiations or at least give notice of renewal. If we do this *after* Washington, it will seem a concession to American pressure. Churchill goes on about the Sudan. But if (as we all think) we must get the British army out of Egypt, it wd have been better to have started the operation with the support of his prestige. If we do it after he has gone, the Waterhouse–Amerys pressure will be all the harder to withstand . . . .

25 June

. . . . [T]he American press is now more hostile than I can ever remember. The antipathy between Dulles and Eden is becoming more and more a feature of the American–British rift . . . . One of the difficulties is the weakness and amateurishness of the American administration. Eisenhower is a generous and noble figure. But he is not a strong character – perhaps not so strong as Dulles, who has all the old Presbyterian rigidity. The Republicans have put up a poor show against McCarthy. Eisenhower has treated the problem as Charles 2nd treated Titus Oates[19] – let the plague run its course. (But a lot of innocent victims are sacrificed meantime)

. . . . On Thursday, P.M. announced – with great dignity and much forebearance under the storm of abuse which followed – the Govt's decision *not* to increase members' salaries. Attlee was dignified too. We had warned our people to be quiet; they had done the same. But,

---

19. Oates was the fabricator of a supposed conspiracy that led to a wave of anti-Catholic hysteria in the 1670s. Like McCarthy, he was eventually discredited.

of course, their irresponsibles got going and tried to move the adjournment of the House and so on. The Opposition met later in the day, and are said to have refused any alternative – such as expenses in some form or another. If this is true, it will save us a great deal of trouble. We may not have to expose the various weaknesses of our scheme. It is also said that it is to be 'total war' i.e. no 'pairing'. None of this will go well in the country.

25 June [sic]
. . . . Read an amusing and interesting book which I have just acquired '*Anecdotes of the Life of Lord Chatham*'. It's in 3 volumes, published 1797. It gives the best account of the speeches I have ever seen. The speeches are taken from the various reports wh were alone available – a sort of re-write by various compilers who got accounts after the debate in the coffee houses or sometimes managed to get into the gallery. No doubt the diction is often not the speaker's, altho' the arguments are pretty near the original. Some splendid phrases remain, which must be genuine. 'Without their virtue' (that is the true spirit of freedom and constitutionalism of the army) 'should the Lords, the Commons, and the people of England entrench themselves behind parchment up to the teeth, the sword will find a passage to the vitals of the constitution' (Mutiny Bill debate 1748) . . . .

27 June
. . . . According to the Sunday papers, the Washington discussions have made a good start. Churchill has obviously tried to use all his authority and all his charm. Dulles and Eden are back on speaking terms . . . .

28 June
The Opposition are still very angry about the salaries. I am not sure that it is the loss of the money wh worries them most. They thought that we had fallen into the trap! The public would certainly blame the Tories, and whatever may be the argument for and against an increase, the timing cd not have been worse. The Budget of 1954 was, no doubt by intention, a disappointing budget – no relief to any taxpayer and no benefits to any class (e.g. old age pensioners) It would have been a fantasy if the only piece of social reform in this year had been to increase members' salaries by 50%. Meanwhile, the Crichel Down controversy gathers in strength. It hardly seems possible for Dugdale (Minister of Agriculture) to survive. But it will depend more on

Churchill's general intentions than anything else. If he decides to declare the innings closed, Dugdale shd be able to remain 'not out' till the end. *The Times* has a very critical leading article today. 'Too many ministers . . . . have been content in recent years to trot like obedient spaniels at the heels of their advisers'. I have cut this out and sent it to the Secretary (Sir Thomas Sheepshanks)

The following is a quotation from a personal letter to the Secretary of State from the British ambassador in Paris – dated June 19th.

'Hence, though it is perhaps rather too early to say this absolutely definitely, I think we may now assume that EDC, in its present form, is dead. Anyhow, if it were . . . . put to the vote . . . . before the end of July it would almost certainly be rejected'. He goes on (does Sir Gladwyn Jebb) 'The best way. . . . would be for us to say, immediately we come to the conclusion that EDC is really dead, that in principle we are prepared to join with France, with Germany, and with the Low Countries, in a simplified and reconstituted Defence Community designed, within the framework of NATO, to be the bulwark of our defence against Communism in Europe.'

After 2½ years! For this is the gist of my first paper to the Cabinet in Feb 1952. Yet Sir Gladwyn and his like have been all this time telling the opposite story to the Foreign Secretary, and all Europe has been persuaded to live in this world of make-believe . . . .

30 June

Guildhall; Mansion House[20] etc etc for their Swedish majesties. Impressive, but too long. We managed (Harry Crookshank, Lyttelton and I) to slip away about 3pm from the luncheon. D did not get away till 4pm. At 8.45 opera – '*Le Coq d'Or*'[21] by Rimsky-Korsakov – quite good fun, tho' a strange choice, since its purpose is to vindicate monarchy! What with Gloriana for the Coronation and *Le Coq d'Or* for their Swedish majesties, our musical authorities have surpassed themselves.

The Town and Country Planning Bill is causing a lot of trouble. We shall have to 'table' nearly 20pp of amendments. I have had long sessions with our own people and with the Opposition also. I hope this will make Report stage a lot easier.

The P.M. is obviously feeling triumphant. Wherever he has been –

---

20. Official residence of the Lord Mayor of London.
21. 'The Golden Cockerel'.

in Washington and in Ottawa – he has charmed and delighted his audiences . . . . I suspect that there are [a] lot of difficulties wh have been glossed over. We have had little by way of telegrams, except the draft of a new version of the Atlantic Charter.[22] It was full of pitfalls as we received it – with that dreadful word 'self-determination' and other phrases which cd be used against the Colonial Empire. However, all the Cabinet amendments were in fact accepted by the Americans . . . .

The new order about Housing Subsidies was published today (June 30th) It 'cuts' the subsidy by the amount of the fall in the Bank Rate and Public Works Loan Board rate – or thereabouts. But it does *not* become effective till April 1955 (which is generous)

2 July

D and I went to a dance at Petworth.[25] We stayed till 3am. The house looked quite lovely. The ball was a tremendous success and seemed like a return (for a few hours) almost to the pre-1914 world. Many old friends – from all over England; all the jewels out of the banks (or out of pawn) champagne; two bands (dancing indoors and out) and the glorious pictures, statues, furniture – all looking superb. It was really a most welcome change from drab political life . . . .

5 July

Our Housing programme is going on well. We shall get well over 350,000 this year, of which 100,000 will be unsubsidised. Next year, I hope for 150,000 unsubsidised. The Chief Whip told me tonight that he thinks Churchill has decided to stay till January! It is queer how these dates continually move forward. My row with him (only a week or two ago) was about September! . . . .

10 July (Sat)

I got down to Birch Grove for luncheon and afterwards went to bed, quite exhausted. These last 4 days have been the most extraordinary which I can remember since the Govt was formed – or indeed at any time which I can recall.

---

22. The result of Churchill's meeting with Roosevelt in August 1941, this document denounced territorial aggression, called for the restoration of self-government for occupied Europe, and proposed various forms of international cooperation.
23. John Wyndham's stately home in Sussex.

Tuesday 6 July

I got back early from the House, after the 10 o'clock division. I was just getting into bed, when the telephone rang in the flat. Could I go to No 10 at once. I asked to be excused, thinking it was just a party to welcome the P.M. and the For Sec and nothing wd happen but cigars, whisky, and desultory talk. However, a message came back 'The P.M. wd be greatly obliged if you cd come'. So I dressed and went. In the Cabinet room were the P.M., Eden, Salisbury, and Butler. The atmosphere was rather strained. I sensed at once that 'something was up'. I was then given two telegrams to read – the first, a telegram despatched from the ship (they came back by ship, not by air) from Churchill to Molotov. This suggested, in rather too fulsome terms, a meeting between himself and Malenkov and his principal colleagues. The telegram made it clear that the Americans were not committed. It could only be a 2 Power meeting to start with. But it might develop into a 3 Power meeting. The question of time and place would have to be settled, but this was a preliminary enquiry to find out what the Russians wd feel, *before* despatching an official suggestion. The second telegram was Molotov's reply. This was very cordial but a little puzzled (I thought) . . . .

In addition, in this file, there was the first draft of the telegram to Molotov, sent from the boat to Butler; his reply, with some drafting amendments. There was another impatient telegram from the ship to Butler (which crossed his reply with amendments) demanding to know whether the Molotov telegram had been sent off.

When I had read the telegrams, (or while I was reading them) the talk turned about the President. To my horror, I learned that the President knew nothing about all this – altho' the P.M. had been his guest only a few days before. In the course of that evening (for we went from Downing Street just after midnight to the F.O., where Anthony explained what had happened to Bobbety Salisbury and myself) I was able to piece the whole story together, partly from things the P.M. said – more or less in self-defence – partly from Eden's account. Further corroboration has come from Colville (P.M.'s private secretary) and others. Ever since the famous – and perhaps fatal, anyway fateful speech of May 11th 1953, Churchill has never concealed his determination to make a journey for a meeting with Russian statesmen, the successors to Stalin . . . .

He would, of course, prefer a 3 Power meeting, or even a 4 Power meeting. But, if that is impossible, he wants a 2 Power meeting. He has repeated this several times in the HofCommons. He repeated it to the President, who said that he (the President) would not come, but still it was Churchill's affair. P.M. says that the President was not 'shocked'. He even spoke of the possibility, in certain circumstances, of his joining a meeting in London . . . .

All this seems very queer. I learned subsequently from Harold Caccia (deputy under-secretary F.O.) who was in Washington, that some such conversation did take place, but that Eisenhower treated it all rather lightly, if not jocularly. He hates all these telegrams and visits from Churchill, and is acutely embarrassed by them. However, since it seems that Eisenhower passionately wants to be asked by the Queen to a State visit to London, there is this simple explanation of his rather light references to the matter. It will not be for the *beaux yeux*[24] either of Malenkov or of Churchill that Eisenhower may come to London, but for the Queen's! . . . .

Once safely on the sea, away from the Americans and the British Embassy and not yet subject to the pressure of the London Cabinet and the Foreign Office, Churchill decided to act. He drafted the Molotov telegram – in rather more unsuitable and sentimental terms than the form which ultimately went, but substantially the same. He was induced by his personal staff to show it to Anthony Eden. He objected in the strongest terms. They wrangled for hours. For one whole day they refused to meet. All communication was by written minute, from one 'suite' on the ship to another. Colville and Christopher Soames (who urged delay) were almost 'thrown out of the port hole' (Colville's words) At last, under the pressure of the tremendous force of this old man's character, Eden gave way – at least to this extent. He did not say 'I will resign if you send that telegram, it will be contrary to the advice of your Foreign Secretary'. That was enough for Churchill! However, Eden made a desperate effort, which only failed by mischance. He was able to secure that the Molotov telegram should not be sent to Moscow until the text had been sent to Butler. This was done. It reached Butler on Saturday afternoon (July 3), 'personal and very secret'. He assumed it to be for himself only. Eden thought he would impart it to the Cabinet. Butler sent back some suggested amendments. Since his telegram with the alterations crossed with an imperious telegram from P.M. 'Has my telegram to Molotov been despatched. It must go at once', he was justified in concluding

---

24. 'Beautiful eyes'.

17. Macmillan and John Foster Dulles, 10 May 1955, at the NATO meeting in Paris.

18. The signing of the Austrian State Treaty in the Belvedere Palace, Vienna, 15 May 1955, with Dulles far left, Molotov signing, Macmillan leaning forward and Pinay far right.

19. An undated picture, probably from the 1955 general election, shows (left to right) Iain Macleod, Rab Butler, Anthony Eden and Macmillan with interviewer Leslie Mitchell at the BBC's Lime Grove Studios.

20. 'Ah, Harold, sometimes I think back to the good old days when I dealt with *foreign* affairs . . . ' – The cartoonist Vicky in the Labour-supporting *Daily Mirror* 15 June 1955) clearly shared Macmillan's apprehensions that Eden sought to be his own Foreign Secretary.

"AH HAROLD, SOMETIMES I THINK BACK TO THE GOOD OLD DAYS WHEN I DEALT WITH <u>FOREIGN</u> AFFAIRS . . . "

21. Western ministers meet in New York, 20 June 1955. Left to right are John Foster Dulles, Macmillan, Konrad Adenauer and Antoine Pinay.

22. Opening the Cyprus talks at Lancaster House in London on 29 August 1955. On Macmillan's left is Stephanos Stephanopoulos and on his right F. R. Zorlu.

23. 'One moment everybody – the Foreign Secretary has had a terrible, terrible shock!' – Michael Cummings' view, in the imperially minded *Daily Express*, of the Cyprus imbroglio on 8 September 1955.

24. 'Spirit of Geneva – are *you* there?' – A satirical view of the Geneva spirit of détente from Vicky in the *Daily Mirror* on 24 October 1955.

25. 'Sensation at the big top. Swapping horses in the mid-stream.'
Vicky's reaction to Macmillan's switch to the Treasury, in the *Daily Mirror*,
22 December 1955.

26. Macmillan leaves 11 Downing Street to go and deliver his Budget speech,
17 April 1956.

27. Chancellor Macmillan buys a National Savings Certificate from Lord Mackintosh, 31 July 1956.

28. A shooting party on the grouse moors above Bolton Abbey, 13 August 1956, in a few days' respite from the Suez Crisis. On horseback are Macmillan and the Duchess of Devonshire, whilst the Duke of Devonshire is the walker on the far left.

29. In the gardens at Birch Grove, summer 1956, with Lady Dorothy and the (then) nine grandchildren who are, left to right, Joshua Macmillan, Adam Macmillan, Louise Amery, Theresa Amery, Anne Faber, Alexander Macmillan, Rachel Macmillan, Michael Faber and Mark Faber.

30. An emphatic moment at the Conservative Party Conference at Llandudno, 22 October 1956. The *Picture Post* caption commented that the Conference made clear 'that Sir Anthony Eden now stands unchallenged and unchallengeable as leader of the party'.

31. Macmillan launches the
new Premium Bonds,
1 November 1956.

32. Chancellor
Macmillan en route
to the Commons
to make a statement
on the cost of the
Suez venture,
4 December 1956.

that Eden had agreed this plan, and took no further action himself. Of course, it never even occurred to him that the President had not been informed. Eden made two serious errors. He ought to have said 'I will resign, if you send that telegram', or – 'I will resign if you send that telegram without informing and securing consent of the Cabinet' or 'I will resign if you send that telegram without at least informing the President'. But he allowed P.M. to overwhelm him, partly with the strength and partly with the weakness of his appeal. He was absolutely determined; nothing would shake him; he would go on alone; if his colleagues abandoned him, he would appeal to the country, who would support him. All this from strength. It was his last passionate wish – an old man's dream – an old man's folly, perhaps, but it might save the world . . . .

. . . . The curious thing is that he has made no plan as to what he will talk about. He is, of course, physically and mentally incapable of a serious negotiation. In Washington or in Ottawa, among friends, they tolerate the endless repetitions and the frightful waste of time, out of loyalty and respect. (Although Eisenhower did say to Eden 'I don't understand how you do any business at all') But with the Russians up against him, he would, of course, be absolutely lost.

I return now to the story of Tuesday evening. It had been a hard day – starting with a Cabinet under Butler, where we finally settled the Members' Pay solution – and with the usual routine of meetings, discussions, paper all through till the House rose at 10am. Eden looked very tired; Rab was sleepy; Salisbury was clearly much upset. The purpose of our being summoned was ostensibly to help to draft a telegram to the President. I think it was really to try to lessen the shock to the Cabinet by breaking it first to the leading members. Churchill was of course in a fine tactical position. Eden is committed; Butler also – they are both 'accessories before the crime'. Now Salisbury and I am made 'accessories after'. One cannot very well make a loud protest at midnight in the Cabinet room. One can't walk out. Anyway, the harm is done. We must try to minimise it. Moreover, there is the undoubted fact that the British people wd applaud the gesture. Owing to all the faults of Dulles, McCarthy and co, even moderate opinion in UK has become more and more anti-American. Of course it will suit the Russians to exploit the position to the full. After a great deal of talk a fairly simple telegram was compiled to the President, giving a précis of Churchill's telegram to Molotov and Molotov's reply in full. Churchill, of course, says that he is confident that the President will quite understand the position. When they had discussed it, Dulles had said 'You are to be a go-between?' 'No' replied Churchill. 'For I know on which side I stand. I will be a "reconnoitring patrol"'. Anyway, Eisenhower always said 'You have a perfect right to act alone'. Churchill accepts, according to his own account, that his will be a 'solitary pilgrimage'. But if he fails, there is no great loss (That, of course, is where he is wrong) . . . .

On Wed 7 July. . . .

At 11.30am the Cabinet met. There was a good deal of business, before we came to the 'bomb-shell'. It was rather dramatic. Eden; Butler; Salisbury and I knew what was coming. The others, blithely unconscious, were full of congratulations and praise on the success of the Canadian visit. Members' expenses, in the form finally agreed, were reported on . . . .

Next Egypt. The whole Cabinet unanimously agreed the new proposal, which the Americans have also undertaken to support diplomatically – and with American 'aid' – in Cairo. We try for 20 years, and hope for 12.[25] We shall try to include Persia, and expect to get Turkey (that is, the right to re-activate the base if these countries are attacked. At present, the list only contains Egypt herself, and the Arab League countries) The troops will leave [the Canal Zone] *altogether* – not even a brigade will be left behind. The base will be looked after by civilian contractors.

On the political side, it was asked what was the strength of the Waterhouse group. Perhaps 40? But the Chief Whip felt that many could be appealed to by argument – especially the overwhelming military argument. There would, of course, remain a hard core.

Churchill said that there was a completely new military situation. First, the right wing of NATO now rested on Turkey and even on Pakistan. Secondly, in an *atomic* war, it had been really unlikely that the Russians wd be able to drive south through the Middle East. In a *hydrogen* war, it was impossible to conceive that they should be able to do so, or that we could 'reopen' the base and send troops to operate from there. The value of the base was doubtful – at least till the

---

25. The agreement finally signed with the Egyptians in October 1954 was only for seven years, during which time civilian technicians were to maintain the base in case of an emergency need for the British to re-occupy it (an attack on an Arab state or Turkey).

thermo-nuclear phase of the war had been settled one way or the other. Meanwhile, the army was rotting away on the Suez Canal, at a cost of £50 millions a year. There was nothing to do; no real training; men were being killed;[26] there were no amenities (in the narrower or the more expansive sense of the word) He (Churchill) wd defend the new proposals, on purely military grounds, whether in or out of office.

FM Lord Alexander strongly supported this view, as did the Chiefs of Staff. It was well known (said Ld A) to all serious soldiers. P.M. said that both FM Lord Montgomery and General Keightley held this view also . . . .

So far all went well. But at about twenty minutes to 1, the P.M. began to unfold his tale. He was obviously nervous. He prefaced it by an account of how he had chaffed the Americans about Guatemala.[27] 'You must have been studying the Jamieson Raid'[28] he told them. As he proceeded, the general look of blank surprise was strange to see. Harry Crookshank sits (on the P.M.'s side) opposite me. His look of disgust was a picture! After P.M. had finished, he asked Eden to say something. Eden said there were obviously great dangers. First, the reaction in USA itself if the plan were followed out; secondly the effect on Germany; thirdly, the effect on France. The first, the P.M.'s personal prestige and the affection felt for him might carry. But the effects in Europe were really more dangerous. (With great chivalry, Eden did not actually say that he had opposed the whole idea) Salisbury, who spoke with a very tense [sic] and carefully prepared phrases, said he thought the Cabinet should reserve the discussion until the President's reply was known. This was agreed. I suggested that the full text of the telegrams shd be circulated to the Cabinet in the special secret box. This was agreed. Then followed a most extraordinary scene. It was by now about 1.20pm. Ld Cherwell had been asked to attend to tell the Cabinet what had happened at Washington in connection with the exchange of information on thermo-nuclear matters, as far as and even a little farther than the law allowed. This he did. It all appeared very satisfactory. Then P.M. [dropped] his second bomb. He told us that the decision had been taken to make the hydrogen bomb in England, and the preliminaries were in hand. Harry Crookshank at once made

---

26. Five British servicemen were killed in spring 1954 in the Canal Zone by Egyptian terrorists.
27. A reference to the recent CIA-backed coup.
28. The failed incursion into the Boer republics in 1895.

a most vigorous protest at such a momentous decision being communicated to the Cabinet in so cavalier a way, and started to walk out of the room. We all did the same and the Cabinet broke up – if not in disorder – in a somewhat ragged fashion. Walter Monckton and Woolton seemed especially shocked! Not, I think, at the decision, (which is probably right) but at the odd way in which things are being done. At 8.15 on this same evening (July 7th) I dined at No 10; a party in honour of Ld Ismay . . . . After dinner, I had a talk with Colville. He told me a good deal of the story of the Molotov telegram (already recorded) and the drama on the ship. He asked me what I thought the effect on the Cabinet had been. I said 'Terrible'. He said 'The P.M. has definitely decided to resign in the middle of September and has so informed Eden'. I said 'But the Government, and probably the Party will have broken up before that. He must go at once, on grounds of health, to avoid a disaster.' He said 'You are very severe'. I said 'As you know, I am devoted to Winston and admire him more than any man. But he is not fit. He cannot function. If there were a strong monarch, of great experience, he would be told so by the Palace.' He said, 'What will happen in Cabinet tomorrow'. I said 'I beg of you to urge him not to try to ride this one off too easily. He must take it seriously and realise how deeply he has hurt us'.

8 July

Cabinet met at 11.30am. We began on the hydrogen bomb. P.M. said that only the first preliminaries were decided. It was, we recognised, a hideous decision. He wd ask Lord S to state the position, since he was responsible, as Lord President, for these developments. This he did. A short, but valuable, discussion followed. Lord Chancellor could see no *moral* distinction between the atomic and the hydrogen – but it was none the less a grave collective decision to make. Monckton agreed. So did Swinton and Stuart. Harry Crookshank was asked to speak first and rather 'put on the spot' by Churchill. But he had not really criticised the actual decision, but the manner of making it and telling the Cabinet. When it came to my turn, I strongly supported Harry (for which he was grateful) I thought the decision too grave to be taken by 3 or 4 ministers, without informing the others. Either we were a responsible Cabinet or not. Anyway, what were we going to say about this? So far the P.M. had got away by answering a P.Q. on the subject that 'it would not be in the public interest etc'. Will this last? How many people will know?

P.M. then suggested that we should take a fortnight to think it over. This was agreed. P.M. then read Eisenhower's reply. It was a polite, but a 'dusty' answer. It started 'you have certainly not let the grass grow under your feet etc'. It was a fine answer – generous and noble, but clearly refusing to accept any responsibility. He was particularly worried about the date – a day or two after leaving Washington and yet no prior warning from the P.M. . . . . P.M. read us his reply, a soft answer trying to turn away wrath. 'Dear friend: I am very sorry you are vexed with me' it began. P.M. takes the full responsibility. He is 'expendable'; his will be the 'solitary pilgrimage' etc etc. Eden has already been working on Churchill. Moscow seems less likely. Why not propose Stockholm or Vienna. Either would be good. Or Berne? Berne would be good. Anywhere, if he can only see his Malenkov and carry out his great plan. Of course, the 2 Power must lead on to the 3 Power – or 4 Power (including France) He will suggest that Russia shd make a great gesture of good faith. She will sign the Austrian treaty, which is all agreed. Then Eisenhower will come to London. So the old man's dream will come true. (Meanwhile, he has of course forgotten that the Russians will certainly ask for a 5 power meeting – that is, China)

The Cabinet were very quiet, but rather grim . . . . Eden said nothing. The Cabinet ended, on the understanding that no action towards Molotov shd be taken until the President replied to Churchill's reply . . . .

9 July (Friday)
. . . . [A]t 12.30, Cabinet. This was held in the P.M.'s room in the HofCommons. It was the most dramatic Cabinet which I have attended. I should have stated that the chief discussion yesterday was not on the merits of the Molotov telegram but on the action of the P.M. He had really given this turn to the discussion, by a very firm statement of his view. He claimed the right to correspond direct with heads of state or government abroad, so long as the Foreign Secy was fully informed. (Here, of course, he had poor Eden in a trap. He *had* been informed and had allowed the telegram to go – altho' it only got past Butler in error) He could not continue as head of a Government which denied him that right. Much of the debate or discussion yesterday was on the corresponding duty of ministers either to accept the corresponding collective responsibility, or to resign. It is, of course, the Chamberlain issue again. It is curious that Eden shd have to suffer this treatment from 2 Prime Ministers, at intervals!

. . . . The President's telegram in reply to the P.M.'s reply was a masterpiece. He scarcely referred to the Russian visit . . . .

The whole of the rest of the telegram was to beseech Churchill, whatever he might do about his Russian meeting, not to urge or even allow by default the admission of China to U. Nations. Since this does not interest Churchill at all, not being related to his Russian mono-mania, he is not at all put out and claims the President's reply as altogether satisfactory.

When he had read this out (with comments) Salisbury opened the discussion. The pros and cons of the telegram to Moscow he wd not discuss. But he was concerned with the method. Of course, he accepted the right of the P.M. to communicate with heads of state or of Govts. But this involved, as the P.M. wd be the first to admit, a corresponding obligation upon other members of the Cabinet either to accept the collective responsibility or to resign. In this case, the P.M. had chosen an unfortunate moment. Two days at sea, he had left the President uninformed. Two days from home, he had kept his colleagues in the dark. He (Salisbury) had the special task, as Leader of the House of Lords, of expounding and defending Govt policy. To do so properly, he must believe in it. He could not undertake to expound or defend this plan. If therefore it was pursued, he must leave the Govt. Churchill was very much moved. At one moment his face went dead white – at the next it was puce. I really thought he was going to have another stroke. As Salisbury spoke, there was a tense, dramatic silence. When he finished nobody spoke. After a few moments, P.M. said – with great dignity and much emotion – 'I should deeply regret a severance. But I hope our private friendship wd survive'.

Later on, Eden expounded the theme that perhaps everything still depended on Geneva . . . .

Any 'settlement' in Indo-China meant the loss of Hanoi. The only question was, wd it be conquered or ceded. As regards a general ceasefire, there was one line proposed, favourable to the Vietminh. Another, further north, favourable to France and Vietnam. The Americans might agree to accept one, but not the other . . . .

. . . . At 2.30, a meeting with Butler, Thorneycroft and Swinton on immense questions – the monetary and trade policy of UK. Or, in other words, (i) shd we have a convertible currency (ii) shd we denounce GATT or stay in it. All to be settled in half an hour! I'm afraid I rather ridiculed the whole meeting, and everyone joined in agreeing that we just couldn't talk about it at the moment. A Salisbury resignation is bound to disintegrate the Govt. All these academic discussions seemed very unreal.

After this, I had a stiff hour with my advisers on the vast mass of amendments which are necessary for the report stage of the Town and Country Planning Bill. It was difficult to keep my mind on these intricate and very technical problems.

At 4.45 I went to F.O to see Eden (at his request) He was very charming, but obviously very worried. Churchill has begun to get him down again. He knows, in his heart, that he ought to have resigned on the boat . . . .

. . . . We talked over the Salisbury position and it seemed that the most important thing was to try to hold this for the present. I undertook to see Bobbety (Salisbury) at once.

So I went back to the Ministry; rang Hatfield[29] (where S had gone); finished my work at the Ministry, and set off for Hatfield by car, arriving about 7pm. We had a long and useful talk before dinner. This is the problem into which Churchill has landed us

1. *If Churchill goes* to Moscow (except with approval of the President) Salisbury goes.

2. If Salisbury goes, the Govt breaks up under the worst possible conditions.

3. *If Churchill doesn't go*, the Russians can blackmail us at any time they like, by leaking the invitation. It's a sort of Zinoviev letter[30] in reverse.

for a) it will be said that Peace-Maker Churchill was prevented from saving the peace of the world by his reactionary Tory colleagues

or b) that the British Govt – including Churchill – gave up the peace on American orders.

It follows that *we* must get into a position where we would not mind a leak or wd leak ourselves.

It seems certain that Molotov will ask Eden at Geneva[31] about the Moscow visit. E will have to say that it must to some extent depend on the outcome of Geneva. If the Russians and Chinese are very intransigent, we might be able to get out of the whole thing. If it goes

---

29. Hatfield House, Hertfordshire, the country seat of the Marquesses of Salisbury.
30. The Zinoviev letter was allegedly written by the head of the Comintern to the Communist Party of Great Britain, calling on them to foment dissension in the armed forces. It was published to great effect just before the 1924 general election.
31. The conference on the future of Indo-China.

very well, we might propose Geneva or Berne as an *immediate* follow up.

I begged Salisbury to hold his hand until Geneva became more clear or perhaps Eden returned to report to the Cabinet. This he more or less agreed to do. He gave me a *firm* undertaking that he would not resign without talking again to *me*. This at least is satisfactory. Dined at Hatfield, with Bobbety and Betty. Motored back to London and went to bed (exhausted) about 1am, as there was a lot of stuff from the Ministry to get finished.

10 July
Harold Caccia (who used to be with me . . . . in Algiers and Italy) rang me at the flat. He wished to see me. He came to the Ministry about 10.15am. He told me his version of the whole story (from which I was able to fill in some of the gaps) We discussed the best tactics to pursue (or for his beloved chief Eden to pursue) as regards a) the Americans b) the Russians c) Salisbury d) Churchill . . . .

Harold C told me that he had heard a vague rumour that the Queen was considering some intervention to get Churchill to resign. I told him that I had discussed with S[alisbury] the possibility of four or five of us going to the Queen. (S said that it was such a pity not to have 'Tommy' [Alan] Lascelles)

I left the Ministry at 11.30am and came home by train. In thinking all this over, I am persuaded that Churchill is now quite incapable – mentally, as well as physically, of remaining Prime Minister. Like many men who have had their strokes, his judgment is distorted. He thinks about one thing all the time – this Russian visit and his chance of saving the world – till it has become an obsession . . . . Of course, with his brilliance and charm and gallantry and astonishing resilience, he can still put in a performance – parliamentary questions, an after-dinner speech (as at the Ismay dinner, when he made a charming little address to Pug) or even a press conference (as at Washington) But it's a tremendous effort and takes more and more out of him. For a great part of the day, he doesn't really function. He postpones everything he can, so that the machine of Govt is retarded and clogged . . . .

13 July
Cabinet at 11.30. P.M. read two telegrams, which have since (like the others) been circulated in the special box. Eden had [had] a talk with Molotov.

(i) He broke to him that C[hurchill] wd not want to go to Moscow. What about Berne, after a happy finish to Geneva.

(ii) There must be a good finish to Geneva. M[olotov] did not seem unduly put out, altho' he said they wd prefer somewhere in the Soviet Union. It is not clear (a) whether the Russians have really thought much about the details or (b) whether they are so pleased at this 'wedge' that they will agree to anything. Eden seems to have mentioned London, as well as Berne. The advantage of London wd be that the President might come after all!

The second telegram was from Eisenhower. He is very friendly, and promises to do his best to 'minimise' the effect on American opinion. I thought the general feeling in the Cabinet was one of relief. But S looked glum and worried . . . .

14 July

Crichel Down was discussed at yesterday's Cabinet and a small committee (of wh I fortunately am *not* one) appointed to write or 'vet' the Minister's speech. He wd have been much better advised to resign.

Lunched with Lord S[alisbury]. As I rather feared, he has determined to resign. This is partly on the ground that he does not like the Russian visit and its reactions on the Anglo-American alliance, partly that he feels that the Prime Minister's methods (like Neville Chamberlain's and Lloyd George's) are intolerable and destructive of full Cabinet responsibility. This is very awkward, but (as I did not oppose his decision too strongly) I felt that he was not too sure of its wisdom. He promised to write to Eden first – this he will do tonight . . . .

16 July

10am to 12 noon. The longest meeting of the Home Affairs Committee that I can remember. It is hoped next session to abolish altogether the War Emergency Regulations and the power of making them in the future. In other words, to revert to government by the established law of the land, instead of Government by decree (or Order in Council or Regulation or call it what you will) But this involves embodying into the statute law certain necessary powers – such as compulsory purchase of land for certain purposes. Such legislation will be particularly tricky in the atmosphere of Crichel Down.

At noon I went to see Lady Churchill (Clemmy) I told her about the Salisbury situation, and discussed with her generally the whole problem. She was charming, and pleased to know accurately what she had only heard partly by rumour and partly by what Winston had told her. She has for a long time thought that Winston ought to resign. Indeed, the strain of it all has made her ill. She feels that he ought to go; but he is like a child in many ways. If he wants something, he must have it. This Russian visit has been a sort of obsession for a long time. She would speak to Winston at luncheon . . . .

Churchill rang up just as I was leaving; so I went along. I found him in the drawing room at No. 10, playing bezique with Jock Colville. He plunged into a long and often violent defence of his conduct. (He was obviously conscious that it was indefensible!) He had a perfect right to send 'private and personal' messages. The Foreign Secretary had agreed; so had the Chancellor of the Ex to the Molotov telegram. In any case, the whole public would support him. If Salisbury, Crookshank or any others resigned, he would form another and more powerful administration. He was now far better in health, quite capable of going on indefinitely and leading the party into the next election. It was only his affection for Eden that made him even contemplate resignation before the General Election. Salisbury's resignation would be as foolish and ill-timed as was his father's (Randolph Churchill's)[32] Now he held all the cards. The public cared nothing for these constitutional niceties. The issue would be – 'Is a top-level talk with Malenkov a good thing or not?' Of course, on this issue he was impregnable. He would express no regret to S or to the Cabinet. After about an hour of this sort of thing, repeated over and over again, and with special reference to the weakness of Salisbury's position (who had himself been party to concealment from the Cabinet of just as grave a matter – indeed far *more* grave a matter (the hydrogen bomb) than a paltry telegram) he began to calm down.

I forced him to admit that these resignations would do us much injury, esp with so many other weak points – from Crichel Down to Suez. 'What do you want me to do? Resign myself?' 'I will never apologise to S or anyone. Do you understand?'

After he had talked all the time for about ¾ hour (with some very fine and eloquent passages about War, Peace, Russia, the future of the World etc) Clemmy came in. She made him listen a little, while I told him just how matters stood and what I had done, including my letter to Eden. While we were talking a message came from Eden, of a personal character. Molotov had said nothing more about the

32. From the Chancellorship of the Exchequer in 1887.

Churchill visit; the conference was going very badly, with the Communists very intransigent. 'If Geneva succeeds, the Russian visit is made easier. If it fails, it becomes all the more necessary'.

P.M. was very nice and took quite well some pretty tough things wh I said (whenever I got the chance!) e.g. that he treated his Cabinet very badly, that he should inform us of the date of his resignation; that it should be *before* the Party Conference in October. The only way that I can find to treat him is in a half-bantering way, with a good deal of chaff. As I went out, Clemmy followed me. She expressed great gratitude. I thought she was going to break down. The whole thing is obviously a very heavy burden on her. His resignation will be her liberation . . . .

18 July
Woke early; read and wrote my diary. Really, this has been a very strange week. It would be stranger still if the public knew what was going on. Curiously, the press has got very little – so far . . . .

20 July
A fairly quiet Cabinet, but a very long agenda. The great question is being postponed till Eden returns. The Geneva conference has ended in a settlement far more satisfactory than one could have hoped. Laos and Cambodia are given a chance to live a separate non-Communist life. Vietnam is partitioned – the French leave Hanoi and the north – rather a tragic event for the great Catholic community. But they could not have held on, and retreat or evacuation is better than a massacre. The south (including all Cochin China) remains free. But there is a general expectation that at the elections which are to be held in 2 years time the south will vote 'nationalist' or 'communist', unless some local figure can be built up on the other side. The Americans will 'respect' the agreement, tho' standing aloof from the struggle to get it – all this fell on Eden. He must have worked with extraordinary patience and skill. Altho' there are already some murmurs of 'Munich' (foolish, because there is no parallel at all) yet I think Eden's prestige and authority will be much increased.

A typical House of Commons day. At the morning Cabinet, Dugdale told us that he proposed to offer his resignation and make the announcement at the end of his speech. It is very sad (for he has been a charming and loyal colleague) but absolutely right and in accordance with the best tradition. In the House – for the secret was well kept –

there was a curious gasp of astonishment and dismay when he announced this at the end of a long and excellent speech. The speech gave an account of the past; a defence, but not a self-justification of his actions; the decision taken about the civil servants concerned (wise and firm but not savage or unfair) the policy that wd be followed about the disposal of land in the future. All this, of course, had been carefully prepared by a strong committee of Ministers, under the Home Secretary, and was the best speech that Tommy Dugdale has ever made.

He is such a particularly open, honourable and popular figure that even the hunters seemed a little taken aback. I remember when Dalton resigned, Nigel Birch called out 'Oh Lord – they've shot our fox!'[33] I think the 1922 pack (that is, the leading spirits in the 1922 or back-benchers committee) have the same feeling now . . . .

21 July

A very long day . . . . A debate at 3.30 on 'Old Age Pensions' initiated by the Opposition. Dr Summerskill opened with a short and unexpec-tedly moderate (though rather acid) speech . . . . The whole debate was pure politics (or impure politics) The Opposition know that the statutory quinquennial valuation is going on, as well as the important investigation under Sir Thomas Philipps (with Trade Unions giving evidence etc) They also know that we shall almost certainly be putting the pension up in a few months. So they demand 'immediate' action; force the Tories to vote against it – and hope to have useful ammu-nition for the Election. I was told on Monday night to 'wind up' the debate for the Govt – the under-secretaries being hardly strong enough.

After sitting through rather a dreary debate, ending in a splendidly old-fashioned, sob-stuff, insincere speech by Jim Griffiths (it would have made a Welsh audience hysterical with false emotion) I got up at 9.30. It was a good 'debating' reply – generally voted the best I have done. The Opposition listened pretty well, considering how severely I trounced them. They reached just the degree of noise and disorder one wants to provoke on such an occasion, without ever getting out of hand. I had one or two phrases, which seemed to please the House. After describing Griffiths' declaration in 1946 'the Chancellor of the Exchequer *intends* to keep the cost of living 31% above 1939' and

---

33. Dalton resigned as Chancellor of the Exchequer on 13 November 1947 after an indiscretion to the press about the Budget.

playing around with his absurdly unsuccessful and boastful promise, (the figure rose rapidly to 70%) I exclaimed 'Unlucky statesmen! They missed their vocation. They should have been cast as Courtiers to Canute!'[34] We won by 30 votes. It is always easy to tell when one can be severe and even wounding in reply. It is when they know in their hearts that they are just 'playing politics'. Then they do not at all resent – indeed they rather enjoy a good stinging reply. Many Socialist members came up to me afterwards with congratulations. But when they *really* feel deeply about something, one shd not offend their susceptibilities. It's quite easy to tell – from their faces. Happily, these occasions are very rare. We won by 30 or so – good, considering that the Liberals were hostile or neutral.

23 July

.... Cabinet at 11am (in P.M.'s room at HofCommons) lasting for 2½ hours. A most painful morning, even shattering.

P.M. I will now ask the Cabinet for approval for the following telegram to M Molotov – copies are before you.

The telegram was then read out, and we followed it, like schoolboys, from the text which we were given for the lesson. It was taken away afterwards, as too dangerous ....

There was no interval for silence, as often occurs. Salisbury took up the argument at once. He spoke from notes, carefully prepared, with restraint, but white and tense. He reverted to the domestic question, as he called it – the constitutional propriety in the P.M.'s sending the first telegram from the ship. He maintained vigorously, but courteously, his view of this matter.

He then passed to the international aspect. He felt that, by a curious paradox, during the next few years the danger to the peace of the world came from America, not Russia. Russia knew that she could be attacked with terrible power by America, with no power of retaliation (except in Europe) America knew that for an interval of some years, she herself was safe. She might be tempted or provoked into rash action. If we were to act alone, without full agreement with US Govt, sending secret messages to the Russians and generally going behind the backs of our ally, what wd be the effect of public opinion in America. There was a new fact wh had emerged since our meeting.

---

34. According to legend, Canute (or Cnut, King of England 1016–35) reprimanded his flattering courtiers by showing that the tide would not turn at his command.

The Moscow Govt had put out an official statement of the situation after Geneva. This maintained all the positions taken at the Berlin conference, and ended with a violent attack on America.

P.M. I altogether deny that American Govt has been kept in the dark. I discussed this in full as a possible action of mine, when in Washington. Dulles called me a 'go-between'. Eisenhower called it 'a noble experiment' in his telegram. His telegram of July 13th pledges him to do all he can to calm American opinion.

On the constitutional question, I absolutely deny the validity of Lord Salisbury's argument. I have always, in all my years as P.M. claimed the right to correspond with Heads of State or Heads of Government, friendly or unfriendly. I could not relinquish this right. Of course, I have always acted after full consultation with the Foreign Secretary, and with his agreement.

Eden You really cannot say this. You know that I did everything possible to dissuade you for one whole day at least on the voyage. I told you that if you sent the telegram 'it would be against the advice of the Foreign Secretary'. I told you that it ought to be referred to the Cabinet. What else could I do? Resign on board the ship, I suppose? (I have never known Anthony make such an outburst in public. The fact is that being a man of the highest integrity, he was really shocked at Winston's *suppressio veri, suggestio falsi.*[35] He told me afterwards in his room 'But the old man is really a crook! He hasn't told the truth' – and he was really distressed at such an end to so long a reverence for him. I suggested that this almost child-like determination to get his way at all costs and regardless of other results must be, partly at any rate, a result of his mental illness. But it is of course characteristic of Churchills all through history.)

This outburst was rather a shock to C, who turned very white then very red. But he went on gallantly enough.

P.M. Yes, yes. But you *did* agree, and on that the Cabinet have no complaint. After all, I don't understand Ld S's position. He acted in just the same [way], when he connived, or really promoted, a similar concealment from the Cabinet about the H bomb. He authorised going into production, four months before the Cabinet was informed . . . .

S (interrupting) I cannot accept that. There was no question of entering production. The materials are not in our possession. It was

---

35. 'Concealment of truth, hint of falsehood'.

not 4 months but 4 days, and it was agreed to tell the Cabinet after your return from Canada . . . .

Eden then went on to express his fears as regards France and Germany. He did not think (though one cd never be absolutely certain) that the Russians wd change their Berlin policy in any way at all. In Europe, they wd propose their defence system; this of course would be the end of NATO or EDC. They would want a seat for China in UNO . . . . On the other hand, the previous telegram had gone; the situation must be dealt with. An invitation of some kind (unless this new Russian statement cd provide a reason to cancel it) must be sent. He felt that something on the lines of this draft wd do the least harm.

There was now a long and very painful pause.

P.M. Has anyone anything to say?

Another long pause.

Since no one wd begin, I broke the ice. I said that at this point I wd only say that I thought we had better work on the F.S.'s last remark. 'What are we to do now'. The future was more important than the past. The future of the Govt; the party; and the country; and of our whole foreign relations, esp with America, was at stake. Nothing could be worse than for the Govt to break up now. Let us think over the whole matter until after the week-end . . . .

Home Secretary (Fyfe) What about EDC and Germany.

The Foreign Secy repeated his anxieties. The only hope would be that the secret would really be kept by the Russians about the proposed meeting. But he wd have to tell the French and the Germans.

P.M. I agree. It may be that the new Soviet statement, if it really is official, is not enough to withdraw the invitation. But it is a sufficient ground for delaying its renewal . . . .

Thorneycroft Your telegram mentioned 'suitable time'. Perhaps, for a number of reasons, including the new Soviet declaration, this is not a suitable time.

Miss Horsburgh I agree. It's a question of timing.

P.M. Something has got to be said. I will take it on my own shoulders.

Ld Woolton But, with respect, that's not possible. Whatever the case may have been before, this cannot be a personal and private telegram. The Cabinet cannot be ignorant of what they have been discussing for 2 hours. They are collectively responsible.

S I am content to leave the past for the future, so long as it is quite clear that the responsibility of the Cabinet will be respected. I cannot accept, tho' I understand, the P.M.'s doctrine.

P.M.   I will not apologise. I cannot change my opinion. If I have lost the confidence of my colleagues there can only be one end to it.

Butler   I have not spoken up to now. If we are to go back to the past, I have written, and deposited with the Cabinet secretariat, a minute setting out what happened about the telegram and why I acted as I did. But surely we must now all consider what is to be done.

Crookshank   I agree. Let us pass to the future. But in saying that, I must make it clear that I support the Lord President's protest. I would not like him to think that he was alone (P.M. looked very angry)

HM   I must, in loyalty to Lord S, say that I think his protest justified. But do let us pass to the problem before us. There is a further point on the telegram wh shd be considered. Many of us, (including, in a way, the P.M.) will be rather relieved if the Russians refuse. Those who dislike the whole idea will be comforted; (he will have done his duty) It will also be very good politics at home if the gesture is made and rebuffed. But if it's on a personal and private basis, it cannot be published. Should not the next telegram be formal and not in any way confidential?

Eden   Yes: this is certainly a point.

Lyttelton   I must also tell the P.M. that I share Ld Salisbury's view about the past. But let's think only now of what is to be done.

P.M.   Very well. We will meet at 11am on Monday, to resume the discussion. If it is to be my last Cabinet, I shd like it to be at Downing St, not here. (in House) Will that suit Lord Salisbury.

S   Certainly, if I am to be there.

P.M.   (flaring up angrily) What do you mean? 'If I am to be there'. Will you resign before that. I hope if you do you will send me your reasons, in writing too.

S   (with a wry smile) I only said 'If'. Of course I know that I cannot publish my reasons without publishing the whole story. That's one of the difficulties.

After this, it being about 1pm, the Cabinet passed on to the next item, the proposed Egyptian treaty .... Almost everything in the agreement is now approved except the time for the evacuation[36] and the length of the treaty itself. The Egyptians want 15 months and 7

---

36. Of the Suez Canal base.

years; we would like 20 years, or anyway 10. If we could get 7 years from the end of the evacuation, it would be good . . . .

24 July
. . . . After Crichel Down, we have a new row to face with this Commander Marten, about an airfield on his property. It is, of course, primarily for the Air Ministry. But somehow 'planning' is brought in. It will be difficult to avoid more trouble unless we tread very warily and I fear Ld de L'Isle has already made the cardinal error of seeing Cdr Marten and having a row with him! The husbands of very rich women are always difficult to handle. A consort is always either jealous or sensitive . . . .

. . . . Anthony rang me up about tea-time . . . . He thinks that we must let Churchill send his telegram but he thinks (as I suggested) that we can stiffen the terms. We might ask for some 'act of faith' (like the Austrian treaty) before the meeting. Salisbury is to see Eden tomorrow (Sunday) night. E hopes that he will be persuaded to withhold his resignation. Before dinner, Eden rang me up again. A completely new situation has been created by an identical [Russian] note to China, UK, France, and US suggesting a meeting of all European powers. This (embarrassing as it may be to answer) is obviously to wreck EDC (and ultimately NATO) But it makes a completely new problem to be solved on Monday and (by a strange paradox) may serve at least to unite the British Cabinet . . . .

31 July (Saturday)
This has been a terrible week. We have had four Cabinet meetings, as well as Home Affairs, Economic Committee and various 'ad hoc' committees. The idea is to 'clear the decks' and prepare for the autumn. But as the party is altogether without any effective leadership and since Cabinet meetings are becoming more and more painful, very little progress has been made. The Foreign Secretary, alone, is strong in the party and the country. Churchill is now often speechless in Cabinet; alternatively, he rambles on about nothing. Sometimes he looks as if he were going to have another stroke.

The great event of the week has been the initialling of heads of agreement in Cairo. There can be no doubt at all that we have acted wisely. 80,000 men in Suez are no strength to us at all. The Army is suffering in morale. We must either get out – into action stations – nearer the front (that is Turkey and Asia Minor and the Persian Gulf) or re-occupy Cairo and Alexandria. Moreover, the Chiefs' of Staff appreciation of the strategic position and the effect of thermo-nuclear warfare, makes it clear that old ideas need to be revised. Of course, this is hard for the Party (and for Churchill) to swallow. It has been a great advantage to get the agreement – and the debate in the HofCommons – before the recess. Eden's 'wind-up' was masterly, and convinced many waverers. In the end, the Socialists abstained and only 26 Tories voted against the Government resolution. My son-in-law, Julian Amery, was of course, one of these. He is able, but unduly influenced by his old father. Leo Amery is generally wrong about everything.

We have had several meetings of leading ministers, but no solution seems likely about Churchill. Anthony Eden, Butler and I (the 'trium-virate', Eden calls it – which I suppose means that he will run affairs in this way if ever he becomes P.M.) are agreed – but helpless. For the moment, the Russian visit is 'off' – until the powers have agreed or despatched their reply to the last Russian note . . . .

We must all oppose an action which might destroy altogether (or at the best wound and weaken) the alliance. But if Churchill persists, the nation – esp the left and moderate left – will be on his side. He will break up the Cabinet and the Conservative Party. But he will not mind this. His present mood is so self-centred as to amount almost to mania. It is, no doubt, the result of his disease. If he were a monarch, we shd be talking of a regency. If he were chairman, of a Company, the Board wd be thinking of a special meeting of shareholders to secure his removal. But as a Prime Minister, he can laugh at all of us – and enjoy it. At the same time, the Party in the House is rapidly disintegrating into small and discontented groups. We must have a completely new Cabinet and Government, representative of the party. The present Cabinet does *not* represent the party. It is a Churchill creation, and based on the practice of war, not of peace . . . .

We also need a new theme. If all the present faces and the old policies go on, we are bound to be beaten at the General Election. 'You cannot ask me' says Churchill (these are his very words) 'to sign my death warrant'. But, as Butler observed, he has no objection to signing ours. All this is a tragic situation. All of us, who really have loved as well as admired him, are being slowly driven into something like hatred . . . .

His performance in the Suez debate was terrible. He intervened to speak about the Hydrogen bomb. If he talks much more in this strain, the whole country will go defeatist and prefer to surrender to Communism. It breaks my heart to see the lion-hearted Churchill begin to sink into a sort of Pétain.[37] This sounds exaggerated – and is – but there is a terrible truth in it too . . . .

Sunday 1 August

. . . . I fear Oliver Lyttelton's leaving us is a great blow. He was always so sensible in Cabinet. He stood up to officialdom, esp our Treasury officials, with their narrow and jealous minds. The civil servants are really more dangerous when they are good (as at the Treasury) They are all 'gown-men' none 'sword and cloak men'. They are against the aristocracy; the successful business-man; and the adventurer (in the widest sense) They are like the clergy in the pre-reformation times. It was against them, rather than against any theological doctrine, that our ancestors revolted. The 'Crichel Down' episode, viewed from this angle, is quite significant. One assumes nowadays that any department starts with a prejudice *against* a landowner, esp of a large and ancient estate. It is curious. The aristocracy destroyed the mediaeval civil servants (the clergy, esp the regular clergy) and seized their property. Now, after 400 years, the new clergy (the civil servants) are destroying the descendants of these sacriligious individualists. So it goes on. But I fear that the new priesthood (like the old) cannot create wealth. It can only flourish as a parasite on enterprise and production. All this Lyttelton understood. Without his help and encouragement I could not have defied the Treasury and the so-called Cabinet decisions. I think it is still on the record that we might only build 260,000 houses in 1953 (our second year) We got 318,000. We are supposed now to reduce to 300,000. 1954 will, all being well, give us 360,000. In 1955 the Cabinet decision is to 'stabilise' down to 300,000. I am hoping for 380,000. At the same time, more offices, more schools, more factories are being built than ever before. The Treasury believe that demand should be reduced to supply. We know that demand creates supply . . . .

Eden rang up . . . . Molotov's answer has come, and has excited the P.M. very much. As far as I could understand from a guarded telephone conversation, the Russian reply, ... is not unfriendly to the idea of the personal visit, without waiting for the 3 power reply to

---

37. Marshal Pétain was the head of the puppet Vichy French government during the Second World War.

the last Russian note . . . . The P.M.'s proposed answer was (it seems) very unwise. The F.O. suggested some amendments. Eden says the Cabinet shd be informed – the text shd be sent round and if anyone objects, a meeting shd be called. P.M. refused this procedure. Eden also wishes a memorandum of his views on the reply to be circulated. P.M. objects. In other words, Churchill is re-playing the drama . . . . The Russians are trying desperately to prevent the German link-up with the West. It will be tragic if Churchill helps them unwittingly . . . .

2 August

Eden rang up at about 11am (I was resting in bed) to say that Churchill had agreed to the proposed reply to Russia *and* Eden's memorandum being circulated to the Cabinet . . . .

. . . . I have never been quite sure myself that if Churchill and Eden had not both got ill together (last summer) something might have been done, in one direction or the other. But, by pure bad luck, some precious months were lost . . . .

7 August

. . . . The Russians, it seems, have now followed up their formal note, asking for a conference of all European powers, with a new and less formal suggestion. They want a 4 power meeting – of a more or less informal kind – USSR; UK; France; and USA (no mention of China) This proposal has now to be considered, presumably with the other. The view is that they felt that the first note had rather misfired – at any rate, it had not prevented Mendes-France from trying to get EDC dealt with in the French assembly during this month. So the 4 power suggestion is now put as a result. Hayter (our ambassador in Moscow) thinks that they fear that the note of July 24 has had a sort of boomerang result, and increased rather than decreased the chance of the French accepting EDC . . . .

The American paper 'Time' seems to have got hold of a pretty accurate story about the recent drama in the British Cabinet. The *Express*; the *Evening News*; and the *News Chronicle* have quoted this, but not conspicuously or with any head-lines or leading article comment. So little harm has been done. It wd be interesting to know how 'Time' got on to a story about which no hint of any kind has got into our press, in spite of a fairly large number of people involved. 'Time' is the publisher of the Churchill memoirs, and (knowing how indiscreet he can be) they may have picked up something from him. Actually, I have never known anything which has happened in this Cabinet kept so completely dark. Many things have leaked but not this . . . .

8 August (Sunday)

. . . . We have been very worried about Maurice, whose nerves are in a bad way. But we have found a new doctor from whom we hope much. He is now in a nursing home for treatment and hopes in a week or two to be well enough to go to France with Katie and the boys. This shd do him a lot of good. The truth is that his nervous system has never quite recovered from a particularly strenuous war, (began when he was 19 only) with a very early marriage and all the cares of a family . . . .

10 August

The American ambassador asked to see me . . . . The Americans are very anxious about the future. But I did think it right to tell him that Churchill's policy had the support of the country . . . . The Ambassador told me an amusing remark of Herbert Morrison. Answering a criticism about Attlee and Bevan going to Moscow and Peking, he replied 'Well, one has to run jolly fast to keep to the left of Churchill nowadays'.

Salisbury came to see me. He is still in a resigning mood . . . .

11 August

To Bolton Abbey. It is very nice to be back, but rather sad. Andrew [Devonshire] has a party of young friends, who are very pleasant. But I cannot understand much of what they talk about, being chiefly racing – or else stocks and shares. They seem to gamble on anything and everything. But they are very polite . . . .

17 August

. . . . The news is bad; the Communists seem to be winning all along the line. Attlee and Bevan and co, after being feted in Moscow, are now drinking down compliments in Peking. Mendes-France (the French Prime Minister) has made a new plan for EDC, wh looks like pleasing neither the 'Europeans' nor the nationalists in France or elsewhere. It seems unlikely to be acceptable to the other EDC powers . . . . I had a letter from Anthony Eden this morning . . . . he has asked Churchill to hand over *before* the Party Conference (October 7th) . . . .

18 August

Left Bolton Abbey for Hardwick Hall. I arrived for luncheon, in terrible weather. There has been no hay harvest and if the rain goes on there will be no corn harvest either. Even when there is no rain, there is no sun. It may be as bad as the summer of 1879, which wrecked Mr Disraeli's last government . . . .

23 August

The Brussels conference is dead and it seems that Mendes-France (at his own suggestion) has gone to Chartwell to see the P.M . . . .

24 August

. . . . I had arranged to see Rab (Butler) today. But, owing to my visit to Chartwell, I had to put him off. He rang up at 10am. From what I cd gather from a conversation necessarily guarded, we were in for trouble. He (Butler) had spent a night at Chartwell a week ago. He found the P.M. thoroughly rested; believing himself to be fully recovered; enjoying his tenure of the F.O. (during Eden's holiday) and generally convinced of his own importance to the world during this critical period. Just as Rab rang off, I got a message asking me to go over to F.O. There I found Eden, obviously rather worried about future plans. It seems that P.M. really said nothing and achieved nothing with Mendes-France. He very nearly gave the game away by referring to what ought to be done *when* EDC has been thrown out by the French assembly. But Eden was able to stop him. For (officially, at any rate) our line is that, like the Americans, we are strongly in favour of EDC.

Mendes-France did not do very well at Brussels. He infuriated the Italians; he was not too polite to Spaak (who really did try) Many of the 5 EDC powers suspect him of having wanted to sabotage EDC all along, and even of having made a deal about it with Molotov at Geneva, in return for the Indo-China agreement. (This last I do *not* believe)

P.M. was very tired after the French had left. He said nothing to Eden about plans. I told Eden what Butler had said to me, which seemed ominous.

I left the F.O. at noon and arrived for luncheon at Chartwell just after 1pm. P.M. was in bed – so I had to wait 20 minutes till he had got up and put on his 'rompers' . . . .

Luncheon lasted till nearly 4pm. After a certain amount of desultory discussion about Soviet policy; EDC; NATO; Adenauer's position; the French confusion, and the like, we get to the real point. Churchill feels better; he has good reports from his doctors; he means to stay as Prime Minister just as long as he can. In favour of this plan, he adduced a number of arguments. First, he (and he alone in the world) might be able to steer through the complications of foreign policy and international problems. He had a unique position. He could talk to anybody, on either side of the iron curtain, either by personal message or face to face. Having now fully recovered his health, he could not abandon the commission which he held from Crown and Parliament .... Secondly, a 'fag end' Government, formed at the end of a Parliament, could never succeed. Such brilliant figures as Lord Rosebery and Mr Arthur Balfour had been swept away, in spite of their talents and their charm, when they had to succeed to Gladstone and Salisbury.[38] It would be much better for Eden if he (Churchill) were to go on till the Election. Or, perhaps, it might be wise to let Eden become P.M. just *before* the election. That could be decided later. Thirdly, he was P.M. and nothing could drive him out of his office, so long as he cd form and control a Govt and have the confidence of the House. This continual chatter in the lobbies and the press about his resignation was intolerable. It arose, of course, from his illness last year. But he was now recovered. Naturally, like any man of nearly 80, who had had *two* strokes, he might die at any moment. But he could not undertake to die at any particular moment! Meanwhile, he did not propose to resign. No Prime Minister has been so treated in the past, and continually badgered about resignation. It was a great shame. Anyway, he could not be ejected.

Of course, all this did not pour out in a single flood of rhetoric. There were pauses; and rhetorical questions; and broodings in silence . . . .

At last, the plan was unfolded. If Eden will agree, he shall be Deputy Prime Minister, Leader of the House, responsible for the 'Home Front', etc etc. He can 'manage' the House of Commons and the party in the HofC (like Pelham and Newcastle for Pitt)[39] He can speak in the country. He can take control of the Party machine. He can 'plan' the programme for the next election. In other words, he can

---

38. In 1894–5 and 1902–5 respectively.
39. In the mid-eighteenth century.

be the sort of 'managing director' of the show, so long as he supports Churchill as 'chairman'.

If Eden agrees to all this, it's plain sailing and I (Macmillan) will become F.S.

Of course, Eden may prefer to remain F.S. It's quite likely. In that case, Macmillan shall be Leader of the House and 'boss' of the Home Front. The game can be played either way, as Anthony may prefer. What did I think?

I said that I thought that when he heard of Churchill's intention to stay, it would be a tremendous shock to Anthony, especially after his long appearance (over many years) in the role of 'heir-apparent' and Churchill's categorical promises in the letter of June 11th (1954) I thought it very possible that Anthony wd decide to retire altogether and forever from public life. He could follow Oliver Lyttelton into the City. In any case, even if he accepts the new situation, will he not prefer to stay in the F.O.? In that case, I cannot play the part. I cannot 'preside' over the Economic Committee (where Rab now rules) or the Home Affairs Ctee (which Ld Salisbury runs) or any other such Committee, permanent or 'ad hoc', without causing an impossible situation. No one could possibly do the job *except* a man who is 'practically' leader of the Party – anyway, the leader-designate. Any-way, I cd not possibly replace Crookshank.

. . . . On my return from Chartwell, as I informed P.M. I would do (and he was pleased) I went to see Anthony at his flat. I broke the news to him of Churchill's decision. At first he could scarcely credit it. It was really incredible, after such assurances, so recently and so categorically given to him . . . .

25 August (Wednesday)

I had arranged a full day at the Ministry, to deal with a large amount of administrative problems, including the road through Cambridge (which has excited city and university alike) The only interruption in this sequence of interviews with my officials was a call to the F.O. at 12 noon.

I found Anthony (quite naturally) pretty sore . . . .

But, of course, the real difficulty is not between Churchill and Eden – and the Premiership must not be treated like an 'estate' wh a father had undertaken to 'hand over' to his son. The truth is that the Cabinet does not function; many of the ministers are unsuited to their jobs; no one coordinates policy; grave errors are continually being made through lack of direction (e.g. the muddle over MPs' pay; the two years unnecessary delay over Suez; the keeping of a whole division in Korea, because Churchill is unable to sign an order; the confusion over the Cyprus announcement) Indeed, the miracle is that we have been able to get along as well as we have. Then, these interminable Cabinets, full of reminiscences and monologues, are becoming an intolerable burden. Meanwhile, the Party in the house is in a state of confusion and broken up into groups and cabals; the Party machine in the country lacks grip and guidance. We are just drifting along to trouble and electoral disaster.

After a good deal of discussion, it seemed clear what are the alternatives.

(1) We could perhaps *force* Churchill to resign. This would require a mass resignation of his leading colleagues; including Butler. The Queen might, in this way, be brought to exercise some influence upon him.

I expressed the view that Churchill wd fight. He would try to reform his Govt and he would get quite a number of ambitious younger men to join. He might even try a coalition on a 'peace' ticket (following the speech of May 11th 1953)

Anyway, this would split the party (as the Asquith–Lloyd George controversy had split the Liberal Party)[40] and ultimately perhaps destroy it (as the Liberal Party had been destroyed) With our nicely balanced national situation, it would make a defeat in the General Election certain.

(2) Eden and I and others who felt exhausted and 'fed up' (e.g. Salisbury, Crookshank etc) could retire, quietly and unostentatiously, into private life. This is the course which Eden professed to prefer. Certainly, the long years of waiting and the cynical deception (or what amounts to it) with which Churchill appears to have treated him, are enough to make him lose patience and lose heart.

But I told him that one really cannot resign because one is not made Prime Minister!

(3) We can try to get – with a number of leading Ministers – a discussion of the machinery by which our affairs could be managed, at least better than now, even under a Churchill Premiership. He will refuse to discuss whether or not he shall resign. But he will not refuse to discuss the 'reorganisation' or 'reconstruction' of the Government.

---

40. In December 1916.

From that, we can get to a discussion of the conditions under which he shall carry on. If he is not alarmed about the possibility of (1) or (2), he will, of course, be obstinate and intransigent. So he shd be left guessing. After an hour's talk, Anthony and I drafted together the letter he should send. It ran something like this. 'I have received your letter. You will understand that after your repeated assurances to me and your very definite letter of June 11th this year, the terms of your letter are rather a shock to me. However, these should not be regarded as personal matters by any of us. It is simply a question as to how the work of the government can best be carried on in the interests of the country and the Party.

No doubt you will be willing to discuss these problems with the same group of your senior colleagues with whom you discussed them some months ago' . . . .

After finishing my work (including the final draft of my broadcast for tomorrow) I got the 5.20 train to Haywards Heath . . . . Finished volume 1 and 2 of Justin McCarthy's '*History of our Times*'.[41] Very slight and superficial – but very good reading all the same. What fun Palmerston was! How the Liberals despised the Tories as the 'stupid' party! How they hated Disraeli! How small they were compared to him, the great political genius and prophet of the 19th century. All the same, what a pleasant century to live in, if you were rich or even of moderate means! . . . .

27 August
. . . . At 11am I went to F.O. Butler came also. We had a discussion between the 3 of us for 1 hour, when Eden was to see Churchill (at noon)

Butler (who has obviously thought a good deal about all this) said that he had been summoned to Chartwell a week ago. Then Churchill had considered three possibilities. (a) He would retire, and speak on great issues from his seat in the HofCommons. He could not promise not to be critical. (b) He would serve in a Eden Govt – as Paymaster General. (c) He would carry on – offering a real position to Eden as 'Deputy P.M.' with control of Home Affairs, leadership of the House and of the Party machine etc.

---

41. Justin McCarthy MP, *A History of Our Own Times, from the Accession of Queen Victoria to the General Election of 1880* (Leipzig: Bernhard Tauchnitz, 1879).

If Eden preferred to stay at F.O. Macmillan shd run the 'Home Front'. Churchill had made it clear, that in view of his restored health and the degeneration of world affairs, he would choose the third (c)

In Butler's view, from the national point of view this could be made to work if Eden wd do it. (It could not work unless he did) I interjected, that I could not do the job. No one cd do it without the authority of the 'second figure' or 'deputy leader'. Anyway, nothing wd induce me to turn out Harry Crookshank, my oldest personal friend for over 50 years, from the leadership of the House . . . .

It was agreed that Eden (who was to see Churchill at noon) should (a) express considerable concern at C's behaviour, and his own preference for resigning from public life shd be hinted at (b) there shd be a meeting of leading Ministers to discuss what, if any, plan wd work. Eden, I must add, seems now more inclined to just staying at the F.O. This would certainly suit him best. The trouble is that it would be taken as 'no change'. Without some dramatic change, I doubt if we can face Parlt and the Country. But, of course, I cannot argue this because it looks as if I want to grab the F.O. at all costs.

Just before the Cabinet (at 3.30pm) the P.M. got hold of me for a moment. 'Eden had been very nice – charming. All was going well. Of course, he might prefer to stay at the F.O. In that case, I would get the Home Front'. Before I cd say anything, the others trooped in . . . .

During the Cabinet, Anthony passed me a note, asking me to come to F.O. after the meeting. This I did. He seemed rather distraught. Obviously Churchill has won, with hardly a struggle. But what could poor Anthony do? It was also clear to me that he will want to stay at the F.O. and just let things rip. C may die. If he doesn't, it just means that he must carry the responsibility for the electoral disaster of 1955. I merely discussed with him the meeting of ministers . . . . I left the F.O. for Euston, and got the 7.15pm for Inverness.

28 August

. . . . [T]o Findhorn, to luncheon with James and Rachel Stuart . . . . I told James about the week's activities. His views are clear (altho' he had not heard of the latest developments, he had expected something like this) He feels

(1) That it is impossible to *remove* Churchill. It would be too risky; he has all the cards. It would damage the Party in the country and in the HofC.

(2) C may last or drop down dead at any minute.

(3) We must prepare for him lasting a full year.

(4) The *only* possible plan is for Eden to take the 'deputy premiership' instead of the F.O. and make a real job of it.

(5) Harry shd continue to 'lead the House'.

(6) C shd publicly say that is making preparations for his final withdrawal. No need to cover it up.

(7) A complete 'reconstruction' of the Govt – to last till General Election. Eden shd really arrange this. Churchill will accept his guidance, except perhaps over the very leading posts.

(8) Macmillan to go to F.O. The alternative – M to do 'Home Front' is impossible. We want some one to preside over Economic Ctee etc. How can M do this, over the head of Butler? Only Eden can do so.

(9) It wd be better still if M went to the Treasury and Butler to the F.O. (Salisbury, Lyttelton, and many others hold this view) Anyway, this is only a variant of the main theme.

(10) He (James) would come up for the meeting. Salisbury *must* be asked or he will resign. He is in a very funny mood. Fyfe needn't be asked. Woolton can be told. F only cares about the woolsack.[42] W agrees to anything that anyone decides. Chief whip shd not be asked to *first* meeting . . . .

3 September

. . . . Churchill called a Cabinet for yesterday. Fortunately, the message reached me at a time when even air travel made attendance impossible. But I have written some suggestions about the problem which results from the French rejection of EDC. The assembly finally defeated it by 60 votes or so. It is curious how (after all the speculation and estimates over the last 2 years) my original view has been confirmed. I looked up again my Cabinet paper on the subject in Feb 1952, when I foretold that it would not pass. I still think that it's a good result for us. 'Federation' of Europe means 'Germanisation' of Europe. 'Confederation' (if we play our cards properly), should be British leadership of Europe . . . .

The F.O. telegrams, telling the whole story of EDC and the French political crisis as reflected in every capital in the world, were very interesting . . . . Reading between the lines, it wd seem that a great deal

---

42. That is, the office of the Lord Chancellor, who sits on a woolsack in the House of Lords.

of the French opposition to EDC was not nationalism but defeatism. Herriot's speech was pure Pétainism . . . .

The Rent Act (Housing Rents and Repairs) has now come into force . . . . From the press cuttings, the left-wing press is trying desperately to whip up a campaign of hatred and misrepresentation . . . . However, by Christmas we shall get a pretty good idea of what is really happening. Will it be a burning issue by next November?

4 September

. . . . [A] mass of telegrams giving a further story of the European crisis. The British policy seems to be – *tout court*[43] – put Germany in NATO. My paper, suggesting a European box inside an Atlantic box, based on Churchill's 1950 plan at Strasbourg, had not reached Anthony before the Cabinet. I hope he will at least consider it . . . . There is, no doubt, however that *we* ought to take the lead, and not just follow meekly in the American track. Anyway, the Americans must surely by now realise how wrong they have been about EDC (and our F.O. also) France has resented the American pressure, almost amounting to blackmail and sometimes bribery . . . .

6 September

A quiet morning – reading and writing and clearing up correspondence. Read Buchan's '*Glencoe*', an essay in book form – very well done. Left Inverness for London . . . .

8 September

. . . . Cabinet at 3pm, with a large agenda and a fairly good attendance of ministers. The most important item was the F.Secretary's statement of policy. He has accepted the idea of using the Brussels Pact[44] as the way out [of the EDC wreckage] . . . .

9 September

Further talks with Eden and Butler at the F.O. Eden is very depressed and so is Butler. Churchill seems to have told Butler that we can't win the next election anyway. This has upset Butler very much . . . .

---

43. 'All and in brief'.
44. A defence pact signed with France, Belgium, the Netherlands and Luxembourg in 1948.

10 September

After seeing the agent for the B.G. estate (Mr Streatfield) motored to London in time for luncheon with the French ambassador . . . . Anthony had earlier warned me to say nothing about the idea of reviving the Brussels pact, but just before luncheon I heard from him that he had 'thrown a fly' over Massigli the day before. Anyway, the ambassador knew all about it, and liked it. By a strange coincidence, the same idea had occurred to Mendes-France and so there is perhaps a chance of French support . . . .

14 September

. . . . A good deal of routine work at the ministry, but not excessive. The usual problems and the usual papers. But the thrill and excitement of the first years have gone. We no longer wait anxiously for the monthly housing score. We have passed the 300,000 and shall pass it again in 1954. There is a lot of trouble brewing (as I expected) about the Housing Repairs and Rents Act. The tenants are being whipped up to complain of its partiality. The landlords are holding meetings of protest that it doesn't give them enough. I still hope that things will settle down pretty well by next year. In the course of the morning, I got a summons to luncheon with P.M. Since No 10 is really shut up, we went to Buck's Club. I must say I love the old man, altho' he *is* so selfish and so difficult. But he certainly has courage and panache. The great car, flying the standard of the Warden of the Cinque Ports; the bows and smiles to the crowd; the hat, cigar, and stick – superb showman. As we drove along a gaping St James's Street to the club in Clifford St, he was recognised and cheered. The luncheon – which was chosen with a great deal of care and detailed criticism of this or that dish or wine – was not a bad one for a man of 80. A dozen oysters; cream soup; chicken pie; vanilla and strawberry ice. Moselle and Brandy washed this down. I'm afraid I cd not manage the soup or the ice-cream. There were 3 or 4 important, but highly confidential, subjects about which he wished to consult me. I must say that this presented some difficulties. He had *not* got his hearing aid and it was really difficult to discuss any of the points intelligently without doing so in what amounted to a general meeting of the members! . . . .

18 September

Burglars got into B.G. last night. All the silver in ordinary use was taken – to the value of £300–£400 or so. They were interrupted before they 'blew' the safe. But far too much good silver – candlesticks, tankards, salvers etc – were out in the dining room and pantry . . . .

21 September
. . . . I lunched with Ld Woolton – who is in despair about the future of the party. There has been a sudden turn against us, everywhere. It's partly irritation and fear, but (he is convinced) mostly a sense that our task is accomplished and our mandate exhausted. I told him to paint it in the worst possible colours to the P.M.! . . . . Eden is now beginning to despair and will want (I suppose) to stay at the F.O. to the end. If there is a swing to the Socialists (as seems probable) it will mean that both he (and I) will be too old after another 5 years . . . .

22 September
. . . . Ld W[oolton] rang up. There has been a careful survey of the position by the most experienced agents – each area working as a team. The result of this exercise confirms the Gallup poll etc. An election now, under the present Govt, wd lead to a disaster electorally. The margin might not be large (like 1945) but it wd be decisive. A further examination confirms the view that nothing can avoid this result *next* year, except a complete change in the structure of the Govt and a new P.M.

. . . . I think the truth is, that we are missing an essential part of our constitutional mechanism – the effective working depends on the power and authority of the Sovereign being revived and used. A king or queen alone could say to Churchill what needs to be said in his interest as well as in ours . . . .

24 September
At the F.O. again – Anthony [Eden], Bobbety [Salisbury] and I. The usual talk round and round. But it was finally agreed that Anthony shd write a letter to P.M. strongly urging – almost demanding – a proper reconstruction. It's clear to me that Eden doesn't want to take the Deputy Premiership (with Leadership of the Commons) I think he is wrong, both from his point of view and from that of the party. A stronger man wd have no difficulty in gradually taking hold of affairs, leaving Churchill as a kind of 'President' of the Company – which is what he wd soon accept – and taking over the active management . . . . But S says 'he is too nice and too weak'. He is too nice to go beyond the letter and spirit of an understanding; he shrinks (and

quite naturally) from leaving an office where everthing is ready-made
– a splendid position, a fine and loyal and intelligent staff – for a job
which doesn't really exist officially and where one wd have to make
the job oneself, with the help of the P.S.! There was some discussion
among the 3 of us of my position. S raised this, very generously. AE
seemed to assume that I wd be glad to take the Ministry of Defence. I
explained that I thought this a bad idea. (i) There was nothing to do –
the whole programme having just been fixed – a day or two ago – for
[the] next 3 years (ii) The public would think either, that Ld Alexander
had made a mess of it, and that I was being sent to clean it up; or, that
we had more or less given up hope of peace and were desperately
preparing for war – or both! . . . .
     . . . . All this very tiresome business interferes with normal work.
However, I had a meeting of my regional officers this morning. We
discussed the problem of the Local Authority programmes. As we hope
to see some 150,000 private enterprise (unsubsidised) houses completed in 1956, it becomes necessary to curtail the allocation for L.A.
building. This is not an easy operation, and will lead to political
trouble. All the same, it is certainly right – politically as well as from
the economic pt of view – to let the unsubsidised go ahead as fast as
they are able and willing to do . . . .

25 September

Worked in bed all the morning, having brought back two immense
bags from the Ministry. The problems change, but do not diminish.
Now we have solved the production problem, we have to start to do
slum clearance, while at the same time giving free play to 'private
enterprise' housing. Of course, the only way to do this is a differential
subsidy – more for slum clearance and less (or nothing) for general
needs. But we haven't time for a Bill this year and (anyway) we hardly
dare face it in an election year . . . .

27 September

Much telephoning between F.O. and Birch Grove (where I stayed for
a day's rest) Anthony feels it necessary to give a new pledge to Europe
– as indeed we have often discussed together but for which formal
Cabinet approval has never been asked. We must undertake to keep 4
divisions (or their equivalent) and tactical air force under SACEUR's
command and on the continent of Europe. If we offer this (he feels) we
may get agreement at the 9 power conference. If not, the whole western

alliance may collapse and US revert to 'peripheral defence' or (worse still) 'Fortress America' . . . .

28 September

. . . . Bobbety [Salisbury], Harry Crookshank and I met at 6pm. It was agreed that Bobbety shd write to Winston asking for a very thorough reconstruction of the Govt – not just a minor reshuffle. It seems now generally agreed that Winston must stay, because no one can find any method (other than a suicidal split in the party) for getting him out! . . . .

29 September

. . . . Our ministerial council in the afternoon. We had a very interesting discussion. The Housing problem is really now in a period of transition. We have solved the material problem – that is, we know we can build about 350,000 houses a year, without too heavy a strain on the building industry. Now we must try to get the right proportion between subsidised and unsubsidised, and concentrate the subsidised on the right people and places . . . .

1 October

. . . . After the Cabinet, P.M. kept me back. He said that he understood from Bobbety [Salisbury] that I shared his view that there shd be a large reconstruction of the Govt – amounting to a new administration. I said – certainly. Then he told me that he must keep Swinton and Woolton . . . . This is his plan – Deputy PM and Leader of House – Eden: Lord Chancellor – Maxwell-Fyfe: For Sec – Macmillan: Chancellor of Ex – Butler: Minister of Education – Eccles: Minister of Housing – Thorneycroft: Board of Trade – Sandys: Min of Labour – Lloyd George: Home Secretary and Deputy Leader of House – Crookshank: this would leave (without other changes) Minister of Defence, Office of Works, and Ministry of Supply to be filled . . . . Went home for dinner. D and I are alone, since Maurice and Katie have left for Wakefield, where M is to stand at the bye-election (against a good Socialist majority) . . . .

2 October

Anthony rang me up from F.O. He seemed rather distressed. He says he really cannot go on unless Churchill will agree to fix *some* definite date for the hand-over. He wants me to tell this to Churchill. This I agreed to do. This prolonged internal crisis of the Government must be resolved soon, or we shall all get completely on each other's nerves – all but Winston, who really rather enjoys it! . . . .

3 October

. . . . The 9 power agreement was signed after a great struggle . . . . It is a *tremendous* triumph for Eden.[45]

4 October

Worked with Marples on the Blackpool speech. We are trying to get some really effective way of setting out the figures of *school* building, to counteract the false propaganda that we have obtained our houses at the expense of schools. I opened an exhibition of carpets in the morning – why, I don't really know . . . .

6 October

. . . . I have got to prepare a speech for next week, for the Wakefield by-election. It's not easy; I shall try to do particularly well, because of Maurice being the candidate, and end up in a flop! Also, I find it very difficult to get down to the second speech, when the first is not yet delivered. My Blackpool speech (to the whole conference) does not (unfortunately) come on till Friday . . . .

8 October

. . . . We had our housing debate in the afternoon. I had nothing in particular to say but said it well enough to please the audience. Like Eden and Butler, I had the compliment of the audience rising and cheering at the end . . . .

10 October

Churchill rang up at 10am . . . . It's all 'settled', after three weeks of struggle. Churchill has won on every point, and Eden capitulated completely. Churchill remains P.M., without any commitment, written or verbal, as to date. Eden stays at F.O. Rab, naturally and properly,

---

45. A conference in London of Belgium, Canada, France, Italy, Luxembourg, the Netherlands, the UK, the US and West Germany, fortified by Eden's pledge not to withdraw Britain's four divisions and air squadrons in Germany without the agreement of her allies, agreed to expand the Brussels Pact into what became the Western European Union as a means of enabling German rearmament.

at Exchequer. Fyfe replaces Simonds as Lord Chancellor – and a few other changes. I am to [be] asked to 'supplant' Harry Crookshank as Ld Privy Seal and Leader of the House. He is to be Home Secretary (as he is my oldest friend, this is pretty difficult) Swinton is to stay – and Woolton. No change at BofTrade. In fact, the 'reconstruction' consists in the retirement of Lords Alexander and Simonds . . . .

. . . . According to Churchill, the change at the F.O. is only 'temporarily delayed'. Eden feels that he must 'see it through', so far as the London conference is concerned. After that, he will exchange with me, taking the Leadership of the House as well as Deputy P.M. I don't believe a word of this . . . .

Looking back over three weeks, it is remarkable with what skill and tenacity Churchill has played his hand. Of course, the holder of the Queen's commission has a very good starting position. Nevertheless, he has timed his management of the affair supremely well . . . . He has refused ever (or practically so) to see any of us except separately. He has played off one against the other – and he has come off triumphant.

11 October

Eden rang up. I told him that P.M. was pressing me very hard to become Leader of the House and Ld Privy Seal. I said that my difficulty was with Harry – my oldest friend. If he was not hurt, or wd like the change, it wd suit me. Eden did not like this at all. 'But when I am P.M. and want you to be F.S., who will lead the House? We can't bring Harry back again.' I said that in my judgment Churchill has no intention at all of resigning, until a few weeks before the poll. So the question wd not arise at any rate in this Parliament. If we won the General Election, we cd see how things worked out. Eden seemed rather put out . . . .

. . . . I motored to London (during luncheon hour) and saw Harry at 4pm. He was quite clear as to his views. He thought Churchill ought to go, and had said so repeatedly to Eden, Salisbury and the rest. But since Eden had allowed C to remain, he cd not be *plus royaliste que le Roi*.[46] But he did not want to be Home Secretary . . . . I said at once that this settled it. After some talk with Eden and Butler, I sent my reply by telephone to Churchill (who was still at Chartwell) I said that Harry refused to be Home Secy. If C wanted him to resign, he was

---

46. 'More royalist than the king'.

ready to go. I cd not possibly agree, in these circumstances, to take his place. I wd take Defence, if he offered it. (This Eden said he wd like, as it would give him help on NATO and Brussels Treaty work. It wd leave Harry in a job he does very well) Churchill seemed put out on the telephone and rather sulky. But he soon recovers.

12 October

.... The labour situation, which (under Monckton's guidance) has been relatively stable for 3 years, seems now rather ugly. The Printers' unions (in a silly inter-union dispute) caused a general stoppage in the newspaper offices on Sunday night. None of the later (London) editions of the dailies were printed. This is now settled. The docks strike goes on, and looks like spreading. This is really directed agst Deakin and the Transport and General Workers. It is got up by the extremists. It looks like spreading to other ports, and developing into a really serious affair. We may have to use troops to do the work.

There was a Cabinet at 4.15. Monckton explained the general situation to us. It seems that the bus drivers are going out as well. At present, the Minister of Labour has not intervened. He wants to wait till after the Albert Hall meeting on Thursday, to which the T&GW union have summoned their chaps. Deakin is going to try to persuade them to go back to work, pending negotiations. He will probably fail. Then, the minister will probably prepare a Court of Enquiry. If the men will not load and unload the ships while it is sitting, we shall have to use troops.

After Cabinet, P.M. kept Harry back for a word alone. Then I came back into the Cabinet room. Everything is settled, at last? (Of course, it may be *un*settled in another hour or two) Harry will remain Leader of House and Privy Seal. I will go to Defence. Monckton agrees to stay, at least through the winter. So Lloyd George can be Home Secretary and Minister for Wales (very good) David Maxwell Fyfe to be Lord Chancellor. Eccles to Education, vice Miss Horsburgh (very good) Sandys to Ministry of Housing. Selwyn Lloyd to Supply. It will be just about 3 years since I took Housing and Local Govt. I shall be quite glad to pass it on. I have done all I can . . . .

13 October

. . . . I stayed in the flat through most of morning, composing a speech for the Wakefield by-election. I go there tomorrow. Maurice is the candidate, facing an adverse majority of 7000 or more. I ought to have recorded that Maurice came over to Blackpool on the second day of the conference and made a very good little speech, just before Butler. It was, he thought, good publicity. Anyway, it was very well received. Carol (Faber) has gone to Wakefield to help. There is a general view that the T.V. of the conference has not done much good. It's said that the P.M. looks terrible – old and almost 'ga-ga'.

I was summoned to No 10 at 6pm . . . . The Cabinet list is more or less complete. I am still at Defence. Harry remains Leader of the House. Duncan Sandys succeeds me. A very long session, arguing about under-secretaries. The whips want the safe men, as they have always done in every party. But they don't make the future leaders of the party. I reminded Winston again that it took Hitler to make him P.M. and me an under-secretary. The Tory Party wd do neither . . . .

14 October

A morning at the Ministry 'tidying up' . . . . Arrived Wakefield about 6pm. I found Maurice in very good form and apparently enjoying himself. Being a by-election, there's a whole posse of agents from the neighbouring constituencies. Of course, he stands no chance; but it's an opportunity for a good spirited campaign . . . . Maurice has got a piper, which makes a good stunt. A very good meeting – crowded, and good questions. Caught the night train to London . . . .

16 October

Cabinet at 11am. The strike situation is worsening. *All* the dockers will be out on Monday; also the bargemen and lightermen. This means no coal; no petrol; no handling of refuse. So the troops will have to go in next week . . . .

18 October

. . . . The dock strike continues, but a new review of stocks makes it possible to avoid using troops. This is an interesting result of economic freedom. Meat, petrol etc are in good supply and since Smithfield is working and the lorry drivers also, we can hold out for a bit without taking a step wh wd inevitably lead to fresh withdrawals of labour.

19 October

I have taken over my new Ministry, after a most moving farewell from my old. All the chaps have really been most kind, and I have the task of answering literally hundreds of letters from all over the country . . . .

21 October

Left by air for Paris, with Sir Harold Parker (Secretary of the Dept) and Mr Hanna (Private Secretary) . . . .

All the complicated questions involved in the new European settlement have miraculously been solved – all but the Saar . . . .

22 October

According to reports, ... If the French cannot get satisfaction over the Saar,[47] they will bring down the whole fabric of Western European Union, the Germans in NATO, and all the rest. It's hard to say how much of all this is serious and how much is bluff . . . .

The Wakefield figures have come through. Maurice has done very well, slightly increasing the Conservative proportion of the poll[48] . . . .

Dinner was with M Temple – Minister of National Defence – at the Hôtel de Brienne. . . . A long and disappointingly dull dinner. My neighbours were M Longchambon (whom I knew at Strasbourg) a rather dreary scientist, and General – well I forget his name – who is their new chief of staff. He was interesting enough, but never drew breath at all, before or after dinner.

23 October

It seems that quite a lot *did* happen after dinner at the British Embassy. The French Prime Minister and the German Chancellor were left in the library after dinner alone. 'Experts' were available in various other rooms. Neither Dulles nor Eden took any part. When the conference broke up at about 2am, it was clear that great progress had been made . . . .

24 October

I got back from Paris late last night, and managed to get a train to H.H. [Haywards Heath] The Germans and the French came to terms over the Saar, and the full series of agreements were signed yesterday afternoon . . . . So the great plan is launched for which we have worked

---

47. Saarland had been put under special administration by France in 1945. In October 1955 a plebiscite rejected the effective separation of Saarland from Germany and, after further negotiations, it became part of the Federal German Republic in 1957 (see *HMM* IV p. 70).
48. By 0.2 per cent. Wakefield by-election 21 December 1954: Lab: 21,882; C: 15,714.

at Strasbourg and elsewhere for more than 5 years. The federal system of EDC is dead; the confederal system of Western European Union is very much alive . . . . It has been a real pleasure to see England leading Europe . . . .

29 October

This has been a hectic week. This new Ministry of mine is a queer kind of affair. I have no power; yet I am responsible for everything – esp if it goes wrong. The P.M. is always busy about defence affairs – on Wednesday the Defence Committee sat under his Chairmanship for nearly 6 hours. (It's true that it cd all have been done in 20 minutes) When I ask for a small meeting with the Service ministers, about 40 to 50 people turn up! I made my first appearance in the HofC (as defence minister) on Wed, and had rather a rough quarter of an hour. It was on the financial consequences of the London–Paris agreements. In the interests of the Treasury and the F.O I maintained some rather difficult positions. We must not admit that it will cost us £80m a year, either on the Budget or on the Exchange a/c. For we are still bargaining with the Germans about future contributions.[49] I got through fairly well, and by seeing the Lobby afterwards, got a reasonably good press.

As I see it the three major *political* problems on the defence front are (a) the new financial burden and commitment in Europe (b) civil defence (c) the use of manpower and the 2 years period of [national] service. I can defend (a) on high moral and policy grounds. But I believe us to be most vulnerable on (b) and (c) . . . .

30 October

. . . . It looks as if the dock strike is ending at last. We shall know later today whether ['Dickie'] Barrett and his committee are prepared to recommend the stevedores to return to work. If so, the Transport and General Workers Union men (who are on strike *against* their leaders and in support of the stevedores) will certainly go back.[50] The loss, in exports, imports, lost time and lost profit for shipping etc, will be enormous. But if it really means a set-back for the Communists and 'fellow-travellers', it may prove worth while all the trouble . . . .

---

49. Towards the costs of stationing British troops in Germany.
50. The successful strike, which began on 4 October, was against compulsory overtime. See Jack Dash, *Good Morning Brothers* (London: Lawrence and Wishart, 1969), pp. 88–90.

1 November

Dined alone with P.M. at No 10. He seemed very tired and white. But he revived gradually. He eats much less now. I put my plan before him, by which he seemed much interested. It is this. We shd introduce and pass the Pensions Bill in December and January. Then (as soon as the Commonwealth Premiers have left – about Feb 10th) Churchill shd resign; Eden shd form a Govt (in wh Churchill shd serve) and dissolve. A General Election held then wd give us these advantages

    a) strategic initiative and tactical surprise

    b) full advantage of the glamour and excitement of the change-over

    c) no 'lame duck' months for Eden

    d) Pensions passed and Budget gains or benefits to come. Anticipation, in politics as in love, is better than satisfaction

    e) things are fairly steady now. They cannot get better; they may get worse e.g. strikes, campaign agst national service, etc.

Christopher Soames came in at the end of the evening, supported this plan (which indeed is largely his own) Churchill seemed much attracted and enjoined absolute secrecy. One thing is important – the redistribution of seats.[51] When does that take effect? . . . .

11 November

A long Cabinet. We decided our pension policy. The increases will be good – very good. The Bill will be introduced and (if at all possible) passed before Christmas. Then the various benefits will begin – from February to end of April – as fast as the adminstrative machine can do the job.

I left for Liverpool, for the West Derby by-election, at 2.30. My first meeting (at 8pm) was very well attended – over 400 crowded into a school-room. I did a piece (wh I gave to the national press) on pensions. This seemed quite acceptable. It will be a very exciting and significant contest. We have a good young candidate – a local boy of very humble origin. I got the midnight train back.

12 November

. . . . Peake talked a greal deal about the retiring age – should it be 65 – or even put off till 67. 'Not compulsory, I suppose?' asked Churchill.

---

51. There was a minor revision of Parliamentary boundaries in 1954, which took effect with the 1955 election. It has been estimated that it helped the Conservatives to win an extra 2–10 seats.

'Well, no man is really fit for work after 67 or 68'. 'Oh!' Poor Norman Brook (secy of the Cabinet) cd scarcely contain himself . . . .

16 November

The pensions vote of censure passed off well enough for the Govt. We got a majority of 19 on the first vote and 24 or so on the second. Dr Summerskill opened in a very poor speech. Osbert Peake made a fine reply. The debate meandered on till Griffiths' wind up. He was, as usual, a mixture of Stiggins, Chadband and Pecksniff.[52] My wind-up was not successful. The first half was good (My phrase about Griffiths' milk of human kindness, bottled and labelled, and left on the door-steps of all the houses in West Derby, went well) But I got shouted at so much in the second half, that I lost my head somewhat, sat down too soon, and allowed one or two awkward interventions by question before the Division. It was a pity. I had taken a lot of trouble, but it did not come off. Of course, the higher the standard you set yourself in the HofC, the more dangerous it is. I felt very concerned at the obvious disappointment of our people – altho' they were very kind about it.

17 November

Another long day in the House. Eden opened the debate on the London and Paris agreements in a very fine speech – well constructed and well argued . . . .

18 November

. . . . My speech was purposely kept on a very low note – without jokes, epigrams, or any other decoration – in order to try to retrieve Tuesday's failure. I think I succeed[ed]. If you want to be thought a serious person (*homme sérieux*) in England, it is necessary to make a long, dull, and flat speech, with a lot of statistics. I got in a bit or two about the European movement. But the rest was a departmental brief, re-written by myself into my own language. It was well received. Then followed the best debate I have heard in the HofC since the Prayer Book debate.[53] The House was full all day, and passionately interested, even excited. The Socialists were split from top to bottom; each speaker really tried to answer the one before. It was genuine debating. Bevan

---

52. Dickensian characters.
53. When the Commons rejected a revised Anglican Prayer Book in 1927.

was very good up to a point, but unfortunately lost his temper when Maclay answered, and 'flounced' out of the House. Paget (Soc[ialist]) attacked the Bevanites and specially Crossman. Boothby made a brilliant speech – better than Walter Elliot yesterday. Attlee wound up with a very fine speech – one of the best I have heard from him. Then Eden, in a brilliant 35 minutes, with scarcely a note, summed up the whole two days discussion. At 10pm the motion was put, and challenged by a few voices. These voted *for* – all the Conservatives and Liberals, and *one* Socialist, McGovern. Against, 7 Pacifists and Communists (or Cryptos) The whole of the Labour party, front bench and back bench, sat in their places throughout the 10 minutes of the division, looking incredibly self-conscious and foolish.

19 November
The result of the Liverpool election (West Derby) is a great triumph for the Govt, and a corresponding set-back for the Opposition. They have tried cost of living; they have tried abolition of food subsidies; they have tried rents; they have tried pensions – none of these have proved winners . . . .

The Conservative majority has gone up from 1700 to 2500 on a much reduced poll, in spite of the new housing estates, which were supposed to be so dangerous. (Perhaps they are going to be a bit grateful for their houses after all!) . . . .[54]

20 November
. . . . Worked all the evening on papers etc. There is not the volume of stuff I used to get from the Ministry of Housing. But every problem is of the highest importance; none can be dealt with by my own authority; most are insoluble . . . .

24 November
. . . . We discussed at my meeting whether or not to put £4m or £5m into developing a new sea-plane, to replace the Sunderland. (Incidentally, I was told that this discussion has lasted for about 4 years, off and on) Since it wd take 5 more years before the machine cd be ready, and no-one seemed to have any very clear idea what it was for, we decided to recommend against it. (Sir Frederick Brundrett, my chief

---

54. Liverpool, West Derby by-election (18 November 1954), C: 21,158; Lab: 18,650.

science man, observed afterwards that it was almost the first decision he had known taken for a long time!) . . . .

25 November

In this morning's papers is an account of a speech made by the P.M. at a party in his constituency. In the course of some 'off the cuff' reminiscences, he referred to the end of the war, when the Russians looked like sweeping across Europe, and to a telegram wh he had sent to FM Montgomery about the possible use of *German* (!) arms and troops to repel it. This is going to make a tremendous row and will be an absolute god-send to the socialists. It may even serve to heal their wounds . . . . At 2.30 to 4, a tremendous meeting with SofS Air, Admiralty, and Minister of Supply about the state of the air-craft programme. It revealed (what I had suspected) that everything is in a terrible mess. Everything seems to be behind schedule, and some of the new planes have turned out very badly, others require great modifications, others are just no good . . . . What to do, remains to be seen. I believe we shd have the courage to stop throwing good money after bad . . . .

Then a meeting about the 'directive' for SACEUR. . . . I fear that the public will be rather alarmed to discover that we really cannot fight any war *except* a nuclear war. It is quite impossible to arm our forces with *two* sorts of weapons – conventional and unconventional. The Air Force and in course of time, the Army will be largely equipped with nuclear weapons of one sort or another. This means that if the Russians attacked (which is *very* unlikely) with conventional weapons only, in the first instance, we should be forced into the position of *starting* the nuclear war, with all that is implied – including the counter-attack on UK. From a purely military point of view, there is no way out. We should be utterly crushed in a conventional war. But, politically, it is full of danger, at home or abroad, and may lead to a fresh outburst of defeatism or neutralism. (And what a chance for the *Daily Mirror* on polling day!) . . . .

29 November

. . . . By contrast with my former dept, every question here is one of high policy, and affects several depts (always including the Treasury and generally the Foreign Office) and requiring the approval of the P.M. Cabinet at 5.30. P.M. . . . . told the Cabinet that he had seen Attlee – or rather had him to luncheon. He had suggested some informal and confidential discussions on defence (as they had with us in former Parliaments) He had also told him about our proposed abolition of A[nti]A[ircraft] command. 'You are quite right', said Attlee . . . .

30 November
What a day! St Andrew's day; the opening of Parlt by the Queen; Churchill's 80th birthday. I did not go to the opening, as I had a Chiefs of Staff meeting at 10. (We met again at 4.30) This was for a general talk – a sort of survey of the whole field of endeavour. I think they found it useful. It was certainly helpful to me. The urgent problem is the 'cold war'. No one is wholly responsible – it's partly Defence, partly Colonial Office, partly Foreign Office. There's no central anti-communist organisation with any drive to it. 'Cold war' alarms me more than 'hot war'. For we are not really winning it, and the Russians have a central position (like the Vatican and [Holy Roman] Empire in old days) and a well-directed effort, with strong representation (through the communist party) in every country.

At 12 noon, the Churchill presentation in Westminster Hall – a very fine ceremony: dignified, restrained and noble. At 6pm we had the Conservative Party presentation (two lovely Queen Anne silver jugs, wh had belonged to General Churchill, Marlborough's younger brother, who commanded the infantry at Blenheim). The Royal Gallery was packed with people for the ceremony – all the retired MPs (as well as present ones) National Liberals etc . . . .

1 December
A very interesting Parliamentary day. At 2.30 Osbert Peake (Minister for Pensions) announced the long-awaited scheme, with all its complications, as well as the time-table. The new rates of pensions are generous increases and will be popular – so will the new war pension rates . . . .

After this statement, the general debate was continued by Emmanuel Shinwell, with a clever, but good-humoured, speech about the Woodford gaffe.[55] His probing questions were searching, but seldom ill-natured. Nevertheless, it was a strange scene to see the hero of yesterday more or less the accused prisoner in the Parliamentary dock. P.M. more or less got off his trouble by admitting his mistake; blaming

---

55. See above, page 367. Woodford was Churchill's constituency.

the fallibility of human memory (it was doubtful if he ever sent the famous telegram) defending (to the delight of the Tories and winning the reluctant approval of many of the Opposition) his general motives at the time. The whole thing was a strange performance, esp as P.M. ended up by inviting Attlee and his principal colleagues to secret talks on defence. After this, attempts by Wigg, Usborne and other squalid or mad figures on the Opposition benches fell very flat. But we had a good little debate on defence, and at 7pm I rose to announce our decisions on various changes and economies – the abolition of AA command and most of the batteries; the disbanding of many Army units; the new plans for R[oyal] Auxiliary Air Squadrons, in view of the arming of the new aeroplanes – Hunters and Swifts. On the whole, this was well received . . . .

11 December

This has been a terrible week – 3 meetings of the Cabinet (very long drawn out) a long meeting with Churchill and a few ministers about the railways situation. Walter Monckton has asked me to help him with this, and it is very tricky. (a) P.M. will certainly want to give in at the end and pay any blackmail to stop the strike (as last year) (b) General Robertson taking a rather precise view of the obligations may refuse to pay the extra wage demand. (c) Can the govt 'direct' him (d) If they do, and he resigns, what will the people say? (e) If they don't, if there is a strike and a coal crisis and a tremendous economic set-back, what do the people say then? (f) what are the consequences on other industries of giving in? (g) Anyway, what are we to do.

I have always felt that the whole railway financial structure was illusory. Really, they are worth nothing, for they cannot make a profit. The interest on the stock is £28m a year; the deficit about £15–20m. So, if it was an equity stock and not a fixed interests stock, income and expenditure would balance and allow another few millions for wages. Wages are not high; against this, there are too many men employed and the unions refuse to contemplate or allow dismissals (at a time of 'full employment' this is absurd)

The rolling stock, engines etc are out of date and worn out. A great scheme of capital expenditure is necessary. The way out is to combine (i) the unions to allow redundancy to be dealt with (ii) the govt to back a scheme of capital development (iii) fair wages, even if this involves additional deficits meanwhile.

Apart from railways, the more I work at Defence the more

confusing and difficult it is. We have many meetings, but little result. I can do very little, having responsibility without power. The P.M.; the Foreign Office; the 3 service ministers; the Ministry of Supply – all have to be dealt with, and I can give no orders. It's a bad set-up and I begin to wish I had never taken on the job . . . .

13 December

. . . . Meeting with Monckton (Ministry of Labour) and Head (War) about man-power. Can we cut the 2 years [national service] to 21 or 18 months? This is certainly worth careful thought. Politically, it wd be very advantageous . . . .

15 December

. . . . Cabinet at 11.30 – a mass of miscellaneous business. A very lively discussion on East West trade (perennial topic) The American attitude is still very difficult and very foolish. To stop trade with Russia (or to hamper trade) except in weapons or critically short materials, has very little effect. Anyway, they usually get what they want; either one of the countries doesn't keep its engagements, or they can trade with countries outside the Paris group.[56]

Luncheon with Daniel. M&Co seems still to be flourishing – for which we must be thankful. A good profit this year – mostly (as usual) put to reserve . . . .

The Speaker gave a dinner for Churchill (as part of the birthday celebrations) All the HofC members of the coalition govt were the guests. Attlee told me a good story of the Russian who had been in the gallery during question time. After listening to the interrogation of successive ministers, he asked 'Who are the accused? What are they guilty of? What will be their punishment?'

16 December

Left 90 Picc[adilly] at 7.45 for London airport, ...

Very shortly after we got to the [Paris] embassy, Dulles and his American team (including Anderson, who is deputy defence minister under Wilson) came for a conference. Also Mike [scil. Lester] Pearson, [Brooke] Claxton (Defence Minister) and Wilgress, for the Canadians.

The problem was how to deal with the 'planning' paper of the NATO military committee, wh requires that the plans shall be prepared

---

56. Presumably a reference either to NATO, or to OEEC.

on the basis of using atomic *and* thermo-nuclear weapons in the case of a Russian attack.

This has caused a lot of talk in the press – and the Parliaments – of most countries, esp as a result of FM Ld Montgomery in recent lectures. We had proposed a formula (to wh HMG had agreed) The Americans proposed a somewhat different one. Theirs suited us still better. I admired Eden's skill. He did not jump at it, but accepted it gracefully, as if we were making quite a concession. Actually, it was a safer formula (politically) than our draft . . . .

. . . . After the meeting in the British Embassy, we all went along to the Quai d'Orsay, where we were received by M Mendes-France, (who is now both Prime Minister and Foreign Secretary)

The conference took place in one of the many magnificent rooms in the palace – attended nominally by 3, in fact by about 50 people. Mendes-France (who looked very tired) was most friendly and agreed to everything without demur – until the conference reached the Saar . . . .

17 December

The NATO meeting took place at 10am. The same scene as last time – nominally 3 ministers from each country and the secretariat – in fact, several hundreds present in the great hall . . . .

Dulles, Eden, Mike [Lester] Pearson (Canada) Spaak, Mendes-France all took part in the discussions. Dulles speaks very slowly and quietly, but effectively and sensibly. He seems very friendly and much less assertive. Probably he is more confident, as he learns his job.

. . . . The afternoon session at 3. (This was obviously a severe strain on the delegates, after the luncheon of which they had severely partaken) I delivered my speech on the item of the contributions of each member state. It seemed well received . . . .

18 December

. . . . There was the usual long discussion about the 'communiqué'. Spaak made a useful intervention. The whole problem is how to retain the political control of NATO forces, and yet be able to deal with a 'bolt from the blue'. Too much precision is clearly inadvisable, as far as public statements are concerned. Yet we *must* have a plan . . . .

20 December

I have received a little poem from the British ambassador in Paris – it runs as follows:

Oriental Impasse

The rottenness of Indo-China
Is not believed until it's seen
The Ministers assembled all
Observe no ray of light at all
Should they remove the obstinate Diem?
The Senate simply worships him
Should they advance the worthy Quat?
The Francophiles won't hear of that.
Well, then, there's always Mr Tam:
Alas! He comes from North Annam
Pardon, maybe, for General Hinh?
No Democrat compounds with Sin
The wife of Emperor Bao Dai
(The Emperor no one will even try)
Apparently a pearl of pearls
Might do; but Cao Dai bars the girls
And as for little Ngo Dinh Do
He's Communist and Viet Minh too!

(dedicated to the Rt Hon H.M. to celebrate his entry into high diplomacy, Dec 18 1954) . . . .

21 December

Cabinets all day. The railway strike is now arranged for January 9th. But I still hope something better can be arranged. It's too stupid that such injury shd be done to a prosperous nation except for the principle – which is that agreements shd be kept – a few millions to the railways wd be well spent. We give the farmers subsidies to the tune of £250 million a year! . . . .

22 December

. . . . A very queer meeting took place at 3pm. Churchill, Eden, Salisbury, Woolton, Butler, Crookshank, Stuart, H.M. It was the most painful affair. Nominally it was to discuss an election. Actually, it was to discuss how long Churchill should stay. He now suggests July 1955! Eden is in despair. The Government business creaks along. Stuart thinks he will never make any decision again about anything, and will stay till he dies or the Parlt ends in 1956! . . . .

1955

1 January 1955

Dorothy and I were alone at Birch Grove to see the New Year in . . . . We have the little Amery girls (3 years and 3 months respectively) with us. Louise is a delightful child, full of character, and pays a visit to my bedroom with a great air. It has been a good week, with *no* Cabinets, but a lot of work done. I feel now that we are really beginning to make progress. But the problems are terrible – and I have to rely on other departments, which I cannot control. If I try to give them orders, they stand on their constitutional powers and antics. If I try to give them advice, it is sometimes welcome, sometimes resented. The weaker the minister, the more sensitive he generally is . . . .

. . . . I have . . . . read the second volume of General Spear's account of the fall of France – a terrible and cruel book, but very well written and as exciting as a romance. No doubt the present French hesitations, contradictions, and vacillations arise from shame. They have no longer any confidence in themselves. I am now starting on Bagehot (of which I have recently acquired the collected edition) . . . .

All this week I have suffered from lumbago. I took one day off and we had a little shoot (Thursday Dec 30th) and got about 35 pheasants – there are very few this year, and mostly old birds. The terrible storms in the summer drowned all the young chicks.

Walter Monckton (Minister of Labour) came to see me twice. I told him not to give in either to the P.M. (who wants to settle at all costs) or the F.S. (who is inclined to fight) Anyway, the impression given by Campbell (N.U.R.) to the Court of Enquiry and the public has been pretty favourable to the railwaymen. They are *not* too well paid; they are rather underpaid. It's really not their fault that the railways don't pay, *except* so far as they (a) insist on redundant men being kept on (b) have obsolete restrictive practices. If the Court is wise, it will give them a flat rise of 5/- or 6/- (in spite of all the arguments about the October agreement made and then rejected) *on condition* that the unions accept a proper use of labour. (10,000 men

= at least £3m a year in wages. It is alleged by the *Economist* newspaper that 100,000 men cd be spared) . . . .

2 January

. . . . A lot of desultory talk, reading, writing. My lumbago is worse. More Bagehot, including '*The English Constitution*' – these essays or books are *very* interesting to read in the light of the next 90 or 100 years. The Victorians were great people, but how certain they were that they were right. Bagehot, a typical Liberal, has a magnificent contempt for everyone, except the middle classes. How short their rule has been! . . . .

3 January

I have settled the Defence Estimates with the Chancellor of the Exchequer. £1520m (instead of £1550m wh depts asked for) I don't think I have really 'cut' them; for I don't think more production is really possible. Every year, since rearmament began, the service departments have 'underspent', because they have always taken too optimistic a view of production possibilities . . . .

4 January

Cabinet at 11.30 . . . . The Court's judgment (of which we were given a summary) will be published tomorrow (Wednesday) The Minister will see both sides and try to get them to resume negotiations. In effect, the Court rebukes both sides – particularly the NUR. The unions have behaved badly in making an agreement and then repudiating it – and then trying to get more by threat of a strike, instead of by making a new claim. The [Transport] Commission have erred in too rigid an interpretation of their 'statutory obligation'. The phrase 'taking one year with another' means you can operate 'in the red', if you see a reasonable chance of getting out of it at a not too distant date. Anyway, the nationalised industries must not plead poverty to avoid paying proper wages. The Cabinet agreed to accept the report (so far as they are involved) as a correct interpretation of the Commission's duty. It remains to be seen whether Walter M can get a negotiations going and the strike called off. I shd hope that he will at least get a postponement . . . . *Then* will come the time for sound and progressive Government policy, and a real overhaul of the whole railway structure. A proper freight and fare structure; a modernisation of equipment; and a proper use of labour – these together might get the railways out of the red. After all, the turnover is £700m, so a loss of £8m or £10m is not a large percentage. I went to St Thomas' hospital after the Cabinet, to see Dr Richardson. If my back continues to be troublesome, I will have to get some treatment . . . .

The 'strike' news doesn't look very good tonight. The NUR 'spokesman' demands 'the Bill, the whole Bill, and nothing but the Bill'.[1] This may be bluff, but it really looks as if there was a pretty strong element (Communist led) who want trouble at all costs. A railway strike has such tremendous repercussions throughout the whole economic system, that this is the best of all instruments for them – better even than docks. In a week, there will be a more or less general standstill . . . .

6 January (Epiphany)

Cabinet at 11.30. The efforts of the Minister of Labour yesterday were not very successful. The report of the Court of Enquiry was really so favourable to the NUR, that there shd have been no difficulty. Unfortunately, half at least of the executive (but not including Campbell (the secretary)) want a row. Six of the twenty are actual admitted Communists – and 4 or 5 are 'left wingers'. So all day yesterday there was no real advance. The men refuse to call off the strike until their claim is accepted. The Transport Commission cannot (even according to the Court's proposal) negotiate 'under duress'. There is thus a complete deadlock. All the arrangements were made for the 'emergency' – a council at Sandringham;[2] the proclamation; the meeting of Parlt next week. The Minister of Labour will try to get a formula which wd allow negotiations to be rescued . . . .

The sequel is interesting. The Commission produced a most reasonable and generous formula. It could only be refused by people who want a row, not a wage increase, yet poor Campbell had to spend from 7.30pm till midnight before he could carry his way with his executive. Eventually, it was decided (14 to 6) in favour of calling off the strike and resuming negotiations on the basis of the formula . . . .

---

1. This appears to be a reference not to legislation but to the need to sort out railway finance that the Court of Inquiry report in January 1955 was also to point to.
2. The Queen's Norfolk residence. A meeting of the Privy Council would have been necessary to proclaim a state of emergency.

7 January

Of course, all the 'highbrow' papers – the *Economist*, the *Manchester Guardian* and the *Times* – are deeply shocked. They wd prefer (and no doubt sincerely) a respectable industrial dispute (however damaging to the nation's economy) to a bad precedent. They pretend that to give the lowest paid railwaymen another 6/- a week is so great a surrender as to undermine the whole industrial structure. I believe this to be a great nonsense. We are enjoying the greatest boom in history. Stock exchange prices have almost doubled in a year. The rate of unemployment is the lowest since records began. Exports are still increasing. How can 700,000 industrial workers be asked to forego their share? Cripps or Cobden (and these papers are really half Socialist, half Manchester laisser-faire Liberals) might do so – because, at bottom, they despised the working classes. But Tory democracy shd stand for a general share in general prosperity.

What is really bad is being blackmailed. Negotiating under duress – the breach of the agreement wh the union had accepted – the failure to follow established rules and procedures – all that is very bad. But I don't think the blame is all on one side. Compared to the old railway general managers (Sir James Milne and co) the Transport Commission is a very unwieldy and bureaucratic affair. Negotiations drag on for months and months. And things are not improved by so many members of the Commission being ex-trades union leaders – poachers turned gamekeeper. This never works. (Actually Benstead – the old NUR secretary – is one of the nicest and most charming of men. But it won't do) Anyway, in spite of the press, the public will be relieved. But, of course, we can't let things rest where they are, with a repetition of this every Christmas . . . .

I had to decide last night whether to authorise cancellation of week-end leave for the troops. I decided not to do so – at least until today. This proved lucky – as it wd have got into the press or BBC and perhaps added to the trouble and tension. Incidentally, I think that if the strike had gone on – or even stayed on as a threat beyond today – it might well have led to the fall of the Govt and in a particularly ignominious way. Once the proclamation of the emergency had been made by Order in Council (planned for today – Friday) Parliament would have had to meet . . . . Even if it met only to adjourn, a motion to adjourn wd have to be put and carried. But (according to Ted Heath, deputy chief whip) it's very doubtful whether we would have a majority. More of our chaps are abroad than theirs. We might easily have been defeated on a motion to adjourn (or on a motion of confidence, if the strike were going on) We must remember that the Opposition can make a fairly plausible case about the 'sabotaging of the integrated transport system' i.e. depriving the Transport Commission of £8m wh they made on the roads and cd use to subsidise the railways. I am certainly relieved and I feel sure that we have been wise to play the hand this way – esp in an election year . . . .

I have still a bad throat and the lumbago is no better. I feel rather depressed. Once one gets these colds, it's hard to shake them off. I went home by car, soon after luncheon. D alone at B.G., but the 3 Macmillan boys have returned, which is very good. Alexander (10 years) explained to me in great detail the characteristics; strengths and weaknesses, and general performance of the various fighters and bombers which are to me 'Top Secret'! He was also well-informed about the future plans and designs – P.1.,[3] and all the rest. (It seems that all this is published in the popular papers like *Aeroplane* etc in great detail. Also, the boys discuss the points of airplanes among themselves, as once they did the 'form' of horses)

I have finished the 9 volumes of *Bagehot*. It has been amusing, as well as instructive, to read them – all so confident and often so wrong. Bagehot edited and wrote in the *Economist* for many years. Crowther (the present editor) is as complacent, as confident, and as sadly wrong as his great predecessor. Liberalism had fine things about it, but it was too sanctimonious and too patronising. The toughs and the toff have combined against it. It's a pity, for with the end of Liberalism has come the elimination of the economic strength and political power of the middle classes . . . .

8 January

I cannot shake off my cold or my lumbago. I have drunk no wine or spirits since the beginning of the year, and shall continue this treatment, to see if it will help. For I think lumbago and wine acid are closely allied . . . .

John Grey, managing director of the Macmillan Co of Toronto, came in the evening, to stay over till Monday. He is a fine fellow and has done a good job. He is having trouble (as was to be expected since

---

3. P1 was the development number of the jet which became the English Electric Lightning, which replaced the Hunter as Britain's principal frontline air-defence fighter.

we sold the control of the American company) with Mr Brett (of New York) . . . . Read *Tristram Shandy* – what a masterpiece!

9 January
A good party in Church. D and I; John Grey; Julian Faber; 3 Macmillan children; 3 Faber children . . . .

A lovely sunny day – cold but little wind. Ld and Lady Moran and Lord and Ly Waverley to luncheon. Moran (whom I have known for many years as Churchill's medical adviser – then Sir Charles Wilson) is a man of great shrewdness and wit . . . .

. . . . M thought Eden wd have great difficulty in standing the strain. The state of his inside is not good, and he ought to be careful. If the artificial bile channel (or whatever it is) 'silts up again' (so M said) it will be very serious. M has watched both of them for so long, that he has a very shrewd idea of the whole position. One of Eden's weaknesses, he thinks, is that he has really no interests, except politics. His mind is never off them. He has no home, no roots, no obligations and really no life, except politics . . . .

The *Sunday Express* is devoted to 'Macmillan among the muddlers' – contrasting my happy luck of success as Housing Minister with my depression and difficulty as Defence Minister. It is not really an attack on me, but on the muddlers – Thomas, Head, de L'Isle. Characteristically, it does not say a word about Churchill or Duncan Sandys! If anyone is responsible for the aircraft situation, they are . . . .

11 January
A busy day at the Ministry . . . . Came home (to B.G.) for dinner etc. Maurice was there, in good form. He was selected last night for Halifax. (Labour seat – but by under 1000) . . . .

. . . . Lunched with Andrew *Devonshire*, to discuss the everlasting problem of the Chatsworth estate. Some final settlement will have to be made soon. Meanwhile, the rise in stock prices has helped to off-set the fall in land values. One of the problems is the timber valuation. He will have to pay 80% duty on (say) £300,000, but is not allowed to cut any timber! He must really fight on this; for it is very unfair . . . .

12 January
M Georgakis called to see me. He was, when I knew him, 'chef de

cabinet' or 'personal assistant' to Archbishop Damaskinos of Athens,[4] during the Communist revolution. He was then a clever and agreeable young man, and *very* intelligent. He did an excellent job, and was of great assistance to Leeper and me . . . .

He spoke about Cyprus. He felt that we had not handled it well. I said that I did not understand why this had flared up at all.[5] There was no feeling about it when I was in Greece . . . .

14 January

Rather a formidable meeting in the morning – Home Secretary (L George) Sir Norman Brook and Sir Thomas Padmore (both of Cabinet Secretariat) Sir H Parker and myself. The problem was what shd be done with the central Govt (and the Queen) in the event of war under the new thermo-nuclear concept. The more I see of Brook, the more impressed I am by his commonsense. L.G. was very good and practical. The plans must now be somewhat recast, but only really on lines already considered. It is necessary to contemplate no central government emerging as an effective unit till *after* the battle for air supremacy. Local devolution and local initiative must be our hope. Here, perhaps, we shall be better off than the monolithic Communist system . . . .

A long and fascinating discussion in the afternoon with the Chiefs of Staff and Sir F Brundrett on the research and development programme. What fighters and what bombers are we to try to make in 7 to 10 years time (I should be happier about all this if the present ones were more successful!) . . . .

---

4. On Macmillan's role in the appointment of the Archbishop as Regent of Greece in 1944 and his later relations with Georgakis see *WD* pp. 602f.

5. Cyprus, having been Turkish since 1571, had been occupied by Britain as a result of the 1878 Treaty of Berlin and formally annexed in 1914, a development both Greece and Turkey recognized in the 1923 Treaty of Lausanne. The majority (about 80 per cent) of the population were Greek, with a substantial Turkish minority. Macmillan, who had no formal dealings with the island during the Second World War, seems to have overlooked the history of calls for *enosis* (union with Greece) in Cyprus, such as the rioting in 1931 which led to the suspension of the Legislative Council. Repeated constitutional offers after 1945 by the British foundered on the hostility of the Greek population to anything which did not include *enosis*, until eventually there was a resort to terrorism early in 1955.

17 January

. . . . After luncheon, I went to the H.Q. of the Joint Intelligence Board, which operates under Kenneth Strong (who ran our intelligence at AFHQ in the Mediterranean campaign) The work is really fascinating, and seems efficient, so far as one can judge.

Sciatica got very painful. I went to the hospital for some treatment and am to continue all the week . . . .

18 January

The hospital treatment – I am put on a sort of 'rack' and extended by mechanical methods till my spine seems about to disintegrate – is rather exhausting. I am to have it for a week. I went at 10.45 to the Economic Ctee (over which Butler presides) We had a useful discussion on the plan for modernising the railways . . . .

Dinner with Selwyn Lloyd (the new Minister of Supply) and Percy Mills. We had a long discussion about the Supply Department and various ways of improving it as an instrument to supply the needs of the services. I am sure that the first thing is to shed its extraneous functions . . . .

20 January

. . . . We had a report from Kenya. It is too early yet to say whether there will be any response from the Mau-Mau to the surrender offer. Some of the white settlers are annoyed – even incensed. Anyway, the surrender offer has enabled us to give an amnesty to those of the loyal police and Kikuyu Home Guard who are accused of different forms of brutality. General Erskine is a good man. I am not so sure that the Governor (Evelyn Baring) is really up to the job. He is a good diplomat – but this is a very rough assignment and needs guts as well as brains.

More discussion about the West Indian immigrants. A Bill is being drafted – but it's not an easy problem. P.M. thinks 'Keep England White' a good slogan! Foreign Secretary explained the very tricky situation which is boiling up in the China–Formosa contest. The Chinese Communists are attacking the Tachen islands. This has upset the Americans, and things are getting rather tense. More discussion of railways. There is really a great opportunity here of doing a big thing. We *must* – at all costs – get the Unions on our side from the start, if we are to get the benefit of modernisation. Electrification, and the substitution of diesel for steam engines – the two main proposals – will pay if – and only if – the savings in man-power per train mile are really made effective. This depends on trade union cooperation . . . .

21 January

First Lord [of the Admiralty] in the morning. He is worried about the proposed agreement with S Africa, which involves abandoning (or rather giving over to joint use) the port and naval dockyard of Simonstown. Of course, if we get the '*quid pro quo*' loyally carried out, we gain enormously. We are to have a British flag officer, with H.Q. at Durban, and an integrated S Atlantic command, in which S Africa will join. For this S Africa Govt even to contemplate joining with us in war against Communist Russia, instead of opposing us or sulking, is a real advance. But Jim Thomas fears that the 'Suez Group'[6] in the Tory party will be hostile and that the Socialists will be against any truck with the reactionary S African government.

I discussed this later with Swinton – who is convinced that it is right to try to get the agreement. If we miss the chance, it won't come again.

Luncheon at Carlton Gardens for Mr C R Swart (Deputy P.M. of S Africa) and Mrs Swart. They were very agreeable and seemed quite friendly . . . .

24 January

. . . . The Chinese crisis is boiling up. The Americans are being very sensible and have accepted much of the wise advice wh Eden has sent them. The real problem is whether they can accept and induce the Chinese nationalists to accept, the evacuation of the Tachen islands, without at the same time guaranteeing the defence of the Matsu islands and of Quemoy.[7] But can these be defended without an atomic counter-attack? There is therefore the risk of war, and 'unlimited' war. The President is being moderate and restrained. But Makins reports the possibility of a wave of emotion in Congress and throughout the country wh may be difficult to control. Meanwhile, it is agreed that the matter shd be brought before the United Nations in the

---

6. The Suez group consisted of about forty imperially-minded Tory backbenchers led by Charles Waterhouse and Macmillan's son-in-law Julian Amery. It first met at Leo Amery's house on 5 October 1953.

7. Islands over which, along with Formosa (now Taiwan), the nationalist Chinese retained control after being expelled from the Chinese mainland in 1949.

most conciliatory form possible, with the hope that the Communist Chinese may agree to attend a meeting to find a way of arranging a cease-fire.

But the fact that the President must (under their constitution) go to Congress to get authority to act in an emergency (an authority which our Govt has through the power inherent in the Crown) will not be understood and will seem rather provocative. The reaction of the Chinese to a cease-fire is, of course, likely to be the claim that all the islands *and* Formosa are part of China. Formosa, of course, can be defended by the Americans without nuclear weapons being employed . . . .

The next item was a long and inconclusive discussion on Japan and GATT. This is a most difficult problem. On the one hand we risk turning Japan towards China and the Communists. On the other, we risk losing Lancashire and the election. I observed that it was like the dilemma which Mr Bennett explained to Miss Bennett on the problem of Mr Collins's proposal of marriage . . . .[8]

After the Cabinet, Rab and I had a useful talk about 'slimming' the Ministry of Supply. Anyway, Iron and Steel shd go to Board of Trade; Electronics shd stay. But what to do with engineering. This is still not settled.

Dined alone with the P.M. He was in a most agreeable mood, and is, I think, reconciled now to resigning fairly soon . . . .

We had much talk about the situation in China. He feels that we must stick with America in the last resort. He is not afraid of Russia joining in (the Chiefs of Staff feel that their opposite numbers in Moscow are just as worried as they are!) . . . .

25 January
. . . . Left for Manchester after luncheon – for a by-election at Stockport. A fair meeting, but no enthusiasm either way. There were about 600 people. I made the same speech as usual! The candidate was good and answered the questions well.

Dorothy rang up this morning from Birch Grove to tell me that the safe had been 'blown' by thieves in the night and *all* the remaining silver (much had been stolen in September) had gone. The value is about £700. But the sentimental value is very great – I am really

---

8. Mr Collins was a suitor favoured by Mrs Bennet but not by Mr Bennet in Jane Austen's *Pride and Prejudice*. Macmillan misspells the name.

distressed. My grandfather's first purchases; my grandmother's; my father's; mother's own pieces and much that had been given to her; Dorothy's presents for tenants etc; my Stockton on Tees presentations – all gone! What is of more practical and immediate importance – nothing to eat with! No forks, no spoons, total eclipse!

26 January

Back from Manchester on the night train. Churchill rang up at 9am to express his sympathy over the burglary (now in all the papers) He asked me to go round to No 10, which I did (about 9.30) I found him in bed, with a little green 'budgerigar' (is that the spelling) sitting on his head! A very strange sight. He had the cage on the bed (from which the bird had come out) and a cigar in his hand. A whisky and soda was by his side – of this, the little bird took sips later on. Miss Portal sat by the bed – he was dictating. Really, he is a unique, dear man with all his qualities and faults . . . .

He had just got a letter from the President, about the atomic and hydrogen bombs . . . .

The bird flew about the room; perched on my shoulder and pecked (or kissed) my neck; flew to Miss Portal's arm; back to the P.M.'s head, while all the time sonorous 'Gibbonesque' sentences were rolling out of the maestro's mouth on the most terrible and destructive engine of mass warfare yet known to mankind. The bird says a few words, in a husky voice like an American actress, (I did not know that budgerigars cd be trained to speak) and occasionally sips a little whisky. A bizarre scene!

27 January

. . . . All this afternoon and early evening (4.30–7.30) we had Defence Committee. The main item was the Defence White Paper. We got it through with very few amendments. The vital points are reserved for the full Cabinet on Feb 8th. These include a) telling the public of the effects of thermo-nuclear war b) that we are making hydrogen bomb c) two years national service to continue d) naval construction programme. About the 'aircraft scandal' (as it is now being called in the Opposition press) we decided to publish a full White Paper, telling the whole story, to come out on the same day as the defence paper. In this (or just before it) the final decision will be announced about the *Swift* fighter. (I'm afraid this has got to go) I don't know whether all this is Duncan Sandys's fault. But he is certainly much to blame for concealing his difficulties from his colleagues, including his father-in-law, the P.M . . . .

28 January

. . . . At noon Sir Ronald Weeks called. He wanted to tell me about Mr Wallis and his secret aeroplane,[9]. . . . This machine is a design. If it is to be developed properly, £2m are needed (at present we supply £50,000 for research) It works on absolutely novel lines – the designer (a man named Wallis) has had some great engineering successes and is undoubtedly a genius. Should we back it or not? It's perhaps a chance of one in three or one in five that it will come off. But if it does, the prize is very great. 1800 miles an hour, and ½ or ⅓ cost of any other such machine. £2m for research and development. If you lose (as is likely) a dead loss. If you win, a huge gain. Weeks (Chairman of Vickers is very keen) But what am I to do? The first thing is to arrange a talk with the best of our advisers . . . .

. . . . At 8pm public meeting in Bromley (Girls Secondary School – Nightingale Lane) Quite a good audience, with about half a dozen Communists who asked questions about German re-armament; American militarism; and the recent brutal attack by the police upon peaceful citizens in the neighbourhood of Westminster. (One of my female Communist constituents was bitten by a police horse) This last affair was a party arranged by the Communist Party. They brought 4000 toughs from all over Britain (including motor coaches from Glasgow) for a mass 'lobbying' of MPs against German re-armament. The police, of course, had to clear the approaches to Westminster, and did it (as always) as tolerantly and good-humouredly as possible. D came to [the] meeting and motored me home. We got back at midnight. I have been utterly exhausted by this week. I'm afraid I am getting older and less resilient. Added to other things, there have been a good deal of family and Macmillan business to arrange. Daniel, John Archibald (our family solicitor) and I lunched at St Martin's St on Wednesday and made a good deal of progress about Canada. We have also to discuss the capital position at home, for we are beginning to accumu-

---

9. Barnes Wallis, who is most famous for the wartime bouncing bomb, to be immortalized later in the year with the release of the film *The Dam Busters*, was then working on a new type of aeroplane with variable-geometry wings and no tailplane for use as a high-speed, high-altitude bomber. However, nothing eventually came from this project.

late rather large cash reserves. Finished Clarendon volume 1.[10] It is a fine, rolling, noble style. I had no idea of what the Stuart HofCommons was really like. Of course, it was hardly different from now. But (never having read Clarendon – or at least not having done more than dip into it 30 years ago) I had no idea how badly and unscrupulously Pym and Hampden and co behaved. Whig historians have told only one side – and that very partially – of a tangled story. Of course, the truth is that (all unconsciously) an immense new principle was being born – viz, that ministers should really be responsible to Parlt, not to the King. To any Tudor monarch, such an idea was absurd. James I had not recognised such a thing – why should Charles I? Indeed, even the Parliamentary leaders hardly realised the revolutionary demand they were making . . . . by a strange paradox, the Monarchy has become more and more popular, and the Parliament more and more con-temned. Now (in effect) power has passed from Parliament to the mass electorate. Once every 4 or 5 years these elect a Government, to last till the next General Election. But during the life of a Parlt, it is largely impotent. The Party system has killed Parliament and debate. The machines of both sides are in control (and any struggle is internal *within* the parties, rather than between them). We never have a debate nowadays at which any vote is influenced by the discussion. Except for the Prayer Book (which did not affect parties) and the debates which drove Oliver Stanley from the Ministry of Labour (on a minor point) and Neville Chamberlain from the Premiership (on a vast issue)[11] I have never taken part in a division in the House which turned on anything but the effective attendance, not the views of members.

Of course, this must not be exaggerated. This refers to debates on the floor of the House. Members exert great pressure behind the scenes – at the Labour Party weekly meetings; at our 1922 committee. Owing to the practice of public reporting (Hansard) which has extended to Standing Committees, very little of importance is *said* in public. Anything important has to be in private. Sometimes, on minor points in a committee on a Bill, argument brings result. But in all great issues, our speeches are declaratory exercises, like those of schoolboys. We

---

10. Macmillan was reading *The History of the Rebellion and Civil Wars in England, Begun in 1641* 3v (Oxford: at the Theater, 1702–4), a memoir by Edward Hyde, first Earl of Clarendon, who was Charles II's Lord Chancellor 1658–67.
11. In December 1927, June 1935 and May 1940 respectively.

scarcely know what is their purpose. Votes of members are not affected, altho' sometimes their spirits are elevated or depressed by the performance of their respective champions. Nobody *reads* the debates; the newspapers scarcely report them. TV ignores them. BBC has reports to wh (I suppose) a few listen moodily. All one can say is, that a debate – if very much to the advantage of one side or the other – has some vague (but quite indefensible) effect on 'public opinion' – that God what (in an age of scepticism) we all worship with true devotion . . . .

29 January

. . . . There was a very convivial scene in the Cabinet a few days ago. There was a discussion on what are called 'Horror comics' – nause-ating and sadistic paperbound and crudely illustrated booklets, of American origin. (They are the successors to the 'Penny dreadful') There is great pressure for legislation to make them illegal. A sample number of copies were produced and handed round by the Home Secretary. The members of the Cabinet devoured them eagerly. There were not quite enough copies for us all – so cries were heard 'Come on now, David, let's have a look' or 'I say; Fred, you might give a chap a chance' and so on . . . .

31 January

The Commonwealth Prime Ministers' Conference met at 3pm. After a welcome by Churchill, we went straight into an account of the Far Eastern situation in Formosa etc by Eden. This was very well done. Nehru followed with a moderately phrased speech, but very anti-American and pro-Chinese in sentiment. Menzies and Holland (for Australia and N Zealand) were (naturally) more favourable to America. St Laurent quiet and moderate. Everyone really agreed (even Nehru) on the line that Eden was taking. Get the Security Council going; get China there; get an evacuation of all the off-shore islands; stop attacks – whether from Communist or from Chiang's side – and if a cease-fire can be arranged,[12] at least a sort of Korean truce may follow. There are some encouraging signs, esp in Moscow. It is clear that the Russians don't want a war in wh they will be engaged. They might not mind a limited war (except that China wd be smashed *too*

---

12. Between the Nationalist Chinese on Formosa (now Taiwan) and the People's Republic of China on the mainland.

completely) But they fear that no war could be limited. Indeed both Moscow and London are working (somewhat paradoxically) on the same lines and trying to restrain their friends . . . .

2 February

Early at the Ministry and got through a fair amount before the Conference began at 11am.

. . . . The P.M. (Churchill) told the Conference about our decision to manufacture the Thermo-nuclear (Hydrogen) bomb (which I had told the restricted meeting [about] yesterday afternoon)

At the afternoon session, we had the most practical discussion we have had so far. I opened shortly – on Middle East (which was the theme of this session) Pakistan and South Africa and Rhodesia were the directly interested countries; Australia and New Zealand had watching briefs. The CAS (Dixon [sic])[13] gave an admirable sketch of the forward strategy now made possible by the nuclear. Just as in Europe we must hold the Elbe and not the Rhine; so in Middle East we may be able (by the delaying effect of the bomb and the prevention of large armies from deploying) to hold the line of the Taurus mountains etc. For this, *small* forces ready at the start are far more important than larger forces later on . . . .

. . . . The present S African plan is to have a division ready to send to Egypt at D + 1 year [sic]. Now we tell them it would be far more helpful to fly a brigade to the Taurus mountains at D + 14. The effects of thermo-nuclear as a defence screen, and the possibility of countering the Russian invasion with quite small forces (*if* they got to their stations in time) constitute a new strategic plan.

In the same way, we are trying to persuade the Pakistanis to send even a brigade to Basra (where a timely reinforcement to the Iraquis might save the Persian gulf) in spite of the more obvious (but much smaller) threat from Afghanistan.

Muhammad Ali[14] mentioned on this question that Pakistan was already much stretched. They were spending 60% of their Budget on defence. They needed more help, from UK or USA, esp for equipment. They had also to remember their Eastern province and the threat from China.

This led Churchill into a long disquisition on the real weakness of

---

13. Sir W. Dickson.
14. Chaudhary Muhammad Ali became Prime Minister of Pakistan, 1955–6.

China. He produced his diagrams to show the tiny industrial resources of China, for instance in steel, compared to the Great Powers. No need to be afraid of China – they were now puffing themselves out again, (just as FDR had puffed out Chiang during the war) They were an ingenious people – clever enough to have an alphabet and a system of learning so complicated that it took years to learn even to read – thus protecting the upper classes from the sanctuary of the civil service ever being invaded from the ranks of the people. That was the true Chinese wall elevated to defend the educated classes from the intrusion of the poor.

Muhammad Ali neatly retorted with the story of the man who was frightened of a barking dog. 'Oh, don't be alarmed' said his friend 'Dogs that bark seldom bite'. 'Yes' he replied 'but does the dog know that'.

Mr Swart was friendly but guarded. He did not oppose the new strategic concept, but of course talked a good deal about 'the defence of Africa' and internal security. Of course on the first point, it is naturally difficult to grasp that S Africa can best be defended from the Russians in Turkey. After all, Charles Waterhouse, the Amerys (père et fils)[15] and all the rest of the Tory die-hards failed to understand it (altho' it was explained to them in great detail by Lord Alexander and by the P.M.) . . . .

3 February

. . . . There was another heavy attack on the aircraft position in the House yesterday. The questions (all from the back benches) were to Geordie Ward. He did very well. I have now announced that we shall publish a separate white paper on military aircraft. This will give the whole story and I don't think the Opposition Front Bench will like it . . . .

8 February

The Conference is over – and, altho' it has been very interesting and in a way enjoyable, I am glad. For it has been very fatiguing. In spite of the newspapers (and the Opposition) the country seems to have remained pretty calm about the Formosa crisis . . . .

The defence meetings have gone pretty well, and we really got fairly close to some of the practical problems. I hope to do more

---

15. 'Father and son'.

business with Menzies and Holland later in the week. But the effort to keep all the routine work going, as well as compose *two* white papers (altho' Selwyn Lloyd has really done the work of the second) has been quite exhausting . . . .

9 February

. . . . Cabinet at 11.30. An immense discussion about Prince Ernst of Hanover. This is really a most curious story. This minor German princeling (who fought against us in the War and who has no claims on our interest) has property in Austria. If he can prove his British citizenship, he stands a good chance of bringing an action to recover against either the British or the American authorities. How is he to do this? Why, by asking an English court for a declaration under an Act of 1705, declaring *all* Protestant descendants of the Electress Sophia to be British subjects. Well – is there any harm in this, except the nuisance of having to pay? There is indeed. For if *all* descendants (wherever they may live and of whatever other nationality they may believe themselves to be) are British subjects, then they are all subject also to George 3rd's 'Royal Marriages Act'. Unless they marry with the express consent of the Crown, recorded in Council, their marriages are void. Therefore a host of such marriages down the centuries are void, including that of the Battenburgs. Therefore the Battenburgs are bastards! What a lawyers' treat all this can be, it is easy to imagine. But did not Queen Victoria get advice from the law officers of the Crown about these marriages? Indeed she did – but they gave the wrong advice. What then is to be done? The Home Sec; the Ld Chancellor, and the Attorney General want to get the case called off, by giving the Hanoverian prince a 'certificate of doubt' (that is to remove doubt) and thereby making him a British subject by administrative act. The Foreign Sec opposes this. All sorts of other people will try the same approach. Many of very disreputable [nature]; many (like the Hanoverian) enemies. There will be a row in Parl, and we shall not be able to reveal the true reason why we object to the 1705 Act being used – that is the prospective illegitimacy of the Battenburgs. Much debate – so much that it takes half the morning. The other half was consumed by an extraordinary idea, which seems to have started with the Court, that some special title shd be given to the Duke of Edinburgh. For obvious reasons, neither the Queen nor the Duke are very much attracted by the title 'Prince Consort'. The suggestion has been made about 'Prince of the Commonwealth'. My personal view is that this will never do. But I said nothing in Cabinet, for I am sure that the Commonwealth P.M.s will never accept it . . . .

10 February

My 61st Birthday. How awful to be so old! How short a time it seems since I was 21! I have much for wh to be thankful – my dear wife; my 4 children; my 9 (latest score) grandchildren. A heavy day – and the morning, we had Mr Menzies – the Australian P.M. – and in the afternoon, Mr Holland, the New Zealand P.M. We made great progress with detailed plans for their contribution to Malaya.[16]

Of course, all this is new ground for them. Always before in the century, their commitment has been to the Middle East. Now it is to the Far East. But, since the Australians have bitter memories of the Singapore story in the last war,[17] all this needs rather delicate handling . . . .

11 February

A tremendous day. Selwyn Lloyd and I had completed our defence white paper no 2 (that on aircraft production) In effect, this paper has three purposes –

a) to give the facts as objectively as possible

b) to whitewash the Churchill, Alexander, Duncan Sandys regime

c) to put any blame for shortage or failures of latest types of aircraft firmly on the present Opposition Front Bench

Of these, b) is what interests Churchill. He has been really alarmed about it all and about his son-in-law (as indeed he had good cause to be) But he is so delighted at the skilful way in which b) and c) have been done – without any injury to a), that he can hardly contain his pleasure. Even so, the Cabinet began with a further discussion of the problem of the Hanoverian Prince. It was decided to let the case go on – and *not* try to get him to withdraw it, in exchange for nationalisation by certificate. In other words, the Foreign Secretary's view prevailed (I had supported him strongly) This conclusion was made all the easier by a subsequent revelation by the lawyers that *not all* the Battenburgs wd be bastardised – only, for some queer reason, Ld Milford Haven

---

16. A defence pact with Australia and New Zealand for the support of Malaya was concluded in 1957, the same year that Malaya became independent.

17. Singapore fell to the Japanese in February 1942. 130,000 troops were captured, including 15,000 Australians.

and Ld Mountbatten. But since Ld M (the next First Sea Lord) was a peer by creation, it didn't matter his being a bastard. (Admirals of the Fleet, it seemed, are bastards anyway) As for Lord Milford Haven – he might lose his seat in the HofLords – but he was a bad lot, so nobody seemed to mind. The Duke of Edinburgh's mother's marriage was somehow not affected after all. Anyway, the whole thing is a pure piece of legal pedantry, and cd be put right in one day (if necessary) by a single clause Act of Parl.

We next heard that Canada was concerned about the 'Prince of the Commonwealth' title. S Africa was altogether opposed. Churchill had made a submission accordingly to the Queen, who of course accepted the result. But she still hankers after *some* distinctive title for the Duke of Edinburgh. Churchill thought 'Prince of England' (to which, in spite of Edinburgh being the Dukedom, Ld Home, deputising for James Stuart, objected) Salisbury suggested just 'The Prince'. It would certainly make a good toast 'Her Majesty the Queen, and His Royal Highness, the Prince'. (Not many people wd think it a bit reminiscent of Machiavelli) After the preliminaries, we started on the White Paper (no 2) and got it approved. Cabinet ended at 2pm . . . .

One of the complications has been the position of the Swift. No 1, 2, and 3 marks are hopeless – and we must announce their rejection. Nos 4–6 we know, in our hearts, will never be any good. But Vickers Supermarine are still trying to get it right and further tests are going on. Nos 5 and 7 *may* be good enough for certain specialised roles. How then are we going to say all this; keep the firm's loyalty and that of the employees; finish enough Swifts (half-made) not to inflict a fatal industrial injury on the firm, who must keep their men in order to 'lead in' to the new *naval* aircraft, due to follow the Swift in the workshops? All these problems arose and were resolved as best we could. But (owing to the way the Cabinet only meets at 11.30 – instead of 10 – and dillies and dallies) we were *not* able to reach our paper on the future of the Swifts! . . . .

The great excitement of the week has been the fall of Malenkov. This typically Russian affair has been staged with the usual melodramatic effects. Malenkov has fallen. But why was he not shot? Because he is brother-in-law to Kruschev? What weakness? What deviation into bourgeois sentimentality? Well, perhaps he *will* be shot – later on. At present he has been made Minister of Fuel and Power!

But what's it all about? M admitted his guilt. He had neglected agriculture. But he had nothing to do with agriculture. That was

Kruschev's job, who now succeeds to the job of boss. It's all very odd . . . .

. . . . The general view is that the new regime will be tougher than Malenkov. I don't really think there is much difference except as to method. M may have tried to wheedle us a little, instead of always using the bludgeon. Personally, I am more frightened of the Russians when they coo than when they roar.

15 February

. . . . Cabinet at 11.30. The Foreign Secy is much concerned about a speech which Dulles is to make in a day or two. The language (as usual with Dulles) is legalistic and obscure but will seem to mean a definite decision not to evacuate the 'off-shore islands' – Matsu and Quemoy. During the discussion he passed me a note as follows 'It would be interesting to know what our Chiefs of Staff think about value of Formosa'. I scribbled a reply 'I did circulate a paper, and will send it round again, bringing still more up to date. They don't really think much of its *strategic* importance, (nothing like American chiefs) but they would not deny the psychological effect in SE Asia of being pushed out now'.

A strong telegram to Makins, asking Dulles to alter his speech – or modify it – and stating quite bluntly that UK opinion cd not approve holding these islands, was approved.

. . . . What it all comes to is that we think they have a right to hold Formosa and Pescadores (at least in present situation in Far East and world in general) but not repeat not the 'off-shore islands'. As P.M. said, Americans are falling into a trap. Russia and China are bound to keep this question of the islands to the fore, in order to divide Western opinion . . . .

In the afternoon, I saw (together with de la Warr, PMG) Cadogan and Ian Jacob. A rather foolish exchange of letters has taken place between them (on P.M.'s instigation) about B.B.C. treatment of the atomic and nuclear problem. De la Warr (weakly, I think) agreed to P.M.'s demand that he shd send them a formal letter, ordering them to cancel a projected series of talks on the bomb and its effects. B.B.C. (led by Jacob) got on its high horse and raised the highest issues of its freedom from Govt control etc (Milton's *Areopagitica* and all that) Norman Brook (in great distress and from love and affection for P.M.) had asked me to try to smooth it out (He has not shewn the B.B.C.'s reply to PMG to the P.M. for fear of an explosion) I think the interview was successful and the lines of future cooperation were laid down. It was generally agreed about the letters that 'this correspondence must now cease' . . . .

17 February
Cabinet at 11.30 . . . . P.M. in very merry mood. I think now that he has taken the final decision to go (though this is known only to Eden, Salisbury, Butler and myself) he is resigned to it and is beginning to plan a future and quite agreeable life for himself . . . . P.M. talked about Nehru, and how much changed he seems. He has behaved very well about the Anglo-American difficulties in the Far East and made no attempt to exploit it. He is now attacked in *Pravda*, wh accuses him of being under Churchill's influence.

P.M. had long talks with Nehru. He said 'I call you now "The Light of Asia". You must reconcile East and West'. Nehru seemed gratified . . . .

Luncheon with Lady Pamela Berry. I reproved her for the *D.T.* attack on our White Paper on aircraft. The press generally has been so-so. It was bound to be a critical press, because of the disappointment. But it was in some cases (esp *D Telegraph*) rather wounding. I think that this is due to the influence of the air correspondents. These feel cheated. They wanted a victim – a head on a charger – and some dramatic change of policy. But we have tried in this paper to be (a) objective (b) fair (c) loyal. So all the correspondents are like a disappointed pack of hounds, when the hunted fox has got up a tree . . . .

22 February
An interesting Cabinet. It began by reading to the Cabinet a letter from General Eisenhower to Churchill, in reply to Churchill's suggestion that the Americans shd definitely evacuate the 'off-shore' islands, and stand on Formosa etc. The President's letter was a powerfully argued and persuasive document. His reasons are (1) that Formosa, if nationalist morale is destroyed, may fall out of their hands – a useless instrument of defence, if the Chinese attack and internally Chiang collapses 2) the whole of SE Asia will be affected by any more Chinese and Communist advances 3) it would be a Munich – but even Hitler at Munich promised not to have any more aggression. He did not, in fact, keep his promise. But the Chinese absolutely refuse to make any such promise. It seems to me clear that (as Makins, our ambassador in Washington, had suggested) Eisenhower is taking a stronger view

on all this than Dulles. There was a reference to Hong Kong and Malaya in the President's letter, which was rather encouraging . . . .

. . . . [T]he CofE began to tell us about the situation of the economy. It is clear that the basis of credit has been expanded too far; there has been too much spending on imports; and stock markets have gone too high, starting too low. Bank rate has been put up already ½% – another action may be necessary. Meanwhile, the transferable sterling rate will be supported by the exchange equalisation account. (If this is limited to an occasional raid, it's all right. But if it's general, it really amounts to convertibility, without flexibility – and may be dangerous) Hire purchase will have to be reduced, partly by squeezing credit, and partly be re-imposing some rules about deposits. 'I understand' said P.M. 'That the ardent suitor of today dare not approach the young lady of his choice without the promise if not of a refrigerator, at least of a washing machine'.

I had luncheon with Mr Cecil King and Mr Hugh Cudlipp (*Daily Mirror – Sunday Pictorial*) and tried to explain to them the significance of the White Paper. I don't think I've ever seen a more unpleasant type than Mr King. Mr Cudlipp (I wd say) though quite reckless, was not without a certain bias towards the interests of his country, always supposing that his personal interests were not involved.

M Chauvel (ambassador of France in place of René Massigli) called – a long talk. No government yet, Mendes-France having been thrown out, 3 Prime Ministers have tried and failed. It may now be M Faure (It will be remembered that Madame Faure is, or has been, Mendes-France's mistress. But what the precise significance of this may be, is obscure) . . . .

23 February
Cabinet at 4pm; Chancellor wants to raise Bank Rate by 1%; put back 15% minimum deposit on Hire Purchase; support the transferable sterling rate; and, (a new point) increase the prices of coal. All this was accepted, except the last point. Even this was not opposed in principle, but only as part of an operation on the balance of payments. Coal was duly postponed . . . .

25 February
I called in to see Rab at 11am. He was rather tired after his exertions yesterday, which were pretty formidable . . . . To add to all this, Churchill had sent for him. He is now trying to run out of his

engagement with Anthony! Rab said that he was almost disgusted at his absolute lack of any sense of honour about his promise. Poor old man! He can be the nicest, noblest, kindest of men. He can be unscrupulous, with a child's lack of any sense of doing wrong. His line is that in view of the financial crisis he cannot leave a sinking ship! . . . .

26 February

. . . . I motored to Chartwell, arriving at 4pm and had 2 hours with Churchill. He was in a very mellow mood, and very charming – but weak and old. (I think Thursday's scene with Rab must have been a momentary flaring up of his insatiable grip on power) He said he could not leave on a note of trouble or failure. So he must hear the Budget as P.M. I agreed, and said it could easily be put to March 28th (or whatever the date is) He said he had in mind April 5th as the day he wd tender his resignation. There shd be one day's interval (to preserve the reality of the Royal prerogative – this he thought very important) before the Queen sent for Anthony. He was very apologetic for speaking first on Tuesday. He felt he must do so. It might be his last big speech; and since he had taken the burden of responsibility on himself about the Hydrogen bomb, he should open the debate. He also did not feel up to sitting through the debate and intervening later on. There was nothing to be done except acquiesce gracefully – although it will mean that the White Paper will never be properly expounded to the House (However, they may have read it!)

. . . . He did read me out his speech. There are some fine passages in it; but there is one fatal flaw. Almost at the beginning, he throws doubts on the practicality of *any* disarmament plan, because enough of the plutonium stuff can be put (and hidden away from inspectors) to blow up most of the world.

I told him a) that if he put this terrific 'news value' point in at the beginning, no one wd listen to a word of the rest of his speech b) that he must not, in his last speech, seem to kill outright the last hope of the world – disarmament. After very little thought, he agreed. He wd make the point at the end – and soften its impact. (This is really vital – or we shall have a terrible Socialist cry at the election – 'The Tories killed the Disarmament Conference')

27 February

Worked in bed till luncheon, trying to re-cast my speech (jettisoning about half) as a 'wind-up' speech . . . .

28 February

The PM's speech appeared in draft this morning. It's still *very* confused and still has the fatal passage throwing doubt on all possibility of disarmament. I sent him at once a minute protesting. I also got into touch with Sir Norman Brook, who is seeing him with Plowden (the atomic boss) this afternoon. If he doesn't alter the passage, I am determined to ask P.M. to call a Cabinet on it. If he says it as it stands, it will be fatal.

I have now heard (nearly midnight) from one of the secretaries that PM has taken my minute well and altered the passage. I must confirm this tomorrow . . . .

1 March

P.M.'s speech was a great success. I had been summoned at 9am to No 10 and got there about 9.30 from Piccadilly. The budgerigar; the whisky and soda; Miss Gilliat; and Christopher Soames. He agreed to a number of amendments – above all, the passages about disarmament are now all right . . . .

. . . . Shinwell followed with a deplorable effort. He was supposed to be moving the official Opposition amendment. This took the line that (broadly) they agreed with our policy, but censured our methods. They accepted the H bomb as a deterrent to prevent war, until disarmament was agreed. But they censured us on three grounds (1) no proper estimate of ultimate cost (2) no plan for 'reorganisation' of forces in light of nuclear war (3) the armaments muddle, esp in aircraft. Shinwell appeared, at the end of his speech, to throw doubt on the preamble to his own amendment, by attacking FM Montgomery and saying that we ought not to use the bomb unless they do – which, with the overwhelming Russian superiority in conventional weapons, is absurd.

2 March

This has been an extraordinary day – the fullest I can remember and one of the most exciting Parliamentary scenes since the fall of Chamberlain . . . .

The debate was resumed by Strachey. He made an effective speech, but in the attempt to bring all the party under the umbrella, he appeared to abandon Attlee. The most skilful part of his speech was that about disarmament – crammed full of blatant lies about Eden and the Government's record, but the kind of lies they like. When he got on to the use of nuclear weapons, he was on dangerous ground.

Selwyn Lloyd replied with a devastating speech. It completely destroyed the vote of censure, as far as the 'armaments muddle' is concerned. At one time, he had Shinwell, Strauss, Henderson, Strachey, and Wyatt, all getting together (usually interrupting each other) and demanding a clean bill of health from the Tories 'It wasn't my fault, was it', 'You must admit I took the right decision', 'You must agree, I had the best advice' and so on. As Selwyn Lloyd observed at one moment, they seemed to behave not as prosecutors, but as accused. If he could not find them 'not guilty', he wd at least find them 'not proven'. His speech was very long – 1½ hours – but the interruptions took up a great part of it. Anyway, he exhausted the subject and his audience, and really killed the vote of censure. After this point, the interest and importance of the debate took a sudden, new, and exciting form.

Bevan got up after Selwyn Lloyd and made a most skilful and effective speech. I thought it the ablest I have heard him make. He attacked Churchill violently. He had one good and telling phrase 'The magnificence of his language serves to conceal the mediocrity of his thought' (a fair hit) All this preliminary tactical exercise – great praise for Strachey and Shinwell, with great attack on Tories – succeeded rather too well. For (as soon appeared) it was not the real purpose of the exercise. But Churchill was stung into an interruption. He got up and began to tell us about the inner story of his desire to have a top-level meeting with the Russians. I sat next [to] him on the bench, trembling with anxiety as to what he might say. Christopher Soames, in his agony, bit his thumb till it bled! He began with his talk with Eisenhower; the President's reluctance; and then his own illness – 'I was struck down – paralysed'. He 'stroked' his left arm, side, and leg with a most moving gesture. The House sat in absolute silence. Then he told the story of this summer. How would it end, I thought? All this is 'off the cuff'. He seems hardly himself. Shall we get on to Eden's reluctance, Salisbury's refusal to agree and the prospect of the whole Cabinet breaking up. No: he had slid successfully past these traps. It was Russian intransigeance and campaign against E.D.C. which had made him wait. Now we must wait till after the London–Paris agreements have been ratified.

After this dramatic and tense incident (in which the first mention of the paralytic stroke caused more interest than the story of the negotiations with Russia) Bevan took up his speech. Naturally, after such an interruption, it was difficult for him to pick up the thread of his own speech. But he did so, and very skilfully began to reveal his real purpose.

He associated himself with Shinwell in the point about 'Should we use nuclear warfare if they didn't?' What did para 22 of the White Paper mean, about defending ourselves with nuclear against Russian conventional superiority? He had supported the bomb as a deterrent. He wd support its use if the enemy began it. But this was something he and his friends could not support. If the Labour motion really meant this, he and his friends must abstain. Would Attlee give his interpretation? Wd he answer his question? On his answer must depend their decision. At one moment during all this, Churchill shewed signs of giving an answer himself. This would have been fatal. It would have relieved Attlee greatly and probably enabled him to keep his party together. However I was able to stop him saying more than 'Minister of Defence will answer this in his winding-up speech'. Why not now, cried the loyal Attleeites, hoping to be helpful. I got up and said I thought it would be more courteous on my part to wait until Mr Attlee had spoken. So Bevan resumed his speech. At the end, it was obvious that this debate, intended to demonstrate the unity of the party, would end up in a shattering display of disunion and confusion.

Attlee wound up the debate, without answering the question posed by Bevan. It seems that his shadow cabinet met at 7pm but cd not agree. So Attlee, like Brer Rabbit, tried to 'lie low and say nuffin'. The rest of his speech was quite inappropriate to a vote of censure. It said nothing at all. When Attlee sat down, the Speaker called on me. But I rose very slowly, so as to give time to Bevan to get up, which he did. Preremptorily, and offensively (seeing that he was parading so openly this quarrel inside the party) he asked him to reply categorically to his question. Attlee shuffled and hedged. 'I was speaking in general terms'. Bevan, with a sarcastic gesture, threw up his hands.

I then made my wind-up. After my failure in the pensions debate, I was rather anxious. I kept it very serious (only allowing myself two or three little digs at the Opposition) and I think succeeded in answering the Bevan question sensibly and effectively. It was a great success as a speech; as great as the other was a disappointment. D was in the gallery . . . .

5 March

Stayed in bed all morning and early afternoon. It started about midday to snow – very hard. Wrote, dozed, and read de Gaulle's *Mémoires de Guerre*. Ld Chancellor and Lady Kilmuir (Maxwell Fyfe) to tea. He thought that we ought to take advantage of the present situation, and have an election in May . . . .

6 March (Sunday)

Church in morning. Very cold and some snow. The sun came out in the afternoon. Finished de Gaulle – a very fine book. I look forward to volume 2, when he gets to Algiers.[18]

7 March

. . . . Eden gave an interesting account of his reception in Delhi. A banquet was given for him in Viceroy's House – now the Governor General's House – where all the old pomp is present. Nehru toasted 'the Queen' and made a most friendly speech, emphasising the 'new relationship', and dwelling on the value of India's inheritance from the British – freedom, the rule of law, a civil service, a Parliamentary system. What was less agreeable in the past, was best forgotten. Even the pictures of British governors and Viceroys are untouched . . . . In Malaya, the soldiers are in good heart. The elections are a worry; it is interesting that (except for India) Malaya is the only country in SE Asia where elections are allowed. So much for 'colonialism'! . . . .

Dined with Ld Woolton, Lady W and Harry Crookshank. We are all in favour of an early election. The *Daily Mirror* and *Sunday Pictorial* publish at great length accounts of Princess Margaret's 'romance' with Capt Townsend – a horrible breach of good manners. All this is very sad, and does not help the institution of royalty in these days. Nothing seems finally settled.

8 March

. . . . The rumour about Princess Margaret's decision to marry Capt T (in spite of his divorce and unsuitability) was all round the House. I suppose this will mean a Bill, for her to renounce her claims to the Succession. More trouble! The Labour 'Shadow Cabinet' are said to

---

18. Where one of Macmillan's tasks was to try to reconcile de Gaulle to the other French leaders (see *WD*, p. 10).

have decided by a large majority (Dalton, Wilson and perhaps 2 others against) to expel Bevan from the Party. This has to go to a Party meeting – the Parliamentary Party and then to the National Executive. Of course, they will carry it, but what may be the effect on the party remains to be seen . . . .

9 March

I lunched yesterday with Eden – only Clarissa there. It seems settled that Churchill will resign on April 5th. We discussed details – e.g. meeting of Parlt, date of Budget etc. He is definite that I am to be Foreign Secy. (I begin to have nerves about it. A terribly difficult task) . . . .

I argued strongly for an immediate dissolution. a) October may be worse and cannot be better b) a certain glamour in a new Govt, wh will soon wear off c) financial position will get worse, whatever we do, as General Election, and all its uncertainties, draws nearer d) there may be a Chinese–American war in June e) Lancashire, GATT and all that needs time and more power to handle f) from AE's personal p[oin]t of view, it's better to get it over – win or lose g) the shadow of an election is preventing us from governing.

We had a good example of the last at today's Cabinet. We have been blackmailed by the Farmers into giving them too much in the annual review, and we are shrinking from the increase in coal prices.

. . . . A Conservative member . . . . introduced a Bill under the ten minutes rule to alter the law of treason. (It seems that the enemies of the United Nations are not, in a legal sense, Her Majesty's enemies) Some of the Labour Party voted for the Bill; 39 against. Ministers did not vote, except a few for. Seeing Attlee and Morrison voting for, I did also and got the service ministers to do the same. Of course, the Bill is only a demonstration and will make no further progress. Sidney Silverman opposed the Bill. When he got up to do so, one of our fellows said in a loud voice 'I hope he'll declare his interest!'

10 March

. . . . D and I motored to London airport and took off for Belfast at 7.20pm.[19] Read Rousseau's '*Confessions*', (in French) which I had begun late last night . . . .

---

19. To speak at the conference of the Northern Ireland Unionists, then affiliated to the Conservative Party.

11 March

. . . . The speech (which corresponds to the speech of the leader of the party at the end of our Conservative conference), is by tradition given at a luncheon, in the Ulster Hall. About 600 delegates eat the luncheon. After 2pm the galleries are filled up by non-eaters. It's a strange affair. The speech is expected to last ¾ hour or so, and as everyone has eaten and drunk pretty well, there is a certain atmosphere of somnolence – except, of course, in the gallery. However, it was a very attentive and easy audience, quick to pick up a point, recognise an allusion, or take up a joke. The chief problem of Northern Ireland is the 6% rate of unemployment. This wd not be so serious, if it did not contrast with England's over-employment. Their industrial problems are not unlike those of Scotland – but worsened by the fact that they have no coal and even more expensive freights. Diversification (that is, not to rely only on shipyards and linen) and specialisation are their best hope. A good deal has been done – the Comets and Britannias are built at Shorts; Courtaulds have put down a fine factory, and British Thompson-Houston another . . . .

12 March

Drove to Hillsborough – now 'Government House'. It is the old Dower House – the present Marquess [of Londonderry] has sold or leased it to the N Ireland Govt. It is a fine 18th century, Palladian affair – with spacial [sic] rooms, a good position, a noble garden, some very magnificent timber.

. . . . The local general was at luncheon, Woodall by name. He told me about the IRA border raids which are at present only tiresome but might provoke reprisals and thus become dangerous.

. . . . Dulles and Eisenhower have had an idea, partly for encouraging the French to ratify the London–Paris agreements; partly to boost up French morale; partly to increase the prestige of NATO; partly to discuss what is the next step with Russia. This wd involve a visit to Paris of President Eisenhower, and – of course, of Adenauer and Churchill. The date wd be May 8th – the 10th anniversary of VE day. German occupation wd cease; the entry of Germany into NATO wd take place with great solemnity; representatives – heads of states or Prime Ministers – of 15 nations would collect in Paris – including President Eisenhower – and there wd be a tremendous jamboree. Meanwhile, the Foreign Secretaries of USA, UK, France and Germany wd take counsel together as to the next step to be taken vis-à-vis Russia.

It was obvious that all this wd excite Winston tremendously – and it has done so. According to AE he immediately withdrew his offer (now a definite plan) to resign on April 5th. He must – in the interest of the nation and the world – continue in office. AE replied in a sharp note and got a very sharp reply – Chequers and Dorneywood[20] are not on telephoning terms at the moment.

AE explained to me on the phone . . . . that he had consulted Rab (Butler) and Bobbety (Salisbury) who both felt very strongly that Churchill ought to stick to his promise. All three feel that, apart from questions of personality and fair dealing, there are 3 points of vital importance. (1) *May* does not suit us. We almost certainly want a General Election in May. June *would* suit us; there wd be a new Govt (whether Conservative or Socialist) and this wd be much better if we are seriously to consider a new approach to Russia (2) Churchill is quite unfit to undertake any negotiation, and Eden would positively refuse to be associated with it . . . . (3) He feels that *if* (and it all depends on this) the French ratify at the end of this month, the Russians will be very sore for a bit. May is too soon to talk. The situation is much complicated by (1) the Attlee–Bevan row; which may develop into a great Socialist schism, of wh we shd be mad not to take advantage (2) a debate on Monday on foreign affairs – Russia and the H Bomb and all that.

13 March

. . . . Another talk with Anthony. Churchill has not communicated again with him and relations are clearly very strained . . . . But, in order to get one move ahead in this desperate attempt to hold on to power, he has made a submission to the Queen – presumably about inviting the President to London. This is smart work! The whole thing is very painful. It is almost a form of advanced megalomania. According to AE, Rab and Bobbety [Salisbury] are firm, but it will be very difficult; nor can one tell what the Cabinet as whole will feel.

I rang up Bobbety . . . . The real point is that we *must* have the option to dissolve the Parlt in May. If we don't, I feel sure we shall get

---

20. Gifted by Lord Courtauld-Thomson in 1954 to be used as an official ministerial residence, Dorneywood was then being used by the Foreign Secretary.

into trouble – either an American–Chinese war or a financial crisis or something. Bobbety also feared that Anthony wd not be able to stand the strain . . . .

14 March
Left Mount Stewart at 7.45am. The plane left Belfast airport at 9.10 and got punctually to London airport at 10.50 . . . . We raced to London, with a police outrider, and got to the F.O. at 11.30. There I found Eden, Salisbury, Butler, and Crookshank – all very disconsolate. Eden was very disturbed, but calm. We all agreed that we must stand together – not on the ground that Churchill should go, because of any loss of power or even because of his pledge to Eden, but for the really vital reason that we must be able to have a May election. Cabinet met at 12 noon to discuss the Washington telegram. The atmosphere was queer. Churchill was in a sombre mood; the ministers 'in the know' were very unhappy, in view of the painful situation; those *almost* 'in the know' (like Woolton and Swinton) were anxious; the rest were puzzled. The discussion was carried on for over an hour, rather formally, on the questions arising from the telegram itself. (1) Was it a good idea to dangle a Presidential visit as a bait to the French (if they were good boys and took their medicine – viz, ratification)? Or might it have the opposite effect (I argued this) (2) Was Victory Day . . . . a very tactful choice, in view of the fact that the Russians were then our allies and the Germans our enemies. (3) Would not this date for the President's visit make an election impossible, even if it were really necessary to maintain confidence in sterling . . . . It looked as if the meeting wd end without the real issue being dealt with. As so often with our countrymen, it was too awkward and painful for anyone to say anything about it. Then a dramatic moment came when Eden said, slowly and without evident emotion 'does that mean, Prime Minister, that the arrangements you have made with me are at an end?' Churchill seemed rather staggered and mumbled something about national interest. 'But does that mean, Prime Minister, that if such meetings are to be held, there is no one capable of conducting them?' Churchill replied 'It has always been my ambition – this is too great a national and international opportunity to yield to personal considerations'. Eden then blurted out 'I have been Foreign Secretary for 10 years. Am I not to be trusted?' Churchill replied 'All this is very unusual. These matters are not in my long experience, discussed in Cabinets'. There was a long and difficult silence. Salisbury then said 'It is clear

that certain plans are known to some members of the Cabinet; would it not be better if they were known to all?' Churchill said 'I cannot assent to such a discussion. I know my duty and will perform it. If any member of the Cabinet dissents, his way is open'. After another pause, Butler made a useful intervention saying 'It's not a question of loyalty to you or your leadership, Prime Minister. It's a question of whether an election may become necessary. You have always said that you wd not lead the party at another election. We must consider all these dates simply from the national interest. In my view, another Labour government now wd be a disaster from which the country might never recover'. Little more was said on this issue, but Churchill led back the discussion to the telegram. The answer must be made. It had been sent off on March 10th. Could not a draft be prepared and discussed at (say) 5.30 at another Cabinet? This was agreed . . . .

At 2.30 I had to meet Swinton, about a telegram to High Commissioner in S Africa. A message from Anthony came and I went to his room at the HofC. Several ministers were there, including Butler and Salisbury. Norman Brook had prepared a draft telegram, but altho' it was excellent on the issues of France, Germany etc, it left the vital question of date open. Anthony, who had to wind up the debate and had made no preparations, was rather distraught. We felt we must try to get the Cabinet postponed till tomorrow and this was done. I did not hear the opening of the debate,[21] as I had much to do at the Ministry. Attlee was very weak – not censure, but mild suggestions about disarmament. Churchill made a good speech in matter, but haltingly delivered. He told the whole story of the telegram to and from Molotov, and somehow managed to give sufficient reason for not going on with the attempt to get a meeting by calling in aid the *official* Russian note while all this private correspondence was going on. (He did not, of course, say that this Russian note averted a Cabinet crisis here)

Noel Baker wound up with the usual disarmament and League of Nations speech. He knows it well, for it has not changed since 1918. Eden made, with very few notes, an admirable debating reply. All day, except when the main speakers were orating, the House was empty.

---

21. This was on an Opposition motion moved by Attlee calling for an immediate meeting with the USA and the Soviet Union, in view of the need to reduce world tension because of the H-bomb.

The whole Labour Party is engaged in lobbying, arguing, plotting about the Bevan crisis. Fortunately, they know nothing about our crisis! . . . .

16 March
FM Ld Montgomery came to see me at 10am today. He was in fascinating form – simple, clear, direct. He is pessimistic about the present NATO situation, and the loss of energy since the earlier years. It is run by Foreign Ministers, not Defence Ministers. He repeated his views about 'Joint Defence' – that is, continental Europe shd guard the Front Door, Britain and America, with air power, the back door. As things are, our front door wd be pushed in at once . . . .

Cabinet at 11.30. A reply from our ambassador in Washington made it clear that the President was *not* thinking of High Level talks with Russia. He merely thought that while he was in Europe, useful discussions cd take place with a view to a note to the Russians suggesting a meeting in October. At this word, Churchill made a gesture of disappointment. The Cabinet crisis is over . . . .

. . . . The great Bevan debate took place this morning. An amendment 'censuring' but not 'excluding' Bevan was defeated by only 14 votes – 138 to 124. Then the motion was put to withdraw the whip. This was carried by 141 to 112. These seem very narrow margins for Attlee . . . .

17 March
Lunch with P.M. and FM Ld Montgomery. P.M. seemed rather low. It is now certain that the crisis of indecision is over. He will retire before Easter. Monty was in good form and did his best to cheer things up. We talked about the future organisation of defence. P.M. was against a Minister of Defence taking control of *all* the services. He still thinks in terms of his war-time experiences. Dined at the Other Club – a large company. I sat next to Louis Spears, who talked about France. He asked me if I thought his books on 1940 etc too cruel. I said, 'cruel, but I fear true'. Nor has anything really changed yet. France is tied up in an agony of indecision, caused by her absurd and unworkable constitution.

23 March
I have begun to clear up my work at the Ministry of Defence. We have done quite a lot, and started more. I have got the Chiefs of Staff to

begin a serious review of the role and composition of *reserve* forces (including the Territorial Army) in the new concept of nuclear war. I'm convinced that we can save money in man-power. I have also got them to begin a proper study of what we can do or ought to do if a Chinese–American war shd begin during the summer. This raises most difficult problems . . . .

24 March

. . . . Finished Rousseau [*Confessions*]. What a wonderful book! I had never read it before (at least not as a whole and not in French) It has an extraordinary fascination and is a most curious picture not only of himself but of the literary and social world of his time . . . .

25 March

. . . . In the afternoon, a long meeting in the F.S.'s room, with Eden, Butler, Salisbury – drafting the party manifesto in the event of an election. Bromley annual general meeting at 8pm. We have now just under 10,000 members, as against about 250 in 1945 . . . .

26 March

. . . . Read Morley's *Rousseau* – a very good book, and amusingly 'dated'. Poor John Morley[22] ('Honest John') believed in Progress but not in God; in science and democracy, and in a sort of strange philosophy called 'Positivism'. To him Rousseau (who believed passionately in God) is a reactionary as bad (in his way) as de Maitre . . . .

27 March

The newspapers are all on strike – or rather the engineers who work in newspaper offices. There have been no papers obtainable for two days except the *Manchester Guardian* and the *Yorkshire Post*. No Sunday papers – an immense relief! . . . .

28 March

. . . . Luncheon party for Herr Blank (the Minister of Defence elect of Western Germany) who is here with a team of advisers to study our methods. The afternoon was taken up with a conference, which I

---

22. Liberal cabinet minister 1905–14.

opened with a sketch of the history of our armed forces and the methods by which Parliamentary control was exercised. During the conference, I passed a note to Carrington as follows 'If anyone had told us in the spring of 1940 how we shd be spending this afternoon in 1955, we shd have been very much surprised'. He replied 'I am still rather surprised!' . . . .

30 March

. . . . It is unfortunate that there are no newspapers – and this is worrying Churchill a lot. It will indeed be strange if there are no papers to write about so immense an event as his retirement . . . .

31 March

The strike of electricians in the newspaper offices still continues. No London 'dailies' have appeared since last Friday – no Sunday newspapers this week and perhaps next. The *Manchester Guardian*; the *Yorkshire Post*, and other provincials are available, but in very small numbers. Today, I am told, the whole London consignment of the *Yorkshire Post* was stolen at Kings X,[23] by some ingenious speculator, for re-sale at an enhanced price . . . .

Dined with the German representative and quasi-ambassador, Schlange-Schöningen. Herr Blank (Minister of Defence designate) was the chief guest. It seemed queer to attend, as the sole Englishman, a dinner party of Germans.

1 April

. . . . I gave dinner for Dorothy, 'Moucher' Devonshire, Walter and Biddy Monckton at the Turf Club, before going to a party at No 10 for Lady Churchill's birthday. Anthony Eden and Clarissa are in the North – he had a great meeting at Newcastle last night. A very pleasant party, with many old friends. Ld Moran (the doctor) was chuckling away in a corner. I asked him what progress he was making in his projected book 'The effect of power on personality?' He replied that it was running now into several volumes.

No newspaper settlement has been reached. Monckton has decided to appoint a Court of Enquiry. This means, I suppose, no newspapers while the Court sits – altho' he has appealed to them to go back to

---

23. King's Cross railway station.

work while the Court sits. The Electricians (who are Communist led) merely want trouble. Since there are only some 700 men involved, they can keep them without much cost to the union. Anyway, their earnings are between £15 and £17 a week, so they must have some resources. The newspaper proprietors are losing heavily. Those which have great range of papers, periodicals etc (like Amalgamated Press etc) are sound enough. The *Daily Chronicle* [sic] is said to be rocky. And the *Daily Herald* too. So perhaps the only tangible result of the strike may be to silence the Socialist and Radical press! . . . .

2 April

Lady Churchill's secretary rang up to say that the Queen thought it wd be nice to wear tiaras on Monday. I happened to answer, and said that this was a body blow to me. Must I go out and buy one for Lady Dorothy? She giggled and rang off . . . .

. . . . Hamilton Kerr (my P.P.S.) . . . . (who is *very* shrewd and *very* intelligent) is *against* an election. These are his grounds 1) there is no real reason for one, except the desire to 'cash in' on a good position 2) it will seem 'unfair' to take advantage of the Labour split 3) it will look as if we were afraid of the future – moving away from trouble. His instinct is *against*. I have felt this also, but the reasons *for* going are also very strong and not all selfish or partisan. The *shadow* of the election is really bad for government and for trade and commerce . . . .

3 April

. . . . From lack of the newspapers (*News of the World; Sunday Pictorial* etc) people are being driven to church! We had quite a good congregation for today – Palm Sunday. Cold, but sunny. Everything is very backward – scarcely a daffodil yet in flower. Very bad news from Cyprus. In spite of the confidence of the Governor and the Colonial Office that there would be no trouble, there have been serious bomb outrages, involving the destruction of the new wireless station, (wh has cost HMG an immense sum) The C.O. (which is the *worst* of all Govt departments) and the Colonial Secretary – Lennox-Boyd – (who is a great overgrown boy, without judgment or profundity) are surprised and mildly pained . . . . Yet (knowing the Greeks) I feel sure a lot could be done if we had proper intelligence and security services. It should be possible to organise a pro-British party among the Greeks. After all,

Xerxes[24] had no difficulty. Some of the ablest of them used to 'medize' in ancient days, and would again for modest rewards.

. . . . Motored to London to see Anthony Eden, at his request, arriving about 9pm. We talked about (1) the Election (2) the Cabinets. About (1), his instinct is for going on, as the bolder and more honourable course. The problem is, till what date? If till October or November of the year, it's not long enough. Is Feb 1956 possible? But what about the register? When will the new valuations for rating come out? These points must be studied tomorrow. What AE wd like to do wd be to go to the broadcast and the T.V. and announce 'No election this year'. I agreed, subject to the points above and Rab's report on the financial and monetary position. AE asked me whether I wd like to be Chancellor of the Ex instead of For Secy. I said it was bit near the Budget and might seem a reflection on Rab; but perh we cd exchange later on. I wd do whatever he wished. About the Cabinet, he suggested Richard Law (Ld Coleraine) for Commonwealth Secretary. I made a plea for bringing in Quintin Hogg (Ld Hailsham) He is the leading intellectual exponent of Tory philosophy. Cd he be Paymaster General? Or even SofS Air? We thought Walter [Monckton] cd go to defence, and Selwyn Lloyd to Board of Trade – he is a Lancashire member and wd be more diplomatic than Thorneycroft. Then perhaps Lloyd George wd take Labour (lower in rank but superior in importance to Home Office) Present Solicitor General cd go to Home Office (Hylton-Foster) Thorneycroft to Transport (with seat in Cabinet) Boyd-Carpenter to Supply . . . .

4 April

. . . . The news about valuation for rating is bad. The lists are given to the local authorities by the Inland Revenue in December; the Labour councillors will 'leak' (altho' in theory they are not to be published till April). So even January 1956 seems doubtful . . . .

A historic dinner party was given by P.M. tonight. It was very kind of him to include us among the guests. Now that he has really decided to go, we are all miserable! Happily, we shall forget the last few months (which have been very trying and nerve-racking, esp for Eden) and we shall only remember the greatness and grandeur of this unique man. He will be ranked as the greatest of all Englishmen . . . .

After dinner, Churchill, in defiance of all precedent, proposed the

---

24. Xerxes I, Emperor of Persia and the Medes 486–465 BC, who is best known for his abortive invasion of Greece in 480–479 BC.

health of the Queen. Having drunk the toast of the Queen, as a cavalry subaltern, in the last century – Queen Victoria, Her Majesty's great great grandmother – having served in the House of Commons and in the Government under five sovereigns – he trusted this novelty wd not likely to prove an inconvenient precedent. He went on to a touching tribute to the Queen and her work for the people and the position of the Crown. It was quite beautifully done . . . .

I sat at dinner between Clarissa Eden and Lady Brook. Clarissa is *against* election. (This is important and may prove decisive) . . . .

Still no newspapers (in London) and none expected till April 15th at least. Monckton made a good statement at question time (in answer to a private notice question from Robens) The Opposition behaved very well, esp Robens, whose 'supplementaries' were all helpful. The T.U.C. leaders are of course very angry with the Electrical Union (which is Communist controlled) about the whole affair . . . .

5 April

. . . . Cabinet at 12 noon. Churchill said goodbye to us in firm but very moving terms. Anthony Eden made a most charming and appropriate reply for us all. This took place after the discussion of one or two items, and a short, inconclusive talk about the advantages and disadvantages of an election. Eden was not to be drawn about this. We then went upstairs to the big drawing room, where a photograph of the Cabinet was taken, as is customary.

This was rather a trying morning for us all, but Churchill stood it very well. When he had to see all the ministers not in the Cabinet and the undersecretaries he rather broke down. But I thought he felt relieved that he had made the decision at last.

Rab Butler came to luncheon with me at Macmillans (where we could talk quietly) He is now all *for* an election and really convinced me that it was prudent, if not necessary . . . .

We had a meeting at the F.O. of the leading ministers, to discuss the Election and the changes. Eden made it clear to me that I was to go to the F.O. and Rab stay at the Treasury. It's too late now to change. The real problem is the Board of Trade. Peter Thorneycroft has done very well and behaved with great courage. Should he be sacrificed to Lancashire? I believe better not . . . .

6 April

Churchill had an audience last night. Eden was sent for at noon today.

So the old P.M. is out, and the new one in. It is a pretty tough assignment to follow the greatest Englishman of history, but I feel sure Eden will make a good job of it . . . .

Another meeting in Eden's room at the House after questions (with Rab, Stuart, Chief Whip, and myself) finally settled the Cabinet. Thorneycroft is to stay at BofT; Selwyn Lloyd becomes Minister of Defence; Maudling becomes Minister of Supply. Lord Home becomes Commonwealth Secretary in place of Ld Swinton, who is now pretty old, though still very clever. I shall miss him because he is a very good and useful colleague. But it is absolutely necessary to promote some younger peers. Someone will eventually be needed to lead the House of Lords . . . .

7 April

Spent the whole morning saying goodbye – 10.30 to 12.30 – to all my leading officials. They were all charming and seemed really sorry. At 12.30 Harold Caccia came from F.O. to arrange a few things and put me a little in the picture . . . .

At 3pm Eden's first Cabinet – all present except Ld Home.

. . . . All seemed to be for an early Election, except Peake. Rab was emphatic. It was more or less decided to dissolve on May 6th and to announce the fact next week . . . .

The dowager Duchess [of Devonshire] is here for Easter – over 80 but remarkably lively. She said how pleased Victor Devonshire wd have been at my becoming Foreign Secretary. So would my poor mother. I owe *everything* to her. What extraordinary ups and downs there are in political life! Before the war, I was a rebel agst the party; resigned the Whip, and was generally regarded as one of the many young men of whom much had been expected but had failed. Churchill rightly said 'It's not a flat-race, it's a steeple-chase' . . . .

12 April

I arrived at F.O. at 10am. It was not a very impressive introduction, as the lift at the ambassadors' entrance was out of order, and I got lost in the strange basement passages! A pretty heavy morning – on Formosa, and Mr Menzies' suggestion of a 'guarantee' of aid to be given by the Commonwealth to US if they got out of the off-shore islands.

Left London by car for Windsor at 2pm. Eden was sworn as 'First Lord of the Treasury'. Lord Home and I kissed hands as Secretaries of

State, and got our seals of office. Maudling and Hill were sworn of the Privy Council, and as Minister of Supply and Postmaster General.

I heard a good story of Churchill. He is supposed to have said meditatively to Eden, after his final decision to resign the Premiership 'And then, of course, if there is an election I shall stand at Woodford, *probably as a Conservative*!'

Cabinet at 5.30. I put forward my alternative plan, which Cabinet agreed I shd put to Menzies – (a) not a 'guarantee' but an undertaking that if they got out of the islands and then the Chinese Communists attacked Formosa, we should support action in assembly of UNO against the aggressor (b) to try to get the 4 (or 5) power talks extended to include a negotiations for settlement in Far East.

Cabinet discussed at some length the printing (or rather newspaper) strike, and the threatened trouble in the B.B.C. It was agreed *not* to try to influence the proprietors to give any concession. This is a test case, against unions which are largely controlled by the Communists. We must try to support the T.U.C. There was a long discussion about Lancashire. The Chancellor of the Ex seems now inclined to make a concession on purchase tax, calculated to help Lancashire and Northern Ireland. There was then some talk about the Election. Everyone seemed to favour an immediate appeal to the country, chiefly on the ground that next year was impossible (largely because of the new valuation for rating) . . . .

14 April

. . . . One of the minor troubles of my new life is being followed about everywhere by a detective. I find it a great bore. There are, in fact, *two* of them; they are both charming, but it worries me. I have so far managed to prevent them from coming to Birch Grove – but I fear not for long.

18 April

Budget Cabinet in afternoon. Everyone enthusiastic about the general plan – 6d off the income tax; no relief from indirect taxation. It's an 'incentive' Budget – not too mean and not too generous.

The only other change is to cut in half (50% to 25%) the purchase tax on Irish linen and on certain Lancashire cotton. The Cabinet were not at all enthusiastic about this proposal; nor do I think Lancashire will be. The Inland Revenue say that it is not possible to remove the tax altogether without 'endangering the structure of purchase tax on all textiles'. It's not a question of money (£3m for half; £6m for the whole) It's a question of drawing the frontier. If this breaks down, it will cost £30m or more.

19 April (Primrose Day)
This was my father's birthday. The children used always to gather little bunches of primroses for him. Cabinet at 11. Walter Monckton (who came down to B.G. last Saturday and Sunday) told us about our new industrial trouble. He does not see any great hope of avoiding the strike of the railway footplate staff (ASLEF) . . . .

. . . . I managed to persuade 'my colleagues' to put off the Cyprus question till after the General Election. I have some ideas, and would like time to develop them.

Rab made an excellent speech introducing the Budget. Of course, they will call it 'a rich man's Budget' – but I doubt if that will cut much ice. It takes over 2 million people out of income tax altogether . . . .

21 April
Anthony Eden was this morning elected leader of the Conservative and Unionist Party at a meeting of Peers, Members, and Candidates. A vote of homage to Churchill was also passed . . . . At 3.30 we had M Pinay, the French Foreign Minister, whom I had invited to come to London for a talk . . . .

The chief immediate problem seemed to be the hesitation of the French about 'depositing' all the documents arising from the Paris agreements. They are still determined to keep the possibility of bargaining with the Germans about the famous Roeschling steel works . . . .[25]

The discussion led to an agreement on a deposit programme. Experts (including German experts) to begin their talks in London on April 27th. Deposit of the agreements on May 5th. Meetings in Paris, to bring Western Union formally into being on May 7, 8, 9, 10, and 11th – also to admit Germany to NATO – also for 3 Power talks (sometimes including Germany to make 4) to discuss and prepare an invitation to Russia for a conference . . . .

Our talks were very useful throughout. They were conducted in French when I spoke with M Pinay alone. When we had the advisers

---

25. Although the Paris agreements on allowing German rearmament had been reached in 1954, French footdragging was still preventing final agreement on the Saarland.

present I spoke sometimes in English (with Lebel – of the French embassy – acting as translator) . . . .

22 April

Cabinet at 10. The railway strike is still looming over us and there seems little chance of its being called off, altho' the TUC may still be able to do something. They are trying hard. After the Cabinet, a Defence Committee. The problem of the Argentine encroachments in the Antarctic was the main problem for decision . . . .

24 April

. . . . Chou-en-lai has made a speech offering 'negotiations'. The State Dept made rather a cold reply. We have given F.O. instructions to give a cautious welcome. Bulganin has made a speech in favour of a 'top-level' meeting . . . .

. . . . At 6.30 I had 'an audience'. The Queen uses the room which Queen Victoria used. She shewed extraordinary knowledge of all that is going on, and obviously reads the F.O. telegrams very carefully . . . .

25 April

My first important appearance as Foreign Secretary was at question time today. I was able to announce the programme – as agreed with Pinay, and during week-end with US. This went very well, and rather spiked the Opposition guns. My welcome of 'top-level' talks upset their plans . . . .

26 April

Nuri Pasha (Iraq) to luncheon. He is over here primarily to get medical treatment for his deafness. He is great fun, and talks a great deal. Jack Wheeler-Bennett came to see me in the afternoon. He fears Germany, most of all if united and neutral . . . . There was a Cabinet this morning, at which I explained (and got approval for) my 'top-level' plan . . . .

27 April

. . . . At 11am Cabinet met. We are really having too many Cabinets, but there is a lot to be done. After the usual discussion on Parl business, we heard an account from Walter Monckton of his plan (or rather the TUC's plan) for trying to get the strike of locomotive drivers etc called off. Since the approach comes from the TUC and there is no 'weakness' by the Govt, this seems a good idea.

A long discussion followed on Lancashire and cotton. The general view of the Cabinet was clear (1) Hope for a favourable response from India about *lower* tariffs. There seems a good chance of this. (2) No quota on imports if (1) is achieved (3) In spite of some administrative risks, abolition of the other half of the purchase tax on cotton cloth manufactured at home. The CofEx strongly resisted this, but seemed to be ready to give in to the general wish of the Cabinet. I could not help feeling that he was being very hard pressed by his officials. There was a F.O. paper on Austria. I got authority to deal with (a) neutrality (b) guarantee as I might think best, undertaking to report before accepting any obligation or commitment wh might prove onerous to UK in future years.

The great event of the day was the account in the morning papers of Dulles' change of front about Formosa etc. Instead of the very damping communiqué put out by Herbert Hoover on Saturday (in his absence) he made a very forthcoming series of remarks to a press conference. We had already sent a telegram to our man in Peking (Trevelyan) telling him to try to find out the real implications of Chou-en-lai's statement at Bandoeung about direct negotiation with US. I also sent a telegram to Washington, offering any help we might be able to give to the new move. I also sent personal messages to Nehru, Muhammad Ali, and the P.M. of Ceylon. It seemed a good opportunity to get on terms with them. It really looks as if some good might come out of this Bandoeung conference.[26] Chou has wanted to pose as a 'peacemaker' and we may be able to keep him on this line. We had a curious scene at questions. The better news wh I was able to give of the Far Eastern situation was not at all to the taste of the Opposition. Even Denis Healey (a right wing Socialist) tried to trap me into a 'commitment' on Formosa. How wise we have been to resist the Australian idea of a 'guarantee'! It would be fatal politically, in present circumstances .... At 5.15 the American ambassador called (at my request) .... I told him about our view on 'top-level' talks .... He did not seem unduly alarmed, 'but of course I knew the problem about the President'. Incidentally, he shewed me a telegram from

---

26. The Bandung conference in April 1955 was originally intended to promote Asian solidarity and neutralism, but with six African nations amongst its twenty-nine participants it became a more general expression of the non-aligned movement.

Dulles to Dillon (American ambassador in Paris) expressing great pleasure at my handling of Pinay and instructing him to give full support to my proposal for settling the Roeschling affair by negotiation, or – if necessary – by arbitration . . . .

29 April
10am. Cabinet. More argument about cotton. The Treasury and the Bd of Trade are clearly *not* in agreement. None of us can really understand the purchase tax mystery. Why can't we have 'the other half'? There seems little chance now of avoiding the railway strike. Eden has been *very* good and calm. His only real fear is lest we shd weaken (or appear to do so) But none of the various formulae yet proposed amount to anything but a complete climb-down from the ASLEF point of view . . . . The only hope now is that the men are bluffing and will give in at the last minute . . . .

30 April
. . . . We heard on the 9 o'clock news that the strike is 'off'. But since there has been no concession – only a change of words – it really means that the union's bluff has been called successfully. This is *very* good, and coming after the breakdown of the newspaper strike, will have a good effect on the inflationary cycle of wage claims and wage concessions. There has been a lot of discussion as to the electoral effects of a strike, had it come off. Some said it wd injure the Socialists (because of the growing irritation of the general public) some said it would injure the Government. I have no doubt at all what the result of this last minute cancellation will be. It will be another feather in Monckton's cap. I went to see Churchill on Thursday (28th) He was at the Hyde Park Hotel, both his London and his country house being in hands of decorators . . . . He was pleased with a new *mot*: Sir Hartley Shawcross (formerly in Labour Cabinet) is the most successful QC at the Bar, earning immense sums and making more and more 'right-wing' speeches. Churchill calls him 'Sir Shortly Floor-cross!' . . . .

1 May
I am still very tired and slept late. We did not go to Church. I wrote, read, and dozed till nearly noon. There is a terrible 4 weeks ahead, so it is as well to prepare for it. Maurice goes off to Halifax tomorrow. He tells me that it will now definitely be a straight fight – with no Liberal. The position in Vietnam is very bad; a sort of civil war has

broken out and the flimsy fabric of the Geneva treaties looks like being torn in shreds. It's all very confusing for us – there is the Emperor Bao Dai (who lives in Cannes) there is M Diem (Catholic – American trained and supported) who is Prime Minister, stubborn, unpopular, and more or less impotent; there are the so-called 'sects' – private armies, sometimes semi-religious, sometimes pure bandits; there is a French General, General Ely, and an American general, General Collins; there are several potential prime ministers, especially one Quat – and there are the powerful and efficiently governed Communist force in Vietminh [sic], waiting to absorb them. Not a pleasant look-out . . . .

2 May
Defence Committee (a long and rather ineffectual meeting) and then a vital meeting of PM, Chancellor of Ex, Woolton, Thorneycroft and myself on cotton. The Indians have come on well and agreed to cut their duties on *imports* by *half* (also preserving the preference) Butler has agreed to take off 'the other half' of the purchase tax on cotton textiles. This is very good . . . .

4 May
Mrs Pandit (Nehru's sister and Indian High Commissioner in London) called at the F.O. at 12 noon. She had nothing very much to say, but said it very graciously. Her views are clearly more conservative than her brother's.

In the afternoon I had a press conference with all the diplomatic correspondents. It was 'off the record', but could be used with discretion. My object was really to get across our present hopes for talks with Russia – at whatever level it might be. The public have made a sort of 'mystique' of so-called 'top-level' talks and won't be happy till they get them.

5 May
A very good press. The *D.T.* especially have given just the kind of presentation which I wanted.

All day today (with various intervals for telephones from and visits to No 10) was filled up with meetings of F.O. staff, going through the programme for Paris. This is going to be a very difficult (and very exhausting) conference. There is a great deal to be done in the various meetings – the foundation of Western European Union; the introduction of Germany into NATO; the routine NATO meetings etc. There is also the *real* work – the private meetings that (with the luncheons and dinners) will fill every minute of the day. All this needs great preparation.

French ambassador called. It's pretty clear that the French want to do business with Russia, at the expense of Germany. They wd really like the partition to be permanent. At 6.30 I went to see P.M. with a plan which I have been turning over in my mind for some days. I tried it on the correspondents yesterday, and some of the press gave it a run today. I think the 'top-level' talks (meetings of Heads of Government) have all been wrongly conceived up to now. Churchill had (or gave) the impression that he wanted something like the Casablanca, Cairo, Quebec, or Yalta conferences. Here in an atmosphere of fervid rush and hurry vast decisions were reached in a few crowded days. This may have been right among allies, in dealing with war. (It was a failure and a disaster at Yalta, which was chiefly about post-war problems) Eden naturally opposed this very unbusinesslike and hurried procedure, as unsuitable to peace conditions. It has also been expected that great and almost final decisions wd be reached at a 'top-level' conference with Russia. If not 'final' or at any rate, pretty vital decisions were reached, the conference wd be a failure. The public wd be correspondingly disillusioned.

But why not think of a 'top-level' meeting as the 'beginning', not the end? Lines of fruitful approach wd be discussed, and then handed on to Foreign Secretaries and experts to explore further . . . . I felt so strongly that we must think of a 'prolonged' period of negotiation – perhaps over years and generations – not a single meeting (wh wd almost certainly fail, and therefore become a disaster) that I drafted a telegram for Eden to send to President Eisenhower, with this plan outlined. I shewed it to him at 6.30, and finally settled it at 10pm, at a second visit. I sent a copy for Dulles, with suggestions to Roger Makins (our ambassador) about handling it in a way that might attract them both . . . .

I ought to have recorded that I went to Chartwell yesterday, to persuade Churchill to join in my T.V. performance on Tuesday next . . . . He made one sly dig at Anthony 'How much more attractive a top level meeting seems when one has reached the top!'

6 May

A long and rather hectic day. We had a useful office meeting on my 'top-level' plan etc, and I have got them to work on a number of different variations . . . . Winthrop Aldrich (American ambassador) came in the afternoon and we had a long talk. He was quite sympathetic, and believed that a formula might well be found which the President might accept. He gave me a useful sketch of Dulles' character (whom he has known since they were young men together) and hints on how to handle him . . . .

I went to Bromley for the adoption meeting at 8pm – quite a good crowd and all seemed very keen.

No one can tell how this election will turn out. If there is no marked swing either way, we may just pull it off, with the help of the seats we gain by redistribution. But there are bound to have [sic] *some* losses, and we can't afford many. I think we shall do well if we get as much as a 20 majority. There is, of course, a lot of luck in it – as to just how the cards fall. I do not believe the confident prophesies of 50 majority. According to the latest Gallup poll, the parties are practically equal . . . .

Dorothy could not come with me to Bromley. It's the only time she has not been present at my adoption meetings, now 10 in all – 1923, 1924, 1929, 1931, 1935, 1945, 1946 (by-election) 1950, and 1951, and 1955. She had to go to York, to be with her sister Blanche Cobbold, whose son, Patrick, has had a terrible accident at Catterick. He was shot, at point blank range, by a private soldier letting off a loaded rifle in error.

The Parlt was dissolved today, but I was too busy to get to the House of Commons. Whatever happens on May 26, it has been a good Parlt and a good Govt and we have the right to be proud of our work. If the Socialists win, we shall have to do a lot of it all over again!

7 May

Left London for Paris. We arrived at the Embassy in time for late luncheon . . . . At 4pm I went to see Foster Dulles, Secretary of State, at the American embassy . . . .

. . . . I found Dulles much more gracious than I had expected. He sometimes seems to be rather dreamy – as if he were thinking about something else. Then he does not look at you – or else 'through' you. But he has a pleasant smile and character. I unfolded to him in due course my plan for talks with Russia. I took great care (as I had done in London with Aldrich) to put it forward as entirely new and on a new basis from the Churchill plan. I did not believe that a meeting of heads of government shd be regarded as the *end* of a negotiation, but as the beginning. I envisaged one or two meetings of the 4 Foreign Secretaries to make preliminary arrangements and discuss the main line in which the problems shd be approached. Then the meetings of heads of government – to last a few days (not more than a week) – then more meetings – perhaps in different groups so as to include different powers, according as to whether the East or West was under discussion (Germany or Indo-China) I said that I felt we were entering on a period when a whole series of such meetings (sometimes at the top, sometimes at a lower level) would be required if a gradual progress was to be made towards a solution of world problems by negotiations instead of by force. Eden and I were very anxious that this plan shd be considered on its merits. It would, of course, help us in our elections – but it was not just an election stunt. It responded to a deep feeling in the hearts of our people (and we believed of other European peoples) and in addition was a practical approach to the problem before us.

All this Dulles took very well – doodling incessantly (for he is almost as great a doodler as Attlee) and occasionally asking a question . . . .

. . . . Our people had meanwhile been trying to 'sell' the idea to their American counterparts (as we learnt later with some success) . . . .

6pm. Meeting at the Matignon – *Dulles*, with his team; Faure (French P.M.) and Pinay (French Foreign Minister) and their teams; myself and my team. This slightly ridiculous, but quite effective, method is now the recognised technique for international discussions of this kind. The only trouble is that the supporting teams tend to become rather too large.

After a short discussion on Europe, in which there was a general agreement to suggest 4 Power talks to Russia but the question of level was only rather lightly touched on, the question of Vietnam was debated at some length. It was very clear that the Americans and the French are exasperated with each other. The French complain of continual anti-French propaganda by the Vietnamese (under the Premiership of Diem) and by American agencies on the spot. The Americans complain that the French cannot reconcile themselves to the new situation after so many years of 'colonialism' and are therefore hampering the chances of a genuine Vietnamese movement growing up, patriotic and *non* Communist.

The meeting was rather painful. M Faure suggested that the French shd withdraw altogether from any further interest in SE Asia; repatriate their expeditionary corps of 90,000 men; and write the whole thing off. Dulles (who evidently regarded this as a *threat* but wd like perhaps to feel that it was a *promise*) offered instead to cancel all American support (to the sum of some $300,000,000 a year) and withdraw. I said that although we were only *indirectly* interested in Vietnam, yet it was a very real interest a) because of the Geneva Treaty b) because of the effect on Malaya etc. I thought we ought all to sleep on this and meet again. This was agreed.

8.15. Dinner at British Embassy – Foreign Ministers of the countries who are to form the new Western European Union – that is, the old Brussels Pact powers, *plus* Germany and Italy. We got the new organisation safely launched by 11.30pm. I presided, and was complimented on the speed with which we got through . . . .

8 May (Sunday)

I went round to the American Embassy to see Dulles. He had been thinking about my proposal. Without committing himself even to recommend it to the President, he had been struck with my idea . . . .

At 11.30 I went to call on the German Chancellor, Dr Adenauer, at the Hotel Bristol . . . .

. . . . He took the view that the Russians were weaker internally than we supposed; were really afraid of being dragged into war by the Chinese; and could be made to make big concessions to the West so long as we remained united and firm. He then talked (rather sadly) about his relations with France. He was really anxious to make all possible concessions. He was very grateful for my pressure on Pinay, before the meeting at Bonn. He had settled everything about the Saar etc with Pinay. Now he heard that Pinay wished to re-open certain points. I said I wd do my best to help . . . .

Luncheon in my honour at the Quai d'Orsay. My abstention from all alcohol (since January 1st this year) is a great blessing. Otherwise I shd not be able to stand these tremendous meals without immediately falling asleep . . . .

At 8 o'clock I went to a dinner given by the Danes . . . . I was very glad to go to this, as it enabled me to expound (at their request) my general plans for the Big Four meetings, making it clear a) that the 3 Powers did not wish to arrogate to ourselves any right to manage the affairs of other nations or to make arrangements over their heads. NATO powers esp must be kept informed all the time and no decisions

affecting various countries of Europe taken without their approval
b) What is already called in the French press *'le plan Macmillan'* – that
is, the beginning and *not* the end conception . . . .

9 May
We all assembled at the formal plenary session of NATO at 10.30 (or
so) This was really a solemn and moving scene. Apart from formalities,
the only business was the admission of Germany. After a preliminary
oration in rather bad French from the Chairman (M Stephanopoulos)
each representative of the 14 powers made a short speech of welcome
to the newcomer – the latest joined member of our club. We sit in
alphabetical order round the table – (or rather oblong) I spoke last but
one – Mr Dulles (US) coming after me . . . .

. . . . At 1pm there was a small luncheon given at the Matignon by
the French P.M. (Faure) for Dulles, Pearson and myself. After luncheon, Faure (who is [a] shifty, plausible and very intelligent little Jew)
began to attack me, not offensively but in bad taste before all the
others, about the Fezzan, the misdoings of the Libyan Govt, and our
African policy[27]. . . . Since I was supposed to be France's best friend,
I object to being more or less insulted in public and I told this to
Massigli afterwards. Anyway, at this half-hour or so (after the others
had gone) they asked for my help with the Americans about Vietnam . . . . (It became clear in the course of this talk that the French
threat of withdrawal was really a bluff, and they had been rather taken
aback by Dulles calling their bluff) . . . .

At 8pm we had to go to an immense dinner – about 150 people or
more present – in the great state dining room of the Quai d'Orsay.
I was next to Spaak, who is always interesting and agreeable. The
only trouble of all this junketing, is that one has to sit up very late to
get through the ordinary work of the office – routine etc as well as
'political' work for the election – articles to write, letters to answer etc
etc . . . .

---

27. French concern was fuelled by the revolt that had broken out in their neighbouring
colony of Algeria in 1954. The Fezzan in southern Libya had been administered
by France from 1942 until Libya became independent under King Idris in 1951.
Faure's bluster was probably tactical as that same year France concluded an
agreement – similar to those already signed with Britain (1953) and the US (1954)
– giving it military facilities in Libya for the defence of its African territories.

10 May

Dulles and I met (alone, except for Caccia) at the Palais Chaillot (where NATO meets) at 10am. Before Pinay came in, he asked me whether I wd think it wd do if the Vice-President came instead of the President. Thinking this was a joke, I told him of the famous music-hall joke 'Poor Mrs Jones, what a terrible thing has happened to her?' 'Why! Haven't you heard?' 'No, I haven't heard'. 'Why, she had two fine sons. One of them went down in the Titanic, the other became Vice-President of the United States. Neither of them was ever heard of again'.

Harold Caccia told me that while I made reply, Foster Dulles put on a look of Queen Victoria saying 'We are not amused'. (It seems that the President made this proposal quite seriously!) However, when the story was over, he laughed out-right (rare for him) and said 'I guess poor Nixon wdn't like that'.

So it was dropped. The President will come. So we have brought off the first 'grand coup' . . . .

I left for the airport at 12.45 and we arrived back at the F.O. about 4pm. There was a lot to do. F.O. business to transact; the T.V. experts to see and rehearse with; Dorothy came, with plans for the Bromley campaign; . . . . I got to Lime Grove[28] about 7pm. We rehearsed the T.V. and it came on at 7.45. I was terribly nervous, for I had a most difficult 'part' to perform and I really hadn't had time to learn my lines. However, I got through it somehow. I could not annouce the form of the invitation to Russia, except in general terms, since the release time had been fixed for midnight. However, this part of the talk was quite effective. I also said I hoped to go to Vienna on Friday, to sign the Austrian treaty and talk with Molotov.[29] We went straight from Lime Grove to the airport, and I was back at the embassy by 10.30 . . . .

11 May

The whole press was full of the 'top-level' decision and the invitation. The English press and the French press were both favourable (as a whole) . . . . At 4pm there was a further meeting of Western European Union, at which I had again to preside. It lasted till 8.15pm. After

---

28. BBC studios.
29. The treaty ended the post-war occupation of Austria and guaranteed Austrian neutrality.

immense efforts we got an agreement on all the points outstanding between the French and the Germans on the Saar statute. It was a tough job, and I was very anxious at some moments. Pinay fought hard (but quite fairly) for his clients, the present Govt of the Saar (which is pro-French) Part of the compromise was suggested by me – that I shd see the Saar Prime Minister tomorrow – whether to get his agreement or to inform him of the agreement reached was left rather vague.

At 10pm I went (with my team) to another meeting on Vietnam. M Faure behaved reasonably; so did Foster Dulles. But, oh, how long! At midnight it was clear that an agreement had been reached, if only someone wd put it into words. This I finally did – on one sheet of paper, and it was accepted as a fair summary . . . .

13 May

Saw French journalists (I had seen the British journalists after luncheon yesterday) and then left for airport. We left at 11am and arrived at Vienna at 3.30. Yesterday Dulles was threatening to refuse to go, owing to the negotiations being still unfinished and the Russians refusing to yield on two important articles (33 and 35) But late last night we heard that the Russians had yielded on both . . . .

. . . . Sir W Hayter (from Moscow) is here. He gave us an interesting account of how the Russians have suddenly became so compliant, and he gave his view of their motives. He thinks they genuinely want (and need) a period of reduced tension in the short term. In the long, their purposes are unchanged. They are frightened of America, now, and of the prospect of war brought on by China or a re-armed Germany . . . .

14 May

. . . . [A]ltho' the pace is terrific, I am missing some of the election and living in great comfort . . . . The weather is perfect; bright sun, but not too hot. The people (who seem very pleasant) are in a very gay mood, owing to the prospect of the end of the occupation after 10 years. Wherever our car goes (with the Union Jack) they cheer or wave or bow. It's rather like an Election! The British have only a token force here now – one battalion. But the Americans have 20,000 and the Russians 40,000 men.

Sir W Hayter kept emphasising that there is no change of heart in Russia, only of method. They still believe in Communism, some devoutly, others from tradition. He compared it to the religious beliefs of the average educated Englishman. All have been brought up in the Anglican background of the English public school. Some are devout Christians; some conforming; others sceptical; but all have a sense of reverence for the traditional faith and ceremonies familiar to them from early youth. Thus it is, after 35 years, with the religion of antichrist. It is respectable to conform; disreputable, as well as dangerous, to be a heretic. On the subject of the leadership, Sir W H thought that altho' they were trying to run on a 'Cabinet' system at the moment, the autocratic principle was so strong, that it was likely that ultimately a new Caesar wd emerge. He did not think it would be Kruschev, who didn't seem to 'carry the guns' . . . . 'How do they feel about the future of Communism?' (I asked) 'They are so certain that it is the right way to run a country, that they feel sure everyone will become communist in the end'. (Absenteeism is punished by 3 months work *without* wages! Poor Yorkshire miners!)

10.30am. Went with British ambassador to call on the Austrian Chancellor – Herr Raab, ... housed in Marie Theresa's old palace – a lovely building. Foreign Minister Figl was with the Chancellor. Both were in a state of barely suppressed excitement. Could it really be true that the Russians (with their 40–60,000 troops in this small country) could perhaps be gone before the autumn? They were most friendly and delighted to see Harold Caccia, who was here as High Commissioner for 4 years . . . . We were shewn round the lovely rooms of this palace, including the room where the Peace Treaty of Vienna was actually signed.[30] This is the room with the 5 doors, specially built so that the Tsar and the Emperor of Austria and 3 Kings could enter the room simultaneously – a splendid solution to the problem of precedence . . . . At 4.30 or so, we left the Embassy for the meeting of the 4 occupying powers and Austria. A lovely sunny day; the streets full of happy people; cheers and hand-waving as our car passes, with the Union Jack. Great crowds outside the Allied Control building. They cheered, clapped and waved, as I got out . . . .

Mr Dulles moved that Mr Molotov do take the chair. This was agreed. The business was short, but took over an hour and a half, because of the translators, Russian, French, English, German.

The business of agreeing to the text of the Treaty was soon over. Then, rather unexpectedly, Molotov began an elaborate exposé about

---

30. In 1815.

the Moscow agreement between the Russians and the Austrians, insisting on having the first five paragraphs read (in all languages) M then produced (or read out) a draft declaration for the 4 Powers to sign, on the neutrality of Austria.

Of course, we all pointed out that (a) we had not got the text of the Austrian declaration (b) that we had not got the text of his proposed 4 power declaration . . . .

Seeing (I think) that we all said the same thing, and that there did not seem any chance of getting through the allied guard, he dropped it and with that (and some formalities) the session closed.

Molotov was some distance from me, and I could not observe him closely. He seemed to me smaller than I had supposed and older (we are all older!) He is grey, not black any more; a very pale, pasty face; a large forehead; closely cut grey hair. He wore a very respectable black suit – and looked rather like a head gardener in his Sunday clothes (actually, he is very like Barnard, the old keeper at Hardwick)[31] . . . .

Dinner at the American Embassy at 7.45. About 5 or 6 small talks were arranged in a large room in this modern house, built in the sort of Algerian villa style. At our table were Dulles, Molotov, Pinay, HM, and M's interpreter (Russian–English) and Pinay's interpreter (Russian–French) . . . .

In talking alone to Foster Dulles, M seems to have made quite sensible remarks about the need to find some peaceful solution of the Formosa problem. At dinner, nothing of very great importance was said, but M was going out of his way to be pleasant – kept talking about the need for mutual understanding and the 'reduction of tension'. (The American ambassador at Moscow – Bohlen – says (a) his own position is not as strong as it was (b) the Russians are very much more frightened by the American strategic air force and the hydrogen bomb (c) are anxious about the economic strain upon their economy by the double demands of armaments and providing heavy industry for China).

After dinner, and the usual toasts, we all sat in easy chairs in the lounge. The conversation was very easy, although very slow – owing to the translations.

It took 3 hours; but not more business was done than cd be transacted among normal people in 30 minutes. This, apart from the

---

31. One of the Devonshire properties.

translation problem, was partly because Dulles is very slow; M was rather 'cagey' and Pinay very irrelevant. I said very little. M asked for elucidation of our invitation. Dulles explained '*le plan Macmillan*' and the idea of the Heads of Government giving an impulse to a continual process of negotiation through the Foreign Secretaries and other suitable agencies. M was very insistent on the Heads meeting and did not seem to like the meeting of Foreign Secretaries *before* the Heads. Dulles explained that it shd all be *one* meeting, with Foreign Ministers perhaps arriving a day or two before to fix final arrangements. M hoped there wd be no agenda. D agreed. The meeting was really intended to leave agenda behind or for further work. Both agreed that public opinion in all our countries shd not be led to expect a spectacular success, but rather the imagination of a new system of patient pursuit of peaceful solution . . . .

As to place, M was very keen on Vienna – as symbol of neutralism . . . . D said categorically that the President wd *not* come to an occupied country . . . . We want Switzerland.

As to time, D explained that the President must be at home in the last week or 10 days of this session of Congress . . . . There was a good deal of discussion about San Francisco, and the United Nations meetings on June 20 for a week. Wd it not be useful for us four to go there for a further talk. M seemed rather keen on this . . . .

15 May

The Treaty was signed at a ceremony which began at 11.30am. The signing took place in the large central hall or salon on the first floor of the Belvedere. (This magnificent palace and garden was the gift of the Emperor to Prince Eugene, just as Blenheim was Queen Anne's gift to Marlborough)[32]

We had all agreed to make short speeches, but Molotov cheated. He offended those present by a long piece of propaganda, about how Austria shd serve as a model for Germany – and about European security etc. After the signing, we all went repeatedly on the balcony facing the gardens. The immense crowd greeted all the Foreign Ministers (at their various appearances) with wild applause. (I thought M got the most applause! Perhaps because they will be so glad when the

---

32. Prince Eugene of Savoy (1663–1736), imperial field marshal of the Holy Roman Empire, who fought alongside Churchill's ancestor, the first Duke of Marlborough, at Blenheim, Oudenaarde and Malplaquet.

Russians – all 60,000 of them – finally go away. Or it may have been that the Communist Party had organised a special 'claque' to cheer for him. Anyway, it was all very emotional. A lot of champagne was drunk *inside* the Belvedere, and the crowd was intoxicated with joy in the gardens *outside*.)

An immense and magnificent luncheon was served in the royal palace – in the old wing occupied by Maria Theresa. We drove in a long procession from the Belvedere to the palace. This began at about 2pm and ended at 4pm. M Pinay and I (not Dulles or Molotov!) then went to the Te Deum, which was beautifully sung before all the civil and ecclesiastical notables, in the Cathedral Church of St Stephen.

After a short interval, we all had to start off again, in evening clothes, to a great dinner at the Schönbrunn palace, at 7pm! This was in a splendid hall, again with lovely gold plate (we had much of this at the luncheon) and lovely china – belonging, I suppose, to the Imperial House. The flowers were wonderful also. (This is a specially good time for Vienna – the lilacs are all out in the city streets and gardens, and much other blossom as well) The toasts were short. We each gave one in turn. I was last and cd not quite think of a toast, as most subjects had been taken. The American ambassador (Thompson) had given me a hint. So I rose and said 'After so many toasts, there is only one left for me to propose. But I believe you will think it the most important. I ask you to rise and drink with me to "the early ratification of the Treaty"'. This brought the house down . . . .

16 May
Left airport at 9.30. Chancellor Raab and Foreign Minister Figl come to see me off . . . .

17 May
A curious experiment in T.V. (much easier for this performance than solo) 10 newspaper editors asked questions; 5 ministers answered them. (Eden; Butler; Monckton, McLeod, and HM) It was said to be a success. I saw Ld Woolton afterwards. Everything is going well, but the Liberals have set us a difficult task. Their intervention has been so planned as to lose us 15 seats to Labour – unless there is a swing. We shall then be *out* by 8 or 10. But there *may* be a swing . . . .

20 May
Another day of electioneering – canvassing and a meeting in the

evening. It's all very tiring, altho' I do much less than I used to do in the old days.

I am made to write a large number of newspaper articles for the election. I find it very difficult to compose anything that is not very banal . . . .

22 May

I have not been able to go very much to the F.O. these last days – but the work has to be done nevertheless, and the stream of 'boxes' never ceases. It is strange to feel on how little turns one's personal life. I may be back at St Martin's St in a week – or at the F.O. for several years (unless I make a fool of myself!) No one seems to know what is happening. There has never been a 'quieter' election – a little too quiet for my taste. Anything may happen. I don't think the Labour Party will get a large majority – but that doesn't seem to matter nowadays. We may scrape in by 15 (in spite of the Liberal intervention being so carefully calculated to lose us 10–15 precious marginal seats) or there *may* be (it seems not impossible) quite a big 'slide' towards us. I do not feel much confidence in the Gallup polls, because they give only a *general* picture, and each constituency has such different features . . . .

24 May

The *Daily Mirror* 'bombshell' has burst. It is just a very scurrilous attack on Tories and Toryism. I doubt if it will do much harm. But, of course, it has a huge circulation.[33] The chief idea is to say that the Tories are bound to get in, so 'vote Labour' and keep their majority small.

I left Kings X at 12 noon, arriving Leeds at 3.15pm, where I was met by Donald Kaberry. We toured several constituencies . . . . I then went on to Halifax, where Maurice is standing. The hall was packed – I shd think 1500 – and Maurice was speaking (very well, I thought) when I arrived. I spoke for ¾ hour and had a tremendous reception. Then we had questions – which everybody enjoyed very much, because we parcelled them out between us and it was a good 'turn'. After seeing his loyal workers and having some supper, I returned to Leeds and got the night train to London . . . .

---

33. The circulation of this Labour-supporting newspaper was then over 4.5 million, easily the largest of the national newspapers.

26 May

Polling day – fine all day, till about 6pm. Then some very heavy storms. D and I went round all the committee rooms and polling stations as usual. Everything very quiet. We got to the Savoy by 8.15 – dinner given by the *Daily Telegraph*. The results began to come through about 10.15. Salford was the first – a 'Tory' swing of 2000 votes or so. I hate this part of it more than anything else. It's too exciting! By midnight, altho' there were very few seats gained, it was clear that we would win. No 'landslide', but a very real swing to us – or rather, away from the Socialists. Their polls fell away in almost every seat. As I had hoped, some of them abstained.

At 1am I went to Conservative Central Office. When I got into Lord Woolton's room, where the results were coming out and being analysed, Halifax came through. Maurice *in*, by 1500.[34] I was so excited that I dashed back to the Savoy, where I found Dorothy, almost in tears, the centre of congratulations from all sides. It is really splendid – so good that he has *won* a seat, and all on his own. This is far better for him than a safe suburban or county seat which he had not earned.

We left the Savoy about 3.30am and came to Carlton Gardens – which will now be our home for 4 or 5 years, I suppose (unless I am turned out of the F.O.) We rang Maurice at 4am. He was just going to bed – his celebrations over. It looks like a majority of 70 or 80.

27 May

. . . . We went to Bromley for the count. My majority is 1000 up.[35] We might have done a bit better, perhaps, but we sent all our canvassers to Bexley and Chislehurst. All the afternoon the results came in. We have been very unlucky this time in the 'fall of the cards'. In 1951 we were very lucky. Reading, Faversham, Norfolk [South West], Barons Court, Blackburn and many other seats are *just not* won – a few hundreds out. The county seats are *not* good. The towns, esp the industrial towns, have done splendidly. Lancashire solid. We even kept Oldham. The total votes cast are *down*. We have ½ million less; they have 1½ million less. (Liberals about the same and did not injure us as much as we had feared) Chislehurst (Miss Hornsby Smith) retained by

---

34. M. V. Macmillan (C): 28,306; D. Brook (Lab): 26,771.
35. M. H. Macmillan (C): 24,612; G. B. Kaufman (Lab): 11,473.

over 3000! Bexley good too. The NE good. The West Riding good. The final majority is 60 . . . .[36]

Dined with 'Rab' Butler at the Turf. I fear the railway strike is on . . . . 'Transport' is the great failure of the last 3 years. No one has grasped the problem at all. Maclay, Lennox-Boyd, and now Boyd-Carpenter – none of them suitable ministers for the job. It needs a big man to take hold of the railways . . . .

After dinner, we went round to see P.M. He was in fine form. He has certainly been first-class during the election. He hasn't put a foot wrong. We decided to attempt no major reconstruction of the Govt till the end of July . . . .

30 May

. . . . The Lord Chancellor and Lady Kilmuir came to luncheon. We 'gossiped' all the afternoon, sitting in the garden. Julian and Catherine Amery came and at last, the triumphant victor, Maurice and Katie, both radiantly happy and looking very well. We talked over all the election incidents and exchanged anecdotes till late. 'We have a wonderful candidate. He is going to do wonderful things for the old people. He cares very much for the pensioners. He is going to put them "out of their misery"!' . . . .

3 June

. . . . A long meeting with Krishna Menon (Nehru's personal representative) at No 10. Eden was very good; but I frankly failed to follow Menon's very involved subtleties. He has been engaged in a number of long conversations with Chou-en-lai in Peking, and thinks that there may be a chance of a negotiation being started directly between the Communist Chinese and the American Government . . . .

7 June

. . . . At this morning's Cabinet, there was an explanation by Walter Monckton of the present strike situation. He passed me a note 'Tomorrow, or the next day may be the next critical day. If Robertson will wear some "token" payment for the drivers and perhaps some firemen, we might get away with it – and treat it as a basis of negotiation. I shall want help when I come to that'. There *is* however

---

36. Conservatives 344, Labour 277, Liberals 6, Others 3.

a certain misunderstanding growing up in the Press about the Government's demand for a return to work *before* negotiation.

The P.M. made it clear – but not abundantly clear, in his broadcast on Sunday. I referred to this, and was supported by Salisbury. We are not, I said, asking for 'unconditional surrender'. We are asking for three stages. (1) agreement on a *basis* for negotiation (2) return to work (3) the negotiation proper – which may take several weeks. We had an interesting discussion on (i) industrial relations (ii) monopolies – on both these vast topics the Cabinet ought to think a great deal. P.M. accepted my suggestion to have a committee of ministers on (i) On (ii) there will be further discussion . . . .

8 June
Field Marshal Phibul (Thailand) who is also Prime Minister, called formally at F.O. . . . .

. . . . At the P.M.'s dinner for the Siamese, I had a long talk with . . . . Mr Geddes (of T.U.C.) about the strike and about the future of industrial relations. On the second point, he thought we shd take advantage of the present state of public opinion to get some discipline restored into the Trade Unions! The problem was, how to act in full alliance with a Tory govt, without the cry of betrayal being raised by the extremists. Geddes wd like a private talk with P.M., and (he said) with me, as soon as the railway strike is over. I said 'When will this be?' He replied 'I *think* by the end of the week' . . . .

9 June
. . . . Colonial Secy and I have agreed a plan for Cyprus. We will put it to the Cabinet next week and I earnestly hope they will agree – at least in principle. The general idea is to start by asking the Greeks and the Turks to talk it over with us. If the Greeks refuse, their position in UNO will be correspondingly injured. If we cd get some kind of a settlement, it wd be a great blessing . . . .

10 June
The strike still continues; I do feel that we ought not to stand too much on 'face' and have said so rather strongly in the Cabinet. I gave a luncheon party for M Mollet (French Minister for Europe) and we had a long and useful discussion about the plans for Strasbourg. This time there will, in addition, be the meeting of the assembly

of Western European Union. It is very important that there shd be no friction between this new organisation and the Council of Europe . . . .

Dined with Walter and Biddy Monckton. He was very tired, but in good heart. If Robertson wd make a 'token' offer in cash, however small, the strike might be settled. But he fears that P.M. and Cabinet will not approve. I said I thought that Robertson (as head of Transport Commission) shd decide on commercial, not on political grounds . . . .

12 June

I have now 4 speeches to prepare. One for the House of Commons on Wednesday; one for the Pilgrims in New York; one for the United Nations meeting in San Francisco; one for the Commonwealth Club in S Francisco.

I had a stenographer and typist down to B.G. and worked all day till about 4pm. After tea, D and I went for a walk in the woods and saw Blake . . . .

13 June

. . . . The Cabinet is beginning to have doubts about 'face'. The P.M. (as I feared) is beginning to be embarassed by his broadcast last Sunday. It is very dangerous to take up too firm a position in these affairs. Actually, ASLEF, led by Mr Baty, are so pig-headed that it's almost impossible to get anything sensible out of them. But I feel that Walter [Monckton] cd get a reasonable settlement (wh wd *not* be thought a victory for the strikers) if he was allowed to bring a little pressure on the Transport Commisson and on Genl Robertson. Woolton made a sensible suggestion. Cd not the total sum (£1 million or whatever it was) wh Robertson offered *before* the strike be offered again, to be divided as ASLEF proposed, but on condition that it does *not* lead to a substantial payment to equivalent NUR grades . . . .

. . . . 3.15–4.30, a most important meeting with Kirkpatrick and Pat Dean, preparatory to a meeting of ministers on the great international problem. At my request, a special ctee of ministers has been constituted to advise on all this – Russia, Germany, disarmament etc. The Chiefs of Staff are also in attendance. P.M.; Butler; Salisbury; Selwyn Lloyd (defence) and myself. The circulation of these deadly papers (all possible plans are canvassed and debated) is severely limited. The code name is CANUTE.[37]

We shall start, of course, with the 'Eden plan' of last year – the Berlin conference. But we may have to add something for the Russians, if there is to be any chance of their leaving E Germany. Perhaps a neutral strip; perh a reduction of British and American troops in *Germany*, or even the evacuation of Germany (at the end of 5 years) by the British and Americans. All this must be studied and the cards ready to be played if the prize is high enough. But, we must a) keep Germany in NATO b) not disarm except in such a way as to keep a balance of conventional forces in Europe c) keep America in Europe. We had a most useful and helpful discussion. P.M. positively brilliant. He really understands all this, and speaks with authority. He backed my suggestion of exploring whether we cd agree a neutral *strip* in E Germany, if [the] Russians evacuated their zone. He also agreed that the first thing was to find out in New York what Dr Adenauer's ideas are. Hoyer Millar (our ambassador in Bonn) is not at all sure that the western Germans are as keen as they have to pretend to be on re-unification . . . .

14 June

. . . . My proposals on Cyprus (which Colonial Secretary supported) had a sort of trial run this morning. The Cabinet did not accept them – indeed some members (as I expected) were definitely hostile. But I was not too discouraged. P.M. was very generous (and it is not easy for him, since he had told Papagos (Greek premier) a year ago that Cyprus was not 'discussable') Anyway, a committee of ministers is to go on working at my plan, with a view to further discussion when I return in a fortnight. We had a rather inconclusive discussion about whether or not to vote for the inclusion of Japan in GATT. Since we all agree that she will have to be elected, both on commercial and political grounds, it seems rather a discreditable line to abstain (which means a negative vote under the GATT procedure) and yet hope that others will vote 'yes'. (I told Cabinet that it reminded me of the Liberals in the 1929–31 Parlt) The question was postponed for a week . . . .

---

37. Both Canute and the preceding Eden plan envisaged limited demilitarization in East Germany.

The Israeli and the Egyptian ambassadors called – in succession. I appealed to them to cooperate with General Burns about Gaza. Both ambassadors disclaimed any intention of going to war. So I said – why then allow a situation to continue on the frontier which may well lead to war? . . . .[38]

Sir F Roberts, back from Jugoslavia, gave me a fascinating picture of the situation there and of the Russian visits. We must do something to counter-act the Russian influence. Tito is very suspicious of them still, but of course he *is* a Communist, altho' Jugoslavia is looking more and more to the West. I shd like to go there myself. I heard a joke current in Moscow. They say that the Russians have invited Adenauer to Moscow in order to show them how a country can be governed firmly. They have had no proper dictator since Stalin died! . . . .

I have written to P.M. to say that I don't think I ought to have 'Dorneywood'. I much prefer to go to B.G. whenever I get a spare day . . . .

15 June

The railway strike is over – on what seems satisfactory terms. But 17 days is too long. Much harm will have been done to the economy, some of which will not be revealed till the months go by. For instance, a heavy importation of coal will be necessary. This will mean $60m or $70m on the exchange.

On the other hand, the fact that (a) industrial and general life cd stand up to at least a ⅘ stoppage of trains without collapse (b) that the men got virtually nothing more than they cd have had at the beginning, may have a deflationary effect and do something to stop the see-saw of wages and prices which has begun to show itself in the last year or two. Whether a lot of traffic will be lost permanently to the roads, remains to be seen.

16 June

After landing to refuel at Gander (Newfoundland), we arrived at New York about 8.45am (New York time; nearly 2pm London time) My

---

38. General Burns was the head of the United Nations Truce Supervision Organisation policing the Arab–Israeli borders. Commando raids into Israel from the Egyptian-occupied Gaza strip had earlier led the Israelis to retaliate with the Gaza raid of 28 February 1955.

party was rather large – Harold Caccia, Pat Dean, General Brownjohn, Lord Hood, Rumbold, Andrew Stark (dep P.S.) typists, detective etc. We were met by Roger Makins (ambassador Washington) Bob Dixon (ambassador United Nations) Consul General etc etc. A great battery of a) still photographers b) movies c) television etc . . . .

At 12 noon, Foster Dulles and his team arrived to visit us. We are all (or mostly) staying at a lovely house, about 15–20 minutes from N York, on the Hudson (West River) which Gladwyn Jebb originally hired and Dixon has taken on. It's most comfortable, and rather old-fashioned. How infinitely nicer than an apartment in Park Avenue! But, of course, the servant problem is formidable. We soon settled down to the usual procedure – each principal, like a boxer, with his second and trainers crowded behind him. (After luncheon, to which the French came, including M Pinay, Foreign Minister, Couve de Murville, M Hoppenot etc.) the game changed (as it were) to three-handed cribbage.

It was useful to have a preliminary talk with F.D. This included Gaza and operation 'Alpha';[39] nuclear warfare; how to handle Adenauer; what concessions we might ultimately offer the Russians as the price for German re-unification. To my delight, I found that what is called 'our thinking' had been proceeding on almost the same lines as the Americans . . . .

After luncheon, a general conference, chiefly on the procedure and content of the July meeting. It was slow batting (not as good as a run a minute) but very safe play. Stumps were drawn for the day about 5pm. At 6pm George Brett (the Macmillan Company) called to see me. (I had called him up when I arrived) He was very frank and quite friendly. He explained to me his point of view about Canada. He must either revert to 50% partnership, or he means to start on his own. I will write to Daniel tomorrow about this. I have always liked George and got on with him. He seemed to me to have developed in stability and dignity since I saw him last. Perhaps independence has done him good!

Pilgrim dinner at the Waldorf, 500 people present. More T.V.; more radio; more 'stills', more news reporters etc etc. What is so odd about it, is that the photographs never seem to appear anywhere!

---

39. 'Alpha', on which Eden and Dulles had already been working, proposed to resolve Arab–Israeli differences by providing a land corridor between Jordan and Egypt across the Israeli-held Negev.

. . . . Jack McCloy made a speech about me; then Foster Dulles made a speech about me. Then I made my own speech (30 minutes) then it was 11pm – and 80 to 90 degrees (But then everything or almost everything is artificially air-conditioned, wh has really altered the whole life and may alter the character of the American people. They used to get very short-tempered and jumpy every summer in N.Y. and Washington owing to the intolerable heat. On the other hand, one is very apt to get a cold or chill, passing from the heat of the street or a room which is *not* conditioned, into the colder temperature of the controlled rooms) My speech seemed to be well received; better than my speech in the HofCommons yesterday. But then the Americans like speeches; they like oratory; and they like a lot of it. They like long speeches; long sermons; long lectures. Altogether, from the point of view of the speaker, they are most satisfactory.

17 June
We met at the so-called 'Presidential Suite' in the Waldorf Astoria hotel. Mr Dulles, (with his advisers) Mr Pinay (with his advisers) HM (with his advisers) . . . . Then Adenauer came to join us . . . .

After luncheon, Adenauer gave us his ideas – rather 'cagily' (as it subsequently proved) but very sensibly. 1) He wants some further 'disarmament' move by the Western powers for propaganda purposes. (He is on dangerous ground here; but then he does not understand the nuclear problem) 2) He is absolutely determined that Germany shd stay in NATO 3) The Americans and Canadians must stay in Europe 4) But he believes the position in Russia to be such that they want a 'détente' and might be got to give up E Germany in exchange for some security in Europe . . . . The conference ended about 4pm. We did some telegrams home and then I went to the United Nations building – an astonishing great glass affair, immensely high, at the top of wh I met the Secretary General, M Hammarskjöld. We had a short talk – mostly about China. He dislikes Krishna Menon, who has interfered with the U.N. approach. So (according to H) nothing more will be done, while the Chinese await the result of Menon's diplomacy. Judging from what Foster Dulles has said about China, there is not likely to be any real development at present. The Americans could not understand Menon's plan, and didn't like it, as far as they did understand it . . . .

At 6pm, Dr Adenauer called to see me . . . . He has his own plan for 'disengagement' in Europe – not at all unlike (though more drastic

and more ambitious) the plan which (among others) we discussed at
CANUTE. It has . . . .

. . . . A de-militarised zone (zone 1) in the middle, where no forces
or installations wd be allowed. Then on each side . . . . another (zone
2) where certain weapons and forces allowed, but not others. Then
another (zone 3) where less restriction. The general idea would be (1)
equality of forces in Europe (2) disengagement (3) control of types of
armaments allowed *within* the controlled areas.

All this was extremely interesting and I encouraged him to discuss
his plan in detail with P.M. and Sir Ivone Kirkpatrick on Sunday in
England (he goes to England tomorrow) I told him that our minds
were working on the same sort of lines. I enjoined on him the greatest
secrecy. If the Russians found out prematurely, it would spoil our
playing of this or similar cards in such a way as to get full value . . . .
(Unfortunately, German 'security' is very bad) I asked him what about
the French. A said he would tell Pinay in very general terms, for he
knew the dangers. They would 'leak'. With every protestation of
admiration and friendship for the French, I confirmed this and begged
him to be careful . . . .

18 June
Woke at 8pm [sic], after eight hours or so of deep sleep. Wrote up
diary and read '*Catherine the Great's Memoirs*' . . . .

. . . . People of importance used to disappear suddenly then, as they
do now in Russia, from a high position in the Council chamber, to the
torturer and to exile or the block.

19 June
Left the house at 7.30am for the airport.[40] An astonishing flight over
the whole of America – coast to coast. What a country! Fortunately it
was clear all the way; so we had excellent views of the Rockies – of
the Salt Lake and the forest, and of the Sierras . . . .

20 June
. . . . Lunch with Mike [Lester] Pearson (Canadian Foreign Minister)
He will continue to do his bit to bring pressure on Dulles about the
Far East. He is alarmed (as I am) that if nothing happens as a result
of Krishna Menon's invitation, the Chinese may think (wrongly, as it

---

40. To fly to San Francisco.

happens) that American opinion is hardening. Then they may precipitate a crisis by an attack on the off-shore islands.

As regards Europe, P has the opposite fear. He feels that if they can't get some kind of a settlement in any other way, the Americans (instinctively isolationist) may 'pull out'. This, of course, has always been Churchill's chief anxiety.

At 3pm we all went to the great opera house where the meeting of UN took place. The delegations filled the stalls; the rest of the house was packed by the general public. (About 3000–4000 in all, I shd say) The President (whom I had not seen for 4 years or so) does not look older. But he looked strained . . . .

I drove back with Foster, to his rooms at the hotel and we had a good talk. He really began to 'let his hair down' about the Far East. He doesn't know what to do. He really wants to get Chiang off the coastal islands, but he can't do it. He sent Robertson and Admiral Radford to do it – some weeks ago – but they failed. He then started a long account of his early experience with émigrés (at Paris conference in 1918) and they always let you down . . . .

The President is taking the line that he will not dine or give dinners. This is very foolish, but is a 'hang-over' from the political odium wh has built up agst Yalta etc. Anthony [Eden] will, of course, want to entertain; and I reserved all his entertaining rights! But it will not be the same thing, if the President is conspicuously absent. (Actually, he likes to go to bed about 9.30pm)

21 June

. . . . In the afternoon, I was able to resume the interrupted talk with Foster Dulles (at his suggestion) But I did not really get much further. The Americans don't really know what to do about China. They know, in their hearts, that their policy has no future – except the risk of disaster. They haven't the courage to take over Formosa themselves. That wd be 'colonialism'. So they have to support a cruel and corrupt administration, which may 'double-cross' them and come to terms with the Communists at any minute . . . .

I motored out to the villa which Molotov and his party have taken – about 45 minutes by car from the centre of the city. It's a typical 'millionaire' place – with large cool rooms – fake furniture – swimming pool etc. Rent $4000 for 10 days. A garden – a fence – plenty of room for all the Russians.

. . . . The Russians, I think, *do* want a 'détente'. They are frightened by the American bases in Europe; they wd like to reduce the expenditure of effort on armaments. But will they pay the price? Anyway, will they pay *any* price for something that doesn't really achieve their purpose? Operation CANUTE doesn't really give them what they want – which is the break-up of NATO *and* the withdrawal of the Americans . . . .

22 June

General Romulo opened today – a great little speaker from the Philippines. He succeeded in torpedoing Molotov's great plan for a peace '*declaration*', about which he talked to us on Monday and to me again yesterday, and for which he has been making great propaganda. Any 'resolution' wd be 'out of order' at this, purely commemorative meeting;[41] it wd of course be drawn up to embarrass us . . . .

Left at midnight, on the Scandinavian air line, for Copenhagen . . . .

24 June

. . . . After some difficulties, a small Dakota plane took off, we landed at Goteburg (Sweden) We then changed into another plane. We got to Oslo about 4.30pm and drove to the Palace. A state dinner and reception. The Queen looked lovely . . . .

25 June

A morning's sight-seeing; a quiet luncheon with Dr Lange (Norwegian Foreign Minister) at wh I unfortunately fell asleep! But he was very nice about it . . . . The Norwegians are tremendously enthusiastic about the Queen, who has charmed them all. They are anyway very fond of us and very easy to get on with. This visit has given them immense pleasure. They hate Germans and Russians – almost equally. Quisling occupied the palace, under the Germans. We were shewn the room in which the Cabinet met. He had a strange idea that he wd be justified by public opinion after the war, and was found here when the Norwegian Govt returned. He was shot.

26 June (Sunday)

. . . . We all drove out to luncheon at the Crown Prince's home in the country – an immense party. I had some conversation with the Indian

---

41. To mark the tenth anniversary of the founding conference in San Francisco.

envoy (who came from Paris) and with the Pakistani. We went aboard the *Britannia* at about 6pm . . . .

27 June

. . . . We have not had much news from England in the last few days. Anthony has taken control of the F.O. and is no doubt enjoying himself. I see we have sent a further note of protest to the Greek government about their Cyprus broadcasts. I fear greatly that recent events will make the Cabinet less willing to adopt my plan . . . .

28 June

The *Britannia* reached Dundee about 9am. The Queen went ashore at 10am – a very pretty scene, with Scottish archers, guard of honour, Band of Royal Marines (landed from yacht) and so on . . . .

After the Queen had left for her visits, we went ashore (Rumbold and I) and motored to Arbroath. There we got a small RAF plane (a Dove?) and got to Northholt about 2.30pm . . . .

We found plenty to do in the office. The chief (and rather surprising news) was that the Cabinet had *accepted* my suggestion on Cyprus . . . .

29 June

10.30. Office meeting about Strasbourg . . . . The F.O. (so strong is tradition) is – from the time of Ernest Bevin and Eden – hostile to the European movement – as a Churchill stunt! I keep trying to persuade them that I favour it – as one of its founders! This has not yet reached the 'lower levels' . . . .

3.30. I moved the 2nd reading of the Austrian State Treaty Bill. Why we had to have a Bill at all was obscure to me, and (by the time I had finished speaking from my brief) was equally obscure to the House! However, we got all stages by 5.30pm! . . . .

30 June

. . . . Cabinet at 11.30. The dock strike looks like breaking up at last – at least in London. We had the usual inconclusive argument about electing the Japanese to GATT. My argument is that as we have no intention of voting against them, and as they will be elected anyhow, we may as well get the credit of voting for them and 'voting early'. But Board of Trade are obstinate and ministers bored by the whole thing – so it was again postponed. There was an interesting discussion about

Malta, who want to join the UK! This extraordinary request has taken everybody by surprise! If we don't accept we shall be shooting the Cypriots for wanting to leave us and the Maltese for wanting to join us! The trouble is that I suppose it will mean 3 Labour seats! I was in favour of this novel (and dramatic idea) so was P.M., Colonial Secy, and strangely enough Ld Salisbury . . . .

P.M. made his statement about Cyprus after questions. The invitation to a meeting for talks (for that is all it is) was well received . . . .

Dinner (at Norwegian Embassy) for Dr and Mrs Lange. I sat between the ambassadress and Mrs Lloyd George – which was pleasant enough, only I cd scarcely keep awake. (This is a sort of fate when I lunch or dine with Norwegians) The truth is that there is so much to do in interviews etc by day, that all the paper work has to be done at night. It has been between 2am and 3am each night this week, since I returned.

1 July

At No 10, for a short talk on Cyprus. The press is good. The Turks have accepted 'in principle',[42] but asked some questions. The Greeks are thrown into alarm and confusion, and have not answered yet. I doubt if they will do so (altho' I have had a nice *personal* message from the King [of Greece]) We decided to take a detached attitude . . . . AE, Lennox-Boyd, and I had a further talk about Malta. We *must* accept, at least in principle. The effect in the world will be great and this is the moment.

Lunched at St Martin's St. DM and Maurice. We discussed George Brett's attitude on the question of the Canadian company. I reported my conversation in New York with Brett. It is not easy to know what it's best to do, but we will wait for his next letter, which is to make a proposal for implementing the idea of 'full partnership' . . . .

4 July

Strasbourg. We arrived here last night, by special aircraft. Dorothy came with me; the rest were F.O. officials . . . . It's fun to be back in Strasbourg, where I spent so many weeks 6 years ago, with Churchill, Sandys, Maxwell-Fyfe, and all the rest; in the early formation years of the European movement. Altho' it hasn't all worked out quite as we

---

42. The conference invitation.

had hoped, yet in one way or another, tremendous steps have been taken towards practical co-operation in European affairs. The instruments have varied; NATO, WEU, OEEC and so on. But the work has been done. The problem is to re-state the precise function of the Council of Europe in all this. I think it has two main functions (a) to keep under review and discuss the political aspect of these *technical* European organs (b) to debate, in the only *Parliamentary European* forum that exists, the great questions of the day. In addition, it represents the concept of Europe as a whole; even tho' now divided ideologically, Europe is a historical and cultural whole. I shall develop this theme in the speech wh I have prepared . . . .

5 July

. . . . In the afternoon, the Greek Foreign Minister, M Stephanopoulos, called on me at my request. We were all teed up in my sitting room – Caccia and Rumbold supporting me – to expect a rather difficult interview. . . . However, to our astonishment, S announced the acceptance of our invitation to the proposed conference by the Greek government, without any conditions or reservations. They even said that they would be glad to meet their friends the Turks for this purpose. The only point wh the Greeks made was that the Turks had surrendered their rights in Cyprus by the Treaty of Lausanne. This hardly seemed very relevant; for the Greeks have never had any rights in Cyprus at all. The only thing the Greeks pressed for was that the conference shd be as early as possible. After the Greeks had gone, and agreed the communiqué to be issued immediately in Strasbourg, the Turkish ambassador in Paris (M Menemenocioglu) – who is acting for the Turkish Govt at the Council of Europe meetings called – also at my invitation. Since the Turkish Govt had already accepted, there was only polite conversation to be made. M Menemenocioglu is a charming and very shrewd old man – who was Turkish Foreign Minister during the last war – and pretty clever then at keeping his country out of trouble. He said that he hoped that we wd not sell our wares too cheap at Geneva, for he believed the Russians to be very anxious to buy.

The Icelandic Minister gave a dinner for all the Foreign Ministers. I sat next to old Bech (Luxembourg) who was as gay and witty as ever. On my other side, the new German Foreign Minister – von Brentano. He told me that he thought the Russians would *not* do business at Geneva. But they wd get Adenauer to Moscow *after* Geneva, and try to make (over his head) a very attractive offer to the German people, promising re-unification in exchange for neutrality.

6 July

I made my speech before the Consultative Assembly this morning.[43] It was a curious experience to be speaking again in this hall – this time from the ministerial rostrum. I had prepared it carefully and knew it by heart. So I was able to deliver it as a speech – in contrast to the usual declarations which are read out without even lifting the head from the manuscript . . . .

We left the airfield at about 8.30pm and got back safely to London airport . . . .

7 July

We had a Cabinet this morning. I gave a report on foreign affairs, including the acceptance by the Greeks and Turks of our invitations and the way in wh we expected the situation to develop. It will not really be possible to have this conference before the third week in August. Geneva will take up all July, and perhaps run on into August. (All hopes for a holiday are beginning to disappear!) . . . .

In the afternoon, further talk with P.M. about reconstructing the Govt – Butler and Chief Whip (Buchan Hepburn) were there. As usual, one starts very firmly – cut out the dead wood and all that – and ends rather weakly . . . .

8 July

A further meeting – 10.30am – on Canute . . . . From what Massigli told me in Strasbourg the other day . . . . the French are likely to make suggestions very much in line with our Canute ideas – that is, a demilitarised strip in E Germany, and some thinning out behind. Of course, the Americans are very nervous about going too far; but they accept the position now that we cannot be quite negative . . . .

9 July

Motored to Chequers – arriving at 9.45am. I found a large party of Indians . . . . Nehru has swallowed a lot of Russian propaganda – I think quite innocently. The most penetrating thing he said was that he

---

43. On relations between the Council of Europe and WEU.

found the Russians and the Americans very much alike – a materialist, mechanically minded view of life . . . .

12 July

Motored to London in time for Cabinet. A very long agenda. The chief problem on the home front is the steadily increasing 'inflationary pressure'. The immense rise in coal prices (nearly 20%) means a corresponding increase in gas, electricity etc. Wages will probably go up again this autumn. The Stock Exchange boom continues, partly depending on the Wall Street boom, partly on conditions at home. But the American boom is much healthier than ours. For altho' wages and profits continue to rise in US, prices have remained remarkably steady over the last 2 or 3 years. In other words, there has been a genuine rise in productivity. That's what has gone wrong at home. There is a lot of talk about 'monopolies'; but little is said about restrictive practices in the Trade Unions.

Rab gave an interesting picture of the situation and of possible remedies. The chief things seem to be a further squeeze on credit, particularly on 'hire-purchase' credit . . . .

13 July

. . . . 10.45. Mr Louw – Foreign Minister of S Africa. Fortunately, I had been polite to him somewhere, at some time, which I had forgotten.

11am. Godfrey Nicholson. He wants us to free the rest of the Japanese war criminals. I did not, happily, tell him that I intended to make this proposal to the Cabinet . . . .

12.30. Office meeting on Far East and SE Asia. To my great satisfaction, the Americans (according to a message received thro' the American ambassador in London) have accepted our suggestions about the invitation to Chou-en-lai . . . . I am now asking O'Neill (who has just arrived in Peking as chargé d'affaires) to deliver the invitation. I have also asked our P.M. to send a personal message to Nehru, asking him to give it a fair wind in Peking. I can only hope that the Chinese will accept. If they do, it will gain still more time, for tempers to cool, and help us materially in repelling a Russian attack at Geneva. The position in Laos is bad – but information is not very clear as to how far Pathet Lao rebels are making progress . . . .

6.15–7.15. Mr Krishna Menon. At the moment, he is my principal 'cross'. I'm sure he is sincere, but he is vain and a bore. He is a sort of oriental Lionel Curtis.[44] He is, of course, very much offended that the Americans have sent their message to Chou-en-lai through us, instead of through the Indians. He says he is not at all offended – so it is clear that he must feel deeply injured. Then he thinks that the Chinese will not accept. Finally, he thinks that unless the Americans can get Chiang out of the offshore islands, there will be war before the end of the year. The trouble is that he may well be right over this.

8pm. Dinner with Robertson (Canadian High Commissioner) to meet Mike [Lester] Pearson (Canadian Foreign Minister) Kirkpatrick, Norman Brook, and Alec Home (Commonwealth Secretary) We had a very good talk about Geneva, about disarmament, and about the Far East. Both Kirk and I were rather shocked at the way Robertson was talking about German neutrality. He seemed to think we ought at least to consider it. I said that it wd be much easier to disrupt NATO than to put it together again. Pearson told us that he had talked a good deal to Fawzi (Egyptian Foreign Secretary) about a possible Arab–Israel settlement. F had said that there ought to be a settlement and that the Great Powers ought to impose it. Pearson asked, on what basis. F then gave a general description of a possible settlement. Pearson told us the details – which showed that F was aware of our 'Alpha' proposals – and their main features. (This is secret from Pearson) It was encouraging (as Kirk and I agreed later) that F was talking sense. It was also clear that Byroade (American ambassador in Cairo) had told F much more about 'Alpha' than we had been led to believe . . . .

14 July
. . . . The Sultan of Muscat – a good old boy – to luncheon at No 1. He takes a robust view of life and will not (if it can be helped) be bullied by the Saudi Arabians . . . .

4pm – left for Paris. D came with me – also Rumbold, Caccia, etc. We arrived at Le Bourget about 6.30, met by Gladwyn Jebb etc. The Embassy is a most lovely house and very comfortable to stay in. It was very hot, even hotter than in London, where we have had a heat wave for a week or more. Dinner at the American Embassy – no French; only an Anglo-American affair. After dinner, I had a go with Dulles on

44. One of the founders of the Royal Institute of International Affairs in 1920–21, Curtis had an important background influence on British foreign and Imperial policy for more than fifty years until his death in 1955.

Alpha – Shuckburgh (F.O.) and Russell (State Dept) present. These two are great friends and have worked for quite a time together on Alpha. I put strongly to Dulles the difficulties which we felt. He explained that he must really say something to keep the American Jews quiet. If he spoke now, he cd still talk sense. In a year's time, it wd be electioneering. I said that if the whole Middle East went up in flames as the result, we wd have to carry the baby. We had been left with the Turco-Iraqui pact, wh the Americans started, and then ran out of.[45] Cd he help us with Nuri Pasha in two ways (a) promising to join the Turco-Iraqui pact *after* Alpha had been launched (b) by buying Centurion tanks from us – as off-shore purchase – to give to the Iraquis. It was agreed that Shuckburgh and Russell shd try to work out an agreed plan tomorrow . . . .

15 July
. . . . At 6pm I had to go to a very long and tedious meeting of the Western European Union Council – the French and the Germans argued for 2½ hours (in excessive heat) about the last stages of the arrangements for carrying out the Saar referendum. Spaak presided brilliantly, and by infinite patience and resource at last got a 'formula' on which agreement was reached . . . .

16 July
10–1. NATO ministerial meeting at the Palais Chaillot. Dulles, Pinay and I (in accordance with an arranged allocation of parts) explained (as well as we could) what we meant to do at Geneva, and how we wd keep the other members of NATO informed throughout – esp. after this conference and before the next. No one made any trouble, except the usual (and quite mild) Italian bleat. They wd like to rank as a great power . . . . I had a talk with M Stephanos Stephanopoulos (Greek Minister of F.A.) about the conference in London. He was very put out about the date – August 29th – and said that he cd not prevent his Govt from 'inscribing' Cyprus on the 'order paper' for U.N. in

---

45. The US had been pressing for cooperation between the so-called Northern Tier countries to confront any attempted Soviet moves against the Middle East. In February 1955 Iraq and Turkey signed a treaty. This became the Baghdad Pact in April 1955 with the adherence of Britain and Pakistan. Iran joined in November 1955. The Americans, however, declined to join, not least because of Saudi and Israeli concern that the Pact might be directed against them.

September. I told him that I thought he wd be making a great error, and that my Govt; the H of Commons, and the British people wd be very concerned. This was not the way to get concessions out of us. He was very apologetic, but said that the Greek Govt was torn apart already about the Conference. Only the influence of Papagos (it was really the King acting on P) had persuaded them to accept . . . . We left the airport about 5pm and got to Geneva at 6.30. D and I are installed in a great suite of rooms in the Beau Rivage – the Edens are in a villa, a few minutes away. We did a lot of telegrams etc and then went to dinner with the Edens . . . .

17 July (Sunday)

. . . . It is very hot; and a great haze lies over the whole valley. At 11am we had a meeting at the President's villa. 'Ike' was in very happy mood and seemed really glad to see me again. He took me for a little talk alone – but about old times, not about present day problems.

The conference took place in the library of his villa. Eden and I; Faure and Pinay, President and Dulles; and 2 advisers each – (we had Kirkpatrick and Norman Brook) The President's speech – or rather a summary of it was passed round . . . . Faure then gave a long exposé of his ideas. We had already been supplied with a copy of his speech. F was quite sound on Germany (or appeared to be so) rejecting neutrality. But he was much more interested in his ideas about disarmament. He has prepared an elaborate plan by which an international body shd be set up to which we should all pay the sums we are going to save by disarmament. The money will then be re-distributed to help 'backward areas'. He claims that this obligation to pay is the only real sanction to make sure that the disarmament really takes place. Neither the Americans nor the British seemed very keen about it. (I can just imagine the Treasury's reaction!) Then Eden put forward the outline of his plan. We did not go into any detail. It is still necessary to conform to the American theory that we are not to put forward any precise 'plans' here; only illustrative suggestions. Of course, once the Conference starts, all this will go by the board.

With translations (for Pinay's benefit) the morning was taken up with this interchange. Faure speaks English, Russian and Italian (or rather understands all three languages) He is clever, but quite untrustworthy – I am sure of that. Eden then explained our point of view, but he did not read a prepared speech. He gave only the headings. We all lunched with the President – a disgusting meal, of large meat slices, hacked out by Filipinos and served by them, with marmalade and jam. The French were appalled . . . .

18 July

The Conference opened with the usual photographing and T.V. stuff . . . . The President opened, on broad and generous lines. Faure followed, with a long and ingenious speech. These two speeches, (with the absurd method of *both* simultaneous *and* consecutive translation in two languages) took up the whole morning. After luncheon, Eden spoke. It sounded well, and will read well. It really ended up as a fine document, which proposed a plan which ought to be acceptable to the Russians. Bulganin then made his speech – very friendly in manner, very stiff in matter. I passed a note to Kirkpatrick saying 'The Russians feel that time is on their side'. He replied 'I'd qualify this. Time is on their side in one sense. But in another sense they wd like to save the money and spare the effort *now*. Also they wd like the appearance of some success at Geneva now. When we reach thermo-nuclear saturation point time is on nobody's side' . . . .

In his summing up, the President said some friendly things about all the speeches . . . .

I went off with Eden, and we had a talk with our advisers as to our policy for the next day. Our anxiety is of course to get German reunification 'at the head of the list' and keep it there as long as possible . . . .

19 July

. . . . The Heads of Governments met in the afternoon. There is a verbatim report taken, so again I will only record impressions. (The room in which we meet in the old League of Nations building is 'air-conditioned'. Outside it is very hot and sultry. There is so much haze that we have only once or twice got a glimpse of the high alps)

Edgar Faure (French Prime Minister) was in the chair.

FIRST ROUND

AE: What about safeguards?

Bulganin: We are strong; we don't want safeguards. Abolish NATO.

Pres: I assure you NATO is for peace.

F: We must unite Germany.

2ND ROUND

AE: You say you don't want safeguards. Why don't you propose
    a European pact?

B: Abolish NATO. No more to say about Germany.

Pres: I've said my piece.

AE: (*interrupting*) The question of Germany is not exhausted.
    We must think about it.

B: Let's get on to the question of European security.

F: All right. But the two questions are interlocked.

Then we all went away.

During Bulganin's speech (on first round) Sir IK passed me this
note. 'B is getting close to the old Soviet position on Austria. I won't
argue – I'm telling you. We won't have it.'

During Eisenhower's rather moving defence of NATO, particularly
addressed to the Russian Marshal Zhukov – as one soldier to another
– he passed me another note. 'This, I think, is a deliberate attempt to
educate these antichristian monsters'.

It was clear, after this meeting, that we are now getting to grips –
altho' the deep division between the two sides is covered over with
great courtesy and friendliness – in talk. After each meeting we go off
and drink together in the buffet. Everyone is very cheerful (or pretends
to be) that there is no progress . . . .

The Russians came to dinner at the P.M.'s villa. It was a purely
Anglo-Russian affair and we had told them that we wanted to talk
business, which they had accepted, seemingly with alacrity. *Bulganin*
looks like a Radical-Socialist mayor of a French industrial town.
He might be '*un bon papa*'.[46] He affects a jolly, friendly, but not
undignified style. He is fat, about 60, and is a good figure-head. All
his observations at the formal meetings have been read from a text. At
dinner, and afterwards, he talked pretty freely. *Kruschev* is an obscene
figure; very fat, with a great paunch; eats and drinks greedily; inter-
rupts boisterously and rudely; but did not hold the entire conversation
in his hands, as he had done with the dinner at the Americans. *Molotov*
was more like he was in Vienna, and less sure of himself than in San
Francisco. He was a bad colour; talked very little; and behaved more
like a civil servant than like a political chief. *Marshal Zhukov* was a
good, soldierly and agreeable figure. He told me about his daughters –

---

46. 'A fine father'.

both of whom had married the sons of marshals – regular Aldershot talk . . . .

Eden conducted the whole affair brilliantly. He exerted all his charm, both at and after dinner. I got certain impressions as follows (a) They are very relaxed, after the removal of the tyrant, Stalin. (They said, with glee, that since 1953, they worked a normal day, instead of all night!) (b) They don't want another Stalin – a bloody and uncertain tyrant. (c) K is the boss, but *not* another Stalin. He controls the party and thus, in a country where there is no Parliament, he controls the Govt. (d) They are unable to accept the re-unification of Germany in NATO, and will fight it as long as they can. This is partly because their public wd be horrified. After all, the Germans treated them terribly and they hate them. (e) They do not fear war; they don't really believe that the Americans are going to attack them. (f) They are anxious about China. They told us so. They (like us) wish that Quemoy and Matsu cd sink beneath the sea. (g) They may fear – in the long run – that China will be a danger to them on their Eastern flank. I think they might prefer a weak nationalist or capitalist China, wh they cd plunder, to a Communist China, wh they have to assist. (h) They don't want the conference to fail. They will play for a draw.

. . . . With all this bonhomie, it is sometimes hard to remember what ruthless and merciless men they are.

20 July

8.30. Eden and I went to breakfast with President and Dulles. We discussed the general situation of the Conference. Eisenhower is determined to get something wh can be called a success, if he can. He is much in favour of our plans for European security, and still hopes we may get our way in Germany if we are patient. We also discussed Alpha (Israel–Arab plan) the Far East; and France. On the Far East, he is stuck. He can't get Chiang out of the islands, and dare not push him too far for fear of pushing him over altogether.

. . . . I was in the chair at 4 Foreign Ministers meeting. We had a discussion for nearly two hours – friendly, but barren . . . .

. . . . [W]e could only agree to leave it to the Heads of Govts to go on with the talk. This afternoon they should complete the talk on the first two items (1) German re-unification (2) European security. The Russians try to say they are separate issues. We say that they are all mixed up together . . . .

This afternoon's debate was short 4–5.30. Everyone agreed to disagree . . . .

21 July
. . . . The Heads of Govts met at 4pm, Bulganin in the chair.

B 'cheated' as chairman. First of all he began a long speech of his own – nominally on 'disarmament' which was the subject of debate, but in reality about European security, NATO, and all the rest. He produced text of a new European treaty, between NATO and Warsaw.[47] (All this, of course, is part of the great propaganda and political game of keeping Germany divided, and making NATO the excuse for it) . . . . After starting on this, B launched into a new theme, nearer the subject of the debate – disarmament. He gave the usual stuff about American bases, nuclear warfare, etc – and produced at the end another long draft treaty which he tabled – nominally on disarmament, but really embodying absurd and unworkable plans for immediate abolition of nuclear weapons, without any effective control system.

Eisenhower spoke next – a very moving, tho' not very coherent address. He proposed to throw open everything, on both sides of the iron curtain, to full inspection by anyone. Faure followed – a clever, well-phrased, very interesting speech – but without much reality. Eden made another, modest, but practical suggestion, wh we had worked out. Why not inspection, first 100 miles, then 200 miles, then still further – with the present line as the centre.

While the President was speaking, I noted to Kirkpatrick 'It seems a long way from the terms of the original invitation – to identify problems but not to discuss them'. A little later on, I minuted 'It would in fact do the exact opposite (that is to abolish the nuclear) To abolish the nuclear now, wd spread terror throughout Europe'. This is the strange, but obvious fact wh stares us in the face. For today's atmosphere of relaxed nerves and greater confidence, is the result of nuclear weapons . . . .

22 July
Eden and I breakfasted together; Dulles came and ate boiled eggs, one after another. We tried to get him to talk about (a) Alpha (b) Far East. But he ate and talked so slowly, that we got little out of him which we

---

47. The Warsaw Pact of the Soviet Union and its Eastern European satellites was signed in May 1955, to counterbalance NATO.

did not know before . . . . But P.M. went along to see the President, who gave him more satisfaction on both. If we will *give* 10 Centurion tanks to Nuri Pasha, USA will give him 70 or more. This will be by 'off-shore' purchase – a good transaction for us, for we shall get a good whack of dollars . . . .

We had a dreary morning – 10–1.15, arguing about the directives.

FIRST ROUND
Mol: put forward his draft.
Dulles: our draft.
Pinay: Germany is the key.
HM: a compromise solution.

2ND ROUND
Mol: perhaps a compromise cd be arranged. One never knows.
D: yes.
P: perhaps.
HM: I hope so.

These are rough summaries. Altogether, after 2 rounds (and trans-lations) it was time for luncheon! Actually, we *have* made progress. The *text* of the directive on *European Security* is agreed. The text on *Germany* is agreed, except for the point about Eastern and Western govts of Germany having a 'right' to participate. This Adenauer can never accept. He will never sit at the same table with the Communist Govt of Eastern Germany, wh is just a Russian puppet. Nor must we ask him to do so. But, in addition to this, the Russians insist on European Security being put on the agenda for the Foreign Ministers in October as Item 1. Then they want disarmament. Then Germany. We know that they will then argue that nothing can be said or done about Item 3 (Germany) until Items 1 and 2 are agreed! They did this before – in one case (Austria) blocking all discussion for 2 years, on the ground that the item in front of it had not been settled!

At the luncheon adjournment, poor Pinay (whose first experience this is of Russian stonewalling tactics) got very cross. M teasingly proposed that we shd meet again at 2.30. P indignantly cried out 'What about lunch!'. He proposed 3.30. I admitted that I was going to lunch with the French, and was looking forward to it; but I thought perhaps 3pm might do. M said 'Mr Macmillan always makes compro-mises – and good ones. Let it be 3pm'. So it was agreed. The French luncheon was certainly superb . . . .

The French are very anxious to go on pretending to be a Great Power. They know that we are doing the same. But they tell us that it's no good. The world is bound to be dominated by the new barbarians, in the West and in the East. Let us, if we can, be the Greeks of this new Roman Empire. (I think the French believe that the Russians and Americans must eventually coalesce. They are already so alike! This is just what Nehru said. Even Sir Ivone K remarked how difficult it is to tell apart the American and Russian thugs, who act as body-guards to their respective Emperors.) . . . .

8.15. Russian dinner for the British (return for Tuesday) The atmosphere was very relaxed and easy. The Russians, who are very hospitable, enjoy parties. We had all the usual things – caviar, smoked salmon, sturgeon etc; with lashings of vodka and continual toasts. Then soup; fish; meat; ice and fruit. White wine, red wine, champagne – all of Russian brands and not at all good. I prefer the vodka, if one must drink with them. Lots of toasts – toasts to everyone present in turn and a lot of rather sentimental speeches about the last war; about comradeship; about future cooperation, combined with a great deal of chaff. *Bulganin* – who looks a sort of French bourgeois mayor (but has a cruel look occasionally peeping through the mask of bonhomie) is nominally head. *Molotov* is sick; white-faced; and weary, but still very efficient. *Kruschev* is the mystery. How can this fat, vulgar man, with his pig eyes and his ceaseless flow of talk, really be the head – the aspirant Tsar – of all these millions of people and this vast country. *Marshal Zhukov* is a pleasant man, and looks a good man. He is a regular soldier, whereas Bulganin is not. Z might have been an officer in the old Russian army (such as are described in Tolstoy) or in the British Army (of the [Sir Brian] Robertson type) Eden has invited B and K to come to England next spring. They are delighted. Z wants to come too.

The impressions of the talk are as follows
1) They don't want war. So long as nuclear weapons exist, they know it to be impossible. Of course, they wd dearly like to get the western powers to abandon nuclear weapons 2) They are not very keen on their *Chinese* connection. It's a convenience now to have such an ally; but it is drawing very heavily upon their resources, both industrial and military. Moreover, they look ahead and wonder whether China may not be a danger 3) Altho' they brag about the agricultural situation, they are alarmed about it. 4) They hate and fear the Germans. They will do everything to stop German reunification, so long as NATO exists . . . .

23 July

. . . . We sat (in restricted session) in a smaller room, where it was much easier to talk together. We met at 11am till 1.15, when we adjourned. The directive on European unification is agreed. Nothing more. But after luncheon (wh took only 45 minutes – in the buffet) the Russians accepted everything in the text. They agreed to our text for the disarmament resolution. They agreed to omitting the mention of the Eastern German Govt and its right to be consulted, and accepted the amendment which I had proposed, giving the Foreign Ministers a right to calling any interested party before them, but naming no particular parties and giving no one a right to be heard. They accepted 'demoting' the disarmament resolution to the third place; they accepted words which linked together, as part of a single problem, European security *and* German reunification . . . . But beyond that the Russians would not go. They obviously thought that by making these concessions, we ought at once to have accepted the 'package deal'. I thought so too, as did Eden. However, the President (obviously prompted by Dulles) obviously thought that in this game of poker, we could win if he held out.

From 2pm to 5pm this situation of deadlock continued. It was rather embarrassing, because the President got so deeply involved in his position that I feared he wd not be able to retreat. We had several 'recesses' for consultation. All sorts of variations of language and order, including mixing up the whole thing in a single paragraph, were suggested. But the Russians stood firm. Finally, at a 'recess' at about 4.45, Eden persuaded the President that we really had got all we cd reasonably look for. Indeed, we were likely to get away with the disarmament directive in our words. (The Americans now realise that nuclear weapons cannot be abolished without disaster. But neither we nor they want to have to say so) . . . .

When we resumed at 5pm, the President, in a little speech of great dignity, got out of a position in which neither he nor we ought ever to have been placed. The agreement was made. Anthony passed me a note 'Foster looks like a bear with a sore head – rather a stupid bear'. I replied 'It's hard to get 2 bears into the same cage'. I also passed him this note at one stage as follows – 'As a practical measure we are much more likely to get German reunification through the medium of European security than by any other means. Indeed, it is the only hope the Germans have'. P.M. agreed, and asked me to keep this formula, for a possible HofC debate . . . .

The conference thus ended – after 6 days of very hard work, both at the table and behind the scenes.

The President and Dulles went straight to the airfield, after suitable personal leave-takings. We also made our farewells to the French, and went back to dinner. The Russians we were to meet again later. Anthony paid a little tribute to Churchill in his speech; this was a happy touch. He seemed very pleased with the result. After all the alarums and excursions of the afternoon, it was certainly a relief to get as good a result. I feel that it is more than we undertook at the General Election . . . . At 9.30, P.M. and I went off to see the Russians. We had a talk on Indo-China. The Russians did not press any point. We told them how we were trying to influence Diem in S Vietnam. We asked their help in Laos. The Russians seemed only concerned to make a suitable reply, on the same lines as ourselves, to Nehru. N had appealed to the co-chairman in identical terms for their support to the International Commission. B then began to talk about his visit to England. K broke in and seemed quite delighted with the prospect. It was agreed that they wd 'discuss it with their colleagues' in Moscow. They hoped to be ready for an announcement to be made in HofCommons on Wednesday.

They then raised the question of other visits – military missions, naval visits etc. It is obvious that Marshal Zhukov wants a trip on his own! Everything went very swimmingly . . . . P.M. did raise the question of prisoners. Couldn't they release them? At this, they all rose together, like immense fish. They all talked at once and the translators were momentarily baffled. They denied that they had *any* Italian prisoners of war – not even war criminals. (They are believed to have 200,000) They protested vigorously their denial. K told a long story to prove that he had tried to get one particular Italian sent back some years ago – but he was dead – at Irkutsk – in Silesia.

If what they said is true (which none of us believe) then hundreds of thousands of these poor people must be dead . . . .

24 July
D and I, and all the F.O. staff, left at 8am, in a Viscount. We had a good flight; and got to Birch Grove by 1pm. It was grand to be back. The garden is really lovely, and it's wonderful to be home . . . .

25 July
One of the chief impressions which we all have of Geneva is this. 'War

– modern war – nuclear war, just isn't on'. All the great nations, esp the 3 nations which are in the nuclear 'game' know this. It's important that other nations, like China, shd know it too. 'Peace' say all the under-writers etc 'is now assumed because everyone knows that there can be no victor in war today'. Then, after a few intervening paragraphs, they go on to say 'Ban the nuclear bomb'. But is this syllogism sound? Is the deduction correct? If we abolish the nuclear bomb (which has abolished war) shall we not bring back war? This is a danger, even if we succeeded in a water-tight system of control, inspection and all the rest, which is impossible. Ought we not to make it compulsory, rather than forbidden, for all great powers shd have a reasonable number of H bombs and the means to deliver them, in order to put other great powers out of any temptation? A few years ago, it seemed possible to devise a workable system of control. Now that is said by the scientists to be impossible. It would be too easy to cheat. Then we thought we might control the means of delivery – the great bombers, wh wd be difficult to hide. I was told by a scientist the other day that the Russians cd fill a small merchant ship with the stuff, blow it up in the North Sea, and the cloud would drift over England (with the right wind) and kill millions of our people. 2 or 3 ships might kill them all. A ship in the western approaches wd do the trick for a west wind. They cd do the same in the Atlantic for America. So why not rest (this is where the argument is drawing us) on the *good* results of all this. It makes war a farce and impossible. Why strive to get back to 'respectable' war, with 1 million Russians, 600,000 British etc – well matched, but almost as disastrous and almost as certain as the 1914–18 and the 1939–45 wars? All this is very confusing, but we really must try to think it all out again . . . .

26 July
. . . . The Parliamentary Committee on Malta has been more or less arranged. It will, I fear, work out that *all* the Socialists and only about *half* the Tories will be in favour of the union plan. This will put HMG in a difficulty.

P.M. gave the Cabinet an account of all we had done, said and heard at Geneva . . . . Then a number of other items were dealt with, including the question which we have discussed so often and so inconclusively – shall we vote for Japan being elected to GATT. It is now obvious that she will get elected, whether we vote or not. So it's really a question of whether to upset the Tory Party (or some of it) or win a little credit with the Japanese. I remarked 'I have never asked my colleagues to put a national above a party interest and hope never to have to do so, nevertheless . . . . '. We decided to vote *for* Japan.

The last item on the agenda was an F.O. item – the vast and complicated problem of Arab/Israel relations; the Anglo-American plan on which we have long been working (known as Alpha) and the proposed date for starting it off, and the proposed method (a speech by Mr Dulles early in Sept) However, the item in front was the suggested road changes at Hyde Park Corner. So we never got as far as Egypt or Palestine.

27 July

Debate in HofC on Geneva. P.M. began – with a very good, clear, and well-argued speech. Morrison followed, full of generous praise. The debate rather limped on after that, altho' it was always interesting. The left of the Labour Party could say nothing against us. Even Crossman was relatively approving. I wound up with a 30 minute speech, which was apparently much to the taste of the House, since I was able to introduce a few light touches and some solid argument. I find HofC speaking as Foreign Secy very difficult. As I said to the House, a F.S. is always caught by a cruel dilemma – hovering between the cliché and the indiscretion. He is either dull or dangerous . . . .

29 July

Krishna Menon came to see me. He is very sore, but it is mostly jealousy. Nehru wouldn't let him go to Geneva. The Chinese–American negotiation has been arranged through us and not through him. So Krishna is human enough to be peeved . . . .

30 July

. . . . *The Times* newspaper has reproved me with almost Trollopian self-importance (Jupiter) for having said 'There ain't gonna to be any war'. Herbert Morrison tried this, but it fell flat. The *New Statesman* and the rest of the pompous week-end press have taken it up. 'Inept exuberance' the *Times* calls it. But only the *Daily Mirror* (which splashed it on Monday morning) quoted me correctly. I said at the airport to the journalists, 'So long as there is the threat of nuclear warfare, "there ain't going to be no war"' . . . .

31 July (Sunday)

We have not been to church at home for a long time. There was quite a good attendance today. Since the Cypriot troubles, I have to go about with detectives even at home, and uniformed police hang about everywhere as well. This gives infinite pleasure to my grandsons . . . .

6 August

. . . . Sir Michael and Lady Wright, and Lord and Lady Waverley came to luncheon. I had an hour's talk with Sir M.W. (who is our ambassador in Iraq) about the probable effects of 'Alpha' on Iraqui opinion and particularly on Nuri. I am beginning to feel more and more doubtful about the whole plan. Yet it will not be possible to stop Dulles. Even if we could do so, American policy will yield more and more to the pressure of the 'Jewish lobby' as the election grows nearer . . . .

8 August

Worked all morning – partly on a further paper on 'Alpha'; partly on a paper on disarmament (for a Cabinet next Monday) partly on the speech with which I am to open the Cyprus conference, and on a new version of the 'British plan'; wh we will table at an appropriate moment. A typist came in the afternoon, and I worked with her on tidying all this up. She left at 5.30 with all these papers. Walked in the garden after tea and read Mrs Arbuthnot. The picture she gives of the Duke is very remarkable. Canning she hates . . . .[48]

10 August

. . . . This morning, I had a good walk in the woods. The chauffeurs and detectives, who swarm now about the place, are very kind and play cricket with the Fabers . . . .

11 August

. . . . The P.M. has started to interfere in a way which I must not allow. Churchill tried it and Eden weakly allowed it – that is, telephoning direct to Sir Ivone Kirkpatrick or to some other official . . . .

---

48. Mrs Arbuthnot's diaries are a major source for early nineteenth-century politics. George Canning was briefly Prime Minister in 1827, and the first Duke of Wellington held the same office 1828–30.

12 August

It is sad to write these words and not be going out to the moor. But I have been lucky . . . . Perhaps I *may* go out again some day before I am too old to shoot – but not, I fear, while I am Foreign Secretary. The truth is that it is not possible to have a holiday at all – without formally handing over control to another minister. This would not be wise for me – at least at this stage . . . .

17 August

. . . . Lunched with Daniel at Macmillans. We discussed the Canadian company. I'm afraid it looks as if G Brett will start on his own, in competition with the Canadian Co. It is tiresome but I think we can survive the loss of the American agency. Of course, all this was inevitable when we sold our control of the American business. However, there was no alternative.

Oliver Lyttelton – now Ld Chandos – came to see me in the afternoon – as gay and amusing as ever. I miss him terribly from the Cabinet. He was one of the few of us who had any practical knowledge of business.

He is very disturbed about the financial position. We need a dynamic policy. We cannot go back to physical controls, high taxation (to skim off purchasing power) and all the Socialist nostrums. We have freed everything, except the key thing – sterling. Free sterling, and the exchange will take and carry the burden of adjustment. Of course, it is harder now than it would have been a year ago. But with as much of a deflationary policy as a govt can do – housing subsidies; post-ponement of roads etc; cancellation of useless defence weapons (like fighters) to give confidence abroad, combined with methods for the 'artificial stimulus of savings', it could still be done . . . .

Got home for dinner. Ernest Marples came for the night. He has a most interesting mind and is a *very* capable man. It is really very wrong that he shd be an under-secretary for Pensions . . . .

18 August

. . . . We have been trying to bring pressure on the Hungarian Govt (who have had a bad relapse into barbarism) to give up the new 'reign of terror' – deportations, imprisonments etc. which began a few months ago. Our protests (renewed after Geneva) seem to have had some effect – or, at any rate, the policy has been changed.

The Egyptians, who have been hoping for a great success in the

Sudan, and have spent lavishly in bribes, seem likely to be disappointed . . . .[49]

. . . . Read Aldous Huxley's new book – *The Genius and the Goddess*. It is a 'long short story'. Not so good as usual, I thought.

20 August

. . . . The weather is unbroken – hot, sunny and dry. Found a lot of work and more troubles. A rebellion (no doubt got up by the Egyptians) has now broken out in Southern Sudan . . . .

23 August

. . . . I have thought a good deal about Goa.[50] The only possible way out wd be a plebescite and self-determination. But then, what about Cyprus? Or (Nehru might think) what about Kashmir? On the other hand, I doubt whether the Portuguese Govt (even under a dictator) can go out except under compulsion. Force they might accept (even 'token' force) But Nehru don't believe in force . . . .

25 August

I did a tour of the F.O. building . . . . going into a number of departments, especially the more mechanical – like telegrams, decoding, filing etc. I think the people like you to come round occasionally as if it were a business. Of course 2 hours is a very short time. I will go on with the job again when I can.

A lot of telegrams from Dulles about Alpha. Also a most secret message from Cairo to say that the Egyptians are to attack the Jews at Gaza today or tomorrow. The scale of the attack seems unknown.

I had Sir Robert Armitage (Governor of Cyprus) to luncheon. Henry Hopkinson (Minister of State, Colonial Office) and Kirkpatrick came. We had luncheon (sent in from the pastry cooks!) at No 1 Carlton Gardens. I was not impressed by Armitage. He is a nice, respectable, well-intentioned and fair-minded Wykehamist.[51] But he has no fire in his belly. He will never ride the storm.

26 August

. . . . Eden and Butler came to luncheon with me at the flat . . . .

---

49. The Egyptians had been trying to persuade Sudan to favour union with Egypt.
50. A Portuguese enclave in India that Nehru eventually annexed in 1961.
51. That is, a product of Winchester, one of the leading public schools.

Both P.M. and Chancellor of Ex liked my paper on the economic situation and the remedies to be applied. I thought P.M. in good heart, but Butler seemed very tired and rather more *'distrait'*[52] than usual. But I have no doubt that he will rise to the new challenge. In my view it needs only some firm, but not vastly extended, measures to get the economy back into balance. The chief thing is to reduce government expenditure (this shd be possible on defence, on housing and bread subsidies and perhaps on school meals. At the same time, we might reduce or abolish the tax on undistributed profits and raise the rate of tax on distributed profits)

Driving back in the car to the Cabinet (which met at 2.30) P.M. told me that he had been warned by the Queen that Princess Margaret *might* decide in October on her marriage with Commander Townsend. She has *not* absolutely decided. It will be a thousand pities if she does go on with this marriage to a divorced man and not a very suitable match in any case. It cannot aid and may injure the prestige of the Royal Family. The present law – under the Royal Marriages Act – is very unsatisfactory. She gives notice and if after a year, Parlt does not object, the marriage takes place legally and her children – if any – are in the succession. It would be much better to pass a new Act, giving her the right to marry, but excluding her and her issue from the succession. But this means an Act in every Commonwealth Parlt as well as ours, and a great deal of talk and controversy . . . .

27 August

. . . . At 11am M Stephanos Stephanopoulos and his ambassador came. We only discussed the procedure for the conference. At noon, the Turks came. M Zorlu was determined to get on to the *'question de fond'*[53] and said they would never agree to Cyprus being in Greek hands. The fact is, they are already surrounded by Greek islands; Cyprus is at their back door, and they are afraid that sooner or later, the Greeks will go 'fellow traveller' or Communist. I am bound to say that I don't feel very hopeful about the outcome, altho' I have wracked my poor brain to find some formula which will mean 'soon' to the Greeks and 'never' to the Turks. The House of Commons wd be content with 'wait and see'! . . . .

---

52. 'Absentminded'.
53. 'Fundamental question'.

28 August (Sunday)

Arthur and Peggy Macmillan (who have been staying here for a week) came to Church with me this morning. D was busy packing. She leaves for Scotland tomorrow. We have had some rain at last, but mostly storms – not much steady rain. However, as my barley is cut and stooked but not stacked, I want a few more sunny days . . . .

29 August

. . . . I lunched with Henry Hopkinson at Bucks. We had a good talk about Cyprus and the conference. I think the Colonial Office will move a little towards my proposals for a really liberal measure of self-government. But what most worries me is the sort of dead hand of despair that seems to clutch the C.O. by the throat. This, in turn, reacts upon all, except a few, Colonial Governors and Governments. The Governor of Hong Kong is a notable exception.

The 'Eastern Mediterranean and Cyprus' conference met at 4pm at Lancaster House. All the introductions were made and the delegates were given tea etc in one of the superb salons of this fine (if ornate) example of late Regency building . . . .

30 August

At 11am we met for the first real business of the conference. As arranged, the British started and I made a portentous speech, lasting nearly an hour, setting out the whole military, historical, economic, and geographical complex of the Eastern Mediterranean and the island of Cyprus. (Everything was included, except a tribute to Aphrodite) This had been prepared in 3 departments (F.O., C.O., Min of Defence) and was a very weighty affair. We had been preparing it for a long time. All I had to do was to turn it into English and put in a few lighter touches. The translation followed, lasting another hour. This concluded the business of the day. This leisurely approach may seem rather absurd. But I think it is wise. It allows the delegates to meet each other. A lot of coffee-housing and even intriguing goes on. The atmosphere of London and the larger problems of the great world begin to influence them. Tomorrow, we are to have the Greek, then – on Thursday – the Turkish position stated.

I gave a luncheon party for the Lebanese ambassador, who – after eleven years in London – is leaving us for Washington. He is a cynical, but amusing, type. He took the gloomiest view of the future of the

Arab–Israel conflict, and was contemptuous of Mr Dulles, and by implication of HMG for their naiveté . . . .

31 August

. . . . M Stephanopoulos spoke for about 35 minutes. The translator played up nobly, and was very slow. He spoke in French. It was after 12.30, one way or another, before the session was over – so we were not disgraced! On the whole, the Greek case was very moderately argued. They blandly abandoned *Enosis* altogether. For *enosis* means that Cyprus shd be tranferred to Greek sovereignty without more ado. The Greeks now said that the principle of 'self-determination' must be applied, and that in accordance with that principle 'free government' should now be established in Cyprus, with a right to decide its future in 3 years time. They then went on to say that *when* (not if) Cyprus was united with Greece, the Greek Govt wd make all necessary arrangements for our base, and wd protect the interests of the minority – i.e. Turks.

There had been a great row among the Greeks (so Charles Peake our ambassador, told us) but the moderates won the day. But I have no doubt that they will continue the struggle later on. Fundamentally, the division, among laymen, is between the older Greek politicians and civil servants and soldiers, (who look back with pride to generations of friendship with England) and the younger men who are beginning to revive some old and foolish dreams of expansion. They *are* foolish, because if 7 or 8 million Greeks come up against 20 million (and more) Turks, they will get a bloody nose. Of course, the Church is unrepentant and chauvinist. This is, in a way, understandable. For, with all its faults, the Ethnarchy[54] kept alive the concept of Greek nationhood and Greek civilisation through 400 years of Turkish domination.

1 September

The Turks made their declaration today. M Zorlu spoke in English. Since he speaks much better French than English, it would have been better had he spoken French. I assume that it was a delicate compliment to us – as well as a wish to be different from the Greeks. His speech was largely judicial and technical. He argued that in accordance

---

54. The leadership of the Greek community by the senior Orthodox cleric (in keeping with the Ottoman *millet* system) on the island.

with the terms of the Treaty of Lausanne, the sovereignty of Cyprus must remain with Britain or revert to Turkey. He had a well argued passage about the historical connection of Cyprus with the mainland, which he claimed was the one thing common to Cyprus throughout all its changes. Whoever held the Anatolian peninsula must, because of geographical and strategical considerations, hold Cyprus. It was the back door to Anatolia. M Zorlu made it pretty plain to the Greeks that in starting off 'the so-called Cyprus question' they were playing with fire . . . .

The Greeks seemed very depressed by the Turkish attitude. However, with that mercurial temperament which makes them so charming, they cheered up at luncheon. The Greek ambassador gave a tremendous affair (though in the best taste, with delicious food) in my honour. This conference is taking a lot of time. But I was giving it first preference in all my work. We *must* try to get some 'détente'. But, although I write a new plan every night, I am not at all confident. The Turks are too tough; the Greeks are too weak, to make a concession. So poor old England will get the blame – and the bombs . . . .

We had a meeting (in restricted session) with the Greeks and Turks this afternoon at 6pm. The secretaries and the officials of all three delegations had managed to agree the text of a long communiqué setting out the positions taken by the three Governments. These summaries were couched in firm, but not offensive terms. I think the advantage to us is considerable in getting their maximum claims set out and officially subscribed to. We can now begin to see whether we can do any trading . . . . The Greeks are clearly alarmed at the prospect of breaking up the Balkan alliance, and possibly some counter-claims by Turkey in Thrace etc. They realise that they have sown the wind, and they don't relish the whirlwind . . . .

2 September

. . . . I think our plan is sensible – self-government at once, on a liberal basis, with Greek and Turkish co-operation and association. On 'self-determination' we must 'agree to differ'. But the Conference should remain in being. It should help to guide the development of 'self-government'. It should meet again, when this is fairly in train, to consider the position. The Turks will not like it, but I believe they will accept. The Greeks will *not* accept, but may agree to take home to discuss with their colleagues . . . .

The alarming feature of the Cyprus problem is the gradual revelations of the utter rottenness of the local government and the almost Byzantine incompetence of the Colonial Office.

The C.O. in London seem to be victims of a kind of moral paralysis. They have neither vision, nor energy, nor courage. The local govt in Cyprus appears to have more or less broken down. There is no proper intelligence or security system. The police are terrorised. Even the ordinary precautions of guarding a wireless station are neglected. The Governor himself has made a very bad impression on all of us during these days. Kirkpatrick can hardly speak for rage and contempt. He seems to be ineffective, even for a Wykehamist, and without any faith in the sacredness of his mission. In his heart, he believes, I feel sure, that we ought to give the island to the Greeks, abandoning it to civil war; breaking up NATO; and precipitating a Greeko[sic]-Turkish conflict; while at the same time abdicating finally our position in Asia, the Middle East and the Persian Gulf.

I keep begging the P.M. to get a new Governor. But nothing can, alas, give us a new Colonial Office.

General Keightley (who commands the Middle East H.Q. who are tenants in Cyprus, without of course any authority in the island) came to see me yesterday. He is [a] splendid soldier. I knew him in Italy[55] and he has done a fine job wherever he has been. He feels that we could 'ride out the storm' if we could get a proper show going. We need a Gerald Templer for Cyprus.[56]

3 September

M Stephanopoulos (Greek Foreign Minister) M Mostras (Greek ambassador in London) and Sir Charles Peake (British ambassador in Athens) came to Birch Grove to luncheon . . . .

. . . . I think (in spite of his extreme nervousness) that M St enjoyed his visit . . . . He complained bitterly of the Turks. They had never before taken so stiff a line about Cyprus. This wd break up the Balkan alliance and cause a most dangerous rift in Turko-Greek relations. Moreover, even the Archbishop Makarios was beginning to lose control to more extreme, and Communist inspired forces. A great disaster was impending. We alone could help.

. . . . The Greeks are beginning to get frightened of all the trouble they have started . . . . I'm afraid I feel very discouraged. These men

---

55. See WD p. 757.
56. To replicate Templer's recent success against communist terrorists in Malaya.

will never face any unpleasant decision. They will always throw the blame for everything that goes wrong on somebody else . . . .

4 September (Sunday)
Church at 11 . . . . At 1pm the Turks arrived. M Zorlu (Foreign Minister) and M Birgi (Director General) The same performance was repeated – walk in the garden before luncheon; the Amerys to luncheon; talk in the library afterwards, and then another walk. The Turks were a great contrast to the Greeks – confident, assertive, and tough . . . .

They beg us not to give way an inch. They wd regard it as an unfriendly act if we did. They don't like 'self-government' very much. But 'self-determination' is an abomination. They feel that the conference has done a lot of good, because it has enabled them to publicise their case, which up to now has gone by default. But they feel that the conference ought to end now. We should all three agree to a moratorium – say five years – before the subject is mentioned again. Meanwhile, Cyprus shd be firmly governed. This is a turning point. If we are feeble now, we are lost. As for UN actions, they are confident that we need take no notice of them. Anyway, this time we ought to be able to rally more support.

In reply, I pointed out that we too had difficulties. We had Parliament and the British people, who might have to endure a rough time in Cyprus, with many casualties. We had world public opinion. Mediterranean peoples cd not be refused any kind of self-government, as if they were primitive savages. While we had no intention of yielding on the essential issue of sovereignty, we must try to keep the conference in being, and give the Greeks a chance of escaping (should they wish to do so) without too much loss of face. M Zorlu got rather heated and even truculent in reply. But M Birgi (who is a much more practical and experienced diplomat) soothed him down, and really admitted the need to try to make some move, in order to keep the [NATO] alliance together. (I feel that the Turks will be very stiff but will in the end accept our formula) M Zorlu would like us to shoot the Archbishop! (He is always reverting to type!) Perhaps we shall have to arrest him – but not quite yet.

. . . . At 8pm I left by car for London, arriving at No 10 Downing St at 9.45 (I had a sandwich on the road) I found P.M. and Chancellor of the Exchequer and we discussed the economic situation etc till midnight. Rab had moved a certain way towards what Anthony and I want – that is a package deal which is something more imaginative than just the old Crippsian idea of 'mopping up purchasing power'. The essential thing is to stop the causes of the inflation – which is [sic] too much capital spending (as well as spending on consumption) both by private and public sectors of the economy. The Bank rate etc will deal with the first; we must deal ourselves with the second.

We had some talk about the reconstruction of the government. I am very anxious to get a good job for *Marples* and some job for *Julian Amery* and I pleaded for both. Rab will help, but the Chief Whip [Buchan-Hepburn] is very prejudiced against both . . . .

5 September
. . . . The Cabinet approved the line which I proposed to take over Cyprus. I really think it is imaginative as well as sensible. The offer of the Tripartite Committee and a real partnership between the 3 powers shd appeal to any reasonable people. However, I am not at all sanguine of success. Later in the day we had a meeting of the Defence Committee and decided on substantial reinforcements – 2 Naval commandos; 1 Infantry Battalion and some oddments to go at once. 1 Infantry Brigade to be at 14 days notice at home. The rest of the discussion in Cabinet this afternoon (it lasted over 3 hours) was taken up with the economic situation. I thought the various contributions were sensible and practical. The chief problem is how to make a 'balanced political package'. A Capital Gains Tax wd undoubtedly have the best political effect – but it is not a very good plan for Tory Govts to start new taxes, and it is said to require a 30–40 Clause Bill. We have got to do the job (at least in essentials) in 5 Parliamentary days.

6 September
We met at Lancaster House at 11am. I made an 'exposé' of the British compromise plan. With translations, this took nearly 2 hours. We adjourned for luncheon – the Turks coming to No 1 Carlton Gardens. The text of the formal British proposal was circulated in [the] afternoon.

It was obvious, while I was developing the British plan, that it was equally distasteful to Greeks and Turks! (Perhaps that proves that it is not a bad plan) The Turks were really angry (or pretended to be) because they thought it weak to have any truck with *'self-government'*. So they staged a scene with me after lunch, pretending to be uncertain as to our views about *'self-determination'*. Actually, my speech had been perfectly clear. I have discovered now, with the Turks, that unless you speak to them very loudly and angrily, with a touch of brutality, they don't think you are serious. They are rather a fine people, but not a subtle one . . . .

7 September
I saw Zorlu at 11am in my room in Lancaster House, and had a row with him. This seemed to have a good effect, for according to the ambassador's information, he had intended to reject utterly our proposals in brutal and even in offensive tones. It is certainly true that you must shout and get angry with the Turks. They are strong but stupid – or at least, without normal perceptiveness. Nature seems to have made them the precise opposite of the Greeks in every respect. After seeing Zorlu, I saw Stephanopoulos, and talked encouragingly to him. He is in a state of jitters.

Meanwhile (whether as a result of our Conference or not – the critics will certainly say 'yes' to this question) trouble is starting. A bomb was thrown in Salonika at the Turkish Embassy and Atatürk's house damaged.[57] In reprisal, there have been serious anti-Greek riots, with a good deal of looting, in Smyrna[58] and Istanbul. It seems as if the police were unable, and perhaps unwilling, to interfere.

In these preliminary talks, I was endeavouring finally to persuade the Greeks *and* the Turks merely to *take note* of the British proposal and then send us the considered reply of their respective Govts. All yesterday afternoon we had been trying to influence them. With the Greeks we were more than partially successful. When we met (at about noon instead of 11am, owing to these private talks) the Greek Foreign Minister contented himself with a very short statement. He said that they were disappointed by our stiff attitude about 'self-determination'. Nevertheless, they would consult their government and let me have their more considered reply to the proposal I had made on behalf of HMG. This was just what we wanted, for I was determined (if at all possible) to keep the Conference in being, even if in a state of suspended animation.

The Turk was less truculent than he had intended to be (or than

57. Kemal Atatürk was the founder and first president (1923–38) of the Republic of Turkey.
58. Now Izmir.

he had been ordered to be by Menderes, the Turkish P.M. – as we knew) But he made what he called a 'full' reply, altho' (under my pressure before the session began) he altered the whole tone of his speech. I could see that he did not follow the English text which had been prepared for him. He spoke in French (which he speaks more fluently than English) and he spoke more or less extempore. He said that the Turkish govt wd send me in due course any additions to their reply.

This just enabled me to say that I would await the *full* Greek reply, and the text of the *final* Turkish reply, before HMG wd decide on another proposal or another search for compromise. Meanwhile I declared the conference to be 'suspended'. We just got away with this, without protest from the Turk, who looked rather anxious to please, for once. Meanwhile, in question and answer, I had repeated (which pleased the Turk) HMG's views on 'self-determination'. The formula, which was partly mine and partly Kirk[patrick]'s, will (I think) stand the test. 'Self-determination' cannot be a principle of universal application to all communities, whatever their size, location, history, strategical importance and all the rest. Even Austria, with her 6 million people, is denied 'self-determination'. She may *not* have *ENOSIS* with Germany and is specifically deprived of that right by Treaty. We broke off at 2am and decided to meet at 7pm to decide the communiqué, publication of documents and all the rest . . . .

At 8pm I had the diplomatic correspondents at the F.O. Lennox-Boyd was with me. I felt it best to have them right away, in the hope of influencing tomorrow's press – which will no doubt incline to be hostile or peevish. The news of reinforcements going to Cyprus broke this morning. On the whole, I feel that the Conference, which cd never have succeeded, has been worth while. It has at least proved that Cyprus is not a 'colonial' problem but a great international issue. The Turkish position has never been understood, most English people do not look at maps and few have realised its key position both for us and for the Turks. Whoever holds Cyprus commands the port of Alexandretta and the back door to Turkey.

8 September
The Press is on the whole pretty good. *The Times*, esp in its leading article, is sympathetic and even flattering. The *D.T.* is good. Even the *Manchester Guardian* doesn't know what to say. Only the *Herald* is critical . . . .

11 September (Sunday)

The Sunday press, even the *Observer*, is quite good about Cyprus. There is a general view that our offer was fair and generous and ought to have been accepted. I took part in a cricket match (the first for 40 years!) this afternoon. It was Politicians (captained by Lord de la Warr) against actors (captained by Rex Harrison) The Lord Chancellor, the Foreign Secretary, the Home Secretary, the Minister of Labour were the stars. The Actors were partly real actors, and partly film and T.V. notabilities. It was quite an amusing performance – my gay (and patched) trousers (I had no white ones) seemed to amuse the press and public. The match was to raise money for Sackville College and was played at East Grinstead. I made 2 runs, and then hit my own wicket – which amused everyone . . . .

12 September

The Press is full of our cricketing exploits! My trousers fill the headlines. Disarmament, Israel and Egypt, the Sudan, Greece Turkey and Cyprus – they are all running along, with varying degrees of 'crisis'. Lunched with Beddington Behrens. He had some interesting ideas about how to curb inflation. He thinks the excess of building of shops, offices etc cd be reduced by asking the insurance companies to hold off this sort of finance.

I had to go tonight to Covent Garden to see the Japanese 'Kabuki' dancers. I sat between the Japanese ambassador and the ambassadress. Altho' colourful, and with a certain dignity, I found this rather barbaric performance insufferably tedious – for 3 hours. Fortunately, I got away in the intervals to Ava Waverley's box, where I found the American ambassador and Mrs Aldrich just back from leave in US. They were very pleasant, as always. Worked late tonight – till after 2am.

13 September

I spent most of the day – till 4pm – at the flat, with a biscuit for luncheon. The prospect of about 4 major speeches during the next 10 days has begun to frighten me. I finished the first draft of one for the Foreign Press Association next week. This is a big affair – with radio and television. It is terribly hard not to make either a very dull or an injudicious speech . . . . Alan Lennox-Boyd came to the flat at 7pm. He wants to arrest – or banish – one of the Cypriot Bishops (not Makarios) but I persuaded [him] to bring this to the Cabinet. I gave an official dinner for Alan [sic] Dulles (head of C.I.A.) the brother of the Secretary of State. We had a large and interesting party and it went off very well. Alan Dulles has as much brain and more charm than his brother – altho' I like them both. Foster is a good friend of ours and so is Alan.

Another late night – till 2am – on boxes. There is really too much work in this office! Yet everything (except mere formalities and signatures) is important. One must see the telegrams which go out in one's name on all important visits.

14 September

Our ambassadors in Abyssinia and in Teheran (both on leave) called to see me. I was very much impressed by Stevens (Teheran) He has done a very good job. He told me that in 3 years time (if all goes well) the Persians will draw £100m in oil income, as against about £12–15m before the row. Yet they are and will continue to be persistent beggars . . . .

I'm afraid the riots in Istanbul (and to a lesser extent in Smyrna) have done the Turks a lot of harm. It seems that the police didn't interfere at first (no doubt believing or having been told that a little beating up wd do the Greeks no harm) Then the mobs got quite out of hand and in Istanbul a great deal of damage has been done (tho' little or no loss of life) There is a most sensational account in today's *Daily Mail*. Their correspondent talks of £100 million of damage. All this is a great pity, for it will put U.N. against the Turks. Nevertheless it proves our case – that this is not a 'colonial' problem but the oldest international and inter-racial dispute in the world. The Greeks seem in a great flap and no doubt the present Govt will fall. Perhaps Papagos is half-dead anyway. The Greeks talk of abandoning NATO and switching to the Soviets. I don't believe it. The only thing for us to do now is to go quickly on our course. We have heard (from the Americans) that altho' the Greeks will continue to refuse a 'tripartite' Committee on preparing for self-government in Cyprus, they will be ready to talk to us. We can, at the right moment, agree to this and then ask the Turks for their views . . . .

The economic and financial position is not improving. August exports are up – really splendid. But imports continue to grow at a still greater rate. I have just seen a return of the reserves. In the first fortnight of Sept we have lost nearly $170m. About half of this, I am told, is 'hot money'. The sooner Parlt meets and our measures are put through, the better it will be. I wish we didn't have to wait another fortnight. Yet I am still convinced that the margin of inflation is not so great as to be beyond control. Only we must act quickly and fearlessly. The political row will not matter, if we can convince the public, including the trade unions and their members, that we are doing the right thing.

The immediate crisis over, we may have to reconsider all our policies. We have made a genuine effort for liberalising trade in Europe and all over the world. We have made sterling in effect convertible.[59] But if America continues to follow her high protectionist policy, we may be forced to the alternative – our old Strasbourg policy – that is, to organise round sterling a non-dollar, non-rouble, group which can isolate itself from American policy. There wd be immense difficulties, and it may be too late. But we may be forced on to this path. Meanwhile, we must do everything we can to make sense of the line of policy wh we have chosen to pursue during the last 4 years . . . .

15 September

A very long day, beginning with the Israeli ambassador – a very pleasant man. Some think him too plausible; but I think him sincere. He has (what is rare with the Israelites) the power of philosophising about the position. He comes to speak about 'Alpha' – Mr Dulles' plan. On instructions, he asked certain questions (which I knew he wd ask) and I gave certain replies (which he expected me to give) After that, we had a most helpful talk about the situation. Mr Elath painted a very realistic and impressive picture of the situation in Israel today. The population is a strange mixture, ranging from sophisticated and highly educated Jews from Hamburg and Vienna, to the latest arrivals from the miserable life of Rabat or Algiers. The party system is hopelessly confused; the electoral system (P.R.) makes it almost impossible to get a Govt of any authority; the extremist views have undue weight. Meanwhile, the determination, or apparent determination, of the Arabs to keep the nominal state of war and the economic boycott permanently going, makes many Israelis despair and therefore lean to violent measures.

The arming of Egypt (partly with our arms) has worried them. The Centurion tanks are the real grievance. Many Israelis feel that their

---

59. From February, for non-British holders.

best chance is to force the issue now, when they believe they could defeat the cowardly Egyptians.

However, the ambassador genuinely feels himself (and I suppose speaks for his Government, which is in the process of formation after the elections) in welcoming the Dulles declaration and our decision to support it . . . .

Defence Committee all the morning. I agreed (in spite of F.O. views) to reducing garrison of Hong Kong. We must take a realist view. It is impossible to meet at the same time the troubles where they occur (like Cyprus) and where they are prospective (like Hong Kong) Whether we have one or two brigades at Hong Kong really does not matter. We hold Berlin with one battalion. But in either case, an attack means general war. A short discussion on Selwyn Lloyd's paper on national service. The decision must, of course, be taken by the Cabinet. But even if we postpone the call-up by 3 months (which is an alleviation to industry but not help to the individual) I don't believe we can hold on to 2 years much longer.[60]

I went to luncheon (having been put off No 10) with Colonial Secretary (Lennox-Boyd) and Solicitor-General. The Governor of Cyprus now passionately wants to arrest the Bishop of Kyrenia for 'seditious language and incitement to murder'. He is, of course, guilty. But that is not really the point. He cannot be tried (altho' there is no trial by jury in Cyprus, yet even the Cypriot judges wd be too frightened to condemn him) so a special ordinance has to be passed giving the Governor the right to deport him and lock him up in the Seychelles. This seems to me very foolish, but I must not offend the Col Secy (who is a most likeable and loyal soul) by saying so too openly. Cabinet at 2.30, lasting till 5pm. Lord Salisbury in the chair. (Eden and Butler being absent) A very long agenda, and a very discursive Cabinet. What a change from Churchill's early Cabinets in 1951 and 2, when scarcely anyone dared speak. They all chatter now. With great difficulty (in spite of Ld S) I carried the view that we had better not arrest the Bishop as long as there was any chance of getting the U.N. steering committee to refuse to *inscribe* the question of Cyprus on the agenda. There is *a* chance, altho' not more than a fair chance at present. It will depend largely on the attitude of the US. I have sent a long personal message to Dulles, but I fear he will find

---

60. National service of twelve months had been introduced in 1947, and was extended to eighteen months in 1948 and to two years in 1950.

some excuse for letting us down. If we were to arrest the Bishop now, it wd give him exactly the 'get-out' he is looking for . . . .

The P.M. (hearing the result of the Cabinet from Salisbury) started telephoning about the Bishop, whom he wants to arrest. We had rather a fierce interchange on the (scrambled) telephone. But as he had a temperature of over 100 I thought I had better ring off. Even P.M. cannot go behind a Cabinet decision, and I had to tell him so.

16 September

. . . . Lunch with Ava (Waverley) and then to Chapel St to try to persuade Lennox-Boyd to forget about the Bishop. He shewed me a telegram to say that

(i) Archbishop Makarios (who opposes terrorism) is now split from the Bishop of Kyrenia (who supports terrorism) From this the Governor makes the strange deduction that it wd help the Archbp if we arrested the Bp!

(ii) The guilty Bishop hasn't opened his mouth for a week – so he ought at once to be arrested and granted the inestimable boon of martyrdom . . . .

Poor Leo Amery died in his sleep last night. He was 81. He had a fine record of devoted and sincere service to the causes in which he believed. He had also great dignity and nobility of mind, as was evidenced when he had to face the appalling tragedy of his younger son's treason, arrest, and execution after the war.[61] Catherine rang up and said she wd leave the children with me for a bit . . . .

17 September

. . . . I had to motor from home to Chequers (3 hours) motor and train from Chequers here (3½ hours) all for the pleasure of 30 minutes talk with a sick P.M. and a jittery Colonial Secretary . . . .

I find a packet of trouble on getting back. The Buraimi arbitration is going wrong. The Saudi Arabians, not content with bribing everybody in the area, have now (apparently) begun to bribe the arbitrators! . . . .[62]

---

61. John Amery broadcast anti-Russian propaganda from Berlin during the Second World War. His father's response is reproduced in John Barnes and David Nicholson (eds), *The Empire at Bay: The Leo Amery Diaries 1929–1945* (London: Hutchinson, 1988), pp. 1071f.

62. The arbitration was into Saudi claims to the Buraimi oasis, hitherto the territory

18 September

. . . . Rather a 'wobbling' telegram from Foster Dulles in reply to my personal message on Cyprus . . . . Meanwhile a riot (of small character) in Cyprus and a very interesting interview in the *Sunday Express* with Archbishop Makarios, who speaks of a settlement and saying that violence must cease . . . .

19 September

A great storm has broken in the Press as a result of Petrov (the Russian agent to come over in Australia) having published his memoirs serially in the *People*. The first instalment appeared yesterday. Even the more reputable journals are in a 'hue and cry' against the Foreign Office. The *Express*, the *Mirror* and the *Sketch* lead the baser part of the pack. We shall now have to publish a White Paper about it, and of course we shall be attacked for having kept silent all these years about Maclean and Burgess . . . .

. . . . I went to dine at the Carlton Club, where I saw the Chief Whip, who walked back with me to Carlton Gardens. We discussed the pros and cons of a special meeting of Parl to deal with the 'economic crisis'. If we can honourably wait to the regular meeting (which might be advanced a week) it would be much better, from the political angle.

(I shd add that I gave a luncheon party at Carlton Gardens for M René Mayer, who has succeeded M Monnet as head of the Iron and Steel Community [sic: ECSC]. I think he will be much easier to deal with than his predecessor) . . . .

21 September

I got an early train to London, and did some work at F.O. before the Cabinet, which was at 10.30. Altho' the Press assumed that we discussed nothing but Burgess and Maclean, they were not mentioned. The whole discussion (apart from a few minor items) was on the economic measures and the proposed meeting of Parl next Tuesday. On the substance of the measures proposed by the Chancellor of the Ex,[63] there was general agreement. The only exception was the aboli-

---

of the Sultan of Muscat and the Sheikh of Abu Dhabi, both of whom were under British protection.

63. To tackle the deteriorating balance of payments position.

tion of the bread subsidy. Altho' it is really absurd to keep it nowadays, it means another 1½% on the cost of living and may have a bad effect on wage claims.

On the meeting of Parlt, there was an admirably conducted discussion, with all the arguments for and against honourably and fairly set out by all the members who spoke (and nearly all did) There was a general agreement that we must not be swayed by what the Opposition would say, or what might be the effect on our own party. The question was, what was our duty. Would the special summoning of an extraordinary session add to or detract from confidence in sterling. The measures could not, of themselves, have an immediate effect. They would take time to act. Certainly, 3 weeks delay wd not matter – since we did not mean either to devalue sterling or to make it fully convertible forthwith. The Chancellor of the Ex was very fair and convincing. He argued *for* the early date at first, but seemed affected by the arguments against. Everyone agreed that we ought to support him in whatever *final* decision he wanted us to make. The discussion was adjourned till 9.45 tomorrow . . . .

Back to No 10 at 3. P.M., Ld Salisbury, Colonial Secy, Minister of Defence. After a long discussion it was decided (I am sure rightly) to offer the Governorship of Cyprus to Field Marshal Sir John Harding,[64] who is just about to end his term as C.I.G.S. If he will accept, we shall have a first-class man . . . . After this meeting, I got P.M. to agree final text of the White Paper on Maclean and Burgess (the F.O. men who deserted to the Soviet Union and are now known to have been spies in their employ. A terribly shaming story) The gutter press (esp *Mirror* and *Sketch*) have violent attacks on me today. Herbert Morrison has given a disgraceful interview to the *Daily Herald*. He has the impudence to say that when he was Foreign Minister (and the worst in history, except perhaps John Simon)[65] he had a poor opinion of the Office . . . .

Dulles has agreed! Wonderful news! I have sent him and Cabot Lodge messages of thanks. The committee of U.N. meets tonight, and we may now succeed in defeating the [Cyprus] inscription – but it will be a near thing . . . .

---

64. Harding was also appointed Commander-in-Chief on the island. Macmillan had at first advised Eden not to appoint a soldier.
65. Foreign Secretary 1931–5.

22 September

Cabinet at 9.45. There was a long and useful discussion on National Service. Most ministers seemed to be ready to accept the Service Ministers and Chiefs of Staff argument for 24 months, with 3 months postponement, to be repeated in such a way as gradually to advance the age. (Arrangements wd be made for University students to be called up earlier if they wished) I spoke last. While I said this made my task as Foreign Secy easier, I was not happy about the finality of this decision. The National Service Act was due to expire in 1958. I thought it a wonderful thing that all parties had accepted the *principle* of national service. But I did not believe that the country wd accept 2 years for ever. Moreover, the whole conception of national service had changed. The original idea was to create large reserves, to be called up on mobilisation and used through a long war. The new nuclear strategy had altered all that. It was becoming apparent that we needed national service men only during their service, to fill the gaps in voluntary recruitment. The final answer was to make voluntary recruiting more attractive. We might approach this by steps. But ought we not now to accept it as our objective. P.M. summing up in fact accepted my argument . . . .

4.30–6 – a film (T.V.) was made of me answering questions to Mr Robert Mackenzie. This is for use in U.S. I went back to F.O., where we had a long meeting (Caccia, Shuckburgh etc) to discuss a new and most dangerous development in Egypt. Nasser has made a bargain with the Russians, for 100 Migs, 100 tanks and other weapons, and a team of Russian technicians. This is a most alarming and perilous success for the Russians, and we *must* stop it somehow . . . .[66]

Dined at Bucks with James Stuart and Jim Thomas. James, from his long experience, supports the idea of a debate on Maclean as soon as possible. This will clear the air, and stop the daily stream of innuendo by Parl Questions.

. . . . [T]his wretched spy business dominates everything for the moment . . . .

---

66. A reference to the recent agreement for a large supply of arms to Egypt, nominally from Czechoslovakia. This stirred anxieties not only about Russian ambitions in the Middle East, but also about the prospects of renewed Arab–Israeli conflict into which Britain, with its extensive Middle Eastern interests and its role, with France and the US, as guarantor of the Israeli borders under the 1950 Tripartite Agreement, would inevitably be drawn.

23 September

. . . . Went at 12 noon to see the P.M. I shewed him the telegram wh we propose to send to Dulles on Egypt's agreement with Russia. I am proposing to Dulles a *very* stiff and almost threatening protest, in the name of the President and the P.M., to Nasser. We really cannot allow this man, who has neither the authority of a throne nor of a Parliament, to destroy our base and threaten our rear.

We then talked about Maclean and Burgess. We agreed that No 10 shd put out, with the White Paper wh is published today, a statement that we shd afford opportunity for early debate.

Then Cyprus. To my delight, it is at last agreed to remove the present Governor. The CIGS (whose term is about to end) F.M. Sir John Harding, has been offered the post and has accepted. This is splendid news. Just as I was leaving, P.M. threw a bombshell. 'How wd I like to leave the F.O. and go to the Treasury?'

I confess I was somewhat staggered. 'When?' 'At once'. 'What about Rab?' 'He can be Ld Privy Seal and Leader of the House'. 'Have you spoken to him?' 'Yes, last night. He seemed rather to like the idea'. We then discussed the effect on Rab's position and the prestige of the Govt. Wd it not seem a confession of failure? Wd not the whole Govt suffer accordingly? What about the autumn Budget? P.M. seemed in a great hurry to settle it, but I said I must think about it . . . .

The American ambassador came at 3pm. The Americans are getting windy about Cyprus and U.N. They fear that the Greeks, if thwarted, will turn nasty. The Greek Govt may fall, and they may 'go to the Left'. I told him that they shd have more courage. The Greeks will never desert their 'sugar-daddy'. They only exist at all by American aid. The Austrian ambassador came next. He wanted our views about the 'guarantee'. Then the Egyptian ambassador – his first visit, on appointment. Altho' this is normally a 'courtesy' visit, I gave him hell about the Russian contract. He said it was not yet completed. I said that it had better not be. Then the C.I.G.S. We had a long talk about Cyprus. I urged him to insist on the right of direct communication with the PM and with me. I thanked him most warmly for his patriotism. Poor man! He was looking forward to a quiet life in Devonshire!

. . . . Sir Harold Caccia – to talk about the P.M.'s astonishing suggestion this morning. He said that P.M. was worried about the economic front. He felt Rab had lost grip of it and was tired and depressed. The death of his wife had got him down. He depended on her for advice and strength. 'But what will the country say? What about "invest in success", and all that?'[67] Chief Whip felt the force of the argument. It cannot really be done in a hurry (if at all) because all the other changes depend on it. P.M. wd, of course, put Selwyn Lloyd at F.O. and run the F.O. himself, through his old subordinates. I asked if P.M.'s purpose was really to get back control of the F.O. Chief Whip thought not. But he was happy about Foreign Affairs and he understood them. He thought I was the only person whom he cd trust with finance, economics etc. The last few weeks had shaken his confidence in the Treasury . . . .

24 September

. . . . Motored to London airport and left for New York at 8pm. American ambassador came to the airport to see me off.

25 September

Arrived in New York about 11am New York time . . . . Sir Pierson Dixon (Bob) who used to be with me in Algiers and is now H.M. ambassador to U.N. came to meet me at the airport. He came on board, after the other passengers had left, to tell me the news of President Eisenhower's attack of coronary thrombosis, which took place in the early hours of Saturday morning at Denver . . . .

. . . . It is too soon to make an estimate of the political results of this very sad event. I shd assume that it means that Ike will not run for a second term, even if he recovers from this attack . . . . If he doesn't run again, it means that the Democrats are almost sure to carry it. In any case, it means that the Republicans will be fighting for their lives, instead of having the 'walk-over' wh they have been expecting. This in turn will reflect itself in their foreign policy. They will be much more sensitive to pressure groups, like the Jews . . . .

We drove from the airport to Ware Hill, the delightful house wh the ambassador to UN – first Gladwyn Jebb, now Bob Dixon, occupies – some 30 minutes out of New York, beautifully situated on the Hudson River . . . .

26 September

. . . . At 12 noon, Dick Casey came in, as pleasant and friendly as ever.

---

67. Gaitskell was shortly to accuse Butler of having stoked up balance of payments problems with an electioneering Budget in April.

He told us what had happened – or rather had not happened – at the ANZUS meeting. The Americans had no detailed plans for the defence of SE Asia. They wd rely on massive air attack, and expect local forces (British and Australian) to deal with local ground attack . . . .

A large dinner at Ware Hill . . . . Unfortunately, I had to leave soon after 9pm to go into town to see Foster Dulles. He was very pleasant and forthcoming. I spoke about the President's illness. D hoped for a very speedy recovery, but said nothing about the implications for the future. Then I thanked him about Cyprus. He seemed very pleased that they had brought off a victory in U.N. . . . . We then got on to Egypt, and the Russian arms contract. He told me that he had spoken strongly to Molotov about it and told him that the President and he both took a most serious view of it. M tried to pass it off as a purely commercial transaction, but D wd not have that. We talked all round the question, and what we might do to bring pressure on Nasser, either by stick or carrot, or a combination of both treatments . . . .

27 September

. . . . After dinner there was the usual conference – four arm-chairs for the protagonists in the middle of the room, with all the seconds, trainers etc ranged behind. Everything went off very smoothly about the arrangements for Geneva. Then D asked if anyone wanted to raise any other questions. Fortunately, Molotov opened with an enquiry about the election of new members to U.N. What did we feel about his proposal to elect all 16 applicants 'en bloc', and thus overcome the complete ice-jam of recent years? D said he thought the number was 18 – there was Japan; and now Spain to be added. M said that these applications were very recent, but were no doubt a matter for consideration. But what did D think of the principle of no discrimination? D said very deliberately and distinctly – 'We feel that each country shd be voted on individually. But if that leads to a deadlock, some arrangement could be made.' But the public opinion of US will not allow us to vote for Bulgaria, Rumania, or Hungary. The U.N. has condemned them for their disregard of Human Rights. After a pause, D repeated the last part, again the great emphasis. Then he said 'Perhaps we could elect the 7 Bandung countries – *and* Italy, Austria, and Finland'. M said 'That wd be good. 10 would be good, but it would still be discrimination' . . . .

After this, D asked if there was any other question which anyone wished to raise. I then started, very quietly and slowly, about the problem of Palestine. It was in our interest to keep things quiet in the world, esp among small countries, while we were trying to negotiate on really large issues. In the Palestine area, there was a vast tense and delicate situation between Egypt and Israel. We had tried to keep some kind of balance in their rearmament, and prevent an arms race. I had heard rumours of a very large sale of armaments by Russia to Egypt. This would have very grave effects throughout the Middle East. M replied on rather different lines to what he had said to Dulles. He said he knew little about the matter, but would enquire. He agreed that tension shd be kept low. But how could a balance be maintained. Perhaps through an interchange of information? Dulles then weighed in, with a very powerful plea and protest. Molotov seemed rather embarrassed when I opened the subject.

28 September

. . . . Luncheon by Alphand (French ambassador to U.N. – a most able and witty diplomat) At one of the various parties, Molotov said, more or less in chaff, to A 'France and Russia should really be friends. We have much between us'. 'Yes' replied Alphand 'all Germany'. Rather taken aback, Molotov said 'Why do you put so much faith in the Germans?' A said in answer 'I thought it was you who trusted them so much in 1939'. M did not like it.

4.30. Molotov called on me at the Waldorf. We had an hour's talk. It began on Vietnam, where M gently took me to task, because Diem had not yet carried out the Geneva agreement. I said we must have patience, but we were doing our best, and swiched to Laos, where the Communist Pathet Lao are in default. M was in a position of great advantage, but did not choose to press it. I was able to ask for the same joint effort to keep the Middle East quiet, without seeming to drag in this matter. We also discussed the membership of U.N., and one or two other questions. All this was duly reported to F.O., where it will be on the files, I suppose for ever. It is rather terrifying to feel that every word we use will be on the record. The Russians no doubt send home their version; we send back ours. Future historians will write about these conversations, and the slightest false move pilloried and traduced! . . . .

7pm. Council of Foreign Relations gave me a dinner; . . . . a much more powerful and influential body than Chatham House. When we got back to the Waldorf we found a mass of telegrams, including one

33. Anglo-French talks between foreign ministers Robert Schuman (left) and Ernest Bevin, 7 March 1950.

34. Herbert Morrison, taken on his becoming Foreign Secretary, 12 March 1951.

35. Aneurin Bevan, on his resignation from the Labour government over prescription charges, April 1951.

36. Oliver Lyttelton arriving at Churchill's house at Hyde Park Gate, London, for a Conservative Shadow Cabinet meeting, 22 September 1951.

37. Sir Hartley Shawcross (left) and Hugh Dalton leaving 10 Downing Street on 27 September 1951, shortly before the end of the Labour government.

38. Labour leader Clement Attlee on the campaign trail, 24 October 1951.

39. Macmillan's brother-in-law James
Stuart (right) with his new Minister of
State at the Scottish Office, Lord Home,
10 November 1951.

40. Antoine Pinay, pictured
in March 1952 when he was French
Prime Minister.

41. Bulganin, Eden, Khruschev and Selwyn Lloyd at 10 Downing Street during the Russians' visit, 19 April 1956.

42. Two founders of the European Movement, but with rather different ideas of where they wanted to go. Macmillan greets Paul-Henri Spaak at 11 Downing Street, 4 September 1956.

43. Macmillan visits the grave of his grandfather Joshua Belles, 23 September 1956, on his first trip to his mother's home town of Spencer, Indiana.

44. Sir Roger Makins on becoming Joint Permanent Under-Secretary of the Treasury, 15 October 1956.

45. Catherine and Julian Amery (with Louise and Theresa) at the christening of the twins Alexandra and Leopold at St Peter's, Eaton Square, 17 December 1956.

46. Sir Percy Mills, en route to Buckingham Palace to be confirmed as Minister of Power, 14 January 1957.

47. The new Premier en route for the Palace to confirm his Cabinet, 14 January 1957.

from Eden, who wants to intervene in the arms for Egypt affair by a 'personal appeal' to Bulganin (in the best Churchill manner!) offering to take up Molotov's suggestion for an interchange of information on arms contracts between us and the Russians. There are, of course, some attractions in this idea, but great dangers also. If we invite the Russians in on Palestine, shall we be able to narrow the issue to Palestine only. In other words, once the Russians have got their foot in the door, how can we keep them out of the whole house?

29 September
9.30. Went to see Averill Harriman (by invitation) at his house in New York. (A lovely little house, with some fine things in it) As in England, multi-millionaires have no chance in politics unless they are on the left. The Democrats might well adopt Harriman as their presidential candidate. The Republicans (who are popularly connected with Wall Street) could not possibly do so. Averill Harriman is a man of considerable charm, and great determination. He is very ambitious. The President's illness has produced, for men like Harriman, a dramatic development in their chance. Averill was very direct about all this to me. He is very critical of the Republicans and their foreign and domestic policy. Eisenhower he admires and likes as a man, but despises as a politician. He should have been a Democrat. He tries to be a liberal Republican, but cannot control the old guard. The Democrats' general position is about that [of] the Tory Party of today. Averill thinks we have done a fine job at home and that we have not had the material or moral support that we shd have had from the American administration . . . .

. . . . Luncheon (at the Racquet Club) given by John Russell, who manages British Information Services. There were present the proprietors, executive directors, or writers in almost every important chain of newspapers and magazines in US. Luce; Scripps Howard; Alsop; Hearst; Ed Murrow; and the rest – about 30 in all. They asked questions (off the record) for nearly three quarters of an hour. No punches pulled – no baloney. It was quite an ordeal, but they seemed fairly satisfied. Roger Makins was there, but no other 'Britisher'. Of course, *if* you should make a good impression, it's worth more than the propaganda of the B.I.S. or F.O. For these men really influence the opinions of the whole American people . . . .

8.30. Dinner by the Russians. I sat next [to] Molotov . . . . On the whole, I shd judge that the Russians will not be cajoled out of this new move by Eden or anyone else. They are approaching Syria, Saudi Arabia, Libya – and other countries. It is really the opening of a new offensive in the Middle East, while Europe is 'contained' by the Geneva spirit, and the Far East has become temporarily stabilised. Nor does this cost them anything. The weapons they will distribute will be obsolete or obsolescent, and will soon be replaced in any case.

The French are terribly worried and excited about the debate on whether Algeria should be 'inscribed' on the agenda.[68] (Of course, we shall support them, for it raises the same principles as Cyprus – the breach of the rule that the Assembly is not to discuss the internal affairs of member states) They threaten to resign altogether from U.N. if the Arab and Asiatic insist on inscription and win their way.

30 September

The life here is terribly exhausting. Except for the Russian dinner (where it wd not be understood) I have managed to keep 'teetotal'. But it is impossible not to eat some of the vast amount of food provided at these endless meals. I fear I shall have put back all the fat I got rid of so carefully at home.

One sees people all day and we work from one morning till the early hours of the next. I am beginning to feel the strain. All the main work of the F.O. has to be carried on as usual, and a mass of telegrams has to be answered, without the staff to do the work . . . .

10.30. My speech in the Assembly. It was quite fun, for I spoke 'in the English manner' – that is, not looking at the notes, but as if in the HofC or an English public meeting. This greatly impresses the foreigners, who normally (with their heads le[a]nt over the ms) gabble through a prepared text . . . . I had a talk with the Secretary General (Mr Hammarskjöld) afterwards. I am not very favourably impressed by him. He is agreeable, and means well, and is highly intelligent. But, the more you see of him, the more you feel that he is suffering from the endemic disease of Scandinavia (esp Sweden) – gutlessness. I suppose after another generation or two of the Welfare State we shall be the same! . . . .

Mr Fawzi (Egyptian Foreign Minister) called, at his own request. He is a pretty smooth customer, sly and insinuating. I made afterwards a very complete record to send home and a short telegram. He called

---

68. That is, so that the UN Assembly could debate the nationalist insurrection against France in Algeria.

the 'arms episode' a 'most regrettable matter'. We ought to sit down and study the position quietly together. The situation was still 'flexible'. I am not sure why he came. It may have been (a) to spy out the ground (b) to make it clear that he was willing to be bribed, either in prestige or by arms. On the question of a 'settlement' with Israel (on the Dulles lines) he was very intransigeant [sic]. He asked for the whole of the Negeb. (Perh this is the result of striking oil near the Gaza strip) But this may only be the opening bid. I did not like Mr Fawzi at all. I took a frigidly correct note of his 'approach', and expressed our amazement at the Russian agreement, quite contrary to the whole spirit of the Suez Treaty last year, and full of dangers for Egypt.

I asked if he had seen Mr Dulles. We work absolutely hand-in-hand with the Americans. He smiled rather weakly, and said that he had not been able to contact Mr Dulles! (They had been in New York together for a week or more!) My next (and last) visitor before dinner was Krishna Menon. He was in a very different mood to the last time I saw him in London . . . . When Krishna Menon forgets to be a Cassandra,[69] he is really very good company . . . .

1 October

Our last day in N York. Being quite exhausted, I insisted on staying in bed till late in the morning, dozing and reading, and trying to think out what we ought to *do* about the Russian move into the Middle East. All the growing evidence put together seems to indicate the opening of a large scale campaign.

The French are in a terrible state of indignation and confusion, so Bob Dixon reports. The vote went against them on Algeria (28–27, with 5 abstentions) They walked out of the U.N. Assembly and seem determined to walk out of the U.N. organisation altogether. But I don't believe they will . . . .

I have had no news at all from home, but I assume that all is well. We have a lot to do when we get back – the Conservative Conference will waste two days at least. As far as I can judge, the gutter press (ably assisted by the independent T.V.) has rather overplayed its hand about Maclean and Burgess and people are getting rather disgusted. I have had one or two letters from Labour MPs urging me to stand firm

---

69. In Greek mythology a prophetess who, though she always told the truth, was doomed to be disbelieved.

in resisting an enquiry into the F.O. Herbert Morrison was now publicly demanding an enquiry. He is a poor creature really – *faux bonhomie*[70] – and without any principles, except opportunism . . . .

. . . . I had asked to see M Pinay before leaving, and met at the Waldorf at 3pm. He has received instructions from Paris that *all* the representatives at U.N., including the permanent mission headed by Alphand shall return to Paris. M Faure intends to introduce next week a '*projet de loi*'[71] wh will mean their *resignation* from U.N. He (Pinay) agreed with the policy of abstention from all activities in the Assembly. But he was against resigning altogether, for he thought that they shd continue on such bodies as the disarmament sub-committee, where M Moch did such good work. I urged him strongly to stand up for this . . . . France was a permanent member of the Security Council, as a great power. It was one thing to resign, another to get back. I sympathised with their disgust at the misuse of the Assembly. We had suffered from it also over such issues as Cyprus. But I hope they wd not separate themselves altogether from the U.N., bearing the future in mind . . . .

Left NY for Washington in a Heron – 8 seater aeroplane, belonging to the Embassy . . . .

We had a good flight (1hr 20 minutes) and a fine view of all the famous Washington landmarks as we circled the city. Drove to the Embassy – which is quite an impressive, but almost inconceivably inconvenient building – by Lutyens. We find there Evelyn Shuckburgh, and a lot more telegrams, including one from P.M. He generally agrees with our proposed plan of action over Egypt and the Russian arms, but still hankers after his message to Bulganin. I don't mind the first 3 paragraphs of his text – which is just an appeal to the Marshal's better nature and the Geneva spirit. It may do something to worry the Russians, and will anyway do for the record. But the proposed fourth para – the offer to sit down and exchange information about what arms we are all sending to Israel and her neighbours – seems to me very dangerous. I am against it; and the Americans will never agree and only have the worse opinion of the PM's judgment if I put it forward. Yet I can hardly suppress it altogether, esp as P.M. thinks that my purpose in coming to Washington is to sell it to Dulles and Co . . . .

---

70. 'False good nature'.
71. 'Legal instrument'.

2 October
The dinner party consisted of Foster Dulles, the Vice President (Nixon) Doug McArthur, Roger and me. Alan [sic] Dulles came in after dinner. I was interested to meet Nixon – in the present situation he plays an important role. I was rather favourably impressed. He struck me as intelligent and not without force and dignity . . . .

. . . . Dulles . . . . took the gravest and most pessimistic view. The evidence was piling up – the Egyptian deal was not an isolated event. The Russians were corrupting also Syria, Saudi Arabia and trying Libya. They would soon start on Iraq. He thought that we might follow up the protest which he and I had already made to Molotov. The President might be able – in say a week – to do some business and he might consider sending the letter to Bulganin on which he was engaged when he was stricken. Vice President Nixon thought this would be a very good plan. It would be rather dramatic if this shd be his first public act on convalescence. This enabled me to mention Eden's idea (tho' not its content, except in the most general terms) of his own message. It was quite well received. We then discussed what pressure could be put at the receiving end. In general, altho' we had not yet got the reports from Cairo of our formal protests, we agreed *not* to take drastic measures. Dulles asked if we had enough troops to re-occupy Egypt and I said, 'not in Suez. They are moving out fast. But it could be done from Cyprus, no doubt'. However, at this stage, this did not seem practical. So it comes to a mild squeeze on Egypt, and benefits to the loyal Arabs – Jordan, Iraq etc. Let unpleasant things begin to happen to Nasser, and pleasant things to the others . . . .

Bedell Smith (my old friend who used to be Chief of Staff in Algiers) came to luncheon with his wife . . . . Bedell said that Ike was offered *both* the Democrat and the Republican nominations! He hesitated a long time, for he was temperamentally more in sympathy with Democrats. But he thought that unless the Republicans got in again (after 20 years and more of Democrat supremacy) the two-party system and with it good and clean government would vanish from US. He thought it his duty to win the hard way with the Republicans. Bedell Smith described his own political position as follows 'I am an Eisenhower Democrat!'

3 October
Roger, Shuckburgh and I went to the State Dept at 10am. Foster Dulles received us, with 3 or 4 of his advisers . . . .

In the end, we reached a complete agreement as to measures to be taken in Egypt and in the other states. We must try to make Nasser uncomfortable, and build up the Northern States. The question of the messages to Bulganin remains. I thought Foster Dulles didn't seem so keen today about the idea of the President. 'He could not commit' the President. I said that P.M. was keen on the idea, but did not press it. I shd have recorded the fact that by the telegram which he sent yesterday (and we received and replied to last night) Eden has really met my major objection . . . . Nevertheless, I am not sure that it ought to go. The peremptory, and quite unacceptable, telegram received this morning no doubt reflects his disappointment at my not immediately agreeing, now that he has accepted my major criticism. Nevertheless, I must not yield without more discussion or he will be For Secy from now on . . . .

. . . . If he sends off the telegram tonight, contrary to my request, I shall resign.

. . . . It seems that the French are going to accept our advice. They will absent themselves from the Assembly, but *not* resign from the U.N. We left at 5pm (10pm British time) After an hour or so, we were told that one of the engines was wrong. So we had to go to Gander (in Newfoundland) and wait there. Fortunately, after an hour or two, we got places in another BOAC plane (tourist class) and left for London . . . .

4 October

However, we arrived at London airport at *11.20am* (our time) and got immediately into a waiting helicopter, reaching No 10 (where the Cabinet was sitting) at 11.45am. Rather good going! (The evening press was full of the story) As I got into the Cabinet, I got a note from Harold Caccia, to say that the P.M.'s telegram to Bulganin had been held up, for the Cabinet to decide! This was an important moral victory . . . . I think the policy is beginning to take shape. I want to get Persia into the Baghdad Pact; to give *all* we can to Irak and get US to do the same. I want to declare for the immediate independence of the Sudan (Nasser will not relish this) get Americans to reduce economic aid to Egypt and transfer it to Irak . . . .

I lunched with Harry Crookshank at his house in Pont St. We were alone. Harry is mildly peeved because he has not had 5 minutes conversation with the P.M. since the Govt was formed. He reads all the time in the newspapers that he is to become a peer; whether in or out of office seems obscure . . . . Of course, the difficulty really rests on the question of the Treasury. If Rab really wants to give it up and become Leader of the House, there is no room for Harry in the Commons.

Left for Bournemouth on 4.35 train.[72] I found D at the hotel, and we had a pleasant dinner with the Wooltons. Then to the Mayor's reception, the Conference Ball, and the Young Conservatives' Ball . . . .

8 October

Lord Woolton made his farewell speech – and a very good one. The ceremony was most touching – for the whole party has a real affection for him and his wife. He will not be easy to replace. Oliver Poole (who has been selected for the job)[73] is an able and attractive man – in the early 40s – and will do well. But 'Uncle Fred' is unique. Eden's speech (about an hour) was very well done – no fireworks, but good common-sense, with a fine appeal for the progressive Tory idea at the end. Eden never makes a really remarkable speech, since he never says anything memorable. But he never makes a bad speech. His only mistake was that he made no mention of agriculture . . . . Eden spoke to me again about the Treasury, and asked me if I had yet been able to decide. I said 'no'. He thought it could wait till early December. I also warned him that I felt we should have to *do* something about the Burgess and Maclean affair. I don't, of course, want an enquiry into the past. But I think something is needed to satisfy the HofC and the public about the future . . . .

12 October

. . . . The Lord Chancellor came at 5.30 and was most helpful about Burgess and Maclean. He feels (as I do) that we shall have to propose some kind of inquiry. I want [it] to be about the problem of 'security in a free society' – for the future. I want, if possible, to avoid a muck-raking enquiry into the past . . . .

15 October

. . . . The Labour Party conference at Margate has not done them much good. They have no policy and are still squabbling. The Trade Unions have ruthlessly asserted their power, and Bevan has been overwhelmed

---

72. For the party conference.
73. Replacing Woolton as Conservative Party chairman.

by the block vote. But he is still the darling of the constituency organisations . . . .

18 October

A long Cabinet. The Butler proposals for the autumn Budget were agreed in general terms. On Housing Subsidies, he and Sandys have reached agreement. The lines more or less follow what we had envisaged as the next step when I put forward my last Cabinet paper as Housing Minister – that is, the reduction of the General Housing Subsidy to an almost nominal figure (say £10) while keeping a subsidy at £22 to £24 for slum clearance. As for Rents, the completion of the revaluation of all domestic property by the Inland Revenue (as opposed to Local Authorities) will be done by the end of this year, and becomes effective in April. My Rents Act was admittedly a 'stop-gap'. It has done some good, but has great drawbacks and complications. It should now be possible (after next April) to base a system of maximum rent on the actual valuation. I had two papers, both of great importance. The first was a paper about Middle East and oil. It was a plea for spending a bit more, in propaganda etc, in defence of this vast investment wh has grown up in Arabia and the Persian Gulf – the last, and greatest, of our overseas assets. The second paper (connected with this) was to seek permission a) to repudiate the arbitration agreement with the Saudis about Buraimi. The Saudis have both bribed the population (to the tune of £30 millions – an incredible figure, but true) and bribed the Arbitration Court. After denouncing the agreement, we shall establish our rights (or rather those of the Trucial States, whom we protect) by a small military expedition. The legal position is rather tricky (the Attorney General was rather wet about this) but the political situation is urgent. We must act, firmly and quickly, if we are to retain our prestige and hopes of more oil in this area . . . .

A long office meeting about the next steps in the Middle East. The chief thing now is to get on with the Northern [Baghdad] Pact, *and* to give some assistance (for instance, the High Dam at Assouan)[74] not in arms but in the economic field . . . .

---

74. The scheme to build a new dam at Aswan across the Nile to improve irrigation and develop hydro-electric power. Britain, France, West Germany, the US and the World Bank were all offering financial assistance.

20 October

I find the very late hours over the boxes getting me down. I do not finish till 1 or 2 am (if I dine out, it's worse) Nor is there much chance of reading . . . .

Cabinet 11–1.15. Buraimi approved politically, as well as militarily. Let's hope it comes off! We decided to tell no one – even old Commonwealth countries or US until it has been put into operation.

The Budget proposals are all now approved – except the abolition of the Bread Subsidy (£30m) It ought to be done, but two considerations made the Cabinet nervous a) effect on wage claims outstanding b) effect on National Assistance. (It makes, of course, a difference of 1.5 points on the cost of living figure) It is said, however, to amount to a trifling sum for men and women earning normal wages – 5d a week. This was held over till next week . . . .

. . . . At 4, Burgess and Maclean, a perennial and sordid topic. It takes up a lot of time and we get nowhere. I shall be glad when the debate is over. Then a meeting with Kirk[patrick] and Evelyn Shuckburgh . . . . We are going to try hard to get the contract for the Anglo-German-French consortium approved – helped by US for Assouan Dam. If we get this, it will regain western prestige in Egypt. It matters much more to them than arms. But it will be very bad if we miss the chance, and let the Russians slip in again. We got off a telegram to Washington (agreed with Treasury) which was good. Other urgent questions are (a) strengthening the Northern [Baghdad] Pact (b) keeping Syria quiet (c) the Sudan (d) Israel. Will she attack Egypt *before* the Russian arms arrive? If so, what do we do? If she attacks Jordan, we are bound by treaty to Jordan (e) the follies of Jordan – esp the King, who is young and wastes his (or rather our money) He wants to buy jet-planes, which none of his air force could maintain, let alone fly . . . .

23 October

. . . . I have now composed (and Dorothy has typed for me) a letter to the P.M. about the proposal that I should move to the Treasury. I have accepted – on certain conditions, the chief one of which is that I must have the same power and position as the present Chancellor of the Ex occupies. I have copied out the letter and taken it with me to Paris. I will sleep on it and (if I finally decide to do so) will send it from Paris by bag . . . .

24 October (Paris)

Here is the letter wh I have sent to the P.M.

'Dear Anthony:

I have thought, for several weeks, over yr proposal that I shd leave the F.O. and go to the Treasury.

Naturally, I am not at all anxious, to do so, for I love the F.O. – the work and the people. It is the fulfilment of a long ambition.

I would like to be clear about certain points from the start, because you are asking me to take over a very difficult job, which may involve some rather painful decisions.

(1) I may want to make considerable changes in the set-up

(2) I may want to bring in outside advisers

(3) The organisation of the Bank of England may require attention

(4) I may want to recommend radical changes in policy, which might affect other departments.

For there is no point in my leaving the F.O. to be an orthodox Chancellor of the Exchequer. I must be, if not a revolutionary, something of a reformer. However, to reform the Treasury, is like trying to reform the Kremlin or the Vatican. These institutions are apt to have the last laugh.

So I must ask for certain conditions without which it wd be hopeless to try

(1) Your firm support, esp through the early troubles

(2) A position in the Govt not inferior to that held by the present Chancellor.

As For Secy, I am the head of the foreign front, under you as P.M. As Chancellor, I must be undisputed head of the home front, under you.

If Rab (Butler) becomes Leader of the House and Ld Privy Seal, that will be fine. But I could not agree that he should be Deputy Prime Minister. (Incidentally, this post does not exist constitutionally, and was invented by Churchill to suit quite exceptional situations)

You will realise that the presence of a much respected ex-Chancellor of the Ex, with all that this implies in the Cabinet and in Whitehall, must somewhat add to my difficulties, however loyal he will try to be.

If he were also Deputy P.M., my task would be impossible.

(3) I should like to be consulted about the Board of Trade. Treasury and Board of Trade must be partners (like Housing and Works, to get the 300,000 houses) Otherwise, it won't work.

I thought it best to be quite frank. If you don't agree, I shall quite understand. If you do, I am willing to try.

Yours ever, Harold.' . . . .

10.30 Tripartite meeting at the Quai d'Orsay . . . . joined by von Brentano (German For Minister) at 5. This went on till 7pm. Everything was agreed, except the P.M.'s plan for inspection of forces, against wh everyone reacted. This was not because of the idea, but because it was based on the 'status quo' – that is, the present line of demarcation, which divides Germany into two . . . .

25 October

NATO meeting, at the Palais de Chaillot. Dulles introduced Item 1 (our plans for German Reunification and European Security). He did not give a very clear picture of the proposed security pact. Most of the foreign ministers obviously thought that to [be] a member of this would confer a benefit or privilege. Actually, it entails a new obligation. It means that we guarantee to go to the aid of *Russia* if she is attacked by a re-unified Germany, which has rearmed . . . .

. . . . At 6.30, the Greek Foreign Minister, M Theotokis, came to see me at the British Embassy. He seemed a much better type than his predecessor, Stephanopoulos. He professed (and I think felt) a real desire to find a way out. The Greek ambassador to London, M Mostras, came with him and seemed much relieved at the change of masters. The Russian move into Egypt has also frightened them. M. T. proposed, and I agreed, that we shd try to find a method of reopening the talks between the Field Marshal and the Archbishop. After all, the gap between them did not seem very great . . . .

26 October

. . . . 10–12. Foster Dulles, with a large number of supporters, including the American ambassadors in Cairo and Tel-Aviv, came to the Embassy. We had rather a rambling, but not unsatisfactory talk. The Americans will definitely send a political *and* a military observer to the Baghdad pact meeting on November 20th. They cannot adhere to the pact without a ⅔ Senate majority, for it counts as a Treaty. But they might ask for a 'Congressional resolution' in support.

They will send more Centurion tanks next year to Iraq.[75] They will study with us more military help in other weapons or supplies. About

---

75. See below, 9 February 1956.

Israel, they will *not* send arms, to compensate for the Egyptian purchase. Such an arms race wd be useless. They will *not* give a guarantee, but the pressure will not be easy to resist as the Election gets nearer. They *will* agree to a restatement of the Tripartite declaration of 1950.[76] I said that this might perhaps be the price to Israel for USA 'adhering' to (by Treaty) or 'supporting' (by Congress resolution) the Baghdad pact.

We talked about the bad behaviour of the Saudis. This gave me an opportunity of telling Dulles about our operation at Buraimi, which took place successfully this morning. He did not say much at first, but later on expressed some fear that the Saudis might take it out on ARAMCO, the American oil company, which they already blackmail and bully unmercifully.

This brought me to Syria, which is also moving into the Moscow–Cairo axis. (I noticed that ambassador Byroade – who seemed to me rather a foolish fellow – did not share these apprehensions, but was slapped down by Dulles) Altho' there are grave objections to an Iraqui coup to take over Syria, there are equal (perhaps greater) dangers in allowing Syria to go Communist. The American thinking has moved a good deal on this since Washington. We next talked of Egypt, and decided to try to get the Assouan dam for a western group, by some means or other. He read me a telegram giving an account of a meeting in Washington between the [World] Bank and the State Dept, and asked if we wd join. I said 'Of course we will' and left Shuckburgh to arrange it. This was a most useful and friendly talk. It went rather slowly; but Dulles is slow. However, he moves on (if almost imperceptibly) and one can gradually get him towards what one wants. It needs patience. What I like about him is his really cooperative attitude – much more so, I am certain, than appears from his manner.

At 12 noon Mr Sharrett, Prime Minister of Israel, came. He talked, almost without drawing breath, till 1.30. It was a very good exposition of his case. Of course, he wanted arms, a guarantee, and strong action against Russia. As he talked so much, and so fast, I did not have to do much more than listen. But I did tell him (a) that while we stood by the Tripartite Declaration of 1950, we wd *not* give a guarantee except *after* a settlement (b) that we wd *not* step up arms to match the Russian deliveries (c) that he must not make a preventive war (d) that he ought to accept our idea for a final Arab/Israel settlement. Till

---

76. See footnote 66.

that was made, we shd all be easy prey to Russian intrigue. Curiously enough, he took this very well. I think he is one of those men who is more interested in what he *says* than in what he hears in reply . . . . Left about 4pm and flew to Geneva. They gave us a Viscount, which brought some of the party from London, and picked us up at Le Bourget. A glorious day – absolutely clear, with a splendid view of the Alps, all uncovered. We were met by the usual photographers and radio apparatus. I said a few words, and then drove to the villa which has been got for my use . . . .

27 October

I went, with my staff, to the French villa – rather inconveniently far from the city – for a meeting with Pinay and Co and Dulles and Co at 11am. We ran through the procedure etc for this afternoon. I got a chance for a talk with Foster about the Middle East. I urged him to give US aid to Lebanon. This small state, half Moslem half Xtian, is quite well disposed. But the Russians are opening a campaign on them, as well as the rest of Arabia and Asia Minor.

We also talked about Syria. The US advisers are divided. Foster said he had never seen such a division. Some thought they were completely gone over to the Soviets. Others thought they cd be saved. I was interested in Foster's changes of mind about this. I don't think he wd be unduly shocked by an Iraqui coup to take over Syria. I must think more about this. Then he told me of M Zorlu's visit to him, who strongly urged that nothing shd be done for Egypt, even on the economic front, like the Assouan dam. He seemed to sympathise with this – for it may be more important not to discourage the loyal Arabs (like Jordan and Iraq) than to try to conciliate Nasser. This too wants consideration. With regard to Sharrett (Israeli P.M.) whom I saw (or rather listened to) yesterday, Foster had also had over an hour's lecture. He had begged 5 minutes in return. He told him (a) that an arms race was absurd – because the Israelis must lose out (b) that a *preventive war* must on no account be allowed. The Tripartite Declaration worked both ways (c) that the Israelis wd get modest arms deliveries from US but only on the normal basis (d) that Israel needed above all a settlement with the Arabs, and wd have to make concessions for it. All these grave warnings the Israeli P.M. promised to ponder deeply. We also talked about Jordan. Cd we not influence her to join the Baghdad pact? Also, perhaps, to make a unilateral settlement with Israel?

It is clear that the Americans are becoming as worried as we are about situation in the M.E. The difficulty is to get them to act with any speed. Yet, without them, with our slender resources, there is little that we can do.

.... The London papers are full of Rab's Budget speech. He seems to have done very well. The actual proposals are not badly received by the right and centre press, and the rage and fury of the Socialist papers seems rather synthetic. It will be interesting to see the score after a week's debating. I think the most damaging and the most lasting attack will be on Rab personally – that the April Budget, with its tax remissions, was a swindle – for the Election. Rab has always rather paraded his virtue (sometimes to the disgust of his colleagues) so this sort of attack he will find very wounding . . . .

28 October
.... Luncheon for Mr Goonewardine (Ceylon ambassador in Washington) a very talkative but friendly gentleman. His chief concern is that Ceylon shd be invited to the United Nations. This implies (for it is the only hope of getting over the Russian veto) that the principle of universality shd be followed, and all 18 nations on the waiting list shd be elected. Altho' this means admitting a lot of trouble-makers (like Ireland) and some fake nations (like outer Mongolia) HMG are reconciled to it and I have told Bob Dixon so . . . .

29 October
.... At 3pm the third meeting of the Conference took place. Molotov was in the chair and 'passed' – as we had expected. Dulles, Pinay and I then spoke – taking (as we had arranged) various aspects of the western proposals. Of course, the weak point (from a presentation point of view) is that our security assurance to Russia only comes into effect if Germany (when united and free) joins NATO. The *News Chronicle* . . . . had falsely represented our plan as being that Germany *must* join NATO. Even the *Manchester Guardian* (in one of those petty moods wh it occasionally falls into) makes almost the same mistake. Our position is that Germany should be free – as of right. This is the right of any nation 10 years after war. If, when free, she joins the Warsaw pact, it is rather we who need additional guarantees. If she is neutral, there is no additional risk to Russia over the present position, where ¾ of Germany by population and ⅔ by area, is already

in NATO. But to compensate Russia for the Eastern zone *also* joining NATO (if Russia is willing to liberate it) we offer this Treaty of Assurance. When it came to Molotov to speak he made a reply (rather feeble) to our points, by wh he seemed rather shaken. (I had reminded him that it was the Russians who had armed 100,000 men in Eastern Germany, with tanks etc. There was not yet a single soldier in Western Germany) Then he got going on a prepared speech which he read out, with the same old stuff, refusing to discuss 'Germany' until we had disposed of 'European Security'. This took us till 6pm, when we adjourned for 20 minutes. After resuming, Dulles stuck to our point, and I elaborated it. The directive instructed us to discuss German reunification *and* security as part of a single item. The western powers had spoken and deposited a written document covering *both* subjects. The Russians had, in speech and in their document, only dealt with *one*. Would they not let us have their views on German reunification? Then we cd discuss the item as a whole, as we were instructed to do? Molotov seemed rather puzzled. He mumbled an offer to make some new proposals on *security*. We repeated that we wanted their proposals on *Germany*. About 6.30 we gave it up, and on M's proposal, the session ended. At 7pm, I made a call on M (at my request) and made a formal protest at the Soviet action in promoting an arms race in Levant. I reminded him of our talk in New York, (where he had disclaimed any special knowledge of these transactions) and of the Prime Minister's appeal and protest to Marshal Bulganin. I reminded Molotov that yesterday and the day before, he had (in his speeches at the Conference) deplored the arms race in Europe. Why did he want to promote it in the Levant? We did not see how the Soviets cd preach the Geneva spirit in one part of the world, and promote strife in another.

M's reply was very lame. He denied any knowledge of the arms situation in the area. He regarded the deal as a purely commercial affair. We also sold arms to Egypt and Israel. He also spoke of the Baghdad pact, and said that while Soviet policy was the same all over the world – to promote peace, the British policy seemed to vary. I merely repeated that I wished to make a formal and stern protest on behalf of P.M. and HMG and bid him good night . . . .

Sunday 30 October
According to the English papers, the Labour Opposition is working itself up into a great state of excitement, attacking Rab and his

'honour'. His colleagues (who are often rather bored with Rab's appeal to what is 'honourable' in Cabinet) will not be able to avoid a certain amusement. But I am sure everyone will rally round, and the party (after the first shock of having to do some unpopular things) will also realise that we *must* do the difficult things early in the Parl. (I wish we had done the Bread Subsidy as well) If these measures succeed in reducing the inflation to a reasonable degree (without producing deflation and unemployment) all will be well . . . .

31 October

This Maclean–Burgess business never ends. The *Daily Express* now alleges that Roger Makins (our ambassador in Washington) 'checked and cleared' Maclean. This is quite untrue. Poor Roger is terribly upset. I have sent him a telegram, assuring him that I will do my best to put the matter right in the debate.

A telegram from P.M. suggesting that we shd agree to exchange information about our arms deliveries to Egypt and Israel with the Russians. This is a reversion to the idea which made so much trouble when we were in Washington. I am still very averse from 'inviting' the Russians into the Middle East. We can't perhaps prevent them from insinuating themselves (altho' the game is by no means lost yet) But need we ask them in? However, it is certainly worth while seeing whether we could confine our offer to Egypt–Israel deliveries. I rather doubt it.

The biggest problem is what to say to Israel. If we give them arms on a scale at all equivalent to the new Egyptian receipts from Czecho-slovakia, we shall so anger the Arab world as to lose all influence with them. We shall be falling into the trap laid for us by the Soviets. If we refuse, we may make them desperate, and they may start a preventive war. Then Jordan may come in, and we are in great trouble. It may be that the right thing is to try to soothe them with enough arms to keep them quiet, but not enough to upset the Arabs. Is this possible? In any event, it all turns on the Centurions. If we give them these tanks, we must give more to the Jordanians, (whom we finance) and so it goes on.

. . . . At 3pm, the Conference met. Item 3 was under discussion – that is, 'Contacts between East and West'. We each delivered our little speech; each side tabled its formal paper; we appointed our committee of experts. This could, of course, be done in ½ hour. With translations and the formality of speaking what cd easily have been tabled, it took 2½ hours.

After a short recess, we reverted to Item 1. Molotov proposed that both East and West German Governments shd be invited to the Conference – Grotewohl and Adenauer, or their representatives. Dulles attacked this, on 2 grounds – that East Germany did not have a 'freely elected' government, and that only West Germany was recognised by all 4 Powers . . . . Molotov, rather nettled, replied and said that the East German Govt was just as freely elected as the West. Since the Conference wd not see one side, it could not invite the other. All positive decisions must be unanimous. Dulles and Pinay said nothing, but before this decision was formally recorded (as of course we knew it must be) I piped up and said – 'Mr Molotov says that the East German Government were elected by free elections. I remember that they were elected by over 99% of the votes. It is 32 years since I first contested an election in my country and I have taken part in 10 contested Parliamentary elections in that time. All I can say is that any man or any party that can get 99% of the votes in a free election aren't politicians – they're walking miracles'. This caused great glee among the Americans; polite amusement among the French. I also observed that the Russians laughed – and then suddenly stopped, looking to Molotov and Gromyko to see whether it was all right to laugh . . . .

The time was now nearly 7pm, and Dulles suggested that perhaps M Molotov wd be ready to circulate the additional proposals on security to which he had referred . . . . The new security Treaty which he suggests is in a way an advance. For it gives up the proposal that NATO is to be wound up. But it has the fatal defect of being based on the permanent partition of Germany . . . .

At 9.30pm (after we had finished dinner) Mr Sharrett, Prime Minister of Israel, called . . . . He gave a very good account of his interview with Molotov, who abandoned the pretence that this was a commercial deal, and admitted frankly that Russia's intervention in M.E. affairs was a deliberate act of policy. Molotov said that it resulted from the formation of the Baghdad pact. Mr Sharett gave a vivid account of his spirited reproaches to Molotov . . . . Finally, he asked what we were going to do. I said that I cd tell him no more than I had done in Paris a few days ago. But I reminded him that, in the new circumstances, if we were to alienate all Arab opinion, we should lose any power we might have to protect or help Israel. It wd just be playing Russia's game . . . .

2 November

. . . . At 8.30 we went to a dinner given by the Russians for the British. It was rather a painful affair, with the usual rather heavy jokes and bonhomie. The food (except the caviare) was uneatable.

In the course of conversation, M asked me what I was going back to England for. I said, 'a debate in the House of Commons'. He said, 'What about'. I said 'On a subject where you can really help me, if you wd do so – on Maclean and Burgess. Can you tell me where they are.' He said, with real or assumed seriousness 'That is a matter wh wd require investigation' . . . .

4 November

An interesting meeting with Molotov at 11.30am. He came to my villa (at his own request) and raised a number of questions – Indo-China; the Security Council and the battle for a place between Philippines and Yugoslavia; the admission of new members to U.N. He said nothing about Egypt and Israel. We fenced elegantly for half-an-hour. Then I went to a meeting of 3 western ministers, with all the officials, and Blankenhorn to represent Federal Govt of Germany. We agreed, after much discussion, to table a motion in the name of the 3 western powers, on behalf of themselves *and* Western Germany, demanding elections in Sept 1956, and a first instalment of the Eden plan . . . .

I left Geneva by train for Paris, with Hancock and George Young.

5 November

Arrived Paris at 7.15, where we were met by Gladwyn Jebb. Motored to Le Bourget and got 8am plane. On reaching London, I went to flat for bath etc, and then to F.O. to see Caccia. At 12.15 I went to report to P.M. and discuss Geneva, Middle East, Cyprus, and other matters. He referred to my letter (wh he had not acknowledged or answered) in rather a vague way. I assumed that he had not yet settled with Rab about his future or mine. Motored to B.G. and had a very pleasant evening at home. Maurice's sons were back from school for half-term and we had a splendid fire-work display and a good bonfire. The guy was generally regarded as representing Molotov! . . . .

6 November (Sunday)

. . . . Motored to London and went to No 10 for a meeting on Cyprus . . . . We agreed a new formula and decided to ask our ambassador in Ankara how he thought the Turks wd take it. If we can get

Archbp Makarios to play with us it will certainly make things easier. But it wd be a cardinal error to antagonise the Turks . . . .

We then had a go at the Maclean–Burgess debate, and I went to F.O. to dictate final version . . . .

7 November

It seems that Molotov has gone back to Moscow for instructions. There are strong rumours that he will return to Geneva with a new plan for Germany . . . .

. . . . At 3.30 I rose in a house as crowded as a Budget Day.

I spoke for an hour – or rather 65 minutes. Morrison followed, with a very ragged speech. I had said that, since the Eden–Bevin reforms were only a few years old, we wd *not* have any enquiry into the F.O. Morrison (who hated Bevin and hates his memory) made a very strong effort to revive this. Otherwise, his speech did not add much. He excused himself and blamed (by implication) Bevin. The debate then flopped until the end . . . . P.M. wound up admirably. He offered the 'Privy Councillor talks'[77] about 'security' – with the implication that it wd be chiefly on the law, and the limitation on security wh the law necessarily involves.

Altogether a great relief that this is over. My speech is said to be the best I have ever made . . . .

8 November

Left London at 8.30 for airport. We got to Geneva for luncheon. The press is on the whole good – except, of course, for the 'gutter press'. Even the *Daily Express* is not too bad. So I hope Maclean and Burgess will be allowed to die.

The afternoon session was delayed till 4pm, as Molotov's aeroplane had difficulty in landing. It started calmly enough – with further mixture of argument and appeal to Molotov by Pinay and myself. Then Molotov threw his bombshell . . . . He refused free elections for Germany altogether. He practically claimed that Germany cd only be united as a Communist and satellite state. After he had finished, Dulles suggested a short recess. After the recess, Dulles said that in his view, Molotov's speech had created so grave a position, that we ought to adjourn till tomorrow. This we did. The French dinner, altho'

---

77. Talks with leading members of the Opposition.

on a splendid scale as regards food and wine, was rather a fiasco, as a consequence of the Molotov bomb . . . .

9 November

. . . . 10.45 – a large meeting at M Pinay's villa (villa Montfleurie) Dulles was in such a depth of despair, that I felt it was rather artificial (like his excessive optimism) Pinay, who is a straightforward little man, was rather triumphant. He loathes Communism; Molotov; and the Geneva spirit in a very simple and sincere way. Finally, after the arrival of von Brentano, we agreed a line for this afternoon. On the whole the note was to be 'More in sorrow than in anger'. Von Brentano came to luncheon with us at the villa, bringing Grewe. He has improved in weight and knowledge since I first met him a year ago. But I thought he took too superficial a view of Geneva. He wants us to break off the Conference with a bang and never have another. I asked him to consider this very carefully. If Geneva was over and done with forever at the first serious hitch the Allies, not the Russians, wd be blamed. Federal Germany wd be under still greater pressure, both internally and from Moscow, to meet and agree with E Germany . . . .

10 November

We had a meeting at 11.30 to decide our plans for this afternoon, when we pass to Item 2 – disarmament. We also discussed the problem of *how* and *when* to bring the Conference to an end. The Russians will try to put the blame for failure on to the western powers. We must avoid this for our own sakes: but it is more important to follow whatever course will ease the position of Dr Adenauer and his friends . . . .

11 November

. . . . M Zehnder (Head of the Swiss Foreign Office) Sir G Jebb (British ambassador, Paris) Sir L Lamb (British ambassador, Berne) and Alan Hare to luncheon. M Z is a clever man, who has made from the vantage point of Geneva, a profound study of Soviet policy. He believes the 'détente' to be, in the long run, something historically inevitable. They must, in time, be dominated by fear of China. Thus, they will try for peace with the West, and special friendship with other Asiatic peoples (like India, Burma etc) who also view China's potential with alarm . . . . With regard to Germany, the Russians are confident. He heard a very high commissar say – 'If we want to, we can always buy the Germans out of the arms of the west. We can offer them E Germany. If that isn't enough, we can offer them the Oder–Neisse territory. If that doesn't do the trick, we can have another partition of Poland'.

Z says that the 'détente' is having a worse effect on our side than we realise. In France, Germany, and Italy, people are going neutralist. We ought to use this conference (and its failure) to shock them into a sense of reality.

At 3pm we had a private meeting (in a small room) and agreed with Molotov a programme for the rest of the Conference. We wd end on Wednesday night. M was very easy over this, so I suppose he has decided that he can't get anything by going on.

At 3.30, we went on with the plenary session – the subject being disarmament . . . . The Russians, however, are merely out for propaganda on this matter. They refuse to face seriously the problems of control and inspection . . . .

What has interested me during these discussions at the plenary sessions is to realise how closely our English left-winger and fellow-travellers follow the Party line. You cd shut your eyes, when M is speaking, and think yrself listening to Silverman, Harold Davies, Crossman, Warbey – or any of that crew. Not only the same arguments, but the same phrases.

12 November

Alan Hare (who has excellent contacts here) believes that the Israelis are now seriously considering an attack on Egypt, to destroy the Egyptian army and bring down Nasser. Everyone seems to think this wd be a great disaster – because of the other Arabs. But there wd certainly be compensations . . . .

3.30. Meeting (tripartite) at Dulles' hotel to discuss M.E., Far East, U.Nations new members, and a number of items. De Margerie acted for the French. We agreed to set up a new organisation to deal with arms supplies to M.E. (Israel and her neighbours) British and French ambassadors wd act with State Dept . . . .

On U.N. elections, I told Americans that we were committed to vote for 18 (the principle of 'universality') in spite of our dislike of Outer Mongolia, Albania, and others. But we could not let down Ceylon, Italy etc. Dulles cannot swallow Outer Mongolia. The French will veto *everyone*, unless the motion on Algeria is withdrawn! . . . . The Turks have reluctantly accepted our proposed new move in

Cyprus. But I don't think it need worry them, for I doubt if Archbishop Makarios will be able to accept the new formula. The German Chancellor seems anxious that the Geneva Conference shd end in a clear break – with no reference to another meeting. He feels that he can best rally the public opinion in Germany by taking advantage of the Russian attitude and getting on with German rearmament etc at full speed . . . .

13 November
. . . . After church, I drove out with John Wyndham to Tholm Les Memises, where I met Foster Dulles, Mrs D, and Mr L Merchant for luncheon. We had a very good luncheon – Foster eats enormously. Janet was calm and sensible as ever.

All through luncheon, Foster told us of his talk with Molotov in the morning, which had lasted for 2 hours and made him miss Church. 'Futile' (pronounced 'footle') he said, over and over again. Actually, they had discussed the new members of U.N. for an hour, Molotov demanding 'Outer Mongolia' and Dulles stoutly refusing to accept it. They had also discussed the conference; the Far East; East/West contacts; and the Middle East. There was no progress on any of these issues. After luncheon, Foster and I drove in my car, Mrs D and the two secretaries in his, to a place called Mémises . . . . We had some talk about the 'China list' and Dulles promised to consider favourably a reduction of the list of embargoed items. I told him that since exports were of no real importance to America, they failed to realise how vital they were to us. Every little extra we could scrape in, made the whole difference. There was nothing about which we cared so much. He said he had heard that we were having difficulties with the balance of payments. (This in a very detached way) I said 'yes – indeed. We are still struggling with the results of having sold all our foreign invest-ments, in two successive wars, before we got American aid'. He said nothing to this, but it seemed to strike him as a new idea.

We arrived at Mémises, and then ascended in a kind of pulley contraption to the top of a peak. We went up in little cars – Mr and Mrs Dulles in one; myself and Mr Merchant in another; John and the detective in a third. Arrived at the top (about 2000 ft above the starting point and some 5000 ft in all) We walked on a grassy slope. There was a fine view of the great mountains, standing out above the clouds which filled the valleys below. But it was very cold.

Dulles and I talked about the future. He felt that it was quite possible that the President wd decide after all to 'run' again. If so, he wd certainly win. Then he (Foster) looked forward to working with me for a long period – 4 years or more. We might together change the history of the world (he grew quite excited and eloquent over this) We must start a 'Counter-Reformation'. We must disprove the slanders against the old western civilisations; shew that 'colonialism' was a fake charge; prove the immense benefit that the British Empire had been and was; and lead the young nations to our side. Much study shd be given to this, and to the philosophic attack on the heresies and falsity of the Communist doctrines. All this was very surprising and rather impressive. Finally, we descended in the same machine and drove back to Geneva.

16 November
Excited telegrams from P.M. arrived during the night, asking me to get Dulles' support for his Guildhall speech on the Arab–Israel conflict. Actually, I had done this yesterday, so John did not wake me up! At 10.15 this morning, I confirmed this with D who gave me the text of the instructions which he had sent to the American ambassador at Tel-Aviv . . . .

At 3pm we met for the final session. The communiqué was agreed. It is very short and objective. It says that the question of future meetings shall be taken up thro' diplomatic channels. Then the final round began – in this order, Dulles, Pinay, HM, Molotov. Molotov was very subdued. My speech was quite effective and I hope will have a good press. Anyway, I can use some of it again in the HofC. We were finished by 6.30 and after all the usual votes of thanks and farewells, back in the villa by 7pm. There was a good deal of normal work to be done, but with so good a staff as I have this is very expeditiously done . . . .

17 November
We left Geneva by air at 8.30am, and got to London in about 2 hours, after a very good flight. It was a clear morning and we got a very good view of the Alps . . . .

Poor James Stuart is in trouble with the West Lothian shale oil industry. This employs 5000 men, but is hopelessly uneconomic. Of course it ought to be shut down; but there is the usual outcry about the men. With overfull employment, they shd be made to go into something else . . . .

18 November

. . . . The Archbp Makarios has not yet returned from Athens to
Cyprus. But I fear there is no hope of his accepting the new formula. I
had a long talk with P.M. about the future. He says Rab has not yet
made up his mind. Wd I still be willing to go to the Treasury? I said
'yes: on the terms wh I put in my letter'. P.M. began to shuffle a bit
on this, wh I took to mean that Rab wd insist on being deputy
premier . . . .

20 November

Arrived at *Baghdad* (after short stops at Rome and Beirut) . . . .[78]
    . . . . Nuri Pasha (P.M. Irak) came to luncheon. He had a bad cold
and was so deaf that conversation was difficult. He is much exercised
about the iniquities of Saudi Arabia. They have an income (in dollars)
from Aramco of some £100m and they spend it in bribery and
subversion all over the Middle East. Syria is almost wholly in their
pay.
    At 3pm we left for the Palace. The King and the Regent received
(at 3.30) all the delegations – that is, UK; Iran; and Pakistan, the Turks
having turned up late. Then a wreath laying ceremony at King Feisal's
tomb[79] and then back to the Embassy. This is a fine old Turkish
house (in the old style) which has been the Residency and is now the
Embassy. It is ugly and comfortable – but its ugliness is pleasant and
traditional. The walls are immensely thick (which keeps it cool in
summer) It rambles about, with lots of buildings (including the old
harem) and has a fine garden. It is *on* the river (Tigris) and in general
position and style reminds me a little of our Embassy in Cairo. The
Office of Works wants to pull it down, in order to build a villa! We
must not allow it . . . .
    . . . . I had been told that it wd be very hot and that Baghdad was
an ugly town. Neither of these prognostications turned out to be true.
The weather is perfect – a June day in England, at its best. The town
is picturesque – the morning and evening lights across the river are
quite lovely.

21 November

The Council meet at 10am. Prime Minister Nuri As-Said (Iraq) was in

---

78. For a meeting of the Baghdad Pact.
79. A key leader of the 1916–19 Arab Revolt and the first King of Iraq 1921–33.

the chair. He was supported by his Foreign Secy (Bashayan) The Prime Ministers of Iran (Hussein Ala) Pakistan (Chaudhary Muhammad Ali) and Turkey (A Menderes) were there. Also the American ambassador and Admiral Cassidy came in (at a later stage) as observers . . . .

The CIGS (Gerald Templer) has a fine position here and in India. It was good to see the friendships between our old Indian army officers and the Pakistan soldiers. I was particularly struck by the Pakistan C of Staff. We lunched with the Pakistan ambassador (a delightful man – a Bhopali) and the Pakistan P.M. and party. Chaudhary Muhammad Ali is a man of high quality, far above his predecessor. He is an old I.C.S. man, and *very* friendly and sincere. He talked frankly to me about Kashmir and his determination to bring Nehru to face the issue – 'Even if it only forces him to abandon some of his insincerity, it will do good. N attacks "imperialism", but practises it!' That is the Pakistani view. The Pakistan P.M. is also much concerned about the Afghan intrigues on the frontier. These are financed and supported by the Russians. They are also egged on by Nehru (so he asserts) But it is a dangerous game. He appeals to us, with USA, to bring pressure on Afghanistan to amend her ways . . . .

22 November

The Council met at 10am. At about 11am there was a pause, while we awaited the reports of the various committees – military, economic, etc. I suggested that we might use the time fruitfully by a private and informal meeting, without the hosts of advisers etc . . . . It was a most useful 2 hours of talk. The general view was (1) that a settlement of the Israel question ought to be got as soon as possible. The Arab states (even those hostile to the Pact, like Egypt) were all coming round in favour of an early settlement. Eden's Mansion House speech (or Guildhall speech) was warmly approved. (2) Until the Israel question cd be settled, the Arab world wd be split over the pact. (3) That Saudi Arabian gold was the cause of endless trouble. The Saudis (whose national income had risen from about £1m to about £100m) were bribing everyone, right and left, and were turning the whole Arab world upside down. If something cd be done to stop this, it would be the biggest possible contribution to peace. Cd the Americans do anything?

The Saudi situation is deplorable. The Americans, who affect to censure colonialism and imperialism, fail to recognise how absolutely irresponsible is their form of capitalism. Money, on this scale, without guidance, is ruinous. Nuri Pasha says that tho' oil may have made the Arabs rich, oil, uncontrolled, will ruin them altogether. We discussed the need to get Lebanon and Jordan to join the pact. Jordan – which we created and still financed with subsidies of about £12m p.a., is turning against us under the influence of Saudi bribery. Egypt is in the same game. The pact powers wd like us to put great pressure on Jordan . . . .

Before this morning's session began – that is at 9.15am – I had a talk with the Turkish P.M. (Menderes) and the Turkish Foreign Minister (Zorlu) They were both quite relaxed, and did not raise any objections to our recent decisions on Cyprus (the new formula etc) But they both deplored the deterioration of their relations with Greece. The work of 20 years has been ruined by the Greek Govt's adoption of *Enosis*, and the violence of their propaganda. Altho' they deplored the riots in Istanbul and wd pay the damage in full, the Greeks were largely to blame. (Actually, we know from secret sources that Menderes stimulated the demonstration, thinking they wd stop at that. They got out of hand, and the wild destruction of that night followed. I think the Turks suspect that we know this, and this makes them a little less truculent than they are apt to be) The Turkish minorities in Thrace had been very badly treated. If this continued, the rich and prosperous Greek minority in Turkey (mostly in Istanbul) would inevitably suffer . . . .

Menderes is agreeable; affable; smiling; voluble – not at all what I expected. But I suspect that behind this exterior, he is a strong character. In his presence, Zorlu says very little – when he does, it is less truculent and '*cassant*'[80] than is usual with him . . . .

The King gave a dinner and reception. The dinner was in the European style and very good. I am (alas) beginning to put on weight again, with all these perpetual banquets! . . . .

23 November

. . . . At 2.30 we left on RAF Valiant for Beirut. Mr Scott (Chargé d'affaires) met me at the airport. I went with him and Shuckburgh, escorted also by the Lebanese Foreign Secy to see the P.M. The F.S. begged me *not* to press the P.M. too hard – or even at all – to join the Baghdad pact. He was a fierce 'Arab' partisan; cared nothing for Communism or the Russian danger; thought only of revenge on

---

80. 'Brusque'.

the Israelis. (When I saw the President of Lebanon – a very good man – he told me that his P.M. had just got another £10,000 from Saudi Arabia. Money talks) The P.M. received me in a large, empty room. He talked at me – a set piece – about the wickedness of the Jews. I replied in a speech in French – about the importance of (a) keeping Soviet influence out of Middle East – hence the Baghdad Pact (b) a settlement in Palestine – hence Sir Anthony Eden's Guildhall speech. It was all rather a waste of time.

Then I went to see the President. He was very civilised (a Maronite Xtian) and very intelligent. He agrees absolutely with us, but repeated the same story – the Saudis have bought up the Middle East! It's really a terrible story . . . .

24 November
Arrived London airport about 9.30am and got a helicopter to South Bank. Got to Cabinet at 11.30. They were all discussing the Budget; all night sittings; obstruction, and all the old things. It was quite refreshing . . . .

25 November
The net result of my impressions in M.E. are as follows (1) We *must* get USA as full members of pact (2) we *must* get a settlement of Arab–Israel problem (3) we *must* somehow stop Saudi Arabians bribing everyone with American (Aramco) money (4) We must meanwhile try to prevent Nasser selling out Egypt to the Communists. (5) We *must* get Jordan – and if possible Lebanon into the pact . . . .

In the morning, I went to a meeting of Colonial Affairs Ctee at No 10. We agreed that Governor shd declare a 'state of emergency' in Cyprus. Our negotiations with Makarios are stuck. But we are still trying to get the Greek govt to bring pressure on him. The Americans (who approve enthusiastically of our new formula) are doing the same. But I fear that the Archbishop is a stronger character than the Greek P.M. or For Secy . . . .

26 November
. . . . At 7pm . . . . I went to a meeting at No 10 called by P.M., Butler, Kirkpatrick and I, with one or two private secretaries. We have got hold of very secret but quite reliable information that Nasser has already agreed (more or less) to allow 'Popular Socialism' (in other words, Communism) in Egypt, as part of the Czech arms deal. This is

to be finally clinched by the Soviets undertaking to build the High Assouan Dam, and take payment over a period of 50 years. Meanwhile Kaissouny (Egyptian Minister of Finance) watched by Hilmi (a stooge of Nasser's) is in Washington negotiating with the World Bank and the US Govt. P.M. was very excited, and wanted us both to go to USA at the end of next week. A large number of telegrams were sent off, asking Americans to help us bring off the dam contract . . . .

Actually, the message which I had already sent to Foster covered all this – the only new thing being the 'secret' information wh confirmed our suspicions. All the same, I am not quite convinced that Nasser has really gone over to the Communists. He may still be playing one side off against the other . . . .

29 November
. . . . Cyprus goes on: neither the Greek Govt nor the Archbishop can be got either to reject finally or to accept our formula. But I feel sure it is a good plan to keep the negotiations going . . . .

30 November
A long day: Mrs Pandit; the French ambassador; the Swiss minister; the Greek ambassador in the morning. None of them had much of interest to say. Mrs P (who is a stout Tory) was terribly upset by the speeches and general behaviour of the Russian leaders (Kruschev and Bulganin) in India . . . .

1 December
10.45 to Palace, for an audience. The Queen had wished to hear about Geneva and Baghdad. I did my best in half an hour to explain the posn to her, without boring her. She showed (as her father used to) an uncanny knowledge of details and personalities. She must read the telegrams very carefully. There was a Cabinet at 11.15; I arrived a little late, to find a tremendous argument going on about the advisability or otherwise of banning the production of 'heroin' – a drug with great advantage but great danger.[81] As usual, the experts have let down the politicians – for the doctors who recommended the ban are beginning to run out . . . .

---

81. First marketed as a medicine in the late nineteenth century, heroin has been controlled since the Misuse of Drugs Act 1971. In the 1950s there was not a serious problem of addiction to this drug in Britain.

4 December

. . . . A mass of telephoning went on between Chequers, F.O. and Birch Grove, which ruined the whole day from luncheon onwards. The P.M. is very nice and friendly, but he does fuss . . . .

5 December

A lot of talk between P.M., Col Secretary and Chief Whip led to a decision that I shd open the Cyprus debate, instead of winding up. I was able to get a re-draft ready, and go through every word with P.M. and Salisbury as well as Lennox Boyd. It is very important that ministers shd really agree to my new plans about self-determination. I summarised our position in the lines of the doggerel – The Greeks say 'This year' – or at least 'Next year'. The Turks say 'Never'. We say 'sometime'. My speech took about 40 minutes, and except at first (when I lost the House and was rather jeered at by some of the Socialists) served as it was intended to do. The fact that there was still a hope of settlement made responsible members unwilling to say things wh wd exacerbate feelings . . . . Half way through the debate, the Socialists decided not to divide.

6 December

The press was unexpectedly kind to my speech. The Greek Govt have now sent an immense telegram (of 14 pages) commenting on our 'formula'. I have set the Dept to work trying to sort it out.

I saw the Greek and Turkish ambassadors for a few moments (at my request) I was relieved to find that the Turk had no protest to make about my speech. He said he realised how lucky they were to find a Conservative Govt in office and that it wd be in their interest to take advantage of this . . . .

11–1. Cabinet. Ld Salisbury wants to cancel the Russian visit. I think it wd not be right to do so. After the Cabinet, P.M. asked me about the change of office. I said 'Why don't you answer my letter?' He said he wd do so . . . .

Office meetings followed. The C.I.G.S. has gone to Jordan. We are authorising him to give £25,000 a year to the King, if this will help . . . .

7 December

. . . . In the course of the evening, the P.M.'s reply was handed to me . . . .

My Dear Harold

I have thought over your letter and worked out a division of duties, which will not be for publication as it stands. But it will be our working guide. Is it acceptable to you?

Anthony.

Enclosure.

The senior members of the Cabinet, under the Prime Minister, will have precedence as follows

Lord President
Lord Privy Seal
Chancellor of the Ex
Foreign Secy

The Lord Privy Seal will be Leader of the HofCommons and will be responsible for planning and carrying through the Govt's programme of legislation and all other Govt business in Parl. He will have responsibility for coordinating the presentation of Govt policy to the public. He will be chairman of the Home Affairs Ctee and the Legislation Ctee of the Cabinet. He will be responsible, on behalf of the Leader of the Party, for the policy direction of the Conservative Central Office. The Chancellor of the Ex, in addition to his control over financial policy, will, under the P.M., have full responsibility for coordinating all aspects of economic policy, both internal and external. He will be Chairman of the Economic Policy Ctee of the Cabinet.

In the absence of the P.M. the Ld Privy Seal and Leader of the HofCommons will act in his place and will preside over meetings of the Cabinet.

It is satisfactory, except in the last paragraph of the enclosure, which begs (or, if you like, raises in a new form) the whole question. I shewed it to D tonight, who suggested that I shd wait a day or two to reply . . . .

9 December

. . . . Sir Percy Mills came to luncheon. After much discussion with him, I sent my reply to P.M.

Dear Anthony

I am grateful to you for sending me your letter of Dec 7th, together with the enclosure.

You will remember that in my letter of Oct 24th, I told you

that I was not anxious to leave the F.O. and take on this thankless task of the Exchequer.

But I undertook to do so, in order to help, on certain conditions.

Roughly, these were:

1) I must have power to make changes in the Treasury set up
2) I might want to bring in outside advisers
3) I might want to look at the Bank of England organisation
4) I might want to recommend some radical changes of policy
5) I shd like to be consulted about the Board of Trade.

I also mentioned that if you want an orthodox Chancellor of the Ex, it wd be better to appoint somebody else. Altho' you have not dealt with any of these points, may I take it that you agree?

Another matter I raised was that of my position in the Govt, and that I cd not agree to the post of Deputy Prime Minister being revived.

I have carefully read the draft you have sent me, and I am very content with the first paragraph; that is, the order of precedence of the senior members of the Cabinet. I also think the allocation of duties is excellent. But the last paragraph does not seem to conform to the first; for in spite of the order of precedence, the Ld Privy Seal is to preside over the Cabinet in yr absence, instead of the Ld President. Surely it wd be better for Ld Salisbury, who by his character and seniority wd be generally acceptable, and, being a Peer, outside all these considerations, to preside in yr absence? This wd be natural according to the table of precedence which you have suggested. I don't press the point, as you know, from personal feelings. But, politically, a great deal is read into these niceties; and this has, as I said in my first letter, an effect on my chances of success in the job you have asked me to undertake.

Percy [Mills] is very keen that I shd go to the Treasury. He says that the business world have quite lost confidence in the present regime . . . .

10 December

Dec 10 1955

My dear Harold:

Thank you for yr letter. I think that we are in full agreement on the essential point that you shd succeed to the full powers of the Chancellor of Exr in the financial and economic field. This implies that you shd examine and reach yr own conclusions on both policy and organisation. If you decide that major changes are necessary, I will certainly consider yr proposals with every desire to help. But I am sure you are not asking me for a blank cheque. Neither you nor I wd wish the move to be presented, or interpreted, as one implying early and important changes of policy. This wd only cause confusion and uncertainty on the exchanges, before you had time to go into matters for yrself. I am not at present inclined to any changes at the Bd of Trade, but I shd certainly consult you whenever any move is contemplated there. There is really nothing new in the practice described in the last para of my draft. You may like to discuss this with me and I shd be very happy to do so, together with any other outstanding points.

Yours ever, Anthony.

11 December

. . . . D and I drove over to see the Kilmuirs . . . . We talked about the political situation, and she (who is very shrewd and has a great knowledge of the party organisation) expressed alarm at how we were slipping. Events have not been kind to us since Churchill left.

David Kilmuir is very anxious that I shd take the Exchequer. He had heard rumours, so I thought it better to tell him the whole story. I had to go to London to meet Sir Ivone Kirkpatrick and Evelyn Shuckburgh to deal with the telegrams which have been arriving from CIGS in Amman. He is striving hard to get Jordan into the Baghdad pact, but it's touch and go. The ministers are mostly timid or bribed by the Saudis. The Prime Minister he describes as a jelly.

13 December

. . . . I saw the P.M. at 7pm and finally accepted to be Chancellor of the Exr. The new govt will be announced in about a week. I have given in about Butler 'presiding' at Cabinet, but have won my point about the position of 'Deputy Prime Minister'. This unconstitutional post will *not* be revived, and the Palace have been so informed. On all other points, P.M. has really met me. After a good deal of thought, we both came to the conclusion that it will be best to keep Peter

Thorneycroft – at least for the present – at the Bd of Trade. There is this Monopolies Bill hanging over us,[82] and he alone seems to understand it . . . .

14 December

. . . . Left London airport at 11am for Paris . . . .

. . . . There was a meeting of Western European Union at the Quai d'Orsay. Beyen (Netherlands) and Spaak (Belgium) opened rather a sharp attack on UK policy regarding the 'Messina' or '6 Power' plans for a common market etc.[83] I replied. I said that always before (e.g. with E.D.C. and steel) we had been accused for concealing our policy till it was too late. Now they complained that we had revealed it prematurely. Of course, there's a good deal behind all this. Neither the Germans nor the French spoke up at all. The French will never go into the 'common market' – the German industrialists and economists equally dislike it, altho' Adenauer is attracted to the idea of closer European unity on political grounds. This of course is very important, and I made it clear that we wd welcome and assist the plan, altho' we cd not join, so long as a proper relation cd be established between the inner and outer circles – the 6 and the 15 – Messina and OEEC.

15 December

Apparently the *Daily Express* and the *Daily Telegraph* (no other papers) have a full account of the proposed changes in the ministry. (I wonder if Lady Pamela [Berry] got them from Rab!)[84] The office of

---

82. The Monopolies Commission had been set up by Labour in 1948. By 1955 there was growing concern at the failure to follow up its reports into, for instance, price-fixing in the tyre industry. This Bill, which became the Restrictive Practices Act 1956, therefore set up a court to police price rings.

83. Despite Macmillan's long involvement in the European movement, there is only one previous fleeting reference in the diary to the Messina conference held in June 1955, at which Belgium, France, Italy, Luxembourg, the Netherlands and West Germany agreed to form what became, in 1957, the European Economic Community. The hostility referred to here was prompted by the British telegrams in November 1955 stressing the divisive effect of a customs union on economic cooperation in Western Europe – in contrast to the role of OEEC – and its negative impact on political cohesion in NATO. These telegrams, both at the time and subsequently, have generally been seen as a deliberate attempt to undermine Messina.

84. Butler was well known for his indiscretions to the press.

Deputy Prime Minister *and* control of the economic front is allotted by these papers to Butler! . . . . Since the French papers carry all this story about my leaving the F.O. I thought it best to tell Foster (in confidence) He was terribly distressed. He wanted to ask the President to call Anthony about it! I was rather touched.

Another long meeting of NATO council, but more constructive, on definite military plans. At 6.30pm, we had a tripartite meeting at the Quai. The chief object of this is to reassure the French, who cannot bear to think of Dulles and me lunching alone together, and are especially worried by the P.M.'s visit to US in January . . . .

16 December

The biggest headache wh we have (UK) is the cost of our troops in Germany in the future, both in *money* and in *balance of payments*. Not only are the Germans refusing any contributions to 'support costs' this year, but they are not making any contribution to the joint effort of defence parallel to our own . . . . My own feeling is that our only hope lies with the Chancellor (Dr Adenauer) No one will take any generous (or indeed any) decision but he.

. . . . A quadripartite argument (French; British; Germans; Americans) took place from 3.30–7.30, with the Germans refusing a penny's contribution, in the toughest way imaginable. (It means something like £30 millions to us on next year's accounts!)

As I expected, the Greeks proved tricky and false. They have now come back with a redraft of the formula. I was very stern with them, and told them that they ought to tell the Archbishop to accept our formula (already redrafted to help them) *with* any necessary glosses by way of explication and elucidation . . . .

The final NATO meeting (in plenary session) ended at last about 9pm having sat from 3.30. I left for the airfield and we finally got to London airport about 11.30pm . . . .

20 December

. . . . There was a Cabinet at 10.30 – rather a sad one, for it was the last for Harry Crookshank and Fred Woolton. Harry has, very wisely, accepted a peerage (which will keep his contacts with his old friends) and refused an office. They wanted him to be Chancellor of the Duchy and 'assistant' to the Leader of the House of Lords. When one has been Leader of the House of Commons for 5 years, this is not a good idea. He talked it all over with me and made his final decision, just before the Cabinet, this morning. P.M. looked ill, but cheerful. I think he is at last getting the administration which he wants, with a complete control over the F.O.

Official luncheon for Egyptian Minister of Finance and Col Hilmi at Carlton Gardens. They were very pleasant and seemed satisfied with what had been done at Washington about the High Assouan Dam. These Egyptians are young, inexperienced, and without much background. But I think they are inspired with a genuine desire to improve their country and help their people. If it means having 60,000 people in prison camps and falling into Russian hands, it can't be helped. They will win through in the end. It is the Young Turks, or even the early Fascist movement over again . . . .

21 December

The list is out today – with a puzzled, but not unfriendly press. My conduct at F.O. is attacked by some; but most of the newspapers say that I was too strong a holder of the office to suit P.M., who has now got his Minister of State, in the shape of Selwyn Lloyd. Butler's position is rather equivocal. The Opposition press is not too bitter, altho' they (with others) hint that he is running away from the trouble. Most of the papers pay a well-deserved tribute to the way he has handled these 4 difficult years . . . .

In the afternoon, I had a series of interviews – saying 'goodbye'. The Heads of Departments; under-secretaries; etc etc. Sir Ivone Kirkpatrick is disappointed; dear Harold Caccia almost in tears. But the Private Secretaries are just angry, for Selwyn Lloyd is going to work all Christmas and Pat Hancock (instead of going home to shoot his pheasants and enjoy a family party) will have to stay in London!

D and I gave a cocktail party to about 200 (of all grades) of F.O. It was a great success, esp since such a thing has never been done within living memory! One man told me that he had been 41 years at the F.O. (in the Library) and never even seen the SofS! . . . .

22 December

. . . . D and I went to look at No 11 Downing St. We were rather appalled at its unsuitability for a residence nowadays. Yet we have nowhere else to go! . . . .

At 3pm I went to the Treasury – for my first visit as Chancellor of the Exr. It seemed very odd and unfamiliar. I have really had rather a raw deal this last year – first with Defence, then with F.O. Just as one is learning one job, one goes off to another. At my age, it is not quite so easy to switch the mind on to a completely new set of problems.

The Private Secy (Petch) is absolutely charming – and, thank God, not too clever! Everyone else is brilliant. It's like going back to Balliol . . . .

28 December
We had a very good day's shooting – the sixth formal day . . . .

P.M. wants me to go to Chequers on Monday, to talk to some Trade Union leaders. But I feel it is too early. I don't know what to say to them. Randolph [Churchill] (who hates Anthony and calls him 'jerk') prophesies an early collapse of the Govt . . . .

30 December
A good morning at the Treasury. I am just beginning to get a glimpse of some of the problems, and how they fall into place. The position is *much worse* than I had expected. Butler has let things drift, and the reserves are steadily falling. If and when they are all expended, we have total collapse, under Harold Macmillan! The best experts do not expect this to happen earlier than 6–12 months from now! . . . .

1956

1 January 1956
. . . . I have finished a paper called 'First Thoughts from a Treasury Window' – it covers all kinds of possible lines of action to deal with our problem. It will be typed and circulated tomorrow.

2 January
. . . . At 3.45 the Governor (Cobbold) came with Mynors (Deputy Governor) and another official. We had a most useful talk for 1½ hours. I encouraged the Governor to blow off his stuff about Government spending etc and then persuaded him to go on *doing his* stuff (i.e. continuance of monetary deflation and credit squeeze) . . . .

3 January
Defence Committee 11.30–2pm. An immense debate. They wanted £70m for civil defence. I got it down to £55m. Then we began the 'pay' debate. The Chiefs of Staff were present, and Ld Mountbatten talked a great deal. Walter Monckton very fair; Head (as usual) aggressive. It was decided to continue the discussion at tomorrow's Cabinet and reach a decision . . . .

Lunched (alone) with P.M. He was in good form and not unduly put out by the heavy press attack upon him[1] and all the trouble about the 'illicit' sale of arms to M.E . . . .

12 January
. . . . I think I have now met *all* the leading officials – down to the middle tier of the Treasury. Many are *very* good; almost all are impressive. Sir Robert Hall (our tame economist) is very inarticulate – even on paper he is not very clear. But I find him sensible. Clem Leslie

---

1. An editorial in that morning's *Daily Telegraph* had fulminated 'Most Conservatives, and almost certainly some of the wiser Trade Union Leaders, are waiting to feel the smack of firm government'.

(alias Lazarus) is an old friend from Ministry of Supply days (in 1940) when he served Herbert Morrison. He went with Morrison to the Home Office and was a considerable figure in the first Labour Government. (He did party propaganda for the Socialists, under the guise of a Treasury official) Now he is rather subdued – shorn of his glory, but still a good servant.

Of the rest – Bridges, Bernard Gilbert, Padmore, Brittain, Alec Johnston, Compton are all 'knights' and senior officials. Leslie Rowan (overseas finance) is of this class. They all seem very good – if a trifle pedestrian. But the efficiency with which they do a job is really remarkable. Turnbull, Playfair, Wilson, are all good too.

Everyone has worked hard at the ideas which I put forward in 'Thoughts from a Treasury Window'. An admirable (if rather critical) set of papers have been produced and all this week we have worked very hard at trying to rule out the 'non-starters' and pick any likely horses for further consideration.

I have put to the Cabinet a short paper, giving my appreciation of the situation. I think ministers were all impressed by the gravity of the position. Indeed, one or two were really shocked. (Rab has really let things slide for over a year, and never told his colleagues into what a mess they were slowly but steadily subsiding)[2]

I have got – before the end of next week – to put forward a short and definite 'rescue' plan. It will be pretty drastic; whether the P.M. and the Cabinet will swallow it, I don't know.

In addition, I have been having a terrible struggle about the new 'pay' structure for the Army, Navy, and Air Force. Altogether, the new plan will cost £70m–£75m a year. But if it succeeds, and we can reduce or even abolish National Service in 1958, it will be worth it – both from the economic and the political point of view. In connection with this, I have had to go to Chequers twice (which is rather an imposition, for it means 3 to 4 hours lost) But it is now all settled. Anthony Head (SofS Army [sic]) has fought very hard and rather unscrupulously. Walter Monckton has been very friendly and very fair. As a Minister of Defence of a few weeks' standing, his posn has been rather difficult.

At the same time, there have been many meetings of a few ministers on Cyprus and the Middle East. I played a big stake to try to get

----

2. In addition to the balance of payments there was also a deteriorating position on the reserves.

Jordan into the Baghdad pact, when I was For Secy. But we have lost – at least we have lost the first round. However, the game is not over yet; and we have *got* to win. For the stakes are very high – no less than the economic survival of Britain. For we lose out in the M. East, we lose the oil. If we lose the oil, we cannot live.

The young King of Jordan is keeping his head and playing up very well. The old feud with the Saudis (now reinforced by American oil money and Egyptian ambition) has taken a new form . . . . [T]hey are trying to buy every leading man and newspaper throughout the M.E. They have also spent large sums in organising sedition in Jordan and elsewhere. After some anxious days, the Arab Legion (under Glubb Pasha) seem to have restored order in Amman and elsewhere.[3] We have sent some reinforcements to Amman from other stations and we have sent a parachute brigade to Cyprus to be ready to go to Jordan if needed.

Meanwhile, our operations in the Persian Gulf have been very successful.[4] The Saudis are complaining and will no doubt stage a protest in United Nations. But they have not reacted and I don't believe they can. The King of Jordan wd like to attack the Saudis, and may do so. All this is disturbing to our public opinion, and our press has been very foolish and defeatist (except, curiously enough, the *Times*) Actually, the struggle for power in the M. East has replaced (for the moment) the struggle in Europe or the Far East . . . .

In Cyprus the position is still obscure. The Governor has undoubtedly succeeded in getting a proper organisation started, altho' it will be a long time before it becomes efficient. 50 or 60 years of Colonial Office neglect have produced a tragically unfavourable situation in an island which is (in many ways) remote from Greece and where we could easily have built up some loyalties to the Commonwealth and Empire had we made any real effort to so. There is still a chance – if we play the hand well – of getting a proper arrangement. The negotiations between the Governor and the Archbishop have been renewed. We had a meeting at Downing St few days ago and agreed to new instructions to the Governor. There are one or two minor changes in the famous 'formula' which may help the Archbp and can do us no

---

3. A reference to the Nasser-inspired riots that had greeted General Templer's attempts in December 1955 to persuade Jordan to join the Baghdad Pact.
4. At Buraimi Oasis.

harm.[5] (Of course, we have had to inform the Turks, who have accepted them with pretty good grace) The talks will now be renewed and we shall see whether the Archbp is really prepared to risk reaching an agreement with us. I feel that the precise terms are not so important as the fact. For a large number of Communist and extremist groups will turn against the Archbp (whatever the terms of any agreement) These forces are revolutionary and cannot be appeased. If Cyprus were to join Greece, they wd either dominate the island or have to be suppressed (if that were possible) by the Greek Govt.

The new Greek Govt (esp M Theotokis) are behaving reasonably well. When the election is safely over, they will be in a stronger position – at least, one hopes so.

We have done a good deal of work in preparing briefs for P.M. and For Secy for Washington. To be quite frank, I don't quite see what we can achieve – unless it cd perhaps be an agreed policy for Middle East. But I fear that the Americans are now only thinking about the Presidential election and whether 'Ike' will run again or not. Dulles seems to be getting into rather deep water with his recent interviews and press conferences. I suspect that the whole administration is leaderless and floundering.

There has been, during the last 10 days or so, an extraordinarily virulent press campaign agst the P.M. This has not only been from the Left (*Herald*; *Tribune*; *News Chronicle* etc) It has been largely from the Right – *Daily Telegraph*; *Daily Mail* etc – usually so loyal. No 10 had even to issue a communiqué last Saturday denying the rumour that P.M. intended to resign. I don't think this campaign will do him much harm in the long run. It may even do him good. But I don't remember anything like it since the days when Beaverbrook and Rothermere were trying to eject Baldwin.[6]

Eden has taken all this pretty well. Indeed, I think he improves as a result of these attacks. He is to make a speech in Yorkshire (I think at Bradford) next week, wh will be important.

---

5. This formula offered 'to discuss the future of the island with representatives of the people of Cyprus when self-government has proved itself a workable proposition and capable of safeguarding the interests of all sections of the community' (*HMM* III, appendix 3).

6. In the early 1930s these press barons led a campaign against Stanley Baldwin, leader of the Conservative Party 1923–37 and Prime Minister 1923–4, 1924–9, and 1935–7, mainly over imperial issues.

. . . . I find the Governor of the Bank rather hard to pin down to any definite decisions. It is essential that the 'credit squeeze' shd be operated with ever increasing effect during the next few weeks . . . .

13 January

Oliver Lyttelton and Clive Baillie came to see me this morning, for a general talk. Each have a different diagnosis of our troubles. O.L. wants us to go on expanding and 'let the exchange rate go'. I cannot feel this to be right. There is too much at risk . . . .

We finished off some more subjects in 'Thoughts from a Treasury Window' at a meeting this morning. We are really beginning to make some progress. The Treasury officials seem a little bewildered at this forcing of the pace. But I think they really rather like it. It's going to be the Housing story over again – I mean, on the personal side . . . .

15 January

. . . . I am getting more and more confused about my affairs. Sometimes a sort of plan forms itself fairly clearly – but almost every part of it is shot down in detail by the Treasury experts! They are particularly critical of any idea of reducing the size of the Civil Service!

Dined with Maurice and Katie at 4 Smith Square – we dined late and it was rather melancholy for Maurice leaves tomorrow for a cure in Switzerland. He is in a thoroughly bad state of health and must try to get put right now.

16 January

. . . . 11.30–1. Treasury meeting. We are working steadily through 'Thoughts from a Treasury Window' – which I wrote at Petworth on Dec 31st–Jan 1st. A large number of very expert papers have been written on all the 'hares' which I started in this, or in 'More Thoughts'. This has resulted in some of the hares being obviously non-starters. Others are put off – as long-term and not any good for the 'crisis' plan. Others are voted runners, and are pursued with vigour . . . . [A]t 10pm to the P.M., to discuss Cyprus. He has had a rather bad idea – which is to go there himself and try to make a deal with Archbp Makarios. I shd have thought this wd merely make him raise his price and infuriate the Turks . . . .

19 January

The plan is in draft. The whole job has taken just about a fortnight –

not bad going. If my colleagues in the Cabinet accept it, I believe we may save the economy from a complete collapse – which otherwise may come in a few months. But the plan is *very tough* and will be politically very unpopular.[7] (But the collapse of Sterling and the capitalist system wd be much worse!) I spent today in giving prior warning of my intentions and asking for support from the ministers most concerned. I thought this more courteous (and better tactics) than letting them get it in the week-end distribution of Cabinet papers . . . .

I gave a dinner party at Carlton Gardens to the following

Governor of Bank (Cobbold)
Chairman of Lloyds Bank (Oliver Franks)
Lazards (Tommy Brand)
Industry (Sir Percy Mills)

I had also Bridges, Boyle (Economic Sec) Hall (our Economic Professor) and Petch (Private Sec) I thus brought into being the Committee of advisers, which I wasn't allowed to have! It was an immense success. There was a most frank, informed, and helpful talk – and almost complete agreement about what ought to be done. (Fortunately, it hardly deviated from the plan) Whether it wd succeed, seemed about even chances. Everyone agreed that if we were to drift on, we shd go on the rocks.

20 January
. . . . The P.M.'s speech at Bradford was a success. Altho' it had been 'written up' rather too much, his calm and dignified reply to his critics was very effective . . . . The only fear to have is that he did *not* sufficiently emphasise the *seriousness* of the position. No doubt he wished to spare Butler. That was right. But we shall have, very soon, to take a more robust line. My guests of last night all thought that the *first week in February* was the date. January would seem 'panicky'; March dilatory.

P.M. rang up about 10.30pm. He had been reading my paper. He seemed very concerned, not to say excited. 'I can never agree to *two* of your proposals. It's absolutely unthinkable'. 'Which do you mean?'

---

7. Particularly, it sought to reduce both public and private consumption, the latter by further raising the Bank Rate to 5 per cent (it had already been increased twice the previous year by Butler), thus effectively ending an era of low interest rates dating back to the early 1930s.

I replied. 'I suppose about the Army in Germany and the ending of Fighter Command'. 'No, no! About bread and milk!'[8] A long conversation followed – chiefly talk by him. It is quite clear that (a) he does not understand the serious character of the crisis (b) will shrink from unpopular measures. Also, to be fair, he cannot follow how taking off a subsidy will help . . . .

22 January

To Bromley, for a church service (at St Mary's) on the occasion of 'standing down' the Home Guard Battalion. The vicar (Rae-Smith) preached an admirable service. There was a parade, with Mayor etc outside the Home Guard Club, followed by sandwiches and beer. The scene was splendidly English – the dear old Home Guard types, covered with medals, and bulging out of their uniforms (to be worn for the last time) were positively Shakespearian . . . .

23 January

A full day. Agricultural ministers (Heathcoat Amory; Stuart; Lloyd George) and Minister of Labour (Macleod) to discuss the abolition of the bread subsidy; the milk increase and the agricultural price review. We reached agreement as to policy.

Then a meeting on Jordan at No 10. Luncheon with Pamela Berry (who is in disgrace owing to the *Daily Telegraph*'s attacks on P.M.) This has made rather an awkward position for her many friends in the Government! However, it seems ridiculous to 'boycott' the proprietors of the *D.T.* Better tactics is to 'laugh it off' and avoid anything but chaff. No serious discussion. James Stuart, Nigel Birch were at luncheon – also Michael Berry. This first rencontre since the newspaper war began passed off very well. My own impression is that the attacks will stop, or gradually cool off, which will be for the general benefit.

. . . . After cabinet, I had a talk with Butler. He is certainly a strange fellow. He seems to have little idea of the state of affairs or of the financial or economic dangers which threaten us. But he promised me support in the Cabinet . . . .

. . . . After dinner, I had to go to No 10, for a talk with Anthony about the situation. This was pleasant enough, but not very profound. He still hankers after 'talks' with T.U. leaders, to 'stabilise' wages, and

---

8. The cuts in bread and milk subsidies were to save £38 million.

does not seem to understand that if we go on pumping money into the system at this rate, neither wages nor prices can possibly be stable.

24 January

Cabinet 10.45–1.15 and 6.30–8. The sole business was my paper, which we took paragraph by paragraph. On the whole, ministers behaved well and seemed ready to co-operate. The P.M. was very anxious (as I expected) about *bread* and *milk*. One or two took the same line. But ultimately everything was agreed 'in principle', subject to agreement later about timing. P.M. and others want everything put off till the Budget. This is not possible (a) because the financial crash may come before that if we do nothing (b) because the Opposition are bound to ask for a debate. So I thought it better to let this go, for the time being, and concentrate on getting agreement on the content of my proposals. It was an exhausting performance; but the P.M. handled it very well, and Butler (except for a natural tendency to minimise the gravity of the situation) backed me up quite loyally. It will now be necessary to have a series of 'unilateral' negotiations with each minister in turn, to try to agree on the precise range and character of the proposed economies, reductions, or postponements.

House reassembled. I had one or two PQs (my first as Chancellor of Ex) and got a friendly reception from our side and from the Opposition. There was rather a 'schoolboy' atmosphere – as there always is on the first day of term. Dr Flemming, who buys strategic reserves for USA and causes us (unwillingly but yielding to Congressional pressure) a lot of trouble about our oil imports into US, came to see me at 5pm. We had a useful talk and I think he will help us. We don't mind the technicalities of GATT etc, so long as we can keep our $200m sales of ME oil (in wh we are interested) to US.

26 January

I am now beginning on the negotiations with individual ministers. Monckton (Defence) and Lloyd George (civil defence). We got £10m cut in civil defence. But the great issues of defence – Fighter Command; the withdrawal of a division from Germany; etc etc remain for further discussion. We also had Postmaster General – got a little out of him – and a preliminary go at Road Transport (Watkinson) . . . .

28 January

Went out with Blake – a dull, misty, drizzly morning, which turned to heavy rain. Got 4 cock pheasants, 2 pigeons, and (*mirabilis dictu*)[9] 1 rabbit.

I find it difficult to reach any very clear conclusions about my work at the Treasury so far . . . . The surgeon's knife is clearly necessary in the short run. But I don't feel I know what to do next – esp in the field of overseas policy. A merely negative attitude to European co-operation (as put forward by the Messina plan and the 6 powers) is not enough. We ought to try to find a constructive alternative . . . .

29 January

I have had a good talk with Walter. What we need most of all now – as an urgent decision – is to reduce the Army by *one* division and to give up Fighter Command, and all that this implies. Everyone really knows that there is *no* defence, yet we go on wasting immense resources on the design, development and production of 'fighters' – up to 1962 and further. This is a great burden on industry, as well as on the Exchequer. It cannot be justified any longer . . . .

31 January

Cabinet. In P.M.'s absence [in Washington] Butler presided (according to the agreement) He is trying (in spite of the agreement) to set himself up as a 'Deputy Prime Minister'. But at present his position in the party is weak and his reputation in the country low . . . .

1 February

My brother Daniel's 70th birthday. The board of M&Co gave him a silver inkstand; the staff a finely bound copy of Lewis and Short[10] (wh he wanted) and I gave him (as a personal gift) a finely bound copy of Oxford Dictionary.

We had a little dinner for him at Carlton Gardens – Daniel and Betty; Arthur and Peggy; Hamish Machelhose: Katie (Maurice being away)

We are working steadily through the ministers, but not scoring quite as many runs as I shd like.

---

9. 'Wonderful to say'.
10. Charlton T. Lewis and Charles Short, *A Latin Dictionary* (Oxford: Clarendon, first published 1879).

2 February

. . . . All the afternoon we worked on the statement. Butler is rather dubious about 'bread and milk' . . . .

. . . . The time table is getting pretty tight, for the statement ought to be made on Feb 15th. Sir Percy Mills came to dine with me at the HofC and we had a good talk later on in my room. He is very sensible and very firm. The delay in settling the demand for more wages in the engineering industry means that the next meeting between the employers and the unions will be on February 17th – two days *after* my proposed announcement. Will this have a good or a bad effect? It is difficult to be certain.

3 February

The Governor came at 10, followed by Deputy Gov and Chief Cashier. So – imperceptibly – the formal meeting between the Treasury and the Bank has come about. We have our talk alone to start with. Then his officials come in and also mine. Of the formal meeting, a minute is taken and a record of decisions.

We had a useful discussion on the technical problem of financing the nationalised industries. It is this immense annual sum which hangs over the market and adds enormously to our funding and other troubles . . . .

D and I left Carlton Gardens this evening for good. We are by way of at least camping in No 11 Downing St on Monday . . . .

5 February

A complete thaw – almost a spring day. I did not go to Church, but worked all the morning on a speech for Gainsboro' by-election . . . . Read 'Blogs' Baldwin's book on his father, Stanley Baldwin. It is an act of filial piety to defend his father's memory and reputation. It is also very well done. Read a life of Sir Francis Burdett by M W Patterson, (2 vols) wh we published in 1931, but I had not read. It is very interesting. I imagine Burdett as being something like my dear friend, Lord Henry Bentinck – half Radical, half Tory – with a genuine hatred of cruelty and corruption. What fun those Middlesex elections must have been.[11]

---

11. Burdett was radical MP for Westminster 1807–37, though he moved to the right and ended his life as Tory MP for North Wiltshire 1837–44.

6 February

. . . . Went to No 11 Downing St – where I slept for the first time. D comes tomorrow. It seems quite comfortable, but is a large house to manage. However, I may be leaving it in a few days' time! . . . .

8 February

10 o'clock. Economic Policy Ctee. A long argument about Hire Purchase. It appears that the legal basis of our right to control hire purchase is very shadowy. Shd we be wise to put any more weight on it? The Attorney General was doubtful. Anyway, to please him, we decided to leave out perambulators! Cabinet at 12 – presided over by Butler. A hum-drum affair. (How one, now that he has gone, sometimes longs for the Churchill Cabinets, wh used sometimes to be called at 11, and only reach the first item on the agenda by 1pm!) . . . .

9 February

The ministers concerned met at 10.30am (under my chairmanship) to discuss the forthcoming agricultural price review.[12] After two hours or more, I just began to learn something about this extraordinary method of arranging the amount of subsidy which is to be paid to the farmers in any one year. But it's really like Alice in Wonderland, and the final figure actually paid bears very little relation to the calculation.

Cabinet at 4, in PM's room at HofC. *PM* looked very fit on his return (he got back this morning) and has obviously enjoyed himself. Selwyn Lloyd (For Sec) looked rather exhausted.

He told us that he had found the President very well, and – as usual – very friendly to us. He really likes England and English people. Foster Dulles was very friendly also . . . .

On Europe, they are 'sold' on Messina – wh they do not understand. It will be the EDC story over again.

On Germany, they are agreed with us about the German contribution[13] – at least for this year. P.M. made it clear that we might have to reduce our burdens – i.e. take away a division.

On Middle East, they want to put teeth into

(a) the Tripartite Declaration (Israel etc) The complication is that

---

12. To fix the support prices for farmers (effectively to bridge the gap between world prices and domestic farm costs). See *HMM* IV, p. 22f.

13. Towards the cost of maintaining troops in Germany.

while, under the American constitution, the President may 'move' forces, he may not 'engage' them without Congressional assent.

(b) on Baghdad pact, US have moved a long way and will give us all support, moral and material, 'short of membership'. (Anyway, till after the election) They will give various sorts of aid to member states – Persia, Pakistan, Iraq, and Turkey. They will buy more Centurion tanks from us to give to Iraq.

(c) On Saudi Arabia, they have moved a bit. They will try to persuade the Saudis to spend their money on roads and schools, instead of on bribery. They will be quiet about Buraimi.

Far East. The President is obviously very disturbed. Chiang-Kai-Shek has 'got him on the raw'. On trade with China, Pres overruled all his advisers and declared that 'something must be done' to meet our point of view.

The real success of the visit was on the atomic and hydrogen front. The President has made decisions to give us (a) information (b) aid, which will save us millions and millions of pounds! (I expressed suitable gratification, and only hope this works out) *Foreign Sec* added that he was impressed by the toughness wh Dulles was prepared to show about Israel, even in the Presidential election year. (This was exactly my experience in Geneva with him) *P.M.* said the only real difficulty was about atom *tests*. The Americans were absolutely convinced now (contrary to their original ideas) that if the bomb was exploded high up in the air, the ill effects were negligible. P.M. thought this might be a nuisance politically, but – as we have more than a year to go before our first test – an ultimate advantage . . . .

10 February

My 62nd birthday. I do *not* feel so old. If my mother and father cd walk into the room, I should feel about 30, and Alexander wd be Maurice!

10am. A talk alone with P.M. and Ld Privy Seal (Butler) about my plans. P.M. still – temperamentally – opposed to bread and milk. He has no conception of the gravity of the financial and economic situation and it's not easy to make him understand it. Butler naturally minimises the crisis – instinctively, since he failed to take any adequate measures in time . . . .

11 February

. . . . David Eccles had kindly written a note for me after the Cabinet.

He said that the talk had gone on for about 35 minutes after I left the Cabinet. The M of Labour was violently against removing the bread subsidy, either now or in the Budget – apparently this shook PM considerably. Macleod (Labour) was supported by his predecessor Monckton (Defence) Butler and Ld Home thought that, if at all, April was the time. (Afterwards, it appeared Butler was for doing it in the Budget) Home Sec said nothing. For Sec was obscure. PM unhappy, his mind concentrated on wages and labour relations. Eccles goes on (in his minute) to estimate the position as follows

against Macleod and Monckton
openly doubtful Butler; Home; P.M.
openly for H Amory; Eccles; Thorneycroft; Sandys
prob for Lennox-Boyd; Stuart; L George; Buchan Hepburn
utterly unknown Ld Chancellor
foxy For Secy . . . .

After reading this and a further note from Bridges, I got hold of Petch (P.S.) and began to compile a letter to P.M. . . . . Not being quite sure what to do, I asked Norman Brook to come in, which he did about 11.30am. He thought it only fair that P.M. shd know that if I cd not carry my proposals, I shd have to resign. I said that I agreed; but I wd not send the letter till I had shewn it to my wife (anyway, it wasn't quite in final form)

About 6pm a messenger arrived, with more work and the text of the letter for me to sign, wh I did . . . .[14]

12 February (Sunday)

P.M. rang up after dinner last night. I warned him that a letter was coming to him wh he would not like. He thought it might be better to postpone the Cabinet till Monday afternoon . . . .

For my part, I shd welcome a delay, because I want it to get round – as it will – to the Cabinet that I shall resign if I cannot get their support. Moreover, another complication has arisen. The National Assistance Board take so calm a view of this rise in bread and milk prices that they are unwilling to raise assistance benefits at all! (Yet it is this 7d a head wh is to cause an uproar among the unions and lead to revolution!) . . . .

Went to London in evening and dined with James Stuart at Whites.

---

14. *HMM* IV, pp. 12–13 makes clear the tactical nature of this resignation.

We came back to No 11 and talked over the situation. I shewed him a copy of my letter to PM, wh he thought correct and fair. He will support me. In his view, I shall win my point – but, like me, he takes a pessimistic view of the situation. Even these measures may be 'too little and too late' . . . . I rang Dorothy before going to bed, to tell her James' verdict, wh pleased her. I don't really see how P.M. and Butler can hold out.

13 February
All the papers yesterday carried a 1000 word statement issued in Moscow by Burgess and Maclean. All the papers claimed 'exclusive' interviews. They explain their motives for going to Russia. They are not agents, but patriots, working for the peace of the world. There is a good deal of speculation about the Russian motive for putting all this out now. (It can't just be to give copy to the Sunday press) The general view is that they want to make dissension between Britain and US . . . .

A Cabinet at 4pm – PM let the discussion run. The Cabinet was roughly as follows: *against* PM, Min of Labour, Defence, Colonies, Ld Chancellor, For Sec. *For* Ld Privy Seal (in principle!) Works, Scotland, Education, Agriculture, Housing, Board of Trade. I made it quite clear that I should not be able to go on if I could not get the support of my colleagues.

14 February
The Governor came to see me at 10. He is very worried, as there are the signs of a flight from the pound and a flight of capital beginning. I hear that P.M. has seen a great deal of Macleod (Minister of Labour) the last 2 days. He sent for him to Chequers when he got my letter. Macleod, as a new Minister of Labour, is quite naturally anxious over the effects on the trade unions of any action wh they may not like. (Of course, in a period of extreme inflation the power of the *moderate* T.U. leader is much reduced).

. . . . Butler, Heathcoat Amory and Thorneycroft came to see me in my room to try to find a solution. They said PM was absolutely determined not to give in on bread and milk. In that case, I replied, he must get another Chancellor. The same ministers came again (after dinner) with the idea of a 'compromise'. Could a formula be devised, which wd make a start? I said I wd consider this, but did not much like compromises! The curious thing about this crisis is (a) that I have hardly had any talk with P.M. He has avoided this; and dealt through emissaries (b) not a word of it has got into the papers. This is really remarkable and shews how friendly and sensible we all are! Actually, the quality and dignity of the discussions in the Cabinet have been remarkable.

I had a talk late tonight with Bridges and with the Governor. I put them the problem fairly and squarely. Which wd do most harm? My resignation or a compromise? Governor had no doubt. My resignation wd cause a panic in the City.

15 February

Macleod (Labour) and Monckton (Defence, formerly Labour) came to see me at the Treasury. Before they arrived, I had a visit from Norman Brook. Brook had prepared a formula – but it was no good at all. I shewed him my letter of resignation.

When the others came, I shewed them a formula which I wd accept. This was 1d off bread subsidy (out of 2½d) at once; rest later. Milk in July, as I proposed originally. After a few verbal changes, they went off to see P.M. (This seems an odd way of doing business – with these emissaries between the two High Contracting Parties – but it is really rather a good way. It saves everybody's face and is less embarrassing) I was summoned to No 10 at 12.45. P.M. accepted the formula, and all was settled. This has been a strange, tense, and very tiring crisis – all the more because it has been, as it were, 'suppressed'. Butler's part in all this has been rather obscure. I feel sorry for him – for he sees his successor 'taking a stand' and all that – which he did *not* do . . . .

. . . . So, after all this effort and excitement, I have managed – by threat of resignation – to get ⅘ of my plan. But will it be enough? Will it do the trick? Or shall we drift into bankruptcy and devaluation in the summer. It's a tremendous gamble, and really worries me. Everyone else (including the PM) seems quite unconscious of the danger. We worked late on the final form of the statement for tomorrow.

The House, untroubled by all these alarms, discussed hanging very happily, and by a small majority voted against it. The Socialists, of course, voted solid. About 30–40 of our chaps (mostly young) voted for abolition . . . .

17 February

I saw Sir G Hayman (FBI) and Sir Vincent Tewson (TUC) *before* making the statement. This was a courtesy, which I think both of them appreciated. Of course, the TUC must make a row about bread and milk. They will also oppose cuts in investment. But if you object to cuts in consumption *and* cuts in investment, it's difficult to see how an inflationary crisis can be overcome. I made the statement to a very full House. I have never seen as many members present on a Friday morning. This was because warning was given yesterday. It took about 20 minutes to deliver. There was a brisk interchange of questions for about 10 minutes . . . .

21 February
The Saturday and Sunday press was unexpectedly good. Today's is better still. I am really very satisfied. The question remains – have we done enough? At 10am Professor Erhard and the German ambassador came to the Treasury for a talk. (He is Minister for Economic Affairs in the German Federal Govt and very able) I tackled him about 'support costs' and he was fairly sympathetic . . . .

22 February
Now that this part of the operation (the political) is more or less over, I must start on new work. It has been a very tiring week or ten days – with the great Cabinet crisis not the least exhausting part. I have now

(1) Further measures to propose, to protect reserves, if these are not enough

(2) Budget

(3) OEEC and a policy for Europe

(4) Economic General Staff – i.e. proper organisation of Govt and Treasury.

(5) Savings – esp in defence expenditure. All these are immense, and urgent problems. Yet there is so much to do, every day, in interviews, speeches, P.Q.s, committees, Cabinet meetings, boxes of papers etc, that one has no real time to think . . . .

23 February
. . . . The whole country seems – perhaps fortunately – more interested in the Death Penalty than in economics. The Govt are in some difficulty about the former, as well as the latter. The HofC has voted – on a motion – against the Death Penalty, and by a substantial majority. But the Govt (altho' allowing a 'Free Vote') advised the House to retain Hanging. What does HMG do? Introduce a Bill of their own (in which

they don't believe) and force it through the HofLords under the Parlt Act? It's a paradoxical and rather perplexing situation.

The 'Cabinet Crisis' – which has caused me great anxiety and mental stress – has been kept a remarkably close secret. I don't remember anything of the kind wh has 'leaked' so little. The press never got on to it at all. It is a curious feeling for me. At one time, Dorothy told the men to stop putting up our pictures etc in No 11, because she thought we wd be moving out again soon! . . . .

27 February

Farm price review. The Farmers will ask for £41m more. We decided to offer £17m and go to somewhere between £20m and £25m. The Minister of Agric is fairly firm; the SofS Scotland very firm. I shd think we shall end up at £22½m. The great thing is to switch them off the immense increase wh they ask for milk and try to get the extra money on feeding stuff (oats and barley) and cattle for beef.

I left for London airport at 1pm[15] with Peter Thorneycroft (B of Trade) and Edward Boyle (my Economic Secy) I am once more the guest of the hospitable British ambassador (Gladwyn Jebb) who came to meet me.

At 5.30 I went to call on M Ramadier. He is Minister of Finance in the new Govt. He is a dear old boy, shrewd and very tenacious. My object was to protest at the flagrant way in wh the French disregard their obligations under OEEC. They pay export subsidies and have special import taxes, against the rules and openly flouting their commitments. I got very smooth words from him, but I doubt if we shall get much action . . . .

I had the same room as before. It was the room in wh I wrote my letter to Eden (wh Pat Hancock copied for me) agreeing to give up the F.O. and go to the Treasury. All very sad.

28 February

M Spaak came to see me at the Chateau [de] la Muette (where OEEC meetings are held) We had half an hour's talk – or more. He was most friendly, but took a very depressing view of Europe. France was no good; Italy hovering on the verge of Communism; Germany becomes more and more aggressive. Cd not UK take the lead? The 6 power movement wd fail, in spite of all his efforts, for France wd never really

---

15. To fly to Paris.

enter a 'common market'. It wd be the story of EDC all over again. I did a record of the talk and sent copy to P.M. and one to For Sec . . . .

1 March
Left Paris at 9.30am. At the London airport I met Winston (leaving for South of France) . . . . In the afternoon, a meeting of ministers to discuss (a) our meeting on Monday with TUC (b) the Russian visit (c) the news that the King of Jordan has suddenly dismissed Glubb Pasha from the command of the Arab Legion. This is a great blow – and seems at present inexplicable. Added to this, the Cyprus negotiations have broken down. The Archbp Makarios keeps raising his price. The only cheerful bit of news is that the reserves will show a good rise this month – perhaps as much as $60m. But of course the true test is the trade balance. We shall not get these figures for a few days . . . .

2 March
. . . . The general view about Jordan seems to be that the King has had a brain storm – like his father. A day or two ago, the ambassador reported everything to be calm and serene . . . .

I lunched at M&Co with Daniel – who seemed very well. We decided to make an offer for the 25% share of the Canadian company which Brett has. (It will cost us £40–£45 thousand, but is worth it for the future) We also discussed the future of the St Martin's Press.[16] It will need more capital if it is to make any progress . . . .

5 March
. . . . I feel sure we ought not to lose our tempers about Jordan and the dismissal of Glubb. One shd not throw away (if there is any chance of rescuing it) the work of 40 years in an afternoon.

The TUC meeting (intended to be the first of two; we are to see them again after we have seen the employers)[17] went off in a strangely subdued atmosphere. They all behaved beautifully and were so respectable, with their dark blue suits and bowlers, that they looked like a lot of undertakers. I had taken a good deal of trouble with my 'exposé' and distributed various 'secret' documents to them – which they seemed to like . . . .

---

16. The new American subsidiary that had recently been set up.
17. These meetings reflected Eden's interest in trying to curb inflationary pressures by agreement with employers and unions.

6 March

.... We spent most of the afternoon at the Treasury in working on the Budget. I am getting more and more confused and alarmed. The field of manoeuvre is very limited; yet people expect so much . . . .

Sir Kenneth Clark came to see me. He wants more money for the Arts Council – wh means for opera, both Covent Garden and Sadler's Wells. Everyone wants more money!

7 March

There was a fascinating discussion this morning at the Econ Policy Ctee (over wh I preside) First, there were two of those curious forms of dealing wh have grown up since the war. In one, the Americans *give* us tobacco; we build houses, to the value, for American soldiers. In another, there is a triangular arrangement, at the end of wh we get a lot of lard for sterling, not dollars, and the Persians get the lard – or other lard – free! Only a well-named Treasury official, called Mr Figgures, fully understands all this. Then we had a long and important discussion (wh must be continued in the Cabinet) about Transport charge. Shall we put the fares and freight up to cover the amount of the recent wage rise? Or shall we have a margin and say to the trade unions – 'Come on boys! Try to earn some of it by working harder and dropping some of the old restrictive rules'. It wd (in my view) be worth trying . . . .

. . . . Then de la Bère, about the future of the Lord Mayor's fund for the Flood disaster.[18] The Treasury agreed to pay £ for £. Now the money isn't wanted! . . . .

8 March

Cabinet 11–1.15. I am glad to find that, since the arrival of Sir D [sic] Kirkbride (formerly ambassador in Jordan) the Cabinet seem to be moving towards the view that we shd try to keep Jordan with us and accept the sort of apology which the King has sent us. Sir D. K. felt sure that if we abandoned Jordan it wd fall into Saudi and/or Egyptian control and that this might easily lead to the collapse of the Hashemite regime in Irak . . . .[19]

---

18. See above, 1–6 February 1953.
19. The Hashemite dynasty had been founded by Hussein Ibn Ali, King of the Hejaz at the time of the Arab Revolt during the First World War. His sons Abdullah and Feisal became respectively kings of Jordan and Iraq.

9 March

. . . . I was relieved to hear that negotiations with the Farmers' unions have ended in an 'agreement to differ'. I don't think they will launch a violent campaign agst the Gov, because Turner is too clever not to realise that, in the present economic climate, the public will think an extra £24m a year is pretty generous . . . .

10 March

. . . . The Socialists *and* the Liberals both express great indignation about the arrests of the Cypriot bishops.[20] So I suppose we shall have a fierce debate next week. But I think it will do the party good, and that people will on the whole approve. There is a chance that Cyprus will settle down, tho' no doubt the Greek Govt will be very angry and appeal to United Nations etc. The Greek ambassador in London has been recalled . . . .

12 March

I hear that Butler has been making trouble over the week-end about the Farm Price Review.[21] All this was settled – as I thought – on Friday, when the Cabinet decided to stand firm on milk etc. Rab rang up P.M. and has persuaded him to try to get a settlement with the Farmers at all cost – or at least at the cost a) of economic wisdom b) of another 2 or 3 millions. Derek [Heathcoat] Amory (who is very sensible over all this) and James Stuart came to see me this morning. We talked it round and round and I agreed that it should be taken to Cabinet for (?) final settlement tomorrow . . . .

All the afternoon was spent in meetings at the Treasury on a number of problems – all urgent and all more or less insoluble! I went over to the House and heard the Home Secy on the Hanging (or rather no-hanging) Bill introduced by Silverman. He made a very fine speech against the Bill. Dined alone at No 11 with Dorothy and then walked back to the House to vote. It was a 'free vote' – but the Socialists voted almost solidly in favour of abolition of hanging. The 2nd Reading of Silverman's Bill was carried by 24 – less than last time.

---

20. Archbishop Makarios and the Bishop of Kyrenia, both of whom had links with the EOKA terrorist organization, were arrested and on 9 March 1956 they were deported to the Seychelles.
21. Butler, unlike Macmillan in suburban Bromley, sat for a rural constituency (Saffron Walden).

The deportation of Archbp Makarios has caused a great furore here – among Socialists and Liberals. The Tories are very pleased. The Americans will have to pretend to be shocked but I hope will back us up in the end. The Greek Govt (wh is anyway in a very weak position) is already much shaken and may fall. Meanwhile, Cyprus is fairly quiet. We can only now await events. The February trade figures are better. Deficit about £49½[m], against £74[m] in January. Exports are up; imports down. But this isn't good enough. We must get a surplus (including 'invisibles') and to do this we need to do better.

The Opposition, who are getting into the habit of moving a vote of censure almost every day, now want a debate next week on 'unemployment in the motor industry' resulting from the 'credit squeeze' and the new Hire Purchase regulation.[22] This is rather a bore, as we are so busy. I suppose I may not be able to avoid speaking . . . .

13 March

A long Cabinet. As Churchill once observed 'At every Cabinet today there are discussed at least two or three problems which would have filled a whole session before the first war'. Cyprus; Malta; Transport Charges and Nationalised Industries Finance; Farm Price Review; Aircraft for India etc etc. The last raised a difficult point. Nehru wants us to make special efforts to supply him with Canberra bombers and the latest devices at a low price. But he also is said to be getting Russian bombers! Are we prepared to see this, and at the same time let him have our secrets?

Then the paradox of Malta, which wants to join UK, while Cyprus wants to join Greece! And so it goes on. I was rather annoyed that the Farm Prices question was re-opened, as the result of Rab's efforts. But I stuck to my guns and won the support of the Cabinet on the real issue – nothing more on pigs, eggs, or milk. I agreed something on the calf subsidy, if restricted to steers and a token figure for silage encouragement. Both of these can be defended from the point of view of sound agricultural economy. So (I hope) it is settled at last at £25.2m, and no one to bother whether Sir James Turner agrees or not . . . .

---

22. Macmillan's February package had increased the deposit that people arranging hire purchase had to pay, to try to reduce demand.

16 March

. . . . Some rather alarming news is reaching us about Nasser. He seems to be aiming at a sort of League of Arab Republics (the monarchies are to go) to include Libya, Tunisia, Algeria, Morocco as well as the Arab states in Asia Minor etc. Egypt wd have a sort of hegemony in this League, wh wd be a strong and immensely rich affair, esp if the oil resources were pooled. To start it off, and gain prestige, Egypt will attack Israel in June (after the last British soldiers have left Egypt under the Treaty) They will seize a part of Israel's territory (Beersheba area) and when called on to stop by United Nations, they will do so. But they will not retreat and hold on to their gain, and establish tremendous popularity etc with all Arabs. Of course, this plan (knowledge of wh comes from fairly good sources and sounds quite plausible) has one defect. If the Egyptians attack the Jews, they will prob (in spite of their superiority in weapons) get a bloody nose. They may even have a shattering defeat, wh wd tumble Nasser off his perch . . . .

17 March

Woke with a cold! This is very tiresome, as I have such a terrific programme ahead. Worked on boxes in bed all morning and afternoon. I seem to have brought a great deal with me, and more will come today. The volume seems during recent weeks to be growing – almost to F.O. proportions. The great difference is that the Treasury leave me alone at week-ends.

19 March

The doctor would not let me go to London. . . . Read D'Israeli [Disraeli's] 'Correspondence with his sister 1832–1852' a fascinating volume, wh I obtained recently from a bookseller's catalogue. Altho' largely drawn on by Buckle and Monypenny, the whole volume is well worth reading. The descriptions of the debates are admirable.

The whole press (all over the world) is full of the accounts of Khruschev's speech (or speeches) attacking Stalin and his memory. He seems to have accused him of almost every known crime. This amounts to the biggest 'volte-face' since the Stalin–Ribbentrop pact in 1939. The *Daily Worker* correspondent in Moscow is in some difficulty. His line now seems to be that 'after a lapse of 20 years time democracy has been restored'. This seems rather thin . . . .

I did some more bits for the Budget speech. The general plan is beginning to take shape; but I am not happy about it as a whole. I want a theme. Will 'savings' be enough? I think we must somehow counter the idea that the Free Society has failed. We must get over the idea that we want an *expanding* economy, but that *self-control* is necessary as well as freedom. Anyway, since the main decisions have been taken in my own mind (unless P.M. dislikes them) we have time. The chief question is how much *more* to raise in taxation in order to keep the deflationary character of the Budget and yet allow for some concessions to the 'saver' and the executive class . . . .

21 March
. . . . Cabinet 11.30–1.15. The Cabinet are getting all tied up about Malta – with the usual shilly-shallying. I urged them to take a lead and if the HofCommons doesn't like it, they can turn us out. Unless we are careful, the question of the integration of Malta will end up like that of the abolition of Hanging – a matter for individual conscience. Trouble with Libya and the usual blackmail. If we won't build them a power station, the Russians will. It is going to be Jordan all over again – huge subsidies and no results . . . .

22 March
We are going to run into a lot of trouble with the Monopolies Bill. The Board of Trade have not realised yet what disruption will be caused. It now appears that the Bill will apply to steel. But this means that until the Tribunal has adjudicated on the steel practices, we can't sell the shares of the nationalised steel companies which we are trying to denationalise! (The 'net book' agreement looks like becoming unenforceable,[23] and so the whole publishing and bookselling business will be disrupted)

I had a meeting with Thorneycroft and his advisers this morning. But I find it rather painful so early in the morning. He shouts at me (with a cockney accent) as if we were a public meeting . . . .

I had a press conference this afternoon in connection with the launching of the White Paper called '*The Economic Implications of Full Employment*'. I thought the press rather hostile. They regard the White Paper as too much of the old policy of exhortation . . . .

23 March
. . . . I have been thinking a lot about the position, wh is (I think)

---

23. This enabled publishers to specify the selling price of books.

deteriorating. So I feel my Budget may have to be still sterner. I had originally felt that 1½% on undistributed profits (£33m) wd be enough. For the surplus will be over £400m. I want about £20m–£30m for my encouragement to saving and help on income tax for middle class. Now I think I ought to be 'tougher'. So I called a meeting of experts, including customs. I have given instructions for all the procedure to be put in hand to increase the Tobacco Tax. Another 2d on each packet of cigarettes wd give us £28m. Then I will increase the undistributed profits tax to 2½% – giving £55[m] – an increase of £83m. This shd cover what I want to do and leave a margin. (The only trouble is the delay, for the profits tax is not actually paid in [19]56–57. However, it is prob 'saved' and that is what matters) . . . .

24 March
. . . . I am now wondering whether to put 6d on the Income Tax (about £90m) which wd be collected this year, instead of 2½% on undistributed profits (£55m) wh doesn't get in to the Exchequer till next year. The Income Tax wd be a shock and *very* unpopular. But perhaps the shock is needed. There is also the political difficulty that Rab took *off* the 6d last year – *hinc illae lacrymae* . . . .[24]

26 March
. . . . P.M. at 9.15, to hear the outline of the Budget. The idea of 6d on the Income Tax didn't seem to shock him very much, altho' he feared the Lord Privy Seal's reactions . . . .

27 March
A long Cabinet. The F.O. and C.O. came back with their ridiculous idea of offering to buy the Haud from the Ethiopians for anything between £5m and £15m, in order to give it to British Somaliland, wh will then become independent and merged in a Greater Somalia. We managed to shoot this down – at least in this crude form . . . .

The TUC Economic Ctee, headed by Mr Heywood came at 5pm. We had a most useful and friendly talk, lasting 90 minutes and agreed on a press communiqué. Mr Geddes (Post Office) summed the whole thing up in a few sentences. 'We want to help. We don't want to be called Tory stooges. You must help us'. (6d on the Income Tax *would* certainly help them) A good evening at the Tuesday Club. Dennis

---

24. 'Hence these tears', a quote from the Roman poet Terence.

Robertson read a paper on Wages and Inflation and a good discussion followed. I did not take part!

28 March

. . . . I am getting fairly clear now about the Budget. The 'savings' package – to encourage private savings – nominally costing £20m must go through. We will abolish the rest of the bread subsidy (£10m this year saved, and £20m next year) We will tax tobacco still more (£27m this year; £28m next) The great question remains – what more to do and if any, by what means? This, in effect, boils down to getting £50m odd through some new arrangements on Profits Tax, or (alternatively) a straight 6d on Income Tax (undoing what Butler did last year) It's a difficult choice, but politically it's going to make a first class row if I have to choose I.T. I heard that Rab is ringing up Sir E Bridges; my P.S. (Petch) and other Treasury officials in a state of considerable excitement. So I thought it best to have a frank talk with him – which I did this evening, in his room in the HofC. He was in rather a queer mood, I thought – almost pathological. He thinks too much about himself – his failures or successes. He feels that his work as a Chancellor will be written down as a failure (wh is absurd. He had 4 years hard labour and did jolly well) He thinks that the Treasury let him down. He feels that a reversal of his (much criticised) decision to take off 6d last year wd be a direct slur on him. He wd have to resign. He might come back later: but he wd have to resign now. 'Yet' he added rather naively, 'I want you to succeed'. I told him that I thought he exaggerated all this. Of course, the Socialists wd crow over us and say that last year's Budget was just 'electioneering'. But we cd hit them back. Their own election promises wd cost £600m. Anyway, all this sort of thing bored the people profoundly. What matters was whether we cd avoid devaluation in the autumn or not. The I.T. proposal must be judged on this. I calmed him a bit – but not (I fear) convinced him. He is in a mood of self-pity. It is the reaction after his wife's death. She was a woman of tremendous character and he depended on her vitality and strength. Now he is alone . . . .

29 March

. . . . We had a tremendous conference this afternoon at the Treasury, and I made them all speak freely. Bernard Gilbert, Herbert Brittain, and (curiously enough) Sir Robert Hall, the chief economist, are *against* Income Tax and *for* Profits Tax. Sir Leslie Rowan (overseas

finance) is strongly – almost passionately – *for* – in order to save the £.
Mr Leslie is *for*. Sir E Bridges is undecided. Of the ministers, F.S.T. (H
Brooke) is strongly *against*. He thinks the Party will rebel. Econ Secy
(Sir E Boyle) is strongly *for*. He thinks this is the only chance (by
impressing world opinion) of avoiding the autumn crash . . . .

8 April

. . . . I think the alternatives are now becoming clear. *Alternative A, or
Press Button A* – A hard Budget, calculated to give a shock to everyone,
and to make foreigners feel we are in earnest. 'The Savings Package'
(£20m) to be balanced by Tobacco, and *6d on standard rate* of Income
Tax, with *no* concessions except an increased Children's Allowance.
This wd give us another £100m *net* for the surplus. *Alternative B or
Press Button B* 'The Savings Package' to be paid for by Tobacco and
Bread (less another 3/- on Family Allowance) giving a margin of £13m
for surplus. £30m on Profits Tax to sweeten it. *But*, a definite undertaking by Govt to *reduce expenditure by £100m*. The first is austere,
Crippsian, and prob right. The second is more in line with Tory
philosophy – savings wd be the theme. But, of course, the deciding
factor (unless I press it to the point of resignation and even perhaps if
I do) will be the memory of last year. Rab, in the flush of his 'invest in
success' campaign, took 6d *off* Income Tax. Anthony and I and all of
us were the beneficiaries of this 'electioneering Budget'. It will be too
much of a cry of '*peccavi*'[25] if we put it back on in the first post-
election Budget . . . .

. . . . If I cd *really* get ministers to face the full implications of
Button B – real economies, with a realistic attitude to defence and
some determination to trim at least the grosser extravagances of the
Welfare State – it would be much better than raising still more taxation
from a people who are already grossly overtaxed. I have sent a very
stiff memorandum to the P.M. demanding Button A, not hinting at
Button B as a possible alternative. I have sent a copy to Rab. Meanwhile, there is the Budget speech – the Budget broadcast – the Budget
T.V. All these have to be prepared, with two endings! Either the happy
ending – £100m economies and no 6d on I.T.; or the tragic ending, 6d
on I.T. and no economies to speak of.

. . . . Today, as a relaxation, I have read *Bleak House* I
remembered Mrs Pardiggle – in Bleak House who gave allowances

---

25. 'I have sinned'.

(pocket money) to her children and then 'boned' it back from them as contributions to her charities. Mrs Pardiggle is Cripps and (if Button A is pressed) *pro tanto* [to that extent] Macmillan. I took down a copy last night – to verify the references – and fell to the temptation. They say nobody reads Dickens nowadays. More's the pity. He is a giant, with all his faults and imperfections . . . .

9 April

I had a long talk with P.M. this evening. He is an enthusiastic supporter of Button B and thinks that we can get the £100m if we force ministers to face the realities.

10 April

. . . . Since it is strictly not part of the Budget proposals, I put my plan for improving the Family Allowance for large families to the Cabinet. It was approved . . . .

14 April

We got home (B.G.) last night, after a dinner at Bromley, a punctured tire [sic] and much delay, at about 2am. Petch and Miss Berry came about 11am and by 6pm we had produced the final version of the Budget speech – after taking account of the mass of criticism – small and great – from different parts of the Treasury. I think now it's as good as we can get it. It's very long, but it is not easy to shorten it without omitting everything that has any style or character. I can't tell how it will be received. Its theme now is at any rate simple. It can be summed up in one word – saving. (1) There is the whole set of proposals for personal saving – new Bonds, concession on Income Tax etc (2) There is the £100m Govt 'saving' (3) There is the public or compulsory saving – the huge Government surplus, fully maintained and even increased by the Tobacco Tax and the Profits Tax.

. . . . All this week has been nothing but the Budget, and I am tired of it! I have to do a Broadcast and a TV performance. 'Statesmen' are now, willy-nilly, turned into second-rate actors.

We have had rather an agitating week with the Bulganin and Kruschev visit.[26] First, the F.O. published (in error [sic] of the police wishes) the full details of each day, hour by hour. This is a gift to the would-be assassin! Secondly, the public are getting rather upset, esp

---

26. The Russian leaders were due to arrive on 18 April 1956.

about their visit to the Queen. Thirdly, some of the Cabinet don't like it. Salisbury is particularly worried – and when he is worried always wants to resign. (This is a great Cecil tradition) . . . .

15 April

. . . . Roger Makins arrived at about 5 and stayed till after dinner. He left Washington on Friday. I put before him my scheme for the Treasury and begged him to consider it favourably. It wd be wonderful for me if I cd get him. But I admit it's asking a lot. At present he has the best embassy in the whole service – Washington – with the excellent chance (if not quite certainty) of succeeding to the headship of the F.O. when Kirkpatrick goes. I want him to give all this up for the bewildering and almost impossible job of restoring British solvency. However Roger is a good patriot, and realised that without a proper financial policy there can be no effective foreign policy . . . .[27]

16 April

. . . . Went to London for Cabinet at 3.45. Ministers seemed to like the plan of the Budget and even accepted the idea of the £100m cut – altho' when it comes to implementing the pledge there will be a lot of trouble . . . .

17 April

Budget day. I stayed in bed most of the morning. Moucher (Devonshire) and Carol Faber came to luncheon. But I cd eat little. The nervous strain of these speeches seems to get worse as one gets older. Anyway, I have never attempted anything of the kind before – 2 hours or so.

D and I left for the House about 3pm. There was a large crowd outside No 11 – and all the usual photographers, radio news people and the rest.

We drove to the House – in the rain. Hamilton Kerr (my PPS) met us and took D to her seat in the gallery.

---

27. Macmillan had thought very highly of Makins since they worked together in North Africa during the Second World War. He now hoped to entice Makins to renew their partnership by taking up the post of Permanent Under-Secretary to the Treasury that Bridges was soon to vacate. Ironically, his success in persuading Makins to leave Washington meant that this crucial embassy was vacant just when the Suez crisis reached its climax, whilst Makins was hardly in the Treasury before Macmillan had left it for the premiership.

Then the agonising wait in my room – alone with the speech.

At 3.27 I went and stood behind the Speaker's Chair. At 3.30 exactly I entered the Chamber. The Conservatives gave me a very good cheer. At the start of my speech (which began, perhaps a little incautiously, with a passage about Churchill and his Budget of 1924) some of the Socialists tried to barrack a bit. They sniggered at any literary turn of phrase or quotation and behaved like rather ill-bred schoolboys. (This was, of course, confined to a few – mostly intellectuals. The old Trade Union types are much too polite to indulge in this kind of thing) However, I went on and soon got them under control. The speech lasted just under two hours. Our people seemed satisfied – particularly with the 'Savings package' . . . .

Gaitskell said a few words – not very gracefully. 'It was not an inspired Budget'. Then I left. The 1922 Ctee was packed with our people at 6pm. There were the usual complainants, but I had a very good reception. Then to No 11, where I went through the broadcast with Archie Gordon (BBC) who is very helpful. Dorothy and I (with Petch and Maude – my Private Secretaries) and Ham Kerr (PPS) went to the BBC place. I delivered the broadcast – and people seem to have liked it . . . .

18 April

The London press is good – the *Times* particularly sympathetic. Curiously enough, the provincials are not so good – except the *Yorkshire Post* and the *Manchester Guardian* . . . .

19 April

. . . . Cabinet 11.45. Singapore; British Guiana; medical views on the dangers of smoking. If we lose Singapore, it's a terrible blow to all our Far Eastern interests. If people really think they will get cancer of the lung from smoking it's the end of the Budget![28]

Bulganin and Kruschev have arrived – and this, with the marriage

---

28. The famous paper by Richard Doll and A. Bradford Hill linking smoking to lung cancer came out in 1950. When the question of whether an information campaign to warn the public of this had come to cabinet Macmillan had asked, in view of the fact that tobacco taxes brought in £670m a year, for any announcement to be postponed until after the Budget. A statement was made to the House by the Minister of Health on 7 May 1956, but a public information campaign had to wait until the 1960s.

of Grace Kelly to the Prince of Monaco, have overshadowed the Budget. There was a luncheon at the Russian Embassy – with glaring lights (for British TV and Russian colour film) there was caviare; and vodka; and those terrible Russian wines. But the unexpected thing was an impromptu (and very interesting speech) by K. The P.M. thinks that he may be able to do some business with them – not about Europe or Germany (wh is hopeless) but about Middle East . . . .

20 April
. . . . I had to go to Bromley to see a deputation of angry shop-keepers – about the new [rating] valuation. This is going to be a troublesome affair for us, all over the country, for some time . . . .

21 April
Our wedding day – 36 years ago. D and I were alone here [BG] today, wh was nice. The Faber children came – the Macmillans are in Italy. An absolutely glorious day – sun and no wind. The garden is quite lovely, the daffodils at their best. I sat about and read. Finished *Sybil* and started *Lothair*. Disraeli's novels, with all their absurdities, are very readable and interesting . . . .

23 April
The debate went on all day. D Jay began for the Opposition – an able speech, but too bitter – at least too bitter all through. He has not learned to vary the tone or the pace of his speaking. Edward Boyle followed – a very good effort but not one of his best. Dalton wound up – a jovial, rollicking kind of speech. I rose at 9.15 – rather nervous. But everything went perfectly, from start to finish. The party were really delighted and I think the Opposition rather discomfited. It was a slashing kind of counter-attack – wh was what our boys needed. Churchill, Eden, Butler etc were all very complimentary.

24 April
The best press I have ever had. D unfortunately didn't go and is now very sad. But she has heard a lot of praise of the speech during the day. Now we must work. I have had a start with a long meeting with Governor on the problem of 'convertibility' – in view of the rapid movement of the rates of official and transferable sterling together. It's rather a good sign really. Owing to greater confidence in UK among foreigners, transferable sterling is rising. Last year the bank had to

spend dollars in buying it in order to sustain the price. Now they are selling transferable sterling and buying dollars in order to depress it! The whole point of the argument is, however, this. Granted that we are '*de facto*' convertible (in the sense in which this word is now used – i.e. for non-resident holders) what are the advantages and disadvantages of becoming '*de jure*' convertible. Can we retain discriminatory import controls. What about capital payments? What about resident sterling? It is a most difficult question. But we must not be rushed by the Bank.

Roger Makins has accepted my offer – subject to his going to F.O. after 3 years at the Treasury. I hope P.M. will agree this. It will [be] wonderful to have him. Altho' Bridges is a most admirable public servant – one of the greatest – he had been through a lot, with the war and the post-war troubles, and he really wants to retire. I hope P.M. will agree to offer him a peerage.

25 April

I felt so tired and exhausted this morning that I cd scarcely get out of bed. However, I dragged myself to a meeting of the Economic Policy Ctee (over wh I preside) Then a luncheon – and speech – at the Constitutional Club. I made a very poor speech.

The Bulganin–Kruschev visit goes on. They had a row with the Labour leaders at a dinner given for them at the HofC by the Labour executive. Our Labour friends asked about the fate of the Social Democrats, now in prison in Russia and the Satellite states, and got a very dusty answer. I gather that the negotiations with Eden and For Secy are pretty sticky. But the visit may have done good. The public have behaved with admirable reticence and discretion. Their sight-seeing visits are being curtailed, in order to give more time to serious talks with our ministers. The British are certainly an odd people. It is said of one of K's speeches that when he talked of capitalism and socialism and so forth, he held the attention of an audience. But he lost them when he began to talk about rockets with H bomb-heads. Then he lost the audience! They were bored!

26 April

B and K have gone to Scotland with James Stuart – a curious party. The Cabinet studied the communiqué and heard an account from PM of the whole negotiation. He clearly thought the visit had been worth while, and some progress made. The Russians understood more what we felt about the M East, and our determination to fight for the oil, if we had to. P.M. of course had obviously enjoyed these talks very much. He excels in all this. Ld Salisbury sat very glum. We had an important discussion about the Rent Bill. It was decided to make it the first Bill of the next session . . . .

The paper work has started to get worse and the number of urgent problems is really appalling. The difficulties wh confront this country are indeed manifold. Yet Archbishops bleat away about Premium Bonds![29]

> Oh that there might in England be
> A duty on Hypocrisy!
> A tax on Humbug; an excise
> On solemn plausibilities!

(I read these lines somewhere, but I forget where) . . . .[30]

The Communist controlled Engineering Union has had the impudence to ask for a further wage increase – 6 weeks after the last settlement. This year, we must really fight these purely disruptive and 'political' claims. If not, there is no hope of stopping an inflation, leading to a devaluation . . . .

28 April

. . . . The gilt-edged market was very strong yesterday: so I hope the Governor has been able to sell some more of the new Treasury stock wh we issued last week. Everything depends on (a) saving and funding (b) firm resistance by employers to fresh wage demands. This of course includes the managements of the nationalised industries . . . .

30 April

I have started a fortnightly meeting of the heads of the different depts – to go through the work to be done and to keep everyone in touch with each other. I think it will be helpful. We had the first meeting this morning. In the afternoon, Mr Governor came with *his* ideas on 'liquidity ratios'.[31] I told him that I was not quite ready with mine.

---

29. One of the centrepieces of Macmillan's Budget, Premium Bonds (an idea which had occasionally been floated before the Second World War) were designed to encourage saving whilst also offering the inducement of modest prize money. It was this element of gambling that provoked ecclesiastical disapproval.
30. Henry Luttrell, *Letters to Julia* (1822), 'Letter II', lines 966–9.
31. For the clearing banks, in order to reduce the supply of credit.

4.30–6.30 – a long, tedious, and rather painful meeting with von Brentano (German Foreign Minister) Dr Hallstein, and a number of German experts. On our side we had Leslie Rowan etc. We made very little headway, but perh left some impressions on him. We are claiming £50m 'support costs' for 1955–6. The Germans are being very difficult and have so far refused even to begin a serious negotiation. After dinner (there was a large party at Carlton Gardens given by For Sec) we got on to the subject again and I gave von B an aide-memoire on lines agreed between us before. He personally, I think, wants to help. But the German Finance Minister is very tough.

1 May
A long Defence Ctee at No 10 – from 11 to 1pm. Apart from the complications of the Jordan situation, the main topic was the German support costs. I made it clear that we must get the £50m somehow. If we can't get it out of the Germans, in whole or in part, we must make economies in our troops in Germany, by hook or crook . . . .

2 May
We *must* get £12m towards the £100[m] out of school meals. So we *must* get the Family Allowances Bill through *before* we announce this economy. I must try to persuade Butler accordingly . . . . Then an hour with Minister of Transport and General Robertson about the future of British Railways – wh are (like coal) hopelessly 'in the red'. A small luncheon at No 10 for von Brentano and Hallstein and more talks about support costs. I think we made some progress. At 4pm another meeting with PM – (Butler and Macleod – Minister of Labour present) about TUC and the next round of wage claims which we *must* resist at all costs. Everything will turn on this year. I think P.M. quite understands this.

3 May
10am. Sir E Compton, Mr Wilson and Petch – on the future agricultural policy – a most difficult subject. The present subsidy system is *not* satisfactory. What is needed is capital improvements, to get more efficient production in the smaller farms. Here the position is easier in Scotland than in England, for the 'crofter' problem is isolated, geographically, from the rest.

11am–1pm Cabinet . . . . A long discussion on MPs' salaries, and ministers' salaries. Altho' everyone admits that junior ministers are underpaid, and in some cases in real distress, there was general agreement that we must do nothing this year – the critical year on the general wages front. Cabinet approved a statement to be made by the Minister of Health about Tobacco and cancer of the lung. It was a much better draft than the original one. I only hope it won't stop people smoking! Coal prices have got to go up, as the result of the last wage increase. But even with *all* the increases due to the last wage increases *and* to removal of subsidies etc, the experts do not expect more than 2 points increase on the cost of living figures altogether. Since wages have gone 7 points *above* prices, there is no justification for a further round of wage increases . . . .

4 May

Michael Fraser – the very intelligent head of the Conservative Research Dept came at 10. I asked him to get his staff working on next year's Budget. If (wh is not more than even chances) we get through this year; overcome the inflation by resisting further wage claims; and surmount the consequent internal strife – what wd be the best way to give away £100–£150m on the Budget? This shd make an interesting exercise . . . .

11.30. Minister of Defence came, with my old friend, Sir Richard Powell. We had a *very* disappointing talk about economies. I heard that the Social Services Ctee (under Butler) had a similiar talk, with similar results. The defence people say that most of the £100m must come off the civil vote. If I don't get what I have promised by the end of June, I must in honour resign and the Govt is lost. Quite a good position, tactically! . . . .

8 May

. . . . After Cabinet, P.M. explained to a few of us the details of the trouble that has arisen over the death of Commander Crabb, while 'spying' on the Russian ships in Portsmouth harbour during the recent visit. It is really a chapter of accidents. First, P.M. was asked by Admiralty about such an undertaking a good few weeks *before* the visit. Next, he wrote a clear and precise minute, expressly forbidding anything of the kind. After that, you wd have thought everything wd have been all right. Not at all. The Secret Service (without proper liaison) and in touch with minor Admiralty officers, arranged this with Crabb (a retired officer, who has specialised in 'frogman' work) The Admiralty agreed – the P.M.'s orders have either been overridden –

evaded, or merely *not* passed down the line. Then this gallant officer does the job – successfully, and without detection. Then, in an excess of zeal, he undertakes another job – and is unsuccessful. He is either killed by the Russians, or drowned by misadventure – we don't know for certain.[32] Then the Russians complain. The Admiral at Portsmouth (knowing nothing about it) denies the charge. Then the commander's relations ask questions. The press begin. The Admiralty issue a denial (the most idiotic thing possible, since otherwise we cd have refused to know anything about it, as is always the rule with Secret Service work) Then the fat is in the fire. What makes it worse is that altho' all this happened on April 17th, nothing was said by officials to ministers until the press story broke. There is a P.Q. to the P.M. for tomorrow. It is most difficult to know just how to handle it. I really feel it a little hard to ask him to take full responsibility . . . .

I had a talk later with Ministers of Labour, Transport, and Fuel and Power. I impressed on them the importance of getting the Boards of the Nationalised Industries to resist all future wage claims. Of course, this cannot be done by any actual authority of ministers; under the strange laws wh control these affairs, the Boards are free to concede what wages they like and then confront us with the consequences. But I think that in most cases – Citrine will perh be the exception – they will follow the wishes of the Govt. If we can call a halt *now* in the nationalised industries, we may get the Engineering employers to follow. Then we might hold the position this year . . . .

9 May
. . . . The P.M. was very firm in the House. Gaitskell behaved very badly. I suppose he thinks that he can 'get back' on us and thereby compensate for his own follies at the Russian dinner. But an aspirant to the post of P.M. ought to know better than discuss 'espionage' and the secret service . . . .

10 May
Cabinet at 11. P.M. now explained his position over the Portsmouth incident to his colleagues. I thought it right to refer to his clear and explicit instructions – a point wh he generously did not mention.

---

32. Crabb was examining the hull of the Soviet cruiser *Ordjonikidze* to find out why it was faster than British warships. His headless body was washed ashore during the summer.

We then had a very good discussion about economic policy and our talk with the TUC, arranged for the afternoon. I made an appeal for help in getting the £100m economies. This exercise is going very 'stickily' at present. Ministers are very good at making suggestions for economies in each others' departments and resisting them in their own . . . .

All the afternoon we worked on the communiqué or declaration of Govt policy wh we hope to come out of the TUC meeting. This took place at 5pm and went very well. In the end, and rather to my surprise, they agreed to quite a good communiqué. This clearly set out the Govt's request for wage restraint and the arguments for it, altho' (of course) it did not commit the unions. Nevertheless, the fact that they agreed to these terms, will certainly help. Of course, the moderate men more or less openly agreed with us. One man said that if only we cd prevent one of them from 'getting in front', they wd all be ready to stand where they are. It is clear that there is hardly any more competitive post than that of a T.U. leader . . . .

11 May

I don't like the signs of the economic times. The trade gap in April is up again to £57m. Building and other activities are going on as fast as ever. 'Short time' has taken the place of 'unemployment' in industry. I have called a meeting for Monday to review the whole position.

'Trial of the Pyx';[33] followed by an immense luncheon at the Goldsmiths Hall; followed by visit to the Mint. 12.45 to 4pm. Very interesting, but very tiring and what a lot of time we spend in these ceremonies. Another speech too, wh has to be carefully prepared, for the company is distinguished . . . .

12 May

. . . . The local election results are bad – but no worse than I expected. The middle classes are exasperated and disillusioned, and the 'revaluation' has worried the shop-keepers. The 'Liberal' candidates have cashed in on this and won a good many votes all over the country. We lost one seat (Plaistow ward) in Bromley, and in Hayes and Keston there was a large Liberal vote. But I feel that all this is very unimportant compared with the great question. Can we save the £ this year? If we can do this and hold the inflation, I can have a Budget next year

---

33. The testing of specimen coin.

which will win back all the middle classes. But I am getting more and more doubtful. The T.U.s are getting into the hands of Communist leaders, and the employers are too weak or too selfish to resist . . . .

14 May
. . . . I strongly advised P.M. to stick to his position about the 'Frog-man' incident and say nothing. I believed he cd put Gaitskell into a difficult position. If he attacked violently, he wd be regarded by serious people as unworthy of the rank of Privy Councillor, aspirant to the Premiership. If he moderated his tone, he wd fail to rouse any enthusiasm among his people. This, in fact, proved to be the case. The Cyprus debate – ending at 8pm, with a bad defeat for the Opposition, in which Alan Lennox-Boyd made mincemeat of Bevan, was a good prelude. Gaitskell started quietly; lost his own people after 5 minutes, and the whole House after 20 minutes. He asked too many questions – which always allows yr opponent to answer none of them. P.M. was short – decisive – and refused to budge an inch. He got the biggest cheer from our side when he sat down that I have ever heard them give him. The debate dragged on till 10. Crossman made a very fine effort to rescue the attack, but it was too late. Gaitskell had muffed it. We got a very large majority – between 80 and 90. Herbert Morrison either abstained or voted with us – a nasty blow to Gaitskell. So did Shinwell . . . .

15 May
. . . . D and I attended a dinner at the HofC of the Plaistow ward (Bromley) About 60 were there. These dinners in the House are becoming very popular. They certainly help the finances of the Kitchen Committee. Unfortunately, through the Liberals putting up a candidate, Ralph Allen lost the seat at the recent local elections. He came to the dinner, and we all gave him the praise he deserves – a fine type. He has done a lot for charities, boys clubs and all the rest in the poorer parts of the town.

16 May
The early part of the morning was spent on discussing the effect of the Restrictive Practices Bill on the Iron and Steel Trade. The President (who is getting a bit rattled) will not make any concession to the Board. But unless we can get this industry taken out of the Bill, I fear that the remaining shares will be unsaleable and the whole purpose of

'Denationalisation' defeated. Peter Thorneycroft came to see me, and offered to resign – wh is odd, as I am not P.M. Had I been so, I wd have been tempted to accept! . . . .

12pm. Speech to the National Savings Assembly, with Lord Mackintosh in the chair. These delegates (200–300) came from all parts of the country. Before I arrived, they had agreed the target of £250m for this year. They also approved Premium Bonds, with one dissentient! I got a tremendous reception, both before and after my speech. It was really quite extraordinary . . . .

We had a long meeting in P.M.'s room – P.M., Ld Privy Seal, Min of Defence, Min of Supply and myself. We are making slow – but *very* slow – progress towards £100m savings. We must get more from defence.

The 'Hanging Bill' was being discussed all day. I voted before dinner in a minority of 12 and then went home to bed. Later on, the abolitionists suffered their first defeat – by 4 votes – on an amendment about 'second murders' by men serving a life sentence. Whether this breach in the 'abolitionist' front will be important or not, I don't know . . . . I am still worried at the economic situation. £1500m a year and 700,000 men in the services is breaking us.

17 May

. . . . Cabinet at 11. The chief question before us was to consider a paper by Salisbury and another by Kilmuir about a possible reform of the HofLords. They have together produced a very ingenious scheme for a chamber of 400 peers, 200 to be 'selected' by a committee of peers (representing all parties) from the 800 or more hereditary peers; 200 to be nominated by the Crown and so built up as to represent all parties. The powers of the HofLords are *not* to be increased. All this is very good, in principle. But what will be the effect in practice. Will the Labour Party boycott the selection committee? Will we be able to carry such a scheme through Parl and the country? Is it worth while? If the powers are *not* to be increased, what is it all for? I ventured to sound this warning note. No decision was reached . . . .

I had the Ministers of Labour, Fuel and Power, and Transport, round to see me in the afternoon. It seems probable that they can prevent the chairmen of the nationalised industries giving in to a new wage claim – at least without proper warning and consultation. I am not so sure about the agricultural position. After them, came Walter Monckton (Defence) with his chief civil servant, Richard Powell. I had

Serpell (of the Treasury) who is excellent. We pressed them hard on economies – which must be of 3 kinds – first, contributions to the £100 million; second, medium term decisions, e.g. on fighter command, maintenance command, warships etc; third, on long-term policy. I think we made some progress. Eden passed me a note at Cabinet wh ran as follows 'I am arranging for Norman Brook to go to see Minister of Supply today (privately – so as not to upset anybody) on my behalf and discuss the list of possible postponements and sales abroad – I am determined that we shall get on with this . . . . '

. . . . I finished up all the work and D and I got the night train for Gleneagles. Our holiday begins! . . . .

20 May

Started our [golf] round at 8.30, and so got off before anyone else. We played round in 2½ hours. I rested till 4, when we played another full round. Read Stendhal. It is wonderful to have no boxes, no telegrams, no telephone calls, no letters. I think the change is doing D good also. It is also pleasant to be physically tired. Normally, one is mentally exhausted at the end of each week, without any physical exercise and fatigue at all . . . .

25 May

I left Drem station at 7.30am for Newcastle. The luncheon at the Newcastle Conservative Club was followed by a speech . . . . The speech 'went' all right with the audience – mostly business men from NE Coast – but it remains to be seen what the general response will be. I made an 'appeal' (wh was nearly a 'threat') for a period of stability in prices and wages.

Motored to Stockton, where D had come direct from Scotland . . . .

26 May

We drove round some of the parts of Stockton which we knew very well and have been much altered by slum clearance etc. The wealth and prosperity of the town is incredible '*Pourvu que ça dure*'[34] . . . .

Drove to Cragthorne, to stay with the Dugdales.

28 May

I came down last night by sleeper from Darlington. D comes by car,

---

34. 'Provided that it lasts'.

stopping one night with her mother at Hardwick. Sir A Fleck (Chairman of ICI) came to luncheon yesterday at Cragthorne. He is a *most* attractive and interesting man. His contribution to the agricultural problem (apart from more and more nitrogen) was interesting. Why a national price settlement? Why not a regional one?

The T.U. leaders have begun to comment on the Newcastle speech. Cousins (Deakin's successor at Transport and General Workers) was critical, but not violent or offensive. Jay said what one might expect and Bevan also. But the Labour politicians don't matter. All the Unions are about to have conferences, and all will recommend increases in wages, with varying degrees of urgency and insistence. But I hope that the Govt lead will bring the employers to the point of resisting these demands. If they do, nobody will be more pleased than the moderate T.U. 'leaders' . . . .

. . . . Worked all the afternoon till 6pm, when there was a meeting about atomic tests. Our troubles are (a) that when the report of the medical committee comes out there will be a fresh agitation to ban tests[35] (b) that since US and USSR *have* completed their tests (while ours is still a year away) they might agree!

Dined with the Moncktons at 2 Harcourt Buildings . . . .

Walter is despondent about the Ministry of Defence. I urged him to bring to an issue the question of his powers over the services. He shall never do any good until the Minister of Defence is either abolished or made really boss. Read and worked late. The boxes seem larger and larger, and the questions to be settled more and more insoluble. 1) Convertibility 2) monetary policy and banking liquidity ratios 3) the £100m cut 4) Britain and the Messina powers 5) tariffs – and the future of empire preference 6) defence etc.

29 May

. . . . The Opposition press is now launched against the Newcastle speech; but the tone is not bitter. One T.U. leader has spoken in favour; most are against. No doubt they are helpless. The test will not

---

35. Prior to announcing Britain's H-bomb tests on 7 June 1956, Eden requested a report from the Medical Research Council, which concluded that the present level of tests was not dangerous, but that increased testing might produce ill-effects 'in a small proportion of the population' (quoted in Eden, *Full Circle* (London: Cassell, 1960), p. 377).

be whether the new wage claims are presented. The test will be how far they will be pressed . . . .

30 May

. . . . In the afternoon, I had a meeting with Enoch Powell (under secy Min of Housing) and Aubrey Jones (Fuel and Power) about miners' houses. The Board are being difficult. I told the Minister that he must get them to revive the Coal Board's Housing Association. In my time it got 20,000 houses built. They cd easily do another 20,000. PM asked me to go to his room to discuss defence. At last he has begun to realise (what I have been telling him for months) that we just cannot stand the pressure of £1500m on the economy . . . .

31 May

. . . . Defence Ctee (restricted meeting) in P.M.'s room. The battle is now joined! The RAF now admit that Fighter Command cannot defend the island. But they still want to spend £1000m over the next 10 years to defend the Bombers – and this on machines alone! I think PM and Salisbury were much shaken by the argument deployed against all this . . . .

5 June

. . . . Lunch with Cecil King (proprietor) and Hugh Cudlipp (editor) of the *Daily Mirror*. They are as good a pair of ruffians as you cd find anywhere. I think King (who cares for money more than anything else) sometimes has a few qualms as to whether he may be digging his own grave. I tried to persuade them to give some support to my 'stability' crusade. But he was very 'cagey'. Cudlipp, of course, does what he's told. Actually, he is rather an attractive fellow . . . .

7 June

. . . . A new horror has suddenly fallen on us. Texas oil company have made a bid (and a very big one too, £63 millions) for all the shares in a company called the Trinidad Oil Co. The shares have more than doubled, and there is wild speculation in the City. Now *I* have to decide whether to allow the deal to go through, or whether to stop it under the Exchange Control Act. Since the deal is obviously beneficial from the economic and financial point of view, this wd seem rather a doubtful course. But of course there is a howl of excitement and fury in the press and the Party. I stalled at question time today . . . .

8 June

. . . . We gave an enormous 'cocktail party' at No 11 to 250 of our Bromley supporters. It was a great success. We got all the old and retired officers as well as the new ones . . . .

9 June

Motored to Chequers in the morning, leaving No 11 at 9am.[36] PM; Ld Salisbury; Walter Monckton; Head (W.O.) Maudling (Supply) and the C.A.S., CIGS and 2nd Sea Lord. We worked away till luncheon and after luncheon till nearly 6pm. The whole of our 'commitments' was the subject of the exercise – from Germany to Singapore. We took also a review of bombers, fighters, and naval forces. No final decisions were taken, but I felt some progress was made. The military are gradually beginning not only to talk about the Hydrogen Bomb strategy but to contemplate putting it into effect . . . .

11 June

. . . . I decided to ask Ld Godber (Shell) and Mr Jackson (B.P.) to come and see me. This they did in the afternoon – separately. I did not want to see them in the HofC, so I had to keep darting across from the Committee Stage of the Finance Bill to the Treasury. I eventually had to miss the P.M.'s meeting with the employers. This was a pity, as I heard afterwards that it went very badly. Both Ld Godber and Mr Jackson were strongly in favour of the Trinidad deal going through. Of course they didn't want to buy, because one of the chief assets of Trinidad is a half share in a distributing system known as Regent. Since BP-Shell run a system of their own, this wd be no use to them . . . .

12 June

The Trinidad affair is developing into a major political crisis. Lord Beaverbrook's *Daily Express*, the *Daily Herald* (Labour) and the *Daily Worker* (Communist) are linked in a somewhat strange alliance – but all against the Govt. I am accused on 'selling out the empire' to the

---

36. This was for the first meeting of the Policy Review Committee. This had been established to review Britain's defence role and commitments, not least in the light of Macmillan's demands for £100m in expenditure cuts, half of which he wanted to fall on defence (see PRO: PREM 11/1778). However, it was effectively rapidly taken over by events in the form of the Suez crisis.

Yankees. It is not yet announced what the Govt decision will be. But I intend to recommend to the Cabinet this morning that, subject to certain conditions, some to protect UK and sterling area interests and some to protect the local inhabitants, permission shall be given . . . .

13 June
. . . . At 5pm, I had to go upstairs to one of the committee rooms, with Aubrey Jones (the new Minister for Fuel and Power) to face an angry and hostile gathering of back benchers. The occasion is the introduction of a Bill to provide more money for coal investment. The cause is a rising indignation against the nationalised industries and their management. We had 2 hours of it, and I think did some good. There are some genuinely disturbed members, and some trouble-makers. One or two of the latter are disappointed officer-seekers . . . .

14 June [37]
I had arranged that Bridges and Rowan shd see Ld Baillieu and Mr Vos (Trinidad Oil Co) and put to them the kind of conditions wh HMG wd require if they were to give their approval to the deal. I was naturally anxious to find out whether these conditions (esp that about the sterling–dollar payments for oil sold in the sterling area in future, and that for the Company being registered in Trinidad) were likely to be accepted by the Texas Co (the purchasers) At the same time, I was anxious to avoid any negotiation with Texas. Nevertheless, the worst political position of all would be to incur all the odium of granting permission, only to find that the deal fell through in the end because of one or other of the conditions. Bridges and Rowan had done this yesterday and I suppose that the vendors discussed it with the purchasers. Just before Cabinet (wh was at 11am) I got a message that the conditions would be accepted by Texas. The Cabinet approved my actions, and the statement wh I was to make at 3.30. We all expected that the Opposition wd move to adjourn. This wd mean a debate at 7pm, and a division at 10. However, I got a hint during the morning that there was some division between them about the course they shd pursue. Wilson is anxious for a row. Gaitskell (who has burnt his fingers once or twice already) is more cautious.

---

37. Macmillan did not mention the withdrawal of the last British troops from the Suez Canal base in conformity with the 1954 agreement.

The rest of the morning in Cabinet was taken up with the search for the £100m saving. This was *not* very successful!

Meanwhile, I have managed to prepare a speech of some kind for the debate this evening, if it shd come off.

I made the statement after questions. It seemed to be pretty well received by our side and the Opposition were clearly rather nonplussed. The sober arguments in favour of HMG giving permission are overwhelming. But, of course, there is a latent xenophobia in every nation, and it is easy to whip up a sense of jealousy and resentment agst the Americans. Actually, we all know that we ought to welcome US investment in UK and in the Commonwealth.

Wilson asked two questions – and very foolish ones. I made rather a long reply and knocked him out. I had put into my statement a promise to publish a White Paper with further details. I thought they might fall for this – and they did. It was an excuse for them to postpone the debate and they grabbed at it. I refused to postpone action till after the debate. I wd send my formal approval at once – after my announcement. If the House wish to censure me, they must do so. Gaitskell tried to bluster a bit but it was clear to everybody that the thing was beginning to 'fizzle' out.

I went up to the Lobby[38] and then to an adjourned Cabinet, about the £100m saving. We made a little more progress but it's now clear that I shall not get the £100m on the first instalment.

After the Cabinet, wh sat for over an hour, we had a meeting of the Policy Review Ctee, and approved a message which we are to send to Washington, asking for an immediate meeting of the ministerial ctee of NATO and a re-assessment of military needs. This means, in plain language, cutting our forces in Germany from 4 divisions to 2 divisions. (The discussion about 'support costs' with the Germans is still going on. But it's clear that we shan't get more than about £30m, and that only for this year . . . .

19 June

Meeting at Treasury on Finance Bill, followed by Cabinet. The chief discussions were a) Cyprus b) the £100m savings. On the latter, my Cabinet colleagues are being sympathetic in principle but very uncooperative in practice. However, I think I shall be able to announce an interim or progress report next week wh will give me £75m or there-

---

38. The parliamentary press corps (known as lobby correspondents).

abouts as the first effort. It may be that this will be received with great derision by the House and the Press. But I think I may be able to present it as a first effort with more to follow.

On Cyprus, the problem of finding a solution acceptable both to Greece and Turkey remains just as intractable as I found it last summer at the Tripartite Conference. This fundamental difficulty cannot be resolved by verbal formulae, however cleverly devised. P.M., F.S., Col Sec, and others are working hard at this. But I am not optimistic. After these subjects, we had a discussion on agricultural wages. I am very disturbed at the prospect of the Arbitration Board giving an increase in a few weeks' time. If they do this, they may touch off a general movement towards wage increases throughout industry, which will damage and perhaps destroy any hope of stability . . . .

20 June

. . . . The debate on the Trinidad oil question took place. It was on the adjournment. I began with rather a dull and serious speech. This was, on the whole, well received. Harold Wilson followed, with a brilliant attack. However, it was not calculated to split our party. On the contrary, it tended to bring the party together. Griffiths wound up for them; Alan Lennox-Boyd for us. The former was lamentable; the latter excellent – only a little too long. We had a good division – 68 majority. I made; in my speech, a direct attack on Ld Beaverbrook and the *Daily Express*. I suppose, from now on, he will pursue me with malignance, by every means, fair and foul.

The debate ended at 7.30pm – wh allowed D and me to dine with the Portuguese ambassador, at Bathurst House (Belgrave Square) This has been transformed into a Portuguese palace. I knew it – only too well – from 1916–18 when I was in hospital in this house . . . .[39]

22 June

. . . . Left for Leeds at 1.28. On arrival at Leeds, addressed a National Savings movement meeting at the City Hall. Then a Conservative meeting at the Town Hall. This was (to my surprise) absolutely packed – 2000 or more. I made rather a dull speech, about the economic situation – with very few quips or jokes. They seemed to stand it fairly well . . . .

---

39. After having been severely wounded at the Battle of the Somme on 15 September 1916.

24 June

I stayed in bed all the morning – missing Church – and finished nearly all the work by luncheon. There was only left over some papers about (1) the £100m saving – to be announced on Tuesday, with a half-time score of £75m odd – and (2) the next move in the climb to the plateau – of wage and price stability. I talked on the telephone to Percy Mills – who is working hard, tho' behind the scenes.

At present, the TUC are lying very low. They are compiling a book or pamphlet on the economic situation, and are not very keen to talk to us for fear of being accused (by the extremists) of falling under Tory and capitalist influence. But the Communist elements (which now more or less control the leading unions, tho' not the TUC) are also organising themselves for this year's decisive struggle. Everything depends on the skill and determination with which we handle the situation.

25 June

Another weary day at the HofC, with Committee stage of the Finance Bill. New clauses are more troublesome than any other part of the procedure. For all new clauses are concessions to the taxpayer, and I have to resist them all.

26 June

We finished the Finance Bill at about 1am. The Ctee stage has run for 8 days in all – 4½ on the Bill; 3½ on new clauses. Entertainment Tax (wh includes Tax on Sport and on Theatre) has been very troublesome. I have been able to defend it in a year where no tax concessions are being made. But I doubt if anyone can keep it together much longer. Yet £40m are involved. I think it will end up as a tax on cinemas and perhaps on T.V.

. . . . After questions – and before the Ctee stage of the Bill began – I made my interim statement on the £100m economies. We were able to get it up to £76m. The House seemed rather uncertain how to take it. The Opposition had a disappointment, for they expected a wide 'attack on the social services' and there was nothing (except the 1d on school meals wh follows precedent) Our side was quiet, but on the whole satisfied . . . . The policy of price stabilisation for the immediate future is beginning to spread. Almost all the National Boards have adopted it. It is now for Private Industry to follow. Of course, it's economic nonsense – prices cannot be stabilised unless costs are. But it's a polite way (and the only way in wh we as a Govt can take a lead) of saying 'no more wages this year'.

27 June

.... [A]nother 'revolt' in the Tory Party is blowing up about Cyprus – the usual gang – Waterhouse, Amery etc. It's all rather silly, as there is so little chance of any settlement. The Turks and Greeks are still a long way from that, (as they were at the Tripartite Conference wh I held in the summer of last year) altho' I think that if we are both firm and patient we may reach a solution in time. I am told that the Greeks are getting anxious – esp the Gk Govt.

At 10.15 we had the first meeting of the reconstructed EPC. It was a useful one, as we cd decide on a line towards this morning's news – further large dismissals and short time in the motor industry. The medicine is beginning to work. The whole thing now turns on the mobility of labour and the strength of mind of HMG.

.... The Engineering Employers are meeting the 40 confederated unions, tomorrow, and are going to warn them against further wage demands. Of course, this will be called 'provocative' but I think it will be salutary.

28 June

The House of Commons was very excited yesterday at question time about the position in the motor industry, but more about the *method* (dismissal *without* discussion with the unions) than about the actual decisions of the managers. It is clear that BMC's action is resented. It is of course explained by the fact that Standard took the other course, and at the end of 3 weeks are still arguing with the unions. It is not easy to tell yet how all this will work out. There may be a strike throughout the industry; altho' I have little doubt that the companies wd not mind 3 or 4 weeks in which to sell their accumulated stocks without adding to them. If we are quite firm, it *will* work out and the excess labour (for the industry has been prodigal in the use of and miserly in the recruitment and retention of labour) will be absorbed in other work. This will take time and meet with a good deal of resistance, esp as the men will prob have to be content with lower wages in other branches of engineering or in general trade and industry.

9.45. Farm Price Review Ctee. The Agricultural Ministers want to enter into negotiations with the Farmers' Union for a 'long-term' agreement. Unfortunately they have no idea of what to propose. A negotiation with Sir James Turner without any clear plan of the goal you want to reach seems to me a very dangerous exercise . . . .

I also put forward, for discussion a plan of my own. This wd be

(1) Guarantee to pay a percentage each year – for say 4 years – of increased costs. Percentage to be variable; say 60% of any wage increase – 70% of other.

(2) No commodity guarantee to be reduced by more than (say) 4%–5% in any year. (Percentage cd vary with commodities)

(3) capital growth up to £Xm for improving land.

Heathcoat-Amory and Stuart seemed to like this general plan and the experts are now to work on the details, with a view to a Cabinet paper and proper Cabinet authority to proceed . . . .

4.45 – Cabinet – a terrible agenda – Cyprus, Malta, Libya, Egypt – all trouble and mostly blackmail. However, we agreed the White Fish subsidy! PM was very hurt at the attitude of Waterhouse and the 'Suez' group over Cyprus and wanted to call a party meeting and ask for a vote of confidence. I don't myself feel that this is necessary – esp as we aren't going to have a Cyprus settlement! . . . .

. . . . [D]inner (with D) at No 10, for Commonwealth P.M.s followed by a reception. All our old friends – Menzies, Holland etc – were very nice and genial. So, I must say, were the new ones. S Africa (Strydom) and Ceylon are on their best behaviour. Australia have given us a knock, with a great cut in their import quotas. But it can't be helped. They have always been like this. When wool prices are high, they are reckless spenders. As soon as these drop, they cut down imports savagely. So it goes on, alternating from year to year . . . .

30 June

. . . . The long negotiation at Bonn on 'support costs' ended on Thursday and was announced yesterday in the House by Walter Monckton. We got £34m odd – £16m short of the estimate . . . .

1 July (Sunday)

. . . . The dismissals and short time working in the motor industry are causing great excitement.[40] The Socialists have put down a motion wh

---

40. Earlier in the year Standard Motors had laid off 2,600 workers because of automation and falling demand (not least because of Macmillan's decision to raise

amounts to a vote of censure . . . . Of course, one has great sympathy for the workers – more, in a way, than for the managements. These have been prodigal of labour and have bribed everybody else's labour away from them. Naturally, it is hard for men to come down from the very high earnings wh they have had to more normal wage-packets . . . .

2 July

We had a great discussion this morning on 'monetary policy'. The Treasury and the Bank have been working on an examination of the whole problem for some months. I managed to get the Governor to agree to this, and I am glad to say that an excellent job of work has resulted. The report is unanimous. Robert Hall and Compton represented the Treasury. As a result, we have decided *not* to ask for a control of liquidity ratios *at present*. (We retain it as a threat) Nor do we think that a control of advances is practicable. But we *shall* ask the Bankers (1) to go on with the squeeze and (2) to *buy* investments. (2) will not be easy, since it is not really in their interests. But it's far the best way in which they can help us – both to restrict credit and to fund the immense sum [of debt repayment] which falls due in August . . . .

3 July

. . . . Harold Wilson opened the debate[41] with a very clever, but rather too 'party-political' a speech. This allowed me to make, in contrast, a speech on very high, national, non-party lines (Anyway, it was prepared on these lines; for I had a shrewd idea what Wilson would do)

It was a good speech and pleased all the House. I saw many Labour members nodding in agreement to large parts of it. Some of our fellows told me that they thought it was the best speech I had made.

4 July

. . . . At 11.30, the President of the Board of Trade and his officials. After a most difficult argument, we agreed on a line for OEEC in Paris,

the deposit for cars bought on hire purchase to 50%), and on 27 June 1956 BMC suddenly sacked 6,000 without warning.

41. On an opposition vote of censure, generally on economic policy.

the week after next – *if* the Cabinet agree. Our problem is to keep both Paris powers and Commonwealth in play, until we have decided on a definite policy towards Europe.

This is an immensely difficult decision – both from the economic and the political point of view. It might make, or mar, the fortunes of the country and those of the party! . . . .

5 July

A three hours Cabinet – 10.30 to 1.30. We dart about from home to abroad – every question gets more difficult. Cyprus, Ceylon, Middle East: then 'Hanging'; a steel strike; the motor car situation, etc. Eden is a good chairman – very fair and very agreeable, but perhaps he allows too much talk on some matters. His own mind is quick and versatile; but I begin to feel without great depth. He does not 'brood' over things, as Churchill did . . . .

We had a long talk about the Aswan dam at No 10 – For Sec and P.M. I gave the F.S. a line, which he promised to work up into a paper. I feel that we should neither abandon the project in a pet, nor be manoeuvred out of it . . . .

6 July

. . . . The whole press this morning has headlines about the Government's plan to 'freeze' wages. There is an account of what the F.B.I. is going to do, and of further meetings between P.M. and T.U.C. I enquired where all this had come from, only to be told that the Lord Privy Seal had talked about it at his meeting with the Lobby correspondents yesterday. It has fairly put the cat among the pigeons. I have had to get Edward Bridges at work to calm things down. Both F.B.I. *and* T.U.C. are very upset. It is really too stupid of Rab to interfere in this way . . . .

7 July

Travelled to Nottingham, for a fete and a speech at Annesley Hall . . . . This is a long day for 35 minutes of a speech! . . . .

10 July

. . . . I went to HofLords to hear Salisbury wind up the debate on Hanging. It was well done. The Lords rejected the 2nd Reading by a large majority . . . .

12 July

A good meeting of the reconstituted Economic Policy Ctee. We have now 3 major problems – and we haven't a plan for any of them; at least, no complete and coherent plan, since they are all inter-connected. These are – 1) UK and Europe 2) UK and Commonwealth – esp urgent in view of Australia's thrust to abolish our preferences and tear up Ottawa 3) British Farm Policy. Somehow or another we have just got to bring these into some harmony. This was subsequently brought by us (Thorneycroft; Amory etc) to Cabinet, who made sympathetic, but not very helpful noises . . . .

I had a luncheon at No 11 for Bowman, the new head of the Coal Board. He is an examiner and miner's leader. I liked him very much – he seemed shrewd and sensible. Whether he has the mental equipment for the job, I don't know. But perhaps, at the moment, the qualities of leadership and courage wh he undoubtedly has are more important . . . .

13 July

10.30. Mr Governor. We are all very angry with Dr Erhardt [sic], with whom I have had a sharp correspondence. Dr E (German Minister of Economics) has been giving some dangerous interviews about currencies, suggesting (in effect) that sterling *shd* or *will* be devalued, within certain limits. I shall remind him in Paris next week of some of the facts of life. Meanwhile, I have had to issue statements to the press – as from the Treasury – denying all this . . . .

At 4.30, long defence meeting about a) civil defence b) National Service and numbers for Forces. We made very little progress. I have got Civil Defence down to £25–£30m. I want it down to £15[m], and the volunteer forces 'stood down'. On numbers for the Forces, I want to get from the present 740,000 to at most 500,000 by April 1958. The meeting was adjourned.

At 6pm, Menzies and McEwen arrived. The latter is a very tough customer indeed. The Australians have made quite preposterous demands – all take and no give at all. They want to abolish (or whittle away to nothing) UK preferences in Australia, but keep – and improve – their favoured position in our market. We had 2 hours or more of very tough negotiation – and got nowhere at all. I thought Bob Menzies seemed rather ashamed, but McEwen (Country Party) was ruthless and unsmiling . . . .

15 July

Slept till noon. I had been quite exhausted and needed the rest. It is fine to be able to sleep for 12 hours on end or more at the age of 62 . . . .

I went to Chequers, arriving at about 6pm. We discussed a number of things – the PM was alone. On the Assouan dam, we were inclined to hold off and give any money to our friends like Irak. We settled the terms of the Govt announcement on wages and prices. But we thought it best that it shd be made from Downing St – as the previous communiqués had been, instead of being made in the House of Commons. PM wd see the heads of the different groups – T.U.C., F.B.I., and Nationalised Industries and explain the plan to them. I hope this will go all right. I agree with P.M. that it's better than a statement in the House, which will only attract a lot of silly and perhaps damaging supplementaries from the extremists of both sides . . . .

16 July

. . . . Policy Review (Defence) at 5.30. A full dress debate on man-power. I fought desperately for a top limit of 450,000. MofDefence supported me. But when? The services want it to be by 1961. I want it to be by 1958 (when the Conscription Act lapses and must be replaced) If we get (say) 350,000 by regular engagement, how do we get [the] odd 100,000[?] . . . . D and I went to the State Banquet in honour of the King of Iraq. It was quite an agreeable party. I had a long talk with Nuri Pasha, with whom I had made great friends last year at Baghdad . . . .

17 July

Left No 11 at 7am. Got the 8am plane to Paris . . . .

I have to preside over OEEC; and this proved very tiring – because of the heat inside and outside the room. 17 ministers manage to bring so many advisers, and the staff is so large, that there must be nearly 200 people packed into the drawing room of the Chateau de la Monatre . . . .

18 July

Another full day's discussion at the Chateau de la Monatre. Luncheon at the Quai d'Orsay. I sat next to M Pineau (Foreign Minister) whom I did not find at all attractive . . . .

19 July

. . . . I gave a press conference at 3.30.[42] We got the 6pm plane to London. There was a full dress debate on Cyprus – but I did not go in till the end. The division was good – 73 majority. Then we had a defence meeting – 10.15pm till 1am at No 11 . . . . It was supposed to be about Air. The RAF seem unwilling to make any great changes. I still want to abolish Fighter Command (as such) on the ground that UK cannot be defended even from Bombers. When the Russians have guided missiles, it cannot be defended at all. But the Air Marshals are demanding 450 fighters now, and quite a lot *even* when the rocket comes. They have managed to invent a new role for them. In addition, they want further work, at full blast, on ground-to-air missiles. All this adds up to £150m a year, or more. Then we went on to the *size* of the Bomber force. We have got it down from 250 to 200.[43] (They cost ¾m each!) But, of course, the *rate* of production is really more important, from the point of view of relief to industry. The Defence Minister wants 7 a month; I want 5 a month. The only item on which some progress was made was about NATO. P.M. has sent a very good telegram to Eisenhower. It looks as if the Americans are beginning to agree that a 'reappraisal' is necessary. The Germans will be difficult, because of Adenauer's personal position.

20 July

. . . . The Cabinet had a long talk about Hanging – but no conclusion. It is not going to be an easy business. The lesson is that a govt shd never allow 'an open question' or a 'free vote'. (Catholic Emancipation caused enough trouble in its day) . . . .[44]

21 July

. . . . The BMC strike is due to start on Monday. Iain Macleod (Minister of Labour) assures me that he does not intend to interfere. It seems that this is the advice of the T. Union leaders (given in private) From the broader pt of view, if we are to have friction – and I don't see how we can have the great readjustments wh we want without *some* friction – it's best to have it in the motor industry, where stocks

---

42. On the need for trade liberalisation.
43. This figure only relates to the nuclear V-force bombers.
44. Having been an open question in cabinet for a number of years before it was finally passed in 1829.

are good and orders not too good. It doesn't seem likely that the strike will last long, because the tactical position of the unions is weak. It isn't easy to get much enthusiasm for a strike against being dismissed. However, the loyalty of the men is very great, and I have no doubt that even *export* orders from stock will be interfered with. Cars will be declared 'black' and the railways and docks prevented from handling them. There is, however, a general feeling that the management of BMC, esp Sir Leonard Lord, have mismanaged the affair. I don't really know the truth; but it wd seem that the 'public relations' part has *not* been well done.

The Government's position is very bad at present. Nothing has gone well. In the M East, we are still teased by Nasser and Co; the Colonial Empire is breaking up, and many people view with anxiety the attempt to introduce Parly Democracy in such places as Nigeria and the Gold Coast. Cyprus is a running sore. The situation regarding Russia is better, but the defence burden goes on. At home, taxation is very high; the inflation has *not* been mastered; no one knows whether the new Chancellor will be a great success or a crashing failure (least of all, does the Chancellor know!) Meanwhile, we see Germany – free of debt, and making little contribution to defence – seizing the trade of the world from under our noses. The people are puzzled; the party is distracted; Eden gives no real leadership in the House (for he is *not* a HofCommons man – he *never* enters the Smoking Room) altho' he is *popular* and respected in the country as a whole. I find it difficult to know whether this picture is too dark, or how it compares with 1952 (the first year of Churchill's last Government) If my memory is right, we were very unpopular at first. It is unfortunate that Butler is ill and does not seem to have been able to do much in the field either of policy or propaganda. The truth is that we have got the public thoroughly mystified. A year ago Butler cried 'Invest in Success'. Now the P.M. makes speeches (without consulting me) about 'moral peril'. This is rather confusing. Nor can the people be blamed for the suspicion that Butler's optimism last year was for election purposes. I do not think it really was that. It was due to ignorance, lack of proper statistical information, bad Treasury advice, a weak Governor of the Bank, and resistance of the Clearing Bankers. I must try not to drift into the same dangers from the same causes . . . .

I had a talk on the telephone with the Lord Chancellor – about the Hanging Bill. It wd be very dangerous for the Govt to try to go back on the HofCommons 'free vote' or to seem to yield to the pressure of the Party Conference .... I think we shd accept the view that the majority of the House is against hanging .... But we shd say (as responsible for Law and Order) that we must have exceptions – not degrees of murder based on moral culpability but on practical grounds.[45] Therefore, poisoning (tho' in a sense the most culpable) will not attract the capital penalty. But shooting policemen will – just as Treason still does (under the Silverman Bill) ....

The Archbishop of Canterbury (who is a silly, weak, vain and muddle-headed man) wants to have degrees of premeditation the test. This is quite wrong. The test shd be (once you accept the HofCommons general view) what exceptions are required in order to preserve the broad structure of a peaceful society. For instance, Highway robbery and murder may not be as wicked – certainly is not so repulsive – as a long prepared poisoning. But – in the 18th century – Highwaymen were more dangerous and troublesome to the guardians of law and order than poisoners ....

Read and finished *Emma*. There is nothing like Miss Austen's novels for a state of fatigue such as I seem now to reach by the end of every week ....

23 July

.... The first day of the strike at BMC has had a queer result. Nearly ½ the total employees (well over 20,000) have defied the pickets and turned up for work. The next two or three days (before the ordinary fortnight's holiday begins) will be decisive. If these powerful unions (AEU, Transport & General Workers etc) cannot get their men out, it will be a great shock to them. But they will probably be able to boycott BMC production at other factories and their shipments at the docks. The management and the unions seem to have behaved with almost equal folly in this affair ....

25 July

No great change at BMC .... The really important thing from my point of view is that no one has seriously questioned the *need* for economic adjustment and industrial mobility, including big changes of labour force. What is in dispute is the method of doing this. Here I have a greal deal of sympathy with the men. BMC ought not to have

---

45. A Bill with different degrees of murder, restricting the death penalty to certain categories, was passed as the Homicide Act 1957.

stood off 6000 with only a few days notice and without discussion (locally) with the union leaders . . . .

11–1. Policy Review Ctee. Now that (in conformity with the American decision)[46] we have withdrawn our offer to help on the Aswan dam, everybody thinks that we have 'saved' millions and my colleagues are full of schemes for spending these 'savings'. But as we really never had the money wh we were proposing to spend on the dam, this is not a helpful exercise . . . .

I had to give a great dinner party tonight to a number of industrialists who help the Party in one way or another. They had many complaints (chiefly of the sort of *Daily Telegraph* kind) but they seemed to enjoy themselves and stayed till 1am!

26 July

. . . . We have reason to believe that both the unions and the [Engineering] Employers Federation (into whose hands the BMC have at last entrusted the affair)[47] wd like to be helped out of an impossible position. The formula by wh the Minister of Labour might assist this process (without a direct intervention) was discussed and agreed at Cabinet this morning . . . .

Before the Cabinet, (at 10.15) PM had asked a few of us to meet to discuss the position of himself and his party. There were present, Salisbury; Ld Chancellor; Chief Whip; Oliver Poole (Chairman of Party) and myself. (Butler is still away, ill) It was a curious discussion, turning almost entirely on the *Daily Telegraph*, and the vendetta wh Pamela Berry (and Editor, Colin Coote) are carrying on against P.M. It's all very unfortunate; Clarissa has tried to 'make up' the blood row wh they had some time ago, but the Lady Pamela is obdurate . . . .

27 July

Nasser has declared his intention to 'nationalise' – that is, seize, the Suez Canal Company. He offers 'compensation at market prices for the shares'. He will 'pay for the Aswan dam from the profits of the Canal'. The speech is very truculent – an Asiatic Mussolini, full of insult and abuse of US and UK. P.M. rang me early and we met just before 11am to agree a short factual statement to be made (it's a

---

46. On 19 July 1956.
47. The dispute finally ended on 10 August 1956 after BMC offered modest compensation and consultation on future redundancies.

Friday) immediately after Prayers. This was all arranged; Gaitskell made polite noises, and there was no great trouble.

The Cabinet went into immediate session and did not break up till after one o'clock. The unanimous view of the Cabinet was in favour of strong and resolute action. As can be imagined, this meant very heavy work for all of us. I spent a hectic afternoon and evening at the Treasury, chiefly on the question of the assets of the Suez Canal Company; the assets of Egyptian Govt and commercial assets in London; and the instructions to be given to shipowners about the payment of dues. In addition, the P.M. has appointed a 'Suez' Ctee of the Cabinet – himself, Salisbury, Home, and myself – with other ministers turning up as required. We met for 2 hours, 7.15–9.15 and settled up a lot of matters. I went off to Pratt's Club to get some food. At 10pm one of the Treasury young men came to me there, with the 'Freezing Orders' to sign – they will be effective from midnight . . . .

Saturday 28 July
I was to have gone to Barnstaple today, to make a speech at a garden fete. Nasser at least saved me from that . . . .

Sunday 29 July
There was so much work to be done that I did not go to Church. I stayed in bed working till luncheon. Maurice is back from his long cure in Switzerland. He looks very well and has put on weight . . . . There was last night and all through today the most violent gale that I ever remember. The wind was terrific and sustained. In addition, there were from time to time violent gusts, which did great damage. We have cut a number of trees in the garden – as well as limbs off many trees. One branch fell on the cottage in the drive, doing some damage to the roof. The bird cherry (near the pond) was split in half. A tall larch – below the pond – was uprooted. A good deal of damage was done to the big oak tree in the yew circle (in front of the house) However, it might have been much worse . . . .

30 July
Bob Murphy arrived yesterday. The Suez Committee met and heard the For Secy's account of the first talk. It is clear that the Americans are going to 'restrain' us all they can. I lunched at No 10 – Bob Murphy, Mr Foster (American chargé) M Pineau (French Foreign Minister) For Secy, Harold Caccia. We had a good talk, and the

P.M. did his part very well. The French are absolutely solid with us, and together we did our best to frighten Murphy all we could . . . . We gave him the impression that our military expedition to Egypt was about to sail. (It will take at least 6 weeks to prepare it, in fact)

31 July

It seems that we have succeeded in thoroughly alarming Murphy. He must have reported in the sense wh we wanted, and Foster Dulles is now coming over post-haste. This is a very good development. The chief problem is how to fill up the time before our striking force can be got ready. Cabinet met at 10.30 and despatched a good deal of routine business, in addition to Suez. Our plan seems to be developing in favour of calling a conference of powers, in order to concoct a plan for the International control of the Canal. But we must begin to take military measures, against any situation wh may develop . . . .

. . . . Dined with Oliver Poole (Chairman of Party in succession to Lord Woolton) He is an able man and a shrewd man. But he has none of the personal qualities wh Ld W had. I think P.M. took a risk in choosing him – like most Conservative leaders nowadays he is a divorcé – and I fear that he will not succeed in getting the same spirit into the party as W did. All the same, he *is* able and absolutely devoted to his task. He is not so perturbed about the *D.T.* and the general campaign agst the Govt as some people are. He admits that it has injured the party *organisation* (wh depends on the 'middle classes' and the readers of the *D.T.*) but he does not think this will a) be permanent b) affect the actual voters.

1 August

. . . . I ought to record that Foster Dulles; the American ambassador; and Bob Murphy all came to see me at Downing St at 6.30. We had an hour's talk. I told Foster, as plainly as I could, that we just could not afford to lose this game. It was a question not of honour only but of survival. We must either get Nasser out by diplomacy or by force. There was no other choice for us. I think he was quite alarmed; for he had hoped to find me less extreme, I think. We *must* keep the Americans really frightened. They must not be allowed any illusion. Then they will help us to get what we want, without the necessity for force. But we must have a) international control of the Canal b) humiliation and collapse of Nasser . . . .

2 August

.... P.M..... spoke – very well indeed – about the whole Canal problem. He could give the House no information – because the 3 Power Conference[48] was still sitting. But he gave a general impression of calm, and determination, wh impressed the House. Gaitskell followed, with quite a helpful speech – except the last part, wh was against the use of force and will weaken the broad position. Later on (I was told) Herbert Morrison made a very good speech, very helpful to the Govt and the national interest.

The Cabinet met again at 5.30 and heard an account from the For Secy of the start of the Tripartite negotiations. It looks like complete agreement and quite a good communiqué. This will a) condemn Nasser b) support international control c) approve a conference of 24 powers in London. (8 will represent 1888 signatories[49] – 8 major users – 8 'pattern of trade' claimants) On the whole, this seems a good result. The Americans have certainly moved a long way. After this, the 'Egypt' Ctee met to discuss the military plan. This was approved, in broad terms. It is not going to be an easy job, and I was rather concerned about the small force available to make the assault, and the extreme difficulty we shall be in for exploiting the position after a landing . . . .

3 August

Cabinet at 11am. The rest of the Cabinet (who are not members of the Egypt Ctee) are naturally a little anxious at so much being done, so quickly and over so wide a field. P.M. gave a broad report and got general approval for all that had been done. After Cabinet, 'Egypt' Committee (I had called it 'Suez' Ctee, but this, it seems, is wrong) sat on. The chief questions were 1) Trade – and the Blockade 2) Canal dues 3) Requisitioning of ships 4) Press. On the first, I had to report a very unpleasant visit wh I had had from the Deputy Chairman and General Manager of the Westminster Bank at 10.30 that morning. They were in doubt as to whether they could pay out to the Suez Canal Company (the legitimate one) moneys in their a/c. I asked 'why not?' Because, they said, it was possible that a court wd hold that Nasser's action was justified and that the money now belonged to the new nationalised authority. I was so angry with them that I turned in

---

48. Britain, the US and France.
49. In the Constantinople Convention of 1888 nine powers undertook to keep the canal open to all shipping and never to blockade it.

fury on them and called them harsh names. They went away saddened; but they promised to do what seemed obviously right and take a chance. They actually had the impudence to ask for an 'indemnity' from the Treasury. I said that I wd much rather issue a decree to nationalise the Westminster Bank. I told this story with particular glee to the Cabinet, because P.M. used to be a director of the Westminster Bank. But I was really shocked by their behaviour. Poor Mr Stirling (the Deputy Chairman) was ashamed; but the manager (whose name I forget) was brazen. On the larger trade question, we have not yet got a general economic blockade (for instance by Germany, Belgium etc) and unless we can get these countries to block Egyptian credits, all the trade will go to them. But I have asked for their help, and we must wait a day or two longer before we decide. Meanwhile, all our credits (and the French) are frozen.

On the second question, it is still quite uncertain what is happening. But it seems as if the Egyptians are still unwilling to refuse to recognise payments in London or Paris, drawn in favour of the old Company, which are of course made into the blocked accounts. But the Americans pay in Cairo (and therefore Nasser gets the control of the money, even if in the a/c of the old company) or pay cash. So do some of our smaller companies. We shall allow this to continue, because it gets the ships through, *without abandoning our position*. (This the Westminster Bank are unable to understand) I had a further meeting later in the day with the Minister of Transport and his people. They think there may be no change. One ship was challenged, but when the master stood firm and said that the dues had been paid in the usual way, the Egyptian authorities climbed down.

On the third question, I am very anxious. The military operations contemplated will, of course, need a lot of shipping. It's on this that the money will go. But I am pressing the Admiralty to let us have all the ships (carriers, old cruisers etc) which they can find. It's tragic having to requisition liners at the height of the tourist season! The fourth problem – the press – is very difficult. We have no censorship powers (these have gone in the general holocaust of wartime regulations) and there is no way of stopping the most detailed accounts of shipping, troop movements and the rest. Appeal to the participation of editors was suggested, and P.M. is to see the leading ones. But this will not deal with the agencies – A.P., U.P., etc. It was decided that Ld Salisbury and I shd see Ian Jacob (B.B.C.) and make an appeal to him. (This we did at 5pm – he was sympathetic, but said that while he could avoid speculation as to the character of operations, 'news' was sacred, and must be reported) Personally, I doubt if we shall get through all this without taking back the old war powers. Before the Egypt Ctee separated, a memorandum was read which I had sent to the P.M. about Israel. I feel that he *must* make use of Israel against Egypt, if the military operation is actually undertaken. The C.I.G.S. feels the same and was very grateful. Of course, there is great danger in this. But if we make no contact with Israel and have no understanding with them, they will probably attack Jordan – which really *will* be embarrassing. Nuri Pasha could not stand that; but I don't believe he wd feel the same about an Israel attack on Egypt . . . .[50]

At 5pm Lord S and I saw Jacob. After that, we had a conference with Gladwyn Jebb and a number of others on a paper wh Jebb had prepared. We have got to get a properly understood arrangement with the French – in writing – as to what is the purpose of the expedition; what contributions – military and financial – we are each to make; the command, by land, sea, and air. We have also to be agreed as to what we are to do *after* the operation is (we hope) successful. This raises a large number of most difficult questions. We don't want to get landed in a long and expensive military occupation. We would much prefer to set up a friendly Govt. Then we have to agree about how the Canal is to be worked *before* the international regime can be brought into being . . . .

I went to dinner with Foreign Secretary at Carlton Gardens. He was tired, but quite cheerful. We did some work on the form of the 'resolution' which we want to 'railroad' (with Dulles' help) through the Conference when it meets. This must *not* be too long (or there will be interminable argument) but it must get in all the salient points, so that we can base the Anglo-French ultimatum to Egypt upon it.

For Secy has had a rough time but has got through well. He is very bitter about the P.M.'s interference, in small as well as in large issues. P.M. invited himself to the French dinner at the Embassy (where he wasn't wanted and held up for 2 hours what was intended to be a business dinner) simply out of vanity and to get photographed. F.S. also feels that P.M. has talked too much in the HofC. But I think he

---

50. It would be embarrassing both because of Britain's treaty obligations to Jordan and the likely effect on Britain's closest ally in the Middle East, Iraq. However, the worrying build-up of tensions on the Israeli–Jordan border seems to have been a ruse to deceive the Egyptians about Israeli intentions.

takes it (as we all do) in good part. Eden will never play Asquith to another man's Grey.[51] He is too much of a prima donna himself . . . .

5 August (Sunday)

I had a talk with Harold Watkinson (Transport) No change on the canal. Nasser has obviously decided not to press the question of 'dues' for the moment. H.W. tells me that only about 3 out of 40–50 ships are paying to Egyptian banks. (This goes for UK) He also gave me better news about requisitioned transport. He hopes to do much more than he expected with air transport, and so spare the liners.

. . . . I went to dinner with Churchill, at Chartwell . . . . C had been shown the plan by the P.M. He asked me what I thought of it. I said that unless we brought in Israel, I didn't think it cd be done. To capture Port Said with a first wave of 400 men; to spend nearly 9 days before a proper 'build-up' or deployment cd be made; to have to go down 30 miles or so of the causeway before ground for deployment cd be reached, all this seemed to me quite hopeless. Besides, what wd we do when we got there? We had had 80000 men on the canal, and yet had been unable to do anything. Surely, if we landed we must seek out the Egyptian forces; destroy them; and bring down Nasser's Govt. Churchill seemed to agree with all this . . . . At 11.30pm Christopher [Soames] rang up, to say that Churchill had decided to go to Chequers tomorrow, and put all the results of our talk and his own thoughts before Eden. Now the fat will be in the fire!

6 August

. . . . Christopher Soames came to luncheon. He told me a good deal about the air side of the plan and was rather worried about some aspects of it. We talked about the general idea, and he agreed that we shd try to seize Alexandria, get a proper 'build-up' in a reasonable time; march on Cairo and destroy the Nasser regime. I am more and more convinced that if we *have* to do a military operation at all, this is the only one that makes any sense at all. Accordingly, I wrote a paper setting all this out, for circulation to the Egypt Committee . . . .

Started to read G Eliot. If I *have* ever read this (almost forgotten) author, I have certainly forgotten too! Read 'Scenes from Clerical Life' – a very queer mixture. The stories are, in a way, moving and hold the

---

51. Sir Edward Grey was Foreign Secretary 1905–16 under H. H. Asquith (Prime Minister 1908–16).

attention. But all the philosophy, and religious verbiage, and strangely dated language (much more completely out of harmony with modern writing than 18th or even 17th century style) make it all very odd reading today.

I shall go on to *Middlemarch*. It will be restful, during the crisis. 3 long volumes of Victorianism should help.

7 August

. . . . The Egypt Ctee met at 3pm. As I expected, the P.M. was in a very bad mood. He had refused to allow my paper to be circulated to the committee, or to the Chiefs of Staff. So I asked that it shd be shewn at least to Cabinet ministers who were on the Committee. This was done. But by a very foolish and petty decision of this strangely sensitive man, copies were not sent to service ministers or to the Chiefs. (However, the Minister of Defence had of course had copies made for them already!)

I discovered later that the source of the trouble was the Churchill visit. Eden no doubt thought that I was conspiring with C against him. After the meeting (which was a very long one) I had it out with him and he was (as he always is) very charming and relaxed about the whole affair. I had arranged many days ago, to go to dine with C, who likes company. I was horrified at the idea that C wd go over to Chequers. Of course, if P.M. had not already discussed the whole plan with C last week, I wd not have said a word. All the same, it *is* a bad plan. P.M. was quite happy in the end about all this, and inclined to agree with my views. I especially urged on him the need to appoint a Supreme Field Commander at once. The planning wd be far better done by those who had to carry it out . . . .

8 August

Morning at Treasury – Minister of Supply came in, about various air projects. We spend very large sums on research and development. We must really make some economies somewhere! What all this Egypt thing is going to cost, one can't guess . . . .

P.M. did a broadcast *and* T.V. at 10pm about the Suez crisis. *This could not have been better done.* It was fair, moderate, convincing and firm. I'm sure it will have a splendid effect, at home and abroad – esp in US. The Liberal and Socialist press here is beginning to get pretty flabby. 'No force, whatever happens'. 'Refer to United Nations' and so on. I have no doubt that the week-end intellectuals (*Economist, New*

Statesman, Observer etc) will be just as bad. So PM's effort is really a blessing, for it will steady moderate opinion. The *Times* has been excellent throughout. Curiously enough, the 'gutter' press (*Mirror* and *Sketch*) have been pretty good. It's the Liberal intellectual who is *always* against his country.

9 August

Egypt Committee sat all the morning; the usual questions, covering a very wide field (but *not* military – here we await a *new* plan, which is now being prepared. It seems that my paper has sunk the old plan, without trace – also, without a word being said about it, to me or anyone else!) . . . .

. . . . If Nasser accepts any plan wh may emerge from the Conference, well and good. If he turns it down flat, we may be able to justify our use of force. (Even so, we need a popular *'casus belli'* – a sort of Jenkins Ear)[52] But if the answer is equivocal? How are we to negotiate, with our invading armada at sea? . . . .

10 August

. . . . Among minor items, I am anxious to get on with a scheme for Petrol Rationing. A full blown scheme, with ration books, will take 3 months to organise. But an interim scheme would help us, from every point of view.

10.30–1.15. A full meeting of 'Egypt' Committee, with Chiefs of Staff – and *maps*! The original plan of landing at Port Said and seizing the Canal (in due course) and staying on it, is utterly and silently abandoned! The plan is now to seize Alexandria (they said last week that this was impossible owing to the powerful defences – now they think it quite feasible) and march on Cairo, to destroy Nasser! This plan was approved. It has two immense advantages, in addition to it being the only way to obtain our purpose quickly. We need *not* stimulate the Israelites to do more than make faces. We need *not* invade Egypt from Libya. On the contrary, we shall take the armoured division by *sea* to Alexandria, when the build-up begins . . . .

I finished off all my Treasury and other business by about 6. P.M. very kindly sent me a message to say that he hoped I wd go to Bolton

---

52. Robert Jenkins, a merchant captain, claimed that his ear had been cut off by Spanish coastguards near Jamaica in 1731, a claim that was used to justify the War of Jenkins' Ear launched eight years later.

Abbey for at least a few days at the beginning of next week, since nothing much more will happen till the Conference starts . . . .

16 August

My 3 days holiday has done me good . . . . It's rather sad, in a way, for me to feel that I gave up the F.O. and am not *directly* responsible. But the P.M. and F.S. seem to rely a good deal on the guidance of the 'Egypt' Ctee . . . . I feel that the financial terms offered to Egypt shd be very favourable – *if*, but only if, Nasser accepts International control of the Canal in its fullest sense.

18 August

The Conference has gone very well so far.[53] Dulles's opening speech was admirable; the general tone of all the speeches was good. Even the Russians were not very intemperate . . . .

Foster told us of his talk with the Russians. They will try to get us to accept nationalisation, with a sort of International Advisory Ctee. This is, of course, useless for us. It wd be a triumph for Nasser. But Foster didn't think the Russians wd press things to extremes.

All the time, the problem remains – how do we act if Nasser refuses and on what 'pretext' or on what 'principle' can we base a *casus belli*. How do we get from the Conference leg to the use of force? British opinion is uncertain – altho' some of the press are very firm. But it remains a tricky operation. Yet, if Nasser 'gets away with it', we are done for. The whole Arab world will despise us. Nuri and our friends will fall. It may well be the end of British influence and strength for ever. So, in the last resort, we must use force and defy opinion, here and overseas. I made this quite clear to Foster who really agreed with our position. But he hopes (and he may be right) that Nasser will have to yield – in due course. This again brings up the frightful problem of how to keep a military expedition, brought together at huge cost, 'all dressed up and nowhere to go'.

Mr Governor tells me that we shall have a very big pressure on sterling, but he believes that we can hold out . . . .

19 August (Sunday)

D and I motored to Hatfield for luncheon. Foster Dulles and Janet; Mr and Mrs Dillon; Winthrop Aldrich; Ld and Lady Salisbury . . . .

---

53. It opened on 16 August.

. . . . Bobbety [Salisbury] and I both got the impression that Foster was getting rather 'sticky'. He won't help us any more with economic sanctions etc. I cannot help feeling that he really wants us to 'go it alone' and has been trying to help us by creating the right atmosphere . . . .

20 August

10.30. Bob Menzies, PM of Australia, called at Treasury. He is getting much firmer in his attitude. (But the Canadians are very wet.) They say that if we use force we shall disrupt the United Nations and the Commonwealth) New Zealand Govt have been splendid from the start. I asked Bob if his govt wd sell us some gold – say £20m. He thought they wd agree. On our side, we shall allow them to try to raise £20m odd of sterling loans on the London market.

11.30. Egypt Ctee. The F.S. gave us the latest news. Pakistan, Iran, with Turkey, want to make some amendments in the Dulles draft. These are quite unacceptable. Whether consciously or not, they are putting forward merely a variant of the Russian formula.

. . . . There are a number of ways in which we cd bring pressure on Nasser – short of force. These must be studied. 1) We could no longer encourage the employees of the Company to stay. The Europeans are anxious to leave 2) We could see to it that Nasser got no dues 3) We could start to move war material out of our base. But the problem still remains – how legally, as well as morally (or how near to legally) – can we take action, even in view of the declaration. Shall we use UN machinery, if only to be able to say that we have appealed to it (Russia wd of course 'veto' almost any resolution) Then there is the difficult question of the recall of Parlt . . . .

21 August

Saw John Foster K.C. (who represents the *old* Company) The legal intricacies of this affair are going to be dreadful. Everyone is claiming money, and wanting a Treasury indemnity! I am taking a very firm line.

Cabinet at 11.30 – Mr Menzies attended. There was rather a mixed bag of business, but Suez and Cyprus filled the bill. The EOKA terrorists have called off the fight.[54] The left wing papers says it's

---

54. The suspension of violence 'in order to facilitate a settlement' proved only temporary.

because they have suddenly been converted and drunk the milk of human kindness in large gulps. A more reasonable view is that Sir J Harding is getting on top of them. We discussed – and agreed – a document in principle about surrender terms . . . .

22 August

. . . . At 11.30 the Egypt Ctee met. It was decided to postpone D day by 4 days. This allows us to put off certain things (like photographing Egyptian ports from the air) until the Conference is finished. The question of certain French ships sailing was put off also for a day or two . . . . It seems now that the signatories to the declaration (17 or 18)[55] can be persuaded to convey it to Nasser through a committee, of wh Menzies is to be chairman. I urged P.M. to bring all possible pressure to get Dulles to be the US member of the committee of 5 (Norway or Sweden; Pakistan; Ethiopia are the others) Even if Dulles has to appoint a substitute for any actual talks, it wd help if he were the titular member . . . . The Admiralty have been very tiresome about the 2 Egyptian frigates. I took a very strong line about this, and I think I have now persuaded P.M. to tell the Admiralty that some physical defects must be found – or made – to prevent them sailing . . . .[56]

23 August

. . . . Egypt Ctee met at 11.30. It looks as if Dulles will now serve – at least formally – on the Ctee of 5. Menzies will be chairman. We decided to let the French ships start from Marseilles. The 'cover plan' can be Algiers, but they will go to Cyprus. Cabinet met at 12. Menzies was present. I put forward [a] Treasury paper about 'compensation' or rather 'lease' of canal etc for Egypt, which shows how attractive the financial terms to Egypt can be. P.M. thought this should be used in any talks with Nasser (if they take place) and also made public. I had to explain that we must get French and American agreement. This was decided upon, and Menzies was very keen on it. We then discussed the pilots. I put forward the plan that Menzies (as chairman of the Ctee)

---

55. The signatories calling for international control were Australia, Denmark, Ethiopia, France, Iran, Italy, Japan, the Netherlands, New Zealand, Norway, Pakistan, Portugal, Spain, Sweden, Turkey, the UK, the US and West Germany.
56. Presumably a reference to the two Z class destroyers, HMS *Wessex* and HMS *Mynges*, sold by the Royal Navy to the Egyptians in 1955, which were being refitted for delivery.

should make it known publicly a) that British, French and other Governments had asked their nationals employed on canal to stay during Conference, as a public duty b) that he and the rest of Ctee hoped they wd stay till Nasser's reply was known. If he refuses all agreement, no further pressure shd be put on them to stay. This was agreed . . . .

24 August

. . . . The Egypt Ctee met at 12 noon. The P.M. told us of his talk with Foster Dulles this morning . . . . He told D that we had no alternative, if we cd not get our way by diplomatic pressure, but [had] to resort to force. The French were equally determined – altho' they really had less at risk than we had. In the long run, they cd feed themselves. Without oil and the profits of oil, we cd not exist. Dulles had not seemed shocked . . . . Dulles had expressed the view that quite a good resolution, in favour of the declaration, could be 'rail-roaded' through the UN Security Council. No very definite conclusion was reached, except not to call Parlt today. (5 days notice are required) Minister of Defence raised the general question. Could we use force? Would British public opinion support us? Of course, if an 'incident' took place, that wd be the way out. P.M. – strongly supported by me and Salisbury – and Home – took the view that we had no alternative. We must secure the defeat of Nasser, by one method or another. If not, we shd rot away. I was left with the impression that Butler was uncertain, altho' he agreed that we must achieve our purpose somehow. He wanted more time, so as to shew that every possible method had been tried, before the final decision to use force. I argued that if D day was postponed too often and too late, it wd never happen. We must be resolved. The Chief Whip was pretty sure about the party, tho' there might be some weaker brethren. Walter Monckton was calm, but obviously distressed . . . .

25 August

. . . . I am working on an economic appreciation of the position, esp from the oil point of view, which is vital. The truth is that we are caught in a terrible dilemma. If we take strong action agst Egypt, and as a result the Canal is closed, the pipe-lines to the Levant are cut, the Persian Gulf revolts and oil production is stopped – then UK and Western Europe have 'had it'. They get 80–90% of their oil supplies from M East. If we suffer a diplomatic defeat: if Nasser 'gets away with it', if Nuri falls, and the M East countries, in a ferment, 'nationalise oil' and so forth, we have equally 'had it'. What then are we to do? It seems clear that we shall take the only chance we have – to take strong action, and hope that thereby our friends in M East will stand, our enemies fall, and the oil be saved. But it is a tremendous decision . . . .

26 August

Poor Dorothy had to take Catherine (Amery) to the hospital in the middle of the night. Julian went with her – so I am alone here, and waiting for news . . . . It is very anxious waiting – for the date is a month too soon and it will be a great strain on her and the babies . . . .

12 noon. D has just rung to say that Catherine's babies have been safely born – a boy and a girl. This splendid news I have given to Louise Amery (the oldest child) to Nannie and the cook and the housemaid and everyone around . . . .

27 August

. . . . The Egypt Ctee met at 6pm. Text of a proposed telegram from PM to US President was approved. It will be followed by a detailed request for further American help, on the question of canal dues and the question of further 'blocking' of Egyptian dollar balances. This will be drafted by Treasury and FO and go through the ambassador. We then discussed, in a F.O. paper, the arguments for and against going to United Nations – Security Council, *before* any forceful action was taken. On the whole, ministers were inclined to favour going to Security Council, 'for the look of the thing'. But it must not mean intolerable delays . . . .

28 August

The Cabinet met at 11. The chief purpose was to give to all those not in the Egypt Ctee, an 'inside story' of what was happening. On the whole, ministers were pretty strong – but all seemed to like the idea of going to the United Nations, if at all possible . . . . Lord President (Salisbury) referred to the 'progressive decline' wh might take place if we did not make a stand. But he was in favour of going to the Security Council, if the Americans wd give us full support. But he added that people seemed to forget that U.N. ought to preserve justice as well as peace. Ld Chancellor (Kilmuir) said the phrase 'force is the last resort' ought to be pressed home. a) It *is* a resort b) the word 'last' means that we must be sure to choose fairly and honourably the point at wh it does arise . . . .

. . . . Another Trinidad oil co [TPD] is for sale and some Americans want to buy! This is hardly the moment, and there will be a great row. I am going to try to persuade Shell to buy . . . .

29 August

I held a press conference this afternoon at the Treasury. The subject was partly the economic effects of the Suez crisis, but mainly the dangers of inflation and a further plea for wage and price stability . . . . I sent a copy to Tewson (Secy of TUC) who was rather alarmed at such a clear appeal to the Congress (which is just about to meet) I made some alterations to help his point of view. Tewson is a good fellow, but a weak and rather timid character . . . .

P.M. telephoned late. Nasser has now accepted a meeting [with Menzies] for Monday Sept 3rd. These delays are really intolerable. Nasser's proposal is put forward in rather an impertinent way. This, combined with the arrest of British subjects on charges of 'espionage', makes me feel that he is getting more and more truculent . . . .

3 September

Back to work. Things actually look pretty grim. On the Home Front, the TUC leaders – out of timidity, not spite – have decided to turn down my appeal . . . . They have attacked the Govt for abandoning 'planning'. This is really rather a battle of words, because (except for the building control) we operate a pretty stringent system of general and even particular planning controls. C.I.C. (wh means that you can't borrow £10,000 without my permission) Hire Purchase; Import licensing; the Credit Squeeze and all the rest . . . . Meanwhile, the Clyde strike looks like being long and bitter. Yet – paradoxically – it's not about wages at all. It's about a guaranteed weekly wage which is far *below* average piece-rate earnings. This makes me think that some way out of our troubles may be found along the line of what American unions call 'fringe benefits'. These wd cost less than average wage increases . . . .

4 September

The press this morning – *Daily Mirror*, *Herald*, *Chronicle* etc are very violent. The PM is accused of deceiving the nation, and of preparing a military expedition wh he has determined to use, at all costs. The

President has sent a very hesitating and defeatist message, urging caution and appeasement. Meanwhile, Menzies seems to be making little progress. There is to be a meeting at 6pm this evening of leading ministers.

Internally the announcement of our loss of \$120m on the reserves comes out this afternoon. It will be a shock to the market. I hope it will also be a shock to the trade unions.

M Spaak came to luncheon and we had a private talk first about Suez. He urges us to be quite firm and not shrink from force if Nasser is obdurate. We then had a long talk (with a host of officials) about OEEC, the Messina plan and the possibility of British association (what we call Plan G) . . . .[57]

6–8.30pm. A long meeting of the Egypt Ctee . . . .

. . . . It was agreed that we shd take the initiative, and if Nasser's reply were to be unsatisfactory, we shd go to the Security Council. Then came the critical problem – the military expedition: I put the problem in this way. There are 3 possible courses. 1) To go to war without going to UN. 2) To go to UN, but continue all the preparations, and face the accusations that we are preparing an invasion. 3) To postpone the final arrangements for the invasion until after UN fails, accepting a further delay of 3 weeks *after* U.N. There was a general agreement that 1) was impossible, in view of public opinion at home and overseas. It was agreed that 3) was unacceptable, because of a) the anti-war pressure that wd build up b) the increasing Russian aid to Egypt of wh we have evidence, wh will make the operation dangerous if we leave it too long. So 2) was clearly the only possible course – on the assumption that we are decided not to let Nasser 'get away with it'. Of course, there is quite another problem which we may have to face – a counter-proposal by Nasser wh is not obviously a negative and will seem to many a reasonable compromise . . . .

5 September

10–1. An excellent meeting of Economic Policy Ctee (over which I preside) to discuss Plan G, before it finally comes to Cabinet. To my surprise, all ministers present (Thorneycroft, Macleod, Heathcoat-Amory, Eccles) were enthusiastic for this great venture. Only Home

---

57. The British plan for a European Free Trade Area (excluding trade in foodstuffs) that would incorporate the Messina Six and other OEEC countries.

(Commonwealth Secy) and David Lloyd (for Colonial Office) rather doubtful. It was an excellent discussion, first on the merits and demerits of the policy; second, on the chances of being able to sell it to the Commonwealth and to the British people. I was much impressed by the combination of knowledge and enthusiasm of these younger ministers. I lunched after with Eccles and Macleod and we continued the talk. But I cannot disguise from myself that it will in fact be very difficult to persuade the whole Cabinet and very hard to sell to the Party and the People . . . .

6 September

The TU Conference has gone very badly so far as 'Wages and Prices' are concerned. Altho' Beard made a good speech on the general debate and Heywood quite a good speech in opening the Economic debates, Cousins (Transport & General Workers) was very violent. He attacked me rather savagely; he attacked the Tory Government; he attacked the Tory Party, and declared that they would have nothing whatever to do with any form of restraint. It should be 'free for all'. Curiously, he made no reply to my arguments about profits; he made no pretence that my plateau *could* not be reached.[58] He said that he and the unions were determined to push us all off it. It was obviously a very effective political speech. Whether it will please the T.U. leaders as a whole, remains to be seen. I think many of them already dislike Cousins, and their attitude will be intensified by this speech. Nor do I think it will help the Labour Party in the country. All elections are really governed by the 'moderate' voter. This outburst will frighten and annoy the 'middle of the road' characters.

Cabinet at 11. The whole discussion was about Suez etc. The chief purpose was to put the rest of the Cabinet in the picture. The general feeling was pretty solid, altho' everyone realises how serious are the decisions which they are asked to take. Judging from Menzies' last telegram, Nasser will prove quite intransigeant. This is anyway better than a delusive show of moderation or a sham compromise proposal . . . .

Dined with Percy Mills – or he with me – at Bucks Club. He thought a conflict on wages inevitable this winter. The Engineers Employers would (he thought) stand firm this time.

---

58. A reference to Macmillan's goal of sustained price stability.

7 September

According to the Press (I have not yet seen the latest telegrams) the Suez talks have broken down. Some say that Dulles is to fly to London again, 'to save peace'. The P.M. has sent a splendid reply to the President, the text of wh was shewn yesterday to the Cabinet.

Saw Hopwood (Shell) and I think we may find a way to keep TPD – at least for the present. I shall have to try it on ministers this afternoon.

Egypt Ctee met at 2.45pm. There was a large and varied agenda – the position of the pilots, who will not want to stay after the failure of the Menzies mission; the new Dulles plan for payment of dues and even operation of the canal by a new organisation;[59] evacuations of British subjects from Egypt and Jordan; the oil problem at home if the canal is closed for any length of time, and other questions of importance. But the most vital of all was the discussion of a new plan wh General Keightley has proposed, at least in embryo, and which has (if it will work) great advantages in flexibility and from the political point of view over the plan wh at present holds the field. It would rely on the forces now assembled in Malta and Cyprus. It would avoid starting the expedition on a fixed date and save a lot of transports (including ocean liners) being requisitioned for the 'build-up' of 5 or 6 divisions (including the 2 French divisions) It was agreed that General K[eightley] and the Chiefs of Staff shd continue their study of this new plan,[60] with a view to a final decision on Monday. One can only hope that this new plan will prove to be feasible, for on the face of it, there are many obvious advantages. Ministers still seem very determined and there is no sign of weakness among those at the Ctee (PM, Ld P, Ld Privy Seal, Colonial Secy, President Bd of Trade, Minister of Defence, Minister of Transport and the 3 Service Ministers) . . . .

9 September

. . . . The President has sent a reply to the P.M. It isn't too bad. The more we can persuade them of our determination to risk everything in

---

59. This was the Suez Canal Users' Association, to be based in Rome and organize its own pilots and take dues, out of which some payment to Egypt would be made.

60. This new plan, Musketeer Revise, envisaged air assaults on military and economic targets along with landings at Port Said to secure the canal. The assault on Alexandria was now deemed to be too inflexible and likely to cause too much loss of life and devastation.

order to beat Nasser, the more help we shall get from them. We shall
be ruined either way; but we shall be more inevitably and finally ruined
if we are humiliated . . . .

10 September
. . . . The financial and economic outlook is very bad. The great
problem remains – what will make the Americans willing to give us
the maximum economic and financial aid? Will it be by conforming
to their wishes or by 'going it alone'. It's a nice point. How I wish
the Presidential election were safely over! . . . .

. . . . The Americans have made proposals for switching us oil from
the Gulf. But it will be dollar oil? Who is going to pay for it?

A long meeting of the Egypt Ctee. More Dulles proposals – on the
'User Club' (CUSA he has christened it) But the scheme is rather
woolly and we *must* have something firm for the House on Wednesday . . . . There was then a long discussion about United Nations.
British public opinion (it is said) demands some reference to U.N. At
present, we are all right, because everything that we have done is in
accordance with Article 33.[61] But force? That is a different matter.
This question will be asked – and must be answered – in the debate.
Dulles will not now undertake to 'railroad' a resolution through the
Security Council. He cannot even promise to vote against a tiresome
addendum, which wd certainly be moved by Russia or Yugoslavia,
deploring the use of force. He might abstain. This makes it very
dangerous for us. To use force *without* going to the Security Council
is really almost better than to use it *after* the Council has passed a
resolution against it. There has been a plan of merely writing a letter
to the President to acquaint him of the situation. But this doesn't seem
a very good plan. It puts the question in the UN court, and leaves the
initiative rather perilously with our critics or enemies . . . .

The French were due to arrive at 6pm – Menzies later tonight. Ld
Pres, Ld Chancellor, and Ld Privy Seal came (at PM's request) to help
me draft the critical passage for P.M.'s speech on the U.N. question.
This we did, and finished by 8pm . . . .

12 September
Telegrams to and from Washington have been pouring out and in

---

61. The UN Charter's Article 33 requires parties to an international dispute to first of
all seek a solution by peaceful means.

during the last 24 hours with increasing intensity. P.M. telephoned me early this morning. The alternatives are still there (1) announce in the debate this afternoon that we are going to take the matter immediately to the Security Council (2) announce the formation of the Users' Club (CUSA) The Americans (who have been rather difficult in the latest exchanges) are against (1) and for (2). This will, of course, make trouble for us in Parlt. But it's worth while, to go for (2) now, since American support is so important – esp in the financial field. So this was agreed at a meeting at No 10 at 11am and the speech was so designed as to be equivocal on (1). There was a good deal of confusion over a phrase in one of Dulles' telegrams, where he spoke of 'compensation' to be paid by the 'Users' Club' to Egypt. This made British ministers very indignant – until I explained to them that in America compensation refers to salary, wages, royalties etc. It does not mean (as in English) payment in respect of a past injury by one party to another, but to present and continuing services from one party to another. This wd be quite reasonable for CUSA to pay, if Egypt provides services etc and the use of the canal for the new organisation. Of course, the whole concept is rather strange, and I cannot see how the Egyptians can possible allow the Users' Club to function.

P.M. made an admirable speech;[62] he had a great ovation. Gaitskell was obviously taken aback by the 'Users' Club' plan and thrown off his balance. The rest of his speech was directed rather to getting off the patriotic line wh he had inadvertently taken in August, on to the 'party' line. It was a nauseating performance . . . .

13 September

This has been a very hectic and confusing day. As we expected – and deliberately risked, in order to get the Americans entangled in CUSA – nearly all the criticism yesterday and today has been about our unwillingness 'to go [to] the United Nations' – whatever this may mean. We say that we are operating under article 33. Our critics say 'Will you promise not to use force without the *consent* of U.N.' We say 'How can this be, seeing that there is a Russian veto?' But, since there is this strange Anglo-Saxon mystique about U.N., they say 'Yes – but *go* to U.N. all the same. Then you will have done the right thing'. Naturally, the Socialists pressed this hard yesterday and today.

---

62. At the start of a two-day debate on Suez for which parliament had been especially recalled.

Equally naturally, the Liberals – Clem Davies and co – and the Archbishop of Canterbury (altho' they must have known why we chose
CUSA, in spite of the delay involved) weighted in on the same side.
This put us in a difficult position, esp as a good many Tories, mostly
young and mostly sons of 'Munichites' – like Richard Wood – began
to rat too. It was all the more annoying because we have every intention of 'going to the Security Council' before the expedition sails, but
have not done so, because Dulles has not yet agreed to vote against,
or even to abstain on a Russian or Yugoslav amendment to our
motion.

Under all this pressure, P.M. naturally began to waver. On the
other hand, the militant wing (Waterhouse–Amery) of the party might
well turn nasty if he were to change his position too noticeably.
Meanwhile, For Secy had moved the vote of confidence at 2.30 – in
a fine speech – but Sir Lionel Heald (an ex Solicitor General) had
declared himself unwilling to vote for the Govt, and other Tories were
following suit. There was a meeting at 6pm. Butler was for giving the
pledge – 'no force, without recourse to U.N.'. I was for standing
firm . . . . If P.M. were to 'climb down' under Socialist pressure, it wd
be fatal to his reputation and position. As we *are* going to Security
Council – as soon as we can rely on US support there – events, not
words, will justify us. However, I thought the form of words wh I
(and Salisbury, Butler, and Kilmuir) had agreed a day or two ago, wd
do . . . . All this – which was interrupted by arrival of reports from
whips, etc etc lasted from 6–7pm or 7.30, and the poor P.M. (already
exhausted with all this 6 weeks crisis and yesterday's debate) had only
a few minutes to prepare his wind-up. When this came to be delivered,
all went well, except for one unlucky phrase, wh he slipped in, I think
by mistake. In answering the question, what wd happen if Egypt
interfered with the operation of our ships under the Users' Club, he
was much embarrassed because of an extraordinary Press Conference
given by Dulles, an account of wh had come over the tape. Dulles,
who had made the *statement* on CUSA quite correctly, and strictly in
accordance with the agreed terms, fell down (as usual) on 'supplementary questions'. He said that, if opposed, American ships wd *not* repeat
not – 'shoot' their way through the canal. No. They would go round
the Cape.

Of course, Gaitskell made great use of this in his wind-up speech
(wh was rather better than his terrible performance yesterday) and
P.M. was a little rattled. So – in reply to interruption – he said 'We

will take it to the Security Council'. There was a roar of applause from the Socialist benches; silence on the Tories, except of course from the waverers – Heald, Walter Elliot, Boothby etc. (Boothby, characteristically, made a fighting speech yesterday and was in full retreat today) I thought that all was lost, and so it nearly was. Fortunately, P.M. stuck to the tougher form of words, wh I had drafted for him, and wh formed the concluding passage of his speech. These words – altho' logically contradictory to what he had just said – seemed to hold the field, and had an air of confidence and determination. P.M. sat down at 9.57. If Gaitskell had risen quietly and said that in view of the assurance given by – or rather dragged out of – the P.M., he would not press the motion. He wd have dealt P.M. and the Govt a mortal blow. But he wasn't quick enough, and the division saved us . . . .

14 September

I woke early – too tired to sleep. The press is *not* too bad . . . . On the whole, the equivocal position created by really contradictory statements, has just got us through. But I fear that it will not increase P.M.'s position to the full degree that his really admirable conduct of the whole crisis and his splendid speech on Wednesday really deserve.

Cabinet at 11, entirely devoted to the G Plan. (European market etc) The documentation of all this is now on a vast scale. But we have tried to get it down to a fairly short summary, to which I have written another summary of the arguments 'for' and 'against'. (My own dept are divided. Edward Boyle (Ec Sec) for whose knowledge and judgment I have great respect, is very doubtful) Peter Thorneycroft introduced the matter – in a good and well-thought out statement. Home put the Commonwealth difficulties. Butler was moderate in putting the UK difficulties, but was on the whole against. So was Salisbury. It was interesting that all the younger men – Heathcoat Amory, Sandys, Eccles, Iain Macleod, were 'for' – in spite of the formidable difficulties . . . .

Egypt Ctee met at 4.15 at No 10. The HofCommons has gone away again (I am happy to say) after debating and voting on Cyprus . . . .

15 September

. . . . It is very difficult indeed to see what the outcome will be over the Canal. It is absolutely vital to humiliate Nasser – or there will be no oil to put through the Canal. We must do it quickly, or our M East friends (like Nuri) will fall. We must also do it quickly, or we shall ourselves be ruined. But we must (if we possibly can) keep the Americans with us, or we shall have no chance of getting out of our financial ruins. At present, they only want to lend us some more money. That isn't really much good to us . . . .

Mr Gaitskell has written a letter to the *Times*, claiming that the Govt's position about the 'use of force' is contradictory and obscure. P.M. rang me about it, and seemed rather concerned. I said that I felt very relieved that Mr G shd take this line, as it entirely destroyed the argument that P.M. had 'climbed down'. My advice was that he shd issue a statement that 'HMG had nothing to add to what PM and For Sec had said in the debate'. The press guidance might be that Mr G seemed a very naive or a very unscrupulous politician. Was it necessary to tell Nasser beforehand how every card in the pack was to be played?

. . . . Maurice and Katie to dinner – with Liz Gore. M in very good form. He confirmed the view that the party is anxious for us to 'go to the United Nations' (whatever that may mean) before force is used . . . .

17 September
Dulles arrives Tuesday. P.M. told me yesterday that he thought we had better 'go to Security Council' at once – as soon as CUSA got going. There is a good deal to be said for this. Indeed, it may be necessary to let it be known in order to get CUSA going at all – which isn't going to be too easy, as many of the 18 powers have begun to get cold feet.

. . . . [T]he effect of the crisis on the exchange market has been very bad. We have lost over $170m from the reserves in 17 days! . . . .

20 September
. . . . I have been reading '*Vanity Fair*'. How good it is! I try to read an hour or two every day, however late. Otherwise, one wd go mad . . . .

The market was better today and we lost no more. But it will be a big shock when the September figures come out – even if we lose no more from the reserves. I had luncheon with Sir Percy Mills and General Brian Robertson. We had a most valuable talk on the industrial situation and the probable Trade Union moves. After this, I saw Iain Macleod (Minister of Labour) and gave him the picture as these two important figures saw it – Engineering and Transport. I am still not without hope that we shall keep the wages position fairly well –

unless, of course, there is a serious increase in prices as the result of Suez and the complete or partial closure of the canal . . . .

. . . . P.M. told me (in great secrecy, for he intends to tell no one else) that the Chief Whip reports a good deal of trouble in the Party. There are three groups. First, the stalwarts, who will support the Govt in strong action, including military action and wd have supported us if we had taken it already; second, those who will support us so long as 'we have been to UN'. This is quite a large number. Thirdly, there are some who are opposed to – or afraid of – force even 'as a last resort' . . . . The Chief Whip cannot estimate the strength of this group. It might be large enough to put us in a minority in a division. P.M. seemed, however, quite determined. It was 1938 over again, and he could not be party to it . . . .

21 September
Arrived New York about 10.15 N.Y. time . . . .

22 September
Left Embassy at 8.15am and flew straight to Indianapolis. Here we were received (ambassador and I) by Mr Pulliam (who owns the [*Indianapolis Star*] newspaper) and seemed to be the big shot . . . . There was a luncheon for 100 'notables', and an 'off the record' speech afterwards. I was given, as my mother's son, a wonderful welcome by these very sincere folks. How I wished this cd have all happened while she was alive! It was what is called 'a true Hoosier welcome'[63] . . . .

After luncheon, we went by air to Bloomington, where we were met by President Wells, the head of the [Indiana] University and other notabilities . . . . After the reception, a dinner at the University building, and then the degree-giving ceremony. This took place in a vast 'auditorium', in the presence of an audience of several thousand students and others. The 'faculty' all marched in, dressed in caps and gowns and hoods, and the ambassador and I marched at the end, with the President. There were a number of prayers, speeches etc, as well as a Brahms something or other played by the University orchestra. Finally, the President made his address, about me and my achievements and my 'Hoosier' connections. I replied in a speech of about

---

63. Hoosier is a nickname (of unknown origin) for natives of Indiana. Macmillan's mother, Helen Artie Tarleton Belles, was born in 1856 in the small town of Spencer, Indiana.

20 minutes. The first half was about my mother and grandparents. The rest was about Anglo-American cooperation, Communism etc. It was enthusiastically received . . . . This was really a most interesting day, and gave me an insight into typical American provincial life – much more the true America than one sees by visits to New York or Washington. The curious thing about these people is their conflicting opinions – held by the same man. For instance, Mr Pulliam's paper – the *Indianapolis Star* – has really bad isolationist leaders, about 'colonialism' and all the rest. For the Middle West is still really isolationist. But he said – and I think sincerely – after my speech (and openly, to the audience) that he admired it and had really been convinced. He had not heard this position put forward before! Of course, I put a lot of stress on the sanctity of contract, on the future interest of underdeveloped countries themselves. I also talked of my personal experience of the dangers of appeasement. This attitude, Makins tells me, is very common and is one of the difficulties of our propaganda effort. They are not impressed by what they read; only by the spoken word. Personality matters to them far more than argument.

23 September (Sunday)

President Wells called for us at 9am and took us for a tour of the University. This is growing at a prodigious rate, with many new buildings of all kinds. We had a walk through the 'campus' – a very pleasant, park-like oasis . . . . We then motored to Spencer, mother's 'home town'. We were then received by an enthusiastic reception committee, including some old people who claimed to remember my mother and grandfather. The Methodist Church – rebuilt in stone since my mother's day but on the same site, was filled with a large congregation of all ages. I read the lesson – the parable of the talents – and made an address to the people about mother and her forbears. I found it rather difficult to get through, without breaking down, and I really felt that my mother was there watching us and enjoying the satisfaction of so many of her hopes and ambitions for me. When I remember all that I owe to her; it's difficult to know how to express what she did for me. It was a most moving ceremony and the people were extraordinarily kind and sympathetic. I stood with the pastor and shook hands with them all as they came out of the church, and they all had a kind word to say. My grandfather's house is still standing, exactly as it was, except that the old timber weather-boarding has been replaced by artificial stone (very ugly) Spencer is a little frontier town – hardly changed since the old pioneer days. The streets are broad and well-planted. The railway still runs through the main street. The houses are the old colonial style.

After the service, we were taken off to the house of one of the leading citizens for refreshment. Then we went to the cemetery; where I laid a wreath on my grandfather's tomb. (He, and my grandmother, and his second wife, and some infant children, are buried together in a sort of family enclosure) The cemetery is by the bank of a river – White River – and was laid out very early in the life of the little community – prob about 1830. This ceremony over, we were taken to a sort of picnic lunch in a 'state park' in the neighbourhood – ham, chicken, apple-pie, cheese etc.

We then motored back to Bloomington and flew back to Washington. We had a terrible storm over the mountains, and I thought at one time that we shd be destroyed by the weight of hail-stones and ice. However, we got through. Dinner with Mr and Mrs Humphrey. He is Secretary of the Treasury – a most charming man, altho' not very easy to persuade of the realities of our economic position . . . .

24 September

Judging from the telegrams and the newspapers, the situation on Suez is calming down a bit, and the general opinion growing that we have chosen the right moment to appeal to U.N . . . .[64]

The state of our reserves and the pressure on Sterling made me very anxious. If this situation goes on too long, it may well over-come us, and we be driven to devaluation or bankruptcy. It is all very sad; because, apart from Suez, we were really beginning to make real progress . . . .

25 September

A message came to the Embassy early this morning from the White House. If we could come at once, the President would be very glad to see me. Since he sees very few people, this is regarded as a great honour. The appointment was kept off his published list of engage-ments, and special arrangements were made to elude the press. Roger Makins and I went in an ordinary car (not the Rolls) and we were taken to a little used and private entrance . . . .

---

64. The discussion at the UN began on 5 October 1956.

His manner cd not have been more cordial. Sitting in his room –
the fine oval study in wh the President works – it was just like talking
to him in the old days at the St George's Hotel in Algiers, at Allied
Force HQs.

. . . . On Suez, he was sure that we must get Nasser down.[65] The
only thing was, how to do it. I made it quite clear that we could *not*
play it long, without aid on a very large scale – that is, if playing it
long involved buying dollar oil. On defence, he said that he had to
contend with his own experts. When he first suggested that they shd
help us in fitting our Canberras to take American A bombs, they
almost went through the ceiling. He himself was clear that we must try
to fit our programmes together, so as to reduce costs on both of us.
About Germany, he was determined to help Adenauer win his election.
But A had obsolete views about armies. We needed fewer soldiers, but
better armed. Hence the importance of tactical atomic weapons. Little
countries cd blackmail us, because we could not use the immense
power of the H bomb, and risk global war. This had happened in the
Formosa trouble; in Indo-China; and was now our trouble in
Egypt . . . .

At 3.30, Roger Makins and I went to the State Dept, for a talk
with Foster Dulles . . . . The Americans are ready to implement their
promise to instruct American ships no longer to pay dues to Nasser.
They will do their best to ensure that American ships sailing under
the Panama and Liberian flags (nearly all oil-tankers) should do the
same. But Dulles warned us that this *might* lead to Nasser closing
the canal . . . . If Nasser lost all (or a greater part) of the dues he
would begin to lose face. This was one of the chief pressures (short
of war) that we could bring on him. Dulles then went on to describe
other measures wh we could take – economic pressures of different
kinds – including the loss of tourism. We must study all this together,
with a view to bringing Nasser down, by overt and covert means,
within 6 months.

There was a good deal of discussion about the Security Council
procedure. Dulles was obviously very upset at the sudden decision
(while he was in the aeroplane going home)[66] to appeal to U.N. He

---

65. Neither Eisenhower nor Makins, in contrast, seem to recollect Suez being dis-
    cussed. See J. Scott Lucas, *Divided We Stand: Britain, the US and the Suez Crisis*
    (London: Hodder and Stoughton, 1991) p. 211.
66. From the London conference of the Users' Club.

had thought that Eden had agreed with him that it was premature and dangerous. There was the Egyptian resolution against force; there was the problem of Israel's request to attend.[67] How were we going to deal with these knotty problems? . . . .

. . . . He reminded me frankly of how he and the President had helped us in May 1955. They had an election now themselves, and like us, were fighting on the cry of 'Peace and Prosperity'. He hoped that Peace could be kept – at least till Nov 6th! But he had been careful in his broadcast to defend the right of Britain and France to use force, if they could not get their rights in any other way.

After this, he turned to our economic position. He thought that, after the election, we should raise the question of our loan payments. He had already spoken to Humphrey (Secretary of the Treasury) about it. I ought to do the same. I was naturally very pleased that this initiative shd come from the American side.

26 September

. . . . There was a meeting in the morning and afternoon of the International Monetary Fund. I delivered a speech which had been prepared for me. One of its objects was to prepare the way for our possible need to draw from it to support the reserves. We haven't got the whole figures – but it looks as if September will show a gain of $50m (this with $175m from sale of Trinidad Oil is of course a *big* loss)

I had a talk with Mr Humphrey this afternoon – of wh I made a record. He suggested that I shd come over after the election and try to make a 'package deal' with them, to include a) a coordinated arms programme b) aid for arms c) the loan. All this is very helpful and may turn out very important – if Eisenhower wins. But this is by no means certain . . . .

28 September

. . . . Luncheon at Overseas Writers Club. I made a 20 minute speech – on Britain's financial and economic position – and answered questions. I was once more struck by the great superiority of American journalists over British . . . .

---

67. Israel had been admitted to the UN in May 1949. This refers to attendance at the Security Council.

Saturday 29 September
Commonwealth Finance Ministers at 10am. This was a most import-
ant meeting. In accordance with the decision of the British Cabinet, we
gave our Commonwealth colleagues a picture of the general plan for
Europe which we have been considering, and its impact on British–
Commonwealth trade relations . . . .

I thought the Ministers and their advisers took the plan very well.
But, of course, there will be trouble when the inevitable press leakages
begin.

30 September
. . . . I ought to have recorded that I went out yesterday evening to pay
a call on my old friend and colleague, Bob Murphy – now under
secretary at the State Dept. We had a good talk and I found him very
sympathetic with our difficulties in Suez etc. He confirmed my view
that all they really cared about is to get the Election over. The growing
strength of the Democrats makes the President's friends and advisers
all the more anxious . . . .

1 October
Left air-port at 10am and flew all day. We got to London at 5am on

2 October
It seems that the press have got a pretty good story of the Washington
talks with the Commonwealth. The Sunday papers carried it as a
headline story, and the Monday and Tuesday papers have a great deal
about the European plan. On the whole, this is to the good, altho'
I fear that many of the papers have got the plan wrong in many
important details . . . . As I rather expected, Rab Butler and Salisbury
are a bit concerned; but they will quiet down . . . .

A meeting of the Defence Committee at 3pm – size of forces at
Singapore was the first item. It is really absurd to keep so many troops
in Malaya now that the Communist terrorism is more or less controlled. Some reduction was agreed. We decided to put an order for a
fighter called P.1 – another £17m. I don't know where it will all end.
I only hope this machine will be a success . . . .

3 October
Having had no sleep for nearly 2 days, and finishing at 3am this

morning, I overslept. However, I got to Cabinet (wh began at 10.45) only a few minutes late.

The two major items (there was a host of small ones) were

a) European plan; British agriculture; Australian trade negotiation

b) Suez.

The discussions were very good on a). Sandys, Eccles, Heathcoat-Amory, Macleod, Lennox-Boyd, Kilmuir, Lloyd George – all enthusiastic. Salisbury expressed no strong view. Butler anxious. I undertook to make it plain that the Cabinet had reached no decision. (In fact, I think we have passed the point of no return!) . . . .

4 October

. . . . The Suez situation is beginning to slip out of our hands. Nothing can now be done till the U.N. exercise is over. But by then the difficulty of 'resort to force' will be greater. I try not to think that we have 'missed the bus' – if we have, it is really due to the long time it has taken to get military arrangements into shape. But we *must*, by one means or another, win this struggle. Nasser may well try to preach Holy War in the Middle East and (even to their own loss) the mob and the demogogues may create a ruinous position for us. *Without oil and without the profits from oil*, neither UK nor western Europe can survive.[68]

---

68. Macmillan's diaries do not exist for the period 4 October 1956 to 3 February 1957. The final stages of the Suez Crisis, the collusion with the Israelis, the launch of the operation and the financial pressures that halted it are all passed over in silence. Macmillan admits he started what would have been volume 23 of his notebook diaries in October 1956. However, rather than losing it, as he claimed at the time, he later told Alistair Horne that he destroyed what he had written, at the specific request of Anthony Eden; see Alistair Horne, *Macmillan 1894–1956* (London: Macmillan, 1988), p. 438. It certainly seems probable that there was a volume covering the period up until Macmillan's accession to the premiership in January 1957 that was subsequently destroyed, whether or no at Eden's behest. The handwritten diary volumes usually cover two to three months, so a volume 23 which finished in January 1957 would fit. Another reason for thinking this was the case is that diary volumes do not run to four months. From January until he took up his pen again on 3 February 1957, Macmillan seems to have been too busy to keep a diary, as was to be the case on a number of occasions during his premiership. With his next entry, however, he reviews the missing period, but not that of Suez – presumably because he had already covered that in the missing volume 23.

1957

3 February (Sunday)

The events of October, November and December 1956, and of the first month of 1957 began to move at such a speed and with such a pressure upon us all, that I was not able to keep up the diary. I mislaid the volume which began somewhere about the beginning of October – and then was caught up by the number of meetings and discussions which followed the Party Conference at Llandudno. At that time, the Prime Minister appeared in good heart – though anxious about the Suez position and the growing rumours of trouble throughout the Middle East. It is quite impossible here to depict all that happened in those weeks, from November till the P.M.'s physical breakdown and departure to Jamaica.[1] After that, I felt that he cd never return and remain P.M. for long. Apart from the appearance of running away from a battlefield (wh was very unfair, since he was really a sick man) the party had been terribly shattered. It became clear by Christmas that the P.M. was really unable to go on. Soon afterwards, the doctors told him the truth. He seemed quite dazed – and was, I suppose, a good deal drugged.

I am sorry now that I did not record the actual changeover, day by day. Since a good deal of nonsense was talked by the Opposition about the influence of the Palace, it may be worth setting down what really happened. The last Cabinet wh Eden held was at 5pm on Wed Jan 9th. (He had told me at 3pm of that day of his final decision. The only others who knew were Salisbury and Butler)

Eden spoke shortly, and with great dignity. The doctors' decision was irrevocable.[2] He must resign. Salisbury spoke – with great

---

1. Not least because of American opposition and financial pressures on Britain's reserves, the Suez operation was called off on 6 November 1956, coincidentally the same day Eisenhower was triumphantly re-elected President in the US. An exhausted Eden left to recuperate in Jamaica from 22 November to 14 December 1956. All British troops were withdrawn from Suez by 23 December 1956.
2. Eden in his memoirs talks of taking his decision in the light of fever attacks

emotion, almost in tears – of his lifelong friendship. Butler spoke next – very appropriately. I said a few words. Then it was all over. It was a dramatic end to an extraordinary, and in many way, unique career. What seemed so dreadful was that he waited so long for the Premiership, and held it for so short a time. For several days past (since Christmas, in fact) many of our colleagues have been very restless. There have been many meetings – no intrigue,[3] but great concern at the apparent inability of the P.M. or anyone else to take hold of the situation. Outside the ranks of the Cabinet etc, MPs have been meeting. There has been a general acceptance of the fact that the Govt could not go on. As soon as Parlt met it wd be in trouble; in a few weeks it wd fall. At the same time, no one has known what to do. For Eden to have left as a result of a political intrigue or split, would have been fatal. The only way out was a resignation on grounds of health. While these ministers and members have been speculating as to whether this could be arranged, or whether any ground for it existed, it happened – suddenly, devastatingly, and beyond dispute. For it became clear that Eden was a very sick man. The strain of recent weeks and months has told on him terribly. The weakness left by the series of operations which he had 2 or 3 years ago has now developed into a serious danger. This therefore was *not* a political excuse. This illness was a reality. To go on with the story; after the Cabinet, I went back to No 11, and spent the evening alone there, working and reading. Butler, I have no doubt, went back to his house. Meanwhile, Salisbury and Kilmuir asked all the members of the Cabinet to see them – one by one. This took place in the Lord President's rooms. I heard afterwards that the opinion was practically unanimous in favour of me, and *not* Butler. The next morning, I stayed at No 11 and did not go to the Treasury. I heard that Ld Salisbury and Sir W Churchill had been sent for by the Queen. But since no one had told me about what had taken place the night before, I had no idea of what advice they wd give. It is since clear that Lord S did not give his own views. He merely informed the Queen of the general view among the leading members of the party

---

relating to the illness that laid him up for much of 1953, on the advice of three medical opinions (*Full Circle*, pp. 581–3).

3. Eisenhower certainly dropped hints that Eden's departure would not be regretted. And Brendan Bracken claimed by early December 1956 that Macmillan was positioning himself for Eden's departure. Bracken, however, had never been one of Harold's admirers.

(i.e. the Cabinet ministers) I think he had also received a message to the effect from John Morrison, Chairman of the 1922 Ctee. Since the Socialists afterwards tried to make out that this was a personal and private effort by the head of the Cecils, it is important to record that Lord S merely acted as a means of conveying to the Queen the general view inside the party. I gathered from Anthony (whom I saw later on Thursday) that he had neither been asked for his advice nor had [he] volunteered it. At about 5 minutes to 1 on Thursday, I was rung by Sir M Adeane and asked to come to the Palace at 2pm. Then I knew.

The Queen was gracious – but brief. I was out of the Palace by 2.30, having accepted her charge and kissed hands as P.M. and First Lord.

As I drove back to No 11, I thought chiefly of my poor mother. The first little note wh I got later in the afternoon was from my sister-in-law (Mary Devonshire) with the same thought. She understood and had a great affection for my mother.

When I got back, I saw first of all Salisbury. I asked him to remain Lord P[resident] and lead the HofL. He agreed; but ever since bombards me with letters about HofL reform; payment of Lords; atomic development and on numbers of other questions, hinting at resignation. But I learnt from the staff here that he always does this. He is very conscientious, but with age has become a little 'pernickety'. But he is a dear and splendid character – a very old friend, with all the Cecil charm wh first attracted me in Oxford days – 45 years ago.

I made up my mind that Butler (whose feelings of disappointment I could imagine only too well) was the key figure. I saw him at once, and offered him whatever office he might wish. (I only tried to steer him off the F.O. to wh he had some leanings, but from wh I think he really shrank in today's circumstances. I was determined to keep Selwyn Lloyd, because I felt one head on a charger should be enough. Two was more than England's honour cd support. Altho' Eden's illness is real, it will be thought in most foreign countries to be 'diplomatic')

Rab was very nice and reciprocated at once the attitude I took. We had preserved the Govt by our loyalty and comradeship before Christmas – during Eden's absence in Jamaica. We must do the same now, or we shd certainly founder. I asked him not to decide immediately. I hoped he wd continue to lead the House, but perh he wd like an office as well. He accepted this idea, and returned about noon the next day with his decision. He wd take the Home Office. I at once agreed, altho' it meant a rather sad parting with Gwilym LG. However, since James Stuart was rather anxious to go too, it was got over without too much difficulty. The chief difficulties came later – not with the Cabinet. I had seen Percy Mills (rather by chance) at luncheon on the Wednesday. I got him to come in on Thursday afternoon (by the garden entrance) and offered him 'Ministry of Power'. I got the message accepting on the Saturday. The Cabinet was completed by Sunday evening, when the Queen came up from Sandringham. My chief problem was the Ministry of Defence. I felt that with Anthony Head it wd not succeed. He was too much of a 'service' man.[4] There was a lot of resistance to my plan of having Duncan Sandys – chiefly from Norman Brook who thought the rows wd be too great. But the Chief Whip felt it was politically an advantage. I also wanted a 'direction' to increase the powers of the defence minister.[5] Brook (who is a tower of strength) drafted them, and I got the 3 service ministers to accept them *before* appointment. By moving Hailsham from the Admiralty to Education a possible danger was avoided. Also I think he will be a first-class Minister of Education. Anyway, he is one of the cleverest, if not always the wisest, men in the country today.

. . . . Henry Brooke was the obvious successor to Sandys at Housing. The Cabinet list was given to the Press for publication on Monday. It got a good reception. The next tack – and rather a tricky one – was the ministers *outside* the Cabinet and ministers of state. I was determined to bring back Ernest Marples, who did so well at Housing, but who was left out by Eden. He is delighted to be P.M.G. Reggie Maudling, with great good feeling and good sense, accepted to be Mill's representative in HofC and genuine deputy. He 'goes down' (nominally) in the hierarchy. But he really is in the interesting part of the game. I hope he will do well. He is very clever; a little lazy; and a trifle vain. But I believe that if he buckles to he *will* do very well. I put

---

4. In other words, he would resist cuts in defence expenditure.

5. Eden had already increased the role of the Minister of Defence to cover pay and managing the balance of forces to fit overall strategy. Following complaints from Sandys about obstruction from the service chiefs Macmillan announced in the Commons on 24 January 1957 that, in view of the need for reductions in manpower and expenditure, he had authorized the minister to give decisions 'on all matters of policy affecting the size, shape, organisation and deposition of the Armed Forces, their equipment (including defence research and development) and their pay and conditions of service' (*House of Commons Debates* 5th ser., vol. 563, col. 396).

David Ormsby-Gore up to Minister of State in F.O. He is young, but very able. After much hesitation, dear Edward Boyle 'rejoined' the Ministry of Education in the Commons.[6] A partnership with Hailsham attracted him. This enabled me to get in Julian Amery – at the other end of the Suez. But the last changes (of course) belonged to the third group – under-secretaries. We got the second group (ministers etc) out on the Thursday and the last (under-secretaries) on Saturday . . . .

The forming of the whole administration took about 10 days. On the whole, it has been well received. It was a *most* difficult and exhausting task. Without the help of Edward Heath, (Chief Whip) who was quite admirable, we couldn't have done it. Norman Brook was also most valuable. The letters which I wrote to retiring colleagues were regarded as out of the ordinary. I took a great deal of trouble with each one, and tried to introduce a personal note into each. The most awkward and difficult job was, naturally, parting with old friends. All of them took it very well, L.G. (who is to become Viscount Tenby) is so old and shrewd a politician that, as soon as he knew that Butler was to succeed him, he realised that I had no option. Patrick Buchan-Hepburn (whom I particularly wanted *out* of the HofC) seemed satisfied with the Barony and a promise of a Governorship in due course. Lord Reading, who is 67, seemed rather aggrieved, and has made it known – or perhaps it is his wife. The Anthony Heads behaved extremely well, husband and wife. I was sorry to lose Fitzroy Maclean; but he is really so hopeless in the House that he is a passenger in an office. It's a great pity, since he is so able.

Altogether, it has gone well. But it has meant seeing nearly a hundred people and trying to say the right thing to each. In the circumstances, many considerations had to be borne in mind – the right, centre, and left of the party; the extreme 'Suez' group; the extreme opposition to Suez; the loyal centre – and last, but not least, U and non-U (to use the jargon that Nancy Mitford has popularised) that is, Eton, Winchester, etc on the one hand; Board School and grammar school on the other.[7]

On Thursday 17th, I had to do a T.V. and broadcast to the Nation.

---

6. Boyle had resigned from the government during the Suez crisis.
7. A reference to the terms coined by Mitford to describe linguistic characteristics in her *Noblesse Oblige: An Inquiry into the Identifiable Characteristics of the English Aristocracy* (London: Hamish Hamilton, 1956).

Dr Hill and George Christ helped me enormously and I think it was a success.

Since we started, I have been struck with two things – the extraordinary efficiency of the Private Secretaries. Dorothy and I have received literally thousands of letters and telegrams, from everyone we have ever known or worked with – from a footman at Government House Ottawa or a driver in Algiers to more exalted and distinguished friends. All these have been sorted out and traced (since many people sign only Christian names this isn't easy) and answers prepared. It has been a tremendous job for me to sign all the answers. The second thing that has struck me is how well everyone has behaved. Politicians are not really cynical and self-seeking. There has been a kind of 1940 spirit abroad. With very few (and rather unexpected) exceptions, everyone has put the public interest and the desire to help me above all other considerations. It has really been quite an exhilarating experience.

The first Cabinet seemed good. I have tried to get the agenda into better shape – with one day Foreign or Colonial questions, and another domestic – financial and economic etc. I have also tried to get the discussions less 'departmental'. We are, after all, comrades in a common enterprise, and stand or fall together.

Dorothy came with me to the meeting of the Party, where I was elected leader in succession to Anthony. We sat behind the platform, in a little room out of sight, where we could not be seen, but could hear the speeches. Lord Salisbury presided. Walter Elliot made a fine speech about Eton – of really classical beauty and dignity. After my unanimous election, we entered the hall. D and the dowager Duchess went to the gallery of the HofC. I had a good reception from our people. The first speeches were again about Eden; then a few preliminary skirmishes.

I have read a good deal in recent weeks – some Trollope, some Henry James, three volumes of Cobbett's *Rural Rides* etc (admirable where country life is described – some of the polemics can be skipped) I have now embarked on R L Stevenson – which I have not read for very many years.

Biographical Notes

Dean Acheson – Lawyer and Democrat who served as Under Secretary of State 1945–47, Deputy Secretary of State 1947–49 and Secretary of State 1949–53.

Sir Michael Adeane – Private Secretary to Queen Elizabeth II 1953–72.

Konrad Adenauer – Chancellor of the Federal Republic of Germany 1949–63.

Winthrop Aldrich – Lawyer and Republican fund-raiser who was one of the people who came to Europe to persuade Eisenhower to run for President. He was US ambassador to London 1953–57.

Lord Alexander of Tunis – Macmillan had worked closely with him when in North Africa, when Alexander was Deputy Commander in Chief. He ended the war as Supreme Allied Commander in the Mediterranean, and was Governor-General of Canada 1946–52 and Minister of Defence 1952–54.

Julian Amery – Son of Leo Amery, like Macmillan he went to Summer Fields preparatory school, Eton and Balliol College, Oxford. In 1950 he married Macmillan's daughter Catherine. Conservative MP 1950–66 and 1969–92. Delegate to the Consultative Assembly of the Council of Europe 1950–53 and 1956, Parliamentary Secretary, War Office 1957–58, Colonial Office 1958–60, Secretary of State for Air 1960–62, Minister of Aviation 1962–64, of Public Building and Works 1970, of Housing and Construction 1970–72, of State at Foreign and Commonwealth Office 1972–74.

Leo Amery – Conservative MP 1911–45, First Lord of the Admiralty 1922–24, Colonial Secretary 1924–29 and Secretary of State for India and Burma 1940–45.

Sir John Anderson – Permanent Secretary, Home Office 1922–32, Governor of Bengal 1932–37, National MP 1938–50, Home Secretary and Minister of Home Security 1939–40, Lord President 1940–43 and

Chancellor of the Exchequer 1943–45. Raised to the peerage as Lord Waverley, he refused to serve in Attlee's or Churchill's second government.

Sir Cyril Asquith – Fourth son of the former Prime Minister, a Lord Justice of Appeal 1946–51 and Lord of Appeal in Ordinary 1951–54.

Ralph Assheton – Conservative MP 1934–45 and 1945–55. Chairman of the Conservative Party 1944–46.

J. J. Astor – Conservative MP 1951–59.

Nancy Astor – Conservative MP 1919–45 and wife of Waldorf.

W. W. (Bill) Astor – Conservative MP 1935–45 and 1951–52 when he succeeded as 3rd Viscount Astor.

Waldorf Astor – 2nd Viscount Astor and proprietor of the *Observer*.

Clement Attlee – Labour MP 1922–55 and party leader 1935–55. Chancellor of the Duchy of Lancaster 1930–31, Postmaster-General 1931, Lord Privy Seal 1940–42, Deputy Prime Minister and Dominions Secretary 1942–45, Prime Minister 1945–51.

Lord Beaverbrook – Press baron, imperialist and maverick Conservative. Max Aitken was born in Canada, sat as a Conservative MP 1910–16, raised to the peerage in 1917 and served as Minister of Information and Chancellor of the Duchy of Lancaster 1918, Minister for Aircraft Production 1940–41, Minister of State 1941, Minister of Production 1941–42 and Lord Privy Seal 1943–45.

Joseph Bech – Luxembourg Prime Minister 1926–37, 1953–58, Foreign Minister 1937–53, 1958–59.

Sir Edward Beddington-Behrens – Founder member of ELEC, executive member of the European Movement and founder, in August 1949, of the section on Central and Eastern Europe.

Peter Bennett – Conservative MP 1940–53. Parliamentary Secretary, Ministry of Labour 1951–52.

Lord Henry Bentinck – A contemporary of Macmillan's at Eton, he was a Conservative MP 1922–43, when he succeeded as the 7th Duke of Portland.

L. P. Beria – Commissar for Internal Affairs in the Soviet Union 1938–45 and Deputy Prime Minister in charge of security 1941–53. After Stalin's death he was arrested, tried and shot.

Michael Berry – Son of Lord Camrose. Chairman and Editor in Chief of the *Daily Telegraph* 1954–87.

Lady Pamela Berry – Wife of Michael Berry. The attacks by the *Daily Telegraph* on the Prime Minister in 1956 have been attributed to bad blood between her and Lady Eden.

Aneurin Bevan – Labour MP 1929–60. Minister of Health 1945–51, Minister of Labour and National Service 1951.

Ernest Bevin – General Secretary of the T&GWU 1921–40. Labour MP 1940–51, serving as Minister of Labour 1940–45, Foreign Secretary 1945–51 and Lord Privy Seal 1951.

Reginald Bevins – Labour councillor in Liverpool in the 1930s. Conservative MP 1950–64. Macmillan's PPS 1951–53, Parliamentary Secretary, Ministry of Works 1953–57, Ministry of Housing and Local Government 1957–59, Postmaster-General 1959–64.

Johan Beyen – Dutch Minister of Foreign Affairs 1952–56.

Georges Bidault – French Foreign Minister 1946–48, 1954, Prime Minister 1946, 1958.

Nigel Birch – Conservative MP 1945–70, Parliamentary Secretary, Air Ministry 1951–52, Ministry of Defence 1952–54, Minister of Works 1954–55, Secretary of State for Air 1955–57, Economic Secretary of the Treasury 1957–58.

Lord Birkenhead – Married to Michael Berry's sister. Author and Tory peer.

Herbert Blankenhorn – Political Director, West German Foreign Ministry 1950–55, German Ambassador to NATO 1955–58, to France 1958–63, to Italy 1963–65, to the UK 1965–70.

W. R. Blyton – Durham miner who became a Labour MP 1945–64. Delegate to the Council of Europe 1949–51.

Lady Violet Bonham Carter – Elder daughter of the former Liberal Prime Minister H. H. Asquith, confidante of Churchill and Liberal politician.

Robert Boothby – Conservative MP 1924–58. From 1930 onwards he had a long-term affair with Macmillan's wife, Dorothy.

John Boyd-Carpenter – Conservative MP 1945–72. FST 1951–54, Minister of Transport and Civil Aviation 1954–55, of Pensions and National Insurance 1955–62, Chief Secretary to the Treasury and Paymaster-General 1962–64.

Edward Boyle – Conservative MP 1950–70. PPS, Air Ministry 1951–52, Parliamentary Secretary, Ministry of Defence 1952–54, Ministry of Supply 1954–55, Economic Secretary of the Treasury 1955–56, Parliamentary Secretary, Ministry of Education 1957–59, FST 1959–62, Minister of Education 1962–64, Minister of State at Department of Education and Science 1964.

Brendan Bracken – Conservative MP 1929–45 and November 1945–51. Minister of Information 1941–45 and First Lord of the Admiralty 1945. Chairman of the *Financial News* and, after the merger in 1945, of the *Financial Times*.

Lord Brand – Former civil servant who was a director of Lazard Bros, Times Publishing and Lloyds Bank.

Heinrich von Brentano – West German Foreign Minister 1955–61.

Sir Edward Bridges – A contemporary of Macmillan at Eton and Oxford. Cabinet Secretary 1938–47, Permanent Secretary of the Treasury and head of the Home Civil Service 1945–56.

Sir Norman Brook – Cabinet Secretary 1947–62, Joint Secretary to the Treasury and head of the Home Civil Service 1956–62, Chairman of the BBC Governors 1964–67.

Henry Brooke – Conservative MP 1938–45, 1950–66. FST 1954–57, Minister of Housing and Local Government and for Welsh Affairs 1957–61, Chief Secretary to the Treasury and Paymaster-General 1961–62, Home Secretary 1962–64.

Sir Nevil Brownjohn – Deputy Military Governor, Control Commission for Germany 1947–49, Vice-CIGS 1950–52, Chief Staff Officer, War Office 1952–55, Quartermaster-General 1956–58.

Sir Frederick Brundrett – Chief Scientific Adviser at the Ministry of Defence 1954–59.

Patrick Buchan-Hepburn – Conservative MP 1931–57. Conservative Chief Whip 1945, 1948–55. Minister of Works 1955–57. Only Governor-General of the Federation of the West Indies 1962.

N. A. Bulganin – Minister of Defence of the Soviet Union 1947–49 and 1953–55 and Chairman of Council of Ministers after Malenkov's fall in 1955 until his dismissal in 1958.

R. A. Butler – Conservative MP 1929–65. President of the Board of Education 1941–44, Minister of Education 1944–45, Chancellor of the Exchequer 1951–55, Leader of the House of Commons 1955–61, Lord Privy Seal 1955–59, Home Secretary 1957–62, First Secretary of State 1962–63, Foreign Secretary 1963–64.

Sir Harold Caccia – Diplomat who served with Macmillan in North Africa. British High Commissioner in Austria 1950–54, Deputy Under-Secretary at the Foreign Office 1954–56, Ambassador to Washington 1956–61, Permanent Secretary of the Foreign Office 1962–65.

Sir Alexander Cadogan – Permanent Secretary of the Foreign Office 1938–46, UK representative to the UN 1946–50, government director of the Suez Canal Company 1951–57, chairman of BBC governors 1952–57.

James Callaghan – Labour MP 1945–87. Parliamentary Secretary, Admiralty 1950–51, Chancellor of the Exchequer 1964–67, Home Secretary 1967–70, Foreign Secretary 1974–76, Prime Minister 1976–79.

Lord Camrose – Editor in Chief of the *Daily Telegraph* 1928–54.

Richard Casey – Australian liaison officer with the Foreign Office 1924–31. Having served in the Australian cabinet 1935–40, he became the UK Minister of State Resident in the Middle East 1942–43, then Governor of Bengal 1944–46. Australian Minister of External Affairs 1951–60 and Governor-General of Australia 1965–70.

Lord Cherwell – Oxford physicist and acolyte of Churchill. Paymaster-General 1942–45 and 1951–53.

Chiang Kai-shek – Head of Chinese Nationalist Government (under various titles) 1928–49, and President of Republic of China (Taiwan) 1949–75.

Chou En-lai – Minister of Foreign Affairs, People's Republic of China 1949–58, Prime Minister 1958–76.

George Christ – Conservative Party parliamentary liaison officer 1945–65.

Randolph Churchill – Son of Winston. Conservative MP 1940–45. Journalist.

Winston Churchill – President of the Board of Trade 1908–10, Home Secretary 1910–11, First Lord of the Admiralty 1911–15, 1939–40, Chancellor of the Duchy of Lancaster 1915, Minister of Munitions 1917–19, Secretary for War and Air 1919–21, for Air and the Colonies 1921, Colonial Secretary 1921–22, Chancellor of the Exchequer 1924–29, Prime Minister 1940–45, 1951–55, Leader of the Conservative Party 1940–55.

James Chuter Ede – Labour MP 1923, 1929–31, 1935–64. Home Secretary 1945–51, Leader of the Commons 1951.

Lord Citrine – General Secretary of the TUC 1926–46, Chairman of Central Electricity Authority 1947–57, and of UK Atomic Energy Authority 1958–62.

Colin Clark – Economist. Director of Oxford University Institute of Research in Agricultural Economics 1953–69 and an early supporter of the Institute of Economic Affairs.

Sir Kenneth Clark – Chairman of the Arts Council of Great Britain 1953–60.

Lord Cobbold – Governor of the Bank of England 1949–61, chairman of commission on Malaysia 1962.

Sir Jock Colville – Diarist and Private Secretary to the Prime Minister 1939–41, 1943–45, 1951–55.

Sir Edmund Compton – Third Secretary in the Treasury 1949–58, Comptroller and Auditor-General 1958–66.

Frank Cousins – General Secretary of the T&GWU 1956–64, 1966–68 and Minister of Technology 1964–66.

Maurice Couve de Murville – With Macmillan in North Africa, when he was a member of the French Committee for National Liberation, 1943. French Ambassador to Italy 1945, Director-General of political affairs in French Foreign Ministry 1946–50, Ambassador to Egypt 1950–54, French representative at NATO 1954–55, Ambassador to Washington

1955–56, to Germany 1956–58, Foreign Minister 1958–68, Economic and Finance Minister 1968, Prime Minister 1968–69.

Sir Stafford Cripps – Labour MP 1931–50. A left-winger in the 1930s, he served as Solicitor-General 1930–31, Ambassador to the Soviet Union 1940–42, Lord Privy Seal and Leader of the Commons 1942, Minister of Aircraft Production 1942–45, President of the Board of Trade 1945–47, Minister of Economic Affairs 1947 and Chancellor of the Exchequer 1947–50.

Harry Crookshank – A friend of Macmillan at Eton and Oxford, and a fellow officer in the Grenadier Guards in 1915–18, he was a Conservative MP 1924–56, Secretary for Mines 1935–39, FST 1939–43, Postmaster-General 1943–45, Minister of Health 1951–52, Leader of the Commons 1951–55, Lord Privy Seal 1952–55.

Richard Crossman – Worked with Macmillan in North Africa. Assistant editor of *New Statesman and Nation* 1938–55, Labour MP 1945–74, Minister of Housing and Local Government 1964–66, Leader of the Commons and Lord President of the Council 1966–68, Secretary of State for Social Services 1968–70.

Hugh Cudlipp – Editor of *Sunday Pictorial* 1937–40, 1946–49, of *Daily Express* 1950–52, editorial director of *Sunday Pictorial* and *Daily Mirror* 1952–63, chairman of Daily Mirror Newspapers 1963–68.

Lionel Curtis – Oxford historian and thinker on federalism.

Hugh Dalton – Labour MP 1924–31, 1935–59. Minister of Economic Warfare 1940–42, President of the Board of Trade 1942–45, Chancellor of the Exchequer 1945–47, Chancellor of the Duchy of Lancaster 1948–50, Minister of Town and Country Planning 1950–51, of Local Government and Planning 1951.

Clement Davies – Liberal MP 1929–62 and Leader of the Liberal Party 1945–56.

Arthur Deakin – General Secretary (Acting until 1946) of the T&GWU 1940–55.

Sir Patrick Dean – Assistant secretary, Foreign Office 1953–56, Deputy Under-Secretary 1956–60, UK representative to UN 1960–64, Ambassador to Washington 1965–69.

Geoffrey de Freitas – Labour MP 1945–61, 1964–79. Under-Secretary for

Air 1946–50, for Home Office 1950–51, High Commissioner to Ghana 1961–63, to Kenya 1963–64.

Earl De La Warr – Served in Labour government 1929–31. Lord Privy Seal 1937–38, President of the Board of Education 1938–40, First Commissioner of Works 1940, Postmaster-General 1951–55.

Viscount De l'Isle – Conservative MP 1944–45. Secretary of State for Air 1951–55, Governor-General of Australia 1961–65.

Moucher Devonshire – Macmillan's sister-in-law, wife of the 10th Duke of Devonshire.

Douglas Dillon – US Ambassador to France 1953–57, Deputy Under-Secretary of State for Economic Affairs 1957–58, Under-Secretary of State 1959–61, Secretary of the Treasury 1961–65.

Sir Pierson Dixon – Served with Macmillan in North Africa. Ambassador to Czechoslovakia 1948–50, Deputy Under-Secretary, Foreign Office 1950–54, UK representative to UN 1954–60, Ambassador to France 1960–64.

A. Duff Cooper – A contemporary of Macmillan at Eton and Oxford. Conservative MP 1924–29, 1931–45. FST 1934–35, War Secretary 1935–37, First Lord of the Admiralty 1937–38, Minister of Information 1940–41, Chancellor of the Duchy of Lancaster 1941–43, UK representative to the French National Committee of Liberation 1943–44, Ambassador to France 1944–47.

Thomas Dugdale – Conservative MP 1929–59. Conservative Party Chairman 1942–44, Minister of Agriculture and Fisheries 1951–54.

Allen Dulles – Director of US Council on Foreign Relations 1942–45, CIA Director 1953–61.

John Foster Dulles – Special representative of the President 1950–51, US Secretary of State 1953–59.

David Eccles – Conservative MP 1943–62. Minister of Works 1951–54, of Education 1954–57, 1959–62, President of the Board of Trade 1957–59, Paymaster-General 1970–73.

Chuter Ede – see James Chuter Ede, above.

Anthony Eden – Conservative MP 1923–57, above. Foreign Secretary 1935–38, 1940–45, 1951–55, Dominions Secretary 1939–40, Secretary of State for War 1940, Leader of the Commons 1942–45, Prime Minister 1955–57.

John Edwards – Labour MP 1945 to February 1950 and May 1950 to 1959. Economic Secretary to the Treasury 1950–51.

Dwight D. Eisenhower – With Macmillan in North Africa, where he was Commander in Chief, Allied Forces 1942–44. Supreme Commander, Allied Expeditionary Force in Western Europe 1944–45, SACEUR 1950–52, US President 1953–61.

Walter Elliot – Conservative MP 1918–23, 1924–45, 1946–58. Minister of Agriculture 1932–36, Scottish Secretary 1936–38, Minister of Health 1938–40.

Ludwig Erhard – West German Minister for Economic Affairs 1949–63, Vice-Chancellor 1957–63, Chancellor 1963–66.

Farouk – King of Egypt from 1935 until his overthrow in 1952. The monarchy was abolished a year later.

Edgar Faure – French Prime Minister 1952, 1955–56.

Feisal II – Succeeded as King of Iraq in 1939, assassinated in 1958.

Sir Oliver Franks – Ambassador to Washington 1948–52, Chairman of Lloyds Bank 1954–62.

Michael Fraser – Joint Director, Conservative Research Department 1951–59, Director 1959–64.

Hugh Gaitskell – Labour MP 1945–63 and party leader 1955–63. Minister of Fuel and Power 1947–50, Chancellor of the Exchequer 1950–51.

Alcide de Gasperi – Italian Foreign Minister 1945–46, 1951–53, Prime Minister 1945–53.

Charles de Gaulle – Worked with Macmillan in North Africa, where he was President of the French Committee of National Liberation 1943. President of the French Provisional Government 1944–46, and founder President of the Fifth Republic 1958–69.

Charles Geddes – General Secretary of the Union of Post Office Workers 1944–57.

Sir Bernard Gilbert – Second Secretary at the Treasury 1944–56.

Sir John Glubb – Head of the Arab Legion (Jordan) 1939–56.

W. G. Grewe – Head of the political department, West German Foreign Ministry.

James Griffiths – Labour MP 1936–70. Minister of National Insurance 1945–50, Colonial Secretary 1950–51, Welsh Secretary 1964–66.

Otto Grotewohl – Leader of East Germany until his death in 1964.

Al Gruenther – With Macmillan in North Africa where he was Deputy Chief of Staff, AFHQ. Chief of Staff at SHAPE 1951–53, SACEUR 1953–56.

Sir William Haley – Director-General of the BBC 1944–52, editor of *The Times* 1952–66.

1st Earl of Halifax – Conservative MP 1910–25. President of the Board of Education 1922–24, 1932–35, Minister of Agriculture 1924–25, Viceroy of India 1925–31, Secretary of State for War 1935, Lord Privy Seal 1935–37, Lord President of the Council 1937–38, Foreign Secretary 1938–40, Ambassador to Washington 1941–46.

W. Glenvil Hall – Labour MP 1929–31 and 1939–62. FST 1945–50.

Sir Robert Hall – Director, Economic Section of the Cabinet Office 1947–53, Economic Adviser to the government 1953–61.

Walter Hallstein – State Secretary in the Federal Chancellery in Germany 1951, and in the German Foreign Ministry 1951–58. President of the Commission of the European Economic Community 1958–67.

Dag Hammarskjöld – UN Secretary-General 1953–61.

Pat Hancock – PPS to the Foreign Secretary 1955, Head of Western Department, Foreign Office 1956–59, Ambassador to Israel 1959–62, to Norway 1963–65, to Italy 1969–74.

Sir John Harding – Commander in Chief, British Army of the Rhine 1951–52, CIGS 1952–55, Governor of Cyprus 1955–57.

Averill Harriman – Democrat politician and millionaire envoy to wartime Britain. US Ambassador to USSR 1943–46, to Britain 1946. US Secretary of Commerce 1946–48, special representative on the Marshall Plan 1948–50, special assistant to the President 1950–51, Governor, New York State, 1955–58, US Ambassador at large 1961, 1965–69,

Under-Secretary of State for Far Eastern Affairs 1961–63, for Political Affairs 1963–65.

Sir Graham Hayman – President of the Federation of British Industries 1955–57.

Sir William Hayter – Ambassador to the USSR 1953–57, Deputy Secretary, Foreign Office 1957–58.

Anthony Head – Conservative MP 1945–60. Secretary of State for War 1951–56, Minister of Defence 1956–57, High Commissioner to Nigeria 1960–63, to Malaysia 1963–66.

Sir Lionel Heald – Conservative MP 1950–70.

Denis Healey – Secretary of the International Section of the Labour Party 1945–52. Labour MP 1952–92. Defence Secretary 1964–70, Chancellor of the Exchequer 1974–79.

Edward Heath – Conservative MP 1950–2001. Government Chief Whip 1955–59, Minister of Labour 1959–60, Lord Privy Seal (with particular responsibility for European negotiations) 1960–63, Secretary of State for Industry, Trade and Regional Development and President of the Board of Trade 1963–64, Prime Minister 1970–74.

Derick Heathcoat Amory – Conservative MP 1945–60. Minister of Pensions 1951–53, Minister of State, Board of Trade 1953–54, Minister of Agriculture and Fisheries (and Food) 1954–58, Chancellor of the Exchequer 1958–60, UK High Commissioner to Canada 1961–63.

Arthur Henderson – Labour MP 1923–24, 1929–31, 1935–66. Commonwealth Relations Secretary 1947, Secretary of State for Air 1947–51.

Edouard Herriot – French Prime Minister 1924–25, 1926, 1932. President of the French National Assembly 1947–54 and leading opponent of the EDC proposals.

Charles Hill – Secretary of the British Medical Association 1944–50. Conservative MP 1950–63. Parliamentary Secretary, Ministry of Food 1951–55, Postmaster-General 1955–57, Chancellor of the Duchy of Lancaster 1957–61, Minister of Housing and Local Government and of Welsh Affairs 1961–62, Chairman of the Independent Broadcasting Authority 1963–67, of governors of the BBC 1967–72.

Quintin Hogg (Lord Hailsham) – Succeeded father in 1950 as Viscount

Hailsham (but disclaimed title for life in 1963). Conservative MP 1938–50, 1963–70. First Lord of the Admiralty 1956–57, Minister of Education 1957, Lord President of the Council 1957–59, 1960–64, Lord Privy Seal 1959–60, Minister for Science and Technology 1959–64, for Sport 1962–64, for the North East 1963–64, for Higher Education 1963–64, Leader of the House of Lords 1960–63, Secretary of State for Education and Science 1964, Lord Chancellor 1970–74, 1979–87.

Sir Sidney Holland – Prime Minister of New Zealand 1949–57.

Christopher Hollis – Conservative MP 1945–55.

14th Earl of Home – Conservative MP 1931–45, 1950–51, 1963–74. PPS to Neville Chamberlain 1937–40, Minister of State, Scottish Office 1951–55, Commonwealth Relations Secretary 1955–60, Leader of the House of Lords and Lord President of the Council 1959–60, Foreign Secretary 1960–63, 1970–74, Prime Minister 1963–64.

6th Viscount Lord Hood – Assistant Under-Secretary, Foreign Office 1951–55, UK representative, WEU 1956, Deputy Secretary, Foreign Office 1962–69.

Herbert Hoover – US Under-Secretary of State 1954–57.

Henry Hopkinson – Joint Director of Conservative Research Department 1940–50, Conservative MP 1950–56. Served with Macmillan during the Second World War, not least as Deputy High Commissioner for Italy 1944–46. Secretary for Overseas Trade 1951–52, Minister of State, Colonial Office 1952–55, Chairman of Anglo-Egyptian Resettlement Board 1957–60, of Joint East and Central Africa Board 1960–65.

Leslie Hore-Belisha – Liberal MP 1923–31, National Liberal MP 1931–42, Independent MP 1942–45. FST 1932–34, Minister of Transport 1934–37, Secretary of State for War 1937–40.

Florence Horsburgh – Conservative MP 1931–45, 1950–59. Parliamentary Secretary, Ministry of Health 1939–45, of Food 1945, Minister of Education 1951–54. Delegate to the Council of Europe and WEU 1955–60.

Sir Frederick Hoyer Millar – UK representative to NATO 1952, UK High Commissioner in Germany 1953–55, Ambassador to Bonn 1955–57, Permanent Under-Secretary, Foreign Office 1957–61.

George Humphrey – US Treasury Secretary 1953–57.

Hussein – King of Jordan 1952–99.

Sir Harry Hylton-Foster – Conservative MP 1950–65. Solicitor-General 1954–59, Speaker of the Commons 1959–65.

Lord Ismay – Secretary, Committee of Imperial Defence 1938–39, Chief of Staff to Prime Minister 1940–45, to last Viceroy of India 1947, Chairman of Council of Festival of Britain 1948–51, Commonwealth Relations Secretary 1951–52, Secretary-General of NATO 1952–57. (Nicknamed Pug.)

Sir Ian Jacob – Military Assistant Secretary to Cabinet 1939–46, 1952, Director of BBC Overseas Service 1947–52, Director-General of BBC 1952–60.

Douglas Jay – Labour MP 1946–83. Economic Secretary to the Treasury 1947–50, FST 1950–51, President of the Board of Trade 1964–67.

Sir Gladwyn Jebb – UK representative to the UN 1950–54, Ambassador to France 1954–60. Created Lord Gladwyn, he became a leading Liberal peer.

Aubrey Jones – Conservative MP 1950–65. Minister of Fuel and Power 1955–57, Minister of Supply 1957–59.

1st Earl Jowitt – Liberal MP 1922–24, Labour MP 1929–31, 1939–45. Attorney-General 1929–32, Solicitor-General 1940–42, Paymaster-General 1942, Minister without Portfolio 1942–44, Minister of National Insurance 1944–45, Lord Chancellor 1945–51.

Donald Kaberry – Conservative MP 1950–83. Vice-Chairman, Conservative Party 1955–61.

Sir Charles Keightley – Commander in Chief, British Army of the Rhine 1948–51, Far East Land Forces 1951–53, Middle East Land Forces (including the Suez operations) 1953–57, Governor of Gibraltar 1958–62.

Sir David Kelly – Ambassador to Argentina 1942, to Turkey 1946–49, to USSR 1949–51.

Hamilton Kerr – Conservative MP 1931–45, 1950–66. PPS to Macmillan 1954–56.

Nikita Khrushchev – Joined Soviet Politburo in 1939. After Stalin's death he achieved ascendancy in 1955, and especially after his defeat of the 'Anti-Party Group' in 1957. Ousted in 1964.

Cecil King – Chairman of Daily Mirror Newspapers Ltd and Sunday Pictorial Newspapers Ltd 1951–63, of International Publishing Corporation 1963–68, of Newspaper Proprietors Association 1961–68.

Sir Ivone Kirkpatrick – UK High Commissioner in Germany 1950–53, Permanent Secretary, Foreign Office 1953–57, Chairman, Independent Television Authority 1957–62.

Ronald Knox – Private tutor to Macmillan 1910, and chaplain at Oxford during his time there. One of the most distinguished English converts to Catholicism, which he joined in 1917.

Viscount Lambton – Conservative MP 1951–73. PPS to Foreign Secretary 1955–57, Under-Secretary, Ministry of Defence 1970–73.

Sir Alan Lascelles – Private Secretary to George VI, 1943–52, to Elizabeth II, 1952–53.

Richard Law – Conservative MP 1931–45, November 1945–54. Minister of Education 1945.

Lord Layton – Editor of *The Economist* 1922–38, Vice-Chairman of the *Daily News* 1930–63, Chairman of the *News Chronicle* 1930–50, the *Star* 1936–50. Deputy leader of the Liberals in the Lords 1952–55 and Vice-President of the Consultative Assembly of the Council of Europe 1949–57.

Lord Leathers – Minister of War Transport 1941–45, Secretary of State for the Co-ordination of Transport, Fuel and Power 1951–53.

Rex Leeper – Worked with Macmillan during the Second World War when he was Ambassador to Greece 1943–46. Ambassador to Argentina 1946–48.

Alan Lennox-Boyd – Conservative MP 1931–60. Minister of State, Colonial Office 1951–52, Minister for Transport and Civil Aviation 1952–54, Colonial Secretary 1954–59.

Sir John Le Rougetel – Ambassador to Persia 1946–50, to Belgium 1950–51. High Commissioner to South Africa 1951–55.

David Lloyd – Under-Secretary, Home Office 1952–54, Colonial Office 1954–57.

Geoffrey Lloyd – Conservative MP 1931–41, 1950–74. Minister of Fuel and Power 1942–45, 1951–55, Minister of Information 1945.

Selwyn Lloyd – Conservative MP 1945–76. Minister of State, Foreign Office 1951–54, Minister of Supply 1954–55, Minister of Defence 1955, Foreign Secretary 1955–60, Chancellor of the Exchequer 1960–62, Lord Privy Seal and Leader of the Commons 1963–64, Speaker of the Commons 1971–76.

Gwilym Lloyd George – Liberal MP 1922–24, 1929–50, Liberal and Conservative MP 1951–57. Minister of Food 1951–54, Home Secretary and Minister for Welsh Affairs 1954–57.

Megan Lloyd George – Liberal MP 1929–51, Labour MP 1957–66.

Oliver Lyttelton – A contemporary of Macmillan at Eton. Conservative MP 1940–54. President of the Board of Trade 1940–41, 1945. Minister of State 1941–42, Minister of Production 1942–45, Chairman of AEI Ltd 1945–51, 1954–63, Colonial Secretary 1951–54, President, Institute of Directors 1954–63.

Douglas MacArthur – Commander in Chief, Allied Forces in South West Pacific 1942–45, Commander in Chief of US Forces in Far East 1945–51, and of UN Forces in Korea 1950–51.

Jack McCloy – US Assistant Secretary of War 1941–45, US Military Governor and High Commissioner for Germany 1949–52.

Malcolm McCorquodale – Conservative MP 1931–45, 1947–55.

Sir John McEwen – Leader of Country Party in Australia, where he held various cabinet posts culminating in Deputy Prime Minister 1958–71.

John McGovern – ILP MP 1930–47, Labour MP 1947–59.

R. W. G. Mackay – Labour MP 1945–51 and keen supporter of the European movement.

Robert Mackenzie – Television political pundit and academic.

Lord Mackintosh – Chocolate manufacturer. Chairman, National Savings Committee 1943–64.

John Maclay – National Liberal MP 1940–64. Minister of Transport and Civil Aviation 1951–52, President, Assembly of WEU 1955–56, Minister of State, Colonial Office 1956–57, Scottish Secretary 1957–62.

Fitzroy MacLean – With Macmillan during the Second World War.

Conservative MP 1941–74. Parliamentary Under-Secretary for War 1954–57.

Iain Macleod – Head of Home Affairs, Conservative Research Department 1948–50. Conservative MP 1950–70. Minister of Health 1952–55, of Labour and National Service 1955–59, Colonial Secretary 1959–61, Chancellor of the Duchy of Lancaster and Leader of the Commons 1961–63, editor of the *Spectator* 1963–65, Chancellor of the Exchequer 1970.

Arthur Macmillan – Elder brother of Macmillan. Lawyer.

Daniel Macmillan – Macmillan's eldest brother. Chairman and Managing Director of Macmillan & Co 1936–63.

Maurice Macmillan – Conservative MP 1955–64, 1966–84. Married Katherine Ormsby-Gore, daughter of 4th Baron Harlech. Followed father to Eton and Balliol. Economic Secretary of the Treasury 1963–64, Chief Secretary 1970–72, Secretary of State for Employment 1972–73, Paymaster-General 1973–74.

Makarios III – Archbishop and Ethnarch of Cyprus 1950–77. A keen supporter of *enosis* and EOKA, he was exiled 1956–59. On its independence in 1960 he became President of Cyprus.

Roger Makins – Assistant to Macmillan in North Africa 1943–44. Deputy Under-Secretary, Foreign Office 1948–52, Ambassador to Washington 1953–56, Joint Permanent Secretary of the Treasury 1956–59, Chairman, UK Atomic Energy Authority 1960–64.

Georgi Malenkov – Member of Soviet politburo 1946–57, Prime Minister 1953–55.

Daniel Malan – National Party leader and Prime Minister of South Africa 1948–54.

J. J. Mallon – Social worker and Warden of Toynbee Hall 1919–54.

Ernest Marples – Conservative MP 1945–74. Parliamentary Secretary, Ministry of Housing and Local Government 1951–54, Ministry of Pensions and National Insurance 1954–55, Postmaster-General 1957–59, Minister of Transport 1959–64.

George Marshall – Chief of Staff of US Army 1939–45, US Secretary of State 1947–49.

Kingsley Martin – Editor of *New Statesman and Nation* 1930–60.

René Massigli – Worked with Macmillan in North Africa, where he was Commissioner for Foreign Affairs in the French Committee of National Liberation. French Ambassador to Britain 1944–55, Secretary-General of French Foreign Ministry 1955–56, French President, Channel Tunnel Study Group 1958–69.

Reginald Maudling – Conservative MP 1950–79. Economic Secretary to the Treasury 1952–55, Minister of Supply 1955–57, Paymaster-General 1957–59, President of the Board of Trade 1959–61, Colonial Secretary 1961–62, Chancellor of the Exchequer 1962–64, Home Secretary 1970–72.

David Maxwell Fyfe – Conservative MP 1935–54, when he was created Viscount (later Earl of) Kilmuir. Solicitor-General 1942–45, Attorney-General 1945, Deputy Chief Prosecutor at the Nuremburg trials, Home Secretary and Minister of Welsh Affairs 1951–54, Lord Chancellor 1954–62.

Adnan Menderes – Prime Minister of Turkey 1950–60.

Pierre Mendes-France – Financial Minister 1943–44, and Minister of National Economy 1944–45 in French Provisional Government. Prime Minister 1954–55.

Krishna Menon – Indian representative at UN General Assembly 1946, 1952–62. Indian Minister without Portfolio 1956–57, Minister for Defence 1957–62.

Robert Menzies – Prime Minister of Australia 1939–41, 1949–66.

Livingston Merchant – US Assistant Secretary of State for European Affairs 1953–56, 1958–59, US Ambassador to Canada 1956–58, 1961–62, Under-Secretary of State for Political Affairs 1959–61.

Sir Percy Mills – Businessman. Controller-General of Machine Tools 1940–44, head of production division for Ministry of Production 1943–44, Chairman, National Research Development Corporation 1950–55, adviser to Ministry of Housing and Local Government 1951–52, Minister of Power 1957–59, Paymaster-General 1959–61, Minister without Portfolio 1961–62.

Guy Mollet – French Minister of State for Council of Europe 1950–51,

President of Consultative Assembly of Council of Europe 1954–56, French Prime Minister 1956–57.

V. M. Molotov – Joined Soviet politburo in 1925 and served as Commissar for Foreign Affairs 1939–49, 1953–57.

Sir Walter Monckton – Conservative MP 1951–57. Solicitor-General 1945, Minister of Labour and National Service 1951–55, of Defence 1955–56, Paymaster-General 1956–57. Chairman, Advisory Commission on Central Africa 1960.

Jean Monnet – Served on Allied supply executives in both world wars, and met Macmillan when he worked with the French Committee of National Liberation in North Africa. Author of Monnet Plan for European recovery 1946. President of European Coal and Steel Community 1952–55, of Action Committee for a United States of Europe 1956–75.

Field Marshal Viscount Montgomery of Alamein – Commander, Eighth Army 1942–44, Commander in Chief, Northern France 1944, CIGS 1946–48, Deputy SACEUR 1951–58.

Lord Moran – Churchill's physician, and political diarist.

Herbert Morrison – Labour MP 1923–24, 1929–31, 1935–59. Minister of Transport 1929–31. Macmillan's chief as Minister of Supply 1940. Home Secretary 1940–45, Lord President and Leader of the Commons 1945–51, Foreign Secretary 1951, Deputy Leader of the Opposition 1951–55.

Muhammad Mossadeq – Nationalist Prime Minister of Iran 1951–53.

Earl Mountbatten of Burma – Supreme Allied Commander, South East Asia 1943–46, Viceroy of India 1947, Governor-General of India 1947–48, Fourth Sea Lord 1950–52, Commander in Chief, Mediterranean 1952–54, First Sea Lord 1955–59, Chief of Defence Staff 1959–65.

Bob Murphy – President Roosevelt's personal representative in French North Africa 1940–42, and worked alongside Macmillan at AFHQ 1942–43. US Ambassador to Japan 1952, Assistant Secretary of State for UN affairs 1953, Deputy Under-Secretary of State 1953–59, Under-Secretary of State for Political Affairs 1959.

Gamal Abdel Nasser – A leader of the 'Free Officers' revolt that overthrew King Farouk of Egypt in July 1952, he became Prime Minister and Military Governor 1954–56 and then President until his death in 1970.

Muhammad Neguib – Prime Minister of Egypt from the July 1952 revolution to 1953, President 1953–54, when he was ousted by Nasser.

Jawaharlal Nehru – Prime Minister and Minister for External Affairs of India 1947–64.

Sir Frank Newsam – Permanent Under-Secretary, Home Office 1948–57.

Godfrey Nicholson – Conservative MP 1931–35, 1937–66.

Philip Noel-Baker – Labour MP 1929–31, 1936–70. Secretary of State for Air 1946–47, Commonwealth Relations Secretary 1947–50, Minister of Fuel and Power 1950–51. Nobel Peace Prize 1959.

Nuri al-Said – The dominant figure in Iraqi politics from the British-led defeat of the 1941 coup until his death during the 1958 revolution.

Anthony Nutting – Conservative MP 1945–56. Parliamentary Secretary, Foreign Office 1951–54, Minister of State, Foreign Office 1954–56.

David Ormsby-Gore – Brother-in-law to Maurice Macmillan. Conservative MP 1950–61. PPS, Foreign Office 1951–54, Under-Secretary, Foreign Office 1956–57, Minister of State, Foreign Office 1957–61, Ambassador to Washington 1961–65.

Sir Thomas Padmore – Second Secretary in the Treasury 1952–62, Permanent Secretary, Ministry of Transport 1962–68.

Alexandros Papagos – Greek Prime Minister 1952–55.

Sir Harold Parker – Permanent Secretary, Ministry of Defence 1948–56.

Osbert Peake – Conservative MP 1929–56. Minister of National Insurance 1951–53, of Pensions and National Insurance 1953–55.

Lester Pearson – Canadian Secretary of State for External Affairs 1948–57, leader of the Liberal Party 1958–68, and Prime Minister 1963–68.

Louis Petch – Private Secretary to the Chancellor of the Exchequer 1953–56, Third Secretary, Treasury 1952–66, Second Secretary, Treasury 1966–68, Second Secretary, Civil Service Department 1968–69, Chairman, Board of Customs and Excise 1969–73.

André Philip – With Macmillan in North Africa, where he was a member of the French Committee for National Liberation. French Minister of Finance 1946–47, of National Economy 1947. Head of French delegation to OEEC 1947–51, and President of Socialist Movement for a United States for Europe.

Antoine Pinay – French Minister of Economic Affairs 1948–49, 1958–59, Prime Minister 1952, Foreign Minister 1955–56.

Christian Pineau – French Finance Minister 1948, Foreign Minister 1956–57.

René Pleven – With Macmillan in North Africa, where he was a member of the French Committee for National Liberation. French Minister of Finance 1944, of Defence 1949, 1952–54, Prime Minister 1950–51, 1951–52, Foreign Minister 1958.

Sir Edwin Plowden – Chief Planning Officer, Treasury 1947–53. Chairman, Atomic Energy Authority 1954–59, Committee of Inquiry into control of public expenditure 1959–61, into organization of representative services overseas 1963–64, into aircraft industry 1964–65.

Oliver Poole – Conservative MP 1950–55. Chairman of the Conservative Party 1955–57.

J. Enoch Powell – Conservative MP 1950–74, Ulster Unionist MP 1974–87. Parliamentary Secretary, Ministry of Housing and Local Government 1955–57, FST 1957–58, Minister of Health 1960–63.

Sir Richard Powell – Deputy Secretary, Ministry of Defence 1950–56, Permanent Secretary, Ministry of Defence 1956–59, Permanent Secretary, Board of Trade 1960–68.

Paul Ramadier – French Prime Minister 1947, Defence Minister 1948–49, Finance Minister 1956–57.

2nd Marquess of Reading – Parliamentary Secretary, Foreign Office 1951–53, Minister of State, Foreign Office 1953–57, Chairman of Council on Tribunals 1958–60.

Patrick Reilly – Deputy Under-Secretary, Foreign Office 1956–57, 1960–64, Ambassador to USSR 1957–60, to France 1965–68.

Joseph Retsinger – Secretary of the International Committee of Movements for European Unity.

Paul Reynaud – French Prime Minister 1940, Chairman of the Economic Committee of the Council of Europe 1952–66.

Syngman Rhee – President of South Korea 1948–60.

Lady Rhys Williams – Liberal. Chairman, ELEC 1948–64, Honorary Secretary, 1947–58, then Chairman 1958–64, of the United Europe Movement. Chairman, Cwmbran Development Corporation 1955–60.

Alfred Robens – Labour MP 1945–60. Minister of Labour and National Service 1951. Chairman, National Coal Board 1961–71.

Sir Frank Roberts – Chargé d'Affaires, Moscow embassy 1946–47, PPS to Foreign Secretary 1947–49, Deputy High Commissioner to India 1949–51, Deputy Under-Secretary, Foreign Office 1951–54, Ambassador to Yugoslavia 1954–57, UK representative to NATO 1957–60, Ambassador to USSR 1960–62, to Germany 1963–68.

Sir Brian Robertson – Worked with Macmillan in North Africa and Italy during the Second World War. Commander in Chief and British Military Governor in Germany 1947–49, UK High Commissioner in Germany 1949–50, Commander in Chief, Middle East Land Forces 1950–53, Chairman, British Transport Commission 1953–61.

Dennis Robertson – Professor of Political Economy at Cambridge 1944–57, Member of Council on Prices, Productivity and Incomes 1957–58.

Franklin D. Roosevelt – US President 1933–45.

Sir Leslie Rowan – Second Secretary in the Treasury 1947–49, 1951–58, Managing Director 1962–67 and Chairman 1967–71 of Vickers Ltd. Chairman of British Council 1971–72.

A. L. Rowse – Labour party activist, professional Cornishman, Tudor historian at Oxford and Macmillan author.

Sir Anthony Rumbold – Assistant Under-Secretary Foreign Office 1954–58, Deputy Under-Secretary, Foreign Office 1958–66.

Louis St Laurent – Canadian Minister of External Affairs 1946–48, Prime Minister 1948–57.

5th Marquess of Salisbury – A contemporary of Macmillan at Eton and Oxford and a kinsman through Macmillan's Cavendish connections. Conservative MP 1929–41. Paymaster-General 1940, Dominions Secretary 1940–42, 1943–45, Colonial Secretary 1942, Lord Privy Seal 1942–43, 1951–52, Leader of the House of Lords 1942–45, 1951–57,

Commonwealth Relations Secretary 1952, Lord President of the Council 1952–57. (Nicknamed Bobbety.)

Sir Arthur Salter – Economist. Independent MP 1937–50, Conservative MP 1951–53. Chancellor of the Duchy of Lancaster 1945, Minister of Economic Affairs 1951–52, of Materials 1952–53.

1st Viscount Samuel – Liberal MP 1902–18, 1929–35. Chancellor of the Duchy of Lancaster 1909–10, 1915–16, Postmaster-General 1910–14, 1915–16, President of the Local Government Board 1914–15, Home Secretary 1916, 1931–32, High Commissioner in Palestine 1920–25, Leader of the Liberal Party 1931–35, Liberal Leader in the House of Lords 1944–55.

Duncan Sandys – Churchill's son-in-law. Conservative MP 1935–45, 1950–74. Chairman, international executive of the European Movement 1947–50. Minister of Works 1944–45, of Supply 1951–54, of Housing and Local Government 1954–57, of Defence 1957–59, of Aviation 1959–60, Commonwealth Relations Secretary 1960–64, Colonial Secretary 1962–64.

Sir Orme Sargent – Permanent Secretary, Foreign Office 1946–49.

Kurt Schumacher – Leader of the German SPD from 1946 until his death in 1952.

Robert Schuman – French Minister of Finance 1946–47, Prime Minister 1947–48, Foreign Minister 1948–52.

Maurice Schumann – French Deputy Foreign Minister 1951–52.

Count Carlo Sforza – Italian Minister of Foreign Affairs 1920–21, 1947–51, Minister Secretary of State 1944–46, 1951–52.

Dame Evelyn Sharp – Permanent Secretary, Minister of Housing and Local Government 1955–66.

Sir Hartley Shawcross – UK Chief Prosecutor at the Nuremburg trials. Labour MP 1945–58. Attorney-General 1945–51, President of the Board of Trade 1951.

Sir Thomas Sheepshanks – Permanent Secretary of the Ministry of Town and Country Planning 1946–51, and of the Ministry of Housing and Local Government 1951–55.

Emmanuel Shinwell – Labour MP 1922–24, 1928–31, 1935–70. Minister of Fuel and Power 1945–47, Secretary of State for War 1947–50, Minister of Defence 1950–51.

Evelyn Shuckburgh – PPS to the Foreign Secretary 1951–54, Assistant Under-Secretary, Foreign Office 1954–56, Assistant Secretary-General of NATO 1958–60, Deputy Under-Secretary Foreign Office 1960–62, UK representative to NATO 1962–66, Ambassador to Italy 1966–69.

Sidney Silverman – Left-wing Labour MP 1935–68.

Archibald Sinclair – Liberal MP 1922–45. Scottish Secretary 1931–32, Secretary of State for Air 1940–45, Leader of the Liberal Party 1935–45.

Walter Bedell Smith – With Macmillan when Chief of Staff, Allied Forces in North Africa, then Italy 1942–44. Chief of Staff, Allied Expeditionary Force in Western Europe 1944–45, US Ambassador to USSR 1946–49, Director, CIA 1950–53, Under-Secretary of State 1953–54.

Jan Christian Smuts – South African Prime Minister 1919–24, 1939–48.

Christopher Soames – Churchill's son-in-law. Conservative MP 1950–66. PPS to the Prime Minister 1952–55, Parliamentary Secretary, Air Ministry 1955–57, Admiralty 1957–58, Secretary of State for War 1958–60, Minister of Agriculture, Fisheries and Food 1960–64, Ambassador to France 1968–72, Governor of Southern Rhodesia 1979–80, Lord President of the Council 1979–81.

Paul-Henri Spaak – Belgian Prime Minister 1938–39, 1947–49, Minister of Foreign Affairs 1936–38, 1939–46, 1947–49, 1954–57, 1961–66. President of the Consultative Assembly of the Council of Europe 1949–51, Chairman of the International Council of the European Movement 1950–55 and of the committee that paved the way for the Treaty of Rome negotiations. Secretary-General of NATO 1957–61.

Josef Stalin – General Secretary of the Central Committee of the Communist Party of the Soviet Union from 1922 until his death in 1953.

Stephanos Stephanopoulos – Greek Finance Minister 1946, Foreign Minister 1952–55, 1966, Prime Minister 1965–66.

Sir Ralph Stevenson – Worked with Macmillan when Ambassador to Yugoslavia 1943–46. Also Ambassador to China 1946–50, to Egypt 1950–55.

Richard Stokes – Labour MP 1938–57. Minister of Works 1950–51, of Materials 1951, Lord Privy Seal 1951.

John Strachey – Labour MP 1929–31, 1945–63. Minister of Food 1946–50, Secretary of State for War 1950–51.

William Strang – Permanent Secretary, Foreign Office 1949–53. Chairman, National Parks Commission 1954–66.

George Strauss – Labour MP 1929–31, 1934–79. Minister of Supply 1947–51.

James Stuart – A younger contemporary of Macmillan at Eton who married Dorothy Macmillan's sister Rachel. Conservative MP 1923–59. Conservative Chief Whip 1941–48. Scottish Secretary 1951–57.

Edith Summerskill – Labour MP 1938–61. Minister of National Insurance 1950–51.

C. R. Swart – South African Minister of Justice 1948–59, Deputy Prime Minister 1954–59, Governor-General 1960–61, President 1961–67.

1st Earl of Swinton – Conservative MP 1918–35. President of the Board of Trade 1922–23, 1924–29, 1931, Colonial Secretary 1931–35, Secretary of State for Air 1935–38, Minister Resident in West Africa 1942–44, for Civil Aviation 1944–45, Chancellor of the Duchy of Lancaster and Minister of Materials 1951–52, Commonwealth Relations Secretary 1952–55.

Lord Tedder – Deputy Supreme Commander, Allied Expeditionary Force in Western Europe 1944–45, Chief of Air Staff 1946–50.

Sir Gerald Templer – GOC, Western Command 1950–52, High Commissioner, Malaya 1952–54, CIGS 1955–58.

Sir Vincent Tewson – General Secretary of the TUC 1946–60.

Ioaanis Theotokis – Greek Prime Minister 1950, Foreign Minister 1955–56.

Jim Thomas – Conservative MP 1931–56. FST 1943–45, First Lord of the Admiralty 1951–56.

Peter Thorneycroft – Conservative MP 1938–66. President of the Board of Trade 1951–57, Chancellor of the Exchequer 1957–58, Minister of

Aviation 1960–62, Defence Secretary 1962–64. Conservative Party Chairman 1975–81.

Josip Broz Tito – Leader of the wartime communist resistance in Yugoslavia who served as Prime Minister from 1945 and President from 1953 until his death in 1980.

Sir Humphrey Trevelyan – Chargé d'Affaires in the Peking embassy 1953–55, Ambassador to Egypt 1955–56, to Iraq 1958–61, Deputy Under-Secretary, Foreign Office 1962, Ambassador to USSR 1962–65, High Commissioner in South Arabia 1967.

Harry S. Truman – US Vice-President 1945, President 1945–53.

Sir James Turner – President of the National Farmers' Union 1945–60.

Lady Tweedsmuir – Conservative MP 1946–66. Delegate to the Council of Europe 1950–52. Under-Secretary for Scotland 1962–64, Minister of State, Scottish Office 1970–72, Foreign Office 1972–74.

William Warbey – Left-wing Labour MP 1945–50, 1953–66.

George Ward – Conservative MP 1945–60. Parliamentary Secretary, Air Ministry 1952–55, Admiralty 1955–57, Secretary of State for Air 1957–60.

Charles Waterhouse – Conservative MP 1924–45, 1950–57. Chairman of the Public Accounts Committee 1950–51, and of the Estimates Committee 1953–57. Leader of the Suez Group.

Harold Watkinson – Conservative MP 1950–64. Parliamentary Secretary, Ministry of Labour and National Insurance 1952–55, Minister of Transport and Civil Aviation 1955–59, of Defence 1959–62.

Jack Wheeler-Bennett – Oxford historian, adviser to the Foreign Office on the publication of captured German diplomatic documents 1948–56 and Macmillan author.

Harold Wilson – Labour MP 1945–83 and party leader 1963–76. Secretary for Overseas Trade 1947, President of the Board of Trade 1947–51, Opposition spokesman on trade and Treasury affairs 1951–61, on foreign affairs 1961–63, Prime Minister 1964–70, 1974–76.

Richard Wood – Son of 1st Earl of Halifax. Conservative MP 1950–79. PPS to Heathcoat Amory 1951–55, Parliamentary Secretary, Ministry of Pensions and National Insurance 1955–58, Ministry of Labour 1958–59,

Minister of Power 1959–63, of Pensions and National Insurance 1963–64, of Overseas Development 1970–74.

Lord Woolton – Conservative Party Chairman 1946–55. Minister of Food 1940–43, of Reconstruction 1943–45, Lord President of the Council 1945, 1951–52, Chancellor of the Duchy of Lancaster 1952–55.

Woodrow Wyatt – Labour MP 1945–55, 1959–70.

John Wyndham – With Macmillan during the Second World War. Private Secretary to Macmillan 1957–63.

Marshal G. K. Zhukov – Soviet Minister of Defence from Stalin's death in 1953 until he was dismissed in 1957.

R. R. Zorlu – Turkish Foreign Minister 1955–60.

Appendix

THE CONSERVATIVE CABINETS 1951–57

CHURCHILL 1951–55

Prime Minister	(Sir) Winston Churchill
Lord President	Lord Woolton 5th Marquess of Salisbury (*Nov 1952*)
Lord Chancellor	Lord Simonds Viscount Kilmuir (*Oct 1954*)
Lord Privy Seal	5th Marquess of Salisbury Harry Crookshank (*May 1952*)
Chancellor of the Exchequer	R. A. Butler
Foreign Secretary	(Sir) Anthony Eden
Home Office (and Welsh Affairs)	Sir David Maxwell Fyfe Gwilym Lloyd George (*Oct 1954*)

Agriculture and Fisheries	Sir Thomas Dugdale (*in cabinet
	   from Sep 1953*)
	Derek Heathcoat Amory
	   (*Jul 1954*)

Colonies	Oliver Lyttelton Alan Lennox-Boyd (*Jul 1954*)
Commonwealth Relations Office	Lord Ismay 5th Marquess of Salisbury (*Mar 1952*) Viscount Swinton (*Nov 1952*)

Co-ordination of Transport	Lord Leathers (*office abolished Sep 1953*)
Defence	(as PM) Earl Alexander of Tunis (*Mar 1952*) Harold Macmillan (*Oct 1954*)
Education	Florence Horsburgh (*in cabinet from Sep 1953*) Sir David Eccles (*Oct 1954*)
Food	Gwilym Lloyd George (*in cabinet from Sep 1953 – combined with Agriculture and Fisheries in Oct 1954*)
Health	Harry Crookshank (*to May 1952 – thereafter office not in cabinet*)
Housing and Local Government	Harold Macmillan Duncan Sandys (*Oct 1954*)
Labour and National Service	Sir Walter Monckton
Duchy of Lancaster (and Materials)	Lord Woolton (*in cabinet from Nov 1952*)
Paymaster-General	Lord Cherwell (*left office and post ceased to be in cabinet, Nov 1953*)
Pensions and National Insurance	Oliver Peake (*in cabinet from Sep 1953*)
Scotland	James Stuart
Board of Trade	Peter Thorneycroft

EDEN 1955–57

Prime Minister	Sir Anthony Eden
Lord President	5th Marquess of Salisbury

Lord Chancellor	Viscount Kilmuir
Lord Privy Seal	Harry Crookshank R. A. Butler (*Dec 1955*)
Chancellor of the Exchequer	R. A. Butler Harold Macmillan (*Dec 1955*)
Foreign Office	Harold Macmillan Selwyn Lloyd (*Dec 1955*)
Home Office and Welsh Affairs	Gwilym Lloyd George
Agriculture, Fisheries and Food	Derek Heathcoat Amory
Colonies	Alan Lennox-Boyd
Commonwealth Relations Office	Earl of Home
Defence	Selwyn Lloyd Sir Walter Monckton (*Dec 1955*) Anthony Head (*Oct 1956*)
Education	Sir David Eccles
Housing and Local Government	Duncan Sandys
Labour and National Service	Sir Walter Monckton Iain Macleod (*Dec 1955*)
Duchy of Lancaster	Lord Woolton Earl of Selkirk (*Dec 1955*)
Paymaster-General	Sir Walter Monckton (*in cabinet from Oct 1956*)
Pensions and National Insurance	Oliver Peake (*left office and post ceased to be in cabinet, Dec 1955*)
Scotland	James Stuart
Board of Trade	Peter Thorneycroft
Works	Patrick Buchan-Hepburn (*in cabinet from Dec 1955*)

Index

www.ingramcontent.com/pod-product-compliance
Ingram Content Group UK Ltd.
Pitfield, Milton Keynes, MK11 3LW, UK
UKHW040641280225
455688UK00002B/62